surviv

london

Edited by Mike Considine, Kate Brady and Marijke Acket

• Alternative Press • London •

acknowledgements

Thanks to our contributors
Cath Felcey (Getting the Place Together, Pets), Gerry McManamon (Jobs), Val Forest (Social Security), David Grace (Poll Tax), Andy Hyatt and Miguel Orgel (Drugs), Sue Shutter (People from Abroad), Anne Warner (Community), Jill Steverson (Green Environment), Tony Day and Jane Clark (Computers), Jane Goodsir (Law), Dillon Rodriguez (Prisons), Kevin Grimwade (NHS, Disabilities), Paul Hobbs (Bicycles), Phillip Grey (Photography), Fiona Graham (Networks, Phone), Matt Thomas and Fiona Sayle (Squatting), Freya Aswynn (Paganism), Maggie Jamieson (Visual Arts), Nik Houghton (Video), Alison Key (Ethnic Minorities), Chris Payne (Gays).

And for help from
Karen Glynn, Derek Langhan, Maisie MacKenzie, Peter Webb, Ruth Grigg (FPA), Dr Sue Mitchell (St Thomas' Hospital).

And for more help from
Martyn Wilkinson, Sion Whellens, Stuart Home, Janet Williams, Dorothy Newton, John Loizou, Peter Webb, Fritz the Dog.

And for other help from
Advisory Service for Squatters, Camden Stop the Poll Tax Campaign, Terrence Higgins Trust, Portobello Project, Release, Wages Due Lesbians, Calverts.

And thanks to those without whom. . .
Mick Laslett, Ken Rees, Michael Brady, Ruth Acket, Aron Gersh, Reinhart Kowalski

Illustrations
Phil Evans for section title page illustrations.

Helen Cusack (cartoons from her book *I'm Not a Feminist But...* - watch out for her new book, *Rocking The Boat*, coming out soon),

Sylvie Legal, Ross and Sean for diagrams in Getting the Place Together section

Diagrams in Sex section courtesy of the Family Planning Association.

Etchings throughout from Dover Publications Copyright Free Books, available from the Dover Bookshop.

Photos (and other things) by Marianne Brady.

Andy and Miguel's note
Thanks to all the people and agencies who helped us put the Drugs section together in such a hurry. Special thanks to Terrence Higgins Trust, Community Drug Project, Institute for the Study of Drug Dependence, Libraries, Harry Shapiro, SCODA, Jane Kennedy, Drug Concern Harrow and Release for all the information and advice.

Published by Alternative Press
BCM Raft, London WC1N 3XX

ISBN 0 9514863 0 6

First published November1989

Printed in Great Britain by
BPCC Wheatons Ltd, Exeter

short contents

expanded contents

somewhere to live 2

getting your place together 17

jobs 36

social security 47

the poll tax 54

food 58

good deals 65

sex 71

travel 130

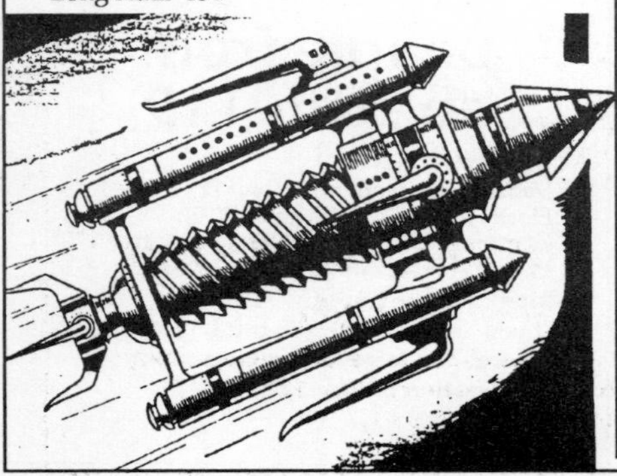

getting around 138

self discovery 146

health 161

martial arts 171

women 175

men 184

lesbian and gay 186

transsexuals/ transvestites192

the law 194

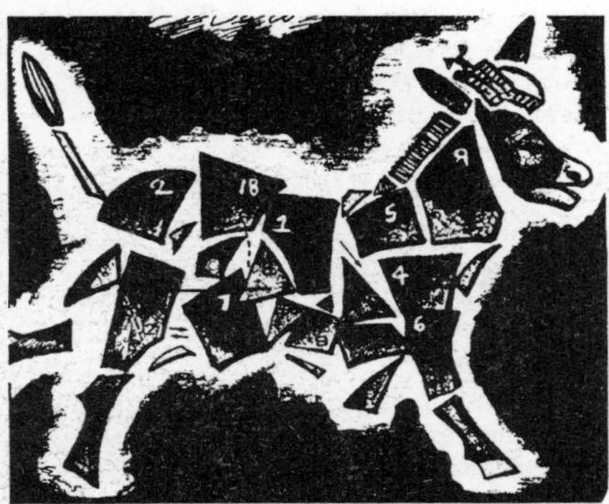

prisons 203

advice centres 207

agitation 215

kids 220

ethnic minorities 231

disabled 235

computers 237

HOUSING: Somewhere to Live, Getting the Place Together

somewhere to live

thousands of people sleep rough or seek accommodation in emergency hostels every night in London. Many are young people who find the task of getting a home especially difficult. The young are often exploited, given meagre wages for their work (if they can find it), or given less than a subsistence wage by the government. Landlords do not want to take them believing they are unreliable or noisy. Thus some face a life on the streets, or in temporary hostels, or on friends' floors. This section tells you where and how to find accommodation and what rights you've got when you're in.

▼CRISIS▼

Reading

Somewhere to Live in London, produced by **SHAC** (see below) is a useful free small booklet. *Housing Rights Guide* (1989) by Geoffrey Randall also produced by SHAC is a more in-depth and comprehensive £5.95 + 50p p&p. *Finding a Place to Live in London*, produced by **HAS** (see below) £2.40 inc p&p is good, and covers most aspects of housing in London. *Women's Housing Handbook* by **Resource Information Service**, *5 Egmont House, 116 Shaftsbury Av, W1 (494 2408)* is well researched and written.

Homelessness

If you are already living in London, then in an emergency, you are supposed to be able to go to your local council and they will rehouse you. In practice they only house you in temporary accommodation if they are obliged to by law. This means that your not likely to get housed unless you're homeless (or are due to be made homeless within 28 days), are not 'intentionally homeless' and have lived in the area for six months and come under one or more of the following categories:

- have dependent kids under 16
- are mentally ill
- are under medication (suffering from diabetes etc)
- are a victim of racial harassment
- are pregnant
- a victim of violence in the home
- over 55 years of age
- have a disability

Warning to Foriegners

Before approaching the council for housing: if you are not a British Citizen and are not sure of your residential status contact the** Joint Council for the Welfare of Immigrants Advisory Service,* **115 Old St, EC1 (251 8706)** ***who will advise you.

Somewhere for the Night

If you need somewhere immediately then the following organisations may help. They will usually refer you to a hostel and may give further help if necessary. Also see section **People From Abroad** (p119).

■ **Housing Advice Switchboard (HAS)**, *47 Charing Cross Rd, WC2 (434 2522)*. Info and advice for people without children, M-F 10-6. Emergency answerphone other times. Publications include *Finding a Place to Live in London* £2.00 +40p p&p, *Housing Association Co-operative Directory* £9.70 inc p&p, *Accommodation in an Emergency* £9.95 inc p&p.

■ **Shelter Housing Action Centre (SHAC)**, *189a Old Brompton Road, SW5 (373 7276)*. M-F 9.30-4.30 (not Wed am). Publications include *Housing Rights Guide* £5.95 + 50p p&p, and a number of publications on rights for home owners, tenants, women who have split from a relationship and are on housing benefit. They produce a housing benefit wall chart, and policy papers and leaflets on housing rights.

■ **Alone in London Service**, *188 King's Cross Rd, WC1 (278 4224 (advice & counselling); 387 6184 (admin))*. M-F 9.30-4. For single people (16-21). Drop in or phone

■ **National Assoc of Voluntary Hostels**, *33 Long Acre, WC2 (836 0193)*. Normally deals with referrals from other agencies (e.g. the DHSS, probation service, hospitals etc) but will sometimes help individuals.

■ **Piccadilly Advice Centre (PAC)**, *(434 3773)*. (see p213). For single homeless people in the West End.

■ **Portobello Project**, *49/51 Porchester Road, W2*

(221 4413). Generally for people in the area, though in practice will help outsiders.

■ **Capital Radio Helpline**, *(388 1288)*. M-F 9.30 - 5.30 and 9.30-9 on Th will refer you to the nearest hostel.

■ **Soho Project**, *12 Adelaide St, WC2 (930 3453 (Soho Project), 930 3440 (London Connection))*. For young homeless. Call in M, Tu, Th & F between 11.30-1 and W 10-12 or phone 10-6 M-F except Wed afternoon. Downstairs the **London Connection** run a cafe which opens early morning and will welcome you. Cheap food and drink and you can sit and talk. **London Connection** also run various youth activities M-F 8-4, M 6-9 women only, Tu, W, Th 6-9. Lesbian and Gay F 7.30-9-30.

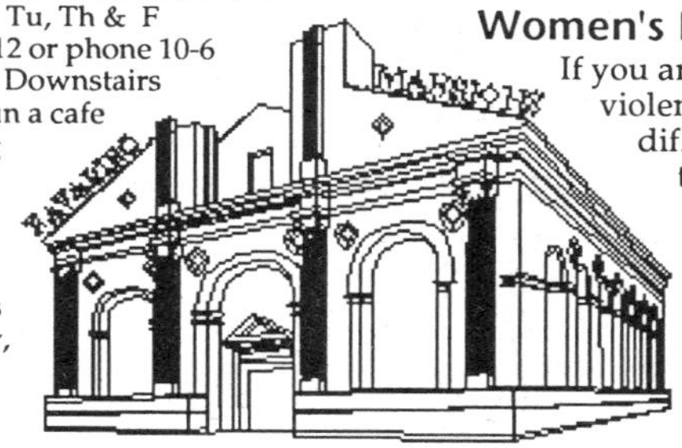

An organisation that campaigns for the homeless is **CHAR (Housing Campaign for Single People)**, *5- 15 Cromer St, WC1 (833 2071)* . They co-ordinate a national campaign for a whole range of single person housing issues, including benefits, civil liberties, health and welfare. They only deal with organisations so if you are homeless use one of the other agencies as they cannot offer direct help to individuals.

The following hostels are short stay (usually 7 days). They can be either single-sex or mixed.

■ **River Point**, *229 King St, W6 (741 2888)*. Mixed 18-60. £70 per wk . Phone first. Breakfast and evening meal. Dormitory (8 people to a room). Charity.

■ **Centrepoint**, *25 Berwick St, W1 (434 2861)*. Males 16-19, females 16-21. Free. Must be at the gate at 8pm. Dormatory. At the time of going to press they are moving. The address given is correct but the phone number may have changed.

■ **Camden Women's Resettlement Unit**, *2/4 Birkenhead St, WC2 (278 6466)*. No children, compulsory shower and hair wash (for lice). Last resort. DHSS. Age 17-60.

■ **London Embankment Mission Council**, *Weber St, W1 (928 1677)*. Sometimes have a few places for men who have been converted to the Christian faith. Free canteen 8.00 am Mon -Fri. 7.00pm Mon and Wed. Free clothing Mon and Thur 2-3.30

Longer stay hostels vary in the comfort they offer. Some are designed for students or working people, others for specific groups such as ex-offenders or those with drinking problems. You will need to join the hostel's waiting list, but it may take some time before they will interview you.

■ **Ada Lewis Women's Hostels**, *(251 6091)*. Three hostels, with a slow turn-round so you may have to wait a long time. About £34 per week single bedsit with shared facilities. Wembley and West Ken and North London.

■ **Beacon House**, *30 Leinster Sq., W2 (229 2220)* and **Beacon House** *Castle Lane, SW1 (828 9137)*. Mixed sexes (but not usually couples). About £56 for a shared room, breakfast and evening meal. 2 meals at weekend. 350 beds.

Women's Refuges

If you are a victim of domestic violence and are having difficulty being housed by the council, it is possible to be accommodated by Women's Refuges. Their address and number is kept secret, but the **London Women's Aid**, *(251 6537)* will refer you, as will advice centres, and the **Chiswick Family Rescue**, *(995 4430 24hr crisis line)* will also find women places in a refuge. See also the section on **Women** (p175).

• Two publications - *A Woman's Place* and *Going It Alone*, both £3.95 + 50p p&p give advice in the event of a relationship breaking down and your rights. Both are available from **SHAC**, *(373 7276)* (see p2).

▼ RENTING ▼

Renting Privately

SEARCHING

If you're in a hurry don't expect to find anything cheap. Rented accommodation in London is expensive, especially in the private sector. The best way to find rented accommodation is by word of mouth. The more people you ask the more likely you will find somewhere. Here is one interesting theory of communication: if you ask 100 people (say friends or acquaintances) if they know of a vacant property, one or two may well be able to tell you. But if instead you ask the same 100 people if they could ask their friends if they had heard of a vacant property then, assuming the 100 friends you ask each ask 100 friends, then the total number of people who will be asked will be 100x100=10,000. Taking this one step further, if you were to ask your 100 friends if any friends of their friends had heard of a flat going, 10,000x100=1,000,000 people would have been asked. This all assumes that the same people don't get asked twice and that you're friends don't mind asking round for you, but it's worth a try. Failing that try the following:

Advertisements

Accommodation is advertised in *City Limits, Time Out, Loot, Evening Standard, Gay Times, The Times, Dalton's Weekly* and local papers. It's best to get the copy as soon as it comes off the press so that you can be first in the queue. Find out where the publication is obtainable earliest by phoning their offices. It is possible to go round to the printers to and buy one as soon as it comes off the press. The first edition of *The Standard* comes out 10.45 am at *118 Fleet St*. Many of the local papers are syndicated and carry the same ads. *Finding a Place to Live in London* (see p2) lists the local papers detailing which are syndicated with publication dates. Otherwise you could put your own 'wanted' ad in a paper.

Advertisements on notice-boards in newsagents shops are good for finding accommodation in the area, so if you want to live in a particular area you should visit the newsagents there. You could also leave an ad seeking accommodation. Also look on noticeboards in community centres, whole food shops, some bookshops (such as **Sisterwrite**, women only) and colleges.

■ **Capital Radio**, *Euston Centre, Euston Rd, NW1 (388 1288)*. Free list of flatshares are available from above address Tues 11am. Get there early. The list is also published in the *Midweek* magazine (on the following Thur, given away free at central London tubes and BR). If you want to advertise your flat/ room phone them on *484 5255* Wed 2-2.30 and Wed and Thur 5.30-6.

Accommodation Agencies

These tend to be oversubscribed around September due to the influx of students into London. They tend to deal with the local area but some cover all London. The usual charge is two weeks rent (plus VAT) if they find you a place. You may lose some of your rights as a tenant when signing so take any contracts with you to a housing advice centre (see p2) beforehand, to get it checked out. Make sure you get a receipt for any money you pay them and make sure as to whether or not it's returnable. They are acting illegally if they charge you a non-returnable 'registration fee'. You only pay if they find you a place. They are on the landlady's side, not yours, so don't use them unless you have to.

When You Meet the Landlady

If you decide to take the flat you may be asked for a deposit. This could be as much as four weeks rent in advance and up to eight weeks non-returnable deposit - a total of twelve weeks rent. Get a receipt saying the deposit is returnable. It is illegal for the landlady to ask for more than two months rent for deposit. The landlady may require some of the deposit there and then so take enough cash with you. It helps if you take an employer's reference and a bank book.

If you do have to leave a deposit, make a list of the flat contents and get the landlady to sign it. Take meter readings too and notify the gas and electricity boards.

Rights of Private Tenants

Your rights as a tenant depend on which category of tenancy you have. The type of tenancy you have will partly depend on when you moved in, your circumstances and the contract you signed with the landlady. The

The Architect at Home

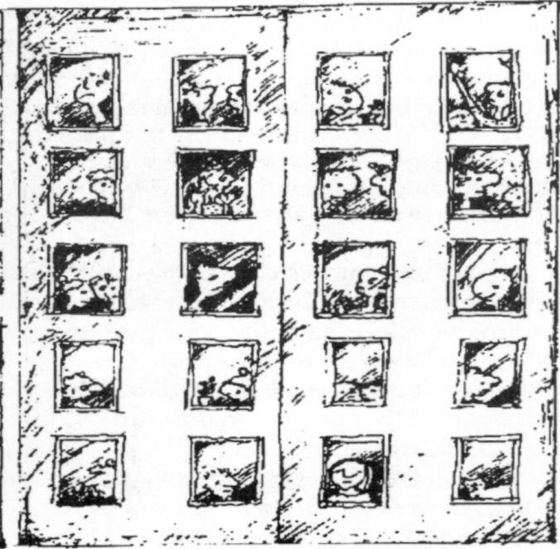

Homes designed by the Architect

law in this area is complicated and it is best to seek advice to determine your status (see **Housing Advice Centres** p212, **Citizens Advice Bureaux** - phone book, or **Law/ General Advice Centres** p207). Since the Rent Act 1988 tenancies started after 15th Jan 1989 are treated differently from those started before that date. **Generally, if you began your tenancy after 15th Jan 1989 you will have less security of tenure than those people who began their tenancies before that date.**

If You Began Your Tenancy Before Jan 15th 1989

Before Jan 15th 1989, as a tenant you could not be evicted without good reason (such as not paying rent) and a court order. This meant that if you did not want leave the landlady could not force you to do so. You were a fully protected tenant

Bogus Arrangements Landladies Used

Landladies were fearful of letting their property and of being stuck with 'sitting tenants'. Many took advantage of loopholes in the law when taking in tenants, such as offering 'company lets' or 'holiday lets'. These type of tenancies offered little security of tenure and as a tenant you could be evicted without good reason (though a court order was needed). The landladies introduced these bogus tenancies to make you a partially protected tenant rather than a fully protected tenant. If however you can prove you have a bogus tenancy, you stand a good chance of becoming a fully protected tenant and of not being evicted.

• **Holiday Let**. This means that the tenancy was of fixed duration for the purposes of a holiday. You were allowed to challenge this agreement if you could show that the landlady knew you were working or that you were not on holiday.

• **Company Let**. An arrangement was made by your company (set up by you) and the landlady.

• **Licenced Let**. You became a licensee rather than a tenant. In this arrangement you must allow others to share the accommodation with anyone the landlady chooses. It was used in genuine instances by hostels.

• **Board services**. You were supposed to receive a moderate amount of food and drink or substantial services such as laundry and cleaning. If you only got some groceries once a week then you could have fought for a protected tenancy.

Proving that there is room to swing a cat

If You Began Your Tenancy after Jan 15th 1989

You will either be an *assured* or *assured shorthold* tenant.

Assured Shorthold Tenancy

The duration of the tenancy is fixed. The period of the tenancy must be for at least six months. To evict you the landlady must give you at least two months notice in writing. A court order is still needed to evict you. This type of tenancy is likely to replace those sham tenancies detailed above.

You are a fully protected tenant for the duration of the tenancy (though there are exceptions).

Assured Tenancy

The duration of the tenancy is not fixed. It is for an indefinite period.

You can only be evicted with a court order. Whether the landlady is able to convince the court that you should be evicted will depend on the grounds for eviction she can put forward. For instance, she may win if a mortgage lender requires vacant possession of the property to sell it. You are a fully protected tenant (though there are exceptions).

Bogus Arrangements

If you have taken one of the bogus arrangements (see above) then you have little security. The landlady can in some cases, put your bags outside and you will not be able to get back in.

Nor are you a fully protected tenant if you have one of the following agreements:

- **Temporary Absence**. The landlady goes away for a short period and lets her accommodation out with intention of returning.
- **Tied**. The accommodation goes with the job. The landlady is also your employer.
- **College**. If you are a student and the college owns your accommodation. In this case you are a licensee rather than a tenant and have to leave when the licence agreement is terminated.
- **Landlady lives on the premises**. You have few rights and the landlady can often evict you without a court order.

Tenant or Licensee?

You may be a licensee rather than a tenant. In most cases a licensee has fewer rights than a tenant. If you are in a flatshare, and you are not the one who signed the tenancy agreement, then you are likely to be a licensee. Check your status and rights with a **Law/Housing Advice Centre**.

Harassment and Illegal Eviction

It is a criminal offence for anyone to force you to leave by intimidating or threatening you. If the landlady interferes with your gas or electricity supply, refuses to take your rent or threatens you then get help from the *Tenancy Relations Officer* at your local Town Hall. You can sue for damages and you can get legal aid for this. If the landlady changes the locks when you are out or refuses to let you back in you can get an injunction (by the next day) to get back in. However, if you began your tenancy after 15th January 1989 and are illegally evicted, and you belong to one of the following you will have difficulties in getting back in: you share your accommodation with the landlady; it's a holiday letting; you are a licensees in a hostel provided by the local council; your rent is free; you are a licensed squatter.

Eviction

If you began your tenancy before 15th Jan 1989 then you do not have to leave any kind of accommodation until a court has granted a possession order to the landlady. So avoid any *Notice to Quit* demand by the landlady. You will be given a chance to be heard in court, but if you have one of the agreements above, where you are not a fully protected tenant then you are likely to lose the case. That is, unless you can prove it was a bogus arrangement. Get advice (see **Housing Advice Centres** p212 or **Law Centres** p207). You will be expected to pay court costs. However it takes a few months for the hearing to come to court so this will give you some time to look around for another place to stay.

If you began your tenancy after 15th Jan 1989 and you are sharing with a landlady and her family, in their only home then, in many cases, the landlady does not need a court order to evict you. The same applies if it is a holiday let.

Rent

You have a right to a rent book if you have a weekly tenancy and if you are not provided with a substantial number of meals. Insist on a rent book if you are a fully protected tenant. See that it is filled in correctly. If the landlady refuses to give you a rent book pay by cheque so that you have a record of payment. This will be useful if the landlady tries to claim you are in arrears when you are not. If the landlady will only take cash try and pay in front of a witness.

'Fair' Rents

If you began your tenancy before 15th Jan 1989 and are a fully protected tenant then you can get the rent fixed to a 'fair and reasonable' rent. Once it is fixed the landlady cannot charge more. If your tenancy began on or after 15th Jan 1989 and your rent is higher than other market rents then you can get it fixed to a comparable market rent. 'Fair' rents are fixed by the Rent Officer (see phone directory). Before applying for a fair rent check the cost of similar properties - the rent could be put up rather than down (though usually it is put down). Also before applying to the rent officer find out if you are a fully protected tenant, because if you are not and the landlady finds out she may deem you a trouble-maker and try to evict you.

Repairs

The landlady is legally obliged to do the repairs. You can get the council to force the landlady to do them if she won't, or you can take the landlady to court to enforce it. Be sure of your tenancy status before you embark on this tactic because if you are not a fully protected tenant you may end up getting evicted (get advice if you are not sure). To get the council to apply pressure phone your local **Environmental Health Officer** (before 10am and after 4pm) and get a home visit. If you wish to take the landlady to court get advice first (see **Law Centres** p207). The second option is the quickest as councils can be slow in forcing the landlady. Do not simply stop paying the rent to force the landlady to do the repairs as rent arrears can be used as an excuse to evict you.

The No Rent Option

Rather than taking the landlady to court or getting the council involved there is another option which is legal - using the rent to pay for the repairs (as long as the cost of repairs is less than a few hundred pounds). This must be done in the following way:

- Give notice in writing to the landlady of the repairs that need doing. Keep a copy of this and all subsequent letters.
- Get an estimate for the repairs from three reputable builders.
- After a reasonable time has elapsed, write another letter stating that the landlady is in breach of obligations and if the work is not done within two weeks you will get the work done and deduct the cost from the rent.
- If there is no response get the work done. Keep all receipts from the contractors. Make sure they are proper receipts.
- Work out how many weeks rent you will be withholding. You will still have to pay other sums due, such as rates and service charges.
- Write to the landlady explaining precisely how the rent deductions will be made.
- Withhold the rent until the cost of repairs has been covered.

You can also withhold some rent for inconvenience and damage done to your property, but don't overdo it.

You must be sure that you are a fully protected tenant before you go ahead with this scheme (seek advice if you are not sure) otherwise it could result in your being evicted.

Council Homes

GETTING A COUNCIL HOME

Council housing is generally cheaper than the private sector and full protection is offered to tenants. Hence there is great demand for this type of housing. The average waiting time is measured in decades, and the problem is getting worse! To get housed you need to score enough 'points'. Points are awarded on the basis of whether you have a family, are old, suffer from ill-health, are overcrowded where you live, etc. If you are young and single you will score hardly any points. The standard of housing varies from a very decent house to a damp flat on a vandalised estate. To be put on the waiting list you must first of all register.

How to Register

The sooner you register the longer the length of time you will have been on the register, and this is taken into account when awarding points. So it is best to register as soon as you can and it is easy to do. Either ring or visit your local town hall and they will tell you how to go about it. You need to be living in the borough to be able to register, but a temporary address is OK. Some boroughs will try to put you off if they think you are low priority, but insist on being registered. Some boroughs require that you re-register every year so ask when you apply.

Waiting

Because councils give priority to those with more points you should remind them of any change in your circumstances. For instance if your health is suffering or you are getting old and vulnerable. If your children have become teenagers and if they are of opposite sex sharing the same bedroom then you could tell the council this is indecent.

Get any official persons or organisations to argue for you. If you are ill get a letter from your GP detailing how your present accommodation is bad for your health. If your present accommodation lacks a bath or inside loo then get you local Environmental Health Officer to write you a letter saying how unhygenic it is. If you are old get a social worker/priest to work for you. The more officials you can muster to argue your case the better. Don't be afraid to make a fuss - this is likely to work in your favour rather than against you.

Each borough has its own allocation policy which is used to decide who gets housed. They are obliged to publish this policy so it's a good idea to get it. You should be able to obtain a copy from the Housing Department.

Other Schemes

Councils irregularly allocate hard-to-let properties to young single people. This type of property is available because others higher up on the waiting list would refuse it as being unsuitable for them. Generally the accommodation is either in high rise blocks (making it unsuitable for children) or on run-down vandalised estates. Enquire at the Housing Department about these schemes.

Some councils offer homes to 'key workers'. These are people that the council wish to keep in the area, perhaps they have skills which are in short supply locally. Ask your council or employer.

Some councils run schemes to keep particular groups in the area, such as sons and daughters of existing council tenants. They may also have some homes available for ex-offenders or those suffering from mental illness.

COUNCIL TENANTS' RIGHTS

Council tenants are fully protected tenants. Those whose tenancies began after 15th Jan 1989 have similar rights to those whose tenancies which began before that date.

To get more information on what your rights contact the **London Housing Unit,** *1st Floor, Berkshire House, 168-173 High Holborn, WC1 (379 7102).* They also have a list of Tenants' Federations who can put you in touch with local Tenants' Associations.

TENANTS' ASSOCIATIONS

Tenants' Associations are often the best way of securing your rights from a large bureaucracy. Each borough has its own tenants federation which keeps a list of local tenants organisations. To find the federation for your borough try **London Housing Unit,** *(379 7102)* (see above) or try the some of the tenants' federations themselves. They should be able to refer you to the federation in your borough. They may also be able to help you set up a tenants' association if you need to. Three of the biggest and most successful are **Hammersmith and Fulham Federation of Tenants and Residents Assoc.,** *217a Ashcroft Square, King St, W6 (748 4114)* , **Camden Federation of Tenants,** *(267 5328)* and **Newham Tenants and Residents Resource Centre,** *7 Queen's Market, E13 (552 5111)* have a good starter pack for those wishing to set up a tenants' association.

■ **Campaign for Homes in Central London,** *5 Dryden St, WC2 (829 8350).* Campaigns for tenants in central London. Seeks to stop the needless office building in the city.

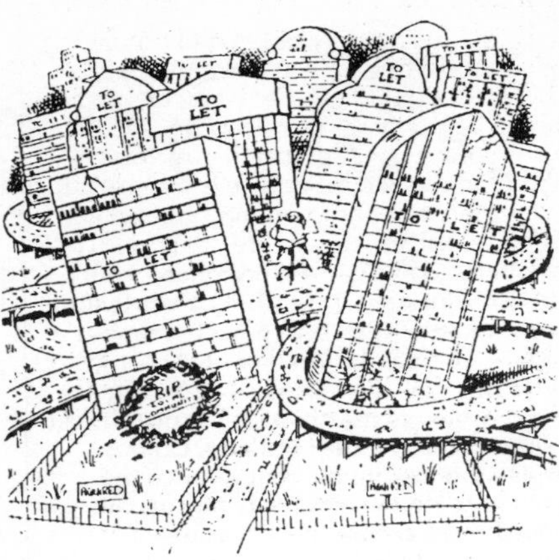

■ **SCAT,** *1 Sidney St, Sheffield S1, (0742 726683).* Keep a database on the privatisation of council housing - for tenants organisations and trade unions. Limited advice but will refer.

REPAIRS

To put pressure on the Council to do repairs you can:

• get your tenants association, or a local councillor to put pressure on them
• take the council to court
• get contractors to do the work and deduct the cost from the rent (see No Rent Option section in Getting a Privately Rented Home)

If the repairs are minor then you can do the work yourself and get reimbursed by the council for this (but take advice first).

Housing Associations

GETTING A HOUSING ASSOCIATION HOME

Housing associations are non-profit making. They get their money from local council and government grants and are all registered with the Housing Corporation, a government body which regulates them. Their allocation policies differ widely because some, for instance, specialise in housing particular groups of people e.g. the elderly, the homeless etc.

They vary in size from those which have only a few properties to those which have several thousands. The rents tend to be only slightly higher than the councils' and tenancy is protected.

They each deal with applications for housing differently. Some will not take you unless you are referred by a council, and others will take you only if you are referred by an an agency e.g. D SS. Yet others will take applications directly. It's worth writing to them yourself. Apply to as many as you wish. The **National Federation of Housing Associations,** *175 Grays Inn Rd, WC1 (278 6571)* sell a directory of Housing Associations and Co-ops in London £10.50 inc p&p as do **HAS,** *(434 1227 (admin no.))* (see p2) £8.95 + 75p p&p.

HOUSING ASSOCIATION TENANTS' RIGHTS

Before the Housing Act 1988 council and housing association tenants had similar rights. Those tenants whose tenancy began after 15th Jan 1989 are treated differently. If your tenancy began before 15th Jan 1989 then you are a fully protected tenant. If your tenancy began after 15th Jan 1989 then you are either an assured tenant or an assured shorthold tenant (depending whether you had and indefinite tenancy or one for a fixed period). Effectively this means that new housing association tenancies are more akin to new private sector tenancies than to council tenancies.

If your tenancy began after 15th Jan 1989 then there is now no guarantee that housing benefit will cover your rent and if you get into arrears it will be easier for the housing association to evict you.

To get information on your rights contact **SHAC,** *(373 7276)* (see p2).

REPAIRS

Housing association tenants have the same rights as tenants of private landlords, but because they are publicly accountable it may be more effective to put pressure on them through a tenants association (see tenants association in **Getting a Council Home** p7). You can carry out minor repairs yourself and get reimbursed (see **Repairs** section in **Getting a Council Home**).

Housing Co-ops

SHORT-LIFE HOUSING

Short-life housing is the name given to the use of property which is awaiting demolition, improvement or repair. Generally the owners are a council or housing association who let the properties on licence to a short-life group. The short-life group then lets the properties on licence to the individuals who comprise the short-life group. The individuals who use the property are therefore licensees rather than tenants.

The life of the property can be as short as six months but usually it ranges from 1-5 years. You do not have any security - you have to move when the landlord wants the property back and you may not be offered alternative accommodation.

The rent tends to be much lower than rents in the private sector, but the property is often in a poor state of repair. You might be expected to put work into repairing the property and bringing it up to a habitable standard, however the property is likely to be in houses with gardens which partly compensates.

It's unlikely that you will get a self-contained property and you will usually have to share a flat/house with others.

Most short life groups only take people without children.

Councils and housing associations prefer to give the property to organisations which are familiar with housing problems such as existing housing co-ops and housing

FOUR MAIN TYPES OF HOUSING CO-OPS

• **Management Co-ops**. Tenants of a HA or Council properties take over and manage their own homes. They can be started by either the landlord proposing to the tenants to take over, or by the tenants themselves making the proposition. Both side however must agree to it. These type of co-ops are presently being encouraged by the government so they are likely to grow in the future.

• **Permanent Private Financed Co-ops.** These co-ops have bought their properties by raising mortgages. The rent covers the mortgage and so may be higher than a fair rent. There are not many of these and the turnover is slow so they don't keep waiting lists. This type is being encouraged by the government so it they likely to grow in the future.

• **Permanent Funded Financed Co-ops.** Financed by a grant system. They tend to be started by existing communities. It takes a long time to get a new one started.

• **Short-Life Co-ops**. These properties are owned by the local Council or HA and the co-op take them over on a temporary basis (see section on **Short-Life Housing**). There are about 200 short-life co-ops in London with an average of 10 to 50 members. Working in short-life can be a useful way of building up experience and skills in managing property and working together in an organisation.

associations, rather than hand them over to a group of individuals who are inexperienced in housing matters (such as those in a squat).

For more information on short-life groups and how to set up a short-life group contact:

■ **Empty Property Unit,** *88 Old St, EC1 (253 0202).* Which helps short life groups establish themselves.

RENTING FROM A HOUSING CO-OPERATIVE

A housing co-operative is a non-profit organisation which runs/owns its properties. It differs from housing associations in that the members comprising the co-op live in the properties they manage.

The rents are used to maintain the property and manage the co-op. The rents are cheaper than in the private sector but it is often difficult to get housed by them as demand is great.

Their membership is open briefly when there is a shortfall in their numbers or when new property becomes available.

Many of them are small and run the day to day business of the co-op on a unpaid basis themselves. So if you write to them don't be surprised if they don't answer. You can assume they don't have any places.

Their allocation policies about who they will house often differ widely from each other. Many positively discriminate towards certain groups, (gays, ethnic minorities, etc). ■ **HAS,** (p2) publish *Housing Association and Co-operative Directory* £8.95 plus 75p p&p which lists the groups the co-ops and HAs gives preference to.

Once invited to a co-op meeting you would be expected to attend several before you could join. This is a useful time for you to see whether it's for you. You may be expected to do co-op work to get housed or to work on one of their properties. If you do work on any of their properties with the hope of being housed it's a gamble. It may not pay off, you might not get housed and there are no consolation prizes.

The other hazard with co-ops is if they end up being poorly managed then the council might revoke the licence on all of the co-op properties and you would end up homeless. Furthermore the co-op is supposed to look after the rights of its members, but if it is poorly managed it may not do so.

SETTING UP A SHORT-LIFE HOUSING CO-OP

To set up a co-op you need at least seven people. They must be prepared to put in a lot of hard work and be committed to working co-operatively. This is the easiest type of co-op to set up, yet it still takes time - at least a few months to get the paperwork together and to gain acceptance. Most short-life co-ops are overseen by secondaries. They help manage the co-ops manage their properties. They act as a go-between between the coop and the council or HA.

■ **Empty Property Unit,** *88 Old St, EC1 (253 0202).* They publish a series of pamphlets explaining various aspects of a co-op with details of how to set up a short life coop, *The Who What Where of Coops, The Legalities of Coops.,* and *Model Agreements for Coops (Tenancies) and Information on the 1988 Housing Act and its Implications for Short-life Housing* (£2.00 + p&p). Provide model rules for coops. Help with negotiating the use of empty property. *Filling the Empties - Short Life Housing and How To Do It* £5.95 + 30p p&p and *Short Life Housing in London - A Guide* £1 +30 p&p.

■ **Housing Corporation,** *149 Tottenham Court Rd, W1 (387 9466).* Provide a free copy of Co-op *Outlines., Tenants' Choice* (free). *Your Power to Choose* (free).

■ **South London Family Housing Association Ltd,** *2 Belvedere Rd, SE19 (653 8833).* are a secondary who will help in setting up co-ops in the South London area.

■ **Solon Co-operative Services,** *233a Kentish Town Rd, NW5 (267 2005)* have tape/slide show: *What is a Housing Co-op?*

■ **National Federation of Housing Co-operatives,** *88 Old St, EC1 (608 2494 or 253 0202).* Provide set of ready made rules for co-ops

■ **Federation of Black Housing Organisations,** *374 Grays Inn Rd, WC1 (837 8288).* Is a national umbrella organisation for Black Housing Projects. It promotes the housing interests of black and other ethnic minority communities; provides advice, training and info to its members and the black community in general.

▼ BUYING ▼

Buying your own home is one solution to the housing crisis. Buying has the advantage that you can claim tax relief (you get this tax relief even if you are not working), you don't have a landlord, and the cost of mortgage repayments may work out cheaper than renting from the private sector. However it can be problematic - repayments, which are fixed to the interest rate vary and they may go up, pushing up your repayments to a sum you cannot afford; you may want to sell and find that there is no demand and either have to wait a long time before finding a buyer or selling off cheap; you will need to let some years lapse before you sell otherwise all the expenses incurred in buying and selling make it unprofitable (unless house prices have gone up dramatically).

Initial costs are high and so you need capital before you begin. You also need to be on a high salary and secure in your job.

At interest rates of 13% and a 25 year mortgage then repayments work out at approximately £10 per £1000 per month, so if you borrow £60,000 you pay back £10 x 60 = £600 per month. With tax relief this works out to £510 per month. On top of this you need to add ground rent, rates, repairs etc.

Because buying a home is likely to be one of the biggest purchases you will ever make you need to be careful because it can be a minefield for the unwary.

See *Which Way to Buy Sell and Move House* (£9.95) **Consumers Association**. *Buying Owning and Selling a Flat* (£6.95) Consumers Association. *Buying a Home* SHAC (£1.70). *Buying Owning and Selling a Flat* (£6.95) Which? and *Where to Live in London* (£7.95) describes the different areas and properties in London.

The size of the loan you will get from a building society or bank will be directly related to your salary. You should be able to get a loan that is 3 times you salary i.e. a £15,000 salary should be able to command a loan of £15,000 x 3 = £45,000. If you are buying with a partner then both your salaries are taken into account. Lenders differ in the formulas they use to compute the size of the loan but a typical sum is three times the larger of your salaries plus the salary of the partner, i.e. If you are on £15,000 and your partner is on £10,000 then you could get a loan of £15,000 x 3 = £45,000 + £10,000 = £55,000.

You will need to have some capital before you begin. It's likely you will only get a 95% mortgage which means that you have to find the other 5% yourself. On a £60,000 flat this would be £3000. You will also have to find money for: registration fees (under £100), stamp duty (£600), solicitors fees (£600 approx), valuation and surveyors fees (£150-£300), insurance (£90 p.a.) and finally setting up costs such as furniture. So unless you can get a 100% mortgage you are likely to need about £5000.

Don't treat buying a house as an investment, think of it as more of a place to live, otherwise it's easy to get euphoric about how much money you will make, and then end up overstretched and repossessed. It's probably better to go for somewhere that's cheap in an unfashionable area than to overstretch yourself by getting too big a mortgage. It could be disastrous if both of you need to work to pay the mortgage and you get pregnant. It makes having a London mortgage the best form of contraception.

The **London Research Centre**, *Parliament House, 81 Black Prince Rd, SE1 (735 4250)* publish *House Price Bulletin* Qtly (£25 pa or £10 per copy) which gives a breakdown of house prices by borough from which you can find out the cheapest area to buy. The cheapest boroughs at the moment are Barking and Newham.

Mortgages

You should choose your mortgage with care. For arguments for and against different types see the latest report in *Which?* magazine (from your local library). *Which Way to Buy Sell and Move House* £9.95 has a good section on mortgages, and is a good comprehensive guide.

There are brokers who specialise in getting mortgages for particular groups such as self-employed. If you are self-employed it is usually harder to get a mortgage and you have to show you are getting regular earnings.

Conveyencing

You can do it yourself. You do not need to consult a solicitor. See *The Conveyencing Fraud*, Michael Joseph. Or you could use one of the cut-price agencies:

- **Ashfords**, *44 London Rd, Kingston-upon-Thames, Surrey, (549 3180).*
- **House Owners' Conveyancers**, *109 Cricklewood Broadway, NW2 (452 6622).*

Shared Home-Ownership

Run by some councils and housing associations. You take out a loan to buy a share in the value of the property (typically between 25 and 90 per cent) and pay rent on the remaining share. Under most schemes you have a right to buy out the remaining share in stages or in one go. These often don't work out any cheaper than buying a cheaper property with a full mortgage and anyway, you're liable for all of the repairs. Contact the **Housing Corporation**, *(387 9466)* (see p10) for details of housing association schemes.

Right To Buy

With certain exceptions council tenants and housing association tenants (before 15th Jan 1989) have a right to buy the property they are living in. You need to have been a tenant for two years (though not necessarily of the property you live in). You get a discount for the length of time you have been a public sector tenant. The discount starts at 32 per cent of the value of the property for the first two years and one per cent for every year thereafter up to a maximum of 60 per cent. It's better still if you are a flat occupier. The discount starts at 44 per cent with an additional two per cent per year thereafter, up to a maximum of 70 per cent. You cannot sell straight away as you lose some/all of the discount.

Homesteading

Run by some local councils. You buy a run-down property and do the work on it to bring it up to standard. Your mortgage payments are deferred for a few years. The cost of the property is low but it will cost a lot for the work unless you do it yourself.

Grants

Grants are given by local councils. They can be claimed by house owners, tenants and landlords, though to qualify you must fulfill a number of conditions. The grant covers a percentage of the cost of the work - between 20 to 65 per cent. You normally can't get a grant for work you have already started.

There are two types of grants - mandatory and discretionary. If you need a basic amenity installed such as an inside toilet, bath, wash basin, hot and cold water then you are likely to get a mandatory grant known as an intermediate grant.

Discretionary grants are given when the council has not run out of funds, which is less often these days. Such grants are: improvement grants - towards major improvements or for converting a house to flats; repair grants - for structural repair to houses built before 1919; special grants - these are for landlords only for installing basic amenities or safety improvements such as fire escapes.

Insulation Grants

Some people can claim towards the cost of insulating lofts, hot water tanks and pipes. You qualify if you are getting income support from the DHSS, Family Credit or Housing Benefit. You can claim 90 per cent towards the cost of the work or £137 whichever is the lower amount. Details from the council or from CABx.

▼ SQUATTING ▼

Squatting can be a solution to the housing problems of people who don't qualify for public housing and can't afford to buy a place or pay the extortionate rents asked by private landladies. It can also be the answer for people who have spent years on council waiting lists without a home of their own. Squatting is a way of using houses that would otherwise stay empty while the bureaucrats quibble over statistics and people stay homeless.

With the present cuts in public spending, housing authorities are finding it hard to carry out many of their planned improvements, resulting in even more houses and flats being left empty. So it's up to us to beat the cuts by squatting houses that would otherwise be left to deteriorate or sold off to speculators.

Most people have no experience of doing house repairs when they first squat, but it's something everyone can learn - the same goes for fighting for rehousing. Squatting gives many people not only the chance of a decent home for the first time, but also the opportunity to develop skills they might not otherwise be able to learn, to increase their confidence in dealing with officialdom and to question the power of those in authority. Often we discover they only wield as much power as we let them have.

Direct action is better than any waiting list. If you are homeless and have tried all the accepted ways of getting a home, don't be afraid of taking matters into your own hands instead of letting the system grind you down.

Everyone has a right to a home, and if others can squat, so can you!

Take control of your own life instead of being pushed around by bureaucrats and property owners who are more concerned with money and status than with the quality of people's lives or their happiness.

Squatting is Still Legal

Squatting is not a crime, with a few exceptions if you can get into a house or flat which is unoccupied you can make it your home.

This section offers you a brief outline of the law and practise involved. If after reading it you decide to squat get hold of a copy of the *Squatters Handbook* which will give you much more information. This and any other advice you need is available from the **Advisory Service for Squatters (A.S.S.)** (see p16)

Finding a Place

Despite the property boom and the sales of council housing stock finding empty places is not that difficult particularly in the boroughs of Inner London.

It can however involve a lot of leg work. Local squatting groups can help you get started with lists of empty property and advice directly related to the area that they operate in. These groups are local squatters coming together to share knowledge and experience. They are not alternative estate agents. They can give you invaluable advice and certainly can point you in the right direction but after that it's up to you. Addresses of these groups available from **A.S.S.** (see p16)

Start walking around estates and streets looking for suitable empties. Council and housing association properties are generally a safer bet, as these authorities are more likely to stick to the law and less likely than private owners to send heavies around to evict you. Also they usually have a lot more squatters and a lot less money so the chances of a longer life in your squat are greatly increased. This is not to say don't squat private places just do so more cautiously. Identifying empty property is easily done, with empties usually secured with either boards or steel doors and shutters on windows and other entrances. Some owners put up curtains and leave lights on to make places look more lived in. Look out for lights that never go out and through net curtains. Once you have found somewhere, find out as much as possible about it before going in. Who are the owners? How long has it been empty? Is it newly renovated, completely trashed or likely to have been allocated? All these factors effect how long your likely to stay in a place.

Property that is newly renovated and in a desirable area is much more likely to be pre-allocated (see P.I.O. p14), than a run down flat on a hard to let estate. Even if you're not P.I.O.ed, the owner will act quicker to get you out of let-able stock than out of places awaiting renovation. You don't have to live in a slum, in fact a lot of people squat to improve their housing conditions, but it's important to realistic. An extra couple days spent doing your own decorating can be worth the trouble.

If you are unsure about who owns the property you can go to the borough planning department, usually at the town hall and ask to see the statutory register of planning consent for the street the property is in. It is a public document and you have the right to see it but if you get hassled tell them you live in the street and you want to know what's happening with the property. This register lists all applications for planning permission and will usually contain the owners name as well as details about work due to commence.

Getting In

Over the last few years, owners (particularly local authorities) have increased their security measures to keep squatters out by using steel doors and shutters and in some cases even security guards! However people are still getting in so don't be deterred, not only are these armours penetrable but a lot of empties are hardly secured at all. Squatters are sometimes arrested or threatened with arrest for Criminal Damage. Criminal damage in its strictest possible interpretation is an offence which almost all squatters commit. Removing steel doors, boards, damaging the front door when changing a lock, even taking out broken parts of the house can be considered to be criminal damage. But don't let all that worry you as only a small amount of squatters ever get busted and with good legal advice they often get off.

Before getting in it's best if you can work out the best way to gain access and the time when you'll get least hassle doing so. Some places are virtually impossible to get into without making a noise and alerting the neighbours. In this case do it at a sensible time of day - most people get a bit jumpy if they hear suspicious noises at night. It can be a good idea to try and get the support of neighbours. Explain why you're homeless, you may get a surprisingly sympathetic response.

When getting in, take as few tools as possible, most importantly a yale lock and a screwdriver. Never open up a place by yourself, get in touch with a local squatting group or **A.S.S.** (see p16) to get others to squat with. Standing up for your rights and cleaning up a filthy flat is much easier with a few of you. Once inside change the lock and secure all entrances. Until you have control over who comes in and out, you do not have possession and can be evicted straight away if the owner or the police come around.

Dealing With The Police

As squatting is a civil matter and not a criminal offence the police should rarely get involved. The one time that they might though, is shortly after you've got into an empty. If they do call don't let them in if you can avoid it. However, the police do have a right to enter and if they suspect that someone inside has committed or is about to commit an 'arrestable offence' (this means most serious offences), they don't even need a warrant. Tell them that you're homeless and that you didn't damage anything when you entered and that your occupation is a civil matter between you and the owner. If you are polite, firm and make it clear that you know what you're talking about hopefully they'll go away. If they persist though you could point out that if they evict you they might be committing an offence under Section 6 Criminal Law Act (below).

Your Legal Position

Section 6, Criminal Law Act

By law you are only squatting when you are actually in occupation of a property. If you go out the owners have the right to break in and repossess the property in your absence. Section 6 protects you from this when you are in. It makes it a possible offence for anyone to use or threaten to use violence to get into any house or flat if there is a person who objects to them coming in, and if they know there is someone who objects.

In principle this means that someone should be in all of the time. In practise this action is used only occasionally, usually against isolated and unorganised squats in the first few days after a squat has been opened. So it is important to have someone in all the time for the first week or so or until some contact is made with the owner. **A.S.S.** (p16) prints a legal warning which outlines the details of the act and warns anyone who may be tempted to break it that they can be prosecuted and receive a sentence of up to six months imprisonment and or a fine of up to £2,000. It might be worth putting one of these up on your door if it seems likely that your going to get hassled. It's a good idea to keep a copy just inside as well, to quote at anyone threatening you with eviction.

PROTECTED INTENDED OCCUPIER (P.I.O.)

Section 7 Criminal Law Act, 1977.

There are two kinds of P.I.O. s - the first kind has to own the property concerned and have bought it or leased it, with at least 21 years of the lease left to run. They must intend to live in the place themselves and not to rent or sell it. If the P.I.O. inherited it or was given it this section doesn't apply. When you are asked to leave, the P.I.O. or person acting on their behalf, has to have with them a written statement, sworn

before a magistrate or solicitor, stating that they have bought the house or flat and intend to live in it. Making a false statement as a P.I.O. is an offence punishable by up to 6 month's in prison and/or a fine of £2,000. Private P.I.O.s are virtually never used.

The second type of P.I.O. is someone who has been allocated a house or flat by a council or housing association.

A genuine P.I.O. is a person who :

• has been 'authorised to occupy' the place 'as a residence'. They must have signed a tenancy agreement or been given a licence to be there.

• has been issued with a certificate by the council or housing association. The certificate must say it has been issued by one of these bodies and that the person named on it has been authorised to occupy the place as a residence.

• is excluded from occupation by someone who entered as a trespasser. This means that someone who previously had permission to live in the place, whether from the council, housing association or an earlier tenant cannot be got out with a P.I.O. certificate. The procedure can only be used against people who have been squatters since the day they moved in.

A person is a P.I.O. only when all these three things apply at the same time. The P.I.O. must be able to move in straight away, this means that if the property has serious structural damage, is due to be renovated or has anything wrong with it that will take longer than a week or so to repair then this Act shouldn't apply.

Usually an officer of the council or housing association comes round on the basis that they are acting on behalf of the P.I.O. Very often this isn't true. Ask to see some form of authorisation signed by the P.I.O. agreeing to the council or housing association acting on their behalf. You don't have a right to see this but at least you can try and determine whether they are acting for a P.I.O. or themselves. You must be shown or posted a copy of the P.I.O. certificate, always insist on seeing this. If you don't leave they can come back with the police and you can be arrested and charged with an offence under Section 7.

P.I.O.s are frequently used and widely abused and fiddled by some councils. Don't be conned, if you have any doubts to its validity stay put and contact **A.S.S.** (p16) immediately.

DISPLACED RESIDENTIAL OCCUPIER (D.R.O.)

Sections 7 & 12 Criminal Law Act, 1977.

If you do not leave a house or flat after being asked to do so by or on behalf of a displaced residential occupier of the premises you could be guilty of an offence.

This part of Section 7 is hardly ever used. It was supposedly brought in to prevent squatters moving into people's homes while they were on holiday or even out shopping! Since squatters don't do this, it shouldn't be a problem. Do check carefully, however, to make sure anywhere you are thinking of squatting really is empty. Some people live with very few possessions and others don't manage or choose to get together the usual sort of domestic arrangements.

An unscrupulous private owner such as a landlord owning several houses may try to claim that they were living in an empty house you have squatted. If this happens get in touch with **A.S.S.** or a law centre immediately. This section doesn't apply if you have, or have ever had, permission to be in the house.

Services

This section explains how to get your Electricity and Gas supplies connected and how to deal with the boards that run these services. For information on getting a water supply and repairs you might have to do on your squat see **Getting the Place Together** (p17).

ELECTRICITY AND GAS

Once you are in, it is important to sign on for electricity and gas supplies quickly, before the owner has time to contact the boards to tell them not to connect you. You do this by going to the nearest showrooms, but there can be problems with this if they suspect you are squatting. The best way to avoid awkward questions is not to have any direct contact with the board's staff. Pick up a connection application form. Fill it in at home and put it through the letterbox after the showroom has closed.

If you do sign in person try to avoid telling the staff that you're squatting, because if they find out they'll probably ask you for a deposit, usually £100. You might be able to get round this by asking to have a budget meter installed or by applying to go on the budget scheme. If at your previous address the account was in your name and there are no outstanding bills, point this out. It should convince them that you're the honest sort.

The law concerning squatters getting connected is extremely uncertain but it's the present policy of most boards to supply unless the owners have given them instructions to the contrary.

Organising

Once you've got you're squat together don't stop there. Get in touch with other squatters. If there's a local group in your area why not get involved. Or if there isn't and there's enough of you - form your own. With over 30,000 squatters in London these groups have their hands full. So obviously, the more people who get involved the better the service they will give.

Evictions

The first warning that you might get of any action being taken against you, could be a visit by the owner or representative. Ask to see their identification and note the name, address and telephone number. They will probably say something like 'You are living here without our permission and you must leave'. Make a note of everything said, and the date. This might be useful evidence in court, especially if you're told that you can stay until a specific time, as this amounts to a licence, and will have to be ended before proceedings can start. More often though, the first warning will be a letter rather than a visit. It will say the same sort of things and that you should leave in 7 days or legal proceedings will be taken against you. Don't panic about such a letter as it has no legal significance and doesn't necessarily mean you'll even be taken to court. Sometimes the first warning will be the summons itself. This is the document that informs you of the hearing and must give you at least 5 days notice.

The hearing is held in a civil court so it's up to you whether you attend or not. The only argument that the judge is likely to listen to is a legal one. The fact that you might have spent a lot of energy, time and money making a 'derry' habitable probably won't get you anywhere. Sometimes you're better off finding another place, than putting energy into a court case that sooner or later will go against you. On the other hand though, if you have got a good legal argument and the hearing gets dismissed, you could get an extra 6 months in your squat.

Whether you fight the case or not it's important to remember that you won't get evicted on the same day that the owners are granted a possession order. This is because in London, due to the high number of actions in the civil courts, there is a waiting list for the bailiffs. Bailiffs carry out the directives of the court e.g. evictions. Owners can't carry out possession orders themselves. Sometimes you'll receive notice of the eviction by way of a letter but you shouldn't depend on this. You can find out when the bailiffs are due, by phoning the court where the hearing took place and asking them. You will need the case number for this information, which is on the summons you've received.

For more information about fighting court cases contact

■ **Advisory Service for Squatters,** *2 St. Pauls Rd, N1 (359 8814).* Open 2-6 Mon-Fri phone or drop in. Legal and practical advice for squatters and homeless people. They will put you in touch with a local squatting group. Get yourself a copy of their essential *Squatters Handbook* (60p, but may be going up slightly in price). Include SAE. Very good value.

▼ HELP WITH HOUSING ▼

■ **Barnet Housing Aid Centre,** *Friern Park Centre, 1 Friern Park, N12 (446 2504).* Mon-Th 9.30-1, Tue 5-7, Fri 1-4 . Most problems inc. homelessness, but especially landlord and tenant. Gujerati spoken.

■ **Brent Housing Aid Centre,** *Hampton House, 1b Dyne Rd, NW6 (908 7401).* Mon-Fri 9.30-12.

■ **Bromley Housing Advice Centre,** *United Reformed Church, Widmore Rd, Bromley, (313 3375).* M-F 9.30-4.30. Refers people needing expert advice.

■ **Croydon Housing Aid Society,** *10a Station Rd, West Croydon, (688 7900).* Mon-Thu 9.30-4. Landlady/tenant, council problems.

■ **Deptford Housing Aid Centre,** *171 Deptford High St, SE8 (691 1602).*

■ **Ealing Housing Aid Service,** *(840 1886).*

■ **Housing Action Centre,** *140 Ladbroke Grove, W10 (969 2433).* Mon 9.30-1, Wed 3-6.30, Fri 1-4.30, Sat 9.30-12. Other times by appointment. Independent. Private and council/housing ass tenants. For tenants in Kensington, Chelsea, Paddington and North Westminster.

■ **Threshold,** *101a Tooting High St, SW17 (682 0321/2).* Mon 10.-12.30, Tue 2.30-6.30, Fri 10-12.30. Similar to HAS but for people in Wandsworth. Advise single homeless people and couples without children.

■ **Threshold,** *126 Uxbridge Rd, W12 (749 2925).* Mon 10-1, Tu 2-6.45, Fri 10-1. As above but for people living or working in Hammersmith.

getting your place together

this section attempts to help the DIY novice to accomplish a few basic installation and repairs commonly needed in short life properties or squatting. It only deals with minor repairs and installation, rather than covering major works.

Tools/Materials for Gas and Water Plumbing

BUYING

Many of these can be bought second hand and in fact it's better to buy good second-hand than cheap brands new. Try Islington second-hand tool shop, **Cross Street**, N1 (Angel Tube); **Brick Lane Market** , **East St. Market** (see p67). *Loot* often advertises second-hand tools for sale and other markets sometimes sell them.

Chinese tools are better than Korean or Taiwanese, which sometimes don't do the job at all. For materials try junk yards and cheap and cheerful shops that look tacky but can offer some real bargains. Also check in skips. It's amazing what people throw away.

SOME BASIC TOOLS NEEDED FOR GAS AND WATER PLUMBING

Diagram 1

WHAT YOU NEED

See diagram 1. Blow torch; Stillson wrench (footprints); adjustable spanners; screwdrivers, Philips (cross) and straight; solder, flux, wire wool or sandpaper; pipe cutters; junior hacksaw; file; bending spring (for 15mm copper pipe); P.T.F.E. tape; plumbers mait (non setting putty); Denso tape (thick green waxy tape for bodge ups); pipe jointing compound (Hawkwhite).

▼ PLUMBING ▼

Water plumbing and gas plumbing are very similar in terms of tools, materials and joints used. Much of what is written on the sections on water plumbing can be applied to gas plumbing- but there is one big difference - it's a lot more dangerous working with gas and great care should be taken. It is best only to carry out gas plumbing when you have familiarised yourself with water plumbing.

Water Plumbing

Plumbing used to be a very lengthy and skilled trade to learn, but in this age of D.I.Y. and new easier and cheaper materials, like copper and plastic, it's much easier for anyone without any experience to have a go.

All you need is a basic understanding of the domestic plumbing layout. When it comes to gas plumbing, more caution and experience is required.

DIRECT/INDIRECT SUPPLY

The cold water supply will come into your home in either a direct or indirect system. All this means is that if the water supply system is direct it will be subject to mains pressure, i.e. there will be no cistern (tank) in the loft or on the roof. This means there is safe drinking water at all the outlets (bathroom as well as kitchen).

If it is an indirect system there will be a cistern in the loft or on the roof, supplying all cold water taps, toilet cisterns etc. except for the kitchen sink, which will be the only source of safe drinking water. The other water will have been stored.

If you live in a block of flats, it will almost certainly have indirect supply, as there is often a large storage cistern in the loft or on the roof, serving all the flats.

If you're not sure and you don't want to go hunting for a cistern in the loft, try and put your thumb under the cold water tap in the bathroom. If you can hold the water back, it is supplied from a cistern. If the pressure is too great, this means it's mains supply and there is no cistern.

This is important to know. For example, if you want to do a repair, you can't just turn the water off under the stairs when there's a cistern full of water in the loft - it will come pouring down. There should be a valve on the outlet from the cistern.

On toilet cisterns there are either high pressure or low pressure ball valves depending on whether it is fed by a direct or indirect system - see ballvalves for more info.

TURNING THE WATER ON/OFF

From Outside the House

The mains stopcock (which is the Water Authority's responsibility) is found outside the garden wall and is under a cast iron cover over a 2-3 foot hole, which can be lifted up using a screwdriver.

The old type and still the most common is a box type end valve.

You need a special key to turn it on or off, which is a box spanner on the end of a rod. See diagram 2. These can be bought from certain plumbing merchants for around a fiver. An alternative is to use an extended socket spanner.

To make a water board key, use a piece of half inch iron pipe. Make a cut accross the end of the pipe, and cut down about 1 inch. Use a cold chisel and hammer, open up this cut and bang into shape so you roughly have a square shape end on the pipe. This should fit over the end of a water board stop cock, and can be turned using a stillsons wrench.

Diagram 2

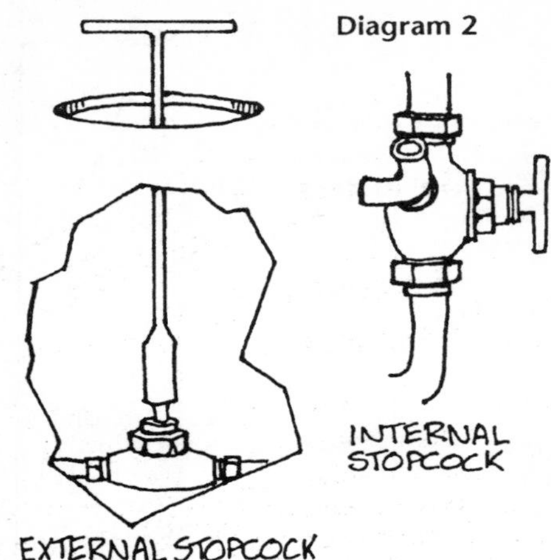

The new type of extended stop valve is called a crutch head and is a similar valve to the inside stop valve. Sometimes it is possible to stretch your arm down and turn it. Otherwise some plumbers' merchants now sell crutch head keys.

A key can be made by cutting a 'V' shape in a long piece of wood.

The inside stop valve is the responsibility of the householder. It can be turned by hand. Sometimes these can get seized up. Don't force it! It may need lubricating by a spray of Plusgas or WD40, or you can use grips.

When turning stop valves full on, turn them clockwise a little (towards 'off' position) so there is a little leverage if they do get stuck.

The Water Board will turn your water on for you once you've registered for water rates.

From Inside the House

When first checking out the cold water supply in the house, make sure there are no open pipe ends. Sometimes councils, housing associations and builders etc, will break off pipes to prevent people from squatting places. See 'Pipes and Fittings' (p 20) for ways of capping off any open ends.

First try the internal stop valve. See diagram 2. If there's no water then try the external one. See 'From Outside the house' (above).

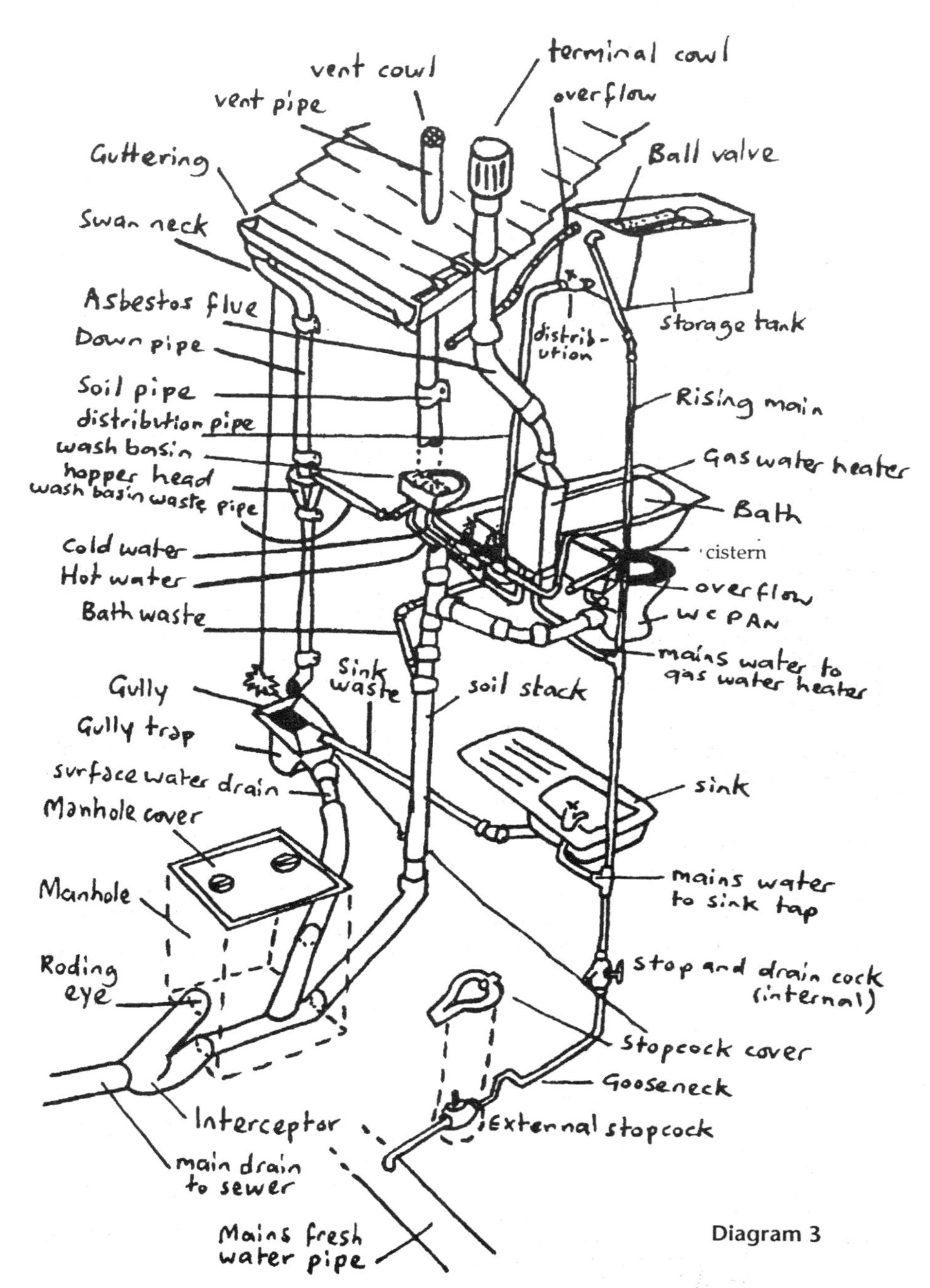
DOMESTIC PLUMBING
vent cowl
terminal cowl
vent pipe
overflow
Guttering
Ball valve
Swan neck
Asbestos flue
storage tank
Down pipe
distribution
Soil pipe
Rising main
distribution pipe
wash basin
Gas water heater
hopper head
wash basin waste pipe
Bath
cistern
Cold water
Hot water
overflow
Bath waste
WC PAN
mains water to gas water heater
Sink waste
Gully
soil stack
Gully trap
sink
surface water drain
Manhole cover
mains water to sink tap
Manhole
Roding eye
stop and drain cock (internal)
Stopcock cover
Gooseneck
Interceptor
External stopcock
main drain to sewer
Mains fresh water pipe

Diagram 3

DIFFERENT TYPES OF PIPE

Copper Pipe

Comes in 3m lengths and costs around £3. Some plumbers merchants sell 1m lengths, so check. Sizes are 15mm, 22m and 28mm upwards. Mostly, you will come across 15mm or perhaps 22m on larger houses and hot water systems. It is used for both hot and cold water supply and gas. Copper can be joined by solder (capillary) or compression joints. See diagram 4. These joints can be straight, elbows, 'Ts' etc. and caps are available for capping off a pipe run. If you've not done soldering before, you can buy the fitting with solder already in (often called 'Yorkshire' fittings) which makes it easier.

Diagram 4

CAPILLARY JOINT

OLIVE

COMPRESSION JOINT

Joining Copper Pipe

1. Clean the ends of the pipes and the inside of the fittings (or joints) with wire wool.
2. Apply a little flux paste over the pipe ends and push the fitting on.
3. Heat the joint with a blow lamp until you see a silver ring appear. Now you know the solder has run and you can take the blowlamp away.

The other types of fittings for soldering are called 'end feed' and are cheaper to buy, but you will have to add your own solder. Clean and flux the pipes as described above. Assemble the joint. Have your blow lamp in one hand and solder in the other. Heat the joint up and then keep touching it with the solder until it is hot enough to run. When you do this, take the flame away as it should be the heat of the metal that makes the solder run, not the flame itself. The solder should run all the way round the joint, through capillary attraction. *Soldered joints will work only if they are* ***clean, dry*** *and if there is enough* ***heat***. Compression joints are far easier for the novice although they are a lot more expensive to buy. See Diagram 5. Clean off the flux from the soldered joint with wire wool.

Bending Copper Pipe

Simple bends can be made by using a bending spring, these cost around £1.50 to buy (for 15mm pipe) (see diagram 6).

Iron pipe (also called 'gas barrel')

Used for gas pipe, it's black and has threaded ends. Threaded fittings are used to join it

Diagram 6

...BEND PIPE OVER KNEE...

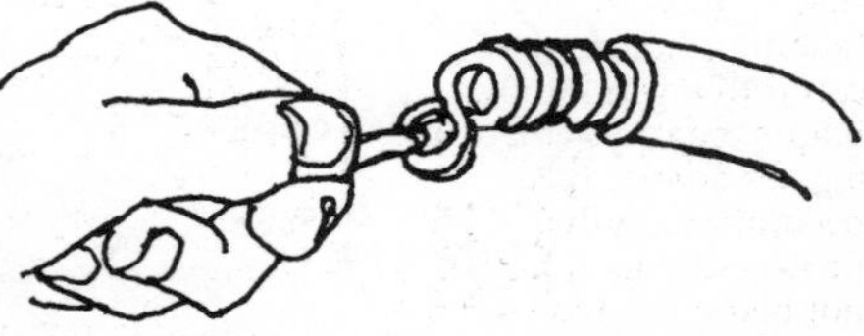

...AND REMOVE SPRING.

together. External threads are known as 'male' and internal 'female'. (See Diagram 2a)

Occasionally in domestic premises,

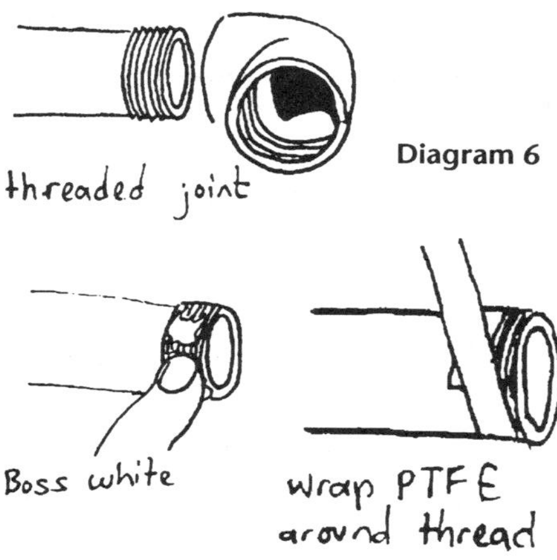

Diagram 6

galvanized steel pipes are used for water (mostly in public or industrial places). These are grey and are zinc coated to protect them from corrosion. Galvanized fittings should be used.

When joining threaded pipes together, a plastic tape called P.T.F.E. tape is used or a jointing paste 'Hawkwhite' to help seal the joint. (See diagram 6). When joining on to gas pipe it is best to continue on with copper

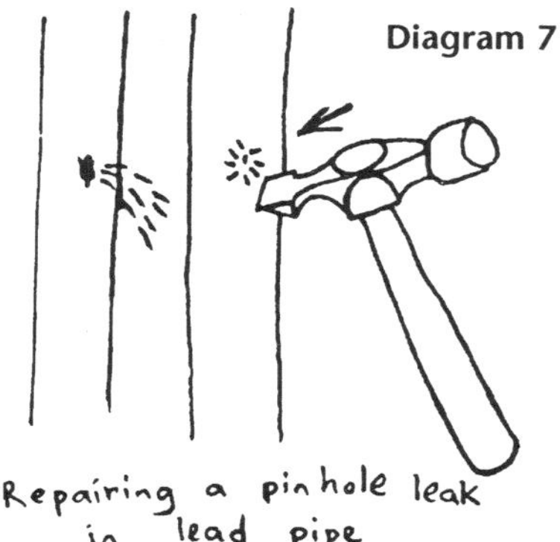

Diagram 7

pipe. An iron to copper connection can be bought from many plumbers merchants to do this.

Lead Pipe

Lead pipe is very soft, heavy grey pipe. Although this is no longer installed there is plenty to be found in old flats and houses on the incoming main.

If a small hole or crack is found on a lead pipe, you can sometimes cover it over by gently tapping the lead with a hammer to 'move' the lead over, as it is very soft and pliable. (See diagram 7). If the lead pipe is leaking or you would like to continue with copper pipe, there is a great new invention used to join lead to copper pipe called a 'leadloc'. It is a compression joint. They cost around £6-£7 to buy and most plumbers' merchants stock them. Lead pipe can be easily cut using a hacksaw and the joints usually come with assembly instructions. (See diagram 5).

Plastic Pipe (poly pipe) - For Cold Water Supply

Blue plastic pipe, which the water board use for main services is very useful for short-life work. It is a good alternative to copper pipe

Diagram 8

compression joint for pol'

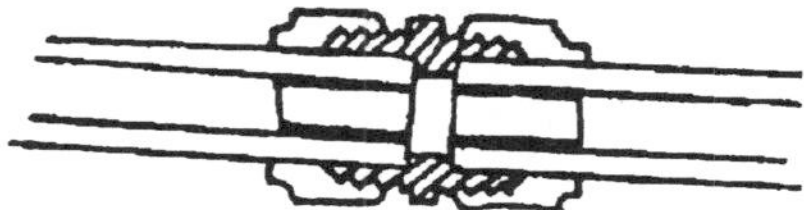

and if there's a lot of work to be done, will work out a lot cheaper. It comes in rigid coils of 25m which cost about £10 available from **Diamond Plumbers Merchants,** *Acre Lane, Brixton SW9*. Some plumbers sell it by the metre, **H.E. Olby** in Lewisham *(690 3401)* charge 65p a metre.

Because it comes in coils you don't have to use many elbow fittings. It's best to buy 20mm diameter pipe which is quite adequate to supply most appliances. It can be clipped using 22mm copper pipe clips (Diagram 8).

Brass compression joints can be used or chunky plastic fittings. The plastic ones are easier to use. They don't need much tightening with a spanner after you've hand-tightened them. Prices of these fittings are:

Inserts (needed for each pipe to be joined) 29p

Straight poly-poly joint £1.59

Poly to 1/2 inch male iron £1.43 (the 'male iron' is an external threaded piece which can be joined on to a copper compression fitting).

Poly to 1/2 inch female iron £1.96 (can be used to connect on to a threaded stem of tap).

Poly pipe - equal 'T' £2.78

Poly pipe - elbow £2.08

For a long pipe run where not many joints are needed poly pipe will work out cheaper, but in other circumstances copper pipe may be better.

Poly pipe can be cut easily with a hacksaw. It should be used only for cold water supply.

Diagram 9

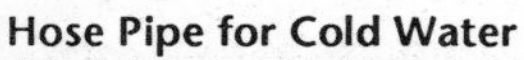

Hose Pipe for Cold Water

A brief, but valuable mention can be made here of using hosepipe in short life properties.

Only use the cross-hatched (thick walled) garden hose. This should take mains pressure, but not forever. You may have to experiment.

You can use special hose pipe joints if you can get hold of them.. But another way is to force a piece of 15mm copper pipe into the hose pipe, and tighten a jubilee clip (available from hardware stores) over it. (If this proves too difficult, dip the hose pipe end into hot water to soften it). Then use soldered/compression joints for copper pipe to join on to it (tees, cap ends) (see diagram 9).

Transparent, flexible plastic pipe can also be used. Joints can be made in a similar way, but use an olive (the brass ring found in compression joints, it can be bought separately for about 10p) and use fine, electrical solder. Solder or stick with Araldite glue. Then force the transparent pipe over the olive and tighten the jubilee clip behind the olive.

Use soldered/compression joints on the copper pipe. This transparent pipe is available in various sizes. Use the size slightly bigger than 15mm copper pipe. You can get transparent pipe from **Camberwell Tool Centre,** *124 Camberwell Rd, SE5.*

FIXING THE LOO

Cracked Pan or Leak

If you find that the pan's cracked or is filled with concrete (a supposed deterrent to squatters) you will have to replace the whole pan. They are quite costly if bought new (about £25-30) but you can get them second-hand. There are two main types: 'S' trap and 'P' trap, which describes the shape of the soil pipe at the back. An 'S' trap is usually needed if the pipe goes into the floor and a 'P' trap if it goes into the wall. You may need a shape that is less common than these. If the pan has to fit in an awkward space and have its pipe running sideways. The best bet is *Loot*, which is good for anything second-hand. Sometimes perfectly good pans can be found on skips.

The pan will either be screwed to the floor or cemented in. The soil pipe connection could also be cemented in.

Using a cold chisel and hammer, carefully break up the pan to remove it. (See diagram 10). Be especially careful not to break the ceramic collar around the soil pipe connection if this is cemented in. If you do break it, you can buy a new one and fit it by inserting the pipe, putting damp brown paper down into the bottom of the gap between the two, and

Diagram 10

filling up with quick-drying cement. When you have got the pan separated from the pipe, put some rags in the pipe to stop any loose pieces falling down and blocking it.

Diagram 11

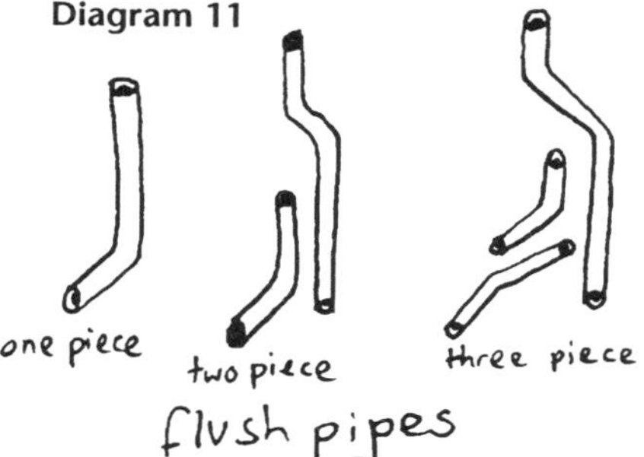

To fit a new pan, you will have to cement it in if the floor is concrete, making a bed of cement under the base. A small bag of Readymix cement will be enough. If the floor is wood, the pan will need to be screwed down. If it is wet or rotten, put a new board down first.

You can now buy a rubber pan connector called 'multi-kwick', which are easy to use. This connects the soil pipe to the pan. Swarfega or washing up liquid can be used to lubricate them if necessary.

The pipe carrying water from the cistern to the pan is called the flush pipe (see diagram 11) and the connection between this pipe and the pan is called the flush cone. They shouldn't leak, but if there are any problems 'Plumbers Mait' is great stuff to seal it. You can also use it for any leak around the soil pipe or for sink wastes, but not for any pipe carrying water under pressure. It's a putty which doesn't set. The surfaces must be clean and dry before applying it. Another good bodge material is 'Denso Tape', which is thick waxy tape and can be wrapped around leaky wastes. It's main use is to protect pipes going through walls from corrosion. (See Diagram 10).

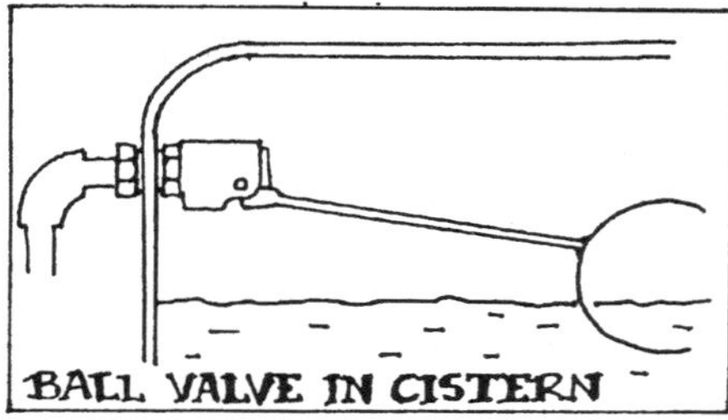

Diagram 12

Cisterns

Ball valves are used on storage cisterns to control the amount of water in the cistern and shut off at the correct level. (See diagram 12).

If the ball on the ball valve is split, the valve will let water pass into the cistern and may overflow. A ball costs about 60p - £1. To change it unscrew the damaged ball and put a new one in its place. If the water level is still too high in the cistern you can bend the arm down, or if it's plastic adjust the screw.

This problem can be caused by a worn washer. Washers can be replaced by firstly turning off water supply to the cistern. Remove the ball valve by undoing the swivel joint. Remove the split pin and take out the arm. There is a cap at the front - unscrew this. A little plug will come out with a washer at one end. Undo the end with pliers and change. Reassemble.

Ball valves will either be low pressure or high pressure depending on whether or not they are fed by mains pressure. See **Indirect and Direct systems** (p 18).

The high pressure valve washer is smaller and the water comes through a smaller hole.

The low pressure washer is larger with a larger hole for the water to come in.

There's lots of new ball valves on the market these days. A lot are plastic and ones for bottom fed cisterns are available too. The old type ball valves come in either low pressure or high pressure, but the newer plastic valves are inter-changeable.

Notes on Washers

In the old days hemp with Hawkwhite (jointing compound) was used instead of washers. Hemp is like horse hair and comes from the hemp plant.

If you have no washer on a connection (e.g. flush pipe to cistern, tap connectors, waste pipes) hemp can be used with a smear of Hawkwhite/jointing compound as it soaks up the water. Make an 'O' ring with it or just wind it round smeared with Hawkwhite jointing compound.

Difficulty Flushing

If a toilet is difficult to flush or continual flushing occurs, the diaphragm washer on the syphon may be split and need replacing.

To check this turn off the water supply or tie the ball valve up to prevent water flowing in. Flush the toilet. Scoop out the rest of the water with a cup to empty the cistern. Unscrew the nut connecting the threaded tail of the syphon to the flush pipe and disconnect flush pipe. Hold a bowl underneath to catch any remaining water. Withdraw the syphon mechanism to reach the syphon.

When buying a new diaphragm (they can be oval shape or circular), buy the largest size available. You can easily shape it to size with a pair of scissors. Remove the old diaphragm. Place the new one so that it covers the metal plate completely and touches, but does not drag on the walls of the syphon. Reassemble the syphon and flush pipe. If you do this and the toilet still won't flush then the plastic syphon may be cracked and will need replacing.

TAPS

The faults that can occur with taps are:

• Leak from the spindle. This is due to a leaking gland nut. Remove the grub screw, handle and cover. Tighten the gland nut, (where the drips are coming from) but not so tight as to make the tap difficult to turn on or off. If leaking persists, wrap some P.T.F.E. tape around underneath the nut or a little grease or petroleum jelly.

• **Water dripping from spout** (when tightly turned off). This is caused by the washer and washer seating not connecting suitably, usually due to an old worn washer. Turn the water supply off. Turn the tap fully on. Unscrew the cover, lift cover and unscrew the head. Remove the retaining nut and old washer. Replace washer with a new one of the same size. Reassemble. Turn the supply back on. 1/2 inch washers are for sink/basin taps 3/4 inch washers are for both taps.

Diagram 13

When fitting a new tap use 'plumbers mait' (see Fixing the Loo) to make it easy and leak proof. See diagram 13. Put it between the basin and base of tap. If you buy a new tap or buy the correct washers you shouldn't need to use this. A special tool is needed for fixing and tightening the tap in place. It has a swivel grip on the end of a bar. It's almost impossible sometimes to connect a tap without one. It's called a *tap spanner* A cheap spanner costs under a fiver (expensive ones about £17). It may be better to hire one for a one-off job.

The other fitting required for installing taps is a tap connector. This comes either bent or straight and has a loose (swivel) nut on one end and a washer. This end screws on to the stem of the pipe and is either a compression or soldered joint. The same fitting is used to connect onto ball valves.

Basin/Sink/W.C. Cistern - 15mm tap connector

Bath/Large Cistern - 22mm tap (with 22mm pipe entering) connector.

If the tap persists to drip after re-washering the tap needs 're-seating' (the seat is what the washer sits on). This can be done using a special tool or preferably buy a new 'seating and washer kit' from plumbing/DIY shops - about 40p.

Push fit joint.

Diagram 14

WASTE PIPES

This section refers to the extraction of dirty water, as opposed to soil pipes which are used in the extraction of toilet waste. See diagram 14.

These days plastic pipe is readily available and fairly cheap. It can be cut easily with a hacksaw and joined by using solvent weld or push fit connections.

Solvent weld is a kind of glue, which actually melts the surface of the fitting and the pipe and welds them together. It is very strong and sets very quickly (it costs about £2 a tin). So make sure pipes and fittings are in position first. It is cheaper to use than push fit. (See diagram 11)

Rubber 'push fit' fittings are made up of an 'O' ring in the fitting which makes the seal. These can be dismantled and used again if need be. Sometimes a little washing up liquid can be used to lubricate them.

Different plastics are made for different methods so check when buying, e.g. some plastics cannot be solvent welded.

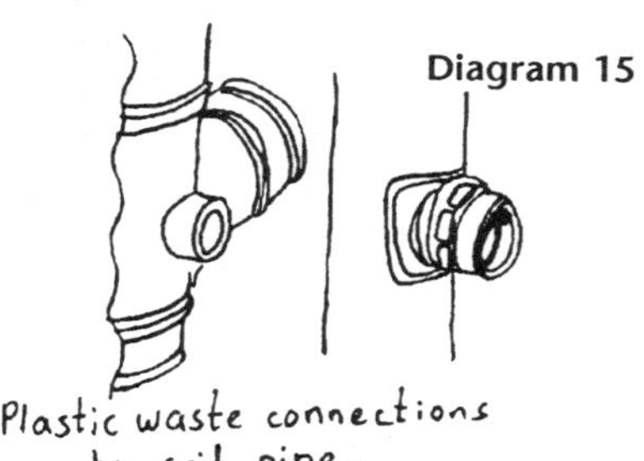

Buy the cheaper, lesser known makes which are quite adequate, e.g. 'polypipe' (not to be confused with blue plastic for mains services) rather than 'Terrain'. Polypipe is available from local plumbing hardware stores.

When fitting waste pipes, only a gradual fall (angle) is needed to make the water flow away. Saddle clips should be used to hold the pipe securely in place.

If you are installing a sink on the ground floor and you have access to a gully, it is quite adequate to overhang the waste over the gully, with a 135 bend at the end of the pipe.

When connecting the waste of a sink, etc, into the main discharge pipe, you use a 'boss' to connect. Cut a hole the size of the boss and file it to size. The surface around the hole and on the boss are solvent welded together. The branch is then connected into this. (See diagram 15).

Waste Pipe Sizes

Sink 1 1/2 inch
Basin 1 1/4 inch
Shower 1 1/2 inch
Bath 1 1/2 inch

Waste fittings are available in straight

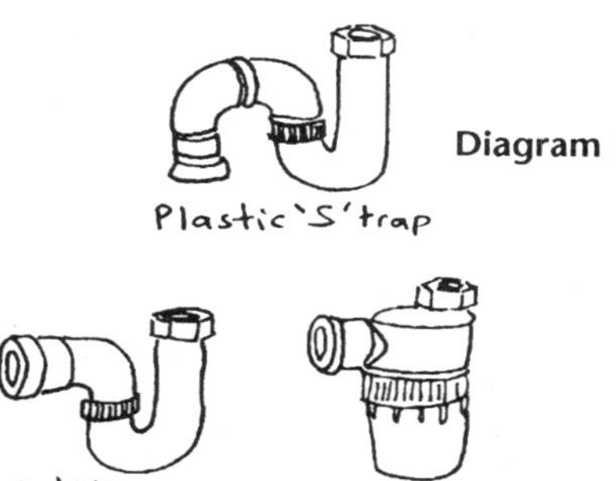

coupling, bends (90 + 135) reducers and tees.

Traps

Traps are fitted to every sanitary appliance. The purpose of a trap is to retain a water seal which prevents bad smells coming up from the drains. See diagram 16.

Gas Plumbing

Gas plumbing is very similar to water plumbing in terms of material and joints used. But there is one big difference. It's a lot more dangerous working with gas and great care should be taken. It is best only to carry out gas plumbing when you have familiarised yourself with water plumbing.

HINTS AND TERMS USED

male thread - external thread
female thread - internal thread
cap - fits over the pipe end or fitting - an internal thread
plug - fits into a fitting, has an external thread

When working with threaded iron gas fittings, two *Stillsons* wrenches are invaluable for grip and leverage.

WARNING

When starting work, not only turn off at the main gas cock, but turn off all appliances, especially those appliances with pilot lights. Otherwise they will go off when you turn the gas off and then when you turn the gas back on - will leak gas and may cause an explosion.

PURGING

When work has been carried out on any new or existing gas pipe work which has been exposed to the air, it is important to carry out purging. If purging is not done an explosion could take place. Natural gas mixed with ten parts air is *highly explosive*, so be warned. Firstly, open all the windows and doors. Turn on the gas at the main gas cock, and then stand by each appliance, turning it on without lighting it, releasing the air, until you can smell gas. Then you must turn off the appliance and wait for the gas to clear. The gas board will always carry out purging when they come to connect the supply.

TURNING ON THE MAIN GAS COCK

The main gas cock is situated on the incoming service pipe on the left side of the meter. It is operated by a handle. If the handle is missing a spanner or wrench can be used or ask the gas board for a new one.

A line stamped on the end of the shank indicates the on/off positions - across the pipe for 'off', in line with the pipe for 'on'.

TYPES OF PIPE

Iron Pipe

Iron pipe uses British Standard threads (B.S.P.) to join to fittings such as elbows, tees, sockets (straight joints) etc. External threads are known as male, internal as female. Just screwing a male thread into a female thread does not give a leak proof fit. It is best to use P.T.F.E. tape around the external thread or jointing paste e.g. 'Hawkwhite' to give a leak proof fit. See 'Different Kinds of Pipe' (p20).

Copper Pipe

When putting in new installations 15mm copper tube is usually adequate for most work. If you have to join on to the existing iron pipe, it is best to buy an iron to copper fitting and carry out the new work in copper.

If you can't find a suitable plug or capped end (plugs fit internally, caps externally), you have to fit a Tee branch. If it's copper pipe you want to tee into, cut into the pipe with a hacksaw and fit a compression or soldered tee, and continue with 15mm copper pipe. If it's iron pipe, cut into the iron pipe with a hacksaw. Unscrew each end from its fitting, and fit an iron to copper connector.

FITTING A GAS COOKER

The supply pipes from the meter should be traced to the nearest intended cooker point. Gas pipes often run underneath the floor boards. If you find the end of the pipe capped or plugged off you can simply convert to copper and run a piece of 15mm copper pipe up the wall about 1m and clip it to the wall. If you have to cut into the pipe, you will have to put in a tee, this is described in 'copper pipe' and 'iron pipe' (p###). Once you've clipped the copper pipe to the wall you can then fit a cooker bayonet fitting (the hose and bayonet fitting), fit together like a light bulb into its holder, this means the hose can be disconnected from the fitting, for the cooker to be cleaned without turning the gas off). The hose on your cooker will fit into this.

Be careful not to fit a pipe where it will be damaged . The hose costs around £6-8. If you can find an undamaged one on a disused cooker, all the better. Older hoses may not have a bayonet fitting, but a 'male' or 'female' threaded end. Take the hose to the plumbers' merchants, explaining that you want to connect it to 15mm copper pipe and they should give you the correct fitting.

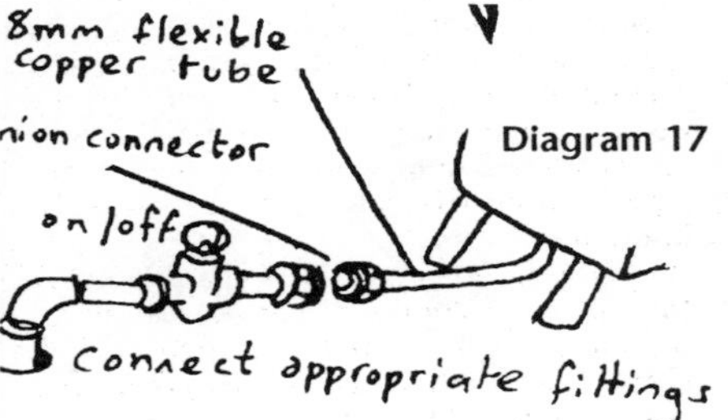

Diagram 17

FITTING A GAS FIRE

Gas fires must have access to a flue. The best place is usually in front of an old fire place.

The chimney should be swept. You can test the chimney is not blocked by lighting a piece of paper and holding it in the chimney. If it burns, you're okay. If it goes out, the chimney is blocked and should not be used until it's swept.

You have to seal the front of the fire place with a piece of aluminium sheet with a slot cut for the gas fires flue and a small slot cut in the bottom. This should be secured to the wall or fire place.

You will often find gas points under the floorboards by the side of the fire. Otherwise you will have to lay a new supply from the nearest gas supply. Turn off at the meter before starting work. If you can find a capped or plugged end you can simply use an iron-to-copper connection and carry on in 15mm copper.(See diagram 17). Otherwise you will have to 'tee' into a gas pipe run (see section on 'Iron and Copper Pipe' (p20).

You should install a gas cock, rather than

connecting the fire directly to the gas pipe. You can use a 'restricter elbow' which does not turn the gas off completely and screws to the floor boards. Then continue on from this in 8mm copper, which can be bought in 1m lengths. You may have to buy a fitting, which links up iron pipe or copper pipe (which may be under the floor) to the gas cock connection. The 8mm copper pipe is flexible and bends around corners and lies close to the wall. Be careful not to crease it, and make sure it is out of the way so it can't be damaged at all.

There will be an elbow connection at the back of the fire to connect onto. Carry out purging and test for leaks before using.

TESTING FOR LEAKS

When you've finished installing new pipe work or appliances, joints must be checked for leaks.

You can check for leaks by looking at your own gas meter. All appliances (including pilot lights) must be turned off. Turn on the gas cock at the meter. If the dial on the meter goes around even a fraction then you have a leak. To find the leak a 50-50 mixture of washing-up liquid and water should be painted on to any suspected joint. If it bubbles you have a leak. Your nose is also a good leak detective, but don't rely on it.

Old iron pipes sometimes start to leak if they are even slightly disturbed. Plumbers used to seal joints with hemp and bosswhite before the switch to natural gas. Natural gas tends to dry out these joints and can cause problems, so check them. If you do find old gas pipes leaking try undoing them and resealing them with Hawkwhite or tape (P.T.F.E. tape) or you may have to replace the iron pipe with a piece of copper. If a gas pipe is leaking before the meter, contact the gas board immediately. It is their responsibility.

If you come home to find a gas leak, switch off at the main gas cock. Open windows to disperse gas. Don't switch on any light as it may cause a spark. Don't smoke. Ring the gas board emergency service immediately.

Put a note on the door warning people of the gas leak.

GAS WATER HEATERS

The Pilot Light Devices

(See diagram). Some heaters may look slightly different from this but the principle is the same. This drawing shows on it a *bimetallic strip*, which is the part next to the pilot light. This opens and closes the main gas valve. When it is heated it allows gas to flow to the main burner, where it is ignited by the pilot flame.

It is a safety device used in case the pilot light is extinguished. The bimetallic strip then cools and closes the gas valve.

In more modern gas water heaters and gas fired boilers a *thermo-couple* is used. This is a flame failure device, the same as the bi-metallic strip.

It is a copper covered cable. One end is attached next to the pilot flame and the other is joined next to an electromagnetic valve. When one end is heated and an electric current is generated the magnetic valve is magnetised and holds open the main gas valve allowing gas to the burners.

Diagram 18

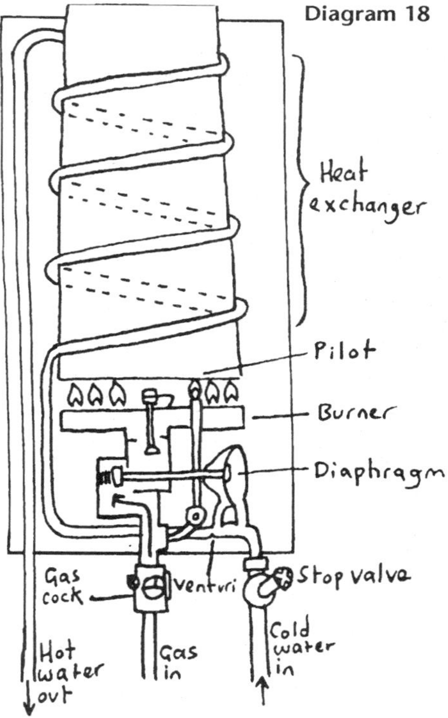

GAS WATER HEATER

If the pilot light was extinguished, the electric current wouldn't be produced and the magnetic valve would spring back, shutting the gas valve, preventing gas flowing to the burner.

Different Types

Gas water heaters are a very convenient and economical way of providing instant hot water. See diagram 18.

There are several different makes but they can be divided up into three types.
Small single points are small wall mounted heaters over a sink or basin; **large single points** which have a spout and are used over a bath or maybe bath plus basin; **multi-point heaters** which can feed several appliances, e.g. bath, basin, sink.

Small Single Point

The small single point heater *does not* require a flue (the flue is a hole cut in an outside wall/chimney to take away the fumes given off by gas appliances.

The single point heaters can be screwed to the wall over the sink or basin. They should not be run for more than 5 minutes continuously.

The multi-point heaters do require a flue. This is very important, as a gas water heater running without any ventilation or flue can be lethal.
The old type of flue (called a conventional flue) is a pipe coming out of the top of the heater and passing through an outside wall where it rises up with a terminal on the top. (See diagram 3).

The new type of flue for multi-points and large single points is called a balanced flue.

This can be fitted to any outside wall, providing there is nothing the other side that will restrict the flow of air, like a tree or another brick wall close by. The flue should always have a terminal and it's best to make sure it's at least 1m off the ground.

There should also be added ventilation in the room, i.e. an air brick or ventilator in the window.

Heaters should never be fixed in cupboards or near combustible materials.

Large Single Points

If you want to use the heater for more than one appliance, position it on the wall, so the spout can be swung from one appliance to another.

You will have to make a hole in an outside wall for the flue, measure the size of the flue hole on the back of the heater. Use a cold chisel and hammer to make the hole. If you've knocked out more than you need, you can cement it up to make it the right size. Take the cover off, there will be screw holes at the back to fix it to the wall.

There will be a flue terminal which fits over the end of the flue outside and will fix on with a chain or some other fixings.

The gas connection to the heater is best done in 22mm copper pipe. If you use 15mm, there may not be enough gas delivered. It's no good running a 22mm supply from a 15mm gas pipe, so if that's all you can connect to, run it in 15mm.

The water supply should preferably be run off the mains in 15mm, or, if off the tank in 22mm. The tank should be at least 2.1m above the heater to give enough pressure.

Multi-point Gas Water Heaters

Secure the heater to an outside wall, fitting the flue and fixing the heater in the same way as for large single points.

Connect the gas inlet to the supply. Use 22mm copper pipe if possible, (see 'Large Single Points' above).

Connect the water inlet and outlet in 15mm copper pipe (or 22mm if fed from the tank).

The water outlet can be run in 22mm and then branch off in 15mm to each outlet. This gives a better flow of water if two taps are operated at the same time.

If you can, install a stopcock on the water inlet and outlet so maintenance will be easier.

Note

If you move into a house where there is one of the old multi-points/single points with a conventional flue, you should run the bath when you're out of the room.

When buying a second-hand gas water heater, lift the outer cover off the heater and look for scorching or damage to the pipes. It is not easy to tell if the water heater works until you connect it up. So get an assurance that it works or that you can take it back if it doesn't.

Installing the Gas Water Heater

Small single point heaters can be positioned on the wall above the sink or basin. They usually have a spout for the hot water to come out of, so just the cold water inlet and gas inlet need to be plumbed.

Remove the cover off the heater. There should be two holes at the back to screw it to the wall.

Identify the pipes; the water inlet should have a tap attached, otherwise you will have to fit a stopcock to it.

15mm copper pipe can be used for the gas and water supply. You can install a gas cock (valve) onto the gas inlet but it is not essential.

'Tee' into the nearest gas supply pipe and take a 'tee' off the mains water supply (which supplies the kitchen sink).

Getting Your Work Checked

It is advisable to have someone from the gas board check over the work you have done. This will cost around £14. If they see the work is unsafe, they will remove the appliance and plug off the pipe.

▼ ELECTRICS ▼

Electricity can be extremely dangerous and frightening, but you don't have to be a qualified electrician to attempt some basic house wiring. However it is best to be over cautious.

You should try and get a 'competent' person who has done wiring before, preferably professionally, to check that what you've done is safe. It will also have to be up to certain standards to reach the electricity boards (EB) approval. If there has not been an electricity supply to your home for quite some time, or it hasn't been checked for years, the EB will insist on inspecting it to see that it's safe.

Safety

There are certain safety precautions when carrying out wiring.
Always remember:
1. Never work on live wires
2. Always switch off at the mains
3. Remove fuses and keep them with you
4. Use a mains tester at every connection to check if it's live.
5. Use insulated tools.
5. Get someone experienced to look over your work.

Even if you have switched off don't make any assumptions, especially in old buildings or half wired up houses.

Follow all the rules and wire up in the standard way. Irregularities could be dangerous if someone else wants to do some wiring later.

Make sure all connections (screws) are tight. A loose connection can cause short circuits or even a fire.

Never join cables with insulation tape. Use junction boxes or terminal strips. These are reasonably cheap and readily available.

Always use the correct cable and fuses for the job.

If you are moving in somewhere with old gas supply, open windows and ventilate the area. A switch can cause a spark.

Treatment for Electric Shock

If someone receives an electric shock:

• turn off the electric current immediately or remove them from the live part by using an insulating material like wood, paper, plastic or rubber. Don't just grab them with bare hands or you,ll get a shock as well.
• be especially careful if they are wet or there is any water around.
• get someone to phone for a doctor or ambulance in the meantime.
• if they have stopped breathing, apply mouth to mouth respiration (see any first aid books for details of this). Apply immediately! No harm can be done. If it is necessary, treat them for shock by lying them down and keeping them warm.

Electrical Terms

Volt (V) unit for measuring the pressure or force which causes an electric current to flow in a circuit.
Watt (W) unit of electrical power an appliance needs.
Amp (A) quantity of electricity - the amount of current a conductor can carry.
Spur a branch cable - connected to a ring circuit.
The Consumer Distribution Board this carries the mains fuse, the meter and a consumer unit (fuse box).
Live (or **line)** wires are sheathed in red plastic insulation. These wires carry the current in a circuit from the power source to the appliance (S) and will therefore be carrying 'live' electricity whether or not the appliance is switched on.
Neutral any cable with black insulation carries the current in a circuit back from the appliance to the power source.

Colour coding for Flex and Cable
Flex (flexible) Live is brown. Neutral is blue. Earth is green.
Cable Live is red. Neutral is black. Earth is green or green/yellow.

Getting Connected

See **Squatting** section (p12) if you are squatting.

If you are not squatting, go down to your local Electricity Board and pick up a form and fill it in. You may be asked for proof of tenancy. If you have just moved address and previously had an account in your name, it can be easily transferred.

They will arrange a date to come and visit and check the wiring and/or fit a meter, or just take the present meter reading. You may have to wait a few days for them to come round.

Diagram 19

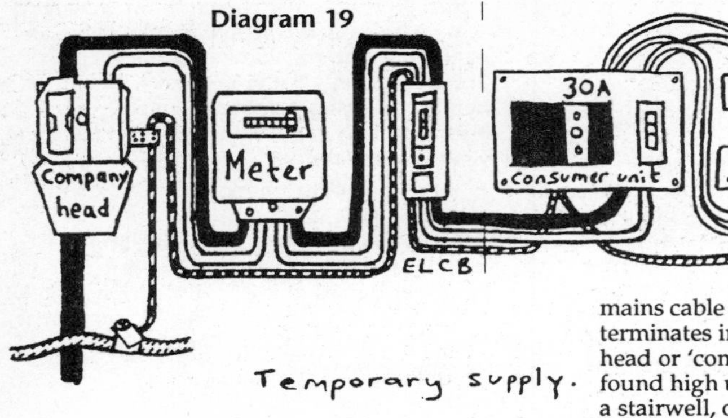

Temporary supply.

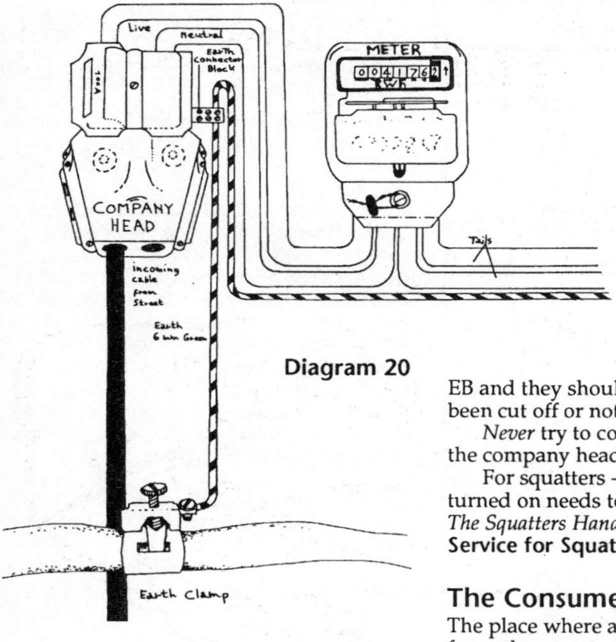

Diagram 20

Temporary Supply

If you write to your local EB asking them for a temporary supply stating your reasons they may connect you. Temporary supplies are given readily if you are are a builder who needs a temporary electricity supply to work - on refurbishing a house for instance, where the original wiring may not be there. You are only allowed a 30amp supply and you have to fit the fuse box yourself. The supply also costs more per unit. (See diagram 19).

Or you might simply consider asking your neighbours to supply you with electricity by running a cable from their house. This is perfectly legal.

The Company Head

The supply or mains cable coming in from the street terminates in a box called the supply head or 'company head'. It's usually found high up near the front door, or in a stairwell, or in a hall or porch cupboard or in a basement. (See diagram 20).

In the company head is a 'mains fuse'. It will either be ceramic re-wireable type or a cartridge type.

The meter and the company head are owned by the EB (The wiring between the two is live!!).

The electricity may be cut off in the street. The mains fuse may be missing, and/or the meter too. Use a mains tester screwdriver on the wires which will light up if there is a supply.

You can also ring the EB and they should tell you if the supply has been cut off or not.

Never try to connect to the mains or touch the company head.

For squatters - getting your electricity turned on needs to be dealt with carefully. See *The Squatters Handbook* or ring the **Advisory Service for Squatters** p16.

The Consumer Unit

The place where all the smaller fuses are kept for each separate circuit. Lighting, sockets, cooker, etc. (See diagram 21).

A typical consumer unit consists of:
5 amp (white) for lighting
15 amp (blue) for immersion heater, electric water heater
20 amp (yellow) for storage heaters and radial circuit
30 amp (red) for ring circuit (sockets) and 30 amp radial circuit
45 amp (green) cooker

It may be a good idea to label the fuses in

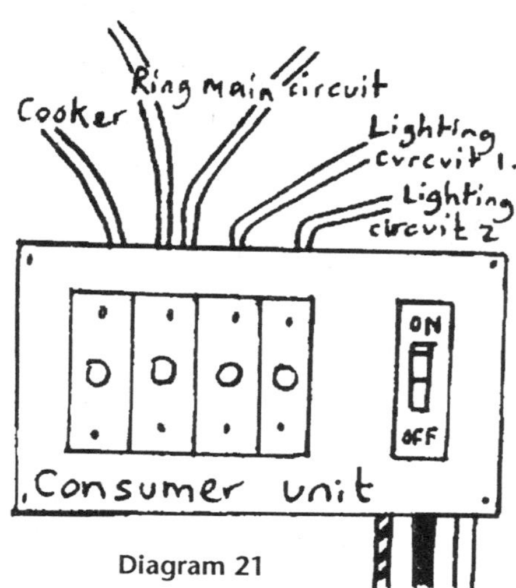

Diagram 21

your CU.
Note: This colour coding is not always conformed to.

Installing a Consumer Unit

If you are installing your own consumer unit, knock holes in it for entry cable and the tails to the meter. These tails are 16mm insulated conductors: red for live connection, black for neutral, yellow/green or green to earth. You also attach this last cable to the earth clamp. The other 2 cables should be left for the EB to connect to the meter.
The EB will provide the meter and cables to connect it to the company head.

Plug Fuses

3 amp (blue, up to 700w). e.g. hair dryer, toaster, fridge, T.V.
13 amp (brown 700w to 3000w). e.g. electric bar heater, kettle.
There are various other sizes too.

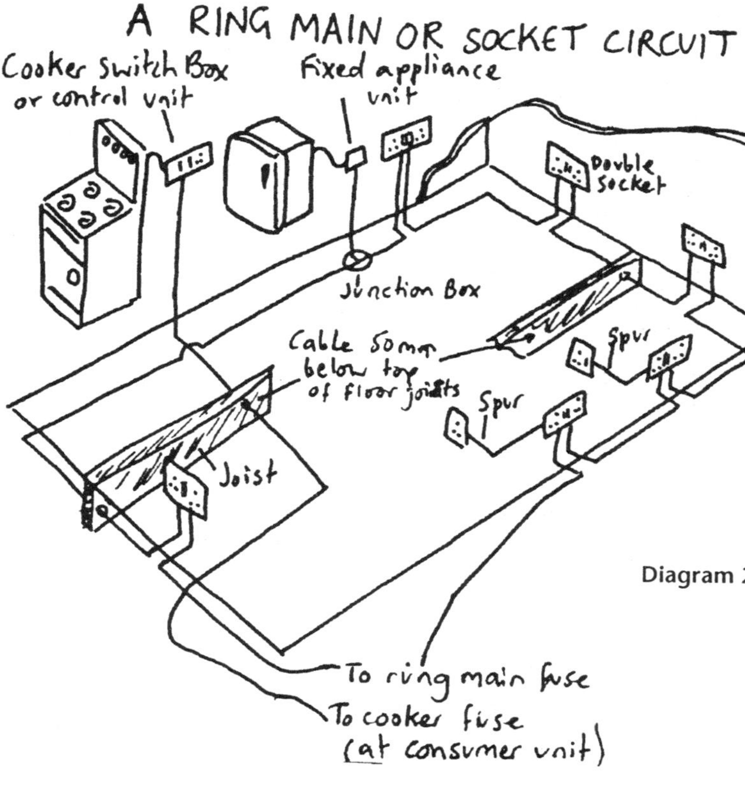

Diagram 22

Earth Bonding

Diagram 23

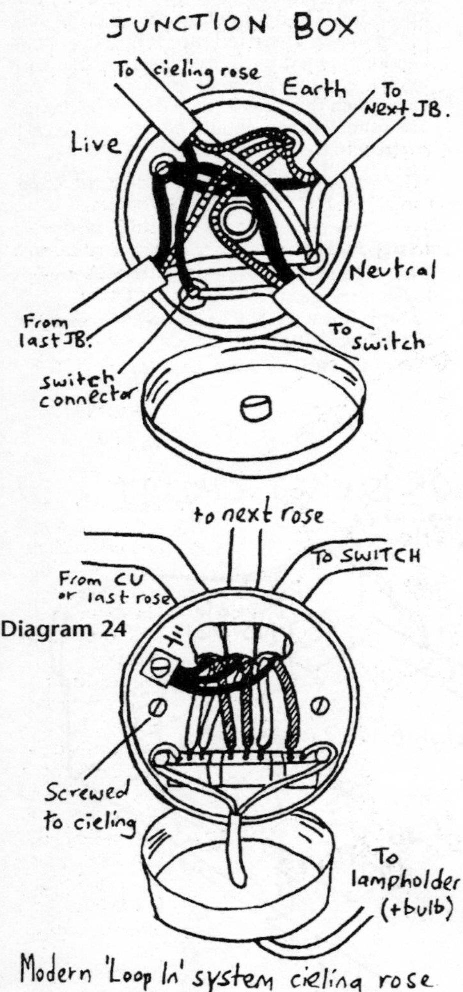

Diagram 24

This is a safely precaution. The earthing offers an alternative route for the electricity to take, rather than going through you! The electricity flows into the ground instead. It's life-saving if you touch a faulty appliance.

One end of the earth wire is connected to the metal service cable or a metal water pipe which gives a good contact with the earth.

The earth wire follows the live and neutral to each appliance where it is securely attached to any metal part of the appliance.

Then if the live part of the appliances shorts onto the metal the electricity is safely carried to earth.

Overload (rewiring fuses etc)

When a circuit is overloaded, the fuse acts as a safely catch.

The old ceramic rewirable type The fuse wire melts and breaks. The old wire can be removed and new wire replaced.

Cartridge The fuse wire is held in a cartridge. When the fuse blow the whole cartridge

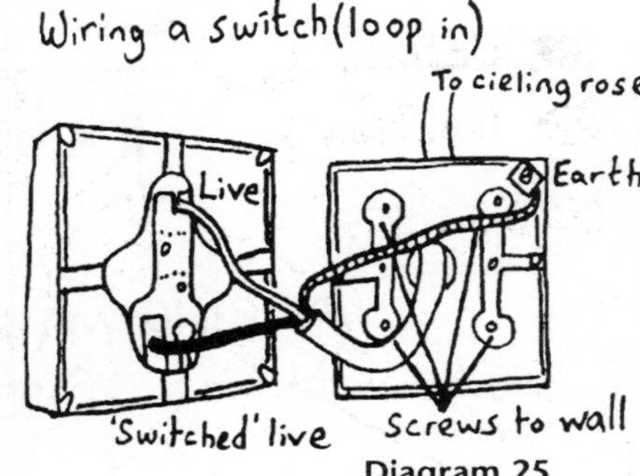

Diagram 25

needs to be replaced. These are like fuses in a 13 Amp plug.

Miniature Circuit Breaker These work on an automatic switch or button which disconnects with any overload.

The switch or buttons can be reset when the overload is removed. Fuses blow for a reason! Check for faults in the circuit otherwise the new fuse will blow again.

Circuits

RING MAINS ETC

The majority of domestic electrical installations are wired in a ring main circuit. In older houses a radial circuit may be installed.

In the radial circuit the cable runs from the fuse box to the first socket, then the second socket and so on, stopping at the last socket outlet.

This is the same in a ring circuit with the addition that the cable returns to the fuse box from the last socket. Thus completing a ring. (See diagram 22).

If there is no existing installation it is best to install a ring circuit, where you connect the sockets in a loop and join both ends to a 30 amp fuse.

You can install extra sockets on 'spurs' from the ring main providing there are more sockets on the ring than spurs. Have no more than two sockets on a spur i.e. one double socket.

A P.V.C. sheathed 2.5mm square cable (twin and earth cable) fitted with a 30 amp fuse can supply 7 1/2 KW of power.

This should be enough for 15 single sockets, unless you use a lot of electric heating. For example, if you have three 2KW heaters and you plug in a kettle as well, the fuse will blow. Add another ring main or don't overload.

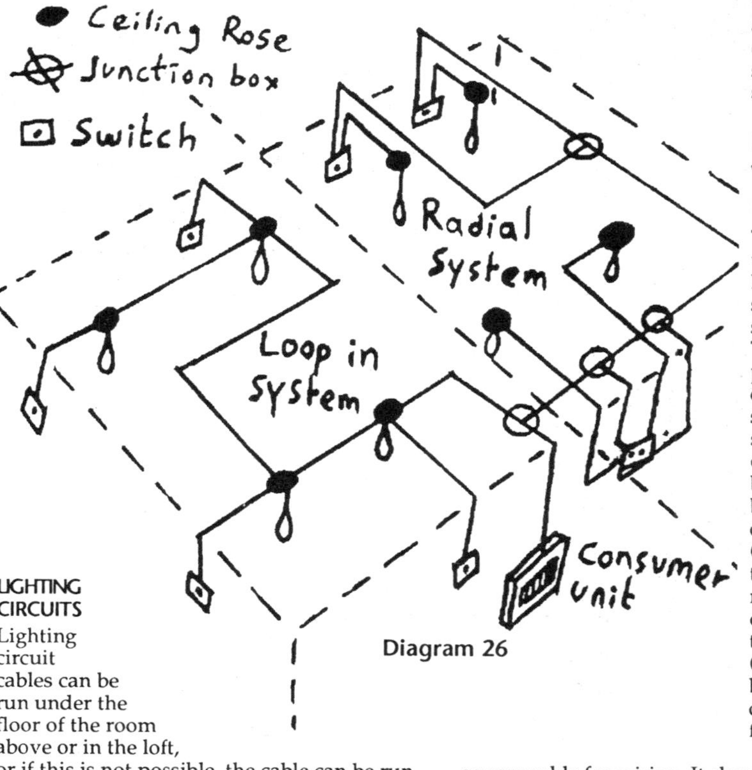

Diagram 26

LIGHTING CIRCUITS

Lighting circuit cables can be run under the floor of the room above or in the loft, or if this is not possible, the cable can be run along the walls. (See diagrams 23, 24, 25, 26).

There are two types of lighting circuits: the radial or junction box, and the 'loop-in'. Both types can be used together in the same circuit.

In the radial circuit the cable runs through a series of junction boxes. From each box one cable runs to the ceiling rose and another cable runs to the switch. Most old lighting circuits are like this. You can recognise them because only one pair of wires runs to each ceiling rose and there is no earthing terminal.

In the loop-in system the cable runs from ceiling rose to ceiling rose by the shortest route. A single cable runs from each light to its switch. New installations are most likely to use the loop-in system.

Cookers

Cookers need their own separate circuit and a 30 amp fuse (45 amp if rated more than 12KW). You need 4mm square cable wired into a cooker socket with a switch on it to turn the cooker on and off. It's often a single socket and switch as well.

Electric Water Heaters

These are small wall mounted heaters with a spout over the sink or basin. They can be picked up fairly cheaply second-hand, still in working order. They can be plumbed in by 'teeing' off a cold water pipe (preferably off the mains) and running a piece of copper pipe to the inlet (which should be a compression fitting).

Use 2.5mm square cable for wiring. It should be on its own circuit with a 15 amp fuse. The cable should be run from the heater to a fused switch (a switch with a light and its own 13 amp fuse).

This will give you instant hot water within a minute or so. Never cover the spout or let it run for too long (it will run cold) and switch off when not in use.

Fixed Appliances

Fridges, washing machines and other appliances which stay in one place can be wired up to a wall mounted 'fixed appliance connector unit' (fused switch). This is cheaper than a plug and socket and has its own switch.

The unit connects up to a socket outlet or a junction box using 2.5mm square cable.

Bathrooms

For safety there should not be any electrical sockets or switches in a bathroom. Any light switches should be the pull cord type or the switch should be outside the room.

Light fittings should be bulb holders attached to the ceiling and you shouldn't be able to touch them while standing in the bath or shower.

You can install heaters but make sure you can't reach them and that they're run from a fitting, fused and switched, preferably outside the bathroom.

Testing the Circuits

POLARITY

In some cases the sockets or lights could be incorrectly wired. The neutral may be in place of the live and vice versa. This should be tested and corrected if necessary.

To test sockets use a normal 13 amp plug. Attach a flex with the live connected to the live pin and the neutral wire to earth pin.

Attach a 240v bulb holder and bulb to the other end. If the live and neutral have been swapped, or the earth is not continuous, then the bulb will not light up.

For checking the polarity of a lighting circuit use a mains tester (an insulated screwdriver with a light in the handle). With the switch off, test both live and neutral terminals. If the polarity is incorrect when the light switch is off one terminal should be live and when the switch is on the bulb will light, but neither of the terminals should be live. (See diagram 25). If it is wired correctly, when the light switch is off, one terminal should be live and when the switch is on the bulb will light and both terminals should be live.

Diagram 27

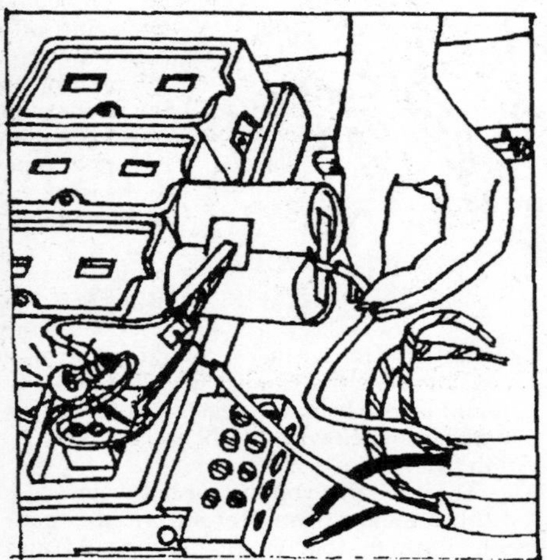

TESTING FOR CONTINUITY IN A RING CIRCUIT

The current should be continuous. To test, first turn the power off and remove the fuses. (See diagram 27). You will need a battery (use a 4.5 volt, large flat 'wonderlight' detachable bike light) with wires and crocodile clips attached to the positive and negative terminals. The circuit to be tested must be disconnected from the Consumer Unit. The battery can then be clipped on with the crocodile clips - negative battery terminal to negative wire and positive battery terminal to positive wire.

You then need a small torch bulb with a wire soldered to the body and another at the bottom of the bulb. Crocodile clips should be attached to each wire. This bulb can then be attached to the other end of the circuit you want to test. Attach the crocodile clips to the positive and negative terminals. If the bulb lights you've got 'continuity'.

Help and Reading

There are lots of good sources. Local reference libraries have many DIY books which you can't take out but you can photocopy the bits you want.

Check out your local adult education institute for classes in DIY plumbing and electrics. **The Building Centre,** *26 Store St, WC1 (637 9001)* has a good bookshop which covers things such as electricity, plumbing and roofing and they have a range of building materials on display. The also carry an index of manufacturers. *The Self Help Housing Repair Manual,*, by Andrew Ingam, is an invaluable source book and although it is now out of print it is available at some libraries.

In general plumbing textbooks are not very good on DIY. Generally, DIY books don't usually have anything about gas.

MAKING A LIVING: Jobs, Social Security, Poll Tax

jobs

from 5 to 16 years old you go to school where you are taught to be obedient, look busy, sit in one spot and keep your hands to yourself. This is the real value of school, so that when you leave you will know how to behave when you find a job.

The main problem with work is that it is boring. You do it because you need the money. Still, the more ***meaning*** *you can find in your work the more bearable it becomes. Usually the more boring, dull, uninteresting the work, the less you get paid for doing it, accountancy being the exception.*

This section outlines some possibilities for making money, learning a new skill, finding work or starting your own business.

▼ LOOKING FOR WORK ▼

First try all the obvious approaches - ask around, look in the papers, contact potential employers directly by using directories like the *Yellow Pages*, or advertise yourself. *What Color Is Your Parachute? A Practical Manual for Job Hunters & Career-Changers* Richard Nelson Bolles (Ten Speed Press £6.95) is good if you are not sure about what type of job is for you.

Right now the government have all sorts of projects designed to get people off the unemployment register but very few of them offer the chance of 'real' work, although there are more job opportunities in London than in other parts of the country. Most of the jobs available in places like job centres offer jobs in the low paid sector such as hotel and catering work or part-time employment in the retail trade.

Not many imaginative initiatives have been encouraged. The few that we know about like job sharing are listed below. There are some places trying to create a more enlightened approach to the world of work such as worker controlled co-ops where, in theory, members have greater control over the decisions that are made.

The important thing is if you have not got a skill and you want to learn one, go ahead and do something about it. *Floodlight* (available in bookshops) lists about every part-time and evening course imaginable. There are also training centres like:

■ **Women's Education in Building (WEB),** *12 Malton Rd, W10 (968 9139)* which has been set up especially to train women over 25 in the building trades.

▼ CASUAL OR ▼ TEMPORARY WORK

This can be for a few days or up to several months. You are paid in cash or by cheque. Sometimes on a daily basis but usually at the end of the week or month. Most employers want your National Insurance number and sometimes a P45.

Seasonal Work

During the Xmas period, post offices take on extra staff. You can get an application form from your local sorting office or by ringing the **Recruitment Centre** on *(239 2000)*. Apply as early as possible (preferably by the end of October).

There is usually work for about 2-3 weeks but the rates of pay are not over generous. They sometimes take on casual staff at other times of the year (same number).

SHOP WORK

Many shops and large stores also take on

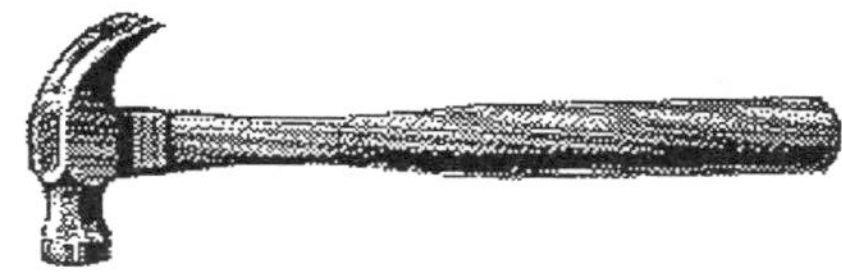

extra staff for the Xmas period and for the Jan and July sales.

A few advertise in Job Centres. It's better to contact them directly. They usually start recruitment at the beginning of November. Some examples are:

■ **Harrods,** *(730 1234).* Go to the Prospect Dept for an application form. The pay is around £130 for a 5 and a half day week. They also take on people for loading in their warehouse.

■ **Selfridges Ltd,** *(629 1234).* Ask for an application form. You must be over 18. Pay is around £139 for 5 day week (including late night on Thur).

PARKS

Seasonal work is available at different times throughout the year, although most of the work in the parks is only available during the summer period. Street cleaning departments in different local councils also occasionally take on temporary staff at different times. Contact your local parks dept or Street Cleansing dept. (see *Yellow Pages*).

Job Centres

For details of full-time and temporary work as well as various government training schemes. You'll find the address under **Manpower Services Commission** in the phone book.

CASUAL JOBS

The following Job Centres have casual work available on a daily basis. (It's mostly heavy work and so it's usually only men that go for it but there's nothing to stop you if you're a woman and have the 'muscle').

■ **Lisson Grove Job Centre,** *46 Lisson Grove, NW1 (262 3477 ext 200).* Mostly kitchen porter jobs and some labouring. They start coming through at about 8am - first come first served. (People start queuing at around 5.30 but it's worth dropping in at any time of the day as jobs come in all the time). Wages paid cash in hand.

■ **Victoria Job Centre** , *119/121 Victoria St, SW1 (828 9231).* Open at 9am, first come first served, cash in hand. People queue from 6.30 am.

■ **Hotel and Catering Casual Job Centre,** *35 Mortimer St, W1 (836 6622 ext 274).* Mostly kitchen portering. First come first served but if you don't get a job they will hold your name over till the next day. Doors open 8.15, queuing starts early. Pay is around £2.50 an hour cash in hand.

Exhibition and Festivals

Large exhibitions often take on temporary staff for setting up, catering and loading and unloading. Sometimes recruited through Job Centres but you can contact them direct or through an agency:

■ **Barbican,** *Silk St, Barbican, EC2 (638 4141).* They don't advertise in job centres. Casual work often available, training given. Write to the house manager stating the hours you want to do (i.e. day-time, evenings or weekends).

■ **Earls Court**, *Warwick Rd, SW5* and **Olympia,** *Hammersmith Rd, W14* both take on staff but their recruitment is done by **Beeton Rumford Ltd** and **M.V. Promotions** (see below).

■ **Royal Festival Hall,** *Belvedere Rd, SE1 (928 3246 catering section)* best to call between 3 and 5pm.

■ **Wembley Stadium Ltd,** *(902 8833 ask for personnel).* Staff are mainly taken on around March. They have a pool of staff who they use regularly, but don't let that put you off, it's worth ringing anytime.

AGENCIES

■ **M.V. Promotions,** *(0932 853751).* They recruit people to help at exhibitions. Ring for info and registration form.

■ **Beeton Rumford Ltd,** they recruit staff for exhibitions at Earls Court, Olympia and sometimes the Royal Festival Hall. Mainly buffet, waitressing or bar work.

Music Venues

■ **Hammersmith Odeon,** *(748 4081).* You'll need to call in to fill an application form, phone first. Regular music venues have staff vacancies for bar work fairly often.

■ **The Camden Palais** *Camden High St, NW1 (387 0428).*

■ **Dingwalls Dance Hall,** *Unit 4, Camden Lock, Chalk Farm Rd, NW1 (485 3129/267 1430).*

■ **Town & Country Club,** *9 Highgate Rd, NW5 (485 4211 after 7pm).*

Market Research

There is a central body that co-ordinates all market research companies. They can send you lots of info about the requirements for the job and how much you can earn as well as a list of 40 companies who do market research.

■ **The Market Research Society,** *175 Oxford St, W1R 1TA (439 2585).*

Television

TV companies sometimes take on temp workers. The BBC have different personnel depts for different work.

■ **Television Film Studios,** *Ealing Green, W5 (743 8000 personnel Dept).* Mostly clerical and cleaning but some messengering and lifting.

■ **Independent Broadcasting Authority** *(Head Office), 4 Sandridge Close, Harrow, (584 7011 Personnel Officer).* Clerical staff only, send CV.

Modelling at Art Colleges

Many art colleges use models for their life drawing classes, usually nude. Models of all shapes and sizes accepted.

■ **Hammersmith and Nth Kensington Adult Education Institute,** *Wornington Rd, W10 (969 0303)* contact Amanda Hayes or Julia Vezza. The art classes may be morning, afternoon or evening. Pay is around £8.50 for a 2 hour session. You must be reliable.

■ **The London Cartoon Centre,** *(969 4562).* Life drawing classes on Thur eve, models usually dress in swimwear.

■ **Chelsea School of Art,** *(Fulham 736 9001).* Apply at the beginning of term, pay is about £4.25 an hour. Other branches only use models occasionally but maybe worth a try: *Chelsea 351 3844, Shepherds Bush 749 3236.*

■ **Royal College of Art,** *Kensington Grove, SW7 (584 5020).* Write to painting Dept enclosing a photo. £4.00 an hour.

■ **Sir John Cass School of Art,** *City of London Polytechnic, (283 1030).* Contact the Arts Faculty Office for info. They use models frequently but you must have a P45 and National Insurance number, even if it's only for one session.

Security Work

Many agencies advertise in *Yellow Pages.* Their requirements and rates of pay vary but they all have a rigorous vetting system. They'll check what you've been doing since you left school (if you're a student you'll need proof) and they check for criminal records. You'll need to be physically fit.
Two examples are:

■ **Argus Shield Ltd,** *College Hse, Wrights Lane, Kensington, W8 (938 2416).* Best to call in to the office (9-5, Mon-Fri). They take women and men. You'll need a National Insurance number and to be 19 or over. All shifts are 12 hours (day or night) and you can work anything from 1 to 7 shifts a week. Pay from £2.50 an hour. You must work a minimum of 1 month.

■ **Securiguard Services (London) Ltd,** *10/12 Emerald St, WC1 (831 7551).* Best to phone if you want work quickly. Minimum of two weeks and 60 hrs a week. If you're under 19 the pay is £2.01 an hour and £2.51 after the first 40 hours. Over 19 it's £2.75 an hour.

Traffic Surveys

Some local Councils offer other sorts of temp work such as traffic surveys. Because this sort of work can be sporadic, it can play havoc with the DSS if you're claiming. You could try your local council or phone the organisation below which organises traffic surveys in different parts of London, for an application form and info.

■ **London Research Centre,** *(627 9682).*

Magazine Distribution

There are several free magazines which need to be distributed every week (usually from outside tube stations). The money varies. You have to be good at getting up early and you *must* be reliable (i.e. don't be late).

Some mags to contact are:

■ **Nine to Five Magazine Ltd,** *9a Margaret St, W1 (637 1377).* Contact Peter Jackson Mon 11-3 or Wed 12-3 for work the following week. They often have vacancies for people on Mons and if you work regularly they will usually give you work on Weds as well. You have to be at the station from 7.30 - 10am. For 2 1/2 hours work the pay if £8, cash in hand. Most of the workers are students and have to sign a form declaring that they are exempt from paying tax.

■ **Girl About Town Magazine Ltd,** *9a Margaret St, W1 (836 4433/2618/3036 ask for Ron or Gordon).* Distribute Mon and Tue, sometimes Wed. 7.30-10am but you all meet up at Oxford Circus first. £7.50 per session plus travelling expenses going up to £8.50 after 8 weeks. You'll need to go to the office to fill in an application form. If you're not a student you'll have to fill on a form P46. Money is paid by cheque which is cashed at their local bank.

Courier Work

There are lots of agencies which need people to deliver, goods, packages or letters. They usually want you to have your own vehicle (bike, car or van). See *Yellow Pages.* Two which use bicycle couriers are:

■ **On Yer Bike!,** *Despatch Co. (Mayfair) Ltd, 5d Shepherd St, W1Y 7LD (493 6632)* work mainly in the West End and City so you'd be expected to know the areas well. Pay is 50% of the jobs.

■ **Hand & Deliver Despatch Co Ltd,** *1-2 Alfred Place, WC1E 7EB (580 2677/436 5944)* (ask for Spike). You're taken on as self-employed. What you earn depends on how fast you are; anything from between £10-£50 a day. You have to hire a radio (£1.50 a day) and buy a bag with their logo on it for £4.

Courier Work Abroad

There are some agencies which will give you a reduced cost flight in return for carrying documents or baggage for them (see **Travel** p130). Try:

■ **Nomad Flights**, *(570 9277)*. At the moment they only go to New York, Montreal, Toronto, Vancouver and Johannesburg. You can stay for a minimum of 1 week to a maximum of 1 month. You will only be able to take hand baggage. Need to book one month in advance, two months for summer and xmas.

Markets

Often Markets (see **Markets** p39) take on casual workers, you have to get there early (around 6am) to offer your services to stall holders. Wages range from £15-20 a day. Supermarkets and fast food restaurants take on temp staff at various times through the year, look in your local Job Centre.

Driving

■ **British Tours**, *(629 5267)* employ people over 25 to take visitors around (£50/day for medium sized car, more for long trips - you must pay running costs but can pick up tips which can be good). Must have taken the London Tourist Board Driver Guide Exam. They will train (£130 +VAT). Car insurance is high if you're under 26.

■ **Drivers Bureau**, *221 Streatham High Rd, SW16 (677 9655)*. References. Over 21.

■ **Hertz**, *35 Edgeware Rd, W2 (723 1692)*. Employ drivers to move cars between branches. You need to be over 23 with a clean licence. The phone number has a recorded message giving the days they will need drivers.

Miscellaneous

■ **Universal Aunts Ltd**, *250 Kings Rd, SW3 (351 5767)*. Link up cleaners, baby-sitters, etc with clients (mainly unskilled work). You must be over 18 and supply two references and go for an interview. Work is on a casual basis, money paid directly from client to worker, £3.50 an hour plus fares, cash in hand.

■ **The Portobello Business Centre**, *249 Kensal Rd, W10 (968 6656)*. **The Portobello Business Trust** runs a small jobs directory of people who are able to offer new work services for a reasonable price. that includes skilled and unskilled work, anything that the public might need. Some jobs are regular but most are one-offs.You must provide two references, complete an application form and pay a membership fee.

■ **Organisation Unlimited**, *(351 0295)* pay about £3.00 and hour (more for skilled work). Cover all sorts of domestic jobs but it's usually cleaning. **Manpower**, *(Notting Hill 229 1200)*, **Extra Man** *(373 3045)* and **Industrial Overload** *(242 5374)* can find you temporary labour jobs. These jobs are often so bad that firms can't get anyone to do them permanently. All pay £3-3.50 hr and take the same amount for themselves.

■ **Lords Cricket Ground** They take on people from April to Sept to work as stewards. and also in the catering section. Stewards are mostly part-time, and they usually work at the test matches.

To work in the catering section contact: The Head Steward (Colin Edwards), **Marylebone Cricket Club**, *Lords Ground, St Johns Wood, NW8 8QN (289 1611)*. To work in the catering section contact: **Mecca Leisure Plc**, *(Fiona Highland Catering Division), 76 Southwark St, SE1 OPP (928 2323)*. They recruit all kinds of catering work at Lords (also the Oval Cricket ground). Usually from April through to Sept.

■ **London Zoo** *(Susan Lacey, 722 3333 ext 541 retail dept)*. Temp work is only available in the cafeteria during the summer period.

■ **Notting Hill Carnival.** The Carnival Arts Committee take on temporary staff to work as stewards or to help with security at the Carnival. Apply in June or July. Tel: *(960 5266/9242)*.

Reading

1989 Directory of Summer Jobs in Britain from **Vacation Work**, *9 Park End St, Oxford, OX1 1HJ, (0865 241978)* it costs £5.95 and lists 30,000 vacancies which include fruit picking, hotels and holiday camps, sports instruction, farming, child care, office work, archeological digs and riding centres. Tells you who to contact as well as details of pay and conditions. You'll find it in most libraries.

▼ TRAINING COURSES ▼

There are a whole range of courses now available called *Access* courses which do not require previous qualifications or experience and they nearly always lead on to a guaranteed place at an institute of higher education such as a polytechnic or university. These courses are organised through the system of Open Colleges.

The Open Colleges are mainly for adults who want to return to study and training. They are also concerned to provide educational opportunities for adults who have, traditionally, been less likely to go into further education. They identify the needs of mature students and priority groups and encourage the development of courses to meet their needs as well as making sure that accurate information is available to adults.

For more info contact:

■ **ALFA (The North London Open College Network)**, *The Marlborough Building, 383 Holloway Rd, N7 ORN (607 9393).*

■ **CAWLOC (Central & West London Open College)**, *35 Marylebone Rd, NW1 5LS (486 5611 Ext 329).*

■ **GLEAN (Greenwich & Lewisham Education for Adults Network)**, *South East London College (Breakspears 329), Lewisham Way, SE4 1UT (629 0353 ext 388).*

■ **OCSL (Open College of South London)** *Manor Hse, 58 Clapham Common North Side, SW4 9RZ (228 2015).*

■ **SCOPE (Second Chance Opportunities for Education)**, *c/o City of London Polytechnic, 117-119 Houndsditch, EC3A 7BU (283 1030 ext 347).*

If you have ever wondered what those TV programmes early in the morning are all about, you might be interested in the courses offered by the Open University. You can find out more by contacting: **The Open University (London Region)**, *Parsifal College, 527 Finchley Rd, Hampstead, NW3 (794 0575).*

▼ PROBLEMS AT WORK ▼

These can come in different forms; from the threat of redundancy to sexual harassment. Often your union will be the first point of contact.

Contacts

ACAS produce a free booklet *Discipline At Work* outlining the steps an employer should take and it makes useful reading. It's available from: **ACAS (Advisory, Conciliation and Arbitration Service)**, *Clifton Hse, 83-117 Euston Rd, NW1 (388 5100).*

If you are Lesbian or Gay **LAGER** (see **Lesbian and Gay** section p186) provide practical support and advice on anything to do with employment at work.

If you are in low paid work there is a Wages Rights Office which will give you advice: **Wages Rights Office**, *Low Pay Unit, 9 Upper Berkley St, W1 (262 7228/9).*

The **Maternity Alliance** (see **Women's** section p181) campaigns for the improvement of rights for parents during and after pregnancy.

Job Share

If you are not able or don't want to work full time you might want to consider job-sharing. This is a way of working where two people share the same, one, full-time job between them. Each sharer does half the work and receives half the pay, holidays and other benefits of the job. All job sharers who work over 16 hours a week have the same employment protection rights as full-time employees.

■ **New Ways to Work**, *409 Upper St, Islington, N7 (226 4026)* produce an introductory guide (£1.50) and a variety of leaflets explaining how the scheme works in detail. There is a job share register which matches people for job share.

Resources

■ **Action Resource Centre**, *Cap Hse, Long Lane, EC1 (629 3826).* Only support inner city community projects with seconded skilled staff to advise on management issues. 'Business skills and resources to community development'.

■ **The Centaur Project**, *313-5 Caledonian Rd, N1 (609 3328).* Educational charity, teach unemployed people basic office skills such as typing, book-keeping and word processing. Government funded. Also building national heritage library for tourists or those engaged in tourist industry.

▼ SELF EMPLOYMENT ▼

More and more people are thinking about starting up in business and working for themselves. There are advantages and disadvantages to being your own boss, compared to being employed, though something like 70% of small businesses go out of business in their first five years and nearly half fail before the end of their first year.

This section gives details of the sources of initial help available for people thinking of starting up in business for themselves, however the opportunities and restriction surrounding self employment are constantly changing.

Check one of the organisations listed below to find out the latest information.

Starting up

SOLE TRADER

This is the simplest form of setting up in business; there are few formalities and no rules about what records you have to keep, but you have to tell your local tax office when you start, and also your local Social Security office for paying National Insurance.

You can trade under your own name, or any other, and you don't have to register this, but if you use a name for your business other than your own, you have to include your own name and address where your business name is printed. This includes all stationary and any sign on your premises. If you do decide to use a trading name other than your own, there are certain words and phrases which you can't use without approval from the Secretary of State for Trade. These include

'British', 'International', 'Society', 'Foundation'. You can check this in a booklet, *Notes for Guidance on Control of Business Names*, from **The Dept of Trade & Industry, The Small Firms Service**, (see **Contacts** p43).

The advantages of starting up as a sole trader are that you can start immediately, there are fewer formalities, and no additional start-up costs.

The disadvantage is that there is no legal distinction between the owner and the business, therefore debts and obligations of the firm are regarded as those of the owner. If things go wrong, creditors can make claims on you and everything you own, and not just on the business.

Small traders are required to pay income tax on the business profit adjusted for taxation purposes

PARTNERSHIP

What you have to do in setting up a partnership is much the same as with a sole trader; there is no distinction between the business and the partners. So if things go wrong *all* the partners are responsible for paying off debts, no matter what agreement has been drawn up between them, and even if the debts were incurred by one partner's mismanagement or dishonesty without the others' knowledge. If you want to use a trading name different from your own name, the procedure is the same as with a sole trader.

However, there can be greater disadvantages with partnerships. The tend to go well when the business is doing well, but when things get difficult, a partnership which isn't on a firm footing can be a lot of trouble. If you have any doubts about the integrity and credibility of your partners, you should also consider starting up your own business as a Limited Company.

To start up properly you must draw up a formal agreement amongst the partners. This should cover every detail of what may crop up in the business between you and your partner(s), and between you and third parties. For instance it should include how profits and losses are to be shared and who should carry out which tasks. It should also set limits on what the partners can draw out each month, how long the partnership is to last, and the procedure for ending it. It should also include details of how policy is decided upon, and how to expel or admit new partners. Partners pay income tax on the business profit adjusted for taxation purposes (see section on **Tax** p46).

LIMITED COMPANY

A limited company is often the most favoured way of setting up in business for the larger small firm, especially in the manufacturing industry. This is because any debts incurred are not taken out of the personal pockets of its directors but out of company funds (unlike with sole traders or partnerships). However, in the early days of trading, or if you were previously a sole trader, the amount you can borrow on a loan may be limited, so you may have to make personal guarantees on top of what the business is worth. In this case, if the business fails your creditors will still be able to make a claim on your own private property.

A limited company costs money to set up (can be as little as £50 though see *Exchange and Mart*). You can do it yourself but it is not advisable. It is best to do it through an accountant or a solicitor (check the fees first). There are also company registration agents who specialise in company formation. The **Small Firms Service** can give you information on agents (see below). The documents have to be filed with:

■ **Companies House**, *55-71 City Rd, EC1 (253 9393).* When you are set up as a limited company you have to make annual returns to the Registrar and your profits will be subject to tax. Also, a limited company is required to be audited each year which is more expensive than accounts prepared for a sole trader or partnership.

CO-OPERATIVE

A workers co-op is a business which is collectively controlled and usually owned by the people who work in it. All the workers can be members and have an equal say in decision making, regardless of length of service or financial stake. This way of working presents a way of avoiding the traditional boss/employee relationship and allows each member a say in how the enterprise is run. Of course there are other problems of how to work out pay structures and decision making. But for many this is a worthwhile compromise. Some of the stages in setting up a workers' co-op are similar to starting as a self-employed business (see p40). You need a business idea and you have to find ways of raising money.

Workers' co-ops have become more popular in recent years as a way of starting up in business and statistically they have greater success in keeping going than the other three ways outlined above. It is a form of organisation which can be applicable to any small-scale manufacturing or service business.

The aims of a co-op differ from other forms of setting up in business, in that the main aim is to provide work for the members, and collective control of that work. Profits are either used to develop or expand the co-op, or are used to the benefit of the community in some way. (See also **Community** section p266).

Most co-operatives register as a corporate body with limited liability. If you don't, your group is legally a partnership, so each member would have personal liability for any debts. Alternatively, it can be registered with the Registrar of Friendly Societies under the Industrial Provident Societies Act. Their address is: **Registrar of Friendly Societies,** *15-17 Gt Marlborough St, W1 (437 9992).*

Advice on setting up co-operatives can be obtained from the head office of the **Co-operative Development Agency (CDA),** *Broadmead Hse, 21 Panton St, SW1 (839 2985)* who will be able to put you in touch with a local advisor who will guide you through the pitfalls.

■ **Community Enterprise Development Agency,** *Palingswick Hse, 241 King St, W6 (741 2304).*

■ **ICOM (Industrial Common Ownership Movement),** *8 Bradbury St, N16 (249 2837 Head Off. 0532 461737)* will give help in setting up a co-op or converting an existing business into a co-op.

■ **ICOF,** *12-14 Gold St, Northampton NN1 1RF, (0604 37563)* will consider applications for loans (rarely 100%).

Business Plan

It is very useful to write out a business plan to clarify for yourself, and any advisers/ potential backers you may have, the strengths and weaknesses of your business proposition. The business plan and cash forecasts need to sell your idea, but the best way it can do this is by being realistic. Would-be backers do not want to know how great you think your idea is, but how well you know your business, what the likely difficulties will be, and how you reckon to deal with them. The business plan must present the business 'warts and all', and include the following sections:

• **Curriculum vitae**

• **Product description** In this section you are describing in a few paragraphs exactly what it is you are going into business to do - whether it's a service or a product. It will affect what you say under the remaining headings, so it's important you get it right. So for example, if you are a fashion designer, you must make it clear whether you are designing ladies', men's or children's clothes, and what type of garments - will it be cheap High Street fashion or exclusive one-off commissions? Keep it simple, be precise, don't get too technical and give the reader a clear picture of your product/service.

• **Market and Marketing** Your proposed customers are your market and your marketing is the way you reach them.
You have already given an exact 'product description' so it should follow that your customer is a certain type of person, of a certain age group, income bracket, and interests.

The way you reach them therefore depends on these factors, and these in turn determine how and where you advertise. Explain what form your advertising will take and justify your analysis of your market. Try also to back up your statements in this section with market research (e.g. questionnaires, surveys etc).

The competition must also be identified in this section. Who are they? Where are they located? How much do they charge? Explain what makes your business different from theirs, the advantages, etc.

• **Skills** This section should draw out aspects of your CV which you then expand on. Here you highlight specific useful elements of any training or experience you may have that will be of direct benefit to your business. If you have no formal training that is relevant, then consider whether your proposed business requires you to work under pressure to meet deadlines, or requires a good telephone manner, etc. If you possess good organisational skills (be they technical or otherwise) necessary to run the kind of business you are proposing.

• **Business location** If your business is running or plans to run from commercial premises, then give a brief description of what you have, i.e. square footage, rent, facilities, location and the advantages and disadvantages. If your business is running from home, then explain how it will operate. It may be that all you need is an answerphone - if so your business overheads will be much reduced.

• **Future Developments** Here you give a brief description of your plans for year two and three - this should be a natural progression from what you expect to achieve in year one, so be realistic about it.

• **Costing** In order to determine your profit margins to get your pricing right, you need to work out the minimum you need to earn a week or an hour in order to break even.
This you do by listing both your personal and business expenses.

Your personal living expenses list should include any regular weekly, monthly or quarterly bills (keep strictly personal though).

Your business expenses should include the same kind of categories, and any other weekly, monthly or quarterly business expenses. Do not include materials for a job, e.g. the fabric for a dress, but include the regular bulk purchase of the cuttings and trimmings which you would have 'around' as a dressmaker.

To work out the annual business expense, multiply the weekly figure by 52 (less any holidays - you'll be lucky!).

You should now have total figures for your personal and business expenses per week. If you add the two together you will get the total amount you need to earn a week. If you then divide this figure by the number of hours you intend to work - 35 or 40, you will get your basic hourly rate. This is the sum you need to earn every hour 35 or 40 hours per week in order to break even - you are not making any money, just breaking even.

If this basic hourly rate is very high, you may find it difficult to compete after you have added on top the cost of materials for individual items if you are making products and what will be your profit. If this is the case, then you need to re-think the viability of your business. If this is not the case, then this exercise gives a solid foundation to your pricing, hence the prices you will charge are not figures simply plucked from the sky.

• **Financial requirements** If you are looking for funding then you need to itemise and justify how much money you want, and what it is to be spent on.

• **Cash flow** The final stage of the business plan is the cash flow.

This section usually seems to be the most difficult, but if you know your business it should not present you with too many problems. Try to remember that all a cash flow represents is a numbers version of what you have already said in words in the Business Plan.

The cash flow sheet is divided both horizontally and vertically.

Horizontally - it is divided into a top and a bottom half. The top half shows your income and the bottom half your expenditure.

Vertically - reading left to right is the list of items under the headings 'Income' and 'Expenditure' and the year divided into 12 months.

Using educated guesswork you then begin to predict both the income and the expenditure that you will incur in the first year of your business. This is done by entering the expected income/expenditure in the appropriate month and against the itemised list on the left of the page.

For example, if on Enterprise Allowance, this is an income which you know you will receive throughout the 12 months of the year, so enter the appropriate figure right across the 12 months having divided £2080 by 12.

Quarterly bills, such as telephone, heating, lighting, etc. should be entered on the cash flow under the month the bill is expected to arrive.

One-off payments, such as accountant's fees at the end of the year, should be entered under the month you expect to be billed.

The important thing to remember is that cash flow forecast is an attempt to predict your cash flow for the coming year. It is for this reason that income and expenditure must be entered under the appropriate month(s), e.g. a healthy bank balance in month three will not mean that you can have a spending spree, as your cash flow reminds you that your quarterly bills are due in month four.

Every London borough now has at least one advice agency which will give you ideas and suggestions for setting up your own business. Most of them also run courses, give grants or loans and run workshop spaces.

Contacts

■ **London Small Firms Centre,** *2-18 Ebury Bridge Rd, SW1 (730 5874/730 6204).* Information and counselling service run by the Department of Trade and Industry. It has a *freephone* service - ring the operator and ask for freephone 2444. Can answer any practical enquiry. If you have a longer and more detailed question, you can make an appointment with one of their counsellors - your first three consultations are free. First session, of one to two hours, is normally held at Small Firms Centre, sometimes at a Job Centre. Second and third sessions could be at your place of business and last half a day or more. Further sessions cost you £30 for unlimited time. Counsellors are seconded from industry. The more clued up you are before you see them, the more useful you'll find the interview. Also publish leaflets.

■ **London Enterprise Agency (LEntA),** *4 Snowhill, EC1 (236 3000/4423).* This is the free market alternative to the government funded Small Firms Service, sponsored by 15 large companies, who provide staff and finance. LEntA offer a free advice and counselling service. The Small Firms Service seems stronger on advice on the formalities and technicalities of setting up a business, and also in advising you in a general way when you're in the early stages of thinking about setting up, whereas LEntA is stronger on advice about marketing, how to improve your project and how to sell your idea, so the further on you are with your business the more helpful they can be. They can also help you prepare your case for funding, help with your cash flow and budget, and help sort out difficulties on the financial side. They have a number of small loans available. They also let out managed workspace for small firms, run the 'LEntA Marriage Bureau' for small businesses looking for capital or management help. Also run courses.

■ **Instant Muscle,** *c/o Wandsworth Youth Enterprise Centre, 28 Tooting High St, SW17 (767 6027).* They work with groups of people (aged 18-30 - but not individuals) from the initial business idea, towards getting set-up and successful. They form part of a network able to help other *Instant Muscle* small businesses. They have four advisers for the Greater London area, and because they work so closely with the groups, there's a limit to the number they can take on. At the moment there are about 60 groups throughout the UK. Although they started up with 'handy person' type businesses, they now work with businesses through a whole range of manufacturing or service provision. Can offer advice to those they don't take on. No money to give away, but can help find sources of funding.

■ **Crafts Council,** *12 Waterloo Pl, SW1 (930 4811).* Give loans and grants for workshops and craft enterprises. These can be for maintenance, starting up, training or bursaries. Worth trying if you've a good skill/ product. Allocated on the basis of the quality of work, require 'a high level of technical ability and design content in your work'. Gallery, regular exhibitions of contemporary crafts.

Also have 'Register of Craftspeople' so that potential customers can get in touch with craft workers.

■ **Industrial Society,** *3 Carlton Hse Terr, SW1 (839 4300)* run *Headstart* courses which offer training in self employment. At the end of the course you are offered a 'business mate'- a local business person who gives on-going support.

■ **Project Fullemploy,** *Unit 20, 131 Clerkenwell Cl, EC1 (251 6037).* Run *Work for Yourself,* a variety of courses for people under 26. Some women only. Tutors available to offer advice to individuals and groups.

■ **Project Fullemploy,** *18 Creekside, Drake Hse, Deptford, SE8 3DZ (692 7141).* As above.

■ **Urban and Economic Development (URBED),** *99 Southwark St, SE1 (928 9515).* Courses including business ideas, business enterprise etc.

■ **Camden Training Centre,** *57 Pratt St, NW1 (482 2103).* Run women only courses on self-employment.

■ **Black Business Development Assn (BBDA),** *51 Hugon Rd, SW6 (736 7399).*

■ **Paul Bogle Enterprise Ltd,** *189 Kentish Town Rd, NW5 2JU (267 0980).* Give business advice to ethnic minorities.

■ **Rastafarian Advisory Service,** *(602 3767)* (see page 234).

Finance

The information listed in this section is not a complete list of sources of finance to new businesses - it is a selection of those schemes and agencies most suitable and useful to young people in the initial stages of thinking about setting themselves up in business.

ENTERPRISE ALLOWANCE SCHEME

If you're about to set up in business, this is the first scheme to look at. It is relatively easy to get on to and you get £80 a fortnight for one year on top of any money you make through your business.

The idea behind the scheme is that it gets round the problem that as soon as you start up in business you can't claim benefit, even though for the first year you may not be earning enough to support yourself. The other advantage of the EAS from the government's point of view is that it cuts down the unemployment figures.

You don't have to convince the EAS that your business is viable, or even show them a business plan. The conditions are:

1. You have to have been unemployed for at least 8 weeks, and be receiving unemployment benefit or income support either yourself or though a member of your family, at time of entry. If you have been on MSC, JTS, etc. or under formal notice of redundancy, this can count toward the 8 weeks.
2. You have to show you have £1,000 available to invest in your business. You need only show that you have access to the money - it could be in the form of a loan or an overdraft (a letter from your bank manager saying you have an overdraft facility can count). Many banks won't give an overdraft for the EAS (in a recent survey Midland, Nat West and Barclays seemed to be the readiest to lend for EAS). Receipts for equipment necessary to your business (car, computer etc) can also be used.
3. You must be 18 or over.
4. You must agree to work in the business for a minimum of 36 hours per week. You can work for someone else for up to 8 hours per week.
5. Your business must be approved by the Department of Employment (in practice this means the EAS staff). For this to happen you have to prove it is:

a) New. You can't take over an existing business. Don't start trading in your business until the EAS say you can (though you can check out premises, cost of supplies, and do any market research necessary).
b) Based in Great Britain
c) Be suitable for public support. This means it must not annoy the neighbours, the police, promote particular religious or political

views, or sell sex or porn. You can't do psychic stuff or astrology. If you're a writer you may be asked to show a chapter by chapter synopsis. Practitioners of alternative medicine or therapy have to be qualified.

If you've been on the EAS once, you may be able to go on it again, but at least 12 months must have passed since you last received any money.

You don't have to be a sole trader. If you go into business with other people, at least half of them must be on the EAS (up to 10 people can be accepted on the scheme), and each person whether on EAS or not, must show they have £1,000 to invest. Slightly different rules apply if you are setting up a limited company.

How to apply

Local Job Centres send you on an EAS *Awareness Day* where they will tell you what's involved in setting up your own business. On the day, you get a form to fill in to send to the EAS office, who will then ask you in to see them. At this interview you have to show you have the £1,000, and sign an agreement.

Other things you should know.

1. EAS money is paid fortnightly *in arrears* by standing order into your business bank account.
2. You may still get some state benefits such as Housing Benefit or Family Credit.
3. You may have to pay National Insurance contributions.
4. You will have to make an Income Tax return to the Inspector of Taxes. You should let the Inland Revenue know when you start your business.
5. You're entitled to three free counselling sessions from the EAS staff. After three months, you either get a visit (they let you know when they are coming) or have to go into the EAS office to tell them what's happening with the business.

GRANTS/LOANS

■ **Prince's Youth Business Trust,** *8 Jockey's Field, WC1 (430 0521).* The Youth Initiative bursary of this organisation is one of the few bodies which offers grants - up to £1,000 for a one-person business, or up to £3,000 for a partnership of up to three people. It is unusual to get the full amount though - grants of £840 are the average. You can only spend it on tools, equipment, transport, fees, insurance and training. You can't use it for working capital, rent, rates or stock. Also give loans on top of grants - up to £2,000 for individuals, £5,000 for groups. Repayment terms are negotiable: 0% year one, 5% year two, 10% for year three. You have to show that an application for a bank loan has been turned down, be 25 or under, unemployed, and their primary concern is to help people who are disadvantaged in some way.

They like you to be in touch with an advice agency, then tell them about your idea and convince them of your need for a grant. You then get an application form which you have to send back with a very detailed business proposal (use an advice agency to help with this). You should have premises when you apply.

If all is well at this stage, you go for an interview or they come to see you. They may tell you to sort out some aspect of your plan if it's not satisfactory. If you're accepted they give you two advisers to guide you through your first year.

■ **London Enterprise Agency,** (see above), have various loan schemes available, or information on who might give you a loan.

■ **Lawrence Atwell's Charity,** *The Clerk, Skinners Hall, 8 Dowgate Hill, EC4 (236 5629).* They can give top-up funding of up to £2,000 to young men aged 17-26.

— USES FOR WOMEN AROUND THE HOUSE —

■ **Thomas Arneways Loan Charity,** *1 Dean Farrar St, SW1 (222 5044)* give loans of up to £1,000.

■ **3i,** *91 Waterloo Rd, SE1 (928 7822)* (which used to be IFCF), was set up by the Bank of England and the clearing banks in 1945 to meet the long term needs of small and medium sized businesses. 3i will also invest amounts of money for a long term - in 1987/8 it lent £537 million to businesses. They'll send you information on starting up, capital for growth, management buy-outs (and buy-ins).

Tax

INCOME TAX

You should to inform your local tax office when you start trading. The address is under*Inland Revenue* in the phone directory. You can fill in form 4IG, which is on the back of a leaflet *Starting Up in Business* IR28 available from tax offices and the **Small Firms Service.**

Tax is payable on the profits of the business, after the appropriate deductions have been made. Some items of business expenditure can be offset against your profits. If you can afford an accountant, she will be able to do this and you could save money. She can also deal with the tax office on your behalf. Even if you've got an accountant, you still need to keep records of income and expenditure for her - and the tax office may want to look at them.

VAT

You have to register for *Value Added Tax* (VAT) if you have reason to believe your future taxable turnover will exceed £22,100 in the current year. Your taxable turnover is the value of your sales or services. You will have to register if your taxable turnover for the last quarter exceeds £7,500. If you leave it too late and register when you have been eligible to pay VAT for some time before, you'll have to pay back the VAT owed.

Once registered, you get a VAT return form every three months. You will need to keep records of all the supplies you make and receive, and VAT charged on both. A pamphlet called *Keeping Records and Accounts,* available form VAT offices, tells you how to adapt business records to give VAT information.

To register you need to fill in form *VAT 1* within ten days of the date that you are liable for VAT. Your local VAT office is in the phone directory under *Customs and Excise.* A useful booklet is *Should I be registered for VAT?* published by them.

National Insurance

As a self employed person you normally have to pay Class 2 National Insurance contributions. From 6th April 1989 these are charged at a flat rate of £4.25 a week. You can arrange with the Department of Social Security to pay by 'direct debit' from your bank. This way you won't have to bother about getting stamps or having a contribution card. Otherwise you can get a card for a year from your local DoSS office, and buy special NI stamps each week from the post office.

You can apply for exemptions from paying Class 2 contributions if your earnings are expected to be less than £2,350 in the tax year starting on 6th April 1989. You need to fill in a small form - CF10, which is in the leaflet *People with small earnings from self-employment* (NI27A).

If you're not sure how much you are likely to be earning, you can apply for deferment of contributions but you should do this before the beginning of the tax year. The leaflet which tells you about this, and contains the application form, is NP18.

By paying Class 2 contributions you will keep up your entitlement to basic retirement pension and sickness benefit. However, you still won't be able to claim unemployment benefit.

If your profits are between £5,050 and £16,900 you have to pay Class 4 contributions as well as Class 2. Class 4 are earnings related - 6.3 per cent of profits. These are normally assessed and collected by Inland Revenue along with income tax.

A useful leaflet is *National Insurance Guide for the Self Employed* NI41, available from tax offices, or you can make enquiries by phoning Freephone Social Security on *(0800 666 555).*

■ **National Research Development Corporation,** *Kingsgate House, 66 Victoria St, SW1 (828 3400)* may provide finance on reasonable terms (a levy on sales) for the development and launch of innovative science-based products and processes.

■ **Small Firm Information Service (SFIS),** *2-18 Ebury Bridge Rd, W1 (dial 100 and ask for Freephone 2444).* Will send you a free pack on how to set up your own business. Can set up free advice sessions, send info, and put you on to local people who can help you (Chamber of Commerce etc). Run by the Dept of Industry.

■ **Association of Independent Businesses,** *133 Copeland Rd, SE15 3SP (277 5158).* Campaigns for the interests of independent businesses. They run an advice line (phone the above number and they'll put you on to an expert). Membership from £45 - £450 depending on number of employees.

■ **The Crafts Council,** *12 Waterloo Pl, SW1 (930 4811).* Can put you in touch with specific craft guild. Gives grants and bursaries.

■ **National Extension College,** *18 Brooklands Ave, Cambridge CB2 2HN, (0223 316644).*

social security

t here have been a lot of changes in the system of social security recently. In theory, social security provides a safety net to stop people falling into poverty, in practise there seem to be quite a few holes. There are more and more exceptions to entitlement and the complexity of the rules means that many people who would be eligible for some money do not claim. Once you've run the gauntlet of the queues and forms and get your money, you'll find your ingenuity tested to the limit to live on the amount you're paid! Patience, politeness and a middle class accent are assets when dealing with the DSS.

Payment is made through ***DSS (Department of Social Security) Offices.*** *There is a two tier system;* ***Unemployment Benefit*** *and* ***income support.*** *You are entitled to unemployment benefit or a pension when you have made enough contributions to* ***National Insurance.*** *This is paid automatically when you are employed or by weekly stamp if you are self-employed (see* ***Jobs*** *p36). Payment of* ***Income Support*** *is worked out according to need, and in some circumstances can be paid even if you are working, and does not depend on the amount of contributions you've made to National Insurance.*

▼ UNEMPLOYMENT BENEFIT ▼

In order to claim unemployment benefit you must 'be eligible for work'. In practise this means that you have to 'sign on' (sign a form declaring that you have not worked and are available for work) at the Unemployment Benefit (dole) Office (see in phone book under *Employment*), usually, every two weeks. To make an initial claim you go the *Fresh Claims* desk. You will be asked to fill in a B1 (which is to assess your entitlement to Income Support) an *availability to work* form which questions you closely on

- what you are doing to find work
- when you are available for work (ie would you be prepared to work shifts/nights/ weekends)
- what work you are willing to do
- how much money you are prepared to earn

Remember when you are filling in this form that you must show that you are available and willing to work, otherwise you will not get any benefit. If you need any help with this or any other form ask your local CABx. It won't look too good if you say you are only looking for work as a stilt walker for £50,000 a year! In future any claimant will not only have to show that they are available for work but also that they are actively seeking work. If you have a professional qualification you can ask to be put on the *Professional Register*, in practice this means you won't be hassled so much about taking any job that is available.

▼ SIGNING ON ▼

When you go to sign on for the first time take:

- your National Insurance number
- Your last pay slip
- Your P 45

There are only two rates of Unemployment benefit:

Under pensionable age	£34.70
over pensionable age	£43.60

Once your claim is sorted out (which may take up to three weeks) you will get a giro every two weeks, two days after you've signed on, and you cash this at your local Post Office (which you will have specified to the dole office) or through your bank.

You will receive this for one year after

which, if you are still unemployed, you will have to claim for income support. You may also be entitled to claim Income Support while you are getting Unemployment benefit if you're needs require it (i.e. if you have kids or a mortgage etc).

If you have left your job 'voluntarily' or have been sacked you will not get any Unemployment Benefit for six months, but you will be able to claim Income Support during this time.

If you earn more than £2 a day you will lose your complete entitlement for that day, (and remember you are supposed to declare any part-time or casual work that you do).

Holidays

If you plan to go away you'll have to fill in a holiday form giving an address or phone number in this country where you can be contacted if a job comes up. You have to declare that you'd be prepared to come back if there was a job. Make sure you fill it in at least a week in advance and hand it in to the office, don't send it. If you don't sign on and they haven't received a holiday form they might assume you've got a job and cancel your benefit.

■ **Freephone Social Security,** *(0800 666 555)* for any enquiries about Unemployment Benefit or Income Support. They won't ask who you are or why you're calling.

▼ INCOME SUPPORT (IS) ▼

Income support is a *means-tested* benefit - i.e. you have to show that you are on a very low income or none at all. It tops up your income (if you have any) to a minimum level laid down by the Parliament each year - it really is a minimum level, so be prepared. Its paid out by the Department of Social Security (there are local offices in your area) you don't have to have made any National Insurance contributions (NI) to get it.

It's for people not in full-time work (24 hours or more a week) and not in full-time education - if in doubt, claim! Couples decide which partner is the claimant. You qualify if you are currently living in G.B. If you are temporarily abroad, benefit may continue for a further four weeks. If you're from another country, you might be able to get IS or at least a reduced rate - *urgent cases payment* - under limited circumstances (see **People From Abroad** p119). No-one with more than £6,000 capital will get it.

School Leavers

As from September 1988, 16 and 17 year olds are no longer entitled to IS. School leavers in this age range who can't find work, or who don't stay on in full-time education are expected to join a Youth Training Scheme (YTS). The Government has guaranteed that a YTS place will be offered to every 16 and 17 year old who wants one. A real *catch* 22 - if you don't take up the YTS place on offer you don't get paid and your not allowed to claim IS - so not a lot of choice.

Like all the Department of Social Security regulations, there are some exceptions - e.g. if you are 16/17 and a single parent, so it's always worth checking the small print - if in doubt, claim and find out. Remember, DSS officials are not programmed to offer advice about benefits you haven't claimed - the onus is on you to claim.

Students

Part-time students 19-21 yrs (less than 21 hrs a week in college) can claim IS if you didn't leave school to take the course, and you can leave it if a job comes up.

You must be under 21 or have been signing on for a year, or claiming IS before the course started.

Full-time students in 'non-advanced education' (up to and including 'A' levels) can't usually claim, but again, some exceptions - if you are living apart from parents, if you are an orphan, taking care of a child, or unlikely to get a job in the next 12 months because of a disability.

Full-time students in 'advanced education' can claim IS during the summer vacation but not Easter nor Christmas holidays.

Sponsored Immigrants

Sponsered Immigrants can claim if your sponsor can't support you any more - but, if your sponsor *could* pay but won't, the DSS will take legal action to get the money back.

▼ HOW TO CLAIM ▼

Anyone under 60 has to go to the Unemployment Benefit Office (UBO) known too as the 'dole' office to *sign on* as available for work (usually once a fortnight).

Addresses and phone numbers are in the phone book under Department of Social Security - or ask in your local library.

Say that you want to claim Income Support and get form B1. Fill this in and send or take it to the Social Security Office - address will be on the form. When/if you get a job, ask the UBO for an earning form (A7) - your IS will automatically carry on for 2 more weeks (and a further 2 in an exceptional emergency).

It tends to be much quicker if you go to the Social Security Office in person, remember to check first that you have the right office and that they deal with your particular address. The offices are open to the public usually 9.30 am - 3.30 pm.

Documents Needed

You will appreciate how useful it is to have with you official documents which you might be asked for when claiming, so take as many of the following as you can find.

- Your last 3 pay slips (and your wife's if relevant)
- National Insurance number
- Rent book (or landlady's letter) water and rates bill/mortgage details
- Post office/bank/buildingsociety book
- Details of hire purchase or other debts
- Child benefit book
- Details of any special expenses
- Children's birth certificatess (if not included in any of the above documents
- Family Credit book (explained later)

Some people can make a claim for IS without having had to sign on first:

- If you are over 60
- A single parent with a child less than 16
- If you're looking after a foster child
- looking after a dependent who is temporarily ill
- If you are pregnant
- If you are a single parent and a student.
- If you're on a government training scheme - YTS and MSC

There are a variety of other exceptions, so always check whether or not you have to sign on - don't apply logic to DSS rules!

If you are in this group, you can fill in form A1 to claim IS.

Earnings Disregarded

You are allowed to earn £5.00 a week without it affecting your IS claim. Single parents and families unemployed for more than two years can earn £15.00 a week and still claim IS.

Capital Cut-Off

If you have more than £6,000 capital you can't get IS, Housing Benefit (HB) or Family Credit (FC).

If your claim is successful, your IS will be paid to you by Girocheque or benefit book which can be cashed at a post office, once a fortnight (in arrears) two days after your signing on day.

▼ CALCULATING ▼ INCOME SUPPORT

The DSS will calculate your benefit on the basis of your 'needs'.

The three stages to work out Income Support are:

- work out your *applicable amount* -i.e. the amount they think you need to live on each week.
- work out your income - the amount you already have from either benefits, part-time work savings etc.
- Take away income you have from amount you need.

The answer you get should be the amount you get.

Income Support is made up of *personal allowance* plus *premiums*. The amount of personal allowance depends on age and is fixed each year by parliament. It's an extremely low rate.

Personal Allowance

(Amounts correct April 1989)

Single People	under 18	£19.40
	18-24	£26.05
	25 and over	£33.40
Couples	under 18	£38.80
	over 18	£51.45

Only mixed sex couples are considered partners.

Single Parent	under 18	£19.40
	over 18	£33.40
Children	under 10	£10.75
	11-15 yrs	£16.10
	16-17 yrs	£19.40
	25 and over	£26.05

Premiums

Family		£6.15
Single Parent		£3.70
Pensioner 60-79 yrs		
	single	£10.65
	couple	£16.25
Higher Pensioner 80+		
	single	£13.05
	couple	£18.60

Disability		
	single	£13.05
	couple	£18.60
Severe Disability		
	single	£24.75
	couple:	
	both disability	£49.50
Disabled child		£6.15

Couples

You are counted as a couple if
• You and your partner are married and living in the same household
• You and your partner are not married but are living together 'as husband and wife'.
A lesbian or gay couple are not counted as partners as far as Social Security is concerned, they are counted as two separate claimants.

Housing Costs

You can get help with housing expenses in addition to basic benefit.

If you are getting Income Support, you can get this in the following ways:
• If you pay rent, you should claim housing benefit (HB) from your local council (see **Somewhere to Live** section p2).
If you pay rates, you can get HB to cover 80% of these. The rest you are expected to pay from your IS.
• If you own your home, you will get help with housing costs (e.g. mortgage interest or interest on a loan for repairs or improvements to the home) from DSS under IS.
• If you pay board and lodging accommodation charges (i.e. hotel, guest house, lodging house or similar type of accommodation, or hostel, residential care or nursing home) or if you pay an amount for accommodation which includes cooked meals, you will get an allowance for meals if you have to eat out. The allowances are:

Lower rate	single	£10.30
	couple	£20.60
Higher rate	single	£11.50
	couple	£23
Dependent children		
	up to 11	£3.45
	11-15	£5.30
	16-17	£6.20
	18 yrs	£10.30

Householders

People solely responsible for the rent or mortgage get the householder rate plus rent and rates. Owner-occupiers get the householder rate and interest payments on a mortgage, plus rates and a maintenance and assurance allowance. It is assumed that any non-dependent people living with you will be paying rent, which is deducted from the allowance paid to you.

JOINT HOUSEHOLDERS

Sharing the cost of a house (gay and lesbian couples come under this section) get the non-householder rate plus your share of the housing costs and the share of the extra that a 'householder' (above) gets.

NON-HOUSEHOLDERS

Those living in someone else's house are always called non-householders. You get a small amount towards rent.

You should be counted as a householder for DSS purposes if you have separate living quarters and separate arrangements for 'buying and storing food'.

▼ HEALTH AND ▼ EDUCATION BENEFITS

School Meals and Milk

If the family is getting IS then school meals and milk are free.

Dental Treatment/ Prescriptions

Dental treatment and prescriptions are free if you are on IS or Family Credit.

Hospital Travelling Expenses

Free if you are on IS. Check with the social worker at the hospital in case there are other funds you might be able to claim e.g. to cover the cost of visiting a relative in hospital.

Education

Apply to your local education authority for school clothing/uniform grant and for maintenance grant for those staying on at school after 16 yrs of age.

▼ DIVORCED/SEPARATED ▼

• If you are separated, your wife/husband is liable to pay maintenance for you and the children. Once divorced, s/he is only liable to pay for the children.
• If s/he hasn't already agreed to pay maintenance, or the DSS think s/he should pay more, they will try to contact her/him.
• If the local office thinks you have enough money to be going on with, they will try and contact your wife/husband before starting to pay you any benefit. But if you are living below IS level you should be paid straight

away, i.e. you should not have to wait for DSS to investigate before paying you.
• If your partner refuses to pay maintenance, you or the DSS can apply for a court order against her/him. See explanatory leaflet (form B0100). Get legal advice if in doubt about what to do.
• If your ex-partner is paying maintenance under a court order, it's a good idea to get the order signed over to DSS so that you get your money regularly.
• If you are single, your child's mother/father is liable to pay maintenance for the child. But benefit should *not* be refused if you are unwilling to give information about the mother/father (if for example you're worried about violence if you give information). If you want to take out a maintenance order, getting the DSS to do it can be easier sometimes.
• An unmarried mother can't take out a maintenance order more than 3 yrs after the child's birth (or the last *voluntary* maintenance payment) but the DSS *can* and they can transfer it to you when/if necessary.
• When a couple makes a claim, it is up to the couple to decide who is to be the claimant and who the money should be paid to. If you separate and still live in the same household, you will probably have to argue long and hard to get the DSS to treat you as separate claimants and they might press you for proof that you are taking out legal proceedings to separate/divorce. Even if you are no longer living in the same household, you might have to convince DSS that you are no longer a couple.
• If you're claiming IS and begin living with a partner (of the opposite sex) your money will be stopped. You can *try* to argue against this.
• If your money is suddenly stopped e.g. because DSS suspect your partner is in full time work and they want to investigate, you don't have the right of appeal.

▼ EXCEPTIONAL EXPENSES ▼ DISCRETIONARY PAYMENTS

Social Fund

The *Social Fund* is a scheme to help with exceptional expenses which your regular income won't stretch to cover. (SF replaces the old Supplementary Benefit). Social Fund Offices are part of local Dept of Social Security offices.

There are six types of payments from the Social Fund
• **Maternity Payments** A flat rate of £85 for each baby expected, born or adopted, for people on IS or Family Credit (see later).
• **Funeral Payments** Payments for funeral expenses can be claimed by people on IS, Family Credit or Housing Benefit.
• **Budgeting Loans** Interest-free loans to help people who have been on IS for six months or more. The idea is to spread the cost of periodic expenses which are difficult to meet out of your weekly benefit. But beware, once you take out this sort of loan, your weekly IS is reduced until the loan is repaid to the DSS. The reduced amount of benefit which you are left to live on is no joke.
• **Crisis Loans** Interest-free loans to help people whether or not on benefit who are faced with an emergency or disaster. Payments are usually made for a specific item or for immediate living expenses not over 14 days.
• **Community Care Grants** These grants are intended to help anyone move back into the community after a period in institutional or residential care. You have to be on IS to claim.
• **Cold Weather Payments** Amount decided when/if cold weather dictates.

Family Credit

Family Credit (FC) is paid to low income families in work - it replaces the old Family Income Supplement (FIS). It is not available to single people nor childless couples.

WHO CAN CLAIM
You can claim FC if your household includes a child or young person and all of the following:

- you (or your partner) usually work 24 hrs or more per week
- you are British residents
- you have less than £6000 capital

HOW MUCH WILL YOU GET?
The amount of FC you get will depend on your income and savings.

HOW TO CLAIM
Get DSS leaflet FC1 from your local post office or nearest social security office. It contains the claim form and a return envelope, so it doesn't cost anything to make a claim. If you have problems getting a claim form phone **Freephone** *(0800 666555)* and ask for a form to be sent to you. The call is free.

A claim for FC can be backdated for a maximum of one year, but you have to have *good cause* for not having claimed earlier. It's in these areas of discretion that you can find difficulty in proving *good cause*.

If you need to contact the **Family Credit Union** you can write/phone them at: **DSS**, *Government Buildings, Warbreck Hill, Blackpool FY2 OYF, (0253 500050/856123)*. It's wise to keep a copy of your letter/details of call, in case you need to write/phone them again. If your claim is agreed, you will be sent an order book which you can cash weekly at your local post office.

Always appeal if you feel you have been unfairly refused a benefit.

▼ GENERAL TIPS ▼

Most benefit offices run on paperwork. Staff are more likely to deal with your query if you put it in writing rather than calling in person or by telephone. Remember to include in your letter your name, address and any reference numbers you've been given. It's a good idea to keep a copy.

If you telephone the benefit office and don't get satisfaction, ask to speak to the supervisor of that department or section.

Remember to check opening times of benefit offices before a visit - if you turn up unexpectedly you might have to wait a long time to be seen. It sometimes helps too to take someone with you for moral support! You're likely to need it.

Emergencies

For example if you have just lost your money/home/possessions and need to contact a benefit office out of normal hours, try your town hall emergency service which will help you contact a social worker who *might* be able to help. Or your local police station should have the telephone number of DSS staff on call outside normal working hours. There are also emergency offices open weekends and evenings. For London contact **DSS Emergency Office,** *Keyworth House, Keyworth St, SE1, (407 2315).*

Lost/Missing Payments

Report it immediately to relevant benefit office. They must issue a replacement (but will want to make some enquiries first). The office has to make sure you get the payments due to you. If you meet resistance from them seek specialist advice (e.g. Citizens Advice, Law Centre, Local Authority Welfare Rights Adviser etc) about how to get your benefit.

▼ HASSLES ▼

Fraud

If you make a false statement deliberately when claiming benefit, you are technically guilty of fraud. If the DSS suspects fraud, they might suspend benefit while they *investigate*. Seek advice before answering any questions.

The Cohabitation Rule

The law says that if an unmarried couple are *living together as husband and wife* they should be treated in the same way as a married couple. The DSS sometimes wrongly accuse couples living in the same household as cohabiting and so try to reduce their benefit. So individuals of opposite sexes who live in the same household, whether there is or is not a sexual relationship, are at risk of falling foul of this rule (e.g. landlady/lodger, tenant/ housekeeper or flat-sharers). So, in the eyes of the DSS, if for example, you have a sexual relationship with a flatmate of the opposite sex, or have a joint arrangement for storing/ cooking food, you might be accused of cohabiting. Women claiming income support or widows benefit are particularly vulnerable.

Get legal advice and appeal if you find your benefit has been stopped for this reason.

Child Poverty Action Group's (CPAG)(see below). *National Welfare Benefits Handbook* has a good section on cohabitation. Also see *The Cohabitation Handbook - A Woman's Guide to the Law* (Pluto Press).

Squatters

You're entitled to IS if you give your full name and address, so appeal if it's refused. Dispute it if they use the ruse that your address is unsafe and make you collect your cheque personally.

Length of Time Before Payment

How soon will you be paid? Once the appropriate officer has made a decision on your claim, payments should start 'as soon as is reasonably practicable'. It's supposed to be within 14 days. Contact the DSS if there is a delay. Seek advice to help you with your claim if necessary (e.g. Citizens Advice, Law Centres etc, see p207). You should be notified in writing of the outcome of your claim - you can ask for a detailed breakdown of how your payment is worked out - ask for form A124.

Reviews and Appeals

If you're unhappy about the amount of payment or if your claim is turned down, you can challenge this by asking for the decision to be reviewed. Ask for a review by writing to your local office. If the Adjudication Officers agrees to change the decision, you can get arrears of benefit going back a year from the date of request for a review.

Appeals If you're still not satisfied, you can appeal to an independent Social Security Tribunal. Write to your local office within three months and say which decision you wish to appeal against, giving reasons why.

It's a good idea to take a friend with you to the appeal hearing - for moral support and strangely enough, it seems to improve the odds for you winning. If you lose, you have a further right of appeal to a Social Security Commissioners, but only if the tribunal has made an error of law.

▼ USEFUL SOURCES OF ▼ FURTHER HELP AND ADVICE

■ **Social Workers** based in local Authority Social Services Departments don't have sufficient staff to help with specific queries but will probably have names and addresses of other agencies which can.

■ **Citizens Advice Bureaux (CABx)** are in most areas (under 'C' in business phone book) as well as independent advice centres (see p207) or local authority welfare rights advisers. You should be able to find out about them from the town halls or libraries.

■ **Claimants' Unions** also give advice. Get details of local groups from **The Federation of Claimants Unions,** *296 Bethnal Green Rd, E2,* and **London and South East Federation of Unemployed, Claimants, and Unwaged Groups,** *c/o 42 Queen Square, WC1.*

■ You can get legal advice from a solicitor under the *Green Form* scheme. Check at your library for the list of solicitors who do legal aid work or from **Legal Aid Head Office,** *8-16 Great New St, EC4.*

■ **Child Poverty Action Group (CPAG)** (and **Citizens Rights Office,** at the same address) publish the *National Welfare Benefits Handbook* (updated every year) as well as other handbooks and guides. For a full catalogue write to **CPAG,** *4th Floor, 1-5 Bath St, EC1 (253 3406).* Will not give help to individuals over the phone, only to welfare advice officers. If you have any benefits queries you should write.

■ **National Youth Bureau,** *17-23 Albion St, Leicester LE1 690.*

■ **Islington People's Rights,** *Whittington Hospital, Highgate Hill, N19 (272 3070 x 4139/4322).* Advice on SS for hospital in-patients and workers.

the poll tax

Unlike the sytem of PAYE tax where the tax rate goes up the more a person earns, the Poll Tax is levied ***regardless of the ability to pay***. This means the poor in our society will be hit the hardest. Many of those who cannot afford to pay will 'disappear' from the electoral register in an attempt to avoid payment. They will then be deprived of the right to vote. Something is going drastically wrong with our society when this happens.*

▼ WHAT IS THE POLL TAX? ▼

The Poll Tax (or Community Charge, as the Government calls it) is a *flat rate tax* on nearly all adults over 18. It will replace rates as a means of paying for council services from 1st Apr 1990 in England and Wales. (The Poll Tax was introduced in Scotland on Apr 1st, 1989).

There are three types of Poll Tax

- **Personal** - paid by all adults over 18.
- **Collective** - paid by owners or landlords/ladies of some short stay accommodation, such as bed+breakfast hotels or hostels. The landlady or owner will collect contributions from residents on a daily basis.
- **Standard** - paid by people with second homes or on property empty for over three months.

Steve Bell

▼ EXEMPTIONS FROM ▼ PAYMENT

- **Prisoners and Detainees** - including both convicted prisoners and those on remand. *But* people imprisoned for non-payment of fines and for non-payment of the poll tax will still be liable.
- **Diplomats,** foreign soldiers and people working for some international organisations.
- **Severely Mentally Disabled** - this will apply to people receiving a severe disablement allowance or invalidity pension, or those over pensionable age who are judged by their G.P. to be *severely mentally impaired*. People who are severely physically disabled *will* have to pay , as will those who become *severely mentally impaired* as a result of a degenerative diseases (e.g. Alzheimer's disease).
- **18 year olds still at school** 19 year olds still at school *will* have to pay.
- **Monks and nuns**
- **Patients in hospitals or homes** - only for those who are resident.
- **Volunteer care workers** - e.g. Community Service Volunteers working for charitable purposes on nominal wages.
- **Residents of short stay charitable hostels and people of no fixed abode.**

Leeds Postcards

▼ WHO COLLECTS ▼ THE POLL TAX?

The Poll Tax will be collected by your local council. The tax is designed to be administered by town hall staff, but it's a charge almost entirely controlled by central government.

▼ THE REGISTER ▼

The *Community Charge Registration Officer* (CCRO) will compile a register of everybody over 18 living in the district or borough (the list includes those who are about to reach their 18th birthday). The CCRO is responsible for updating the register when people leave or move into the borough or district. The initial register is due to be compiled by 1st December 1989. The register will show the type of Poll Tax each person must pay (Personal, Collective or Standard).

How the Council Compiles the Register

Every household will have a person

designated as the *responsible person* for filling in the registration form. Details can also be obtained from the electoral register and other places such as school records, social security and housing benefit records.

Filling in the Registration Form

When the registration form arrives through the post you are supposed to fill this in and return it. *However the council cannot prove you have received it, unless it was sent as recorded delivery.* If, after about three weeks, they have not received your form they will send you another one to complete. Again they cannot prove you have received it, unless you received it as recorded delivery. If they have still not received it, about three weeks later the council will send round a *Poll Tax Canvasser* to get you to fill in the form. *If you say you have received it and did not fill it in then you may be liable for a fine.*

The Poll Tax canvasser will then ask you there and then to fill in a form. Check on the form the date you have to return it by and fill it in and return it by that date.

Checking the Register

You will be sent a copy of your entry when the register has been compiled. You can also check your entry at the Town Hall after 1st December 1989. If your entry is incorrect, you can appeal to a tribunal.

▼ METHODS OF PAYMENT ▼

There are a number of methods.

• A single payment for the whole year (councils prefer this and some are thinking of offering incentives to people to make one-off payments e.g. free sports pass to council facilities).

• Ten instalments per year.

• Some councils (e.g. Camden) are considering weekly instalments to help those least able to pay.

▼ RESPONSIBILITY FOR ▼ SOMEONE ELSE'S POLL TAX

You can be held responsible for someone else's poll tax. If you are married or living with a partner as a married couple, you may be liable for each others' poll tax. So if your partner does not pay, you may have to pay their bill as well as your own. This is called *joint and several liability*. You will not be responsible for your children if they don't pay the poll tax. If you are living in a flatshare with friends the *responsible* person will not be held liable if any of the others fail to pay.

▼ IF YOU REFUSE TO PAY ▼

You will be considered to be in arrears if you fail to pay within seven days of receiving a reminder. The council will then apply to the magistrates court for a *liability order*. This allows a council to gain information about the individual's employment or other source of income, savings and possessions. The council can then get the money by:

• telling your employer to deduct the money from your wages.

• getting the Dept of Social Security to deduct the money from your Income Support payments.

• seizing and selling your possessions (this is called *distraint)*

If the money cannot be collected through distraint, the non-payer can be sent to prison for up to three months.

▼ REBATES ▼

Everybody over 18 will pay *at least 20%* of their poll tax unless they are exempt (see above). If you are on Income Support, or if your income is below the amount you would get if you were on Income Support then you can get a rebate.

If your income is above that level, you can still get a rebate - but it won't be the full amount. For each £1 you receive over and above income support level, your rebate will be reduced by 15p.

Rebates are worked out on the basis of family income - so even if you have no job or income of your own, you may not get a rebate if your partner is working.

If you have savings over £3000 you will

not get the full rebate, if they are over £8000 you will receive no rebate.

People on income support will still have to pay 20% of their poll tax bill - but will receive a benefit top-up. This top-up represents 20% of the national average poll tax and not 20% of the actual local bill which means it will be very much greater in some areas.

▼ VARIATIONS IN PAYMENT ▼

The amount you pay depends on where you live. Poll tax bills in Inner City areas (with higher costs and greater demands for local services) will be much greater than in the 'shire' areas.

▼ THE UNIFIED ▼ BUSINESS RATE

Also known as the *National Non-Domestic Rate (NNDR)*. This is a new tax on local businesses and replaces the present business rate set by a local council. Councils lose the right to set the level at which they tax local businesses - the levels will be set by central government. The money will be collected centrally and then redistributed to councils on the basis of their adult population. This will increase the burden on individual poll tax payers in some boroughs as the council will receive less than under the previous system. To maintain the level of services they will have to charge individuals.

▼ POLITICS OF THE POLL TAX ▼

Is the Poll Tax Fair?

The rich will gain at the expense of the poor. A millionaire will pay the same as a cleaner. The poor will pay a greater proportion of their income than the rich.

Large families will pay more - if there are three or more adults living in a household, all will have to pay the poll tax and this will invariably be greater than the rates bill would have been.

Black people will be worse off, as the majority of black people live in inner cities with the highest poll tax bills and their household sizes tend to be larger.

Women will be hit harder than men, as they tend to be lower paid and because many women at the moment are not directly responsible for paying the rates.

Young people will suffer as they now receive reduced levels of income support (young people between 18-24 yrs will lose entitlement to rebates at lower earnings level than those 25 or over). Many young people live in cramped conditions in flat shares. If there are four of you living in a flat share, you may find yourself paying twice as much as your rates bill would have been.

People who find difficulties in paying will fall behind and will then have money deducted from wages or income support which will further increase financial difficulties. Many will be forced to spend less on essential items - food, heating, clothing in order to pay the tax.

Civil Liberties and the Poll Tax

In order to make collection possible a list of everybody over 16 years will be held on computer. The *responsible* person is expected to inform on everybody who lives in their house. If you move address you must re-register within 21 days. If opposite sex members live at the same address, and they are not registered as a couple, the council will have to snoop to find out whether they are *living as man and wife.*

Civil liberty organisations are opposed to this kind of identifying and tracking of its citizens.

▼ CONTACTS AND GROUPS ▼

■ **Local Government Information Unit,** *2nd Floor, 1-5 Bath St, EC1 (608 1051).* Produce an excellent *Guide to the Poll Tax* £5 (inc. p&p).

■ **Child Poverty Action Group,** *4th Floor, 1-5 Bath St, EC1 (253 3406).* (see p53). Produce a booklet *Ability to Pay,* explaining rebates.

■ **Campaign Against the Poll Tax Resource and Information Centre,** *60b St, Georges Rd, SE1 (928 7636).*

■ **London Against the Poll Tax,** *c/o Harry Barnes MP, House of Commons, SW1*

■ **London Federation of Anti-Poll Tax Groups,** *c/o 72 West Green Rd, N15 (802 9804).*

There are also many groups run by individuals in the London Boroughs, such as

■ **Camden Stop the Poll Tax Campaign,** *13b Murray St, NW1 (485 3690 and 431 2760 (answerphone)).*

■ **Islington APT,** 726 Holloway Rd, N19 (272 3586).

Contact **London Against the Poll Tax** or **London Federation of Anti-Poll Tax Groups** (see above) for the address of your nearest group.

CONSUMING: Food, Good Deals

food

You can spend a fortune on food in London. Or you can buy cheaply if you are choosy and know where to look. You can also eat healthily and cheaply. Eat well - you are what you eat. If you are eating convenience foods and foods which you know are bad for you, you may have to consider adopting a new diet. This may also mean changing your life style which is usually harder to do.

▼ FREE FOOD ▼

• Food markets (see section on **Markets** p66) often throw away fruit and veg at the end of the day. Get there when they're closing.
• Bakeries will often give their unsold daily produce to you if you are a charity or cause.
• Some pubs leave nuts on the counters for their customers to eat.
• Supermarkets often leave food out round the back if they are past the 'sell by' date.
• Sandwich bars and restaurants will often give away food which won't keep overnight.

▼ FREE MEALS ▼

If you are desperate you can get three meals a day if you walk briskly and follow the trail of the so-called 'soup-runs'. There are also day centres, run usually by Christian organisations that do free food. If you have to you can book in at a night shelter and get fed. Contact the **Piccadilly Advice Centre**, *(434 3773)* (see p213) for more info.

■ The **Krishna Consciousness Society**, *(437 3662)* (see p148), do a free 'feast' on Sunday afternoon, but you have to listen to their creed.

▼ CHEAP MEALS ▼

Many companies and colleges run subsidised canteens. If the company or college is large you're likely to be unnoticed as a visitor. Walk straight in, looking confident and head straight for the lifts (canteens are not usually on the ground floor).

▼ GOOD DEALS ▼

Supermarkets are generally cheaper than the corner shop, but once in you can end up buying more than you bargained for because of the cunning way the goods are laid out and the trail you are forced to follow from the entrance to the cash till. Beware the supermarket psychology! Decide what you want to buy before you go and make a list and keep to it.

Supermarkets lose on some of the products they sell. These products are usually on display in the shop window. They are known as 'loss leaders' and they are supposed to entice you into the shop where you will buy other products to make up the difference. So if you buy just these 'loss leaders' from a variety of supermarkets you can end up doing quite well.

Some products are sold off cheaply because they are near their 'sell by' date. Saturday evening is a good time for this.

▼ DIETS ▼

Vegetarianism and Veganism

A vegetarian diet is one which excludes all meat. A vegan diet excludes not only meat but also all animal products, such as milk, eggs and sometimes honey. Most vegans also prefer not to use or wear leather.

The past few years has seen an increasing number of people becoming vegetarian or vegan. A number of different factors have contributed to this change in eating habits. Recent publicity about the possible harmful effects of meat and dairy

products has added to the argument that a vegetarian diet is healthier and has offset the popular and unfounded fear that unless your diet includes a lot of meat you will become undernourished in some way. The saturated fats present in animal products have been found to be contributory to the development of heart disease, and links between high meat consumption and low fibre intake have been found with breast and bowel cancer. Much research shows that a high fibre, vegetable and fruit based diet is also less fattening and promotes healthy functioning of the digestive system.

However, most people who adopt a vegan or vegetarian diet do so for ethical reasons. Since the consumption of meat and dairy products is no longer necessary for our survival, it is argued that the suffering inflicted upon animals in the food creating process is also unnecessary. Factory farming and mass production of meat means that in the modern world animals are subjected to greater suffering than in the days of the smallholding. The publicity which has been given to the way in which meat is produced has left many people feeling that since they cannot condone the process, they cannot eat the product either.

Ecological awareness too has played its part in the change in eating habits. Animal farming tends to use up more resources than plant farming and requires more acres of land for less food production. Forests throughout the world have been cleared for animal grazing and this has led to further ecological problems.

For more information contact the following:

■ **Vegetarian Society,** *Parkdale, Dunham Rd, Altringham, Cheshire, WA14 4QG, (061 928 0793).* Answer queries and publish leaflets, factsheets (including vegetarian diets for pets and infant nutrition). For further info phone the London office (*994 6477*, they are moving so address not supplied). Send three 14p stamps to the above address for info pak). They publish the *Vegetarian Handbook* (£2.99 + 70p p&p) which is a consumer guide to vegetarian foodstuffs, household goods and additive) and *The International Vegetarian Travel Guide* (£3.99 +70p p&p) which lists hotels guesthouses and restaurants through Britain and abroad. Bi-monthly mag *The Vegetarian* and

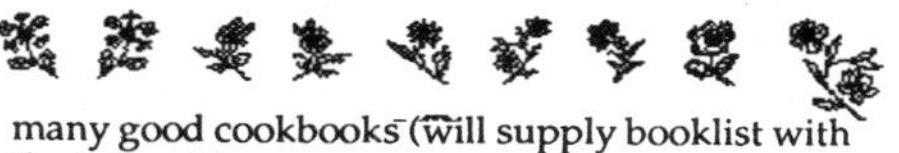

many good cookbooks (will supply booklist with the info pak).

■ **Vegan Society,** *33/35 George St, Oxford OX1 2AY, (0865 722166).* Publishes info pack (SAE); a good recipe book *The Caring Cook* (£1.99); *The Cruelty Free Shopper* (£2.50); publications on child nutrition, infant feeding and veganism; a magazine *The Vegan* (£1) qtly . Send sae for publications list. Membership £10 (less for low incomes).

■ **Gay Vegetarians,** (see p###)

Macrobiotics

Macrobiotics is familiar to most people as a kind of diet. But it is also a whole theory of health and well being based on the balancing of the opposite and complementary energies of Yin and Yang (the Chinese conception of complementary opposites e.g. positive/negative, light/dark, hot/cold). Literally the word Macrobiotics means 'large life'.

Cereals and brown rice form the basis of the Macrobiotic diet because they contain the best balance of Yin and Yang. Yin foods are those which contain a lot of water, grow above the ground and tend to be hot, sour or sweet in taste. Yang foods tend to be hard, dense, dry, grow below ground and are often red or yellow in colour. Different methods of cooking can also increase the tendency towards Yin or Yang: quick cooking increases Yin, and slow cooking, Yang. Foods that will promote this balance depend on the temperament of the eater and his or her environment. It is better to eat local foods too, because there is a natural affinity between the food of a region and its people.

■ **Community Health Foundation,** *188-194 Old St, EC1 (251 4076)* hold workshops on macrobiotics and cooking.

Miscellaneous

■ **Green Farm,** *Burwash Common, E. Sussex, (0435 882 482)* publishes *The Natural Healing Book, Nutrition Handbook, Cleansing the Colon, The Nutrition Program Handbook* and *The Wright Diet.* They supply a wide range of pure dietary supplements. Membership £5 p.a. includes newsletter, a free sub to the mag and varying discount on all orders. Mail order.

■ **Denes Petfoods,** *2 Osmond Rd, Hove BN3 3SD, (0273 25364).* Keep your pet feeling zippy with this range of no additive health food. Herbal remedies too. See the **Pets** section on how to turn your dog into a vegan dog.

▼ BULK BUYING ▼

You really have to buy a lot to make this work, and it only pays if you can consume before the foodstuff perishes. So you either have to eat with gusto or co-operate with friends, workmates, flatmates, your co-op etc, in collective buying. Inevitably buying basic foodstuffs like rice, beans etc, is the safest financial bet.

Where to Go, free from **Farm Shop & PYO Association**, *Agriculture House, Knightsbridge, SW1 (235 5077)* lists farm shops and 'pick your own' places in Great Britain. Good for all kinds of produce from veg to farm eggs to herbs.

Cash and Carry

■ **Capital C&C,** *24 Beaconsfield Rd, NW10 (459 7671).*

▼ BULK SUPPLIERS ▼

Wholefoods

■ **Community Foods,** *Micross Brent Terrace, NW2 (450 9411).* M-S 9-1, 2.30-5.30, Sat 12-4. Cheap bulk suppliers and the largest in London: pulses, nuts grains, dried fruit, spreads, oils, beverages, herbs and spices. 5 kilos a ton: £30 min cash and carry.

■ **Wholesome Trucking,** *Unit 9, Higgs Industrial Estate, 2 Herne Hill Rd, SE24 (737 2658, 733 2614).* M-F 9-5. Bulk suppliers. Pulses, beans, snacks, juices, mueslies, cosmetics, soaps, ecological washing powders. Wholefood delivery in and out of London. £100 min order for delivery. If you pick it up yourself it's £75 min order.

■ **Alara,** *Unit 4 and 5 Camley St, NW1 (387 9303).* M-F 9-5. £30 min cash and carry. £100 min if delivered in London. Beans to toiletries, jams, soya products, comprehensive range.

■ **Aspall Cider,** *Aspall Hall, nr Debenham, Stowmarket. Suffolk , (0728 860510).* Apple-juice, organic cider, and cider-vinegar.

Dairy Produce

■ **Marine Ices,** *8 Haverstock Hill, NW3 (485 8898).* 7 days 10am-11pm Mon-Sat, 11-11 Sun. Ice-cream and fruit sorbet, without additives. Wholesale/ retail.

Vegetarian Products

■ **Marigold Foods,** *Unit 10, St. Pancras Commercial Centre, Pratt St, NW1 (267 7368).* Mostly pre-packed health foods, refrigerated products, vegetarian cheese, yoghourt, seasonings and spices, biscuits and cakes, bread, bouillon, flour and pasta. Mostly sell to wholefood shops but will deal with the odd group/coop. Min order £75.

Grains, Pulses, Pasta

■ **Petty Wood & Co Ltd,** *15 Dufferin St, EC1 (251 2311).* Fruits, epicure dried pulses, honey, sugar etc.

■ **Emco Products,** *71/75 Fortess, NW5 (485 2217).* Beans, pulses, oils, sauces.

■ **Pasta Foods,** *Veruluam Industrial Est, London Rd, St. Albans AL1 1JF, (0727 60461).* Wholegrain pastas (min 15 cases) free delivery. Subsidiary of Rank Hovis McDougall. Worthwhile if buying large quantities.

Bakeries

■ **Goswell Bakeries,** *Caxton St North, E16 (474 6141).* Range of natural breads, Allinsons breads, will deliver.

Drinks

■ **Whittards,** *73 Northcote Rd, SW11 (924 1888).* They have 50 kinds of teas and tisanes, plus 15 coffees. Herbal teas, chocolate.

■ **Monmouth Coffee House,** *27 Monmouth St, WC2 (836 5272).* Cheapest high quality coffee (6 kinds) in London - sampling room so you can taste a cup first. Beans and ground. Mail order.

■ **Costa Coffee,** *30-34 Old Paradise St, SE11 (582 7272).* Roast, blend and pack. Bulk coffee packed in small amounts (minimum of 6 kilos).

■ **Wistbray,** *PO Box 22, W11 (603 9524).* Caffeine-free, low tannin tea (and herbal cigarettes), mail order or collect.

▼ VEGETARIAN RESTAURANTS ▼

See Sarah Brown's *Vegetarian London* (£3.50, Thorson) which reviews the vegetarian restaurants and gives a good description of each.

See also *Time Out Guide to Eating Out in London* (£3.50) which lists all types of restaurants in London.

We've given three gradings: cheap, cheaper and cheapest. Otherwise assume it's going to cost you £7-£14 for a meal, depending on the restaurant.

North

■ **The Fallen Angel,** *65 Graham Street, Islington, N1 (253 3996).* M-Sat 12-12, Sun 12-11.30. Wine bar/ cafe. Phone first.

■ **Something Else,** *49 Cross Street, Islington, N1 (226 6579).* Lunch: Mon-Sat noon-3.30pm. Dinner: Mon-Fri 6-11pm, Sat 6-11.30pm, Sun 6.30-10.30pm. Wholefood.

■ **Rani,** *7 Long Lane, N3 (349 4386).* 12.30-2pm, 6-10.30. Closed Mon and Tues lunch. Indian.

■ **Jai Krishna,** *161 Stroud Green Road, Crouch Hill, N4 (272 1680).* 12-2, 5.30 -10.30, closed Sun. Indian. Cheaper.

■ **Earth Exchange,** *213 Archway Road, Archway, N6 (340 6407).* Th-M 12-10, W 8-10 womens' evening. Cabaret Mon evening. Vegan/wholefood. Community feel.

■ **Milward's,** *97 Stoke Newington Church St, N16 (254 1025).* Mon to Fri 6-12, Sat and Sun 12-12. Vegan/wholefood.

■ **Spices,** *30 Stoke Newington Church St, N16 (254 0528).* 12-3 and 6-12 M-Th, F 12-3 and 6-1, Sat 12-1am, Sun 12-12. Indian.

■ **Jazz Cafe,** *56 Newington Green, N16 (359 4936).* 12-3, 6.30-12 (7-11 Sun). Wholefood. Some vegan. £3 admission evening, £2 concs. Music weekend lunchtimes (no extra).

■ **Raj Bhelpoori House,** *19 Camden High Street, NW1 (388 6663).* 12-11.30 daily. Indian. Cheap.

■ **The Viceroy of India,** *3-5 Glentworth St, NW1 (486 3401).* 12-3, 6-11.30 daily (6-11 Sun). Indian.

■ **Diwana Bhelpoori House,** *121 Drummond Street, Euston, NW1 (387 5556).* 12-11.45 daily. Indian. Cheap.

■ **Chutney's,** *124 Drummond St, NW1 (388 0604).* 12-2.45, 6-11.30 daily. Indian.

■ **Ravi Shankar,** *133 Drummond Street, Euston, NW1 (388 6458).* 12-11 daily. Indian. Cheap.

■ **Manna,** *4 Erskine Road, Chalk Farm, NW3 (722 8028).* 6.30-12 daily. Wholefood. Sometimes vegan.

■ **Sabras,** *263 High Road, Willesden , NW10 (459 0340).* 1-3 and 5-10 Tue to Fri, 1-10 Sat and Sun. Indian.

South

■ **Wilkins Natural Foods,** *61 Marsham Street, SW1 (222 4038).* Mon-Fri 9am-5pm. Vegan/wholefood. Cheaper.

■ **Windmill Wholefoods,** *486 Fulham Road, SW6 (385 1570).* 12-11 Mon to Sun vegan/wholefood.

■ **Jacaranda,** *11-13 Brixton Station Rd, SW9 (274 8383).* T-Sat 10-11. Not strictly vegetarian, but we like the atmosphere and it's fairly cheap.

■ **Wholemeal Cafe,** *1 Shrubbery Road, Streatham , SW16 (769 2423).* 12-10 Mon to Sun. Vegan/wholefood. Cheap.

■ **Dining Room,** *Winchester Walk, London Bridge, SE1 (407 0337).* Tues-Fri 7-10pm. Vegan/wholefood.

■ **Coffee Shak,** *39 Lee High Road, Lewisham, SE13 (852 1084).* Mon-Sat 9am-11pm, Sun 11-8.

East

■ **Cherry Orchard,** *241 Globe Road, Bethnal Green, E2 (980 6678).* 12-10.30, closed Sun and Mon vegan/wholefood. Bring own alcohol (corkage 80p). Run by Buddhists. Cheapest.

■ **Ronak,** *317 Romford Road, Forest Gate, E7 (534 2944).* 11-10, closed Mon.

West

■ **Baba Bhelpoori House,** *29-31 Porchester Rd, W2 (221 7502).* 12- 3, 6- 10.45, closed Mon. Vegan/Indian.

■ **Diwana Bhelpoori House,** *50 Westbourne Grove W2 (221 0721).* 12-3 and 6-10.30 daily. Indian. Cheap.

■ **Angel Gate,** *51 Queen Caroline Street, W6 (748 8388).* Vegan/wholefood/vegetarian.

■ **Hearth Cafe At Earthworks,** *132 Kings Street, Hammersmith, W6 (846 9357).* Mon-Wed 11am-6pm. Thurs, Fri & Sat 11am-11pm.

■ **Ravenscourt Park Tea House,** *Ravenscourt Park (North East Side) Off Padenswick Road , W6* .Winter 8.30 - dusk daily, Summer 8am-6pm daily. Vegan/wholefood.

West End

■ **Country Life,** *1 Heddon Street, W1 (434 2922).* 11.30 - 3.00, Fri 11.30-2. Closed Sat and Sun.Vegan/wholefood. Buffet. Cheapest.

■ **Cranks Health Foods,** *17-18 Great Newport Street, W1 (836 5226).* 8.30-8.30 Mon to Fri, 10-8.30pm Sat, Sun 11-6. Vegan/Wholefood.

■ **Cranks Health Foods,** *8 Marshal Street, W1 (437 9431).* 8-10.30 Mon to Sat. Closed Sun. Vegan/wholefood.

■ **Cranks Health Foods,** *9-11 Tottenham Street, W1 (631 3912).* 8-8 Mon to Fri, 9-8pm Sat, closed Sun. Vegan/wholefood.

■ **Hare Krishna Curry House,** *1 Hanwell Place, W1 (636 5262).* M-Sat 1-10, closed Sun. Cheap.

■ **Nuthouse,** *26 Kingley Street, W1 (437 9471).* 10.30-7.00 Mon to Fri, 10.30-6. Sat, closed Sun. Vegan/wholefood. Cheap.

■ **Raw Deal,** *65 York Street , W1 (262 4841).* 10-10 Mon to Sat, closed Sun. Wholefood. Cheap.

■ **Cranks,** *23 Barrett St, W1 (495 1340).* 8-7, closed Sun. Vegan/wholefood.

■ **Mandeer,** *21 Hanway Place, W1 (323 0660).* 6-10.30 Mon to Sat, closed Sun. Indian. Cheap.

■ **Woodlands Restaurant,** *77 Marylebone Lane, W1*

.(486 3862). 12-2.45 and 6 - 10.30 daily, Sun 6-10.30. Indian.

■ **Woodlands Restaurant,** *37 Panton Street, Off Haymarket , W1 (839 7258).* 12-2.45 and 5.30-10.30 daily. Sun 6-10.30. Indian.

■ **Greenhouse,** *16 Chenies Street, WC1 (637 8038).* 10-6 Mon, 10-10 Tue to Fri, 1-8.30 Sat. Vegan/ wholefood. Cheap.

■ **Cranks,** *10 Adelaide St, WC1 (379 5919).* 10-10.30 (10-6 Sun). Vegan/wholefood.

■ **Cranks Health Foods,** *11 The Market, Covent Garden, WC2 (379 6508).* 9-8pm Mon to Sat, 10-7 Sun. Vegan/wholefood.

■ **Bunjie's Coffee House,** *27 Litchfield Street, WC2 (240 1796).* 12 till 11 every day. Sun 5-11. Wholefood. Cheap.

■ **Food for Thought,** *31 Neal Street, Covent Garden, WC2 (836 0239).* 12-8, Sat 12-8, closed Sun. Vegan/ wholefood. Cheaper.

■ **London Ecology Centre,** *45 Shelton Street, Covent Garden , WC2 (497 2723).* 10.30am-10.30pm, closed Sun. Vegan/wholefood. Cheap. Licensed.

■ **Neal's Yard Bakery and Tea Room,** *6 Neal's Yard, Covent Garden, WC2 (836 5199).* 10.30-7.30 Mon Tue Thur Fri, 10.30-5 Wed, 10.30-4.30 Sat. Vegan/wholefood. Cheap.

■ **Shan,** *200 Shaftesbury Avenue, WC2 (240 3348).* 12-10 Mon to Sat, closed Sun.

The City

■ **East West Restaurant,** *188 Old Street, EC1 (608 0300).* Mon-Fri 11am-10pm. Sat & Sun 11am-3pm. The only macrobiotic restaurant in town.

■ **Slenders,** *41 Cathedral Place, St. Paul's , EC4 (236 5974).* 7.30-6.15 Mon to Fri, closed Sat and Sun. Vegan/wholefood.

▼ WHOLEFOODS AND ▼ ORGANIC PRODUCE

Wholefood is food that is unprocessed - brown rice as opposed to refined white rice (which has has the husk removed) for instance.

Organically grown foods are foods which are grown with no artificial fertilisers or chemical treatment. Foods which are organically grown are likely to be wholefood, and wholefoods are likely to be organically grown. However brown rice in supermarkets is not usually organically grown.

Healthfoods are foods which are supposed to be healthy for you. They may or may not be. Health food shops are often oriented to selling vitamin pills and special diets. Health food shops may be expensive and you may need to shop around and compare prices.

Safeways are good on organic food produce. Sainsburys still have some way to go although their range of wholefoods is growing.

Read the label carefully. Words like 'natural' and 'healthy' do not mean much. Products often say 'without artificial flavourings or additives' when they are full of sugar - which isn't very healthy at all.

Additives

Additives are used to preserve/flavour/keep moist/colour food - and more. Additives are listed on the label. If you want to know what they do and whether they are considered dangerous then read *The New E for Additives* by M. Hanssen (Thorsons, 1987, £3.50).

3

Meat

If you are a meat eater then **Wholefood Butchers,** *31 Paddington St, W1 (486 1390)* is expensive, but the animals have been organically reared without sex hormones or antibiotics. Or try **Unique Butcher,** *217 Holloway Rd, N7 (609 7016)* which is also an 'organic butcher' they also do other organic produce, veg, bread etc.

Wholefood Shops

Below are listed wholefood shops in London. Ring first to check opening hours.

West

■ **Wholefood,** *24 Paddington St, W1 (935 3924).* Good. Wide range. Organic wines. Books on healthy living

■ **Market Place Health Foods,** *8 Market Place, W3 (993 3848)* and bread, cosmetics, vitamins, bookshop.

■ **Cornucopia,** *64 St Mary's Rd, W5 (579 9431).* Also homoeopathic remedies.

■ **Ceres,** *269a Portobello Rd, W11 (229 5571)* and bakery (pizzas, croissants made on premises), herbs, noticeboard - rather expensive, crowded Saturdays.

■ **Friends Foods,** *113 Notting Hill Gate, W11 (221 4700)* and homoeopathic remedies, herbs. Bach flower remedies.

■ **WestKen Health Foods,** *6 Charlesville Rd, W14 (385 0956).*

West Central

■ **Alara,** *58 Marchmont St, WC1 (837 1172).* Herbs, spices, plants, books, cosmetics, remedies, bulk. Take-away. Organic veg.

■ **Plunkett's Farm Shop,** *Neal's Yard, WC2 (836 1066).* Organic stock, veg curry take-away, potted herbs for planting, fruit and veg.

■ **Golden Orient,** *17 Earlham St, WC2 (836 5545).* Grains, pulses, nuts, teas, spices, herbs and homoeopathic remedies and vitamins.

■ **Neal's Yard Wholefood Warehouse,** *21 Shorts Gdns, WC2 (836 5151).* Excellent selection, wide range. Organic, fruit and veg, organic wine and beer, cheese, nuts and dried fruit, peanut butter.

■ **Neal's Yard Bread Shop,** *8 Neal's Yard, WC2 (836 1082).* Organic flour used, whole grain.

South

■ **Wilkins Natural Foods,** *53 Marsham St, SW1 (222 4038),* and freshly prepared fresh foods, veg, vegan wedding cakes and Christmas cakes. Vegan. Publish mag.

■ **Plunket's Farm Shop,** *153 Clapham High St, SW4 (738 8760).* Organic stock, potted herbs for planting, fruit and veg.

■ **Windmill Wholefoods,** *486 Fulham Rd, SW6 (385 1570).* Veg, free range eggs, dried fruit and flour. Also cosmetics, remedies, good range of herbs, wines. Restaurant.

■ **Brixton Wholefoods,** *56/58 Atlantic Rd, SW9 (737 2210).* Also wide range of herbs and spices, veg. Bio-degradable washing materials, water filters, homoeopathic remedies. Noticeboard. Rasta craft shop next door.

■ **South London Bakers Coop,** *639 Garrett Lane, SW18 (947 5264).* Solely a bakery, organic wholewheat loaves, muffins and rolls.

■ **Terrapin Wholefoods,** *76 Effra Rd, SW19 (543 3999).* Also skin-care products, crafts, yoga classes and an exercise studio, beauty salon and solarium, pottery, crafts and jewellery.

South East

■ **Village Health Foods,** *31 Tranquil Vale, SE3 (318 0448).* Also remedies, cosmetics.

■ **G Baldwin & Co,** *173 Walworth Rd, SE17 (703 5550).* Good selection of dried herbs, roots, oils, incense and books.

■ **Provender,** *103 Dartmouth Rd, SE23 (699 4046)* and herbs, spices, cosmetics and bakery.

East

■ **Friends Foods,** *51 Roman Rd, E2 (980 1843)* and homoeopathic remedies, herbs, hot take-away snacks. Veg convenience foods e.g. vegeburgers. Buddhist coop.

■ **Only Natural Foods,** *108 Palmerston Road, E17 (520 5898).* Also homoeopathic and natural remedies, veg, cafe/restaurant next door.

■ **Clearspring Natural Grocer,** *196 Old St, EC1 (250 1708).* Whole and organic foods, veg, bakery, imports, no sugar products. Specialises in macrobiotic and Japanese foods. Homoeopathic, Bach, and herbal remedies, beer and wines, 'New Age' music tapes. Natural cookware. Vegan and vegatarian take away bakery snacks.

North

■ **Barnsbury Health Foods,** *285 Caledonian Rd, N1 (607 7344).* Also herbs, dairy, vitamins, minerals, macrobiotics, books, herbs and spices. Protein foods.

■ **Alara,** *58 Seven Sisters Rd, N7 (609 6875).* Organic veg, nuts, grains, supplements. Books. Recycled Spanish glassware. Essential oils. Frozen foods.

■ **Earth Exchange,** *213 Archway Rd, N6 (340 6407)* and fruit, veg, wine. Cafe. Wide range of essential oils, bio-degradeable cleaning products.

■ **Bumblebee,** *30 Brecknock Rd, N7 (607 1936).* Also dairy, veg, wines, beers.

■ **The Haelen Centre,** *41 The Broadway, N8 (340 4258).* Wholefoods good range of herb extracts, books, cosmetics, organic veg, toiletries, wines and beers.

■ **Food for All,** *3 Cazenove Rd, N16 (806 4138).* Run by Ananda Marga. Also books, herbs, cosmetics, crafts, noticeboard. Profits go to support relief work. They do a breakfast-run. Free advice on health and spiritual growth.

North West

■ **Sesame Health Foods,** *128 Regents Park Rd, NW1 (586 3779).* Also homoeopathic remedies, vitamins.

■ **Abundance Natural Foods,** *246 Belsize Rd, NW6 (328 4781)* and veg, bakery, goat's milk and products, homoeopathic and natural remedies, cosmetics, English and vegetarian cheeses.

■ **Keshava Natural Foods,** *84 Willesden Lane, NW6 (328 9078).* Also vitamins, cosmetics, books, macrobiotics, medicinal herbs, homoepathic remedies.

▼ LATE NIGHT EATING ▼

Open till 3am:

■ **Bill Stickers,** *18 Greek St, W1 (437 0582).* Sun till 11pm. Mexican. Expensive.

■ **Costa Dorada,** *47 & 55 Hanway St, W1 (636 7139).* Sun till 1am. Spanish.

■ **Elysee,** *13 Percy St, W1 (636 4804).* Sun till 2.French/Greek; licensed.

■ **Grecian Grill,** *271 Percy St, W1 (636 6351).* Licensed. Live music and dance. 10-3.

■ **Original Kebabs,** *52 Rupert St, W1 (437 9474).* Sun till 1am. Licensed.

Open till 4am:

■ **Far East Chinese,** *13*

Gerrard St, W1 (437 6148) take away/eat in.

■ **Mayflower,** *58 Shaftsbury Av, W1 (734 9207).* Cantonese. Sit down/take away.

Open till 5am:

■ **Cafe International,** *38 Kensington High St, (937 6968).* Licensed. Mixed menu, Italian.

■ **Sun Luk,** *2 Macclesfield St, W1 (734 5161).* Cantonese. Take away service.

■ **Lido,** *41 Gerrard St, W1 (437 4431).* Chinese; licensed. Does take aways.

■ **The Globe,** *103 Talbot Rd, W11 (727 9559).* International menu and snacks.

Open till 6am:

■ **Emmanuelle's,** *149 Finchley Rd, NW3 (722 3235).* Burgers, kebabs, spaghetti. Licensed.

■ **Gregory's Kebabs,** *365 Green Lanes, N4 (800 2474).* Closed Mon. Licensed.

■ **Rockafellas,** *3 New Burlington St, W1 (734 3075).* Burgers, salads, non-alcoholic cocktails. Licensed.

■ **Toddies,** *241 Old Brompton Rd, SW5 (373 8217).* African/English food, breakfasts. Licensed. Blues singer Fri, Sat after 12. Sun till midnight.

Open till 9am

■ **Harry's,** *19 Kingly St, W1 (734 3140).* 10-6am Sat.

All night or 24 hrs:

■ **Canton,** *11 Newport Place, W1 (437 6220).* Cantonese. Licensed. Does takeaways.

■ **Gt British Success,** *85 Gloucester Rd, SW7 (370 4404)* burgers. Licensed. Takeaways, (other branch at 22 *Terminus Place, SW1).*

■ **Strand Palace,** *Strand, WC2 (836 8080)* (snacks only).

▼ POLITICS ▼

■ **Oxfam,** *274 Banbury Road, Oxford OX2 7DZ, (0865 56777),* is the head office. They can put you in touch with a local group. Publications, relief work and development abroad, educational resources for schools.

■ **World Development Movement,** *Bedford Chambers Covent Gdn, WC2E 8HA (836 3672).* Local groups, publications, info.

■ **Christian Aid,** *PO Box1, SW9 8BH (733 5500).*

■ **Hunger Project,** *77 Cromwell Rd, SW7 (373 9003).* They say hunger is not necessary and ask you to tell your friends this.

■ **Coffee Campaign,** *52 Acre Lane, SW2 (490 1555).* Coffee is one of the most exploitative cash crops. Only a tiny percentage of the price we pay here goes to the county of origin, less still to the plantation workers. The campaign publicises the plight of coffee workers, distributes free pamphlets on how the coffee business works, and sells coffee grown and processed in socialist Tanzania - less exploitative but not much cheaper. Phone to check availability.

■ **Compassion in World Farming,** *20 Lavant St, Petersfield, Hants, GU32 3EW, (0730 64208/68863).* Farmers opposed to battery/intensive animal rearing and pressing for more humane conditions, transport and slaughter. Advocate more arable farming and less reliance on a diet of animal products (92% of agricultural land in Britain is used for growing animal feed). Free leaflets showing the horrors of intensive rearing and a magazine *Ag* (£3).

■ **Farm and Food Society,** *4 Willifield Way, NW11 (455 0634).* Researches farming techniques, and campaigns for less use of toxic chemicals, for 'non-violent' farming and for better, safer food. Newsletter, occasional papers.

■ **The Free-Range Egg Association (FREGG),** *39 Maresfield Gdns, NW3 (435 2596).* Campaigns against battery distributors. Has a 'patchy' list of shops where you can buy free-range eggs, and a list of free-range farmers. Sae for details.

■ **Chickens Lib,** *PO Box 2, Homefirth, Huddesfield, West Yorks HD7 1QT, (0484 861814).* Pressure group trying to outlaw battery farming and broiler production. Leaflets and petition forms. Video.

■ **Soil Association,** 86 Colston St, Bristol BS1 5BB, (0272 290661). Campaigns for the promotion of organically grown food.

▼ COMPLAINTS ▼

Complaints about hygiene should be made to **The Environmental Health Officer** of your local council, though it's best first to complain to the manufacturer as they are more likely to compensate you. Be sure to check the 'sell by' date on perishables, especially in the corner shop as their turnover is slow.

good deals

▼ FREE THINGS ▼

Skips are a good place to look. People throw out fridges with minor faults and replace them with new ones. The same applies to much electrical equipment. So it's possible to find stereos, TV's, spin dryer etc. Fixing the minor repairs of 'finds' will not only save you money, recycling is good for the planet. Though make sure you test it properly before you use it.

The most common find in skips is furniture. It's possible to get shelving, armchairs, tables, pots and pans to furnish your place. Keep your eyes open in your locale.

Look out for stuff dumped in commercial areas by firms. You might need to look around the side of their building or ask them if they have anything they are throwing out. If they are in the clothing business you can get off-cuts. If they are building merchants you may be able to pick up wood off-cuts or damaged units.

You can get a free haircut by being a model at some hairdressing salons. Ask at your hairdressers if they have a model night. Otherwise you can get a cut for greatly reduced prices at modelling schools. **Vidal Sasson** has two schools, one which does experimental haircuts, and the other does regular cuts. **The Ginger Group** also take models. They are both in the telephone directory.

Your local library have all the daily papers and many periodicals.

Half-price tickets (on the day) for West End theatre, ballet and opera shows can be had if you're 14-25. You also get a free magazine. Contact **Youth & Music,** *78 Neal St, WC2 (379 6722).*

▼ SECOND-HAND ▼

Furniture

For household equipment car boot sales are better than jumble sales these days. Look in your local paper for times, they are usually Sat or Sun morning.

Look in *Loot, Exchange and Mart* and noticeboards in newsagents windows for good deals.

There are many second hand furniture stores dotted round London - look under **Furniture - secondhand** in the *Yellow Pages.*

■ **Oxfam,** *570-572 Kingsland Rd, E8 (923 1532)* furniture and second-hand clothes.

Clothes

CHARITY SHOPS

Charity shops are sprinkled around London. You can pick up some bargains and haggle over the price.

■ **Barnardo's,** *72 Turnham Green Terr, W4 (995 2762).* M-Sat 9-5. Other branch at: *3 Parkway Hse, Shene Ln, SW14 (876 5620).*

■ **The Children's Society,** *135 Shene Ln, SW14 (876 2767).* M-Sat 10-4.30. Other branches at: 129 Pitzhanger Ln, W5; 3 Victoria Crescent, SW19, (946 2808).

■ **Hapa,** *57a Fulham High St, SW6 (736 4225).* M-Sat 11-4.30.

■ **The Nearly New Shop,** *20 Camden Rd, NW1 (485 8936).* M-Sat 10-4, Other branches are: 55a Baring Rd, SE12; 33 Heath Rd, Twickenham; 3 Belgrave Gdns, NW8; 22 North End Parade, W14; 64 Sheen Rd, Richmond.

■ **Notting Hill Housing Trust,** *Head Office 26 Paddenswick Rd, W6 (741 1570).* Second hand shops at: 288 Upper Richmond Rd SW15; 57 Kensington Church St W8; 46 Turnham Green Terrace W4; 394 Richmond Rd Twickenham; 166 Acton High St W3; 76 Askew Rd W12; 86 Camden High St NW1; Unit 9, 24 Ealing High St W5; 59 Notting Hill Gate W11; 70 Pitshanger Lane W5; 178 Queensway W2. 36 Tooting High St SW17; 178 Uxbridge High St Middx; 19 The Broadway, Wimbledon SW19.

■ **Oxfam Shop,** *Wilberforce House, Station Rd, Hendon, NW4 (876 3599).* (North London Headquarters not a shop). Branches at: 190 Chiswick High Rd, W4; 166 Kentish Town Rd, NW5; 16 Meymott St, SE1; 34 New Broadway, W5; 149 Putney High St, SW15 (789 3235); 155 Station Rd, Edgware; 246 West End Ln, NW6; 26 Ganton St, W1; 120 Golders Green Rd, NW11; 202 Kensington High St, W8; 91 Marylebone High St, W1; 233 Muswell Hill Broadway, N10; 76 Putney High St, SW15; 61 St.

John's Wood High St., NW8; 68 Tranquil Vale, SE3; 202b Kensington High St, W8 (937 6683); 23 Drury Lane, WC2 (240 3769); 80 Highgate High, N6 (340 3888); 61 Gayton Rd, NW3; 89 Camden High St, NW1; 87 King St, W6 (846 9276); 68 Tranquil Vale, SE3 (852 6884); 7 Astoria Parade, Streatham High Rd, SW16 (769 0515). 58 St. John's Hill, SW11 (585 0220) south London Headquarters (not a shop).

■ **Red Cross,** *67 Old Church St, SW3 (352 8550).* M-Fri 10-4.30.

■ **The Spastic Society,** *73 Camden High St, NW1 (380 1455).* M-Sat 9.30-5.30 Other branches at: 304/304a Green Lanes, N13 (886 3340); 139 Kilburn High Rd, NW6 (624 7798); 46 Seven Sisters Rd, N7 (607 7779); 93 High St, SE15 (639 5646); 210 High St, E17(520 5273); 7 Lewis Grove, SE13 (852 5334); 346 North End Rd, W14 (385 3853); 12 Vivian Av, NW4 (202 2569).

■ **War on Want,** *301 Finchley Rd NW3 (435 3884).* M-Sat 10.30-4.30

VERY CHEAP NON-CHARITY SHOPS

■ **Leslies,** *105 Roman Rd, E2* 9-4.

■ **Second Hand Rose,** *79 Lower Clapton Rd, E5 (985 6766).* 10-5 (closed Th aft.)

▼ MISCELLANEOUS ▼ BARGAINS

■ **Gatto,** *206 Garrat Ln, SW18 (874 2671).* Hand and power tools.

■ **The Cooker Centre,** *420 Edgware Rd, W2 (723 2975).* Fridges and domestic appliances as well.

■ **Reconditioned Gas Appliances,** *387 Hackney Rd, E2 (739 7729).* Water heaters, cookers, wall mounted fires, gas fires.

■ **Buyers and Sellers,** *120 Ladbroke Grv, W10 (229 1947),* is a cheap place for domestic appliances (freezers, fridges washing machines etc). All guaranteed. Will talk knowledgeably over the phone to you.

■ **Henry's,** 303 Edgware Rd, W2 (723 1008), do cheap electronic parts.

■ **No 1 Electronics,** *Kingsgate Workshops, 110 Kingsgate Rd, NW6 (328 3861).* Cheap ionisers, kirlian cameras, organ tuning, time travel machines. Anything electronic to do with healing, or anything electronic that 'will raise people's consciousness'. Sell brain wave machines and IQ increasing machines! etc.

• Discounts Houses can be cheap for new stuff. Ring these numbers for local branches: **Comet,** *(459 8877);* **Argos,** *(637 1869)* look through a catalogue in the showroom and then buy them in the same store.

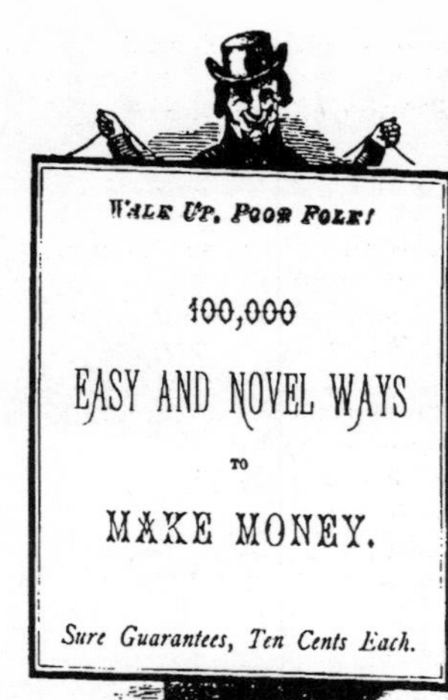

▼ MARKETS OF LONDON ▼

Renting a Stall

If you've got something to sell you can rent a stall on an annual/weekly/daily basis from £2-20 per day (fees vary depending on which day in the week you want the stall). However some pitches are long term only. Other pitches are handed down through the family when the stallholder dies so you can literally wait a lifetime and not get the stall you want. Ring the following for details: **Camden**: Works Dept, (485 4111) ; **Greenwich,** (854 8888 x 2708) ; **Hackney,** (986 3123) ; **Islington,** (226 1234) ; **Lambeth,** (274 7722 x 2530) ; **Petticoat Lane,** (937 1572); **Portobello Rd,** (727 7684) ; **Westminster**: Trading Standards Office, (828 8070 x 1089/ 1090) .

The Markets

The Markets of London Forshaw and Bergstrom (Penguin, updated for 1989, £5.99) gives the rundown on the history and locale of London's markets.

NORTH

■ **Camden Passage,** N1
W 10-2, Sat 10-5
Antiques, objets d'art, jewellery, books

■ **Nags Head,** N7 (Holloway Rd near Enkel St)
W-Sat 9-5.
Clothes, new and second-hand, bric-a-brac. Nylon.

■ **Bell St,** NW1
Sat 9-5.
Second-hand books, clothes, eastern rugs, junk shops. Expensive.

■ **Camden Lock,** NW1 (Commercial Place)
Sat and Sun 10-6
Crafts, bric-a-brac, snacks. Popular and expensive.

■ **Hampstead Community Market,** NW3
Sat 9.30-6.
Food, clothes, jewellery, hardware, crafts, bric-a-brac.

■ **Kilburn Sq,** NW6
F and Sat 9-5
Mostly clothes, fashion ware, jeans, materials. Big.

■ **Church St,** NW8
T-Sat 9-5
General household, fruit and veg,

antiques, bric-a-brac, furniture. Big and good.

■ **Queen's Crescent**, NW5
Th 9-1.30, Sat 9-5
Fruit, Veg, Clothes

SOUTH

■ **Bermondsey**, SE1
F 7-5 (officially, but often finishes earlier)
Antiques, furniture, ceramics, silver.

■ **Lower Marsh and The Cut**, SE1
M-Sat 10.30-2.30
Household, clothing, fruit and veg

■ **Catford Broadway**, SE6
Sat 9-5.30. A few stalls in the day.
Food, clothes, household. New. 'Fallen off the back of lorry' stuff.

■ **Douglas Way**, SE8
F and Sat 8.30-5
Fruit and veg, flowers, hardware, second-hand clothes and junk

■ **Greenwich**, SE10 (south side of College Approach)
Sat and Sun 9-6; wholesale market 6-noon M-F.
Crafts, antiques, second-hand books, wholesale veg, crafts. Good.

■ **Choumert Rd**, SE15
M-Sat 10-4
Fruit and veg

■ **East St**, SE17
T, W, F and Sat 8-5, Sun and Th 8-2
Fruit and veg, clothes, toiletries, hardware, household, luxury goods and plastic junk.

■ **Westmoreland Rd**, SE17
Sun 8.30-12.30, Tu-Sat 9-4
Antiques, furniture and junk on Sun. Small general market weekdays.

■ **Beresford Sq**, SE18
Tu-Sat 8.30-5, Closed Th afternoon.
Fruit and veg, fish, meat, clothes, flowers, jewellery, hardware.

■ **New Covent Garden**, SW8
M-F 4-11am, Sat in summer only
Fruit, veg and flowers. Big.

■ **Brixton**, SW9 (Brixton Station Rd)
M-Sat 9-5.30, closed W aft.
General, fruit and veg, second-hand clothes, fish and meat, textiles. Fun and colourful. Music.

■ **Battersea High St**, SW11
F and Sat 9-5
Fruit and veg, fish, flowers, cassettes, general. Sparse.

■ **Northcote Rd and Clapham Junction**, SW11
M-Sat 9-5 Northcote Rd, F and Sat 9-5 Junction market
Northcote Rd - Fruit and veg, Junction market - clothes and hardware, reggae

■ **Hildreth St**, SW12
M-Sat 9.30-5, closed Th aft.
Food, flowers, haberdashery, household. Eastern flavour.

EAST

■ **Brick Lane**, E1 & E2
Sunday. Dawn to midday
New and second-hand, clothes, furniture, carpets, tools, electrical, shoes, food. Big and fun.

■ **Petticoat Lane**, E1
Sun morn only Middlesex St, 10.30-2.30 M-F Wentworth St
Mostly clothes, some gold and silver in Goulston St. Tourist trap. Expensive and crowded.

■ **Watney St**, E1
M-Sat 9-5
Fruit and veg.

■ **Whitechapel and Mile End**, E1
Whitechapel M-Sat 8.30-5.30 closed Th aft., Mile End 8.30-5.30 Sat.
Whitechapel - fruit and flowers, general. Mile End - household, clothes.

■ **Spitalfields**, E1 (junction Commercial St and Folgate St)
M-Sat 4.30-2.30
Fruit, veg and flowers. Wholesale.

■ **Columbia Rd**, E2
Sun 8-12.30
Flowers, pot plants, shrubs

■ **Roman Rd**, E3
Tu Th Sat 8.30-5.30
Clothes, jewellery, fabrics, discontinued lines. Fresh food and household. Plastic junk.

■ **Chatsworth Rd**, E5
M-Sat 9-4
Food, clothes, household

■ **Broadway Market**, E8 (north of Regent's Row)
F and Sat 9.30-4
Food

■ **Kingsland Waste**, E8 (junction Kingsland Rd, Englefield Rd)
Sat 9-5
Tools, timber, electrical spares, hardware, some clothes and food.

■ **Ridley Rd**, E8
Tu-Sat 9-5
West India n, fruit and veg, clothes, jewellery, hardware.

■ **Well St**, E9
M-Sat 9.30-4
Food and household

WEST

■ **Portobello Rd**, W11
Antiques - Sat 7-5, small general M-Sat 9-5
Antiques, bric-a-brac, junk. Clothes and fresh food

WEST END AND THE CITY

■ **Berwick St**, W1
M-Sat 9-5
Food, fruit and veg, clothing and fabrics. Small.

■ **Jubilee Market and Earlham St**, WC2 (commonly known as Covent Garden Market)
Jubilee - 9-5 daily, Earlham St M-F 10-4
Clothes, crafts, novelties, household, foods, second-hand books (Earlham St)

■ **Bayswater Rd**, W2 and Piccadilly, W1
Sun 9.30-4
Paintings, prints, etchings and reproductions

■ **Exmouth Mkt**, EC1 (between Farringdon Rd and Rosoman St
Tu and F 9.30-4
Second-hand books, bric-a-brac, clothes

■ **Leather Lane**, EC1
M-F 10.30-2
Food, clothes, household

■ **Whitecross St**, EC1
M-F 10.30-2.30
Clothes, food, flowers and novelties

■ **Smithfield**, EC1
M-F 5-9am
Meat, poultry and game. Wholesale.

▼ AUCTIONS ▼

This is a good way to furnish your place out cheaply. You can get most household contents. Don't worry that scratching your nose will accidently buy you a stuffed gorilla. You sometimes need to wave your hand wildly in the air to be noticed at all.

You can usually view on the day before. Examine the goods carefully. Look for woodworm in furniture. There is no guarantee that electrical goods work unless it's stated, in which case you can return them if they don't.

■ **Bonhams,** *65 Lots Rd, SW10 (351 7111).* Household goods Tue from 10.30, view Mon 9-7, Sat 10-1. Cat £1 (or subscription). Every other week (Wed), ceramics alternating with pictures. Textiles and furs, silver, toys and dolls, glass, china, books, maps and misc. Buyer pays 10% and seller pays 12.5%.

■ **Christies,** *85 Old Brompton Rd, SW7 (581 7611).* Furniture - Wed from 1, view Tue 9.30- 4 or morning of sale. It's a mixture of high and low priced stuff. Cat £2.50. There's a regular sale of good quality textiles, costumes and accessories - some Tues in the month (ring) from 2pm, view Mon till 7.30 or Tue am. Cat £2.50 - £5. Also monthly sale of wines for all tastes. Buyer pays 10% vendor's commission and vendor pays 10%. (Lots of other sales of collectables).

■ **Dowell Lloyd,** *118 Putney Bridge Rd, SW15 (788 7777).* Furniture sales fortnightly, Sat 10am, view Fri 9.30 - 7.30 evening. Jewellery sale Tues, view Monday 9.30-3.30. Alternate Saturdays furniture/Met police Lost and Found. Buyer pays 10% premium on furniture, and on Lost and Found 15% CJanVAT.

■ **Forrests,** *79-85 Cobbold Rd, E11 (534 2931).* General furniture and trade stocks and antiques fortnightly. Thur 11am, view Wed 10-5, cat 50p, 80p by post. Good bargains. 10% commission to vendor plus VAT, buyer's premium of 10% which includes VAT. 20p entry fee.

■ **Frank Bown,** *15 Greek St, W1 (437 3244).* Every other Thur.

Office furniture, trade stock, vehicles, occasional household goods and machinery, modern and reproduction office furniture, and office equipment. Phone to find out what's on. Seller pays 15% (£2 min), buyer's premium a commission of 10% + VAT.

■ **General Auctions,** *63 Garrett Lane, SW18 (870 3909),* for unclaimed stolen bikes from the Metropolitan police (Monday 11am -12) followed by secondhand electrical goods, TVs, computers, typewriters, tools. Also cars (see p142). Viewing F and Sat 9-3, buying 11am Monday.

■ **R.F. Greasby,** *211 Longley Rd, SW17 (672 2972).* Cat 50p + p&p. Furniture, clothes, computers, cameras etc. and LT lost property. Every other week on Mon 10am. View Sat before sale 10am-4pm. Buyer pays 10%, seller 15%.

■ **Rosebery's Auctions,** *3-4 Hardwick St, EC1 (240 1464).* Antiques once a month Wed from 11am, view Tue before sale date. They can give you a valuation. Vendor's commission of between 10-15% and buyer's of 10%. General sales are held at *Old Railway Booking Hall, Crystal Palace Station, SE19 (778 4024).* Every other Sat from 12.

■ **Lots Road Galleries,** *71 Lots Rd, SW10 (351 7771).* Two sales a week: Mons 4pm sale of contemporary furniture; 6pm sale of antique and reproduction furniture, rugs, pictures and objects. View Friday from 9 till 3, Sat and Sun 10-1, Mon 9-sale starts. Cat free or can be posted to you for 25p per week. Buyer pays 12% + VAT and seller 15% (negotiable).

■ **Philips Marylebone,** *Hayes Place, NW1 (723 2647).* Paintings - lower range of market. Sale Fri 11am, view Thur 9-7, Fri 9-10.30.

■ **Philips West 2,** *10 Salem Rd, W2 (229 9090).* Modern repro & Victorian Furniture, porcelain and objects, minimal amount of household goods. Thur from 10, view Weds 9-7. Buyers pay 10% and sellers pay 12.5% (£15 min). Both pay VAT. Cat £1. Collectors Dept for collector's items, sales Weds at 11 or 12.

▼ SERVICES ▼

Use *Time Out Guide to Services in London* £4.95 which is comprehensive. From newsagents.
One co-op that is still soldiering on is **Gentle Ghost**, *27 Royal Crescent Mews, W11 (602 3719)* which do removals only, with or without vans.

▼ CONSUMER ▼ LAW

The law states that if the goods you have bought are faulty or are unsuitable for the purposes for which they were described, then you can get your money back or a replacement. If the goods are new and not labelled 'substandard' then ignore any 'Sale goods cannot be returned' signs. Make sure you get a receipt which identifies the goods clearly.

If you have any problems then contact a local **Citizens Advice Bureau** (phone book).

■ **The Office of Fair Trading**, *Field Hse, Breams Bldgs, EC4 (242 2858)* is committed to protecting the consumer against unfair practices. They won't deal with complaints directly, but will send you their free leaflets if you write to them.

■ **The National Consumer Protection Council**, *London , NW4 4NY (202 5787)*. (full address). They handle complaints from irate shoppers. Also do counselling for alleged shop-lifters (over the telephone as well as interview). Send 50p for a factsheet to CCAS at above address.

■ **The National Consumer Council**, (see p164). Set up and funded by the government. It does not deal directly with complaints from the public, but deals mostly with policy issues. They publish reports on consumer affairs.

If all else fails you can take the trader to court. If the item cost a small sum then you can use the **Small Claims Court**. For larger sums you will need to go through the **County Court**. See the **Law** section (p194).

If you're a heavy spender you might consider joining the **Consumers Association**, *2 Marylebone Rd, NW1 (486 5544)* £51 p.a., which entitles you to *Which?* magazine, *Car Buying Guide* and *Tax Saving Guide*. You can get three months free subscription to *Which?* magazine by cancelling your post-dated bankers order after three months and there is no charge. For an extra £20 pa sub you can get the help of their lawyers.

▼ PUBLICATIONS ▼

The Time Out Guide to Shopping in London £3.50 lists specialist and basic shops by subjects and by the area.

The Time Out Guide to Services in London (£4.95) from newsagents lists services by subject and area.

Which? magazine do reviews of products (see **Consumers Association** above). They also produce guides on holidays, tax-saving, money and cars. You can usually view them at your local library.

Citizen Action: Taking Action in Your Community (Longman, 1986)

The User's Guide to the Environment (Kogan Page, 1983)

Glad Rags Debbie Thompson (Wildwood House, 1984, £2.95) lists London's charity shops, period shops, men's shops, fancy dress shops and more.

PLAY: Sex, Drugs, Arts & Media, Pets

sex

despite the sexual revolution of the sixties after which everyone was supposed to have got rid of their 'hang ups' about sex, most people still find it difficult to talk about, especially if there are any problems. Perhaps this isn't helped by the kind of 'perfect' sex often presented on TV and in films which tends to give the impression that we have to be ready to have sex all the time and that when we do we should go through certain set manoeuvres. Most people don't find sex like this. There are as many ways of having sex as there are people, and this includes not *having sex when you don't want it. It's easy to try and get the love and reassurance you might need through having sex, though in fact a good cuddle may be much more satisfying - but strangely enough, it's sometimes much more difficult to ask for.*

Attitudes to sex, and to sexual roles, have changed radically over the past 30 years. During that time we've seen the advent of reliable contraception, the legalisation of abortion and the whole issue of 'a woman's right to choose' with respect to her own fertility raised. The women's movement has questioned sexual roles and the patriarchal (male dominated and hierarchical) way in which society is organised, and the devaluation of what are considered 'feminine' qualities. The gay liberation movement brought into question the assumption that heterosexuality is the norm. There's been a liberalisation of sexual attitudes, with an increase in people living together rather than getting married, women deciding to bring up children on their own, more divorce, more choice in sexual lifestyles, as well as an increase in the amount of pornography available. And lately we've had to contend with the tragedy of Aids, and the change in sexual habits which many people have made as a result. With all this, it's not surprising that in society in general there are many different, and often contradictory ideas about sex. Many people are questioning what it really means to be a woman or a man, and looking for a way of bridging the often difficult gap in communication between the sexes, without resorting to rigid stereotypes or to blaming each other for the ills of the world.

▼ COUNSELLING ▼ AND PROBLEMS

The groups listed below offer counselling and 'training' in sexuality and relationships.

■ **New Grapevine,** *416 St John's St, EC1 (278 9157. Helpline: 278 9147).* For those aged 25 or under. Weds 2.30-6.30 drop in or helpline. Office hours Mon-Thurs 10.30-5. Phone first if possible. Long term counselling also available.

■ **Portobello Project,** *49 Porchester Rd, W2 (221 4413/4425).* 16-25 age range. Mon 10-6, Tues 10-4, Weds, Thur Fri 10-6. Appointment not necessary. Will refer on for long term counselling if required.

■ **Help Advisory Centre,** *3 Adam and Eve Mews, W8 (937 7687).* Weekdays 11-7. Phone or write for appointment. Short term counselling, groups and workshops on various topics including sexuality, abortion etc. Free.

■ **London Youth Advisory Centre,** *26 Prince of Wales Rd, NW5 (267 4792).* Mon, Weds and Thurs 9.30-7.30. Appointments preferred. Drop in centre for medical queries and family planning Thurs 2-7. Mainly for 12-25s. Free.

■ **London Marriage Guidance Council,** *76a New Cavendish St, W1 (580 1087).* offers personal/sexual counselling to single or married people. Contact head office for local branch. Donation for counselling, but this is negotiable. Long waiting lists (can be months) in most areas, except West End (a few weeks).

■ **Portman Clinic,** *8 Fitzjohns Ave, NW3 (794 8262).* Psychotherapy for people who have sexual problems or delinquency. NHS run. Apply in writing.

■ **The Women's Therapy Centre,** *6 Manor Gardens, N7 (263 6200).* Workshops and groups on aspects of women's sexuality as well as other issues. Low cost concessions available. Phone before you visit.

■ **Redwood (Women's Training Association),** *'Invergary', Kitlings Lane, Walton-on-the-Hill, Stafford, ST17 OLE, (0785 662823)*. Do list of assertiveness and sexuality courses run by women.

■ **Spectrum,** *7 Endymion Rd, N4 (341 2277)* runs sexuality courses (eight sessions £105). Basic and intermediate courses are single-sex, advanced is mixed.

▼ CONTRACEPTION ▼

Even though it's been around for a long time - the ancient Egyptians used alligator dung, and in the 17th century they used lambs' intestines as condoms - it's only relatively recently that birth control has been at all reliable. Even so, it's become increasingly evident that there's no perfect method. They all have drawbacks and some have side effects and health risks. Women are still largely responsible for birth control, as they are for child care, and the real 'sexual revolution' will be when men also get fully involved in the issues of fertility. While women still take most of the responsibility for contraception, their fertility is subject to a great deal of control by the medical system and state. Pregnancy and childbirth are on the whole still treated as an 'illness' for which hospitalisation is necessary, rather than as a natural event which modern medical science could make a safer and more satisfying experience. Women are also restricted in their choice of lifestyle if they decide to have children by lack of benefits and childcare facilities, making it particularly difficult for single or separated women.

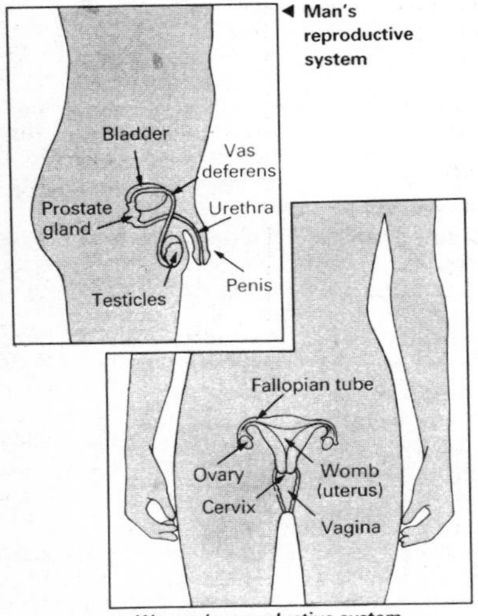

◀ Man's reproductive system

▲ Woman's reproductive system

It is extremely important to find a method of contraception that suits you and you feel you will use - remember there are no easy solutions to an unwanted pregnancy.

Where to go

You can get birth control free from

• A Family Planning Clinic (or Brook Advisory Centre, below, if you are under 22, or 25 for some centres). You can get addresses of local ones either by looking in the phone book or from:

■ **The Family Planning Association,** *Head Office, 27-35 Mortimer St, W1 (636 7866)*. They can put you in touch with your local family planning clinic. Will answer all queries about contraception, sexuality and health over phone, and refer you if you want longer term counselling. Leaflets.

■ **The Brook Advisory Service,** *153a East St, SE17 (323 1522 or 703 9660)* and local branches, is also free (except Tottenham Ct Rd branch which charges for over 21s). Also counselling on relationship problems and abortion, pregnancy testing, post coital contraception.

■ **Marie Stopes Well Woman Centre,** *108 Whitfield St, W1 (388 0662)*. £17 for basic consultation, supplies are extra.

• Your own GP or, if she is not willing to prescribe them, a GP who is.

If you are under 16, your doctor can prescribe contraception for you without your parents' knowledge, but only at her discretion. If you're unsure about your doctor's response, go to a clinic - **Brook Advisory Service** is particularly for young people and will prescribe contraceptives in complete confidence, as will a Family Planning Clinic.

Advice you get about birth control methods is not always completely unbiased - for instance some FPCs and doctors are more 'pro-pill', or 'pro-diaphragm' than others.

Choosing a method

Since no contraceptive is either 100% reliable nor completely convenient *and* side-effect free, choosing a contraceptive can feel like choosing the best of several evils. It's often a case of getting used to a particular method. Most sexually active heterosexuals try a range of different methods throughout their fertile years. Factors you need to consider are: your age; your lifestyle; your health; how important it is to avoid pregnancy; your partner and relationship; safer sex.

For instance, if you're a woman in her late 30s in a stable, long term relationship who has finished her family, you might consider sterilisation. If you're a heterosexual man who moves to different partners you should use condoms, and might consider using spermicide as well.

Methods

PILL

There are two types of pill: the **combination pill** and the **mini pill**. The **combination pill** is a combination of two artificially produced female hormones, oestrogen and progestogen. It prevents conception by preventing the release of an egg from the woman's ovaries. It also thickens the mucus at the cervix and alters the lining of the womb, making it less likely to accept a fertilised egg.

The pill is prescribed by a doctor, and is usually taken every day for three weeks. Then you stop for a week during which you have light bleeding, like a period. Some pills are taken every day and your doctor will tell you how to take them. With some pills you're protected at once - but with others you will need to use an additional method of contraception for a while.

The **mini pill** is a progestogen only pill which must be taken every day at the same time, and every day of the month. It works by thickening the mucus at the neck of the womb, making it hard for sperm to travel through. It also makes the lining of the womb less likely to accept a fertilised egg. It's less effective than the combination pill (if used properly it is probably 96% effective compared to the 99% effectiveness of the combination pill - see table)

Several things can decrease the effectiveness of the combination pill. If you forget to take it for longer than 12 hours you may ovulate. Consult the packet or a doctor for instructions if this happens - what action you take depends on the brand of pill you are taking. Usually you should use another method of contraception for seven days while continuing with the pill. If you have diarrhoea or vomiting even for a day this can cause failure, as can certain antibiotics and anti-epilepsy drugs. The mini pill can stop working if you have a bad bout of vomiting or diarrhoea, which may prevent the hormones being absorbed. If you take your mini-pill more than three hours late you must use another method for the next 48 hours, before you are protected again, *Always* tell your doctor that you are on the pill when you are prescribed other drugs.

The pill can increase the risk of blood clots, heart attacks, high blood pressure and circulatory diseases, though this is less likely with today's low dose pills. Some research suggests it may increase the risk of breast cancer and cervical cancer. Side-effects can be headaches, migraine, vaginal infections, depression, weight gain. Nausea, a common side effect during the first few months, may be helped by taking the pill with a meal or just before going to bed. While many women experience none of these, if you do have unpleasant side effects

Note: *Percentage effectiveness or success rate* is defined as the percentage number out of a 100 women using a particular method for a year that will **not** get pregnant. E.g. if a contraceptive is 98% effective it means that of 100 women using it for a year, 98 will not get pregnant (i.e. 2 **will** get pregnant).

Comparable Effectiveness Rates of Contraceptives

	% success rate used very carefully	**% success rate not used carefully**
Combined pill	more than 99	93-99
Mini pill	99	96-99
IUD	99-97	-
Diaphragm/cap used with spermicide	98	85-98
Condom	98	85-98
Natural Birth Control	98	80-98
Sponge	91	75-91
Female Sterilisation	failure rate 1 in 200 to 1 in 1000	
Male Sterilisation	failure rate 1 in 1000	

which don't go away, consult your doctor who may decide to put you on another brand of pill which may suit you better.

The risks associated with the pill increase if you are over 35, have taken it for over 5 years, or smoke. It can't be used if you have a family history of thrombosis. Afro-caribbean women should have a sickle-cell test first because if they have sickle-cell anaemia they shouldn't take it. Breastfeeding mothers can take the mini pill, but not the combination pill.

The pill is the most reliable and convenient contraceptive available at the moment. Positive side effects may include relief of pre-menstrual tension, less painful and more regular periods, and it doesn't interfere with lovemaking in any way. Research suggests there may be a reduction in ovarian cancer, cancer of the womb and rheumatoid arthritis. But for some women the risks and side-effects are too severe. You have be sure that you will remember to take it regularly. Some women find that they prefer barrier methods because they like being in touch with the rhythm of their natural cycle.

INTRA-UTERINE DEVICE

Intra-uterine devices (IUDs) are small plastic and copper devices which are placed in the womb by a trained person. One or two strings hang down into the upper vagina, so that you can check that the IUD is still in place. IUDs work by preventing the eggs and sperm meeting, and stopping a fertilised egg from settling in the womb.

They are about 97-99% effective. Contraceptive foam or jelly used mid-cycle increases effectiveness. The IUD can be expelled (usually in the first few months after fitting) so it's important to check that the strings are still in place, especially after a period.

An IUD in place

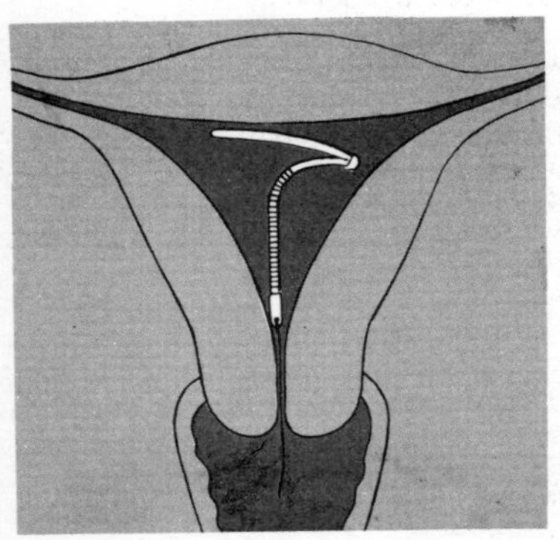

Multi-load Copper 250 (actual size)

Copper-T (actual size)

Novagard and Nova-T (actual size)

Lippes Loop* (actual size)

IUD users may be more likely to get an infection of the womb and fallopian tubes called Pelvic Inflammatory Disease (PID) or salpingitis. This is more likely in young women who move onto new sexual partners, or whose partner has more than one partner. For this reason (as well as the fact that it offers no protection against Aids) it's not the best method for those who aren't in a mutually faithful relationship. Particularly in the first few months, it may cause cramps, back pain and heavier bleeding during your period, though this is less likely as IUDs become more efficiently designed.

There's a slightly higher risk of ectopic pregnancy (where the egg implants in the fallopian tube), which can be dangerous. If you do get pregnant with the IUD in place, there's a higher risk of miscarriage and it should be removed. If you have it removed early in the pregnancy there's less chance of miscarriage than if it's left in place.

The IUD is useful for those who can't remember to take the pill.

VAGINAL DIAPHRAGM AND CERVICAL CAP WITH SPERMICIDE

A **diaphragm** is made of soft rubber and shaped like a dome, with a rim reinforced by a spring. It fits over the cervix, and measures from 5 to 10 cm in diameter - it has to be the right size for you and fitted by a doctor or nurse who will teach you how to put it in properly. *You should always use a spermicidal jelly, cream or pessaries with it* - if you don't get this from your doctor or Family Planning Clinic, read the packet to make sure that it's compatible with your diaphragm or cap. The diaphragm blocks the entrance to the cervix and holds in place the spermicide which kills the sperm. It is 98% effective if used properly, but falls to 85% if not used properly.

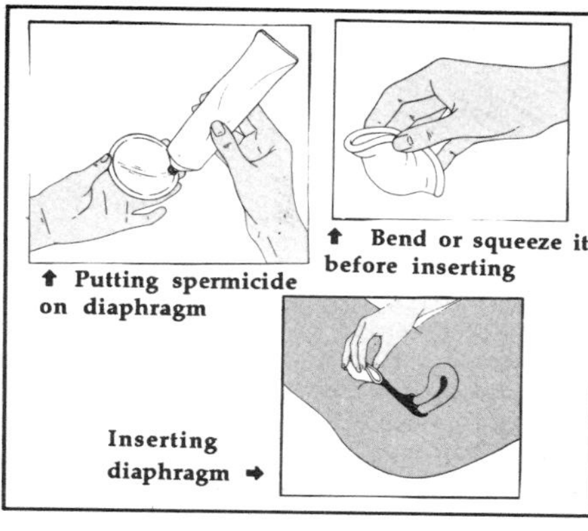

You put five centimetres of spermicide on each side of the diaphragm, and a little on the rim leaving a space for your finger and thumb as this helps with putting it in. Squeeze it with one hand and with the other part the lips of your vagina and insert the diaphragm, squatting, standing with one leg raised or lying down. When in place, check with your fingers to make sure that your cervix is under the cap - you can feel it as a lump under it. You can put it in any time before you have sex, but if you leave it longer than 3 hours before sex you'll need to put in some more spermicide, without removing the diaphragm (you can do this by using pessaries, or with an applicator). It should be left in for at least 6 hours after you last had sex. If you make love again you will need to put in some more spermicide beforehand. Don't have a bath within the 6 hours, and don't use oil based lubricants (such as vaseline) with the diaphragms and caps because they corrode rubber. Vegetable oil based spermicides such as Rendells and Genexols also damage the rubber and some vaginal ointment may also do so - consult your GP, clinic or chemist if in doubt. You can leave it in up to 24 hours.

Cervical caps are smaller than diaphragms and look like thimbles. They fit over the cervix by suction. You put a teaspoon of spermicide inside, but none round the rim.

There is also a sponge available, made of polyurethane, and filled with spermicide which fits over the cervix, but this is only 75-91% effective so isn't recommended if you really want to avoid pregnancy.

Diaphragms and caps need to be checked regularly (every 6 months is best). If you lose or gain 7 pounds you may need a new size, as you may after pregnancy, abortion or miscarriage.

Some people are put off these methods because the spermicides seem messy and off-putting (especially for oral sex since they don't taste very nice), and they are worried that putting it in will be an interruption to their spontaneity. However, once you are used to the diaphragm it isn't as much bother as it sounds - and there are no health risks involved, nor unpleasant side-effects.

CONDOM

Sheath, Durex, Johnny, Rubber etc

A condom is a thin rubber sheath which fits over the erect penis so that the sperm can't get into the vagina. It comes rolled up - squeeze the teat at the end so that there's no air in it, or if you're using a plain condom, expel the air by squeezing the end, and unroll the condom. It must be put on before you have sexual intercourse, not just before the man comes, because sperms can be discharged from the penis long before ejaculation.

Condoms are 98% effective if used carefully and consistently, if not used so carefully they are only 85% effective. Use brands that have a BSI kitemark stamped on the packet - this means they've been tested to the appropriate British Standards and are less likely to tear. If you or your partner are allergic to condoms, Family Planning Clinics stock a special brand which is hypo-allergenic.

The advantages of condoms are that they are readily available (you can get them from shops or slot machines in pubs etc). They give some protection from sexually transmitted infections and HIV - the virus that causes Aids. The disadvantages are that some people feel they interrupt sex and can cut down on the sensation the partners feel.

You can also get condoms in a variety of flavours and colours, ribbed or with various kinds of knobbles - although many of the novelty brands of condom don't have the BSI kitemark. Ordinary condoms are one size but stretch to fit all men - although at a US Government Select Committee in 1978 it was suggested that condoms be packaged in different sizes (labelled

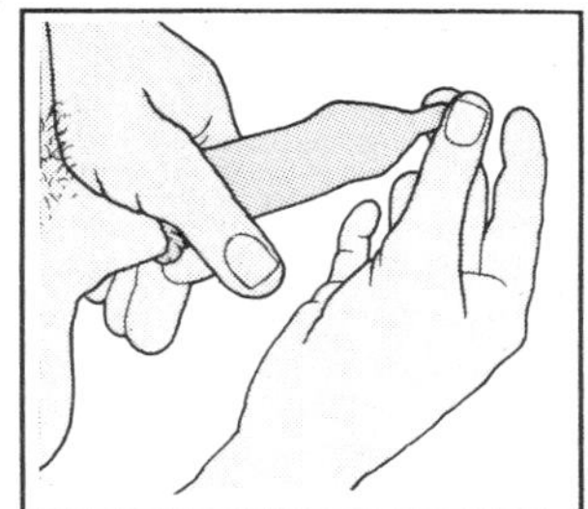

'jumbo', 'colossal' and 'super colossal' so that they don't have to go and ask for 'small'). Now there's a larger size being brought out for the 10% or so of men who need more length, width and 'head room'! Some brands are slightly different shapes. You can buy thicker condoms for safer sex.

SPERMICIDES

You can get spermicides in different forms: cream, jelly, pessaries, foam, film. They are poisonous to sperm and kill them. They aren't very effective at all used on their own, however foam is the most effective. If you are using foam, insert it no longer than 15 minutes before you make love. Foam, cream and jelly has to be inserted with an applicator, pessaries and film can be pushed high into your vagina manually though they need a few minutes to dissolve.

They have no side effects though some people are allergic to them - try another brand if this happens.

INJECTABLE CONTRACEPTION

This is progestogen which is injected into a woman to give contraceptive protection for eight weeks (Noristerat) or 12 weeks (Depo-Provera). A lot of publicity has been given to this method in the radical press as it has been used (particularly in Third World countries) on women without their consent, with reputedly serious side effects in some cases e.g. infertility. Long-term risks are still debatable - but you may have to wait for a year after you stop having the injections for periods to resume. Other side effects are similar to the pill. Best avoided.

STERILISATION

Sterilisation for women usually involves cutting or blocking the fallopian tubes, so that the egg cannot get into the womb, and the sperm can't get to the egg. It usually involves a stay of a day or two in hospital, and some clinics will do it on an day-care (i.e. outpatient) basis. It should be considered a permanent method as reversal is only 20-70% successful. Women are counselled before having the operation to make sure it's really what they want. There are rarely any side effects - periods continue - and the failure rate is only 1 in 200 to 1 in 1,000 depending on the method used.

Sterilisation for men is called a vasectomy, and involves cutting or blocking the two vas deferens - the tubes which carry the sperm from the testes to the penis. It is done under local anaesthetic, and rarely has any side-effects, and is easier to do than female sterilisation. You must use another method of birth control for some months until two sperm counts show that you are infertile. It's possible to have sperm frozen before the operation (BPAS, below, offer facilities for this) so that if you change your mind you can still have children. The failure rate is 1 in 1,000.

NATURAL BIRTH CONTROL

If you don't want to use artificial methods of contraception, natural birth control can be fairly reliable, but only if you use a combination of temperature and noting changes in vaginal mucus, and you get an expert in natural birth control to teach you. They are all based on recognising in various ways the fertile and infertile times (the 'unsafe' and 'safe' period) during a woman's cycle. The unsafe period is a period of ten to fourteen days around ovulation - five to seven days either side. During the unsafe time the partners must use a barrier method of birth control, have sex which does not involve any vagina to penis contact, or abstain from sexual contact altogether. The last two options may require a lot of self control, and in general natural birth control requires a lot of work and commitment. But it can be an opportunity for a woman to get to know her own body and natural cycles more, to share responsibility for contraception and communicate with her partner. Knowledge of these methods can also be used to help you get pregnant if you want to, and possibly to help you determine the sex of your child (see below). You are more likely to avoid conceiving if you have unprotected intercourse only in the time after ovulation up

The Menstrual Cycle

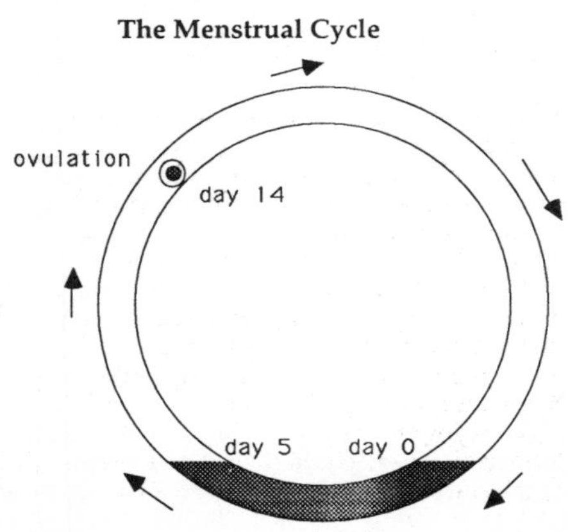

to the next period, than if you have unprotected sex in the time after a period up to ovulation.

■ **National Assoc of Natural Family Planning Teachers,** *NFP Centre, Birmingham Maternity Hospital, Queen Elizabeth Medical Centre, Edgbaston, Birmingham B15 2TG, (021 472 1377 ext 102).* Have lists of Natural Family Planning Teachers throughout the country.

■ **Natural Family Planning Teachers,** *c/o Mrs Rosalind Byrne, 51 Ditton Rd, Surbiton, Surrey, KT 6 6RF, (399 4789).* London co-ordinator for natural family planning.

Mucus Method

This involves observing the changes in quality and quantity of the cervical mucus throughout the menstrual cycle.

During menstruation cervical mucus can't be observed easily, so these are not necessarily safe days. After your period you may have a couple of days of no mucus, and a sensation of dryness in your vagina (however if yours is a very short cycle you may have mucus straight away). Then the mucus will start to become more profuse, starting off whitish or yellowish, thick and tacky and becoming clearer, more slippery and stringy like raw egg white (you can stretch a strand of it between two fingers). These changes start about five days before ovulation and on the most fertile days you may have a sensation of slippery wetness and lubrication. Intercourse should be avoided from the first time you see or feel mucus until four days after the slippery wet sensation has gone. After this, the mucus will resume a whitish, yellowish, cloudy appearance and tacky consistency. You should learn this method from a properly trained natural family planning teacher (see above).

METHODS THAT AREN'T METHODS

• Withdrawal of the penis just before the man comes (sometimes known as *whipping it out)* is most unreliable, as some sperm are released from the penis before the man comes.
• Douching can force sperm even further up the vagina.
• Standing up and jumping up and down is a complete waste of time.
• The woman not having an orgasm is no protection at all, and most unsatisfying for her.
• Spermicides used on their own have a high failure rate.

Basal Body Temperature

Just before ovulation your temperature drops slightly, and after ovulation it rises. By taking your temperature every day at the same time as soon as you wake up with a *basal* fertility thermometer which measures minute temperature changes, you can tell when you have ovulated. When you have recorded a temperature for three days in a row which is higher than all the previous six days the fertile time is over. You can get charts on which you record your temperature and mucus changes from the FPA. Because many things can affects your temperature (even taking aspirin), you may need expert help to interpret your chart. This method by itself will not enable you to find out which are the infertile days before ovulation.

Calendar method

This should only be used as a cross-check with the above two methods. You need to keep a chart of your periods for at least 6 consecutive cycles. Work out the number of days in the shortest cycle and subtract 19 - this gives you the probable first fertile and therefore unsafe day after the first day of your period. Then work out the number of days in the longest cycle and subtract 10 - this gives you the probable last day of the fertile time after which it is safer to have sex again. If your cycle changes you will need to alter your calculations.

Astrological Birth Control

If you are an astrology buff and are happy to get pregnant you could try this! The fertile time according to this method is when the sun and moon are the same distance apart in degrees as they were when the woman was born. This happens once every 291/2 day lunar cycle. It is calculated with an ephemeris (an astrological table of the planets' positions).

Methods of birth control for use after unprotected sex

MORNING AFTER PILL

This is a high combination dose of oestrogen and progestogen which must be taken within 3 days of (but preferably as soon as possible after) unprotected sex. Two special pills are taken immediately and two are taken 12 hours later. It is 96-99% effective. Your period will arrive at the usual time, slightly earlier or later. It may make you feel sick, and if you vomit you may need to take more pills, so tell your doctor. This method is meant for emergencies only and is available from FPCs and GPs.

IUD INSERTION

An IUD inserted up to five days after unprotected sex should also prevent a fertilised egg implanting in the womb. It is almost 100% effective and can be used as an on-going method if appropriate.

▼ CONCEIVING ▼

If you are trying to conceive and you have been using the pill you should allow 2 natural periods for your body to get back to normal, using a barrier method during that time (this makes sure that the hormones are out of your body). You can use the natural birth control methods described above to find out when you are most fertile. You are most likely to conceive if you have sex a few days before and at the time you ovulate. If you're having difficulty conceiving, when you make love, a position which is supposed to help conception is with the man on top, and the woman facing him underneath, a pillow supporting her hips and her knees pulled up towards her chest. When the man comes he should stop thrusting and hold still. Then he should withdraw and the woman should stay in her position for as long as possible - about half an hour is recommended. This encourages as much sperm as possible to make their way into the womb.

Health and nutrition is important - eat fresh foods and cut down or cut out drinking and smoking if you can (both partners) before you conceive.

Determining the Sex of Your Child

There is no certain way to ensure the child is a boy or girl. However, sperms carrying X (female) chromosomes can live longer and are hardier but swim more slowly, and sperms carrying Y (male) chromosomes die faster but swim more quickly. On this basis some people suggest if you want a girl its best to try to conceive by having sex in the two days preceding ovulation, so that only the longer living X chromosome sperms will still be around at ovulation. If you want a boy, have sex on or just after ovulation.

There is also a special diet which is supposed to alter your body chemistry to favour the survival of one or other set of sperms - it's calcium and magnesium rich for girls, potassium and sodium rich for boys. The book to get for this *Girl or Boy Your Chance to Choose* Hazel Phillips and Tessa Hilton (Thorsons). Before embarking on any diet, check with your doctor that it's OK.

Infertility

It's not unusual to go a year before you get pregnant, but if you are having difficulty in conceiving your doctor can refer you to an infertility clinic. Both of you should be tested. You can also get help from various private clinics, although this may be expensive. Around one in ten couples experience problems in conceiving, and over two thirds of them can be helped to have a child of their own.

DONOR INSEMINATION

This is a useful option for women without men partners or for women whose partners are not very fertile. Sometimes this is available on the NHS, if not PAS and BPAS (below) will do it. The success rate is about 40%. They screen donors and try to match their physical characteristics with the couple.

ADOPTING

The British Association of Adoption Agencies (below) publish a booklet *Adopting A Child* (£2.50) which lists all the adoption agencies, run by either the Social Services or on a voluntary basis, to which you can apply. You can't adopt if you have a criminal record, and you have to have a medical check up to ensure that you're healthy. You will also be screened very thoroughly by the adoption agency, who, if they don't like some aspect of your lifestyle, may ask you to consider changing it or turn you down. It's most difficult to adopt babies, and easier to adopt older or handicapped children. It is possible for single and gay people to adopt, but of course much more difficult than for a married heterosexual couple - it can depend on the attitude of your adoption agency and what kind of child you want to adopt. If you're not married only one person can be the legal adoptive parent, though you both may look after the child.

It can be a lengthy process - if you're accepted there can be a long wait for a suitable child.

■ **National Association for the Childless,** *318 Summer Lane, Birmingham B19 3LR, (021 359 4887).* Info on infertility, support, counselling referral. .

■ **Post Adoption Centre,** *15 Wilkin St, NW5 (284 0555).* Post adoption support and counselling for adoptive families, adopted people and parents whose child has been adopted.

■ **Association of British Adoption Agencies,** *4 Southampton Row, WC1, (242 8951).*

■ **The British Agencies for Adoption and Fostering (BAAF),** *11 Southwark St, SE1 (407 8800).* Advice and information about adoption. Can put you in touch with local agencies. Leaflet *Single and Pregnant and Thinking About Adoption* (30p).

■ **The Independent Adoption Service,** *121 Camberwell Rd, SE5 (703 1088).* Write for info.

▼ PREGNANCY ▼

Pregnancy testing

A missed period or a lighter and shorter period than normal is the major sign of pregnancy, and this can be accompanied by enlarged and tender breasts, nausea, tiredness and frequent peeing. Missed periods can be caused by other things (e.g. stress or coming off the pill).

There are different kinds of pregnancy tests. Some GPs offer free tests, but you may have to wait two weeks after your missed period, and the result may take up to a week to come. Some family planning clinics offer a free test with same-day results. Private testing services are available at a price and give quick results (see *Yellow Pages*), and chemists may offer a similar service. Pregnancy counselling charities give tests and on the spot results for a charge. Do it yourself pregnancy test kits are available for £6 or upwards. They give quick results, although it might be wrong if you don't follow the instructions properly. The **Brook Advisory Centres** will do them free, as will some women's groups. For all these tests you will need an early morning urine sample. There is a blood test now (available from private agencies only - see below) which is fairly accurate *before* a missed period.

If you very much want to be pregnant and are considering having a very early test, bear in mind that there's quite a high rate of miscarriage in the first few weeks of pregnancy, so if you have an early test and *do* miscarry you will know about it, rather than just thinking that your period is late.

At the moment it can be quite difficult to get a free pregnancy test. Some GPs are refusing to do urine sample tests because local hospital laboratories aren't doing them anymore. If your GP does agree to do a test, you should *never* be charged for this.

Warning: Urine tests can give a false negative result the first or second time you have them. If you still haven't had a period after 28 days, and it's important for you to know quickly that you're pregnant see your doctor or pregnancy advisory clinic.

NB: There's a number of organisations (e.g. one called **Life**) which offer free pregnancy tests and counselling. They are *very* much against abortion and will try to persuade you to go through with the pregnancy.

Options for unwanted pregnancies

The first thing you need to do on finding that you are pregnant is to decide as quickly as possible whether or not you want to go through with the pregnancy. If you feel you need to talk to someone about it who won't pressurise you either way, the pregnancy advisory clinics listed below offer counselling for pregnant women.

KEEPING THE CHILD

The **National Council for One Parent Families** can give practical advice on housing, the law, Income Support and benefits, maintenance, daycare and other issues. It can be hard being a single parent because you can end up feeling isolated, even though it's much more socially acceptable nowadays to bring a child up on your own. It helps to have the support of friends, family etc. A word of warning about 'shotgun' marriages - think very carefully about getting married or living together *just* because of a pregnancy. Unless you want to do this anyway because you love each other and get on, this kind of partnership can produce stresses which can be damaging to the parents and baby.

ADOPTION

You can either go to your local Welfare unit (part of Social Services) or an adoption agency (voluntary), or contact the National Council for One Parent Families, who will refer you to one of these organisations. You will receive counselling to make sure it's the right decision for you. It's illegal to arrange an adoption through a third party, and you can only arrange it yourself if the adoptive parents are relatives. Six weeks after the baby is born, if you still want the baby adopted, you'll be asked to sign a consent form and hand the baby over to her adoptive parents. If you don't want to look after the baby for the six weeks after birth, the agency can arrange to have her fostered in that time.

When the child is 18, she will have the right to know who her biological mother is, and may try to find you.

■ **Post Adoption Centre,** *(284 0555)* offers counselling for parents whose child is being/has been adopted.

ABORTION

The issue of abortion produces strong feelings both in those who are for women's choice, and in those who are against it being available at all. Women having abortions can feel very differently about them; some don't have strong reactions while others may go through a difficult time where perhaps they have contradictory and painful feelings. Even though you believe that you have the right to choose whether you have a child or not, you may need a period of mourning after an abortion. For this reason counselling to help you make your mind up is very important. Under the 1967 Abortion Act, abortion is allowed under the law if two doctors sign a form saying that having a child would caused physical or emotional damage to the woman greater than that caused by an abortion. If the child might be handicapped, this is also grounds. The legal limit for abortion is 28 weeks, although doctors are very reluctant to perform late abortions. They should be carried out as soon as possible.

Abortions are available on the NHS, but this can sometimes be difficult in practice - only 44% of abortions are done on the NHS. Waiting lists for hospitals are long – if your hospital appointment is set for a date after you will be more than 10 weeks pregnant (i.e. 10 weeks after the first day of your last period) it might be better to go to a private abortion clinic, because NHS hospitals don't do many abortions after 12 weeks, and you may be refused an abortion on the grounds that it is too late. The availability of abortion on the NHS also differs from area to area, depending on the views of GPs and hospital consultants.

In a recent survey, 70% of doctors were found to be in favour of the 1967 Abortion Act, but your doctor is under no obligation to tell you her views on abortion, nor whether the consultant she is referring you to at the hospital is for or against. If your GP will not refer you for an abortion you can try to register with a doctor who is more likely to do so. Your local women's centre may be able to tell you who is sympathetic, or you can try getting a register of doctors from your local Family Practitioner Committee, or your local library and look for the letter 'C' after the doctor's name. This shows that the doctor gives contraceptive advice, and so may be *slightly* more likely to refer you for an abortion than one who doesn't, though this isn't necessarily the case.

The private abortion clinics listed below are non-profit making, and will arrange an abortion for any woman they believe needs one.

Methods of Abortion

Up to 12 weeks Dilation and Evacuation is performed: the cervix (neck of the womb) is dilated and the contents of the womb, including the foetus are sucked out using a vacuum pump. This can be done under a local anaesthetic. Dilation and Curettage is similar, but the contents of the womb are scraped out - this method can be used up to 15 weeks under a general anaesthetic. Usually late abortions are induced using either a saline or prostaglandin (a substance which induces natural labour) solution injected into the womb. Obviously this method carries more risks and is more distressing than early abortion methods.

New Developments

At the time of going to press, a new method of early abortion, using a pill called RU 486, is undergoing tests in this country. It can be used up to 7 weeks after the first day of a woman's last period and is being used in France at the moment, though it isn't available in Britain yet. It doesn't involve surgery or anaesthetic and is straightforward, though to use it you have to make your mind up more quickly about the pregnancy if you are in doubt. You still have to be eligible for an abortion under the '67 Act.

It involves a doctor giving the woman who wants the abortion anti-progesterone steroids (progesterone is a hormone which is needed to keep the lining of the womb intact). 48 hours later a pessary made of prostaglandin, a substance which relaxes the cervix, is inserted into her vagina. This induces contractions and she has what is like a heavier than normal period during which the fetus is expelled.

Methods of Abortion that Don't Work or are Harmful

Pills, potions, drugs and alcohol don't work - if you take enough to affect the fetus you will poison yourself. Lifting heavy weights or jumping from high up will injure you, not abort. NEVER poke anything into your womb - this can cause serious infection and death.

Addresses

■ **PAS,** *11-13 Charlotte St, W1 (637 8962)*. Pregnancy test £7 (accurate 1 day after missed period). Consultation fee £40 including counselling fee. Prices for abortion start at £175. Also do sterilisation, post coital contraception, smear tests, donor insemination.

■ **British Pregnancy Advisory Service (BPAS),** *7 Belgrave Rd, SW1 (222 0985).* £4 test accurate 4-5 days after missed period. Abortion up to 14 weeks £168.

■ **PCC,** *40 Mortimer St, W1 (580 4847).* £5 pregnancy test (accurate 2 weeks after period), £8 for sensitive test accurate 1 day after conception. £40 consultation, under 12 weeks: £140 day care, £160 overnight. 13-15 weeks £190, 16-20 weeks £240. 21-23 weeks £340 .

■ **P & G** , *26 Fouberts Place, W1 (437 7125 - 24 hours).* £5 for pregnancy test or £8 for 'sensitive' test (accurate immediately after conception). Abortion:12 weeks £200; 13-15 weeks £250; 16-19 weeks £280. No extra consultation fee.

■ **Marie Stopes,** *108 Whitfield St, W1 (388 4843).* Pregnancy test accurate one day after missed period £8. £40 consultation. Under 12 weeks: daycare £140; overnight £160. 13-15 weeks £190, 15-20 weeks £240. 21-23 weeks £340.

■ **BCO Laboratory Services,** *144 Harley St , W1 (487 3063).* Do pregnancy test by blood sample which is 100% reliable 10 days after conception (£13). If you go in before 2pm you'll get the results the same day.

■ **Abortion Anonymous,** *(350 2229)* run a counselling helpline M-F 7-9pm for women who have had abortions and need to talk about it with another woman.

Campaigns

■ **National Abortion Campaign,** *Wesley Ho, 4 Wilde Ct, WC2 (405 4801).* Member of the **Pro-Choice Alliance** - affiliated groups campaigning on the issue of a woman's right to choose. Campaigns for better facilities, raising all issues around women's right to control their fertility, in schools, unions etc. Organises conferences, forums and rallies, provides speakers and sells literature and video cassettes mail order. Contact them for addresses of local groups.

■ **A Woman's Right to Choose/Abortion Law Reform Association,** *88a Islington High St, N1 8EG (359 5200).*

▼ CHILDBIRTH ▼

Home or hospital

While the health service is moving towards bigger maternity units and shutting small ones down, more women are questioning the way in which they are expected to give birth, and the treatment of pregnancy and childbirth as an illness, rather than a natural process which the body is capable of completing in most cases without too much intervention.

Home Giving birth at home means that you will be in familiar surroundings, with your partner and/or friends present, will have more control over your labour with less routine medical intervention. However if you are in a high risk group - have certain conditions such as toxaemia, or an illness which is made worse by pregnancy and labour - hospital is probably better. If you are in your mid thirties or over, or under 16 you are more likely to develop complications, so hospital might be better. It also depends on where you will feel more relaxed - some women feel more at ease at home, and some in hospital - and how relaxed you are may play a large part in determining how smoothly the labour goes. Check to see if there's an emergency service 'flying squad' in your area which can cover you if something goes wrong.

It's been assumed that hospital births are safer, but studies have not shown this to be the case. What *has* been shown to be crucial in determining the health of the mother and baby is good ante natal care and nutrition - it's the poor who develop complications most frequently.

You are entitled to have a home birth if you want one, though doctors may try to put you off. If your GP is sympathetic she may have a midwife attached to the practice. If she isn't sympathetic, you should get in touch with your local midwife service to find your own midwife. You can find the address at your local public library. Otherwise write to the Area Nursing Officer or Area Medical Officer asking for names of local midwives. The midwife will be attached to a doctor who can supervise the birth.

If you want a home birth, make sure you have not been booked into a hospital against your will.

■ **The National Childbirth Trust** (p82) publish a booklet, *Giving Birth at Home* (£1 + 25p p&p) which outlines the arguments for and against home birth, and tells you how to set it up.

Hospital: You are entitled to choose a hospital within your local area, though your doctor will refer you to the nearest one. When choosing check on whether they allow the father to be present at the birth; whether they insist you lie down during birth (walking about can help ease pain); whether you have control over what pain relief they give you; whether you can have your baby with you when you want; what the visiting restrictions are, their policy on breastfeeding and demand feeding; and when they will let you go home.

Contact the **Active Birth Centre** (p82) if you want to know what is the attitude of hospitals in your area. There are two other options which *might* make your experience of hopital more pleasant:

GP Units These are small units close to a

hospital run by midwives and supervised by GPs. They *can* be more relaxed and informal than hospitals - but not always. They provide ante natal and neo-natal care too so that there is more continuity.

Early discharge You can pre-arrange a discharge from hospital after 48 hours, but not all women are allowed this - it depends on how straightforward the birth was.

Addresses

■ **International Centre for Active Birth,** *55 Dartmouth Pk Rd, NW5 (267 3006).* Runs classes on aspects of active birth and parenthood including exercise and yoga, preparing for labour, breastfeeding, baby massage, breathing. Supply books and tapes mail order. Pyramid float pool on the premises for relaxation. Variety of natural therapies available (acupuncture, homoeopathy, cranial osteopathy and massage). Portable water pool for birth for hire or purchase.

■ **The National Childbirth Trust (NCT),** *Alexandra House, Oldham Terr, Acton, W3 (992 8637).* Will refer to local branch. Run ante-natal classes, give post-natal support, support or counselling for breastfeeding.

■ **Society to Support Home Confinement,** *c/o Margaret Whyte, Lydgate, Lydgate Ln, Wolsingham, Bishop Auckland, Durham DL13 3HA, (0388 528044).* Leaflets giving advice on how to arrange home confinement. Will also give telephone advice to those having problems doing this. Send large SAE.

■ **La Leche League,** 27 Old Gloucester St, WC1 (242 1278). Promotes and advises on breastfeeding.

▼ MATERNITY AND WORK ▼

Antenatal Care: You have the right to take time off for antenatal care (this includes relaxation classes) without loss of pay whatever hours you work or however long you have worked in your job.

Some jobs are illegal during pregnancy (e.g. using X-rays or working with some chemicals), or harmful (e.g. those involving heavy lifting) and your employer must move you to a different job if there is one, providing you have worked for her a) for two years for more than 16 hours a week, or b) for five years if you have worked 8-16 hours a week.

If there's no similar job you can be dismissed, but you still qualify for maternity leave and pay at the same rate as if you hadn't been dismissed.

Maternity Leave: You're entitled to up to 40 weeks unpaid leave beginning eleven weeks before the week of the birth and finishing 29 weeks from the week of the birth, on condition that

1. Your employer has six or more employees - otherwise it's up to them whether you get maternity leave or not.
2. You have worked for the same employer full time for two years by end of the 12th week before the week the baby is due. If you work part time it must be 5 years.
3. You work until the end of the 12th week before the week the baby is due.
4. You write to your employers at least 21 days before you stop work to say that you're going on maternity leave, and intend to return after the baby's birth. If the baby is premature, write as soon as you can.
5. You write to your employers at least 21 days before you want to return giving them the date you intend to return.

When you go back to work your employer may not give you your old job back, but should give you a *similar* job.

You only have to make up your mind whether you want to go back to your job 21 days before the date you have to return.

Maternity Pay: You're entitled to Statutory Maternity Pay (basic rate £34.25) for 18 weeks in total whether or not you decide to return to work, as long as you've worked for your employers for at least six months. If you've worked for two years full time or five years part time you get 9/10ths of your average pay for six weeks. You have to have worked up to the 15th week before you baby is due, or have had a live baby before this date.

Maternity Allowance: you can claim this if you're not entitled to maternity pay because you're self employed, left or changed your job during pregnancy or your claim for SMP was late. You have to have made 26 National Insurance contributions in the year before the baby is born.

For more information read the leaflet *Pregnant At Work* published by **The Maternity Alliance**, 15 Brittania St, WC1 (837 1265) who give advice on difference aspects of maternity, including benefits, rights at work etc. Leaflets (translation in Bengali).

▼ POST NATAL PROBLEMS ▼

■ **The Association for Post Natal Illness,** *7 Gowan Ave, SW6* has a pamphlet explaining the symptoms and may be able to put you in touch with other groups or with counsellors.

■ **Women's Health Concern,** *17 Earl's Terr, W8*

(602 6669). Staffed by doctors, psychologists, counsellors. Telephone service for all gynaecological problems/queries including menopause, pre-menstrual syndrome, post natal depression. Free leaflets. Study days for nurse counsellors.

■ **Women's Health and Reproductive Rights Information Centre**, *52 Featherstone St, EC1 (251 6580)*. Will answer queries by phone on all aspects of women's health. Also drop in centre open: 11-5 M-F closed Tu. Large library and leaflets covering various topics. (See also **Women's** section p175).

■ **The Stillbirth and Neonatal Death Society**, *28 Portland Pl, W1 (436 5881)*. Support/befriending to parents who have had a baby die around birth. 12 groups in London.

■ **The Foundation for the Study of Infant Deaths**, *14 Belgrave Sq, SW1 (235 1721/0965)*. will put you in touch with local support group for bereaved parents. Gives support over phone as well as practical advice (e.g. on monitors for babies) and fundraises for research into *sudden infant death syndrome (cot death)*.

▼ SEX & HEALTH ▼

Since the advent of Aids (Acquired Immune Deficiency Syndrome), other sexually transmitted diseases have faded into the background. If you practice 'safer sex' (see below) your chances of catching Aids and any of these infections will be less - but it is still possible to catch them if you're sexually active - some of them such as thrush and cystitis aren't technically sexually transmitted diseases, and you can develop them even without having sex.

If you get any symptoms go straight to a clinic, and if you're diagnosed as having any infection, let your partner(s) know. Because women don't always get symptoms when they have caught a Sexually Transmitted Disease (STD), if you're a heterosexual man the only way your partner may know she has one of these infections is if you tell her *you* have it. Don't have sex until you've been given the OK by the clinic. No one should be blamed for catching a sexually transmitted disease, but passing it on either through not bothering to check symptoms out at a clinic or through having sex when you know you've got it is unforgivable.

Where to go for treatment

Hospital STD clinics are listed below. They are often called 'special' clinics, or 'genito-urinary medicine' clinics. They are often 'discreetly' placed outside the hospital, and men and women usually have separate clinics or separate times to attend.

These days the staff at STD clinics treat you as they would a patient witl any other illness - perhaps more considerately since they are keen to encourage people to come when they need to. But there may be some exceptions to this, if you don't like one clinic, you can go to another.

Some operate an appointment system - if you have to wait too long and are desperate, try either turning up and waiting to be seen, or going to another which operates a drop-in system.

When you get to see the doctor she will ask you about your symptoms and medical history and then blood, urine and swabs (from the vagina, penis and anus) will be taken. Clinics don't do the HIV and Aids tests as a matter of routine as they do for all other sexually transmitted diseases - if you want it you will have to ask and have counselling to make sure it's the right decision. Most clinics will give you the results of some of the tests while you're there, but you may have to go back for some - they rarely give you your results over the telephone.

Sexually Transmitted Disease Clinics

■ **Central Middlesex Hosp**, *Special Clinic, Acton La, NW10 (965 5733)*. Walk in M, F 10-12, Tu, W 10-12 & 2-4, Th 2-6.

■ **Croydon General Hosp**, *Special Clinic, London Rd, Croydon, Surrey, (684 6999)*. Walk in. Women: M, F 2-6, Tu, W 9-12, should arrive 1 hour before they close. Men: M, Th, Fri 9-1, Tue 2-6 get there half hour before they close.

■ **Guy's Hosp**, *Lloyd Clinic, SE1 (955 5000)*. Appointment necessary. M-F 9-5.

■ **Hillingdon Hosp**, *Genito-Medical Dept, (0895 38282)*. Men: no appointment necessary M 2-5.45, Tu 4.30-6.15, W, Th 2-3.45, F 4.30-6.15, Women: by appointment only Mon, Tue, W afternoon, Fri morning. No appointment necessary Tu and Fri evening 4.30-5.45.

■ **London Hosp**, *Whitechapel Clinic, Turner St, E1 (247 7310)*. Walk in. M-Th 9.30-5.30, F 10.30-5.30.

■ **Middlesex Hosp**, *James Pringle Ho, 73 Charlotte St, W1 (636 8333)*. Appointment necessary. 8.30-5.

■ **Newham General Hosp**, *Glen Rd, E13 (476 1400 ext 306)*. Appointment necessary.

■ **Oldchurch Hosp**, *The Annexe, Oldchurch Rd, Romford, Essex, (0708 46090 ex 3258)*. Walk in. M 10-

12, 3.30-5.30 (women & men), Tu 9-11 (women), 2-4 (men), Weds 9.30-12 (men), 33.0-5.30 (women), Thu 10-12 (women & men), Fri 9-11 (women & men).

■ **Royal Free Hosp**, *Marlborough Clinic, Pond St, NW3 (794 0500).* Appointment necessary. Open 9am, no new patients seen after 3.30pm. Mon am (men), pm (women), Tu am & pm (men and women). Weds (men), Th am (men). Th pm (men & women), Fri pm (men and women).

■ **Royal Northern Hosp**, *Special Clinic, Holloway Rd, N7 (272 7777).* Appointment necessary. M-Th 10-5.45, F 10-3.45.

■ **St Anne's Hosp**, *St Anne Rd, N15 (800 0121).* Walk in. Tu 3.30-5, W 9-11, Th 9-11, Fri 10.30-12.30, 3.30-5.00.

■ **St Bartholomews Hosp**, *Special Treatment Centre, EC1 (601 8888).* M-F 9-11.45, 1.30-4.15. Walk in every day except Weds when appointment necessary.

■ **St George's Hosp**, *Blackshaw Rd, SW17 (672 1255).* Walk in. M 1-5.45, Tu 2-4, W 10-12, & 2-4, Th 9.30-11.45, 2-5.45.

■ **St Helier Hosp**, *Special Clinic, Wrythe La, Carshalton, Surrey, (644 4343).* No appointment necessary. Men: M 9-12, W 3.30-4.30, Th 3-4.30. Women: Tu 3-4.30, W 1.30-2.20, F 9-10.30 and 1.45-2.45. Doors open 1 hour before clinic starts. HIV testing with counselling Weds 9-11.

■ **St Mary's Hospital,** *Praed St Special Clinic, Praed St, W2 (725 1697).* M-F 9-6, W 10-6. Walk in.

■ **St Paul's Hosp**, *Genito Medical Dept, Endell St, WC2 (836 9611).* Appt necessary (2-3 weeks wait), referral from GP preferred. Men only. Thurs 2-4. No HIV testing.

■ **St Stephens Hosp**, *John Hunter Clinic, Fulham Rd, SW10 (376 4555).* Walk in. M-F 9.30-4.30, (closed Fri 12-2).

■ **St Thomas' Hosp**, *Lydia Dept, SE1 (928 9292).* Walk in. M-F 9-5.30 (Tu closes 4.30).

■ **University College Hosp**, *Special Clinic, Out-patient Bldg, Grafton Way, WC1 (387 9300).* Appointment necessary. 9-11.30, 1-4.30.

■ **West London Hosp**, *Martha & Luke Clinics, Hammersmith Rd, W6 (846 1234). Walk in. 9.30-12.30, 2-5.*

■ **West Middlesex Hosp**, *Genito-Medical Dept, Isleworth, (867 5718).* Women appointment only Mon am, Weds afternoon & eve, Th, F afternoon. Men walk in M 9.30-11.30 & 4.30-7, Fri 2-3. Appt only Th afternoons.

■ **Westminster Hosp**, *(Op 6), Dean Ryle St, SW1 (630 5266).* Appointment necessary M-F 9.30-4.30.

Non Specific Infection

This is often called Non Specific Urethritis in men. Women may get a whitish discharge and abdominal pain (though they rarely have symptoms) and men a thin grey discharge and pain or stinging on peeing. It can recur.

It is curable, but, if not treated properly, can lead to infertility in both men and women.

Genital Warts

These can appear at the bottom of the vagina, the cervix, or the vaginal lips in a woman, and towards the tip of the penis, or under the foreskin in a man. In moist areas they may be large and soft, on dry parts of the genitals they may look more like the same warts you get on hands or feet. They develop a cauliflower like appearance if they grow large. Warts can be treated by chemicals, frozen off or burnt out with a laser. It's best to use a barrier method of birth control - preferably a condom - for a year after treatment because the warts can recur in this time. Women who have warts may have abnormal cervical smear tests, so they should have their test repeated every year.

Gonorrhoea

Gonorrhoea is caught through intimate contact, usually through genital, oral or anal sex.

Most women don't show any symptoms and so have to rely on being told by their partners that they've got it. Any symptoms you do develop will appear from 2 days to 3 weeks after infection: vaginal discharge, irritation of the vagina or anus, painful urination, or sore throat and enlarged glands if the infection has been caught orally. If the disease is untreated at this stage it may progress causing abdominal pain, vomiting, fever and irregular periods. You can become infertile if it isn't treated.

Most men develop symptoms within a week. There's a thick milky discharge from the penis which may form a crusting at the end, and pain or burning on peeing, like 'pissing broken glass'. Uncircumcised men may have reddening or irritation of the penis. Your lymph glands (in the groin) may be enlarged.

Gonorrhoea is treated with antibiotics - go back to the clinic for a follow up visit because the infection may not be cleared up by the first course of treatment, but will be completely cured by subsequent courses of treatment.

Herpes

This is a virus which is similar to the one which causes cold sores. Symptoms are painful sores like blisters or small bumps which can rupture to form open sores or ulcers. They appear on the external genitals, the cervix or inside the vagina in women, and usually on the penis in men. They can also occur near the anus, and on the buttocks and thighs. You may also have enlarged lymph glands, and feel run down. The sores last from a week to a month until they heal by themselves. It's spread through sex, both by genital contact and oral sex. It's only infectious during the time you have the sores.

The first attack is usually the worst. Women are often affected more severely than men, and the first attack should usually be treated by special anti-viral antibiotics, particularly in women. After that it may recur periodically, often at times of stress, or when you are physically run down. To relieve symptoms, wear loose clothing, take painkillers, and if it's painful to pee try doing so in a warm bath. A warm sodium bicarbonate or salt solution can relieve pain.

There may be higher risk of abnormal smear tests in women with herpes, so you should have a smear test every year. If you get pregnant, tell your doctor you have herpes - it can in a few, rare cases cause complications in pregnancy. If you have your first ever attack while pregnant there is a higher risk of miscarriage and of the baby being abnormal in some way. If you are having an attack when labour begins, some doctors will advise a Cesarian section (an operation where the womb is cut open to release the baby at birth). For more information contact

■ **Herpes Assn**, *41 North Rd, N7 (609 9061).* Helpline and counselling for Herpes sufferers. Send 5 first class stamps for general info leaflet.

Trichomoniasis

Is passed on through sex. It doesn't produce symptoms in men, though they can carry it, but in women there's a thin, foamy, yellowish green or grey discharge with a bad smell. Sometimes it itches as well and produces discomfort on peeing.

It's treated with a drug in pill form called Flagyl (Metromidedle). Don't use tampons while you're infected.

Yeast Infections/Candida/Thrush

Thrush is very common, and can be very irritating because it recurs. It mostly affects women, though men can also have symptoms and should be treated if their partner has it. Yeast fungus is present normally in the vagina and anus, but when your system is out of balance or the vagina becomes less acidic, the yeast grows and produces a thick white discharge (like cottage cheese) and irritation. An attack can be set off by allergy to perfumed soaps, slight abrasions to the vagina (caused by using tampons or vigorous sex) or antibiotics, and women who are pregnant or on the pill seem to be more susceptible. It's treated with pessaries and cream. You can sometimes nip it in the bud by bathing the outside of the genitals with diluted vinegar, or putting natural live yoghurt on the outside and inside the vagina - put a tampon into the yoghurt and then insert it.

To prevent attacks, always wipe your bum from front to back to avoid germs spreading from the anus to the vagina. Don't use perfumed soaps. Some women who suffer from recurrent attacks of thrush try alternative medicine, where the treatment usually involves a change of diet.

Cystitis

This is inflammation/infection of the bladder. Symptoms are that you want to pee all the time but nothing comes out though you have a terrible burning sensation. You may have back pain, fever and some women have reported a sensation of 'crawling out of the skin'. You may have blood in your urine. Your doctor will test your urine and then prescribe antibiotics. In women it can come back, sometimes brought on by sex, not being able to pee when you want to, or being run down. It's rare in men.

If you feel an attack coming on, drink a pint of water immediately, and keep drinking as much water as you can - a pint every 20 minutes or more. A teaspoon of sodium bicarbonate taken in water lowers the acidity of the urine and so lessens the burning sensation (not to be taken if you have high blood pressure or heart trouble). A hot water bottle on your back and between you thighs will help the pain. In general, avoid spicy food, perfumed soap, tight trousers or tights, and sex positions which put pressure on the bladder (e.g. rear entry) and pee before and after sex.

Syphilis

Syphilis, caught in the same way as gonorrhoea, goes through several stages. The first sign is a painless sore which looks like a pimple, blister or open sore which may weep or look crusty. This appears on the point of sexual contact - genitals, lips, anus, mouth etc. With women this may develop inside the vagina and so may go unnoticed. After 1 to 5 weeks the sore goes away - but the disease doesn't.

In the next stage which occurs from a week to 6 months later there are a range of symptoms including rashes (particularly on the palms of the hands and soles of the feet), mouth sores, swollen or painful joints, sore throat, slight fever and headache, hair loss, a raised patch around the genitals and enlarged lymph glands. These symptoms may be so slight that they're mistaken for 'flu or other mild infections.

Like Gonorrhoea, Syphilis is treated with antibiotics. It's important to go back to the clinic for a follow up visit because the infection may not be cleared up by the first course of treatment. However, both infections are completely cured at the end of treatment.

If the infection remains untreated after this stage it goes dormant for 10-20 years, after which it can cause blindness, insanity, heart disease and eventually death.

Crabs or Pubic Lice

These are round, crab-like lice which live in the pubic hair, or more rarely the hair of armpits, eyebrows or chest. They are large enough to be seen with the naked eye. You catch them from close physical contact or from bedding or clothes used by someone who has them. They cause intense itching. Get rid of them by using cream, powder or shampoo called Lorexane or Quellada which you can buy at chemists or get free at a clinic. Leave it on for 24 hours then wash off, but meanwhile make sure you either wash your clothes, bedclothes, towels etc in boiling water or don't use them for a week because the crabs' eggs live for 6 days when separated from the body.

Aids

Aids (Acquired Immune Deficiency Syndrome) is caused by a virus called HIV, and leads to a breakdown in the body's immune system. People with Aids are vulnerable to infection which would not normally affect healthy people, such as a particular kind of pneumonia, a rare form of skin cancer, and other infections of the organs.

HOW THE HIV VIRUS IS TRANSMITTED

The HIV virus is transmitted when the body fluids (e.g. blood, semen) of an infected person get into the body of another person through breaks in the skin (cuts, grazes, sores), the vagina or rectum (back passage). You *can't* get it from being in the same room with someone with the virus, using the same toilet or towels, hugging them, sharing cups, eating with them or shaking hands.

In practice most transmission has taken place through the exchange of body fluids during sex and through sharing needles and syringes while injecting drugs. (see **Drugs** section p100 for more information on safer drug use). Though some people were infected through blood transfusions and using blood products (e.g. haemophiliacs) in the past, blood used medically is now treated with heat which kills the virus, so it's most unlikely in this country.

WHO IS AT RISK

Most of the people who have become infected with HIV so far are: gay or bisexual men; injecting drug users who have shared needles and syringes; haemophiliacs; and the sexual partners of people falling into these groups. However, as Aids spreads, heterosexuals who have unsafe, unprotected sex are becoming more at risk all the time. The lowest risk group of those who are sexually active is lesbians.

THE HIV TEST

There is a test you can take to see if you have been infected by the HIV virus - but this is not a test for Aids itself because not everyone who has been infected with the HIV virus goes on to develop full-blown Aids. It involves taking a sample of blood and testing it to see if you have developed *antibodies* (the body's own defence mechanism) to the HIV virus. If you have, the virus is present in the body, and your test is 'positive'. Over a period of 2-5 years, 10-30% of people found to have been infected go on to develop Aids. Because Aids is such a new condition, and because it takes a long time from infection to the development of the disease, it's not known yet how many people infected with the virus will go on to develop Aids. Nor is it clear yet whether some people might recover from the disease - some new evidence from the US may suggest that this is possible in a small number of cases.

If you are considering taking the HIV test, think carefully about the implications before you go ahead. The best place to go is probably a Sexually Transmitted Diseases clinic (see 83) because they offer absolute confidentiality, and they will counsel you before the test (and after if the result is positive). If you are in a high risk group, consider how you would deal with a positive result (in other words if you were found to be infected with the HIV virus). If you're inclined to worry it may be difficult to cope with, but if you're very worried about being infected it may put your mind at rest, particularly if your risk has been very low - but you have to consider the possibility that you *are* infected. If you're in a

Safer Sex - How to Do It

Sexual practices can be rated in terms of risk: 'very low risk' means you've next to no risk of catching HIV as the risk is a theoretical one. 'Low risk' practices *could* transmit HIV but in comparison to those in the 'high risk group' are much less likely to do so.

NO RISK
Masturbating on your own
General body contact such as stroking, massaging (but not on partner's penis, vagina or anus)
Sex toys (e.g. dildos, vibrators etc) if they're not shared with others
Enemas and douches given to yourself

VERY LOW RISK
Mutual masturbation
Kissing your partner's body (but not on the genitals)
Penis/vagina to body contact
Sex toys used with a partner (as long as each one isn't shared)
Bondage, spanking, beating (as long as the skin isn't broken)
Urination ('golden showers' or 'water sports') not on partner's body

LOW RISK
Putting one or more fingers into the vagina or anus (make sure fingernails are short to avoid scratching)
Oral Sex:
Fellatio - a man or woman sucking or licking a man's penis (avoid coming into the mouth itself as this might increase the risk)

LOW RISK CONTINUED
Cunnilingus - a woman or man tongueing a woman's vagina (avoid this during a period as there's more risk, as there is with bleeding gums)
Anilingus (rimming) - tongueing your partner's anal area
Fisting or fist-fucking - putting a hand, fist or forearm into the rectum

HIGH RISK
Vaginal intercourse without using a condom (withdrawal before coming doesn't make it safe either)
Anal intercourse without using a condom (remember to use a strong condom as they are more likely to break, and a lot of water-based lubricant)
Vaginal sex during a period
Any sex act which draws blood from the vagina, penis or anus, or pierces the skin.
Enemas and douches used before or after vaginal or anal sex.

high risk group and considering having children, the test is important because you can pass the infection on to the baby in the womb, or through breastfeeding, and pregnancy can trigger the development of full-blown Aids in infected women.

The issue of whether to have the test or not is complex, and you can get advice and counselling from **Terrence Higgins Trust** (below).

Bear in mind that the results of the test take two to four weeks to come. During that time you may need the support of a friend to talk to, and this is certainly true for afterwards if your test is positive. Be careful who you do tell though - don't tell anyone unless you feel you want to tell them the result. Don't tell your employer, or possibly your work colleagues, because some people have lost their jobs if the test has been positive.

RESOURCES

Terrence Higgins Trust (see below) is the contact point for a large number of support groups for those who are worried about HIV/Aids, are HIV positive, or have Aids:

■ **Body Positive**, *PO Box 493, W14 (373 9124 7pm-10pm daily)*. Self help support group for those who are HIV positive.

■ **Blackliners Helpline**, *(673 1695)*. 1pm-4pm Tue-Fri. Advice for people from the Black community.

■ **Frontliners** , *c/o Terrence Higgins Trust*, self support group for people with Aids.

■ **National Aids Helpline**

English: *0800 567 123 (24 hrs)*

Cantonese and Mandarin: *0800 282 446 (6-10pm Tue and Wed)*

Punjabi, Bengali, Hindu, Urdu, Gujarati: *0800 282 445 (6-10pm Tue and Wed)*

Arabic: *0800 282 447 (24 hrs)*

All calls are free.

■ **'Worried Well' Service**, *(601 7357)*. For those worried about HIV or Aids.

■ **Mainliners**, *(738 7333)*. Helpline for drug users who are HIV positive or with Aids

▼ PREVENTION ▼

Safer Sex

Safer sex is relevant to everyone who's sexually active. It's particularly important for those who are unsure of the sexual history of their partner, and for those who move on from one partner to another. You can't tell who's got the virus - they may be carrying it and look perfectly well. Don't forget, when it comes to Aids, when you have sex with someone, in effect you're having sex with everyone they've ever had sex with.

General: The HIV virus is transmitted in sex when body fluids enter a partner's body through the vagina, rectum, mouth or breaks in the skin, so the general rule is that sexual activity involving penetration by a partner's penis, or exchange of body fluids is high risk. Blood and semen are the main hazards, but all body products such as urine and faeces may contain a slight risk. Saliva is OK unless it contains blood (e.g. from bleeding gums or mouth ulcers), so kissing is relatively safe.

Use a condom for vaginal sex - remember to check that the packet has a BSI kitemark on it, showing that it's been tested to British Standards. For further protection, spermicides which contain a substance called nonoxynol (e.g. Duragel, Orthocreme or Delfen cream) if used with a condom may also help to kill the virus if it's present. Anal sex is best avoided altogether, but if you do have anal sex use a condom - preferably one of the extra strong ones now on the market especially designed for anal sex. Spermicides may irritate the rectum (back passage) so usually can't be used there. Don't use oil based lubricants (e.g. Vaseline, baby oil, cooking oil, Crisco etc) with condoms because they damage the rubber - instead use water based ones (e.g. KY or 1-2-1). **For comparative risk of various practices, see box on p87.**

If you need more advice about safer sex, or on any aspect of Aids and HIV contact

■ **Terrence Higgins Trust**, *BM AIDS, WC1 (242 1010/833 2971 helplines; 831 0330 Admin)* who give telephone advice and counselling, and publish a wide range of leaflets.

Cervical Smear Test

Women should have a cervical smear test *at least* every three years - more frequently is better.

When you have a smear test done, a doctor takes a sample of cells from the cervix (neck of the womb) with a swab. These are examined for any signs of abnormality, which may indicate very early on if there is any likelihood of you developing cancer. If these abnormal cells can be detected early on, treatment and cure are straightforward. The results of the test can take a couple of months to come through. If you are asked back it may be that the doctor wants to repeat the test because it wasn't clear, or you may have an infection, or occasionally because the test showed abnormal cells.

drugs

Drugs play a significant role in society. The majority of us use some sort of substance for recreation, whether it's a joint, a glass of beer, a cup of coffee or a cigarette etc. Drugs are not necessarily illegal because they are more dangerous than legal drugs like alcohol. In writing this we are not condoning or advertising the latest street drug. We have set out to give the information so that if you are taking something, you can find out a bit more about what you are taking, hopefully before you take it.

These are some of the commonly found drugs sold on the street, which will help you with identification.

▼ TYPES OF DRUG ▼

Cannabis (dope, draw, blow, weed, grass, hash, ganga)

Cannabis Sativa is a bushy plant found wild in most parts of the world and easily cultivated in Britain. The plant products seen in London range from the resin which comes in small slabs or chunks, as well as hash oil, and the dried and chopped leafy parts of the plant known as grass, bush etc.

Tetrahydro-cannabis (THC) is the most important psychoactive ingredient, and the amount found in the cannabis products in London varies considerably. These products are generally rolled up in a cigarette or 'joint' often mixed with tobacco and smoked, although some people like to eat it either on its own or as part of a cake or fudge.

The effects of cannabis vary according to the situation, the amount used and the mood of the user. Generally it helps you relax, can cause talkativeness, and a greater appreciation of sensory experiences including sound, colour and touch.

By itself, cannabis is not thought to be physically or psychologically harmful, though there's no conclusive evidence about its long term effects on users' health.

The use of cannabis in this country goes back centuries. It was first brought over here by the Romans who used the fibrous stalks to make rope and sail cloth. Queen Victoria's personal doctor, John Reynolds, was a leading advocate of cannabis; he described it as 'one of the most valuable therapeutic agents we possess'. In the mid nineteenth century the prescription of cannabis was considered the standard treatment for migraine. Even up to 1973 in this country, doctors were still able to prescribe cannabis.

More recently THC, the most important active ingredient in cannabis has been isolated and used to alleviate side effects of chemotherapy in cancer patients. THC tablets are starting to be used in the treatment of anorexia nervosa (the condition in which the sufferer diets compulsively and becomes very thin) and other eating disorders.

Suppression of the use of this drug continues to criminalise large sections of the population, even though there is no medical case against moderate use. Since its use is so widespread, the law can't be enforced systematically against everyone using it. In practice this means that suspect groups like the unemployed and young black people are most likely to be the targets of prosecution.

Prices: Hash £80-120 an ounce
Herb cannabis £40-80 an ounce
Hash oil £6 a gram

■ **Legalise Cannabis Campaign**, *Box No BM Cannabis, London, WC1N 3XX.*

LSD (Acid)

Lysergic Acid Diethylamide (LSD) is derived from ergot, a fungus found growing wild on rye and other grasses. It was first produced in 1938. In the 50s and 60s it was put to therapeutic use, and the CIA became

interested in it for use in warfare and funded research in universities, which inadvertently led to its widespread recreational use.

LSD is a powerful hallucinogenic drug which usually comes in the form of small pills (microdots) or as *tabs* of impregnated paper. The effects of an LSD *trip* can last anything between 5 to 24 hours, though 6-12 is more usual. Sense of time can become distorted, music can be heard more acutely, and strange patterns seen although it is rare to have full-blown hallucinations. Things which are insignificant in normal life can become extraordinarily absorbing, alive and significant on acid e.g. the texture of an orange's skin, the pattern on a carpet, the 'growing' of a tree. Some people also report having insights into themselves and religious experiences while on acid trips. Moods and emotions can swing from intense 'highs' to deep 'lows'. How comfortable you feel in your environment, what kind of mood you are in and who is with you will play a large part in what your experience on an LSD trip will be. It's always best to take it with someone who has experience of the drug themselves. If you feel anxious or depressed this may be intensified by the drug and you may have a *bad trip*. In this case, it can be helpful to remember that any unpleasant feelings are the product either of an unsuitable environment or your own mind, so you can either take yourself off somewhere more pleasant, find a friend to reassure you, or try to absorb yourself in something you know is more pleasant.

People don't get physically addicted to LSD and death by overdose is unknown. There are no known physical health risks attributable to LSD use. Adverse psychological effects are possible after one trip, but are more common in regular use. These usually occur if you have existing or latent mental illness.

Tolerance of LSD develops very quickly and after 3-4 days use further doses are ineffective unless you don't take it for a further 3-4 days.

The street price for a tab of acid is about £3.

Hallucinogenic Mushrooms (Magic Mushrooms)

Hallucinogenic plants have been used for thousands of years by ancient tribes and civilisations to gain a heightened state of consciousness and spiritual insight. Psilocybin mushrooms and other sacred intoxicants were taken by the Aztecs of Mexico at the time of the Spanish invasion in the 1500s. There is no record of use of hallucinogenic mushrooms in European history, although witches used other kinds of hallucinogenic plants.

About a dozen kinds of hallucinogenic mushrooms can be found in this country, some containing the drug psilocybin and another group which contains the more powerful substance, psilocin. There is also a small group of mushrooms called the Amanita group, Fly Agaric is one of these flowering between late July and early December. In America there are many more varieties.

Liberty Cap: This is the most readily available hallucinogenic mushroom in the UK, containing the two drugs psilocybe and semilonceanta. The power of the dose contained in individual mushrooms varies, because of variation in size and the user's body weight and contents of stomach. The effects are increased if taken with alcohol.

Liberty Cap fruits between September and November throughout the UK. It usually grows in groups or long lines. They are a tiny, elegant species with a yellow/brown cap that often comes to a sharp point. The stem is lighter coloured and they are about 4-8cm tall. This is a generalised description, so check a guide.

IDENTIFYING MUSHROOMS

There are about 3,000 species of fungi in the UK and only a small number of these are poisonous and can, and do, kill people. There are some others which can make you unpleasantly ill.

When you go out mushroom hunting for the first time, go with an experienced person, don't go alone. Take a mushroom guide book with you to identify the mushrooms 'in the flesh'. A good one is the *Collins Guide to Mushrooms and Toadstools* which has hand drawn pictures. When trying to identify a mushroom, make sure you identify a mature specimen, because they change rapidly as they grow. Examine all the mushrooms in the area. Different species don't usually grow together, only sometimes.

Examine all the physical features of the *whole* mushroom, and check with your guide book. First look at the shape and colour of the cap to see whether the surface is shiny or dull, and whether it's marked with lines. Break a piece off and see what the flesh looks like and how it smells.

Look at the colour of the gills and the way they are joined to the stem, as well as the colour and shape of the stem to see if it has rings on it or a bulb at the bottom. When you take them home and identify the spores. In the mushroom guide it should tell you the colour of each species' spores.

To test spore colour, take off the cap (top of mushroom) and place it gill (underneath) side down on a piece of paper. With a very small cap, put it into a closed tin with a drop of water.

Leave the mushroom overnight. The next day you should see a print on the paper - if it's not the right colour, throw the mushroom away.

MUSHROOM POISONING

The symptoms of mushroom poisoning can appear from 20 minutes up to 40 hours after eating. The later they come on, the more serious the poisoning is.

If you feel ill a day or two later and then feel better, seek medical advice immediately - it could still be lethal. Since mushrooms are still legal there is no problem in calling a doctor. The most common symptoms are vomiting, diarrhoea, increased saliva, cramp, watery eyes, jaundice, breathing difficulties. Epileptic fits can occur too. If you're with someone who is ill, take them to casualty or dial 999.

It will help the doctor identify the poison if you can give her a specimen of the mushroom, or show her where you picked them from, and if you can, collect any vomit or shit from the person to give to the doctor.

If someone has been poisoned, but hasn't been sick, you could help them to be sick by tickling the back of their throat, or giving them hot salted water to drink. After they have been sick, give them burnt toast.

If they lose consciousness, lie them on their right side with their left leg bent. Make sure their throat is not blocked.

If the person has a fit, clear a space for them and put something in their mouth like a wad of hankies to stop them biting their own tongue. Don't give them anything to eat or induce vomiting.

Mushroom poisoning isn't always due to picking the wrong mushroom, but sometimes to picking the right species in the wrong conditions. Don't pick wet or dirty mushrooms because they go off quickly. Don't pick old mushrooms. If you pick large amounts of mushrooms, they can deteriorate quickly, especially if they are damp or put in a closed container. Check for worms and maggots which leave tiny 1mm holes.

If you eat mushrooms from the Amanita group (fly agaric), make sure they are the non-poisonous ones (check the guide book) and DO NOT eat them raw. They should be cooked in an oven, hung up to dry or boiled in salt water.

Eat a small amount and make sure you don't feel ill. Mushrooms are usually dried or crushed and either eaten or make into a tea which is drunk.

Don't take mushrooms on your own, try to be with a close friend, preferably someone who has taken mushrooms before or is taking some as well. Try and choose somewhere comfortable, like a field or a room. You should feed cheerful, unworried and relaxed before taking them.

A 'trip' can start between half an hour and 2 hours of taking them, and last for between 4 and 9 hours. Mushrooms have a similar effect to LSD. They exaggerate the mood you're already in, heightening your perceptions and senses. Feelings can swing from elation to paranoia. Mushroom eaters may also have profound experiences, and many hippies took them for this reason in the 60s and 70s. Physical effects include numbness of muscles, nausea, diarrhoea and increased heart beat.

THE LAW ON MUSHROOMS

The possession of hallucinogenic mushrooms and their consumption is legal. But any preparation or deliberate treatment of the mushrooms or an attempt to extract the active chemical ingredient is illegal, and for this you could be prosecuted.

The definition of preparation covers any deliberate alteration of the naturally occuring plant material, including drying and crushing to make the mushroom fit for consumption. If the chemical psilocybin (which is the phosphate of psilocin) is extracted, this counts as a controlled drug - under the Misuse of Drugs Act (1971) psilocin is a class A drug. You can be prosecuted if you admit to treating the mushrooms before eating them. The police sometimes try to prosecute for possession even though it's not illegal, because they are confused about the legal status of mushrooms.

Amphetamines (speed, dexies, uppers)

Most speed these days is illicitly manufactured amphetamine sulphate. It's often sniffed up the nose or injected. It boosts energy levels, confidence and the power of concentration - amphetamines stimulate the central nervous system. After the effect has worn off, users feel depressed and exhausted.

Amphetamines were used in the Spanish Civil War to keep soldiers awake and make their reactions keener. In the Second World War, the British Government doled out some 72 million tablets to their forces. Hitler himself was unable to function without his daily 'fix' of speed, which might explain some of his paranoid ravings.

Most occasional users of speed don't become dependent on it, but for those who *do* become psychologically dependant, it can be a very difficult habit to break. To get the same effect you have to take increasingly higher doses. The body needs to recover from lack of food or sleep so if you continue to take it the body's resistance to illness is lowered. Regular use can lead to delusions, hallucinations and feelings of being 'got at', and some people can become seriously mentally ill.

Cocaine (coke, charlie)

Cocaine is a stimulant extracted from the coca plant which grows in South America. The cocaine which is seen in the UK is a treated extract called *cocanium hydrochloride* and comes as white crystals. What you buy in London is around 30-50% pure, the rest being made up of weight additives. It costs around £45-60 a gram, and is sold by the quarter gram upwards.

Cocaine is often snorted or injected but it is difficult to make because of the high temperature at which it will vaporise. Cocaine hydrochloride can be treated with chemicals which free the base cocaine from the hydrochloride. This process is known as 'freebasing'.

Crack is a ready form of freebase cocaine which is easily and inexpensively produced. It need no special apparatus and can be smoked in an ordinary pipe or heated in tin foil and the fumes inhaled. Crack gets its name because when it is smoked the baking powder residue left in it crackles.

The physical effects of cocaine and crack are similar to adrenalin. It can increase the rate of breathing, raise blood pressure, heart rate and body temperature, while suppressing sleep and appetite.

The pleasurable effects people get from cocaine hydrochloride are decreased hunger, indifference to pain and fatigue, feelings of great physical strength and mental ability. This usually happens within about three minutes and lasts for up to an hour.

Freebase cocaine (of which 'crack' is a highly publicised form) takes effect within seconds of being smoked. There is an initial rush of very pleasurable feelings lasting for two minutes. This is followed by an intense high lasting for about thirty minutes. As the effects of crack wear off there are some unpleasant side-effects. It is common to feel tired and depressed. Users may feel irritable, hungry and possibly experience panic attacks. To avoid this, crack users often take more crack as one dose wears off, and this encourages repeated compulsive use which can lead to dependency.

Who uses cocaine? **Release** *News* June 1989 reports 'drug advisors have seen cocaine go from being a drug of the wealthy in the UK three years ago to being a common street drug. Its purity is up and the street price is down. Crack use has been reported in several parts of the UK but currently is not a major problem, although this is not to say that it will not become one in the future'.

MDMA (ecstacy, XTC, E)

Ecstacy was first discovered in 1912 and patented as an appetite supressant in 1914 by a German company. It was used in the 1970s by some American psychotherapists as an aid to therapy (particularly for couples). Ecstacy is a stimulant drug with some of the properties of LSD but does not cause hallucinations. The effects are usually at a peak for about 2 hours.

Problems with ecstacy usually occur if you feel anxious about taking it, or are uncomfortable in your surroundings. It is not physically addictive, although tolerance can develop quite rapidly leaving you vulnerable to toxic side effects. These include nausea, dizziness and jaw tension. Anyone with a heart problem or high blood pressure should avoid taking ecstacy because it increases heart rate and blood pressure.

Tobacco

Cigarettes, loose tobacco, snuff, pipe and cigars.

Tobacco comes form the dried leaves of the tobacco plant which grows in many parts of the world, including England. It came to England in the second half of the 16th century.

It is prohibited to sell tobacco to anyone under 16 years of age, though young people can legally buy, possess and smoke it. Apart from this there are no restrictions on its sale.

Tobacco contains several harmful substances. Cigarette smoke consists of droplets of tar, nicotine, carbon monoxide and other gases. It increases pulse rate and blood pressure and lowers the appetite.

Nicotine is the substance which is addictive, it makes the heart beat faster and pushes up the blood pressure.

Carbon monoxide is a poisonous gas and it cuts down the amount of oxygen the blood can carry.

People who smoke it are more likely to suffer from heart disease, blood clots, heart attacks, lung infections, strokes, bronchitis, bad circulation, lung cancer, cancer of the mouth and throat and ulcers. Once you've stopped smoking you reduce the risk of getting any of these. If you stop before damage has occured to your lungs, they will clear up in a few weeks.

HELPFUL HINTS IF YOU WANT TO GIVE UP

- Take each day as it comes. Don't plan the rest of your life without cigarettes
- Hide any matches/ ashtrays/ lighters
- Avoid other smokers
- Have things to nibble on hand like fruit, nuts etc
- Be especially careful at times where you used to smoke e.g. tea breaks etc.
- Keep busy when you get cravings
- Save up the cash you spend on cigarettes, or use it to buy yourself other 'treats' as a reward for not smoking
- Try other relaxing methods; deep breathing, meditation etc
- Remind yourself about the reasons for giving up
- Don't give in to temptation, not even one!

Depending on how much you were addicted to smoking, craving should ease in the second or third week but it may take longer.

Caffeine

This is a stimulant found in tea, coffee, soft drinks (mostly cola), chocolate and in some headache pills.

Coffee first came to England in 1601 and was used medicinally. Later on, the 'coffee shop' became a focal point for men to gather socially and discuss political activities, until governmental licensing restrictions. Tea, which was introduced into this country in 1661, is made from the dried leaves of shrubs native to South East Asia, and was also first used medicinally.

One cup of coffee contains 115mg per cup if filtered, 80 mg per cup percolated, and 65 mg per cup instant. Tea contains 100mg per cup for loose tea, and 65 mg per tea bag.

Caffeine in soft drinks (cola) is usually equal to 2-3 cups of filter coffee. Because children have a low body weight, one soft drink for a child can be equal to 6 cups of coffee for an adult. Stimulant pills available over the counter usually contain 200 mg of pure caffeine per tablet

In the short term, a small dose acts as a 'pick me up' and allays drowsiness and fatigue. Larger doses can increase the heart and breathing rate, raise blood pressure and constrict blood vessels in the brain (relieving some types of headache). The user will feel alert, but also may feel anxious and irritable.

Too much can cause sweating and shaking. It's addictive and withdrawal symptoms are headaches, and feeling irritable and drowsy.

People who take 8 or more cups a day of drinks containing caffeine can develop peptic ulcers, heart disease or even cancer of the kidney or bladder. Try counting how many cups of tea and/or coffee you drink in a day - it's likely to be more than you think!

	DRUG GROUP	PRINCIPAL DRUGS scientific names	 trade, slang, other names	LEGAL STATUS
DRUGS THAT DEPRESS THE NERVOUS SYSTEM	**Alcoholic Beverages**	Ethyl alcohol or ethanol	**'Booze'** etc Beers, Wines, Spirits, Liqueurs	Can be bought by adults (18+) and drunk outside a pub/bar by children (5+). Need licence to sell.
	Barbiturates and Other Hypnosedatives	**Barbiturates:** Quinalbarbitone Amylobarbitone (combination of above) Pentobarbitone Butobarbitone **Non-Barbiturate Sedatives:** Chlormethiazole Chloral Hydrate	**'Downers', 'Barbs'** and various slang terms derived from trade names or colour of pill/capsule. Seconal Amytal Tuinol Nembutal Soneryl Heminevrin 'Choloral'	Prescription only medicine Controlled drugs Prescription Only Medicines
	Benzodiazepines	**Minor Tranquillisers:** Diazepam Chlordiazepoxide Lorazepam Oxazepam **Benzodiazepine Hypnotics:** Nitrazempam Flurasepam Triazolam Temazepam	**'Tranx':** Valium, Librium, Ativan, Serenid **Sleeping pills:** Mogadon Dalmane Halcion Euphynos	Prescription Only Medicines Controlled drugs but legal to possess without a prescription
	Solvents and Gases	Toluene Acetone Butane Fluorocarbons Trichloroethane	Glues Lighter fuel Aerosols Cleaning fluid	In UK illegal to sell knowingly for inhalation. In Scotland misusers may be taken into care.
DRUGS THAT REDUCE PAIN	**Opiates, Opioids, Narcotic Analgesics**	Diacetylmorphine, diamorphine, or heroin Dipipanone Methadone Pethidine Dextromoramide Dextropropoxyphene	'Junk', 'skag', 'H', 'smack' Diconal, 'dike' Physeptone, 'amps' (injectable', 'linctus' (oral)' Pamergan, Pethilorfan Palfium Distalgesic	Prescription Only Medicines. Controlled drugs.
		Opium Morphine Codeine	Nepenthe, Gee's Linctus* Duromorph, Cyclimorph, kaolin & morphine* Actifed*, Phensedyl*, codeine linctus*	Prescription Only Medicines, except in the form of some very dilute mixtures (*) available without prescription from pharmacies. Controlled drugs, but (*) legal to possess without a prescription.

RECOMMENDED MEDICAL USES	METHODS OF ADMINISTRATION	PREVALENCE AND AVAILABILITY	EFFECTS
	Swallowed as a beverage	Available through over 170,000 licensed premises. Over 9 in 10 adults drink to some extent.	Depress the nervous system, relieve tension and anxiety, promote relaxation, impair the efficiency of mental and physical functioning, and decrease self control. In higher doses there can be 'drunken' behaviour, drowsiness, stupor, sleep/ unconsciousness. With the exception of minor tranquillisers, these effects may be associated with positive feelings of pleasure. Tolerance develops with frequently repeated doses. In high doses there can be strong physical dependence to alcohol or hypnosedatives, less strong to minor tranquilliers, not at all to solvents or gases. Depressant effects may be dangerously augmented if more than one depressant drug is taken at a time, or if depressant drugs are taken with opiate-type drugs.
Promote sleep in severe, intractable insomnia Promote sleep in insomnia, sedation in the elderly.	Swallowed as pills, capsules or elixirs. Injected	Barbiturate pills and capsules produced for medical use are available on the illicit market.	
Relieve anxiety Promote sleep in insomnia.	Swallowed as pills or capsules.	Most commonly prescribed drugs in Britain. Also available on the illicit market	
	Vapours or gases inhaled through nose/mouth.	Widely available in shops, homes and places or work. Some 5-10% or secondary school pupils may have tried them.	
Pain relief, cough suppression, anti-diarrhoea agents. Treatment of opiate dependence (methadone).	Heroin can be smoked, sniffed up the nose, or injected. Most other opiate preparations can be injected or swallowed.	Illicitly produced and imported heroin is the most widely misused of this class of drugs. In many areas heroin is commonly available on the illicit market. Other opiates avaialble from doctors or by theft. Perhaps 70,000 regular users.	Reduce sensitivity and emotional reaction to pain, discomfort and anxiety. Feelings of warmth, contentment. Relatively little interference with mental or physical functioning. Higher doses, sedation, stupor, sleep/unconsciousness. Tolerance and physical dependence with frequently repeated doses. Depressant effects may be dangerously magnified if more than one opiate is taken at a time, or if opiates are taken with other depressant drugs.

This table has been reproduced with the permission of the Institute for the Study of Drug Dependence, from their booklet *Drug Abuse Briefing*.

	DRUG GROUP	PRINCIPAL DRUGS scientific names	 trade, slang, other names	LEGAL STATUS
DRUGS THAT STIMULATE THE NERVOUS SYSTEM	**Amphetamines and amphetamine-like drugs**	**Amphetamines** Amphetamine sulphate Dexamphetamine (combination of the above) **Amphetamine-like Drugs** Methylphenidate Diethylpropion	**'Uppers', 'speed'** 'sulphate', 'sulph', 'whizz' Dexedrine Durophet Ritalin Apisate, Tenuate	Prescription Only Medicines. Controlled Drugs
	Cocaine	Cocaine Hydrochloride Cocaine freebase	'coke', 'snow' 'crack', 'freebase', 'base'.	Prescription Only Medicines. Controlled Drugs
	Caffeine	Caffeine	Coffee Tea Cocoa Soft drinks Chocolate Analgesic pills	Unrestricted.
	Tobacco	**Tobacco** (Contains nicotine) Nicotiana tabacum Nicotiana rustica Nicotiana persica	Tobacco Cigarettes Snuff	Illegal to sell to children under 16. Otherwise unrestricted.
DRUGS THAT ALTER PERCEPTION	**LSD and other synthetic hallucinogens**	Lysergic Acid Diethylamide and Lysergide Phencyclidine	LSD, 'acid' PCP, 'angel dust'	Controlled drugs; LSD not available for medical use.
	Hallucinogenic mushrooms	Psyilocybe Semilanceata (contains psilocybin and psilocin) Amanita muscaria	Liberty Cap 'magic mushrooms' Fly Agaric	If prepared for use may be a controlled drug. Otherwise unrestricted. Unrestricted.
	Cannabis	**Cannabis Sativa** (contains tetrahydrocannabinol) Herbal Cannabis Cannabis resin Cannabis oil	'Pot', dope', 'blow' etc 'grass', 'marihuana', 'ganga', 'weed', 'the herb' etc 'hash', 'hashish'	Controlled drugs; not available for medical use; illegal to allow premises to be used for smoking cannabis.

<table>
<tr><th>RECOMMENDED MEDICAL USES</th><th>METHODS OF ADMINISTRATION</th><th>PREVALENCE AND AVAILABILITY</th><th>EFFECTS</th></tr>
<tr><td>Treatment of narcolepsy and hyperkinesia.

Short term treatment of obsesity.</td><td>Amphetamine sulphate powder sniffed up the nose. PIlls and capsules taken by mouth. Frequently injected.</td><td>Illicitly manufuctured amphetamine sulphate commonly available on the illict market, plus some pills and capsules produced for medical use. After cannabis, probably the most widely used controlled drug.</td><td rowspan="4">Drugs that stimulate the nervous system increase alertness, diminish fatigue, delay sleep, increase ability to maintain vigilance or perform physical tasks over a long period, and elevate mood. Excepting tobacco, high doses can cause nervousness, anxiety and (with the exception of tobacco and caffeine) temporary paranoid psychosis. Withdrawal effects include hunger and fatigue. Although unpleasant, these effects are practically never of the kind that might require medical assistance.</td></tr>
<tr><td>Rarely prescribed. Local anaesthetic</td><td>Cocaine hydrochloride powder sniffed up the nose, sometimes injected.
Cocaine freebase smoked.</td><td>Illictly manufactured and imported hydrocholoride powder available on the illict market, but expensive, so not usually used frequently.</td></tr>
<tr><td></td><td>Swallowed as a beverage, in confectionary, or in pills.</td><td>Freely available in beverages and foodstuffs taken regularly by the great majority of people in Britain.</td></tr>
<tr><td></td><td>Smoked. Snuff is sniffed up the nose.</td><td>Widely available in shops. 38% of UK adults smoke.</td></tr>
<tr><td></td><td>Swallowed as variously formed, illicitly produced paper squares, pills, tablets, capsules etc.</td><td>Illicitly manufactured LSD is commonly available on the illict market. Other hallucinogens relatively rare.</td><td rowspan="3">Heightened appreciation of sensory experiences, perceptual distortions, feelings of dissociation, insight, elevation of mood. Sometimes anxiety or panic, occasionally severe. Relatively little physiological arousal or sedation, and minimal risk of physical dependence. With hallucinogens and hallucinogenic mushrooms, commonly pseudohallucinations. With cannabis, relaxation, drowsiness, talkativeness. With PCP, significant physiological effects including anaesthesia, sedation or stimulation, and relatively high probability of adverse physical and psychological effects.</td></tr>
<tr><td></td><td>Swallowed raw, cooked or brewed into a beverage, often after drying.</td><td>Liberty Caps grow wild in Autumn in many parts of Britain and are commonly taken for hallucinogenic effects. Use of other mushrooms rare.</td></tr>
<tr><td></td><td>Burnt and smoked by itself (herbal cannabis) or with tobacco. Sometimes eaten (resin).</td><td>Most widely used controlled drug in Britain. Probably one million people in UK use cannabis. Smuggled supplies widely available on illicit market.</td></tr>
</table>

Amyl and Butyl Nitrite (poppers)

Both known as amyl nitrites. Amyl nitrite was discovered in 1857 and used medically for chest pains. It was first used recreationally in the 1930s as an aphrodisiac. It became popular again in the 1960s especially with the male gay community because it relaxes the muscles, making anal intercourse easier. It's classified as a pharmacy medicine. Butyl nitrite has no medical use and is sold mainly in the US - it's not classified as a drug.

In London, amyl nitrite is sold in sex shops, clubs, pubs and bars for £2-3 a bottle. It's often used to enhance sexual pleasure, inducing a slowed down sense of time, prolonging orgasm, prevent premature ejaculation and relax the anal sphincter.

Since it reduces blood pressure, it can cause blackout. In rare instances this can cause heart attacks, so it's advisable not to take amyl nitrite if you have heart trouble. Other effects are nausea and vomiting, weakness and headaches. There have been cases of nitrite dermatitis which affects the upper lip, nose and cheeks.

There are no withdrawal symptoms, nor do users develop psychological dependence.

Alcohol

Alcoholic drinks like beer, whisky and wine contain ethyl alcohol (ethnol) which is a by-product of fermented fruits, vegetables and grains. Methyl alcohol contained in methylated spirits is used by some people because it's cheap - luckily this is rare because methyl is poisonous and can be fatal.

Over 90% of the adult population drink alcohol in some way. The consumption of alcohol as a recreational drug almost certainly predates recorded history. Legal restriction on alcohol by the state started with a concern to supress gatherings which might lead to political agitation amongst workers. A 1495 act gave JPs power to close troublesome ale-houses. More recently state control and trafficking of alcohol have brought in a lot of money. Regular moderate drinking is unlikely to cause serious health problems. If you drink more than 21 units (men) or 14 units (women) per week, you increase your chances of developing ulcers, liver disease, heart and circulatory disorders, cancer and brain damage.

A unit is measured by its alcohol content i.e. half a pint of beer or cider is equivalent to one measure of spirits, which is equivalent to one glass of wine (there are seven units in a bottle of wine).

Tolerance to the presence of alcohol in the body develops quite fast. Sudden withdrawal from heavy use can be life-threatening, producing symptoms like sweating, anxiety, trembling, delerium (DTs), and possible convulsions, coma and death.

Symptoms are more serious if other drugs are used in conjunction with drink.

Contacts for help with alcohol problems:

■ **Alcoholics Anonymous,** *11 Redcliffe Gds, SW10 (352 3001).* Longest established alcoholics organisation; has open-door, self-help policy. Will refer to local groups.

■ **ACCEPT (Addictions Community Centres for Education, Prevention, Treatment and Research),** *Richmond Royal Hosp, Kew Foot Rd, Richmond, (940 7542).* Drug treatment centre for users of tranquillisers or alcohol who are wanting to stop. One-to-one counselling and group therapy. Phone for appointment. M-F 9.30-4.30.

■ **ACCEPT,** *The Broadway Clinic, The Broadway, Wealdstone, Harrow, Middx, (427 7700).* Day centre for people using tranquillisers or alcohol and wishing to stop.

■ **ACCEPT,** *200 Seagrave Rd, SW6 (381 3155).* Day treatment clinic, individual counselling. Also deal with tranquillizer addiction. Relatives groups.

■ **ACCEPT,** *470 Harrow Rd, W9 (286 3339). M-F 10-6.* Programme includes relaxation, psychotherapy, art therapy, tranquilliser and dreams group.

■ **Al-Anon,** *61 Gt Dover St, SE1, 403 0888.* Groups for family and friends of problem drinkers.

Benzodiazepines

Benzodiazepines are the most commonly prescribed drugs in Britain, and include such drugs as Librium, Valium and Ativan. Many prescriptions of these drugs are repeated and may be issued without the patient seeing the doctor. They are prescribed for sleeping problems, anxiety or emotional distress.

Tolerance develops quickly with these drugs and they become ineffective as sleeping pills after two weeks, and ineffective against anxiety after four months, so use which continues beyond four months can be due to dependence. Sometimes severe withdrawal symptoms can occur if you stop after you've been taking them for several years. These are not life-threatening but can include nausea, vomiting, insomnia and anxiety. After very high doses convulsions and mental confusion can occur on withdrawal. There has been a lot of publicity recently about these drugs since their addictive potential has been discovered, and self-help groups for those who want to stop taking tranquillisers have formed.

■ **TRANX,** *25a Masons Ave, Wealdstone, Harrow, Middx, HA3 5AH, (427 2065/2827 or 863 9716 (general enquiries)).* Support, advice, one to one counselling and self-help groups for users of tranquillisers and sleeping pills. Will also refer people to groups in other parts of the country if available. Drop in or phone, M-F 10-3.

■ **Women's Tranquillisers Group**, *Women's Centre, 2-6 Peckham High St, SE15 (701 2564).* Women's support group, M 10.30 phone for details.

■ **Hackney Tranquilliser Project**, *c/o City and Hackney Association for Mental Health, 345a Mare St, E8 (533 0822/985 4239).* Weekly self-help group for women coming off tranquillisers. Also phone counselling and support M-F 9.30-5.30.

■ See also **ACCEPT** (p98).

Solvents

Glue, lighter fuel (butane), typewriter correction fluid, nail varnish remover.

Solvents are usually taken by people unable to obtain other drugs like alcohol.

Glue and other solvents are sniffed through the nose and mouth and make you feel light headed, merry and dizzy. The experience is similar to being very drunk. Some people feel sick and drowsy. Unlike alcohol the effects come on gradually and disappear after about 15 minutes to three quarters of an hour if sniffing is stopped.

Afterwards, users fall asleep and wake up with a hangover that can last a whole day. The dangers come mostly from accidents which occur when you are high. There have been cases of choking by inhaling vomit or suffocation by covering the head with a plastic bag. Squirting gas in the mouth can be fatal because the gas can freeze the tubes that lead to the lungs. Using solvents for 10 years or more can cause brain damage.

Barbiturates (barbs, downers)

These have a relaxing effect similar to alcohol. Larger doses send you to sleep, or make make it difficult to talk or to concentrate. Accidents can happen on barbiturates in this state because it's easy to overdose - it only takes a few more pills than normal, and if mixed with alcohol the effects are even stronger. They are very addictive and habit-forming.

Some people mix barbiturates with heroin or speed.

Opium/Morphine/Heroin

The opiate drugs act upon the pain receptors in the brain acting in a way similar to the body's own natural pain killers. There is an effect of relaxed detachment and euphoria. Initially you might feel nauseous and even vomit. (Though this effect soon disappears and your body becomes used to the drug).

Opiates can also depress breathing and the cough reflex.

Opium is the dried milk of the opium poppy. Opium can be chemically processed into morphine and morphine into heroin. Each process produces a stronger drug, with more potential for addiction.

In its pure form heroin is a white powder. But it's often found in London in a brown (sometimes granular) form - *Brown Sugar.*

Street prices range from £60 - £80 a gram. It can also be bought in a wrap for £10-£20. In recent years in London heroin has varied widely in availability from very pure (up to 94%) to very weak (less than 10% pure).

Heroin bought on the street is likely to have been diluted (or adulterated) with a variety of powders of similar appearance, such as caffeine, quinine, flour, glucose powder, chalk dust, and talcum powder, and other drug substances like phenobarbitone powder.

Heroin can be smoked, snorted, or injected. Smoking heroin is called *chasing the dragon*. The fumes are inhaled after heating the heroin on tin foil. Injected heroin is dissolved in water and heated a little before being sucked into a syringe - (see **Safer Injecting** section p100).

The opioid tablets are listed in the **Directory of Tablets** section (p104). These drugs are not meant to be injected. They contain stuff like chalk which won't dissolve. If you inject them they cause abscess and damage your veins. There is also a risk of getting gangrene. There can be other problems when small particles get through the filtering process and block up small veins.

HEROIN USE AND HEALTH

Serious health risks do exist. Fatal reactions to injected adulterants (not to the heroin itself) can and do occur. With the uncertain purity and composition of street heroin, adverse reactions are an ever-present possibility.

Fatal overdoses can occur when users take their usual dose after a break during which tolerance has faded.

Physical withdrawal can occur after as little as several weeks on high, frequent doses. Such withdrawal results in a variable degree of discomfort generally comparable to a bout of 'flu. Effects include tremor, sweating and chills, aches, sneezing and yawning and usually start 8 - 24 hrs after the last

fix. Generally these symptoms fade in 7 to 10 days but feelings of weakness and loss of well-being may last for several months. Sudden opiate withdrawal is rarely life threatening and is considerably less dangerous than withdrawal from alcohol or barbiturates.

There are long term effects of use but these are rarely serious in themselves. They include respiratory complaints, menstrual irregularity, and constipation. Physical damage among regular users is commonly associated with poor hygiene and the injection of adulterants.

Opiate use during pregnancy results on average in smaller babies who may suffer withdrawal symptoms after birth. Help with opiate problems during pregnancy is available in London (See **Help** p105).

Addicts who receive opiates on prescription and who maintain a stable, hygienic lifestyle may be indistinguishable from non-drug users and suffer no physical damage, because opiates in themselves are relatively safe drugs. However as opiates are the most commonly injected street drugs in Britain those users who do inject face a higher risk of becoming infected with the Aids (HIV) virus (see **Aids and HIV** section on the importance of safer injecting and safer sex). The consequences of injecting opiates and of a drug-using lifestyle can be very serious.

SAFER INJECTING

If you are going to inject, it is important to do it in the right part of your body. If you don't you will waste the hit and can do yourself serious damage.

Avoid feet, groin, neck, breast or backs of the knees because these are areas where you may hit an artery. Bleeding doesn't stop easily in these areas and there is greater risk of blood clots developing.

Clean the area where you are going to inject with a sterilised wipe or surgical spirit. This will reduce the risk of infection and abscesses.

Try not to use the same vein too often, because it needs to have a chance to recover.

When you inject you get the full force of the drug in a 'rush' but it's also easier to overdose. Mixing drugs, or having a second hit while you're still 'out of it' is also risky because of the danger of overdosing.

If you get infections or abscesses go to see a doctor - either a sympathetic GP or a hospital casualty department.

If you are going to inject, it's very important not to use unsterile and/or shared needles. Sharing needles increases the chances of you getting infections such as hepatitis B and the HIV virus which can lead to Aids, as well as increasing the risk of abscesses, septicaemia and embolism. There is no known cure for Aids at present and it is almost always fatal, so prevention is of greatest importance. Needles and syringes are legal and can be bought in some chemists. Alternatively use the numerous free needle exchanges in London, some of which are listed on p102.

INJECTING AND HIV/AIDS

(The following section on Injecting and HIV/ Aids has been reproduced with permission of **Terrence Higgins Trust** from their leaflet *More Facts About AIDS for Drug Users*, available from them (p88).

People who watch the way they use drugs stay healthier for longer than people who don't. This applies particularly to people infected with HIV. If you are antibody positive (infected with the HIV virus which can leads to Aids) continue to expose your body to infections by fixing, sharing works and using contaminated street gear, you increase your chance of developing Aids. So look at the way you use and see if you need to make changes. You can do several things, depending on what you want to do and what support and help is available.

You can Stop Sharing

Always try to get your own set of works.
Find a helpful local pharmacist or your nearest syringe exchange.
Some areas are opening needle exchange schemes (see p102) where you can get new works free.
Use a clean set of works every time you fix.
Keep your works safe so they can't be borrowed without your knowledge.
Use you own spoon etc for cooking up.
Use clean water to mix with your gear.
Dispose of your used works safely or through your exchange.

You can, if you have to share, clean your works

Clean used equipment immediately it is last used (see also diagram which shows a method using household bleach)

Separate the needle, barrel and plunger and clean them in hot tap water and household detergent (washing-up liquid)
Remove all traces of blood
Rinse the works thoroughly with clean water.
Do the same with any spoons etc.
After you have used the works, clean them in exactly the same way before anyone else uses them. Then get a new set of works as soon as possible.
NB This method *may* kill any HIV present in the works. It will also help to stop blood clotting inside so that it can be flushed out effectively. However, it is always safer never to share cleaned works, even with partners or close friends.

You can Stop Fixing

You can find lots of alternative ways of taking ANY drug which don't involve fixing or skin-popping
You can smoke or snort heroin
You can snort speed
You can drop pills (all opiate drugs can be found in oral form)
You can freebase or snort coke
You can go over to oral substitutes like methadone (if you want to get a reliable supply you should approach a treatment centre (listed p106) or a doctor: it will mean fewer hassles in the long run.

You can Stop Using

Don't be afraid to ask for help on this one: you don't have to go it alone.
Find a local drugs agency to give you advice on self-help methods of coming off or other available treatment options.
If you're using barbs or tranquillisers on a regular basis don't cut yourself down suddenly: reduce your daily dose very gradually.
Explore the many self-help support groups like **Narcotics Anonymous** (see p105).
Think about what you want in the long term, coming off isn't that difficult, *staying* off can be.
Think about who you're spending your time with: if your friends are users they may have their own problems and won't be able to give you much support.
Consider the possibility of a rehab programme: you may need a break from the scene to get your life together.

Safer Sex

Even if you don't share works HIV can be passed on by certain kinds of sexual activities. You can help protect yourself and your partners by adopting safer sex. (see *Safer Sex* in the **Sex** section p88).

Cleaning used works

- Draw cold water into the syringe and then flush out
- Do this twice
- Draw some household bleach into the syringe and flush it out
- Do this twice as well
- Finally flush it out twice with fresh water

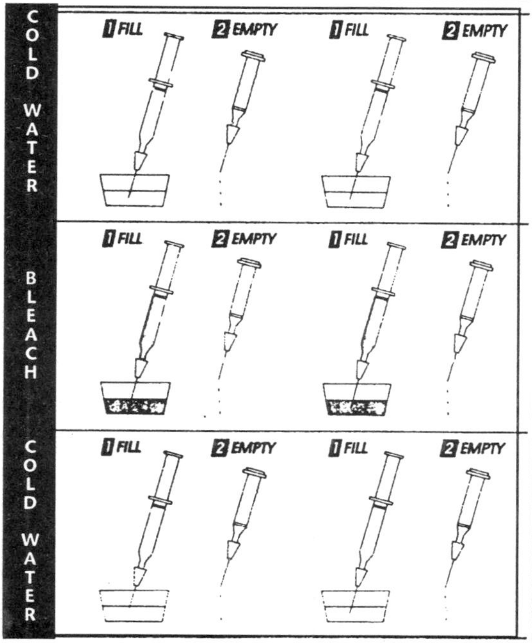

COLD WATER: 1 FILL, 2 EMPTY, 1 FILL, 2 EMPTY

BLEACH: 1 FILL, 2 EMPTY, 1 FILL, 2 EMPTY

COLD WATER: 1 FILL, 2 EMPTY, 1 FILL, 2 EMPTY

NEEDLE EXCHANGES IN LONDON

The majority of needle exchanges offer not only clean needles but also:
• Safe disposal services for used needles and works
• Condoms and safer sex leaflets
• Access to counselling by local drug agencies
• Other practical help and advice to drug users and their friends and relatives

There are two main types of service:
• Chemist based schemes which recruit local pharmacies who normally display a special sign in their window; you can get free or cheap needles from these chemists, depending on local funding and politics
• Special teams of trained workers who either exchange out on the streets in mobile 'buses' or in particular premise

West

■ **The Exchange,** *16a Cleveland St, Bloomsbury, W1 (631 1750/636 8333 x 4595).* M-F 12-6pm. Drop in.

■ **The Caravan Needle Exchange,** *St Mary's Hosp, South Wharf Rd, Paddington,W2 (725 1418).* M-Th 10-8 (6-8 women only), F 10-6. Sat 1-5 drop in. Welfare rights worker on Th.

■ **Hungerford Project,** *26 Craven St, WC2 (930 4688 Tom Finnigan, David Bagott).* Tu & F 2-5 drop in.

OVERDOSE: WHAT TO DO

If someone becomes unconscious due to taking an overdose:

• first check their breathing. If they've stopped breathing you will have to carry out mouth to mouth resuscitation. (Head back to clear throat, make sure airway is clear. Blow into the persons mouth in short intervals, until the chest rises, three to five times, check the pulse, continue until breathing starts. You will have to check in a First Aid book for more detailed description or better still do a First Aid course).

• In the meantime get someone to phone an ambulance, tell them what the person has taken

• If the person is still unconscious lie them in the recovery position, on their right side with their left leg bent, loosen any clothing and clear the mouth of any external obstructions, false teeth etc.

• Don't give them anything to eat or drink

Note: take their pulse from the wrist

South

■ **Basement Youth Project,** *227 Earls Court Rd, SW5 (373 2335 Tom Finnigan, David Bagott, Shareen Sadiq).* Drop in M 2-4.30, F 10-1,Th 1-4 women only.

■ **Drugline,** *9a Brockley Cross, Lewisham, SE4 (692 4975).* M-F 9-5 drop in.

■ **Community Drugs Project,** *30 Manor Place, Walworth Rd,, SE17 (703 0559 Alex).* M-F 2-5 drop in or M, W, F mornings by appointment.

■ **CADA (Campaign Against Drug Abuse),** *359 Old Kent Rd, SE17 (231 1528/237 8784 Eidlish Dickworth).* M,Tu 12-5, W-F 10-5 drop in or by appointment. Choice of needle sizes. Th 2.30-5 health care available.

■ **Balham Needle Exchange,** *St George's Drugs Dependency Unit 110 Balham High Rd, SW12 (871 7192 Jean Laws 767 8711 emergencies).* M 6-8.30pm, Tu, F 2-5pm.

■ **Stockwell Project,** *1-3 Stockwell Gdns, SW9 (274 7013/738 7784).* M 2-5, Tu & W 10-5 (closed lunch), Th 10-1, 2-8, F 2-5.

■ **Lambeth Syringe Exchange Scheme,** *c/o Health Liaison Unit, 138/146 Clapham Park Rd, SW4 (Karen Gowler 622 6655 x 228 Kim Mulji 672 9933 x2185).* The Exchange is run through the following Chemists:

■ **Aron Pharmacy,** *3 Barrett Hse, Rumsey Rd, Stockwell Park Est , SW8.*

■ **Ben's Chemist** *, 7A Victoria Mansions, South Lambeth Rd, SW8.*

■ **Deans Chemist,** *13 The Pavement, Clapham Common, SW8.*

North

■ **Drug Concern Barnet** *, Woodlands, Colindale Hosp Grounds, Colindale Hosp, NW9 (200 9525/9575).*

■ **DASH (Drug Advisory Service Haringey),** *Stuart Crescent Health Centre, Wood Green, N22 (881 6742).* M-F 9-5.

Greater London

■ **Community Drug Advice Service,** *Oxlow Lane Clinic, Oxlow Ln, Dagenham Essex, (592 7748).* M, Th 9.30-5.

■ **SWAP Drug Concern Harrow,** *Siddons Hse, Roxeth Hill, Harrow Middx, HA2 OJJ, (864 9622).* M-F 9.30-5.30.

■ **Substance Abuse Unit,** *Needle Clinic, Accident & Emergency, Hillingdon Hosp, Pied Heath Rd, Hillingdon UB8 3NN, (0895 57285 Stuart Gill).* W 4-6 drop in or appointment. Also Th 4-6 at **Needle Clinic,** *Accident & Emergency, Rickmansworth Rd. Rickmansworth.*

■ **Kaleidoscope Project,** *40-46 Cromwell Rd, Kingston-upon-Thames, Surrey, KT2 6RE, (549 7488/ 2681).* 7am-11pm drop in, daily.

TOLERANCE AND ADDICTION

Tolerance means that your body gets used to a drug so that more has to be taken to get the same effect. As tolerance develops there may be a tendency for some users to move from smoking or snorting heroin to injecting to maximize the effect. Gradual escalation of dose does not in itself lead to risk of death through overdose since tolerance also develops to the drugs effect of suppressing respiration (unlike barbiturates). However *fatal overdoses can occur if the user has not been using it for a while and the body has lost its tolerance.* Overdose may also occur if the drug is purer or stronger than expected and risk of overdose is increased if heroin is used in conjunction with other drugs such as alcohol or barbiturates.

Physical dependence on opiate drugs is often not as significant as the strong **psychological dependence** some long term users develop. Although some people use heroin on an occasional basis and dependence of any kind is not inevitable, many users find themselves quickly developing a tolerance and come to depend on it. If you find this is the case you are *addicted*.

ACUPUNCTURE AND WITHDRAWAL

Acupuncture has been found to be an effective alternative therapy for treating withdrawal from addictive drugs and associated problems such as anxiety, sleeplessness and aches and pains. (See *Acupuncture* in **Health** section p###).

▼ LAW ▼

If arrested (see **Law** section p###)
Say nothing until you have seen a solicitor, you should be offered the duty solicitor, if so accept, say nothing until she arrives. If you have any problems contact **Release**.

The Misuse of Drugs Act

The Misuse of Drugs Act 1971 lists drugs for which it is a criminal offence to possess. The Act also makes it a criminal offence to engage in a number of other activities with drugs in the list which are usually referred to as Controlled Drugs.

You can be prosecuted if the police can prove; you've been in possession, produced, supplied to another, offered to supply another, been concerned in supplying to another, been in possession with intent to supply, exported or imported a controlled drug, or allowed your premises to be used for consumption or supply.

The Act divides controlled drugs into three classes, each carrying a different penalty.

Class A includes: heroin, methadone, morphine, opium, pethadine, psilocin, MDMA (ecstasy), LSD, PCP (angel dust), cocaine and coca leaf.
For possession of a class A drug the maximum penalty of 7 years in prison and and unlimited fine. Only the most serious possession offence would get this penalty and most people charged with their first possession offence can expect a non-custodial sentence. The maximum sentence for supplying Class A drugs is life imprisonment. Anyone found guilty of supplying Class A drugs can expect to go to prison.
Class B includes: amphetamines, barbiturates, cannabis, and cannabis resin. All class B drugs become class A drugs if prepared for injection. For possession the maximum penalty is 5 years in prison and an unlimited fine. The vast majority of people facing their first possession charge can expect a fine if found guilty. The maximum sentence for supplying Class B drugs is 14 years. Anyone found guilty of supplying Class B drugs faces the possibility going to prison although if the amounts involved are small there is a chance of a non custodial sentence.
Class C includes : methaqualone (mandrax), minor tranquillisers such as valium, ativan and mogadon and a number of mild amphetamine like stimulants. For possession of some Class C drugs the maximum sentence is 2 years in prison and for supply offences 3 years. Minor tranquillisers, although Class C drugs, are currently legal to possess even without a prescription, although it is an offence to supply them.

Release, the National Drugs and Legal Helpline: *377 5905 M-F 10-6 24 hour emergency 603 8654, 169 Commercial St E1*
Release is an independent national agency concerned with the welfare of people using drugs, including people with legal problems over their drug use. They offer a confidential advice, information, referral and counselling service to drug users, dealing with: drugs and the law problems , drug use and general criminal legal problems.

If you need help in a hurry or need advice on a legal case Release will help. They also publish a range of pamphlets about most street drugs.

Directory of Tablets

OPIOID PILLS

Diconal
(1 part dipipanone hydrochloride to 3 parts cyclizine hydrochloride). They have a very strong effect on people not used to heroin.

DF 118 (Dihydrocodeine tartrate)
30mg white tablets marked DF 118. A mild narcotic.

DST 1 Continus
(morphine sulphate)
10mg brown tablets
30 mg purple tablets
60 mg orange tablets
100 mg grey tablets
All sustained release film coated.

Palfium (dextramoramide as a tartrate)
Comes in 5mg white scored tablets and 10mg peach scored tablets. The effects are similar to morphine.

Dramoron (leverphonal tartrate)
1.5 mg tablets made by Roche.

Fortral (Pentazocine hydrocholoride)
Tablets film coated 25 mg.
Capsules grey/ yellow 50mg.

Pethidine Hydrochloride
50mg tablets

Tengesic Buprenorphine
Tablets (subligual) 200 micro grammes

BENZODIAZEPINES

Diazepam
Capsules 2mg
Tablets 2 and 5 mg

Alupram
(Diazepam)
Made by Stelnhard
Scored 2mg tablets

Tenzine
(diazepam)
Made by Berk
Scored 2mg tablets

Salis Diazempam
Made by Galen
Capsules 2mg violet/ turquiose
5mg violet/mauve

Valium (diazepam)
Made by Roche
Scored 2mg tablets
5mg yellow tablets
10mg blue tablets

Xanox (Alprozalem)
Made by Upjohn
Scored tablets 250 micrograms
Pink scored tablets 500 micrograms

Lexoton (bramozepam)
Made by Roche
1.5mg lilac tablets

Ativan (lorazepam)
Scored 1mg blue tablets
2.5mg yellow tablets

Librium
(chlordiazepoxide)
Made by Roche
5mg capsules yellow/ green
10mg capsules green/black
Tablets are green 5mg, 10mg and 25mg.

AMPHETAMINES

Dexedrine (Dexamphetamine Sulphate)
Scored 5mg tablets.

Where to go to get help with drug problems

SOUTH

■ **Community Drug Project,** *30 Manor Pl, SE17 (703 0559).* By appointment M-F 10-1 & 2-5, drop in M, W & F 2-5. Needle exchange (see p102). Advice, info, counselling and referral to detoxification and rehabilitation.

■ **Two-Three-Five Project,** *235 Balham High Rd, SW17 (672 9464).* Mixed, age 17 plus. Hostel for ex-drug or alcohol addicts and ex-offenders. Must be drug free.

■ **Lambeth Drugsline,** *(677 9541).* Advice, info, and counselling. 24 hr.

■ **Stockwell Project,** *1/3 Stockwell Gdns, SW9 (274 7013).* Advice and info.

■ **Greenwich Drug Project,** *c/o Memorial Hosp, Shooters Hill, SE18 (856 5511).* Advice, info and counselling for users, family and friends. Home detoxification in conjunction with GP. M-F 9-5.

■ **ADFAM,** *Unit 7, South Thames Studios, 5-11 Lavington St, SE1 (401 2079).*

■ **Oak Lodge,** *136 West Hill, SW15 (788 1648).* Age 18-38, Residential. Drug free on entry (medical withdrawal may be arranged before admission). Self-referral.

■ **The Fulham Connection,** *Bishop Creighton Hse, 378 Lillie Rd, Fulham, SW6 (741 5875).*

Meetings for parents every first and third Thursday of the month at 7.30.

NORTH

■ **Omnibus Work Space**, *30-41 North Rd, N7 (700 4653).* Advice, education and info for women with drug/alcohol problems.

■ **CHOICE**, *608 Holloway Rd, Islington, N19 (272 1551).* Drop-in tranquilliser withdrawal self-help group meets Tu 7-9pm. Phone for details M-F 9.30-5.

■ **Community Drug Team**, *2b Forest Rd, N9 (443 3275).* Assessment, groups, referral. Home visits, home detoxification/withdrawal.

■ **The Angel Project**, *Inner City Action on Drugs, 38-44 Liverpool Rd, N1 (226 3113).* Drop-in and phone advice, info and counselling. Training of non-specialist workers. M & Tu 10-2, W, Th & F 2-8, Sat 10-2.

WEST

■ **The Hungerford**, *First Floor, 26 Craven St, WC2 (930 4688 (24 hr answerphone)).* Advice info and counselling for drug and drug related problems. Drop in M-F 2-5. Phone lines open M & W 2-5pm and Tu, Th & F 10-1 &2-5. Appointments available.

■ **City Roads (Crisis Intervention)**, *356-358 City Rd, EC1 (278 8671/2).* Residential, mixed. Short stay detoxification with counselling and primary health care for drug users in crisis. Accept referrals from all over London, 24 hr advice, info and counselling service.

■ **New Horizon**, *1 Macklin St, WC2 (242 0010)* is a day centre for people 16-21 in the West End. Has self help advice point where you can use phones, directories etc. Help in referring to hostels. Activities programme.

■ **Blenheim Project**, *7 Thorpe Cl, W10 (960 5599 (24 Hr answerphone)).* M-F 10-5 Wed 1-5 by appointment. Advice, support, info and counselling on drug problems for users, friends and relatives.

■ **Great Chapel Street Medical Centre**, *13 Great Chapel Street, W1 (437 9360).* Walk-in for all ages of people not registered with a doctor in London. M-F 12.45-4, Sat 11-12.

■ **Turning Point**, *Bedford Centre, Bedford Hall, Bedford Rd, W13 (567 1215).* Therapeutic day centre for people with alcohol problems. Long term treatment offered with group therapy and individual counselling. Drop-in for those who would like to know more M-F 4-5.

EAST

■ **East London Drug Project**, *Oxford Hse, Derbyshire St, Bethnal Green, E2 (729 8008). M, W & Th 6.30-9.30pm.*

GREATER LONDON

■ **Croydon Youth Counselling Service (Drop in)**, *132 Church St, Croydon, (698 0404 (24 Hr Answerphone)).* Youth counselling service including help with drug problems. Open M, W & F 4-8pm, Tu and Th 12-2pm and 6-8pm.

■ **Drug Concern (Croydon)**, *Lodge Rd Annexe, Lodge Rd, Croydon, (684 4707).*

■ **Kaleidoscope Youth and Community Project**, *40-46 Cromwell Rd, Kingston-upon-Thames, Surrey, KT2 6RE, (549 2681/7488).* Treatment clinic W 7.30-9.30pm and F 10-12am drop in offering health care service to drug users and ex-users, also advice, counselling and info. Hostel, self or professional referral. All night club, F 10pm-6am.

■ **Harrow Community Health Council**, *2 Junction Rd, Harrow, Middx, (836 6432).* Advice, info and counselling.

■ **The Newham Drug Project**, *254 Catherine Rd, E7 (472 0111).* M-F 8.45-4. Advice, support and home visits.

■ **DASH (Drug Advisory Service Haringey)**, *Block H, St Ann's Rd, N15 (802 0443).* Advice, info, counselling and treatment. 9-4.30. Appointments preferred.

■ **Under 21**, *Chestnut Hse, 398 Hoe St, E17 (558 0811/509 1219).* Drop-in and crisis phone line M & Th 10-9, Tu, W & F 9-5.30. Also counselling and info service for young people under 25.

■ **Drugsline Essex**, *Romford, (0708 49151).*

GENERAL HELP

■ **Narcotics Anonymous HQ**, *(351 6794).* Self help group for people with drug problems. Phone for local contact and time and place of meetings.

■ **Mainliners**, *Unit 228, The Enterprise Centre, 444 Brixton Rd, SW9 (274 4000 x 210).* For users worried about HIV or Aids.

■ **Families Anonymous**, *Blackfriars Settlement, 47 Nelson Sq, SE1 (731 8060).* Self-help group for parents, partners and relatives of users. Meets Monday 8-9.30pm.

■ **Drug Advice Workshop**, *145a Putney High St, SW15 (788 1199 (9-5pm) 785 9624/876 5638 (M-F 1-6pm)).* Support group for relatives and friends of users of all types of drugs. Appointment only.

DRUG DEPENDENCY CLINICS AND SERVICES

■ **Beresford Project,** *8 Beresford Sq, Woolwich, SE18 (854 9518).* Advice, info and counselling. Telephone enquiries M-F 9.30-12.30 & 1.30-5.30. Drop in M, W, Th & F 1.30-3.30.

■ **Bexley Hosp (SE Thames RHA),** *Ashdown Ward, Old Bexley Lane, Bexley, Kent DA5 2BW, (0322 526282).* In-patient detoxification only. Broad catchment area. Referral through St Giles Hosp (see below).

■ **Charing Cross Hospital Clinic,** *Drug Dependency Unit, 57 Aspenlea Rd, W6 (385 8834).* Prefer GP to refer but will take self-referral. M, W, Th, F 9-5. Tu 9-7. Out-patient clinic primarily opiate addicts. Drop in or appt, M-F 9-5 and Tu 9-7.

■ **Community Drug Team,** *11 Windsor Walk, SE5 (708 5888).* In and out patient detoxification with community support and home visits. Self or professional referral. Catchment area South Southwark and East Lambeth. Open 10-5. Tranquilliser users support group.

■ **Hackney Hospital,** *Homerton High St, E9 (986 6816 Community Drug Team 985 5555 x 8334).* Drop in M, W & F 9.30-12. By appt other times. Self referral.

■ **Henderson Psychiatric Hospital,** *2 Homeland Drive, Sutton, Surrey, (661 1611).* In-patient treatment of drug related personality disorders. Professional referral from anywhere in the country. Must be drug free & 17 years or over.

■ **Maudsley Hospital,** *Denmark Hill, SE5 (703 6333).* In and out patient. Specialist treatment. GP referral only. For South Southwark and East Lambeth (including Peckham).

■ **Queen Mary's,** *Roehampton Lane, SW15 (789 6611 x 309).* In and out patient.

■ **Rees House Day Hospital,** *Moreland Rd, E Croydon, (654 8100).* Croydon. GP referal only, but can try them without. Mon-Fri 9-6.

■ **St Clements (The London Hospital),** *2a Bow Rd, E3 (377 7975).* Drop in clinic M-F 4-5.

■ **St George's Hospital,** *Drug Dependency Treatment and Alcohol Research Unit, Clare Hse, Blackshaw Rd, SW17 (672 1255 x 4098/4099 or 672 9881).* Out patient service, advice, counselling, assessment, individual and group therapy and support both in the hospital and the communiy for any person with drug related problems. Training courses for professionals. Self or professional referral. Appointments preferred. M, T, Th & F 9-5, W 9-8pm. Non-users group W 6pm, ex-addicts offering mutual support.

■ **St Giles' Hosp (SE Thames RHA),** *Drug Dependency Unit, St Giles Rd, SE5 (703 0898).* Appointment preferred. M 9.30-4, Tu 10-6, W 9.30-4, Thu 9.30-6, Fri 9.30-4. New patients must be in at least 1 hour before clinic closes.

■ **St Giles,***St Giles Rd, SE5 (703 0898).* M 2-6, W 10-12, 2-4.30, F 10-12. For Lewisham, North Southwark, Greenwich, Bexley, parts of North Kent.

■ **St Mary's Hospital,** *Drug Dependency Clinic, Praed St, W2 (723 8829).* Out-patient, drop-in or appointment. M 10-12 noon. Tu & Th 10-4.15, W 11-7.15, F 12-3, closed for lunch 12.30-1.30.

■ **St Stephens,** *SW10 (352 8161).* SW1, SW3, SW5, SW7, SW10, W8, W14. Mon-Fri 10-5 outpatients only. Drop in clinic 10-11.30.

■ **St Thomas' Hospital,** *Drug Dependency Unit Lambeth Palace Rd, SE1 (633 0720).* M 1-8, Tu 12-1, 2-4.30; Wed 2-4.30, Th 10-1; Fri 2-4.30. All referrals through GP, social work agency or Stockwell project. Lambeth.

■ **Tooting Bec Hosp (SE Thames RHA),** *Drug Dependency Unit, Tooting Bec Rd, SW17 (672 9933).* In-patient unit serving patients primarily from South West and South East Thames areas, others only if beds are available. Assessment, stabilisation and detoxification - short, medium and long term - and rehabilitation. Referrals through St Georges and St Thomas's Hospitals. (See above).

■ **West Middlesex Hospital,** *Isleworth, Middx, (867 5070/1/2/3).* Self referral. Mon 2- 9. Weds 9.45 - 1, 2-5. Thurs 9.30-1.30. Hounslow, Spelthorne, Kingston, Richmond. Waiting list.

■ **St Mary's,** *Paddington, W9 (725 6487).* M, T, Th 10-4; W 11-7; F 11-3: for Westminster (W1, W2, W11, NW1, NW6, NW8), Kensington & Chelsea (W8, W10, W11, W14), Harrow and Brent.

■ **University College Hospital,** *Drug Dependency Clinic, 122 Hampstead Rd, NW1 (387 9541/ 9543).* Out-patient. M-Th 9.30-5. New referrals seen M & W 2-3.30, no appointment necessary but letter of referral from GP or professional organisation is asked for.

■ **University College Hospital,** *clinic at: National Temperance Hospital, 122 Hampstead Rd, NW1 (380 9693).* Referral by voluntary or statutory agency. New patients M 2-3.30, W 2-3.30. Bloomsbury, Haringey, Islington and Hampstead. For existing patients M-Th 9-5, Tue 9-7, Fri 9-1.

▼ GENERAL▼ RESOURCES

■ **Release,** *169 Commercial St, E1 6BW (603 8654 (24 hr emergency service); 377 5905).* See box p103.

■ **Institute for the Study of Drug Dependence (ISDD),** *1-4 Hatton Pl, EC1 (430 1991: library/ info service 430 1993).* Very helpful and useful for research. Excellent drug library. Also press cuttings, academic papers, reports etc. Helped in writing this section.

■ **SCODA (Standing Conference on Drug Abuse),** *1 Hatton Pl, EC1 (430 2341).*

arts & media

If you want to consume art, London is a shopper's paradise. To find out what's going on, City Limits, Time Out *and* What's On *have comprehensive weekly listings with reviews. There are also a lot of opportunities for learning the skills of a particular art form, or developing those you already have. Many adult education institutes offer cheap classes, as well as the opportunity to expand your social life* (Floodlight £1) *from your local newsagent for details). Community Arts Centres (listed below) also offer cheap courses .*

The one thing you are unlikely to get however, unless you are very lucky, is a living wage from your art.

▼ ARTS FUNDING ▼

There are quite a few organisations giving funding - for many different purposes: it's not only individual projects which are funded, but sometimes management and skills training too. On the whole it's easier to get money if you are already established. So on starting up, think small at first and raise money from other sources: subscriptions, entrance fees, benefits, running workshops etc. The *Arts Funding Guide* by Anne Marie Doulton (Directory of Social Change) is a list of funding sources, both official and alternative.

The *Guide to Awards & Schemes* available from **Arts Council of Great Britain**, *(ACGB), 105 Piccadilly, W1 (629 9495) who* fund the establishment arts organisations in Britain, but have some money for smaller projects which are of 'national interest' (if your project is more locally based, **Greater London Arts Association** is probably a better bet). Tend to fund organisations rather than individuals. Full details are in the *Guide to Awards and Schemes*, available from

■ **Greater London Arts Assoc (GLAA),** *25 Tavistock Pl, WC1 (837 8808).* GLA give a wide range of funding to arts projects, productions, events, exhibitions as well as some funding towards training (management etc) for those involved in arts groups. They are 'particularly concerned to ensure access to and involvement in the arts for those traditionally excluded by virtue of their age, gender, class, race, disability, sexual orientation or education.' Membership individual £6, orgs £25 for which you get statutory papers as produced, advice packs (e.g. on disability and marketing), and can attend AGM. Mthly mag *First Glance.*

■ **Calouste Gulbenkian Foundation,** *98 Portland Pl, W1 (636 5313).* Funds arts organisations (and some individuals) with charitable status in the area of arts, arts education and social welfare arts projects.

Local Authorities The Arts and Recreation Departments sometimes fund local arts projects, though it varies from borough to borough. It's worth contacting them anyway.

▼ VISUAL ARTS ▼

Studio space

This is expensive and hard to get in London, though like any property it depends where it is. Prices are charged by the square foot and include lighting. You can apply to agencies though waiting lists can be long for reasonably priced space - two which are both registered charities are

■ **Space Studios,** *6 Rosebery Ave, EC1 (278 7795).* Waiting list is closed at time of going to press.

■ **ACME Housing,** *15 Robinson Rd, E2 (981 6821).* provide housing shared with other artists and studio space. Also a waiting list - studio space list is very long, though still open at the time of going to press. Housing waiting list is closed.

Otherwise there's the commercial market - East End is probably the cheapest. You could try getting together with some other people, renting out factory space and converting it into studios.

Getting your work seen and sold

Galleries can take as much as 45-50% of sales which can make it almost not worth the effort, and staggering round them with a portfolio can be demoralising and exhausting. Mostly they just say their 'books are full', whatever that means. Many restaurants and cafes have exhibitions and they take a minimal cut - around 10% of work sold.

Put on your own exhibition Another way of getting your work seen is to rent a gallery (split the cost between 2 or more of you to save money). **British Rail Property,** *(837 5800)* rent out railways archways (though they are getting more expensive now) - paint one white and put on a show.

Advertising is very important. Put your show in the free listings in *City Limits, Time Out* and *What's On*. Harass the Visual Arts editor to come and review it - send her photos of you and your work. Do this *well* in advance.

Railing space You can rent railings to hang your work on in places like Bayswater Road and Green Park. Generally the work is pretty poor, but you can make money if you pitch your work right - remember there's the tourist trade in the summer. Ring **Westminster City Council's Licensing and Enforcement Dept,** *(798 1089)*. You have to go along to show your work to them which must be original. You can sell painting, crafts, sculpture, but not prints of other people's work. Waiting list can be up to 3 months. It costs about £4 per day plus the licence (£46 for 13 weeks). You can opt out at any time and get a refund if it's not working out.

Open shows held by Royal Academy, Whitechapel Art Gallery, South Bank Arts Complex etc. There's a lot of competition (out of about 6000 entries they only hang about 150 at Whitechapel) but it's usually cheap to enter. Get an application form from the gallery and if possible visit before you submit your work to find out what sort of thing is likely to be accepted. For instance at the RA Summer Show etchings, lithos and silk screen prints are the best bet because they sell, they're easy to hang and can be crammed in. Otherwise representational art is where it's at here.

Look out for other 'open submission shows' in Visual Arts section in *City Limits*, and advertised in newspapers etc.

Postcards You can have postcards of your work printed fairly cheaply and take them round shops.

Miscellaneous

■ **SHAPE,** *Thorpe Cl, W10 (960 9245)*. Introduces professional visual artists, musicians, actors, dancers and puppeteers to hospitals, prisons, youth centres, day centres, as well as to elderly, mentally and physically handicapped people, the homeless, disturbed adolescents and offenders.

■ **Artic Places,** *PO Box 23, 20 Villiers St, Sunderland SR1 1EJ , (091 5673589)*. Artists newsletter and a number of publications including comprehensive directory of exhibition spaces in Britain.

Publications

The Artists Directory and the *London Art and Artists Guide* (Art Guide Publications/ A & C Black £8.95). Both give information and contact addresses on all aspects of surviving in the visual arts world.

▼ POETRY ▼

If you want to start writing poetry, but aren't sure how to unblock your latent talents, ILEA **(Local Education Authorities)** run creative writing classes which are supportive and encouraging. If you want to read your poetry and get feedback, the **Poetry Library** or the **Poetry Society** (both below) can supply you with a list of workshops. Criticism can be brisker in these, though they also aim to be supportive.

If you want to get into print, the **Association of Little Presses** (below) offers information and advice, and publishes a booklet *Getting Your Poetry Published* (Peter Finch, 30p + 15p p&p) which details possible markets. They also have a leaflet giving a step-by-step guide to producing a book of your own work. See also **Printing & Publishing** section (p256).

Details of poetry readings can be found in *City Limits* and *Time Out*. If there's a group of you, why not organise your own - back rooms of pubs are traditional venues. Put up leaflets locally and get your friends to come. Charge a very nominal sum for entry and hope that you recoup the cost of the room.

■ **The Association of Little Presses,** *89a Petherton Rd, N5 2QT (226 2657).* Helpful information on getting your own poetry published, particularly on self-publication. Produces*Catalogue of Small Press Books in Print* annually (£2.40 + 60p p&p), and magazine *Poetry and Little Press Information* qtly (£3 for 3 issues) which gives details of recent small press publications; an ALP newsletter; and *Small Presses and Little Magazines in the UK and Ireland* address list of over 1000 publishers (£1.50 + 30p p&p). Organises bookfairs, exhibitions and gatherings. Membership £7.50 a year open to presses, institutions and individuals.

■ **Arts Council Poetry Library,** *Level 5, Royal Festival Hall, South Bank Centre, SE1 (921 0664/0943/ 0940).* Open 7 days a week 11-8pm. Modern poetry in English, or translated into English. Periodicals. Provide a list of poetry groups, workshops, competitions, magazines, bookshops and publishers. Events noticeboard . Regular readings in the *Voice Box,* beside library.

■ **The Poetry Society and National Poetry Centre,** *21 Earls Ct Sq, SW5 (373 7861).* Membership £15 pa, £10 unwaged, includes quarterly *Poetry Review.* Some workshops, regular readings, bookshop (large stock of contemporary British poetry). **Critical Service** offers analysis of a piece of work for a fee. Information leaflets: *Notes on Getting Your Poetry Published.* Send sae.

■ **The Poetry Olympics,** *c/o Michael Horovitz, Piedmont, Bisley, Stroud, Gloucester,* stages performances of radical contemporary poetry for new voices in British poetry who express 'humour, passion and music, a sharp political awareness and outspoken opposition to racism, sexism, war and other pollutions'. Publishes *New Departures,* and is planning new anthology of experimental, protest and performance poets.

■ **Book Trust,** *Book House, 45 East Hill, (870 9055).* Publish a *Guide to Literary Prizes* (£3.25) which lists the major competitions and awards in poetry and prose.

▼ DANCE ▼

Classes

These range from glorified keep fit to body awareness, through to disciplined art form. Some places are big and may have facilities like a sauna, cafe and creche, others just a cramped changing room, though the plus side of a small dance studio is that you get more individual attention. All have classes for the beginner. Adult education institutes also run classes (a cheaper option than studios for those eligible for concessions), as do some local Sports Centres. For information about accredited schools consult the **Council for Dance Education and Training,** *5 Tavistock Pl, WC1 (388 5770)* particularly if you are considering professional training.

■ **Academy of Indian Dance,** *16 Flaxman Terr, WC1 (387 0980).* Classes are held at **The Place Theatre** (Euston), **Riverside Studios** and **Brackenbury Institute** in Hammersmith. Four kinds of dance taught: Kathak, Bharata Natyam, Odissi, Kathakli. Classes for all different levels and age groups. £2 per hour. Also run summer school, intensives, and master classes in Indian classical dance style. Contact Mira Kaushik (director) for further details.

■ **Africa Centre,** *38 King St, WC2 (836 1973).* Runs classes in traditional African dance. Mon 6.30-8.30. £9 per term, (£1 concs) plus membership £5.

■ **All That Jazz,** *The Riding, Golders Green Rd, NW11 (455 8160).* Jazz and contemporary jazz, body conditioning, aerobics, karate, self defence. £3 admission to classes.

■ **Chisenhale Dance Space,** *64 Chisenhale Rd, E3 (981 6617).* Contemporary, Lindy Hop jive, movement, African dance. Membership £3 per year, plus class admission £2.50. (concs available)

■ **Dance Attic,** *212 Putney Br Rd, SW15 (785 2055).* Contemporary, jazz, belly dancing, tap, Spanish, rock 'n' roll, Russian ballet, and also classes in aerobics, yoga, tai chi, roller skating, fencing, martial arts. Creche, art gallery, poetry workshops. Membership £1.50 day, £20 half year, £30 year (reductions for students and members of Equity) plus £2.50 for individual classes.

■ **Dancercise,** *The Barge Durban, Lion Wharf, Richmond Rd, Old Isleworth, Middlesex TW7 7BW, (560 3300).* This is dance as exercise as the name suggests made up of many different dance styles - jazz, contemporary, ballet, disco. Classes are graded, it's about £3.25 for a class.

■ **Dance Works,** *16 Balderton St, W1 (629 6183).* Jazz, ballet, flamenco, belly dancing, yoga, ceroc, body conditioning and aerobics. £75 pa membership, (£22 per month) plus £3.50 admission to classes.

■ **Drill Hall Arts Centre,** *16 Chenies St, WC1 (631 1353).* Modern dance, self-expressive movement, dance theatre, yoga, tai chi, aerobics, acrobatics, self defence. Membership 50p pa, plus £2.50 per class.

■ **English Folk Dance and Song Soc.,** *Cecil Sharp Hse, 2 Regents Park Rd, NW1 (485 2206).* Can put you on touch with Morris dancers, etc. Their *Folk Directory* (£4.50) is comprehensive and *Folk London* (5p) lists events. M'ship £15. Morris, country, clog and sword dance. Public dances at weekends.

■ **Institute of Indian Culture,** *4A Castletown Rd, W14 (381 3086).* Indian dance as well as classes in various aspects of Indian culture. £2.50 admission.

■ **Jackson's Lane Community Centre,** *271 Archway Rd, N6 (340 5226).* Contemporary and jive. Indian dance and music. Classes are cheap - £2 membership plus £1-2 for class.

■ **Jubilee Hall Sports Centre,** *The Piazza, Covent Gdn, WC2 (836 4007).* Contemporary, jazz, yoga, martial arts. £2.50 class admission.

■ **London School of Contemporary Dance,** *The Place, 17 Dukes Rd, WC1 (387 0152 x 243).* Full and part-time courses in contemporary and body conditioning, but also jazz and ballet according to demand. £3.20 a class. Intensive courses at Easter/ Summer include tai chi. **Young Place** for children and teenagers on Saturdays. Contact Karen Burgin.

■ **Islington Arts Factory,** *2 Parkhurst Rd, N7 (607 0561).* Adult classes in ballet, jazz, contemporary, flamenco, raks sharki, lindy hop. **Junior Factory** - ballet for 6-16 yr olds. Two young people's companies meet there on Sundays. Music courses, exhibition space for visual arts and photography, rehearsal space for theatre, dance, bands.

■ **Laban Centre for Movement and Dance,** *Goldsmiths Coll, Laurie Gro, SE14 (692 4070).* Evening classes in jazz, ballet, contemporary, dance history and appreciation (£15-£22 per term). Summer school runs range of courses for beginners through to professionals. Also run courses to BA, MA and PhD level, as well as a range of one year specialist courses.

■ **Oval House,** *(735 2786).* (See page115) do dance classes, theatre, music, self defence, photography.

■ **Pineapple Dance Centre,** *7 Langley St, WC2 (836 4004).* Ballet, jazz, keep fit, aerobics, body conditioning, ceroc, tap, belly dancing, Indian, yoga. £3.50 plus membership (day £3, monthly £18, Yearly £55). Mostly eves, professional dance classes throughout day. They also have centres in Paddington *(487 3444)* and Kensington *(581 0466)*.

Reading

■ **Dance Books,** *9 Cecil Ct, WC2 (836 2314).* Mon-Sat 11-7. Extensive stock including out of print books, mags and posters.

■ **Performance Magazine,** *295 Kentish Town Rd, NW5 (482 3843).* Quarterly £1.75. Broad range of performing arts.

▼ THEATRE WORKSHOPS ▼

The following places run workshops in various performance skills. Drama schools also sometimes run part time courses - ring them to find out.

■ **Albany Empire,** *Douglas Way, SE8 (691 8016).* Run *Second Wave,* young women's drama project for 11-25 yr olds from SE area who haven't had access to drama or arts training - acting, playwriting, video, film etc taught. **Basement Youth Arts** for same age group as well as group for 8-12 yr olds. Workshops for young unemployed.

■ **Common Stock,** *182 Hammersmith Rd, W6 (741 3086).* Youth and Community theatre running workshops in video, music, drama, writing, design and theatre arts for 7-50 yr olds (or older). Free. Hammermith and Fulham area.

■ **The Drill Hall,** *16 Chenies St, WC1 (631 1353).* Run workshops and rent out space for them.

■ **The Actors Centre,** *4 Chenies St, WC1 (631 3599).* Workshops for Equity members only.

■ **Tara Arts Group,** *356 Garratt La, SW18 (871 1458/9).* Run workshops in acting skills, and offer advice and space for theatre groups just starting up.

▼ FILM ▼

A useful guide to training in film and video is *Directions* published 3 times a year, and available from **BFI Publications Dept,** *99 Rathbone St, W1 (636 3289)* £2 + 40p postage, £6 .50 for 1 year's sub. The *British Film Institute Yearbook,* which contains run downs on various groups, is £10.96, £11.95 by post, and also available from them.

Resources

■ **Independent Film-Makers Association,** *79 Wardour St, W1 (439 0460)* are undergoing a radical restructuring - will still lobby TV stations on behalf of independent film makers as they have in the past, but now will probably become more of an access centre with information on funding etc.

■ **Assoc of Black Workshops,** *(359 0302).*

■ **London Film-Makers Co-op,** *42 Gloucester Ave, NW1 (Workshop: 722 1728, distribution: 586 4806).* Workshop, cameras, editing equipment, black and white 16mm printer and processor. Possible to make a 16mm black and white film from beginning to end at co-op. A few courses, and regular skill sharing workshops - go with your needs for tuition and course or help will be worked out. Cinema showing experimental/independent films, last Tues in month open screening when anyone can show their work and get it discussed afterwards. Distribution library with over 2,000 experimental films. Membership of workshop for first year £35 waged, £20 concs. Cinema is *(586 8516).*

■ **Four Corners Films,** *113 Roman Rd, E2 (981 4243; 981 6111 equipment hire.).* Wide range of equipment: 16mm and super 8, plus production facilities. Education courses on use of specific equipment and production process. Small cinema for occasional screenings. Saturdays they have a children's cinema club which includes screenings and practical work.

■ **Cinema Action,** *27 Winchester Rd, NW3 (586 2762).* Facilites for 16mm post production. Editing room, cinema/viewing facilities and small studio. Make features and documentaries.

■ **Greater London Arts Assoc,** *1 White Lion St, N1 (837 8808).* Have film and video dept which funds and gives advice on production, budgeting, how to organise training, exhibitions and screenings. Information on funding for all parts of the process.

■ **British Film Institute,** *21 Stephen St, W1 (255 1444).* Runs many services for the public. Library service and stills library (by appt). Runs **Federation of Film Services Societies** which helps film societies in setting up and running their society. Has distribution library (mainly 16mm). The production and distribution divisions have a small amount of money to give to filmakers starting in business. The **National Film Archive** houses 40,000 titles available to 'bona fide users' . **National Film Theatre** shows films in two cinemas every day, and houses **Museum of the Moving Image.** The Education Dept has an advisory service, slide packs, study guides and a catalogue for schools, conferences, courses etc. Associate membership £10.50 (some concs).

■ **Concord Video & Films Council,** *201 Felixstowe Rd, Ipswich, Suffolk IP3 9BJ, (0473 715754/726012 bookings, 0473 77747 despatch).* Large film and video library of over 4,000 titles, specialise in social documentary, ecology, third world, peace, growth. Catalogue: video only £1, all titles £2.50 inc postage. Average price for borrowing video £10 + post and VAT.

■ **The Other Cinema,** *79 Wardour St, W1 (734 8508).* Documentaries/features, videos/films on human rights, third world, environmental and nuclear issues, world development, TU and labour studies. Send £1 worth stamps for catalogue.

■ **Cinema of Women,** *31 Clerkenwell Close, EC1 (251 4978).* Good selection of feminist films - £5 for catalogue.

■ **CIRCLES Women's Work on Distribution,** *113 Roman Rd, E2 (981 6828).* (See page 182). Distribute women's work on film video, tape/slide.

■ **Arts Council Films,** *105 Piccadilly, W1 (629 9495).* Documentaries on art and artists, only distribute selected films: architecture and dance. 16mm films, 3/4 inch videotape, VHS. Free catalogue.

■ **Educational and Television Films (ETV),** *247a Upper St , Highbury Corner, N1 (226 2298).* General films from E/Europe, particularly GDR, USSR, plus some other films with political themes.

Free films

■ **British Museum,** *Gt Russell St, WC1 (636 1555).* Tue-Fri 3.30 in basement lecture theatre.

■ **The Imperial War Museum,** *Lambeth Rd , SE1 (735 8922).* At weekends, but you have to pay to get into museum.

■ **The Museum of Mankind,** *Burlington Gdns, W1 (437 2224).* Tue-Fri.

■ **Tate Gallery,** *Millbank, SW1 (821 1313).*

▼ VIDEO ▼

Almost twenty years on from its first faltering steps video has recently begun to establish itself as both an art form and, more broadly, a tool for communication with more screenings, exhibitions, training courses and workshops than ever before.

Funding for workshops and centres is being cut, but there is still a wide range of courses on offer from basic VHS production through to video graphics. The emphasis varies from place to place: e.g. some workshops are for women only, some specialise in helping local people produce campaigning videos about local issues. It can be costly to learn, though most places do reductions for the unemployed.

Video Art

There's increasing interest in video as art, a good place to see this is the **ICA**, *The Mall, SW1Y 5AH (930 3647).* Screenings on Suns. It also has a large collection of video art, campaign tapes and pop videos which can be viewed in the cramped confines of the rather grandly titled *Videotecheque*. Cost 50p per half hour - Sundays only 12-5.30. 1000 titles to choose from viewed on three 20" monitors.

Making a Video

Despite rumours to the contrary video is not that cheap a medium to work in. Of course, it depends on what you're doing and what you want the finished product to end up like but in general, while the actual material costs (camera hire, tape costs) are low relative to film, it's the post-production (i.e. what you do *after* you've shot the tape or when you edit it) which can end up costing more than you've bargained for. It's also a fallacy to imagine that video is easier to use than film equipment, and that it's lighter or more portable - not true as many a camera person loaded down with battery belts, tape deck and tripod will probably tell you.

Despite this, video can be a good place to start for the budding director. For equipment hire see organisations listed at the end of the section.

Getting Money

There are two major funding bodies in London:

■ **Greater London Arts,** (see page 107) who tend to sponsor work which deals with political/social/local issues;

■ **Arts Council of Great Britain,** (see page 107) which tends to go for more experimental projects. They both have 'Small Awards' (of up to £500) which are for first time film or video makers, and applications are dealt with about twice a year. (A word of warning - for the first time maker awards are for basic production costs only. You're not supposed to pay anyone who works on the film, and you certainly won't be able to afford a director's chair!)

It may also be worth contacting your local authority. Many boroughs have small sums available for local arts projects although criteria and conditions change from area to area. It can be difficult to find the right person or department to talk to.

Finally there are those who've trod the slippery path of sponsorship and/or fund raising and managed to make a go of it. One group, calling themselves *Build Hollywood,* hired the Hackney Empire and got Jonathan Ross, Nicholas Parsons and a host of cabaret and music artists to appear for free in support of their project.

Courses

There are a great many video and TV production courses around - they are often advertised in the *Guardian* on a Monday in the media pages. They can be expensive, and though they often promise the gateway to a prosperous career, before you commit yourself try to find out as much as possible about the course, the tutors' backgrounds, and just how many of the students who have come through the course were actually able to use what they learned.

The *British Film Institute Yearbook* is an excellent guide to video and film production, distribution groups and workshops, available from **British Film Institute,** *127 Charing Cross Rd, WC2 (437 4355).*

Training/Equipment Hire

The organisations listed below offer facilities, equipment hire and sometimes training courses.

■ **Aphra Workshops for Women,** *99 Leighton Rd, NW5 (485 2105).* Scriptwriting workshops for women in TV drama.

■ **Ceddo Film and Video Workshop,** *South Tottenham Education and Training Centre, Braemar Rd, N15 (802 9034).* All aspects of film and video training - beginners/intermediate/advanced. Sometimes run women only courses according to demand. Though they particularly encourage Black people to get involved in training, courses are for those from all ethnic groups.

■ **Clapham-Battersea Media Centre,** *Latchmere Rd, SW11 (223 3681).* Basic/intermediate/advanced training.

■ **Connections,** *241 King St, W6 (741 1766).* Basic/intermediate/advanced training. Also courses for women, minority groups, disabled, unemployed, and local groups.

■ **Despite TV,** *178 Whitechapel Rd, E1 (377 0737).* For people living and working in East London who are doing non-commercial work. Informal training.

■ **Fantasy Factory,** *42 Theobalds Rd, WC1 (405 6862).* M-F10-8pm. Run short training courses in video editing. Basic/Intermediate/Advanced training.

■ **Film Work Group,** *79-89 Lots Rd, SW10 (352 0538).* Informal training only.

■ **Hackney Media Resources,** *90 De Beauvoir Rd, N1 (241 2162).* Basic and intermediate training.

■ **London Video Access,** *23 Frith St, W1 (734 7410).* Set up to produce, promote and distribute video work, they have a library of over 600 tapes. Main distributor of video art. Training in production and post production. Three edit suites. Training for all levels - beginners to advanced. Some women only courses. One to one tuition for people who want specific skills. Work with **London Deaf Video Project.**

■ **V.E.T. Ltd,** *Unit 15, Tower Workshops, Riley Rd, SE1 (237 6565).* Basic/intermediate/advanced training. Some women only courses.

■ **West London Media Workshop,** *118 Talbot Rd, W11 (221 1859).* Video production and facilities house with subsidised rates for non-commercial uses. Edit and production courses.

■ **Women's Media Resource Project,** *85 Kingsland High St, E8 (254 6536).* Basic/Intermediate/ Advanced training for women.

Publications

■ **Independent Media,** *7 Cambell Ct, Bramley, Basingstoke RG26B 5EG, (0256 882023).* Magazine of video, film etc runs reviews, arts and media section and features up to date information on shows, competitions, grants etc. Mthly £1.50 per issues, Subs £15 pa.

■ **Mediamatic Magazine,** available from *Performance Magazine, 61A Hackney Rd, E2 (739 1577).* Glossy video arts journal published in Amsterdam - all articles are in Dutch and English. Covers international video scene. Qtly £3.

▼ PHOTOGRAPHY ▼

Buying

London offers a wealth of resources for photographers from the keen amateur to the established professional. The beginner could indeed be overawed by the sheer quantity of products on offer.

The cost of materials, and more particularly equipment, can vary considerably, so it pays to shop or phone around. Retail competition is so intense that manufacturers' recommended prices are often undercut. Some companies deal in *grey* imports (goods bought cheaply abroad by individual importers). Don't be rushed into a purchase by an eager sales person; research the equipment carefully to be certain it meets you requirements.

The advantage of buying secondhand equipment from a shop is that generally it carries a guarantee of at least three months. Bargains are more likely to be found in the private market where amateurs occasionally sell virtually unused/unwanted equipment. Always check carefully for dents, scratches or rattles that may indicate damage, and that the aperture and shutter mechanism work properly.

When buying film and other materials it is advisable to use large reputable outlets who will have a regular turnover of stock. Out of date film and paper can be purchased at significant reductions, but with unpredictable results, particularly with colour materials.

■ **City Camera Exchange, Photo Optix, Techno, Jessops** and **Vic Odens** have various branches in the capital offering discounts on new equipment, secondhand and mail order departments. They can suffer from indifferent or over-zealous sales staff, but this is offset by a wide range of stock at competitive prices.

■ **Keith Johnson and Pelling,** *93 Drummond St, NW1 (380 1144)* and *11 Great Marlborough Street, Wl (439 8811),* are both large shops concentrating on the professional market with mainly new, but some secondhand, equipment. They have knowledgeable staff to demonstrate equipment, and offer good after sales service. The Great Marlborough Street branch has a repair department.

■ **Leeds Camera Centre,** *16 Brunswick Centre, WC1 (883 1661/1641).* Similar to Keith **Johnson and Pelling,** and also has a huge equipment hire department.

■ **Process Supplies,** *13-21 Mount Pleasant, WC1 (837 2179).* Extensive supplies of materials and accessories at competitive prices.

■ **Morgans,** *179 Tottenham Court Rd, W1 (636 1138).* Secondhand equipment of all shapes and sizes, prehistoric to the modern day.

■ **Silverprint,** *12b Valentine Place, SE1 (620 0844).* Specialise in black and white print materials, including lots of obscure imports.

■ **A.W. Young,** *51 Atlantic Rd, SW9 (274 1967).* and **Marston and Heard** *378 Lea Bridge Rd, E10 (539 6585)* are now both amalgamated into the **Phototech** group. They deal mainly in secondhand and government surplus equipment and outdated film and paper.

■ **Jessops,** *11 Frognal Parade, Finchley Rd, NW3 (794 8786).* Photography/darkroom equipment. Cheap film.

■ **Phototec 'Brunnings',** *28 Museum St, WC1 (637 0165).* Old established firm selling new and secondhand photographic and scientific equipment inc. obscure pieces.

■ **The Photographers Gallery,** (see p114) has a useful notice board advertising private secondhand equipment for sale.

See also classified section of some photographic magazines.

Breakdowns

If an item of equipment breaks down while under guarantee it is best to take it back to the shop you bought it from and they will send it back to the manufacturer/wholesaler. This usually means you are without the equipment for some weeks. For a speedier service for out-of-guarantee breakdowns it is best to go to outlets with their own repair departments.

If you need a repair the following shops are helpful and reliable:

■ **Keith Johnson and Pelling,** (see p113)

■ **Leeds Camera Centre,** (see p113)

■ **Camera Care,** *32 Tottenham St, W1 (323 0633).*

■ **Sendean,** *105 Oxford St, W1 (439 8418).*

■ **Profix,** *164 Union St, SE1 (261 0412).*

Processing

Getting your films processed is not as hit and miss as it used to be. With colour prints the choice is between high street/mail order rapid machine processing - cheap, but of unpredictable quality; and more expensive laboratory hand printing - this is best reserved for occasions where optimum results are required. Colour transparencies (slides) are best entrusted to specialist colour labs. Black and white printing is a dying skill and good quality work is hard to come by. Don't be surprised if you pay more for black and white than colour prints.

■ **APR,** *2 Iliffe Yard (off Crampton Street), SE17 (708 2728).* Specialist black and white printing and renovation work.

■ **Colour Processing Laboratories (CPL),** *18 Warren St, W1 (388 7836).* Pricey, but good all round lab.

■ **Grove Hardy,** *2 Burrows Mews, SE1 (928 1603).* Quality black and white printing on fibre based paper.

■ **Joe's Basement,** *89-91 Wardour St, W1 (434 9313).* Open 24 hrs, handy for insomniacs, offering a good all round service at competitive prices. They also have a shop selling film and paper round the clock.

■ **Westside,** *27 Hanson St, W1 (637 8201/2757).* A personal favourite for colour work. A good quality, reliable, friendly service.

Although we've recommended only a few, in reality there are hundreds of laboratories (check the classifieds in some photographic magazines), and the best advice is to find one offering a good service locally and then sticking with them as most will ensure good service to regular clients.

DIY Processing

If you fancy doing your own processing and printing but don't have access to a darkroom there are a number of centres offering facilities, many also run courses. It's worth checking the student/equipment ratio before enrolling on a course as some are hopelessly over-subscribed.

All of the following have darkroom facilities and run courses:

■ **Beehive Centre for Photography,** *136 Gloucester Av, NW1 (586 4916).* Studios and darkrooms for hire.

■ **Blackfriars Photography Project,** *The Beormund, 177 Abbey Street, SE1 (237 9312).*

■ **Camerawork,** *121 Roman Rd, E2 (980 6256).* Also have regular lecture series on various aspects of photographic practice and theory, often tied in to current exhibitions.

■ **Photo Co-op,** *61 Webbs Rd, SW11 (228 8949).* Also extensive photo-library.

■ **Photographers Gallery,** *5 & 8 Great Newport St, WC2 (240 5511/5512).* Also have regular lecture series on various aspects of photographic practice and theory, often tied in to current exhibitions.

Education

Many adult education, local community and arts centres offer longer part-time day or evening courses catering for varying degrees of aptitude. *Floodlight* lists most.

Advanced full-time courses are run by the following polytechnics and colleges:

■ **Middlesex Polytechnic,** *114 Chase Side, N14 (886 6599).* Offer B.A. in Graphic Design which covers a broad spectrum of visual communication. Also B.A. in Combined Studies and B.A. in Fine Art. Both of these encourage the student to specialise in a narrower range of disciplines.

■ **North East London Polytechnic,** *Romford Rd, E15 (590 7722).* B.A. (Hons) Fine Art. From a broad start the student chooses an area of specialisation. Also incorporates an element of critical theory.

■ **Polytechnic of Central London,** *309 Regent st, W1 (486 5811).* B.Sc. and B.Sc. (Hons) Photo Science: concentrating on photo scientific theory. B.A. (Hons) Film, Video and Photographic Arts: a non-vocational course in creative practice and academic study of photography and film.

■ **Harrow College** run a B.A. in photography.

■ **London College of Printing** run a B.A. (Hons) similar to the **PCL** course and also a photo-journalism degree.

■ **Paddington College** has a diploma course.

All the above are three year full-time courses, although **PCL**'s B.A. (Hons) can be taken as a four year part-time course. Most colleges also offer programmes of short specialist courses. Many Further Education colleges run Access courses for potential degree students without the necessary entrance qualifications.

Publications

■ *Amateur Photographer, Prospect House, 9-13 Ewell Rd, Cheam, Surrey, (661 4300).* As the name suggests this magazine is pitched at the amateur market. Product tests, useful practical tips and pages of adverts handy for comparing prices.

■ *British Journal of Photography, 244-249 Temple Chambers, Temple Av, EC4 (583 6463).* Broad Coverage of news and events, reviews of shows and publications. Very extensive and exacting product tests. Photography related articles and a comprehensive classified section.

■ *Creative Camera, Battersea Arts Centre, The Old Town Hall, Lavender Hill, SW11* Long standing champion of discursive criticism of various aspects of photography.

■ *The Photographer* is the magazine of the **British Institute of Professional Photographers** and tends towards technical and industrial concerns.

■ *The Photographic Journal* is published by the **Royal Photographic Society** and is similar to the BJP in layout and content.

■ *Ten 8*, news, extended articles and critical analysis of photographic practice.

Galleries

Many other galleries occasionally have photographic exhibitions - check in photographic publications or listings magazines (*Time Out* and *City Limits*).

■ **Camerawork,** *121 Roman Rd, E2 (980 6256).* Concentrates on community, women's, social and political non-mainstream projects. Organises and distributes touring exhibitions.

■ **Barbican,** *Barbican Centre, EC2 (638 4141).* Varied programme from large/international touring exhibitions in the main gallery space, to more obscure works in the concourse spaces.

■ **Institute of Contemporary Arts (ICA),** *The Mall, SW1 (930 3647).* Generally one person shows.

■ **National Portrait Gallery,** *St. Martin's Place, WC2 (930 1552).* Occasional portrait show on various themes.

■ **Photographers Gallery,** *5 & 8 Gt Newport St, WC2 (240 5511/2).* Three exhibition spaces, enabling up to four separate shows at any one time. Organise and distribute travelling exhibitions. They have a print room where original photographs can be purchased and also a library.

■ **Portfolio Gallery,** *345 Portobello Rd, W10 (969 0453).* They also sell original work as well as print and distribute postcards and posters.

■ **Special Photographers Company,** *21 Kensington Park Rd, W11 (221 3489).*

Bookshops

In addition to the **ICA** and **Photographers Gallery** the following bookshops have extensive photography sections:

Dillons, *82 Gower St, WC1 (636 1577)*; **Foyles,** *119 Charing Cross Rd, WC2 (437 5660)* ; **Zwemmers,** *72 Charing Cross Rd, WC2 (240 1559).*

▼ RADIO ▼

■ **Community Radio Association,** *Southbank Ho, Black Prince Rd, SE1 (582 7972).* Advice, development, training. Has 300 members, magazine *Airflash* - bimthly, with London Supplement.

■ **TX-Radio Today,** *Box 225, WC1N3.* Recorded message giving details of pirate stations broadcasting, and those that have been busted as well as information about what's happening in the radio world as a whole. Unfortunately we've just accidentally deleted the phone number!

■ **Local Radio Workshop,** *12 Praed Mews, W2 (402 7651).* Providing training in radio production. Recording studio equipped to make broadcast-quality tapes. Two full-time workers will advise and help groups make their own programmes. They distribute cassettes of programmes (send sae for list) and campaign for airtime access programmes.

■ **Radio Society of GB,** *Lambda Hse, Cranborne Rd, Potters Bar, Herts EN6 3JE, (0707 59015).* M'ship £20.50 pa, includes sub for mthly *Radio Communications.* Access to technical advice. Discounts on publications.

▼ ARTS RESOURCE CENTRES ▼

■ **Battersea Arts Centre,** *Lavender Hill, SW11 (223 8413).* Classes in dance and self defence for adults; dance, drama, movement and photography for children. Youth Theatre for teenagers.

■ **Camden Arts Centre,** *Arkwright Rd, NW3 (431 1292).* Lithography, etching, art classes. Gallery space on approval of work. (Membership £45 for Camden residents, £65 non-residents).

■ **Greenwich Mural Workshop,** *MacBean Centre, MacBean St, SE18 (854 9266/316 7577).* Arts workshop produces murals and banners for community organisations. Some courses on murals and banner making.

■ **Island Arts Centre,** *Tiller Rd, E14 (987 7925).* For use by people living in Tower Hamlets and Isle of Dogs. Workshops, courses and projects for adults and children: pottery, photography, drama, video and screenprinting etc.

■ **Moonshine Community Arts Workshop,** *Victor Rd, NW10 (960 0055).*

■ **Oval House,** *52 Kennington Oval, SE11 (735 2786).* Dance, drama, arts workshops. M'ship £20 per year waged, £5 concs. Rehearsal space, theatre, cafe, noticeboard. Carnival. **Oval Options** serves schools and colleges around issue of employment.

■ **Yaa Asantewaa Arts Centre,** *1 Chippenham Mews,, W9 (286 1656).* Black arts centre, wide range of regular workshops (drama, music, creative writing, arts, crafts, martial arts, sports), cultural events and stage performance area for amateur and professional artists. Cultural exchanges.

p e t s

This section is intended to give some information about alternative pet foods, how to avoid private vets bills when you are hard up, what to do when your pet dies and where to get a new pet.

▼ FOOD ▼

We are becoming more conscious about what we eat, what goes into our food and the dangers of additives. Yet many people still feed their animals ingredients that probably contain harmful additives. There are also many veggies/vegans who would rather not feed their dogs on meat. Dogs can live quite adequately and healthily on a vegan/vegetarian diet. This is not the case with cats as they need particular vitamins and minerals that cat food/meat contains.

Dog Food

Happi-dog pet foods supply both vegan and vegetarian pet dog food. It is dried food made up of soya protein and other ingredients. Boiling water is added to the food, which must be allowed to cool before it is ready to eat. The main brand of Happi-dog is vegan, and there is quite a selection of varieties, some of which are vegetarian. You can order it wholesale, when it can be delivered free to your door. It is much cheaper this way. The address of the main suppliers is **Happidog Pet Foods,** *Bridge End, Brown Hill Lane, Longton, Preston, Lancs PR4 4SJ*. Send a cheque and a letter stating your name and address and amount you require. A 20 Kg of vegan 'Supermeal' (£12.59 inc p&p) sack lasts about 2-3 months (at 1-2 bowls a day), depending on the appetite of your dog. You can also get it in 2kg and 10kg sizes and in tins (min order 24 cans). They sell puppy, gerbil, rabbit and hamster food. You can buy it in smaller amounts from certain pet shops in London listed below:

■ **Jerrard PCW,** *41 Granviller Arcade, SW9 (274 8006).*

■ **Norwoods Pet Store,** *4 Norwood High St, SE27 (670 5160).*

■ **Broadway Pet Stores,** *6 Muswell Hill, Broadway, NW10 (883 3200).*

■ **Barnes Health Food,** *60 Barnes High St, SW13 (876 5476).*

If you do wish your dog to eat a vegan/vegetarian diet, it is advisable to feed it on **Happidog** or other dried 'complete meal' vegetarian dog food.

Cat Food

The only alternative to meat for cats is 'Vegecat'. It comes in a jar and one teaspoon is added to each cat meal of vegetarian leftovers. One jar costs £5.95 and it provides 30 days supply. It provides all the minerals and vitamins needed by a cat that is fed on a meat free diet. Don't use it with kittens. Vegecat is available by mail order from **Wholesome Trucking,** (see p60). Postage free.

▼ FREE/CHEAP HEALTH CARE ▼

If you are unemployed or on a low wage and are on state benefits, there are hospitals which will give emergency treatments for your sick animal. For non-emergency treatment there is a waiting list. They don't do free vaccinations. They are set up as charities and rely on donations to survive, so they will ask you to give something if you can. The three main organisations are the PDSA, RSPCA (they charge a small amount) and the Blue Cross. They are dotted all over London, so it's best either to ring or just go to your local branch.

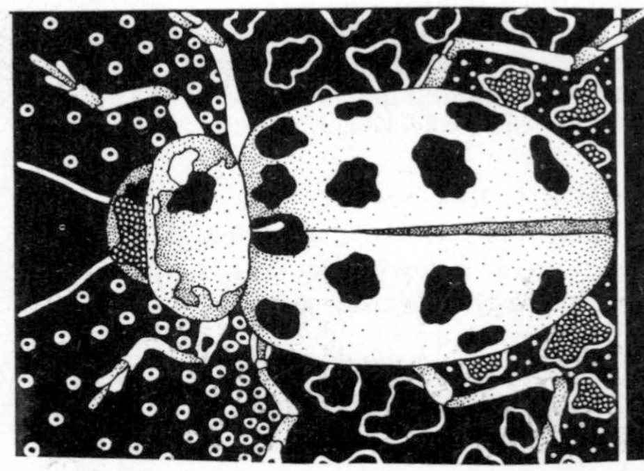

PDSA branches are: *4 Church Terrace, NW4 (203 2090) ; 184 High Rd, NW10 (459 3342, emergency 203 2090) ; 154 St. James Rd, SE1 (237 1206, emergency 686 3972) 2-6 Basildon Rd, SE2 (310 4822) ; 233-235 Lewisham Way, SE4 (691 0577) ; 198 Tulse Hill, SW2 (674 9388, emergency 686 3972) ; 170-172 Merton Rd, SW19 (542 1923) ; 2a Holly Rd, W4 (994 4055, emergency 203 2090)*

RSPCA clinics: *45 Bramley Rd, W10 (969 5836) ; 10 Cambridge Av, NW6 (624 4610) ; 1 Camberwell Station Rd, SE5 (274 6995) ; 79 Church St, N9 (807 3807) ; 48 Uxbridge Rd, W7 (567 1839) ;They have two hospitals: 6 Clarendon Drive, SW15 (789 8252) ; Sir Harold Harmsworth Memorial, Sonderburg Rd, N7 (272 6214).* Their emergency services are For London, North of the Thames, *(272 6214)*, London, South of the Thames, *(789 8252)*.

Blue Cross Branches are: *Argyle Pl, King St, W6 (748 5150) ; 483 Merton Rd, Southfields, SW18 (874 7310).*

▼ GETTING A PET ▼

If you lose your dog or if you wish to purchase a stray dog then contact **Battersea Dogs Home,** *4 Battersea Pk Rd, SW8 (622 3626).* They take in stray dogs, mostly from police stations. They keep them for 7 days for owners to pick them up. On the eight day the dogs are for sale. If you want to see if your dog has been taken there go Sun 2-4. If you wish to buy then go Mon-Sat 10.30-4.15. It costs £25-50 to buy and this includes vaccinations. They do take in a few cats.

▼ CATS ▼

■ **Cats Protection League,** *(... 6009)* will be able to provide you with a cat. No charge, but donation welcome. They will try to get the cat vaccinated and neutered before rehoming. Memb £5 pa. incl *The Cat* bi-monthly mag.

▼ FINDING A HOME FOR YOUR PET ▼

If you cannot look after your pet any more, you will need to find a home for it. The best way is to to find a friend or acquaintance who would be willing to look after it. If you take it to the RSPCA or the PDSA they will destroy it after a short period if no home can be found, so beware. Some organisations have been known to advertise free homes for pets only to use them for vivisection, so it's a good idea to check out the home first. You could advertise in the local papers or shop windows, but be sure to check out the home first by visiting it.

If it's a pedigree then, for dogs at least there are individual welfare homes for different breeds (look in *Exchange and Mart* for someone who breeds your type of dog and ring them, they may know). The **Cats Protection League** (see above) will do their best to find a home for your cat (they inspect the homes beforehand).

▼ PET DEATH ▼

You can dig a hole and bury your pet in the garden (if you're lucky enough to have one). The hole should be at least three feet deep. Do not wrap your pet in plastic or anything that is not bio-degradable.

Both the **PDSA** and the **RSPCA** will cremate your pet for free, if you can get it to one of their branches.

GETTING IN, OUT & AROUND: People From Abroad, Travel, Getting Around

people from abroad

this chapter is for all of you who have come, or are planning to come, from abroad to visit, work, study or settle. The rules are tricky and it's best to know what you'll be up against when you come. This section tells you about immigration rules, what to do if you're refused entry, where to go to find accommodation, work and lots more.*

▼ ACCOMMODATION ▼

Short Term accommodation

■ **London Tourist Information Centre,** *Victoria Station Forecourt, SW1 (730 3488 automatic queuing system).* Open daily 9am-7pm (8.30 in summer). Can tell you about budget hotels (from £14 per person a night sharing), budget hostels (from 10 sharing) and halls of residence (from £10). Send written enquiries to the head office at least 6 weeks in advance. Also have an info centre at Heathrow Underground Station terminal 1, 2 & 3 open 9am-6pm.

HOSTELS

■ **London Hostels Association (LHA),** *54 Eccleston Sq, SW1 (828 3263).* Have 11 hostels around town, B & B, full board and self catering from £38 a week for a double room.

■ **YHA Youth Hostels,** *London Headquarters 14 Southampton St, WC2 (836 8541).* (See p### **Escape** section). You have to be a member and can only stay 4 nights running (adults £7 a night + membership). They have 7 hostels in town. Contact HQ for advanced booking (always full in summer) and membership. Take a sleeping bag. You can also join at the hostels themselves.

■ **YWCA Accommodation and Advisory Service,** *16-22 Great Russell St, WC1 (580 4827).* (Young Men/Women's Christian Associations). Have several hostels - some very central (and expensive), all pretty comfortable. Most are for long stays and heavily booked in the summer. See phone book for addresses.

■ **Lee Abbey Students Club,** *26 Courtfield Gdns, SW5 (373 7286)* 3 months minimum stay.

■ **Dynamic Hotels Ltd,** *49 Princes Sq, W2 (727 5437).* Have four hotels, prices from £8.50 a night in a 6 bed dorm, including breakfast.

■ **Howard Hotel** *64-65 Princes Sq W2, 727 6062.*

■ **Hillbrow Hotel** *48-49 Princes Sq, W2, 229 6305.*

■ **Palace Court Hotel** *12-14 Pembridge Sq, W2.*

■ **Florida Hotel** *23 Argyle Sq, WC1 837 6543.*

■ **Astor Hotel,** *45 Queensborough Terrace , W2 (402 6735).* From £7.50 B & B. Have other branches around London as well.

EVEN CHEAPER

■ **Tent City,** *Old Oak Common Lane East Acton, W3 (743 5708).* Open 24 hrs, 22nd May-3rd Oct. £4 a night. Bunk beds in 14 large tents, women's, men's and mixed (bring sleeping bag or borrow bedding). Showers, toilets and snack bar. Just turn up.

■ **Tonbridge Club,** *120 Cromer St, WC1 (837 4406).* Women's and men's dorms. £2 a night. Book a few days ahead.

■ **Portobello Project,** *49/51 Porchester Rd, W2 (221 4413).* (See p213). Don't do accommodation but can supply you with lists and ideas.

■ **Basement Project,** *227 Earls Court Rd, SW5 (373 2335).* Have lists of cheap accommodation in their area.

CAMPING

For a full list of camp sites in or around London phone the **Tourist Board** (above). Some of the ones closest to central London (they're usually quite far out) are:

■ **Hackney Camping,** *Millfields Rd, E5 (985 7656).* June 18-Aug 25. £2 per night per person kids half price (under 5 free). Book ahead for August.

■ **Crystal Palace Camp Site,** *Crystal Palace Parade, SE19 (778 7155).* More expensive (£3.10). Open all year. Max stay 14 days, 7 days peak period.

■ **Lee Valley Regional Pk,** *Eastway Cycle Circuit, Temple Mills Lane, E15 (534 6085).* April-Oct £2.50 per night (£1.20 for kids) Book in advance.

■ **Lee Valley Pk,** *Picketts Lock Centre, Picketts Lock Ln, N9 (803 4756).* All year. No need to book. £2.50 per tent.

FREE

If you're feeling brave or desperate you could try one of the many parks in London. Don't take any valuables with you, leave as much as you can at a left-luggage office at any railway station. It is illegal so using a tent is out. *Hampstead Heath* has many places to hide away, it's regularly patrolled by the police but they often have more exciting things to do than hassle you and, besides, the Heath on a summer's night is often as busy as in the day. More central; *Russel Park* and *Bloomsbury Park* are said to be good places and *Hyde Park* and *Kensington Gardens* are big enough to be missed by the patrols. *Victoria Park* in east London is easy to get into after closing but it's quite open and not easy to hide away there.

There is what amounts to a virtual city of long-term dossers, young and old, near the entrance to the new **Museum of The Moving Image** at the South Bank, free soup and tea provided (see p58 **Food** section). Or you can find a large cardboard box and join the estimated 60,000 other people who sleep out where they can in London every night. Beware! London changes character at night, muggers abound, trust is a forgotten word and only the tough or blessed survive unscathed. Not an option for the sane.

Tube stations are out, they close around midnight, you'd be thrown out and the seats are too uncomfortable to sit on for more than ten minutes let alone have a good sleep on. Railway stations are patrolled by British Rail Police who will throw you out if you haven't got a ticket.

HOTELS FOR FREE

For those with nerve and acting ability you could try going to a hotel (leave your luggage elsewhere) looking as smart as you can and head for a toilet or bathroom. Lock yourself in for the night and ignore any angry pounding on the door or say your ill. If you're lucky you'll be left alone to get a good sleep and wake up to a bath in the morning.

Long Term Accommodation

If you want to stay for more than a few weeks you could consider renting a flat or a bedsit; it won't necessarily be any cheaper than a hotel (from £45 a week per person) but at least you're free to come and go as you please. Loads of ads in free mags (handed out at most tube stations) and newsagents. You'll need enough money for a deposit and usually one months rent in advance (see **Somewhere to Live** p2).

If you have a valid student ID card, **The University of London Accommodation Office,** *University of London Union 1 Malet St, WC1 (636 2818)* can help you find accommodation between terms; Summer, Christmas and Easter. You have to go in person with your ID card, no appointments. Or contact **Project Tours International,** *67 Wigmore St, W1 (935 9979/637 3250).* Family houses, self catering, B & B from £45 for a single room. Student or not, you can phone or write to individual universities and colleges to see if there is room in their student halls or contact London Tourist Boardabove. It usually costs around £10-£14 (sometimes cheaper). Although it's best to book a few months in advance they're worth trying if you're stuck for somewhere to stay as they often have short notice vacancies.

▼ GETTING INTO ▼ THE COUNTRY

Anyone coming here is subject to the *customs laws* and there are certain things that you must not bring in to the country. If you think you don't have to pay duty on anything you're bringing in, go through the green 'nothing to declare' channel. Customs officers have the right to search your luggage. If you are found bringing in drugs, you will probably be arrested and refused entry to the country (but you will still have to appear in court charged with this offence and can be sent to prison here before being sent back).

■ **Release,** *169 Commercial St , EC1 (603 8654 (24 Hrs))* (see also **Law** section p194). Office 10-6 Mon-Fri. Release offer a confidential advice, info, referral and counselling service to drug users. Will refer people onto specialist groups/agencies if necessary.

You will also have to see an *immigration officer* who decides whether you are subject to immigration control or not, and, if you are, whether you qualify to enter. The immigration laws in force now are the *1971* and the *1988 Immigration Acts,* and there are detailed Immigration Rules which explain how the law is to be interpreted; the current rules are called *HC 388,* published on 14 June 1989. In order to get in, you have to satisfy the immigration officer that you qualify, in whatever category of the rules you are trying to enter. Immigration officers and their treatment of people vary, and it is, in general, harder for black people to satisfy them that they qualify to enter than for white people.

If you are not subject to full immigration control

A British citizen is not subject to British immigration control and can come here at any time. A Commonwealth citizen who had a parent born in Britain, or who is a woman who married a British man before 1983, is also not subject to immigration control, but must get a *certificate of entitlement to the right of abode* from a British high commission overseas, before coming here. A Commonwealth citizen who had a grandparent born here can get permission to come to stay here permanently by proving, through all the birth and marriage certificates, their legitimate descent from a British-born grandparent.

Citizens of European Community (EC) countries are free to travel within EC countries to work (or look for it) or to set up in business or self-employment, or to provide or receive services. This covers almost anything that you can think of doing. You'll be given a piece of paper by immigration officials to say that you have six months in which to establish yourself in one of these ways and then you're supposed to apply to the Home Office for a residence permit, but this is not necessary; you can just stay here. EC countries are Denmark, Holland, Belgium, Luxembourg, Ireland, France, Federal Republic of Germany, Italy, Greece, Spain and Portugal. Spanish and Portuguese citizens are not yet free to come to work here until 1993.

If you are subject to full immigration control

If you intend to stay permanently or to work here you need to get permission from a British embassy or high commission abroad before you come. This is called *entry clearance.* So does anyone who is a *visa national* who is coming here for any purpose whatsoever, including just a visit. The countries whose citizens need visas are being added to all the time - they include all Eastern European countries, most non-Commonwealth Asian and African countries, India, Pakistan, Bangladesh, Nigeria, Ghana and Turkey. Visa nationals who come here without a visa will be sent straight back, so you must find out in advance if you are a visa national. The rules for qualifying to get in are the same whether you are applying at a British post overseas or at the airport here but immigration officials tend to be more thorough abroad.

■ **Joint Council for the Welfare of Immigrants,** *115 Old Street, EC1V 9JR (251 8706).* Independent non-government organisation working against racism and injustice in British immigration and nationality law. Advises individuals and organisations about immigration and nationality law problems, lobbies for change in the law, provides information and trains other advice workers.

■ **UK Immigrants Advisory Service,** *County House, 190 Great Dover Street, SE1 4YB (357 6917 Refugee unit 357 7421).* Advises and represents people with immigration problems, specialising in representing immigration appeals. The Refugee Unit deals specifically with refugees and asylum-seekers.

■ **Migrant Services Unit,** *London Voluntary Service Council, 68 Chalton St, NW1 (388 0241).* Has information about migrants' issues and works closely with migrants' organisations on issues around housing, employment and education. Can give advice to individuals or refer you on. Will be moving early in 1990, contact above number for details.

■ **West London Migrants Unit,** *441 Harrow Road, W10 4RE (960 5746).* Produces information for and works closely with migrant community organisations in West London.

■ **Runnymede Trust,** *11 Princelet St, London, E1 6QH (375 1496).* Is a research organisation on immigration and race relations and has an extensive library.

■ **International Social Service,** *Cranmer Hse, 39 Brixton Rd, SW9 (735 8941).* Gives confidential advice on immigration and emigration problems and repatriation.

▼ COMING TO VISIT ▼

Visitors have to convince the immigration officers that they are:
• coming just for a visit
• for a definite length of time
• that they intend to leave at the end of their visit
and
• that they have the money to live on for the time of their visit without needing to work or to claim benefits here.

It helps to have a return ticket (this can always be cashed in later) and to have enough money to cover the time you want to stay (but not too much, or they may be suspicious that you want to stay longer). If you are going to be supported by friends or relatives, it will help if you have an invitation letter from them and proof that they have the money to support you. The immigration officers may contact them to be sure that the letter is genuine. If you have a definite reason to return home it will help if you have a letter from your employer or college saying when you have to be back.

Visitors are almost always allowed in for six months, even if you say you only want to stay for two weeks. Your passport will be stamped with this time limit and with *employment prohibited* - this means what it says and *any* work that a visitor does is illegal. (Business people are allowed to do business on their visits). A visitor cannot get an extension to a six months visa (the immigration rules won't allow it). People who are not visa nationals may be able to stay on longer as students. Visa nationals cannot change their status in this way and you would have to leave the country and come back again with a new visas as a student.

▼ COMING TO STUDY ▼

Formalities

It is very important to say at the outset to the immigration official that you want to come here to study, even if you have not yet made definite plans or got a college place (see **Staying Here Longer** p125). Students have to prove to immigration officials that they are coming to follow a *full-time* course of study, which means at least 15 hours daytime classes per week and that they:

- have enough money to pay their fees
- have enough money to live here without needing to work or to claim benefits

and

- that they intend to leave the UK at the end of their studies.

You must have a letter from the college where you have been accepted, to confirm the course that you will be doing, and have proof that you have the money to do this. If your country has strict foreign exchange controls, it's important to have made proper arrangements for money to be sent to you here, or to have definite proof that friends or relatives here are both able and willing to support you while you study. Fees for overseas students at recognised and government colleges are very high. Some independent colleges may charge lower fees but may not provide any genuine education - BEWARE! If immigration officers do not believe that you want to leave the UK at the end of your studies - for example, if most of your family already lives here, or if you are studying a subject they do not think you will be able to use in your home country, you can be refused entry.

If you are allowed in, it is usually for the length of the course, or a year, whichever is shorter. You will also be restricted from working; your passport stamp will probably say, 'given leave to enter the UK on condition that the holder does not enter or change employment without the consent of the Secretary of State for Employment, or engage in any business or profession without the consent of the Secretary of State for the Home Department is hereby given for/until ..... (date). This means that you cannot do any work unless your employer first gets a work permit for you (see p124). Working without a permit, even a couple of hours at a weekend, is illegal and could be dangerous.

Scholarships and Grants

To find out about scholarships and grants available from the British government and various charities contact:

■ **Association of Commonwealth Universities,** *36 Gordon Sq, WC1H OPF (387 8572).* Publish *Financial Aid for First Degree Study at Commonwealth Universities* (£3.50) and *Scholarships Guide for Commonwealth Postgraduate Students* (£13.50).

For scholarships and bursaries from the British Council ask at any BC office. And try **Christian Aid,** *PO Box 100, SE1 7RT (620 4444)* who can help with info and also offer some scholarships to foreign nationals (esp African and Asian) who intend to go back to work in their own countries.

■ **World University Service,** *20 Compton Terr, N1 2UN (226 6747).* Give grants to refugees.

The Africa Educational Trust p129 give help mainly to South Africans.

■ **ILEA, (Inner London Education Authority)** *Information Office, County Hall, SE1 (Grants dept 633 6325/633 7864).*

■ **Regional Advisory Council for Technological Education,** *Tavistock Hse South, Tavistock Sq, WC1 (388 0027). A Compendium of Advanced Courses in Colleges of Further and Higher Education* £4.40.

■ **UCCA (Universities Central Council for Admissions),** *PO Box 28, Cheltenham, Glos GL50 1HY, (0242 222444).*

▼ LEARNING ENGLISH ▼

Studying English in London can be exciting and rewarding. But, watch out, it can also be isolating, frustrating and more expensive than it's worth. If you come to a school to learn you might find that you spend most of your time speaking your own language to people from your own country. It takes effort and confidence to go out and meet the English speakers that you need to befriend if your time here is going to be worthwhile. And then you'll probably find that they speak a very different English to the one taught in school. The best way to learn is to immerse yourself in the language as much as possible; get a job, live with English-speaking people, go to British films, read the papers. Be patient too. Some people tend to assume that the best way to help a foreigner understand English is to speak loudly.

If you decide to go ahead and find a school you can get *Learning English,* a list of all government courses and most private schools or colleges from **BTC (British Tourist Centre),** *12 Regents St, SW1Y OBW (730 3400).*

Private Schools

Language schools, like tourists, tend to pop up in the summer and be few and far between at other times. Those that stay open all the year round will be more likely to have a more serious attitude to study. The summer schools mostly cater for young, school age students who, more often than not, are here for a good time. Learning English is not usually high on their list of priorities. Don't hesitate to question the school before you decide whether or not to study there. Take a note of: qualifications and experience of their teachers, size of classes, methods used and past results and whether they teach specialist English (e.g. technical or business English). A string of letters after a name may look impressive but it might not mean much. Here's a guide to some of the most common:

■ **ARELS (Association of Recognised English Language Schools),** *2 Pontypool Place Valentine Place , SE1 8QF (242 3136).*

■ **FELCO (Federation of English Language Course Organisations).** Both have their own inspectors to check on standards in member schools. Their schools are generally considered to be the most reliable.

■ **FIYTO (Federation of Youth Travel Organisations).** This is mainly concerned with travel so membership does not imply any educational status.

■ **BC British Council** (it will usually say 'recognised as efficient by the BC').

Accommodation

Check that your school will arrange accommodation for you - finding a place to stay in London can be a nightmare. Most schools will be able to find you a place with a British family, which is an important part of the learning process, as well as an ideal way to discover what the British are like when not on public view.

A few schools we can recommend are:

■ **Marble Arch Intensive English,** *21 Star St, W2 (402 9273).* Has a good reputation with free places for sponsored political refugees, good facilities, courses at all levels and a friendly atmosphere.

■ **International House,** *106 Piccadilly, W1V 9FL (491 2598).* Also run training courses for TEFL (Teachers of English as a Foreign Language).

■ **Davies School of English,** *56 Eccleston Sq, SW1 (834 4155).*

■ **European Language and Educational Centre,** *36 Honor Oak Rd Forest Hill, SE23 3SN (699 1174).*

Government Courses

You can find various courses in all areas of London run by the ILEA (Inner London Education Authority). They cover English language, customs, history etc. They are very good value, even cheaper if you're from an EEC country, and daytime courses are free to under 18s.

The teaching standards are good though the classes are often large and in cold, old Victorian buildings and you'll have to find your own accommodation. However, you'll be more likely to meet English speaking students there and enjoy facilities such as a students union, and a subsidised cafe and/or bar.

■ **ILEA Information** (see p226), do a free booklet *English Classes for Students from Abroad.* After April 1st 1990 the ILEA will no longer exist but the classes should continue under local education authorities. Find out from the town hall in your area.

■ **The University of London Dept. of Extra-Mural Studies,** *26 Russell Sq, WC1 (636 8000).* Runs two summer schools in English. Accommodation included. You need to book Jan-March.

Other courses

■ **Floodlight,** *Room 77, County Hall, SE1 7PB (633 1066)* (£1) from newsagents gives info on all part-time (day and evening) courses run by local education authorities. You can take a course in anything from Tai Chi to politics, flower arranging to rock climbing.

■ **BTA,** *64 St James' St, SW1 1NF (730 3400)* do a free booklet on *Special Interest Holidays* covering the whole of the country.

■ See also *Young Visitors to Britain* (see p125 **Central Bureau**).

Student Cards

If you are in full time education you can apply for an International Students Card from **NUS,** *461 Holloway Rd, N7 6LJ (272 8900).* You will also receive a discount card which will entitle you to all sorts of discounts - on consumer goods and services, restaurants, theatres and travel - most are listed in the free *Discount Handbook* that comes with the card. **London Student Travel,** *52 Grosvenor Gdns , SW1 (730 3402)* supply the *ISIC (International Student Identity Card)* which can give reductions for travel. Take a passport size photo, and proof that you're a student. Also do a card for non-students under 26. Both £4.

▼ COMING TO WORK ▼

(See also **Jobs** Section p36).
It is extremely difficult to come to settle down here in a permanent job. In order to do this your employer has to get a *work permit* for you before you arrive. She has to show that she cannot find anyone else who is already allowed to work here to do the job instead, and that your experience and qualifications and skills are exactly what are needed. Permits are only given for highly skilled professional jobs and for top-level management transfers within multinational companies.

A small number of specialised jobs do not need work permits. These include missionaries, ministers of religion, monks and nuns, representatives of overseas newspapers, private servants of diplomats and people working for overseas governments. These people must get permission from a British post abroad before travelling.

It may be possible to come to work here temporarily in several ways:

- as an *au pair,*
- as a *working holidaymaker*. This is a provision designed for young Australians and New Zealanders 'doing Europe'; the rules define them as young Commonwealth citizens, between the ages of 17 and 27, with no dependants, who are coming for a holiday but want to do some work incidental to their holiday. You have to show that you have some money, so that you won't need to claim benefits if you can't find a job, and you must appear to be on holiday but may want to to take part-time (or short-term) work occasionally. Two years is the maximum time you can be here as a working holidaymaker. If you are black, you will have more difficulty in convincing immigration officials that you want to be here mainly for a holiday, rather than work.
- for a *work camp*. Some agricultural work camps are able to bring in people from abroad to work for a specified (short) time at the camp. The workers are not allowed to remain here after the camp is over, will never be allowed to stay after 30th November and are not allowed to do any other work.
- as a *trainee* in order to get practical experience in a subject that you have been studying academically, either here or abroad. Your employer needs to get a trainee work permit for you, and show how the experience and training on offer will be helpful to you, and confirm that you intend to leave Britain after your training.
- as a *language assistant* at a school. This has to be as part of an approved scheme for language teaching and two years is the maximum time a person can stay.

■ **BUNAC** , *232 Vauxhall Br Rd, SW1 (630 0344)* organise student exchanges between UK & US.

Au Pairs

By law an au pair must be a single woman (or 'girl' according to the Immigration Authorities) between the ages of 17-27 from a western European country including Malta, Cyprus and Turkey. You can't be an au pair for longer than two years and it's difficult to get a placement for less than 6 months. If you're a man you can be an au pair in other countries but not in Britain, though that may change in 1992.

It can be an excellent way of practising your English and learning about the British way of life. You live as part of a family and help out with light chores and the kids (it helps if you like children and animals). Conditions vary from family to family but officially you should only work for up to 5 hours a day with at least one day off a week and time to attend language classes and 'religious services'. You should be given your own room and get between £18-£25 a week pocket money. Make sure you find out exactly what the conditions will be and what you'll be expected to do before you come or you might have a nasty surprise.

A *demi-pair* is not half an au pair but one who pays the family (about £12 a week) instead of being paid by them but who works less (2 hours a day).

You can find ads for au pairs in *The Lady* magazine and in *The International Herald Tribune* or go through one of the agencies below.

■ **International Catholic Society for Girls (ACISJF),** *St Patrick's International Youth Centre 24 Great Chapel St, W1V 3AF (734 2156).* They mainly offer advice but they can also help out with finding a family. They don't charge and you don't have to be a catholic. They publish a leaflet telling you your rights as an au pair, if you have any problems you can go to them for help.

■ **At Your Service Agency,** *32 Manor Hall Ave, NW4 (203 6885/6862).*

■ **Jolaine Au Pair & Domestic Agency,** *18 Escot Way, Barnet, Hertfordshire, (449 1334).* They won't charge for finding a placement, the families pay.

Beware of agencies that charge a fee. Agencies open up and disappear frequently the ones above have been going a long time and have a good reputation. Don't answer ads in newsagents for an au pair wanted, they're more likely to be men advertising for sex.You can get a leaflet (RON 2(AP)) with info about au pairs from the **Home Office Immigration & Nationality Dept** (p126). (See p121 for Immigration regulations).

Work Camps

See **Jobs** p56 for voluntary work where you'll get food and accommodation, a lot of hard work and fun. With increased mechanisation on farms there are fewer casual jobs available and, what there are,are usually only for a very short period of time. A useful publication which gives details of work camps is *Young Visitors to Britain* (£2.45) see **Central Bureau** below. Or you could try **International Farm Camp**, *Hall Rd Tiptree Colchester Essex, (0621 815496)*. For exhausting, low paid work on their farm. You get about £15 a day usually for fruit picking.

Where to go to find a job.

■ **Angel International Recruitment,** *50 Fleet St, EC4Y 1BE (583 1555 (catering) 583 1661 (office/ nursing))*.

■ **London Hostels Association,** *54 Eccleston Sq, SW1 (834 1545)* residential domestic work.

■ **HF Holidays,** *142 Great North Way, NW4 (0768 67658)*. Provides staff for guest houses (vacancies rare).

■ **Central Bureau for Educational Visits & Exchanges,** *Seymour Mews Hse, Seymour Mews, W1H 9PE (486 5101)*. appoints around 3,000 foreign language assistants to schools in Britain. The jobs are mainly for European students and 'young teachers of English'. You take small conversation classes for approx 12 hours a week. You have to work for a full school year (Sept-July) for about £3,510. Apply to the Education Ministry in your own country - further details from the Bureau. Publish *Young Visitors to Britain* (£2.45 incl, £2.95 Europe, £4.50 the world), a guide to work, study and leisure, which also includes info on welfare.

▼ POLITICAL ASYLUM ▼

The UK is not known for its generosity in granting people asylum. To qualify, you have to show that you have a well-founded fear of persecution in your own country, for reasons of race, religion, nationality or because you belong a certain social group or hold a particular political opinion. If you need asylum here, ask for it immediately and get advice from one of the refugee agencies listed below. Get help as soon as possible. Immigration officers may try to send you back quickly without properly considering your case.

■ **Refugee Arrivals Project,** *Room 205, 2nd floor, Queen's Building, Heathrow Airport, Hounslow, Middx, TW6 1DL, (759 5740/1)*. Advises refugees who arrive at the airport and who have difficulties about being refused entry, accommodation etc.

■ **Refugee Forum,** *54 Tavistock Place, WC1 (482 3829)*. Is a refugee self-help organisation, with many branches throughout the UK and other countries in Europe.

■ **World University Service (WUS),** *20-21 Compton Terrace, N1 2UN (226 6747)*. Gives support and advice on education for refugees as well as running education projects abroad.

■ **British Refugee Council,** *2nd Floor, Bondway Hse, 3-9 Bondway, Vauxhall, SW8 1SJ (582 6922)*.

■ **Amnesty International,** *(278 6000)* give advice and help to refugees.

▼ COMING FOR MARRIAGE ▼

You have get permission in advance from a British post overseas. You'll have to prove that:

- you and your partner have met
- there is a genuine relationship between you
- you intend to stay together permanently as husband and wife
- you did not get married to come here and
- that you and your husband/wife will be able to support and house yourselves without claiming benefit.

These rules are operated very toughly for men coming from the countries of the Indian subcontinent and increasingly so for women from Far Eastern countries like the Philippines and Thailand, but there are rarely problems for people from other countries. If you are allowed in as a fiance(e) it is only for six months and you are forbidden to work. After marriage (or if you are already married) you are allowed in for a year, with no restrictions on working.

▼ STAYING HERE LONGER ▼

If you are not a Commonwealth or an EC citizen and if you are allowed to stay for more than 6 months, you can also be required to register with the police. This means going to the **Aliens Registration Office,** *10 Lamb's Conduit St, WC1 (725 2451)*. (Open 9-4.45). (If you're outside London go to a local Police station) and telling them details about your name, address, occupation, nationality and marital status and paying them £25 to write this in a little green book which they give you. You are supposed to tell the police of any change in these particulars within one week. It is rare for them to check up on this though, unless the police are trying to get you for something else and have failed.

If you are refused entry at the airport you have the right to appeal against this. If you had obtained entry clearance in advance, you can stay in Britain while your appeal is going on, so you may get the holiday you had planned anyway. If you did not have entry clearance in advance, you can only appeal after you have gone back. You fill in the appeal forms that the immigration officers gave you and post them back to the airport. You will hear about the appeal several months later.

Citizens Advice Bureaux are general advice centres, which can advise on most things, or can refer you to other organisations. They are not just for British citizens, but for anybody who wants advice or information. Look in the telephone book under 'Citizens Advice Bureau' to find the nearest one.

Law Centres are set up in order to provide more detailed legal advice and representation for people who could not afford to pay for a lawyer. See Law p194 or contact the **Law Centres Federation,** *Duchess House, 18-19 Warren St, W1P 5DB (387 8570)* to find out if there is one in your area.

Extending Your Stay

If you want to extend your stay, or if you want to change the conditions of your stay, you have to apply to the **Home Office, Immigration and Nationality Dept,** *Lunar House, Wellesley Rd, Croydon CR9 2BY, (686 0688)* to do so. You *must* apply *before* the date stamped on your passport runs out, but not too soon, as the Home Office will not consider an application for an extension when you have more than two months permission left. Get advice before applying to the Home Office, as the staff there are not employed to help you but to implement the immigration law!

The rules say that six months is the longest time you can stay as a visitor. If you need to stay a bit longer it is best to write to the Home Office. They are very slow and very busy and you may not get a reply by the time you want to leave. If there are special reasons for staying longer, e.g. you are too ill to travel or you need to look after a friend or relative who is ill, it is possible for an exception to be made, but usually applications from visitors are refused.

If you are not a visa national, you can apply to stay longer in order to study. You have to show that:

- you have been accepted for a full-time course of study
- you have the money to pay for this and to live here without needing to work or to claim benefit

and

- you will leave at the end of your studies.

Visa nationals cannot switch from being visitors to students. Even for others, it can be risky - the Home Office may ask you whether you had considered studying here before you came and if you had, they may treat you as an *illegal entrant* - someone who did not tell the truth to immigration officers on arrival and who therefore got in to the country under false pretences - and they can be arrest and detain you and send you back. Make sure that you can explain how you changed your plans after your arrival here and that you did genuinely come as a visitor.

If you get married to someone allowed to stay here you can apply to stay with them. This is generally easier than if you are applying from abroad to come to join him/her - provided that it is a relationship that started, or became serious, after you came here. You also have to show all the same things that a person from abroad has to show on marriage (see p125).

If you came here as a visitor or student you will not be allowed to stay on longer to work, because you have to get permission for this outside the country. The only exception to this is people who have studied nursing here and who want to stay on to work as nurses; the hospital that wants to employ them can apply for work permits for them while they are still here.

If it is no longer safe for you to return to your country of origin, you can apply for asylum here. You should write to the Home Office to explain your situation, as fully as possible, and ask them to give you asylum. Get advice from a specialist organisation before making your application. While this application is pending, you are entitled to claim Income Support at the Urgent Cases rate, and if you wait for more than six months without getting a decision from the Home Office, you can get permission to work.

If you are refused permission to stay

As long as you applied to the Home Office before your permission to stay ran out, you have the right to appeal against any refusal. Any appeal has to reach the Home Office within 14 days of their decision - if you don't get the decision in time to appeal because they don't know your address, that is your fault and you have lost your right to appeal. The Home Office will send you a form and you can stay here and are allowed to work while the appeal is pending.

If you applied to the Home Office late, after your permission ran out, you have no right to appeal and will be told to leave the country immediately if your application is refused. If you feel you have good grounds for doing so, it is always possible to continue an argument with the Home Office, urging them to change their minds and allow you to stay, but you are illegally in the country while all this is going on.

Being Thrown Out

There are several ways the Home Office can get rid of you. If you have stayed longer than you were allowed, or have broken another condition on your stay, for example by working without a permit, you can be *deported*. This can be done by the Home Office making its own administrative decision to deport you, and you have the right to appeal against this. However, if you have been in the UK for less than seven years, the only grounds of your appeal can be either that the Home Office has got its facts wrong and you did not really overstay or work, or that you are a refugee. You cannot argue any other reasons why you should not be deported, like having family here, or being in the middle of a course of studies.

You can also be arrested and charged with the criminal offence of breaking the conditions of your stay. If you are found guilty, as well as any other sentence, the court can recommend that you be deported and the Home Office then considers whether to carry out this recommendation. If they do there is no further appeal, apart from the normal one against sentence (see **Law** section p194) but you can appeal against the destination of your deportation. It is up to you to prove that another country will allow you to go there instead.

If the Home Office believes that you entered the country illegally then they can just send you away, without having to go through any court or appeal process - this is called *removal* and can be done very quickly and easily. Often a person is interviewed by immigration officers and is forced into saying something that makes them suspect they didn't tell the truth on arrival. Therefore that person entered by deception.

▼ BRITISH NATIONALITY LAW ▼

British nationality law is now the *1981 British Nationality Act*, which has been in force since 1 January 1983. It changed the way in which people are born British, altered the names of British nationals with different rights and made provisions for how people can become British in future.

PEOPLE BORN BEFORE 1983

Anyone born in Britain before 1983 is automatically a British citizen. The only exception to this is people whose fathers were overseas diplomats here at the time of their birth. People born abroad before 1983 whose father was born or adopted in Britain, or who had become British in Britain, and who was married to their mother, are automatically British citizens through descent from their father.

PEOPLE BORN FROM 1 JANUARY 1983 ONWARDS

People born in Britain from 1983 onwards are only automatically British citizens if either of their parents were either British citizens or settled (allowed to stay permanently) in Britain at the time of their birth. So children born here to overseas students, or to visitors, or to work permit holders, are not automatically British. People born abroad from 1983 onwards, whose mother or father was born or adopted in Britain, or who became British in Britain, are automatically British by descent from either parent. If the parents are not married, only the mother's status counts.

▼ BECOMING BRITISH ▼

Adults (people over 18) can apply for *naturalisation* to become British citizens. People who are married to British citizens qualify for naturalisation if:
• they are allowed to stay here permanently (have lived here for at least 3 years without being out of the country for more than 270 days in that period, and not more than 90 days in the year before applying)
• they intend to continue to live in Britain and
• are of good character.
The fee is £60.
Other adults can apply if they:
• have been allowed to stay here permanently for at least a year,
• have lived here legally for at least five years altogether, without being out of the country for more than 450 days, not more than 90 of those days in the year immediately before applying,
• are of good character,

- intend to continue living in Britain

and

- have a sufficient knowledge of the English, Welsh or Gaelic language.

The fee for this is £170.
Parents of children who want them to become British can apply on their behalf; the fee for a child's application, which is called *registration*, is £60.

Other Kinds of British Nationals

British citizens have full rights to live in Britain and are not subject to immigration control. Other types of British nationals do not have any rights at all. This includes *British Dependent Territories* citizens from current British colonies, who only have any rights in connection with that colony. A new status, *British National (Overseas)* has been invented for people from Hong Kong after it returns to China, still giving them no right to come to Britain. *British Overseas* citizens are people from countries that used to be British colonies, who were not able to gain citizenship of their new countries under their independence laws - mainly people of Indian descent from East African countries and Malaysia. *British subjects* and *British protected persons* are also people from territories previously ruled by or under the protection of Britain, who could not gain a new citizenship on independence. The last three groups have no rights in any country because of their citizenship, but if they do manage to get into Britain, they cannot be deported because no other country can be forced to take them in.

Further Reading

Because immigration rules are altered frequently and because a lot also depends on the way the Home Office and the immigration authorities interpret the rules, it is impossible for any book to stay up-to-date for long. So it is often useful to contact one of the organisations above for advice, as well as reading this or any other book.
Immigration Law and Practice, by Lawrence Grant and Ian Martin, Cobden Trust, 1982, and *First Supplement, 1985.*
Immigration Law and Practice in the United Kingdom, by Ian Macdonald, Butterworths, 2nd edition, 1987.
Worlds Apart: Women under Immigration and Nationality Law, by the Women, Immigration and Nationality Group, 1985.
JCWIs (see p121) *Immigration Factsheets* - a series of 5 leaflets:
How to sponsor your husband, wife, fiance or fiancee to come to the UK.
How to sponsor your children to come to the UK.
How to sponsor someone wanting to visit the UK.
Useful addresses and telephone numbers.
How to sponsor dependent parents for settlement in the UK.
JCWI Bulletin - published quarterly.
British Nationality: the Action Group on Immigration and Nationality's Guide to the New Law, by Ann Dummett and Ian Martin, 2nd edition, 1984.

▼ USING THE NATIONAL ▼ HEALTH SERVICE

(See also p161 on NHS).
The National Health Service (NHS) is open to all people who are *ordinarily resident* in Britain. That means you have to be living here for a particular purpose, for example, working, or coming here to live with your husband. It is assumed that anyone who has been living here for more than a year, who is working here, or who is a student enroled for a course of at least six months is ordinarily resident. Otherwise there are also reciprocal arrangements with several countries which entitle people to free medical treatment, as long as the need arose during their time here. These countries are Anguilla, Australia, Austria, British Virgin Islands, Bulgaria, Czechoslovakia, Falkland Islands, Finland, German Democratic Republic, Gibraltar, Hong Kong, Hungary, Iceland, Malta, Montserrat, New Zealand, Norway, Poland, Romania, St Helena, Sweden, Turkey and Caicos Islands, USSR, Yugoslavia. Citizens of EC countries are also entitled to treatment.

The main groups of people who are not entitled to free NHS medical treatment are visitors from countries with which there is no reciprocal agreement, students on short courses and people who had been receiving treatment for a particular condition before coming here. They can be charged for any medical treatment they receive, except treatment for an immediate emergency in an Accident and Emergency or Casualty department of a hospital and treatment for a specific list of serious infectious diseases. There are centralised laid-down lists of charges and hospitals may demand a deposit before starting treatment, or may present bills weekly. Hospital treatment is very expensive - take out medical insurance before you come; it is very difficult to get it later.
If you need medical treatment, you can either go straight to a hospital casualty department if it is an emergency, or register with a local doctor (known as General Practitioners or GPs). You can get a list of local GPs from the local Family Practitioner Committee or

Community Health Council (See *Yellow Pages*) and then you get in touch with doctors to ask if they will take you on. If the doctor thinks you need more specialist treatment she will refer you to a hospital or another doctor. If you are entitled to use the NHS, this consultation and referral is free, but there are charges for any drugs the doctor prescribes for you and for dental treatment and eye checks.

■ **Emergency Private Dental Service,** *(452 7279).*

▼ CLAIMING WELFARE ▼ BENEFITS

The benefits system is very complicated and it is often worth getting advice from a local **Citizens Advice Bureau** or **Law Centre** (see p207) *before* claiming. In general, visitors are not entitled to claim any benefits as they had to show when they arrived that they had enough money not to need to claim. If you're a student you cannot usually claim benefits unless there has been some short-term emergency, for example delays in money being sent from home, then you can claim Income Support for up to six weeks. (See **Social Security** p47).

If you didn't have to prove that you could support and house yourself when you came into the country you can claim benefit at the Urgent Cases rate while you wait for a decision on your application for Income Support. So can people who are here because they are appealing against a Home Office decision. There are reciprocal agreements between Britain and Iceland, Malta, Norway, Sweden and Turkey so that if you come from one of these countries you can claim Income Support whatever your immigration status here. EC citizens can claim too, but you may receive threatening letters from the Home Office if you do. Although EC citizens cannot be forced to leave Britain for claiming benefits, you can be refused permission to come back in if immigration officers know you've been claiming.

▼ OTHER USEFUL ADDRESSES ▼

■ **The British Council (BC),** *10 Spring Gardens, SW1A 2BN (930 8466).* Funded by the government to promote 'a wider knowledge of Britain and the English Language and develop closer cultural relations between Britain and other countries'. It organises educational exchanges, scholarship programmes, English language teaching and more. They also have some literature for foreigners, including *How to Live in Britain* (though this is only available from foreign offices), which covers aspects of life in the UK, and has a comprehensive index of addresses.

■ **Central Bureau for Educational Visits & Exchanges,** *Seymour Mews Hse, Seymour Mews, W1 (486 5101).* Government-financed, it has info on educational visits (mainly short-term). Their *Young Visitors to Britain* (£2.45) is a good guide to English and other studies, special interest holidays, workcamps, paying guest visits and advice centres. Comes in most European languages. They also publish *Study Holidays* (£6.20 England, £7.00 Europe, £10.25 the world) many of these language courses include special interest and activity options such as sports, riding etc.

■ **National Union of Students,** *461 Holloway Rd, N7 6LJ (272 8900).*

■ **United Kingdom Council for Overseas Student Affairs (UKCOSA),** *60 Westbourne Grove, W2 (299 9268/9).* Advice on finances, immigration, visas etc. Casework service M-F 1-4.

■ **University of London Advisor to Overseas Students,** *Senate Hse, Malet St, WC1E 7HU (636 8000 Ext 3041).* For general advice.

■ **The Institute of Race Relations,** *2 Leeke St, WC1* has a large library and produces the journal *Race and Class.*

■ **International Students' House,** *229 Gt Portland St, W1 (631 3223).* Hostel accommodation (from £8 a night) also open to non-residents. Sport and study facilities, films at weekends, disco, bar restaurant. Accommodation. Membership 3 months £7.50.

■ **Africa Centre,** *38 Kings St Covent Gdn, WC2 (836 1973).* Leisure and cultural facilities, African restaurant. In the same building is the **Africa Educational Trust** *(836 5075)* which offers a counselling and grants service.

■ **Commonwealth Trust,** *18 Northumberland Ave, WC2N 5BJ (930 6733).* Club and events for Commonwealth students. Also hostels and flats.

■ **Indonesian Students Hostel,** *44 Dartmouth Rd , NW2 (452 8936).* Hostel accommodation only.

■ **Malaysian Hall,** *46 Bryanston Sq, W1 (723 9484).* Hostel accommodation only.

■ **Thai Government Students Office,** *28 Princes Gate, SW7 1QF (584 4538).* Advice on welfare, accommodation, visas. Attached to the Embassy.

■ **At Ease,** *c/o St John's Church Waterloo Rd, SE1 (928 2003).* Mon 5.30-6.30. Give advice to draft dodgers and deserters.

■ **International Friendship League,** *3 Creswick Rd, W3 (992 0221).*

■ **Swiss Welfare Office,** *31 Conway St, W1 (387 3608).*

■ **German Welfare Council,** *59 Birkenhead St, WC1 (278 6955).*

travel

This section helps you get away from the bustle of London. You can either find quiet interesting spots within it or perhaps escape from the city into the country or even abroad. What we have included here are cheap, interesting ways of taking a long or short break.

▼ WITHIN LONDON ▼

The cheapest though not always the easiest way of getting away from the whirl of London is to meditate. If you don't know how to meditate you could learn. Once learnt you can take regular excursions in the safety of your own home. The **London Buddhist Centre**, *51 Roman Rd, E2 (981 1225)* (see p147) run cheap, short courses.

If meditation does not satisfy you then look for the green places on the map. London is rich in parks. Most of those within the central area are jammed with joggers or tourists, especially in the summer months. **Holland Park** is pretty and less crowded than **Hyde Park** to which it is adjacent. Look out for the spectacular peacocks. You could take a dip in one of the outdoor ponds at **Hampstead Heath** (rats have been spotted there though, and their piss causes disease) - there are five which are women's, men's and mixed. The heath is easy to get to (Hampstead tube station) and once you're there it's large and easy to get lost in. **Wimbledon Common** is certainly worth a visit. It sprawls and is wild in places, and it's easy to forget you are in London at all. **Epping Forest** is a former royal hunting ground and in early autumn mushroom pickers gather there. It's 6000 acres. Take the tube to Snaresbrook. Deer roam the 2500 acres of **Richmond Park,** which is a former royal hunting ground.

If you fancy a walk by the water then get the tube to Hammersmith and stroll from **Hammersmith Bridge** to **Barnes Bridge** along the north or south side of the Thames. You can get a British Rail train from Barnes Bridge back into town. Or walk the **Grand Union Canal** from Uxbridge to Mile End (you don't have to do a marathon as the tube stops at Uxbridge, Northolt, Greenford, Warwick Avenue, Camden Town, King's Cross, Angel, Mile End and there is access all along the way).

▼ OUTSIDE LONDON ▼

The following places will welcome you to stay for a night to several weeks. They usually require you to become involved in their projects and help out, otherwise they will accommodate you if you pay.

■ **Monkton Wyld Court**, *Nr. Charmouth, Bridport, Dorset DT6 6DQ, (0297 60342).* It is a community of people who run the grounds, tender the organic garden and look after the animals. Good vegetarian wholefood. Pottery and woodwork. Will accommodate groups by arrangement. £14 per person per day full board. £16 at weekends. Play equipment for kids.

■ **WWOOF (Working Weekends on Organic Farms)**, *19 Bradford Rd, Lewes, Sussex BN7 1RB*, is a countrywide exchange network where bed and board and practical experience are given in return for work on organic farms and smallholdings. Midweek, long term and overseas stays are also available. An excellent opportunity for organic training or changing to a rural life. Provides a detailed list of places to members where help is needed each weekend so that you can make your own arrangements. Subs £6 pa, £7 pa (overseas).

■ **Centre for Alternative Technology,** *(0654 2400).* (281). Courses from sun power to organic gardening. To stay you have to do a residential weekend course £55 - £115 which includes full board and lodging. Good wholefood cooking, diverse group of people who work on community basis. Or you could also go as a volunteer for up to 2 weeks (advance arrangements necessary), and you will be asked to contribute to board and lodging. There is also a camp site (0654 2492) which is the cheapest way of visiting the site.

■ **CAER (Centre for Alternative Education & Research)**, *Rosemerryn, Lamorna, Penzance, Cornwall, (0736 810 530).* Self-sufficient centre offering w/end and week-long workshops in therapies such as yoga, bodywork, gestalt and massage.

■ **The Manor House,** *Beaminster, Dorset DT8 3DZ, (0308 862311).* £13-£16.50 per person per night. Home grown veg. Massage and aromatherapy if you wish from private practitioners. Tranquil gardens.

■ **Lower Shaw Farm**, *Shaw, Swindon, Wilts SN5 9PJ, (0793 771080).* W/end and week-long events on a variety of subjects - yoga, massage, crafts, women's events - reasonable prices, less for low-paid. Wholefood vegetarian. Run weekend courses and let out to groups. Also take WWOOFers. Sae for programme and more info.

Some Other Ideas

■ **Youth Hostel Association,** *14 Southampton St, WC2 (836 8541)* are cheap and are dotted throughout the country. They also have no age limit. They can sometimes be plush. There are 260 in Britain. M'ship £7pa (over 21) £3.70 (under 21) plus £2-7 a night. Publish *Youth Hostel Accommodation Guide* £2.95, obtainable at above address, which lists all the youth hostels with details in Britain.

■ **Country Farm Holidays,** *Shaw Mews, Shaw St, Worcs WR1 3QQ, (0905)613744)* arrange cottages from £80-500 p.w.

■ **National Retreat Centre,** *Liddon Hse, 24 South Audley St, W1 (493 3534).* publishes *The Vision* £1.30 p&p yrly. An annual listing of retreat houses, mainly Christian, some in London.

Free Food and Accommodation

For a pleasant life style you could book in at the **The Rowett Research Inst.,** *Greenburn Rd, Bucksburn, Aberdeen AB2 9SD, (0224 712751)* and be put on a controlled test diet. It's a minimum of 4 week's stay. They pay travelling expenses. Entertainment in the form of reading, colour TV and walks, though you are not allowed to stray from the grounds lest you lapse.

Getting There

HITCHING

Some rules

• If you are a woman alone don't get into a car if you are suspicious or if there is more than one man in the car.
• If the driver seems drunk don't get into the car.
• Women should hitch in twos for safety.
• If there is more than three of you, you should consider splitting up, and meeting up later.
• Having some luggage will show you are a genuine hitchhiker whereas having too much might seem like a burden.
• Make eye contact with the driver (sun-glasses prevent this).
• Stand where the traffic is slow and has a chance to stop in safety: traffic islands, roadside restaurants, traffic lights and petrol stations for example.
• Those hitchhikers who use a signs swear by them. They are especially useful if the road junctions ahead are complex.

Some dodges

• Hold up a sign showing the wrong direction e.g. East when the traffic is flowing West. A helpful driver may get out to correct you, or she may think she is going the wrong way and stop to check with you. You can let her in on the wheeze.
• Wear an official looking uniform. You're likely to get a boring lift though.
• Use a CB radio to contact the drivers of lorries. They cost about £70 on top of an annual licence fee. Or ask the lorry driver you are with to contact another driver with his CB who is going your way.
• Ask round at lorry drivers' cafes.
• Hold a number plate in your hands. This is the sign lorry drivers use with each other to get lifts.
• If you are a man, wearing a blue boiler suit gets lifts quickly.

Don't stop at road transport. Try hitching on canals and on the Norfolk broads. The traffic whizzes by at 5 knots which makes it all very pleasant but rather slow. Or you could hitch across the channel.

Hitching Across the Channel

Go to one of the ports that allow the driver to take one passenger across free. A good place to find a lorry driver who can take you across to the continent is **Smithfield Market** (near

St. Pauls Cathedral) or **Stratford International Freight Depot** (tube to Stratford and then a long walk).

Or ask for a lift on a yacht. Go to a yacht marina on the south coast such as Brighton and Dover. It helps if you've sailed before and better still if you exaggerate your experience.

Hitchhiker's Manual Britain Simon Calder (Vacation Work £3.95) contains lots of useful tips, directions for hitching out of 200 towns and cities, and motorway maps.

BUSES AND COACHES

They've advanced a long way from the cold, hold-on-to-your-bladder, jolting ride that used to be the norm. On many coaches you get video, meals, toilet, bar and restaurant. On some coaches they simulate aeroplane travel, providing stewardesses who greet you when you come 'aboard'.

Since recent deregulation of the bus and coach service in 1986 there are a large number of independent services and the situation is chaotic. The main operator for long distance service is still **National Express**, *Victoria Coach Station, Buckingham Palace Rd, (730 0202)*. The coaches leave from this address. Some typical prices: London to Manchester £15, London to Birmingham £10.50, London to Bristol £12, London to Glasgow £16.50. The price of a single is nearly the same as a return so you might as well get a return. Add on approx 25% to these prices if you travel Sat and Sun.

TRAINS

British Rail's ticket pricing is complex. You can often get a cheaper fare then the 'standard' fare. Many of the discounted fares are called 'Savers'. You are quite likely to be eligible for a discount as there are so many types of 'Savers'. Pick up leaflets for what's on offer from the information desk or ask the at the ticket office which is the cheapest permutation for you.

Some typical prices ('savers')
London to Birmingham £18.50* return, £26 return, £19 single.
London to Manchester £28* return, £38 return, £32 single.
London to Bristol £21* return, £28 return, £19.50 single.
London to Glasgow £49* return, £59 return, 47.50 single.
Where * is indicated you cannot travel before 9.30am, nor between 4.30-6pm.

You can also apply to buy a 'rail card' if you belong to a certain category. Rail Cards enable you to buy tickets at two thirds the price. The rail card lasts for one year. There are often restrictions such as only being permitted to travel in non-rush hour periods.

• **Student** £15.
• **Family** £20. You can take three extra adults at two thirds the price, and up to four children for £1 each. You must buy at least one child's ticket.
• **Senior Citizens Railcard** £15. Can take four children for up to £1 each.
• **Disabled** £12. You can take an adult companion at two thirds the price.

You need to go the the correct railway station in London to get to the destination in England that you want. Look in the Business Telephone directory under *British Rail*. The stations are listed, with areas in England they serve; and you can phone their *speaking timetable* to get info on times of trains to your destination.

London's eight main stations are: **Charing Cross** to South East England; **Euston** to North Midlands, North Wales, northwest England, and Scotland (including Glasgow) via the West coast; **King's Cross** to East and North East England, Scotland (including Edinburgh) via East coast; **Liverpool St** to East Anglia and Essex; **Paddington** to West and South West England, South Midlands, and South Wales; **St. Pancras** to North Midlands; **Victoria** to South and South East.

FLYING

■ **British Midland Airways,** *(589 5599)* do a standby single £49. Off-peak Return £79 (you must book ahead two weeks; weekdays flights limited to 9.10, 11.00, 13.10, 21.00, but more flights over the weekend). Flights depart from Heathrow.

▼ GOING ABROAD ▼

Arm yourself with a good book on travel. We recommend the comprehensive and detailed *The Travellers Handbook* ed. Melissa Shales (Wexas, 1988, £9.95). Otherwise browse the stock at the **Travel Bookshop,** *13 Blenheim Crescent, W11 (229 5260)* They've got books, guides, maps both new and old. For those who travel to those who like to travel from the comfort of their armchair.

Hitching

Germany is fast besause of their excellent roads and it's easy to get lifts. Holland is good too. France is a pig due to the police and it's hard to get a lift. It's illegal to hitch from their motorway service stations. Greece is okay as you're likely to get a lift from a tourist as well as locals. There aren't that many people in Ireland so the waits can be long, but they're worth it. Italy is slow and women hitchers shoud be wary of the men. In Belgium the police will keep an eye on you. Portugal and Spain are slow.

■ *Europe - A Manual for Hitchhikers* S. Calder (Vacation Work, £3.95) is good and so is *Hitchhikers*

Guide to Europe K. Walsh (Fontana, 1988, £3.95), though it lacks route directions.

Trains

In Western Europe trains are generally luxurious, efficient and expensive. For the rest of the world this is not always the case. You will find that outside Europe trains are generally slower than buses. In Europe they can be slow if you do not understand the language or the timetable and end up in some forgotten siding.

If you are under 26, an *Interrail* card (£145) will allow you to travel anywhere (valid for one month) in Europe and North Africa. Obtainable from mainline stations.

Buses

The seats may be hard in some countries but it's the cheap way to travel. Don't plan your schedule too tightly as delays are frequent.

Freighter

If you've got the time, travelling on an ocean going cargo ship will cost you about £80 per day. Visit the library and browse through the *ABC Passenger Shipping Guide* which lists all passenger carrying freighter services, giving breakdowns of voyage, duration, ships, fares, passenger capacity, operating company and their agents. Obtainable from **ABC International**, Dunstable, Beds. LU5 4HB, Then contact an agent who specialises in freighter travel for further advice on the shipping company concerned.

Flying

Havoc prevails. Flights to the States can work out cheaper than some European flights. So it's best to shop around. Non-discounted scheduled flights are the most expensive way to travel and you should only fly this way if it is essential that your flight is not delayed or you cannot adhere to restrictions imposed on the discounted flights. If you are going on a package holiday or to a destination in Europe then use a travel agent, who will try to get you a charter flight (which can be as much as 70% discount of the scheduled fare), but phone round to get the best deal. Charter flights account for a big section of the flight market.

If you are willing to go at short notice, (one day to a few weeks) *The Evening Standard* list cheap flights offered by travel agents and bucket shops. Don't be surprised when you ring them if the fare has been bumped up. They have a habit of advertising one price and asking another. Keep ringing round till you get the best price.

Most flights are protected by one of the following bodies: ABTA, CAA, Air Travel Trust, TOSG, so that if travel agent/operator/ airline goes bust you will get your money back. Make sure that the travel agent or 'bucket shop' is protected by ABTA (they should have a sticker on the door).

Pay by credit card if you can, as this gives you double protection. If the tour operator goes bust then you stand a good chance of claiming from the credit card company under the Consumer Credit Act.

OTHER DISCOUNTED FLIGHTS

You can get the following types of flights from a travel agent. We've listed them so you can understand what you are offered.

Apex/Super Apex This is the official discounting for the airline. You book and pay two to four weeks in advance. It must be a round trip except for the Far East where one way fares are available. Up to 60% reduction.

Pex/Super Pex Similar to Apex but you don't have to book so far in advance. Mostly Europe. Must include a Saturday night in the round trip. 50% fee for cancellation.

Excursion For long haul routes. Restrictions on min and max length of stay. 25-30% discount.

Standby Mostly to the USA, peak season, though some European flights. You can buy the ticket up to three months in advance but your flight is not confirmed till the day before departure.

Student Up to 25% discount. Apex is usually a better deal.

Youth Ages 12-21. Up to 25% discount. Apex is usually cheaper.

Round The World The first part of your journey is booked three weeks in advance, but thereafter you book your flight as you go along. You can't backtrack and you have to make a minimum number of stopovers. It's a good deal as the discounts are high.

Point to Point Economy mainly between US and UK, and some Far East and South Africa flights. Up to 50% discount. You cannot stop off.

Eurobudget Similar to Point to Point Economy. Up to 50% discount. Europe only.

Scheduled Consolidation Fares These are charter-priced seats on scheduled flights. 'Consolidators' (bucket shops) buy a number of seats on the aeroplane to take advantage of the hefty discounts given for 'group booking.' They then sell them on an individual basis to travel agents. They are intended as package holidays but end up as flight only tickets (the accommodation is supplied but not intended to be used, and may be as minimal as a shed on a farm).

Airpasses Enables you to travel very cheaply on domestic routes in various countries, notably the US, but also Australia, Brazil, India, and New Zealand. You get unlimited mileage, but usually cannot visit the same city twice. There is a limit to the number of cities you can visit and you may not be allowed to fly at busy periods. For an *Airpass* in the US it may work out best to travel to the US on a particular airline's trans-atlantic service. You need to get the *Airpass* before reaching the US.

LONG HAUL

Slow long-distance flights may be cheaper than a non-stop Apex flight. It is almost always cheaper to fly via various countries on the way to your chosen destination. Stopovers on your outward journey or return are sometimes free so ask when booking. Some of these flights have booking restrictions so check the conditions before travelling.

Bucket shops buy many seats on a flight cheaply from an airline. They then sell these 'dumped' tickets (sometimes 1/3 the scheduled fare) with few travelling restrictions to travel agents. If you go to the bucket shops direct you can avoid the travel agents 10% commission. They may not be members of ABTA, which means you could be ripped off, or if the company you book with goes broke, lose your money. But this doesn't happen often. To find a bucket shop check in the ABC timetables for an airline flying the route you want. It's best if the airline does not usually fly that route. Then contact the Airlines Sales Manger and ask for the name of a 'reputable consolidator' (i.e. bucket shop) who is selling their tickets.

■ **Trailfinders**, *42-48 Earls Court Rd, SW7 (938 3366)* has good prices for flights worldwide and tours to far-flung places. They guarantee a refund if the tour operator goes bust.

Courier Flights

You can sometimes get a free flight by acting as a *courier* (it involves taking a document/parcel to the destination), although many agencies will only give you a discount on the flight. It's possible to pick up a one-way flight to New York for free if you're willing to go on a day's notice. If you want to go on a two week return flight with more notice then you will pay about two thirds of the cost of a charter flight. The best deal you will get is with a company that provides courier service to the business public.

Look in the *Yellow Pages* under 'courier'. One such worldwide courier service is **DHL**, *(890 9393 x 3407)*.

Otherwise use a travel agents that deals in courier flights, such as **Polo Express**, *(759 5383)*, **Shades International Travel**, *(0274 814727)* **The Travel Store**, *(383 7181)*

FREE/CHEAP FLIGHTS

Unusual Free Flights

We have discovered that in some countries, notably Latin America, military planes will take you free. Let us know if you have had experience of this.

It's sometimes possible to get flights on cargo planes in some off-beat parts of the world. You have to talk to the captain at the airport office of the cargo company to see if they take passengers. They often have no timetable to speak of so you have to be on 'standby'.

Vehicles

Take out recovery policies with the **AA** or **RAC** (see below). They both have reciprocal agreements with similar organisations in Europe, so that in the event of a breakdown, you do not end up paying massive recovery charges. For travel outside Europe take out cover with **Europe Assistance**, *252 High St, Croydon CRO 1NF, (680 1234)* and **Campbell Irvine Ltd**. *(937 6981)* will do a worldwide 'Accidental Damage, Fire & Theft'.

Whether by car/van/truck you will need the following

• **International Driving Licence** £2.50. Not needed for Western European countries except Spain. May be needed for countries outside Western Europe. You need to take a full UK driving licence and two passport sized photos to either of these two motoring organisations

■ **AA**, *Leicester Sq, WC1 (839 7077)* - you don't have to be a member. If you're planning a long trip it might be worth joining. As well as free route maps, you get a 'courtesy service' from equivalent organisation in Europe. They also do a 5-star insurance (£14.25) which covers spare parts and getting you back here if necessary.

■ **RAC**, *49 Pall Mall, SW1 (839 7050)* which offers similar services as the AA. They publish *Continental Motoring Guide* which lists the motoring regulations of each of the Western European countries.

• **Insurance**. Get a *Green Card* from your insurance company which extends your cover to include other countries. Costs £10-£15.
• **Carnet** is needed for countries further afield than Europe as a guarantee that you won't sell your vehicle. If you don't have this you will have to leave a sizeable deposit at the border.
• **International Certificate of Motor Vehicles** needed for a few countries. Available from the AA or RAC.

It's best to make two sets of photocopies of all your vehicle documents. Keep the originals with you; one copy in the vehicle and the other copy at home (so that it can be forwarded to you).

OVERLAND BY TRUCK/VAN

If you plan to travel overland you need a reliable vehicle. You can save on accommodation costs if you can live in the vehicle/bring your own camping equipment and you don't have to put up with the filth and bugs found in some cheap accommodation. The major drawback is the red tape of the bureaucracies.

Land/Range rovers, Volkswagon Kombi, Mercedes Unimogs, four ton Bedford M trucks are favourites. But you could save money if you can put up with the cramped conditions of a 2CV panel van. The choice of vehicle is dependent on many factors: terrain covered, interior space, whether the country you are visiting carries the spares/special repair tools for your vehicle, price, payload, reliability, running costs, petrol/diesel, to name a few.

Check in advance whether the countries you are visiting carry the spares for your vehicle.

You can view vehicles at Provost St, N1, Saturdays and Sundays where you will find travellers haggling over battered machines. They range from a few hundred to a few thousand pounds but average out at about £1400. Many of the vehicles are registered abroad, but so long as they are not in this country for longer than 12 months they do not have to incur UK registration. They may, however, need a lot spent on repairs and servicing to bring them up to scratch. A better bet is to try car auctions (see p142) or look in *Complete Car Auction*, *Loot*, or *Exchange and Mart*, all from newsagents.

Money

You are allowed to take as much cash and travellers cheques out of the country as you wish.

If you're travelling regularly to Europe get a Eurocheque card. This will enable you to cash your own cheques in a European country.

Take some cash as well as travellers cheques - both in sterling and in the currency of the country you are going to. Carrying sterling, although it could be stolen, frees you from much of the bureaucracy of the banks. Carrying some cash in the currency of the country you are going to enables you to pay immediately in cash as soon as you get there. This might be especially useful if the banks are closed when you arrive.

Both Heathrow and Gatwick airports have banks that are open 24hrs a day, so you can exchange currency there.

Avoid getting money sent to you through the post if you are in far flung places as it *never comes*. Find a bank that is associated with your bank in England and have your money wired through. Better still - though it is a hassle and only worth it if you are expect to stay in that country for a long period - set up bank accounts with banks in the towns you expect to pass through. Use only those banks that are affiliated to your bank in England.

Don't bring too much money into a country that has a *soft* currency, because if you don't spend it you may have difficulty in getting it out due to currency restrictions. Third world and the Soviet bloc are typically *soft* currency countries.

Set ups are quite common in black market currency deals (especially in Soviet block countries), so don't pre-arrange a meeting with a dealer. Check the notes you exchange are not counterfeit. Some countries ask you to declare all monies you are carrying when you arrive and want you to account for it when you leave. If you want to play the black market you will need to hide it from them on arrival/departure, but if they search you and find it, they will be confiscate it. If a country is riddled with black market currency dealing you should keep receipts of what you buy to validate your spending story.

USA

If you intend to do a lot of travelling in the States consider *Greyhound* coach vouchers. Phone **Greyhound**, *(839 5591)* You can purchase a 30 day voucher for £180 (or 7 days for £80, or 15 days for £125), which allows unlimited travel all across the States they can arrange hotel/motel accommodation, but if you can sleep sitting up you can save on this expense. You must purchase before you go.

Or you could buy an *Airpass* flight ticket before you go which offers you unlimited mileage in the US (see p133).

Some good deals can be had with fly-drive trips. The cars are included at only a nominal fee.

Work Abroad

■ **International House**, *106 Piccadilly, W1V 9FL (491 2598)* run teaching courses (for about £450) and may be able to help you find work abroad. A few local authorities run much cheaper courses, but there's usually a waiting list.

■ **Vacation Work**, *9 Park End St, Oxford, ((0865) 241978)*. Publish *Work Your Way Around the World Summer Jobs Abroad, Summer Employment Directory of the US* as well as a number of other directories on work opportunities abroad. Also *Travellers' Survival Kit* and *Hitch-Hikers* Manuals.

They operate working holidays in France, Switzerland. Members' benefits include free update sheets of Summer jobs, and free information service on work abroad. £10 to join. Mainly a publishers, will supply publications list of work and travel abroad.

■ **Central Bureau for Educational Visits and Exchanges**, *(486 5101)* (see p129) publishes a number of useful directories - *Working Holidays 1989* (£7.70 incl p&p) which lists thousands of short term (2 wks to 1 year) paid and vocation jobs in Britain and overseas; *Home from Home* (£3.95 incl p&p) which is an international guide to home stays and exchange visits with detailed info on organisations who arrange the swap.

■ If you want to spend your summer entertaining American kids then **Camp America**, *(589 3223)* pay your fare and $150-$450 (depending on age and skills). You must register first (£50). You can bum around afterwards. Apply November the year before. You can also work on the camps doing other tasks such as kitchen work (they pay $350 for nine weeks).

Health

Falling ill abroad can be very expensive. If you are visiting a country within the European Economic Community - Denmark, France, West Germany, Belgium, Spain, Ireland, Holland, Greece, Luxembourg, Italy, Greece, Spain and Portugal - then you can get *urgent* treatment free or at a reduced rate if your N.I. contributions are paid up. If you've been unemployed or self-employed your contributions may not have been paid up and you may not qualify. Unfair though it is, if you've been self-employed all your life and have paid all your contributions you still don't qualify.

Some EEC countries, notably France, Luxembourg will only pay 70% of your treatment, and you may have to pay and claim back the 70%.

Continuing treatment of a pre-existing illness, e.g. asthma, diabetes etc. may not fall within the definition of urgent treatment so you may have to pay.

If you are working or living in these countries then these arrangements do not apply, and you should request info on your health rights from **DHSS Overseas Branch**, *Newcastle-upon-Tyne, NE98 1YX*.

So it's worth considering private insurance even if you are only travelling to

AIDS

To avoid getting Aids and Hepatitis B:

■ Don't have sex with a new partner. If you do have sex with a new partner use a condom (see the **Safer Sex** section). Be ultra careful in countries where you know AIDS to be prevalent - in Africa and the Far East for instance.

■ If you are going to a high risk country, in case of emergency take an **AIDS protection pack** from **Thomas Cook Vaccination Centre**, *(499 4000)* (see p137) which includes syringes (but does not include blood). However if you need a blood transfusion and you are in a high risk country then contact the British Embassy who may either supply an Aids free donor or will give you a blood substitute until you can be flown out.

■ You can get Aids from any instrument you use on yourself that has pierced another's skin. So make sure you use fresh/sterilised needles for ear piercing or acupuncture.

Europe, let alone a remote place on the planet. Take out *medical* insurance for at least £100,000. Sounds a lot, but if you need to be flown as a stretcher case from say Asia to the UK, it could cost you £30,000 for this alone. Don't take out a policy that limits how much can be spent on certain services such as ambulance costs - go for *total* cover.

If you are travelling outside of Europe go to an insurance broker who deals in travel insurance. Question in detail what you are covered for. Don't rely on your local travel agent to provide decent insurance.

It's worth taking out some baggage and personal money insurance too.

VACCINATION

Vaccination against diseases other than yellow fever can be given by your GP. A list of centres giving vaccination against yellow fever is given in a leaflet *Notice to Travellers: Health Protection* obtainable from your local DSS office, or you could go to **Thomas Cook Vaccination Centre,** *45 Berkeley Sq, W1 (499 4000)* where you will get vaccinations and certificates on the spot. If you want to know which jabs you need contact **British Airways Immunisation Centre,** *102 Cheapside, EC2 (606 2977),* they give free advice on all health requirements. Ring for an appointment.

■ **Hospital for Tropical Diseases,** *4 St. Pancras Way, NW1 (387 4411).*

If you get bitten by a wild or domestic animal anywhere (except Britain), get medical help as soon as possible. Rabies is normally fatal if untreated and it's a horrible death.

Passports

You can obtain application forms for passports (including instructions) at any main post office. The standard passport costs £17.00 and is valid for 10 years worldwide. Forms should be posted to the appropriate office indicated on the form. Allow at least a month (and three months in summer) for the return of your passport.

You can get a *visitors'* passport direct from a main post office issued on the spot. It's valid for one year and costs £7.50, but only travel to Western Europe is allowed (if you're travelling overland to Greece you pass through Yugoslavia and a visitors passport won't do).

Families can travel on one passport, but only the bearer can travel alone. This kind of passport is slightly more expensive.

Keep a separate note of your passport number and its date and place of issue in case you lose it. Then it's much easier to get a replacement.

■ **Passport Office,** *70 Petty France, SW1 (279 3000).*

You're only allowed one passport although you can sometimes get another if you are travelling to countries where the stamp of one would prohibit you entering another.

Visas

If travelling to an EEC country visas are not necessary as long as you hold a British standard (or visitors') passport. If you hold a non-British passport check first with the appropriate embassy to see if visas are needed for that country. Allow plenty of time before travelling for your visa to be processed. They can ask for your passport and it may take a long time.

Guide to International Travel published by ABC Travel Guides has up-to-date info on passport/visa/vaccination and climate for the world (check with your nearest ABTA travel agent).

Visas for America are not required any longer as long as you fulfil all the following conditions: hold a standard 10 year passport; are travelling to the states for 90 days or less on holiday or business; are travelling in and out on a participating airline carrier; are holding a return or onward ticket.

If you do fulfil the non-visa requirements and decide to travel to the States you will be obliged to fill in a visa-waiver form. Do this before you travel as the queues at the airport can be long.

For some countries outside Europe, getting a visa can be a problem, Africa and the Middle East are notorious.

To list all the tips about dealing with the visa hassles would require another book. Some things to bear in mind: getting your visas at another city may be easier; you may encounter the outstretched palm; carry plenty of spare passport-sized photos; be patient and be prepared for the unexpected. Talk with recent travellers to those countries.

Other Bits

■ **Prisoners Abroad,** *(833 3467).* They will tell you which British prisoners need visiting in the country you are going to.

■ **Servas,** *47 Edgelay Rd, Clapham, SW4 6ES (622 8404).* Not a travel organisation but an international network of hosts and travellers established to build world peace though friendship. Hosts offer two nights accommodation to approved Servas travellers . M'ship (£5 for hosts £12 for travellers) includes newsletter.

getting around

▼ CYCLING ▼

If you already ride a bike around London you'll know that it's the fastest, cheapest and most convenient way to travel in the city. If you don't, then maybe you should consider trying it. Don't be put off by the high noise levels and aggressive drivers; on a bike you can zoom along quiet back streets, cycle paths and through parks. You'll soon find that cycling in London is much faster than any other form of transport; average traffic speed in the centre of London is only 5 mph, so a bike will easily beat a car, bus or taxi, and even the tube on shorter distances, as well as being a great deal more pleasant.

The bicycle will also take you door to door and improve your health and fitness at a gentle pace. As cycling is about five times more efficient than walking you can cover long distances with surprisingly little effort.

Altruistically, the cyclist can feel good where the motorist can't, as bikes don't cause pollution, are silent, don't waste resources and don't need six-lane highways.

Escape

After the rigours of city life, a combination of train and bike will take you on a lone voyage of self discovery or a group outing of decadent indulgence into the quiet country lanes, rounded hills and wealthy commuter villages which surround London.

It is still possible to find hidden tea shops, pubs with horse brasses and roads without traffic within 20-30 miles of the metropolis, near enough for a day's or even an evening cycle.

How to Get a Bike

RENTING

If you think you would like to try cycling you could rent a bike. It's not that cheap (£6-£15 per day). For the price of renting for two weeks you could buy one secondhand.

All require deposits ranging from £15-£200 depending on the bikes value.

■ **De Ver Cycles,** *630 Streatham HIgh Rd, SW16 (679 6197).* 10-speeds sports are best value. £6 day. ID required. One day is the minimum. If hiring for London - Brighton run book early.

■ **On Your Bike,** *52-54 Tooley St, SE1 (407 1309).* From £6 a day, £25 pw.

BUYING

Second Hand

Can be very dodgy, bikes might be stolen or in dangerous condition. Check especially that the frame isn't bent at the front. Street markets are worth avoiding. Shops should give a guarantee (and a receipt). Buying privately is often a good deal, but any second hand bike can cost a lot of money to bring up to a safe and efficient level. In the long run it's best to buy new.

New and Repairs

In the long term a better quality cycle is better value for money. As well as being safer, stronger, faster, more comfortable and more fun.

Avoid really cheap bikes, such as the ones advertised in newspapers and mail order catalogues, and expect to pay the following.

£100- £185 A *3 speed, steel framed heavy old fashioned bike* which is wonderful for a journey of less than three miles with no hills.

£185 - £300 Bikes in this price range are often known as *commuter bikes.* They are a hybrid with the upright riding position of the 3 speed and a light, strong frame with alloy wheels (again lighter and stronger than steel, with more powerful brakes) and 5 or 6 gears. You would be happy to cycle to Brighton on such a bike.

£300-£500 *Racing bikes* are very light, very fast, and frighteningly hard to control and hence not good for city riding. Beware. Under the guise of their originals come pseudo 'racing bikes' or 'sports bikes' which look good and flashy, and which cost a lot less (£125+) than their original, but they are hopeless for town riding, let alone racing.

Touring bikes on the other hand are well equipped for almost any sort of riding; the streets, country lanes or the Pyrenees. They have hand built frames (usually of Reynolds 531 tubing), are light, very strong, with powerful brakes and a wide range of gears for speed or climbing hills. The drop handlebars which are good on long distances can easily be changed for town use.

£300+ *Mountain Bikes* or *All Terrain Bikes (ATB's)* are now very popular as they allow adults to behave as children while looking cool and displaying their disposable income. ATB's are very well suited to London's streets and to country lanes and tracks. They're strong, comfortable and safe, and the better quality ones are light too, hence their popularity with despatch riders.

When you buy a bike make sure that you can straddle the crossbar with your feet flat on the ground and have at least 1 inch clearance (3 inch clearance on a mountain bike).

All the following shops sell new bikes and do repairs unless stated otherwise.

■ **Broadway Bikes,** *242 The Broadway, NW9 (202 4671)* new and second-hand.

■ **Covent Garden Cycles,** *2 Nottingham Court, WC2 (836 1752)* new and second-hand, repairs, accessories, clothing.

■ **Mosquito Bikes,** *10 Bradbury St, N16 (249 7915).* A co-op selling new bikes and a good range of spares and accessories. Do repairs. Also at *123 Essex Rd, N1 (226 8841),* which is bigger and glitzier than the Dalston shop.

■ **Edwardes of Camberwell,** *221-248 Camberwell Rd, SE5 (703 3676).*

■ **Condor Cycles,** *144-148 Grays Inn Rd, WC1 (837 7641).*

■ **Bike Peddlers,** *50 Calthorpe St, WC1 (278 0551).*

■ **Brixton Cycle Co-op,** *433 Coldharbour Lane, SW9 (733 6055).* Sells new touring and mountain bikes, including its own brand of co-op bikes called *The Great Escapist.* Do the repairs for the big bike rides. Well oiled help. Unpretentious and friendly.

■ **Bell St Bikes,** *73 Bell St, NW1 (724 0456).*

■ **Condor Cycles,** *144-148 Grays Inn Rd, WC1 (837 7641).*

■ **Portobello Cycles,** *69 Golborne Rd, W10 (960 0444).* Second hand, new mountain bikes.

ACCESSORIES

Accessories consist of the gimmicky, the dangerous and the useful: *wheel discs* add to the weight of the bike, so-called *safety levers* on the brakes don't work and are better replaced with flat handlebars; and extras like *toe clips, padded shorts, cycling shoes with a stiff sole, mitts, mirrors, helmets* and *puncture-resistant tyres* increase efficiency, comfort, safety and convenience respectively. Don't forget the essential lights and a strong lock.

PROTECTION

Most fatalities are the result of head injuries. **Beta Bikes,** *275 West End Ln, NW6 (794 4133)* do a helmet £30-£100. as do **FW Evans,** *77 The Cut, SE1 (928 4785)* which is good £40.

LUGGAGE

■ **Bike Hod,** *29 Leslie Pk Rd, Croydon, Surrey, (654 7603).* Make trailers with semi-solid wheels, which hitch to the seat post (from £50).

MAINTENANCE

Cycle maintenance is relatively easy as most of the mechanical parts are visible. The **London Cycling Campaign,** (see140) run cycle repair workshops.

A reliable shop will offer to give a new bike it's first service free of charge; this will be necessary within about six weeks of purchase as the parts wear in.

INSURANCE

You can get bike insurance if you have a household contents policy. You pay an extra sum to the normal cost of the policy. But usually the maximum you can insure for is £150, which is too low low a ceiling these days. Contact your broker for details.

Better to contact **Bike Events,** *(0225 310859)* (see p140) who offer good value accident, theft and third party cover and free legal advice. They donate £1.50 from each policy to **Sustrans,** an organisation that has worked for some years towards building a national network of cycle paths in Britain, often along old railways.

BOOKS

On Your Bike £2.50. Lists bike shops. Has a map of London streets showing cycle routes

plus recommended back roads. From bookshops and cycle shops or direct from **London Cycling Campaign** (see below).
Richards Bicycle Book £4.95. Easy to read, funny, very informative, especially on repairs.
Ordinance Survey Cyclists Britain (Pan) give O.S. maps with bike routes and descriptions.
Cyclists Europe (Pan).

CONTACTS

■ **Cyclists Touring Club (CTC),** *69 Meadrow, Godalming, Surrey, (04868 7217).* Membership: over 21 £15, under 21 £7.50, for a household group £24, includes *Cycletouring & Campaigning*, free legal aid, insurance scheme, touring info service, handbook, consumer info.

■ **London Cycling Campaign,** *3 Stamford St, SE1 (928 7220).* Membership £8 pa waged, £4 unwaged; *Daily Cyclist* free to members; third part insurance scheme. Pressure group for urban cyclists. Weekly rides at weekends.

■ **Bike Events,** *PO Box 75, Bath, Avon , (0225 310859).* They organise day bike rides e.g. London to Brighton; and holidays e.g. London to Skye and Bordeaux to Barcelona.

▼ MOTORBIKES ▼

Cheap to run. Easy to park. Can be dangerous depending on how they are ridden - it's the under 21's who make up many of the casualties. Though many accidents are the fault of the other drivers who do not see the biker. British weather is the major drawback; you will need to get the proper clothing.

Regulations

The laws regarding testing and licensing were changing at the time of going to press. Some of the changes take effect from 2nd Oct 1989; others in mid 1990; some are, as of yet, only proposals which are likely to be implemented. So check the information that is given below before acting on it. Form D100 from the post office, will tell you what regulations are in force.

You have to be at least 16 to ride a moped or 17 to ride a bike over 50cc. If you have not passed your test you will be granted a provisional licence. With a provisional licence you can only ride machines under 125cc. You must take part 1 & 2 of the test within one year of holding a provisional licence. If in that time you have taken the test and failed or had a valid reason for cancelling a test you had booked, then you can get another years extension. If after that year you have not passed your test then you will not be entitled to hold a licence for 12 months. If you continue to ride your bike without a licence you are not only riding illegally but your insurance is invalid.

If you intend to ride nothing bigger than a moped then you could take a test for mopeds only. You do not have to take part 1 but must take part 2. If you pass you will get a full licence, but it only covers you to ride a moped. If you wish to ride a bigger bike then you have to take part 1 and part 2 of the test again on a bike greater than 50cc and less than 125cc.

You are required to wear a helmet to British Standard 6658 or a turban (if you are a follower of the Sikh religion).

You must also display L plates.

Learner riders are not allowed to carry a pillion passenger, even if the passenger holds a full motorcycle licence.

Training and testing

Part 1 of the test costs £17.94 and part 2 cost £24. You will be accompanied by the text examiner who will ride with you on her own bike. She will be in one-way radio contact with you, through earphones in your helmet (supplied by the examiner). She will feed you directions and keep an eye on you. (Comes into effect 2nd Oct 1989)

From mid 1990 you will have to do a basic training before you can get a provisional licence.

If you already have a full driving licence for a car, this gives you provisional licence entitlement for a moped, but you will have to take the basic training when it comes into effect in mid 1990.

Buying New

Most dealers will promise you a unique after sales service and then fail to deliver when you return with a faulty machine. Talk with your friends about which dealers give value for money, and which bikes they recommend. You will get more flexibility if you pay cash than part-exchange or use hire purchase. Read the reviews in the motorcycle press, bearing in mind that they are less critical than they could be. You have to read between the lines.

Buying Second-Hand

If you buy second-hand then look in *Motorcycle News* or *Loot* or *Exchange and Mart*. You can often pick up extras such as top box included in the price. Cash, as usual, works well.

THINGS TO CHECK

The chain should not be too slack especially

round the rear wheel sprocket; damage to the ends of the handlebars and footrests (if these are dented you can assume the bike has had a crash or fall); rusty exhausts; engine oil leaks; front forks are not bent; the wheels are in alignment (if you get down on your knees at the front of the bike the front and rear wheels should be parallel); the mileage. Customised racy looking machines sold by youths are likely to have been thrashed.

Old English bikes, eastern European and Italian bikes tend to break down. The Japanese and the German BMW are the most reliable.

Mopeds
Good for heavy London traffic. Easy to manoeuvre and cheap (up to 180 m.p.g.). Many have automatic clutch and gear change. Not much good for long journeys but ideal for commuting. Don't get the sportier versions as they are expensive and likely to have been thrashed.

Insurance
Expensive if you are young, especially if you want to get a big bike. Cheapest we've found is **Devitt (D.A. Insurance Ltd),** *32/66 High St, E15 (555 0711)* who will give you a quote over the phone.

Riding Gear
Get yourself a good helmet. Don't buy one second-hand because you do not know whether it's had a fall (simply dropping it from your hand on to concrete can produce hairline cracks which renders it inefficient). A full face helmet will protect your face as well as your head in the event of a crash.

Rescue
Both the **AA** and the **RAC** (see p###) offer breakdown rescue to bikers. £25.25 and £37 p.a. respectively.

Maintenance and Repairs
Easy to do yourself. First you need to get a good manual (try the Hayes series) and the correct tools. The maintenance is mostly a simple matter of doing the required oil and spark plug changes.

■ **Hamrax,** *328 Ladbroke Grove, W10 (969 5380)* do a good repair service with breakdown facilities. They will fetch your bike in one of their vans. Also specialise in spares for Triumph, AJS and Matchless.

Crashed Bike
■ **Bike Techniques,** *95 North St, SW4 (720 5293).* If you've had a crash they will arrange to have your bike picked up (£15 to recover it) and will repair it.

Hiring
■ **Scootabout,** *59 Albert Embankment, SE1 (582 0055).* Honda and Kawasaki only. Mopeds are Yamahas £12.59 inc a day, 125cc, £14.89; 200cc, £16.68; 500cc, £22.94; 750cc, £28.75. They do repairs and sell second-hand and new machines.

Training
■ **Star Riders London Booking Office,** *Head Office, Cobalt, Federation House, 2309/11 Coventry Rd, Sheldon, Birmingham B26 3PB, (764 7022 London Office).* Good value 4 hour course (called Bronze) £15 inc. VAT. Normally 9-1 Sat morning. For beginners to learn how to get on to the road safely. If you buy new Honda, Yamaha, Kawasaki or MZ then you get this course free.12 hour course (called Silver), times varied to suit. Usually 6 weekends of 2 hour duration. £36 inc. VAT. You can then take the part 1 of the test (£17.75) on their site. Special one-to-one tuition is available at £9 p.h. Weekend training available on request at certain centres. For experienced riders their Gold course, £32 inc. VAT will increase your riding abilities and you can take their own test £15 (some insurance companies will give you up to 25% discount if you have passed this test). Or the Gold course and test combined is £40.

Contacts
■ **British Motorcyclists Federation (BMF),** *129 Seaforth Av, Motspur Pk, Surrey KT3 6JU, (942 7914).* Membership £15 pa gets you discounts on clothing, machines and insurance; legal advice and bi-monthly *Motorcycle Rider*. List of local clubs. Link up with RAC (can save up to £16 on their membership). They train despatch riders and those new to motorbikes. £20-£30 for their beginners training courses. Campaigns for bikers rights.

■ **Wima (Women's International Motorcycle Association)**, *(07918 6524 or 07918 6801)*. 'We aim to promote and encourage women and motorcycling - and consider that we can ALL have lots of fun doing it!'. Monthly newsletter. Organise national and international rallies. Will give details of local clubs. M'ship £8.50.

■ **Motorcycle Action Group**, *PO Box 750 Birmingham B30 3BA, (021 459 5860)*. Promote and protect bikers rights. Campaigning against unnecessary European and national regulations. For info contact *London office, Dorian Mead 0784 462608*.

▼ CARS ▼

Cars are an expensive form of travel and can be a big drain on your resources. It costs you at least £5 a week in tax and insurance before you start calculating other expenses. On top of this there are repairs, AA membership, oil and petrol, parking charges and fines.

The cheapest way of owning a car is to buy an old banger. It may cost you more throughout the year in repairs but you will save from not losing in depreciation. Or you could buy a moderately used car, which will be more reliable but without the big loss in depreciation experienced in buying a new car.

It's best to sell your car privately than part-exchanging for another from a dealer.

If you've an old banger then the repair/ recovery service offered by the RAC and AA will pay for itself in no time. (see p134). Both will now repair your car if it's broken down outside your home. They are a good way of saving petrol - even if you've broken down in Scotland they will take you and the passengers back to London.

Hiring

Car hire companies normally require that you be over 21 and have held a licence for at least a year, though some firms have more stringent regulations than this. You may have to leave a deposit. You can find them in the *Yellow Pages* or the *Evening Standard*.

Vans are cheaper than cars; and long journeys usually work out cheaper if you get a deal with unlimited mileage. Cheapest we've found are: **Practical Used Car Rental**, *111 Bartholomew Rd, NW5 (284 0199)* Min 25 yrs of age (or 23 with penalty). Oldish cars; (AA covered) £5.95 per day +5p per mile. £41 per week +5p per mile (excl VAT). Other branches: *249-253 Cambridge Heath Rd, E2 (729 6276); 43 Gunnesbury Lane, W3 (992 8199)*. Also cheap is **Supercars**, *40 Warner St, EC1 (278 6001)* £19.55 at per day for a small car. £250 deposit and free mileage for the first 100 miles.

Car Auctions

Good if you know something about cars. Depending on the particular organisation, you can view the day before or a couple of hours before it begins. If it's a newish car they will give/sell a warrantee. With an older car you may get several days to test it and can bring it back and get your money back if there is a problem. You have to leave a deposit (usually 10%) and pay the balance within 24 hours.

It's best to bid against a dealer as she will drop out if the bids become too pricey whereas individuals may keep bidding against each other to excess. Dealers can be recognised by the *Glasses Guide* they carry in their hands.

Contact your insurance broker before you go who will give you free cover for that day.

■ **ADT Auctions**, *Harlequin Av, Gt West Rd, Brentford, (560 0303)*. Tue, Thur 9.00 till evening and Sat open at 9am, sale at 11am-1.30.

■ **Belmont**, *Penhall Rd, SE7 (858 5429)*. Tu and Fri 7pm.

■ **Central Motor Auctions**, *Morden Rd, Mitcham, Surrey, (648 9438)*. Mon at 5.30, W and F at 11am.

■ **City Motor Auctions**, *Evelyn St, SE8 (691 0066)*.

■ **British Car Auctions**, *620 Gt. Cambridge Rd, Enfield, Middx, (366 1144)*. Tu Th Sat 9.00am, sales at 11.00am .

■ **Sussex Car Auctions**, *The Market, Heathfield, Sussex, (04352 3059)* on Wed at 7.00pm.

Specialists

For tyres, batteries and exhausts go to the specialists who deal in these - they are usually cheaper. **Associated Tyre Specialist**, *89 Crescent Lane, SW4 (622 4508)*

Branches in E14, E1, E10, SW4, SE18, SW19, N18, NW1, NW10. **London Tyre Warehouse,** *56-60 New Cross Rd, SE14 (639 9491)* tyres, MOT, exhausts. **National Tyre Service,** *245 Brixton Rd, SW9 (274 2237)* branches throughout London. **Wembley Tyre & Battery Service,** *78 Duddenhill Lane, NW10 (459 6191).*

Lead Free Petrol

If you want to know what to do to make your car run on lead free petrol then contact **Campaign for Lead Free Air (CLEAR),** *(387 4970)* who are very willing to provide the information. It may be that your car already runs on lead free petrol or may only need minor modifications to do so.

▼ PARKING ▼

Traffic wardens don't work in the rain (they claim their pens don't write). So if it looks like rain you stand a better chance of not getting booked.

They also tend to be sympathetic to 'Car Broken Down' signs (though you can't break down too often as they make a note of your number and will look for repetition).

There are many instances where a vehicle is parked illegally but a traffic warden is not allowed to issue a ticket, parking on a pavement for instance (good for bikers to know). What they will do instead is stick a label on your machine and make a detailed note of the circumstances. You are supposed to go to the police station with the label and *confess*. You are unlikely to be prosecuted for ignoring the label. The choice is yours. Beware though that you are not causing an obstruction, as the traffic warden may contact the clamping unit or a tow away truck.

Traffic wardens are sympathetic upon seeing a copy of *Police Gazette* on view in the rear windscreen of your car, or for that matter any indications that you are a gas/British Telecom/water board/council employee/nurse/doctor/midwife/traffic warden.

People have been known to carry 'out of order' bags with them and slip them over convenient meters.

Cars with foreign licence plates are unlikely to get a ticket.

If you are parked on a single yellow line check that the grey post with a sign on it (which tells you the parking times) is within reasonable distance of your car (in many cases they have been vandalised). Traffic wardens cannot issue you with a ticket if it's missing.

But.......there's clamping and towing away to be wary of.

▼ PUBLIC TRANSPORT ▼

The buses and underground are run by London Regional Transport. For enquiries phone **London Transport Enquiries,** *(222 1234)* which has 24 hr info on getting about - including night buses. Route info, timetables and free maps from Euston, King's Cross, Oxford Circus, Piccadilly Circus, Victoria, West Croydon and Heathrow.

Tubes finish between 11.30pm and 1am during the week and 11.30 on Sunday. If you miss the tube you can get a late night bus. They all pass through Trafalgar Square (from about midnight) onwards.

Taxis

For a black cab (radio controlled) phone any of the following numbers:

286 0286
272 3030
272 0272
253 5000

COMPLAINTS

Make sure there is a meter and a for hire sign displayed, as people are buying up old cabs and using them for cabby service. Take the plate number (not the vehicle license number), displayed inside and outside of cab. Complain to **Public Carriage Office,** *15 Penton St, N1 (278 1744)* which covers all licensed black cabs.

CAB LOST PROPERTY

■ **Metropolitan Police Lost Property Office,** *15 Penton St, N1 (833 0996).* Mon - Fri 9-4. It is 3 -6 days before they come into possession and they keep it for 3 months.

• Minicabs are ordinary four door saloons driven by their owners who hire their services out. They cost about the same as black cabs for short distances but are cheaper for long runs. Agree on a price before starting journey. See under 'Mini cabs' in *Yellow Pages*.

TAXIS FOR WOMEN BY WOMEN
See under the **Women's** sections (p181).

▼ COMMUNITY TRANSPORT ▼

If you are a voluntary group you might think of buying a minibus for your transport needs. It needs to be organised properly. You should consider the needs of those will use it, legislation, and where funding will come from. You could invest in an information pack by the **National Advisory Unit for Shared Transport,** *35 Fountain St, Manchester M2 2AF, (061 236 5581)* called *Starting Up* £7.50 + £2 p&p. It covers admin, licensing, driving, insurance, legal aspects, constitution. They also provide speakers; give info on needs of those with mobility handicaps. The following groups run community transport and will give you advice on getting and organising transport

■ **Camden Co-operative Transport,** *St. Margeret's, 25 Leighton Rd, NW5 (267 3243).* You need to be a member to hire out a vehicle. M'ship £5.75 pa if funding is less than £5000 else £17.25 . Take and administer bookings.Vehicle can be delovered. Wheelchair. Minibus. Can supply drivers and do driver training.

■ **Community Car Drivers,** *St. Margeret's, 25 Leighton Rd, NW5 (485 3871)* for any Camden resident who cannot use public transport eg invalids, agoraphobia, parents with small children and a complicated journey. Must be Camden residents. The drivers are volunteers using own cars. Can go outside London. Wheelchair. Do not do hospital trips. 25p per mile.

■ **Haringey Community Transport,** *Room 9, Tottenham Green Education Centre, Town Hall Approach Rd, N15 (801 2525).* £10 pa M'ship. £18 per day for vehicle (ex fuel). Minibus (15 seats). Disabled.

■ **Tower Hamlets Community Transport,** *25 Newell St, Limehouse, E14 (987 6447).* Car maintenance courses. Driver training. Summer, day and bank holidays trips. Driver provided. Minibus. Van. Disabled.

■ **Shared Transport Service,** *The Old School, Dixon Rd, Small Heath, Birmingham B10 OBS, (021 773 2858/9068).* They operate a successful vehicle sharing scheme in Birmingham. Provide Minibus and ambulance, for lunch clubs and the elderly and disabled to get about. Will provide free a small number of booklets and give advice on setting up a shared vehicle scheme.

▼ MESSENGERS ▼

If you need some item delivered quickly then you can use a courier service. They charge approx £5- £10 for picking up an item at your door (you can pay the messenger) and delivering it within the London area.

■ **Speedway,** *(701 6222)* use bikes, cars, vans.

■ **Pegasus,** *(622 1111)* bikes.

▼ CONTACTS ▼

■ **Transport 2000 London & South East,** *5 Pembridge Crescent, W11 (727 4689).* Concerned about the impact of transport on society and environment.

■ **Campaign Against the Lorry Menace (CALM),** *62 Oakhurst Grove, SE22 (693 8752).*

Rail

■ **Railway Development Society,** *Reg Snow, 48 The Park, Gt. Bookham, Surrey KT23 3LS, (0372 52863).* Publish *Railwatch*, qrtly; campaigning for more investment and against closures.

Waterways

■ **Inland Waterways Assoc,** *114 Regents Park Rd, NW1 (586 2556).* Promotes the restoratio, retention and development of inland waterways. Their *Inland Waterways Guide* lists boat hire firms. Sell *Imrays Inland Waterways of England and Wales* and the Nicholsons *Guide to Waterways*.

■ **Transport on Water,** *Northside, Royal Albert Dock, E16 (476 2424).*

Pedestrians

■ **Pedestrians' Assoc,** *1 Wandsworth Rd, SW8 (735 3270),* 'safeguards the needs and interests of pedestrians'. Publish *Walk* (3 times a year) £3 p.a.

Air

■ **Civil Aviation News (CAN),** *c/o FCA, The Community Centre, Hanworth Rd, Feltham, Middx,* aims to unite workers in civil aviation. Started at Heathrow by unionists. An infrequent publication.

MIND, BODY, SPIRIT: Self Discovery, Health, Martial Arts

self discovery

In some ways the movement for the exploration of consciousness (whether based in religion or psychotherapy) has grown up over the last twenty years, and become more solid. There's less exuberant guru worship and, in general, a greater sense that a real change in individual consciousness spills out into changing the world for the better, rather than escaping into transcendental bliss-out or group narcissism.

The word 'therapy' originally meant 'attendance on the gods' and the implication of this is perhaps that healing can only take place when we are able to get in touch with whatever is of greatest value to each of us in our life It also shows the link between traditional spiritual practice and the new 'way' of psychotherapy. Both can be a means of developing inner strength and awareness and of finding more loving and truthful ways to relate to others.

Some people are wary of the power of therapy or spiritual groups, and there is some wisdom in this. While there are many benefits to be had from them, it is also as well to have some measure of healthy scepticism. It's easy to fall into thinking that you 'should' do, think or behave in a certain way in the face of any new theory, group or leader who seems to have it all worked out. Value your own point of view and gut feeling about the rightness or wrongness of any idea or situation for you. From this standpoint, you'll be able to tell the 'pearls' from the 'clay'.

▼ PRACTICES ▼

Meditation

There are many different kinds of meditation. Most aim to shift awareness away from both the many external things that demand attention and the internal chatter of the mind, and focus on one thing. This then produces a state of clear perception and calm.

This can be done by focussing on the breath, concentrating on an object such as a candle or stone, paying attention to the body and physical sensations, visualising a colour or a sacred form, just sitting and watching thoughts and feelings arising and disappearing, and so on. Contemplative meditation is slightly different; thought is not stilled but focussed around a particular subject such as love, or a symbol.

Meditation doesn't have to be done sitting down - there are walking and 'dynamic' or whirling dance meditations.

Many of the Buddhist, Hindu and Sufi groups listed in this section teach meditation, as well as some groups listed in the 'other groups' section (a few of which are non-religious).

Yoga

'Yoga' means 'union' - with the divine principle. There are different forms, but *hatha* yoga in which physical postures are used as a way of relaxing and meditating is best known. Other forms include *mantra* yoga - the repetition of a word or phrase, *karma* yoga - spiritual practice through work, *bhakti* yoga - becoming like god by devotion, *raja* yoga - meditation and mental discipline, *jjana* yoga - union through insight into the absolute, and *kundalini* yoga which raises energy through the six chakras (energy centres) towards illumination at the highest centre.

Pranayama or breath control is sometimes used with hatha yoga.

Hindu, and some Buddhist groups teach yoga. There are plenty of ILEA hatha yoga classes (cheap) where the emphasis is on developing fitness and relaxation. Local classes may be advertised in libraries and health food shops. *Yoga and Health* (£1.10 from newsagents) lists courses.

■ **Yoga for Health Foundation,** *Ickwell Bury, Northill, Biggleswade, Beds, (076 727 271).* (£55 per weekend, full board and activities included). Run special courses for the disabled (including MS). Publish *Yoga and Life,* qtly 90p.

■ **Institute of Indian Culture,** *4a Castletown Rd, W14 (381 3086).* Hatha yoga classes Tues 6.30, Advanced Mon 7. Meditation Thurs 6-7.

■ **Bodywise,** *119 Roman Rd, E2 (981 6938).* Lunchtime and evening yoga classes. Also dance, massage, Alexander Technique.

■ **Sivananada Yoga Centre,** *50 Chepstow Villas, W11 (229 7970).* Eve and w/end classes in yoga and meditation.

■ **Yoga Centre**, *13 Hampstead Hill, Gdns, NW3 (794 4119).* Hatha Yoga Tu at 7 and meditation Wed at 7 under the guidance of Sri Nandi.

▼ SPIRITUAL TRADITIONS ▼

It seems to be the fate of 'official' religions to become rigid and institutionalised in their own countries. Certainly over the last 20 years many people in the west have turned to eastern religions to find a living spirituality, and have learned to temper the west's emphasis on 'doing' with the eastern sense of the importance of 'being'. But the challenge of finding a new way of expressing spirituality has not only come from the east - pre-Christian pagan religions are also growing again after nearly 2000 years of underground activity, as is interest in the shamanic tradition (see below). Many Christians are finding fresh ways to make their religion relevant to the modern world, and in general there is more emphasis by followers of different traditions on finding the unifying 'spirit' of all religions.

Buddhism

Dubbed 'the thinking person's religion', Buddhism was founded 2,500 years ago by Guatama Buddha. He taught that human beings try to get and hold onto pleasant experiences and avoid painful experiences, but because everything is impermanent, we are constantly facing the pain of losing what is pleasurable. The state beyond this cycle of holding on and running away is called *Nirvana* or enlightenment, and the way to attain it is through an ethical lifestyle, meditation and profound realisation of the ever-changing nature of existence.

Buddhism emphasises the importance of the individual's own efforts towards growth, and stresses the development of *mindfulness* or awareness of oneself, others and the world. Unlike most religions, there is no creator God in Buddhism.

As it spread to different countries from India where it started, Buddhism adapted itself to different cultures and three main forms developed.

Hinayana, practiced mainly in SE Asia, stresses the importance of morality, the monastic lifestyle, rationality and 'insight' meditation.

Mahayana developed the *Bodhisattva Ideal* where personal enlightenment is renounced so that the practitioner can help others to Nirvana. It stresses the development of compassion as well as wisdom. The Japanese Zen school is of this tradition, where the approach is anti-rational (impossible intellectual problems are struggled with until the rational mind is short-circuited) and the emphasis is on *zazen* (meditation with no object).

Vajrayana, the form practiced by Tibetan Buddhists, is sometimes also called the Tantric school. It is colourful, ritualistic, works with psychic energy and uses chanting, physical prostrations and meditations in which deities are visualised. There are various schools within this tradition which have a different flavour, emphasising a different aspect of practice ie study or meditation.

The **Buddhist Society** (below) publish the *Buddhist Directory* (£2.99 from them), which lists all groups in Britain.

■ **London Buddhist Centre**, *51 Roman Rd, E1 (981 1225).* Centre of the **Friends of the Western Buddhist Order** which was founded by Sangharakshita, an Englishman who spend 20 years in India as a monk. Seek to synthesise elements from all Buddhist traditions and develop a modern, dynamic approach. Have set up communities, and co-operative businesses around the centre to provide ethical work. Large and lively centre. Beginners meditation class Weds 7pm. Courses also run in West End.

■ **Dharmadhatu**, *27 Belmont Cl, SW4 (720 3207).* Founded by the Tibetan teacher, the late Chogyam Trungpa Rinpoche whose books, such as *Cutting Through Spiritual Materialism* and *Shambhala* are an excellent guide to the spirit of Buddhism, framed in western terms. Meditation Weds 7pm.

■ **London Kagyu Centre**, *Unit 5, 21 Perseverance Works, 38 Kingsland Rd, E2 (609 8591).* Small, informal centre under guidance of Lama Chime Rinpoche, who visits once a month. Teachings from difference types of Buddhism. Very informal meditation Weds 7pm. Difficult to find so ring for directions.

■ **Rigpa Fellowship**, *44 St Paul's Cres, NW1 (485 4342).* Set up by Lama Sogyal Rinpoche, a Tibetan teacher with a western approach, they also host visiting teachers of Tibetan and other traditions. Weekend workshops include healing, death and dying, Buddhist psychology. *Tsok* or chanting ceremonies. Meditation Thursday 7.30pm.

■ **Buddhist Society,** *58 Eccleston Sq, SW1 (834 5858).* Longest established British group, tends towards Hinayana and older membership. Summer school, cassettes, library. Publish journal *The Middle Way*. Membership £16 pa.

■ **Buddhapadipa Temple**, *14 Carlonne Rd, SW19 (946 1357).* Run by Thai monks, is traditional Theravada school. Meditation Tues and Thurs 7. Study and Sunday School.

■ **Manjusri Institute,** *10 Finsbury Pk Rd, N4 (359 1394).* Resident teacher is Tibetan Geshe Namgyal Wangchen. Evening and weekend groups on meditation and buddhist philosophy. Large retreat centre in Cumbria.

■ **London Zen Society,** *10 Belmont St, NW1 (485 9576).* Rinzai sect under direction of Sochu Suzuki Roshi and Kyudo Nakagawa Roshi. Daily sittings (meditation). Mon-Fri 6-8 am and pm. Sesshins (prolonged meditation sessions).

■ **London Soto Zen Group,** *c/o Duncan Sellers, 23 Westbere Rd, NW2 (794 3109).* Under direction of Throssel Hole Priory (monastery and retreat centre in Northumberland). Meet Weds 7-9 – ring first to check location.

Hinduism

Hinduism is more a collection of different ideas, schools and sects than a centralised religion. 'Hindu' was originally Persian for Indian, and was used by foreigners to lump together all the religions and cults of India.

There's no central doctrine, though most accept the authority of the Veda scriptures, written over the 5,000 years of the development of Hinduism. The soul is usually seen as passing through countless incarnations, and the struggle for liberation (*Moksha*) from this cycle involves realising the God within or true self (Atman) which is identical with Brahman, the absolute. The idea of Karma - that we suffer the results of all our actions, good and bad, over successive lives - is usually important. Devotion to the guru or teacher, who is seen as the enlightened embodiment of God, is often central. Hindu practices are the different 'yogas' (see **Yoga**) - mantra chanting, meditation, devotional ritual, service or work, asceticism, hatha (physical posture) yoga etc.

■ **Sri Chinmoy Centre,** *c/o Flat 2, 51 Eaton Rise, W5 (991 0222).* 'Love, devotion and surrender' is the teaching of Bengali Sri Chinmoy. He also believes in jogging as a way to keep fit and develop dynamism. Meditation meetings at Quaker Meeting House, Woodville Rd, W5 (Fri at 8).

■ **Raja Yoga Centre,** *98 Tennyson Rd, NW6 (328 2478).* Use meditation and positive thinking, taught individually in series of 7 day 1-hour courses. Committed practitioners wear white and are gentle and non-evangelical.

■ **Krishna Consciousness Society,***10 Soho St, W1 (437 3662).* Famous for their saffron-robed chanting excursions through the West End, and for their sympathisers and devotees in the rock world. Founded by Bhaktivendanta Swami Prabhupada, they adhere closely to the Veda Scriptures, and chant the Hare Krishna mantra. They are *Vaishnavas* -ie worshippers of Vishnu, a Hindu deity. Run a vegetarian restaurant on the premises, and a college for Vedic studies in Herts. 'Monastic' and lay following (who wear white).

■ **Maharishi Corporate Development International (TM),** *2 Douglas St, SW1 (821 1813).* Meditation on personal mantra, founded by the Maharishi Mahesh Yogi. Free introductory courses 4 consecutive days 11/2-2 hrs. £165 or £85 low waged including 3 month follow up.

■ **Satyananda Yoga Centre,** *70 Thurleigh Rd, SW12 (673 4869).* Run by followers of Swami Satyananda. Various yoga classes (including advanced cleansing techniques), pranayama, meditation and satsang. Publish *Yoga Times*. Residential courses in their Ashram in Wales.

■ **Sri Aurobindo Centre,** *8 Sherwood Ave, SW16 (679 0854).* Sri Aurobindo turned to mysticism after political activism. When he died in 1960 his teachings were carried on by a French woman known as *The Mother*. In southern India his devotees are building a model town called Auroville. Yoga, meditation and study meetings.

■ **Meher Baba Assn,** *228 Hammersmith Gr, W6 (743 4408).* Meher Baba was taught by several spiritual masters of different traditions. He promised to reveal the secret of the universe after he had remained silent for 35 years - he died 34 years later, in 1969. He taught by writing on blackboards and the message 'don't worry, be happy' is his.

Kabalah

Teachings of Jewish mysticism which were handed down orally until the 13th century when they were written down, most notably in the *Zohar, Book of Splendour*. The soul finds its way back to its lost union with God through purity and meditation, and must pass through ten planes or centres of power represented symbolically by the Tree of Life and 32 paths corresponding to the vertebrae.

■ **International Order of Kabalists,** *25 Circle Gdns, SW19 3JX (542 3611).* Study mystical Kabalah, esoteric colour psychology, Greek and Egyptian mythology, meditation, Major Arcana of Tarot which correspond to paths of 22 subjective states of being. Correspondence course for those who can't get to meetings (£30 yr). £20 a year subs, monthly meetings, local groups.

■ **Will Parfitt,** (693 9951). Individual and group therapy and tuition in Qabalah, Tarot and Magick. Author of *The Living Qabalah* (Element 1988 £8.95) a practical guide to the Qabalah with many exercises to make its symbolic language more accessible.

Paganism

The word pagan is derived from the latin *paganus* meaning 'countrydweller'. The nearest English word for this would be 'heathen'. Pagans and heathens alike form a variety of religions who have in common care for the earth and an active interest in the ecological welfare of the planet. Pagans see themselves as human beings sharing the natural environment together with the plants and animals and not as the sole owners of the earth's resources.

Paganism rejects the concept of an 'only one', male god, rather they experience divinity as a polarity envisaged as God and Goddess.

Paganism is non-dogmatic and offers scope for a variety of opinions and practices with the one and only rule 'and it harm none to do what thou wilt'. There are various neo-pagan traditions, to name a few; *Wicca*, a revival of the pre-christian native matriarchal religion of Britain involving for the most part Celtic mythology; Odinism or Asatru, the still existing Elder Faith of the Northern European countries based for the most part on the Icelandic Eddas and Germanic folklore and *Druidism*, a revival of the British/Celtic priesthood. *(Freya Aswynn).*

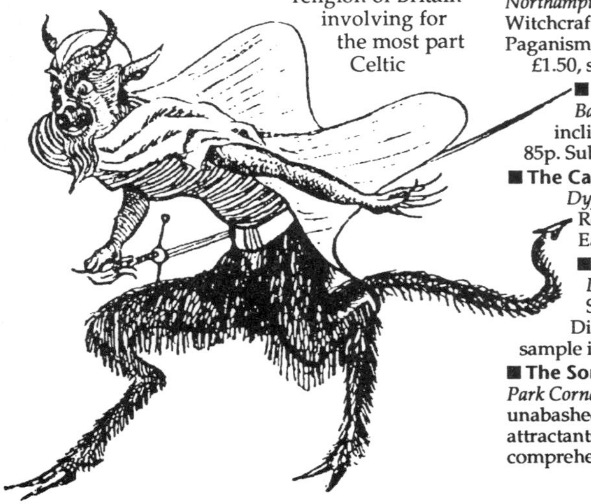

PUBLICATIONS

■ **Crone-Icle,** *c/o 56 Old Oak Rd, Birmingham, B38 9AJ.* Magazine for Women of Spirit 'from Alchemy to Zen' £1.25.

■ **The Deosil Dance,** *Omega Publications, 178 London Rd, Northwich, Cheshire.* 'Revolutionary, freethinking journal of pagan religions today'. Sample £1.25.

■ **Moonshine Magazine,** *498 Bristol Rd, Selly Oak, Birmingham B29 6BD.* Articles on Pagan philosophy and life from a Shamanic and Druidic point of view. Sample copy £1.75 inc. p&p. Subs 8 issues (1 year) £12.

■ **O Fortuna,** *BCM Akademia, WC1N 3XX.* Articles on spiritual, magickal and ecological progress, folklore, poetry, humour, children's pull-out section, and prize crossword. Sample issues £1.50 plus stamp. Subs £6 (payable to S. Bate).

■ **New Dimensions,** *Mark Saunders Publications, 1 Austin Cl, Irchester, Northants, NN9 7AX.* Qabalah, enochian, gematria, mythology, magic, UFOs. 12 issues pa, 75p.

■ **Occultline,** *91 Windmill La, Bushey Heath, Herts WD2 1NE.* Occult contact network for those interested in Wicca, magic and New Age.

■ **Aquarian Arrow,** (same address), 'Represents the radical left wing of the modern Western Mystery tradition'. Does very good book reviews of books from different traditions.

■ **Quest,** *BCM-SCL Quest, London , WC1N 3XX.* Practical information on modern Magic, Astrology, Witchcraft and Occultism. Sample £1.

■ **Sut Anubis,** *Occultique, 73 Kettering Rd, Northampton NN1 4AW.* Original articles on Witchcraft, Crowleyanity, Ceremonial Magic, Paganism, current events, news. Sample copy £1.50, subs £5.75 for 4.

■ **Wood and Water,** *4 High Tor Cl, Babbacombe Rd, Bromley, Kent.* A Goddess-inclined eco-pagan magazine. Sample copies 85p. Subs £3.40 for four issues.

■ **The Cauldron,** *Caemorgan Cottage, Cardigan, Dyfed, SA43 1QU.* Pagan journal of the Old Religion, Wicca, Odinism, Druidism and Earth Mysteries.

■ **Lamp of Thoth,** *4 Burley Lodge Rd, Leeds LS6 1QP.* Features Chaos Magick, Wicca, Shamanism, Thelema, Sub Genius Discordianism and The Sinister. Qtly, sample issue £2.25, subs 6 issues £10.50.

■ **The Sorcerer's Apprentice,** *The Crescent, Hyde Park Corner, Leeds LS6 2NW, (0532 753835).* From unabashed magic spells to occult sexual attractants. Extensive mail order catalogue and comprehensive book list.

GROUPS

■ **Asatru Folk Runic Workshop,** *Freya Aswynn, 43 St Georges Ave, N7 (607 9695).* Northern Mysteries Study Group. Courses in runecraft, lectures, consultations.

■ **Centre for Pagan Studies,** *Flat B, 5 Trinity Rise, SW2 (671 6372).* Provides classes and workshops on European Paganism, Shamanism and Witchcraft. Also mythology, folklore and earth mysteries.

■ **The London Group,** *BM Vixack, WC1N 3XX..* Western mysteries study group, correspondence course on Kaballah and related subjects.

■ **Green Circle,** *Elizabeth Hornby, 43 St Georges Ave, N7 (607 9695).* Open Pagan social fellowship particularly for those who are as yet undecided on a particular path.

■ **Pagan Federation,** *c/o Gareth Evans, 43 St Georges Ave, N7 (607 9695).* Promotes greater contact and awareness among pagans and aims to present the truth about paganism to the world. Publish *The Wiccan* 50p.

■ **Odinic Rite,** *BCM Runic, WC1N 3XX .* Charity promoting the religion and tradition of Northern Europe.

■ **Acca and Abba,** *BCM Academia, WC1N 3XX (677 5837).* Occult tuition centre, witchcraft ritual magic and tarot.

■ **Panakeia,** *1 Ravenstone Rd, N8.* Women's mysteries group, include feminism and ecology.

■ **House of the Goddess,** *33 Oldridge Rd, SW12 (673 6370).* Matriarchal tradition. Run courses. Publish *Craft Circular* qtly, news, events etc. Sample 45p, subs £1.50 pa.

■ **The Magickal Teahouse,** *33 Oldridge Rd, SW12 (673 6370).* Pagan cafe also sells occult paraphernalia and holds events. SAE for programme.

■ **Pagan Funeral Trust,** *BM Box 3337, WC1N 3XX.* Non-profit making organisation dedicated to providing Pagan rites of passage for those of the old and new faith. Newsletter twice yearly, sub 50p.

■ **Servants of the Light,** *PO Box 215, St Helier, Jersey, Channel Islands.* Occult school with origins in the Golden Dawn. Runs correspondence course in mystical Qabalah. Publish *Round Merlin's Table.*

■ **Directory of Occult Resources (DOOR),** *Spiral Publications, 8 King St, Glastonbury, Somerset BA6 9JY.* Lists periodicals, directories, networks, groups, events, services etc. Sample issue £2.50 plus 45p p&p, subs 4 issues £11.

Shamanism

This is found as part of the native cultures of many different societies all over the world e.g. the Aborigines of Australia, Lapplanders, and American Indians. Traditionally the shaman uses rhythmic drumming and chanting, or more rarely, hallucinogenic drugs to alter consciousness and journey into 'non-ordinary reality' (as Carlos Castenada called it in his popular *Don Juan* shamanic books) in order to gain insight, heal the sick or make contact with guides or teachers. It is largely the shamanism of the North American Indians which has made the most impact, with their *sweat lodge* tradition (a sort of do-it-yourself sauna in which participants chant for long periods) and the *medicine wheel* teachings. Ritual, mask-making and a positive relationship with nature are also important elements. Tends to be held as workshops rather than ongoing groups, sometimes led by shamanic teachers visiting the UK from abroad, especially the US.

■ **Eagle's Wing Centre for Shamanic Studies,** *58 Westbere Rd, NW2 (435 8174).* Courses and weekends in shamanism and teachings of North American Indians.

■ **Open Gate,** *6 Goldney Rd, Clifton, Bristol, (0272 7345952).* Occasional workshops in shamanism, awakening the dreambody, as well as on spirituality/psychotherapy. Held in London and Devon.

■ **Medicine Ways,** *Galdraheim, 35 Wilson Ave, Deal, Kent CT14 9NL.* Journal of worldwide shamanism including resources and events, psychotherapy, medicine counselling, energy work, dowsing, healing. Correspondence course in Shamanism.

Sufism

Sufism is sometimes called the mystical wing of Islam. Traditionally undogmatic, the aim of Sufi seekers is direct experience of, and union with, God or as Sufi poets have put it 'intoxication with the Beloved'. It has been called 'the way of the heart', and places emphasis on intuition. One medium of sufi devotion is the arts, particularly music and poetry. Teaching is often through parables. Practices include meditation, guided visualisation, breathing exercises, music and dancing.

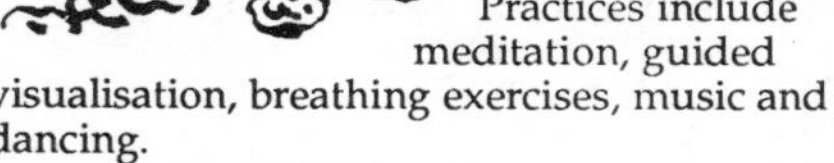

■ **London Sufi Centre,** *21 Lancaster Rd, W11 (221 3215).* Founded by Pir Vilyat Khan. Activities include meditation, sacred dances, Zikr, healing. Run counselling centre at same address, which seeks to synthesise eastern and western traditions.

■ **Nimatullahi Order,** *41 Chepstow Pl, W2 (229 0769).* You have to be initiated by head of order before you attend meetings, who will see you after you've read up on Sufism and initiate you if he thinks you're sincere.

▼ OTHER GROUPS/CENTRES ▼

Below are listed groups and centres which don't fall easily into any particular tradition mentioned above.

■ **Aetherius Society**, *757 Fulham Rd, SW6 (736 4187).* In 1954 Dr George King was given a command to: 'Prepare yourself! You are to become the Voice of Interplanetary Parliament!' His previous practice of Yoga enabled him to go into a trace state and make contact with a Being from the Planet Venus, called Aetherius. The society aims to spread the teachings of this and other interplanetary guides, including Jesus and Buddha who came from Venus. This solar system is believed to be ruled by an interplanetary parliament based on Saturn. Planets are classrooms where we learn various lessons through thousands of lives. A new master is to come shortly in a flying saucer to lead those who are ready into a New World. They practice various kinds of yoga, prayer, mantra yoga, pranayama, spiritual healing. Sun am, Mon eve meetings.

■ **Anthroposophical Society**, *35 Park Rd, NW1 (723 4400).* Founded by Rudolph Steiner who found application for his theories in many areas: there are Steiner, doctors and hospitals using his theories, and agriculturalists. There are also Steiner Schools (see **Kids** section).

■ **Baha'i Faith**, *27 Rutland Gt, SW7 (377 7589).* Founded by Baha'u'llah (born in Persia in 1817), they believe in the oneness and equality of mankind. They have their own scriptures, holy places and parliament. Youth meetings Weds 8, open meeting Thurs at 8.

■ **Barry Long Foundation**, *BCM Box 876, London WC1 (341 3850).* Founded on the teachings of an Australian, straight-talking guru who teaches mainly through tapes and books on topics such as meditation, the way to happiness, how to stop thinking etc (though he sometimes visits this country to give talks and seminars). No religious dogma or group as such - followers practice individually.

■ **Beshara Trust**, *Sherborne Hse Stables, Sherborne, Cheltenham, Glos, (04514 448).* Though their roots were in Sufism, do not align themselves now with any one religious tradition but offer residential study courses covering economics, science, arts, mysticism etc in order to discover the 'eternal truths, accessible to each person'.

■ **Druid Order**, *161 Auckland Rd, SE19 (771 0684).* Perform ancient ceremonies to mark Spring and Autumn Equinoxes in London, and Summer Solstice at Stonehenge. Druidism is an ancient British religion, which, among other things, stresses the interrelation of opposites within and without. Fortnightly meetings, classes of instruction, ritual etc.

■ **Findhorn Foundation**, *Cluny Hill College, Forres, Scotland IU36 0RD, ((0309) 73655).* Educational spiritual centre with strong non-denominational outlook. Guests can visit and participate in the residential community for a few days or weeks. *Experience week* includes meditation, dance, games, nature outings, work and simply being. Also run special events and workshops on various themes; creativity, management, aspects of spirituality. Publish magazine *One Earth* £2.25 qtly.

■ **Free Daist Communion**, *39 Tabley Rd, N19 (607 3235).* Followers of Master Da Free John, western born spiritual adept. Teaching is about happiness - we are already happy but we don't know it because we are so involved in the self-absorbed quest for happiness. You study teachings and then move onto awareness practice of how you separate yourself from happiness and the world around you.

■ **Graigian Society**, *10 Lady Somerset Rd, NW5 (485 1646)* (between 12 noon and 6pm). Eclectic religion containing elements of Gurdjieff, Jung and tarot. Very much concerned with Green issues, they aim to create 'a natural and sensitive world'. Small residential community whose members do pottery, mask-making, puppetry and weaving in a creative environment. Open to visitors, but ring first during times specified above.

■ **International School of the Golden Rosycross**, *45 Woodlands Rd, Earlswood, Redhill, RH1 6HB.* The Rosicrucians are a western mystical tradition founded in about 1425 by Christian Rosenkreutz who visited India disguised as a monk, returning with a secret doctrine gleaned from gurus there, or as another story goes passed down from teacher to pupil from the lost city of Atlantis. They emphasise knowledge, and study esoteric wisdom from different traditions (notably the Kaballah) in order to know 'Divine Truth, Wisdom and Love'.

■ **Krishnamurti Foundation,** *(650 7023).* Krishnamurti, born 1895, was 'discovered' in India at the age of 14 . He was adopted as a leader and brought to the West and educated at Oxford. He denounced all paths to the 'truth', something which did not deter his followers who packed his talks.

■ **Lucis Trust,** *Suite 54, 3 Whitehall Ct, SW1 (839 4512).* Set up in 1923 by Alice Bailey who had 24 books on esoteric subjects dictated telepathically by a Tibetan. Monthly full moon public meetings in Charing Cross Hotel. Run several projects: *World Goodwill* which aims to form international links founded on goodwill, and publishes papers and a newsletter on global problems; *Triangles* where a group of three people form a mental link by meditating for a few minutes each day; *The Arcane School* which runs correspondence courses (donation according to circumstances) and the *Lucis Press* which publishes the books.

■ **Life Training Centre,** *16 Talbot Rd, W2 (727 0652).* Founded by two Americans: a psychotherapist, Bradford Brown, and a Christian minister (an unusually dynamic one by British standards), Roy Whitten, whose gritty but compassionate approach is a synthesis of psychology, therapy and spiritual work in a 35 hour weekend training (£150 inc. VAT). Evening groups on self esteem (£60).

■ **Order of Bards, Ovates & Druids,** *260 Kew Rd, Richmond, Surrey TW9 3EG.* Students learn mostly through correspondence course about Druidry. The student rises through the three grades of *Bard, Ovate* and *Druid.* Aims of the Order are to 'help the individual develop his potential - spiritual, intellectual, emotional, physical and artistic' and ' to work with the natural world, to cherish and protect it, and co-operate with it in every way'. Runs campaign for Individual Ecological Responsibility and Tree Planting Programme.

■ **Purnima Rajneesh Centre for Meditation,** *1st Floor, Spring Ho, Spring Pl, NW5 (284 1415).* New centre run by followers of Shree Rajneesh, whose mixed fortunes since the height of his popularity in the 70s have led him through a large ashram in India, $6m ranch in the US, alleged murder attempts on US citizens by his close followers and now to a change of name (to 'Osho' Rajneesh). They use synthesis of western therapeutic techniques (encounter, bodywork etc) and traditional eastern yoga, meditation, sacred dance. Rajneesh encounter groups in days gone by had a reputation for 'no holds barred' and in a very few cases ended in injury to participants, though things are very different now. Various meditations include 'Dynamic' which involves very vigorous physical and vocal expression - good for those who find 'sitting' meditation difficult. Demonstrations of this and other meditations every day (80p charge). Videos of Shree Rajneesh, workshops.

■ **School of Economic Science,** *90 Queensgate, SW7 (835 1256).* Various courses (philosophy, economics, ethics) which consist of lectures held over 10 or 12 weeks. Emphasis on 'wisdom, truth, consciousness, the powers available to man and what inhibits his development'. £30 per course, £15 FT students.

■ **Theosophical Society,** *50 Gloucester Pl, W1 (935 9261).* Founded by Madame Blavatsky in 1875, Theosophy means 'Divine wisdom', encourages the study of different religions as well as philosophy and science to penetrate the universal truth each holds. Believe all life is one, that it is evolving (through reincarnation), in the brotherhood of all mankind and human perfectibility. Public lectures on Sundays, library and bookshop. Astrological Lodge runs courses and workshops.

■ **Teilhard Centre,** *23 Kensington Sq, W8 (937 5372).* Teilhard de Chardin was a Jesuit priest and a scientist. He saw the principal of evolution towards ultimate unity (the 'Omega'-Point) as underlying everything, both biological and spiritual. Has library, holds seminars, conferences, groups, meditation groups, study, discussion of science.

■ **Saros,** *26 Buckingham Gr, West Timperley, Altrincham, Cheshire WA14 5AH, (061 962 8459),* draws its inspiration from eastern and western religious experience. Practices include study, open-ended discussion groups, exploring myth and movement developed from different disciplines.

■ **School of Meditation,** *158 Holland Park Ave, W11 (603 6116).* Teach meditation using mantra. Instruction over 12 weeks once a week; individual or group tuition available. Cost usually 1 week's wages, £50-£60 concs.

■ **St James's,** *197 Piccadilly, W1 (734 4511).* As well as being a healing centre, run 'Alternatives' programme - a series of talks and workshops on ecology, spirituality, and 'New Age' concerns.

■ **Subud,** *452 Uxbridge Rd, W12.* Can put you in touch with local groups. Bapak is their teacher, though they stress he is not a guru. 'Latihan' is the basic spiritual practice, which involves an hour's worship and purification, which may entail singing, dancing or crying. Not dogmatic and tolerate other religions.

■ **White Eagle Lodge,** *9 St Mary Abbots Pl, W8 (603 7914).* Non denominational Christian church founded 1936 on teachings of spirit guide White Eagle by his contact on earth, Grace Cooke. Services Sun 6.00, spiritual healing Mon and Tue 3.45.

■ **Urasenke Foundation,** *c/o Michael Birch, 4 Langton Way, SE3 (853 2595)* The London representative of a Japanese school, teaches through the performance of the tea ceremony. Sessions are £10, and you have to be a member of the society.

Spiritualism and Psychism

This is a broad area which in general covers all practices where contact is made with spirits or entities either from beyond death or another plane. This contact may be for different purposes: for healing, proving after-death survival, seeing the future, or for advice. A new form of this has developed called *channelling* where a spirit guide is said to send messages (often of a philosophical nature) to one particular person who then becomes the permanent channel for this guide. It is particularly this kind of psychism which has taken off in the US where people even 'channel' dolphins. A number of books have been written in this way. As with all spiritualism and psychism, it tends to provoke strong reactions one way or the other - you either love it or you hate it.

■ **College of Psychic Studies,** *16 Queensberry Pl, SW7 (589 3292).* Courses on various aspects of psychism etc. Non-religious.

■ **Psychic News,***20 Earlham St, WC2 (240 3032).* News and ads for spiritualists (wkly 22p). Bookshop at no. 22.

■ **Spiritualist Association,** *33 Belgrave St, SW1 (235 3351).* Clairvoyance with emphasis on survival after death, not fortune telling. Also do healing. Private appts, public demonstrations at 3.30 and 7.00. Lecture at 7.00. £2 for non members.

■ **National Federation of Spiritual Healers,** *Old Manor Farm Studio, Church St, Sunbury on Thames, Middx, (09327 83164).* Can put you in touch with local member healer.

▼ DIVINATION ▼

Human beings have for a long time been devising ingenious ways to try to make an uncertain world more certain: reading cards, gazing into fires, dropping hot wax into bowls of water and interpreting the shape chicken's entrails take when thrown on the ground, to name but a few. In the past fortune tellers and seers have had enormous power - in some cases they decided matters of state and the fate of whole nations (as did the famous oracle at Delphi in Greece). Divination can be about finding out what's going to happen, or it can attempt to discover the *meaning* of events for an individual. Methods like the I Ching and Tarot place an emphasis on the latter, and, used for the better don't offer predictions so much as clarification about what different courses of action may mean in terms of your life as a whole. Used in this way, the oracles don't look into the future so much as more deeply into the present, bringing greater awareness of the opportunities and challenges presenting themselves in a situation.

Astrology

Not just a matter of 'sun signs' but of working out every planet's position and the relationships between them at the exact time of your birth in order to show character, psychological make-up and attitudes. Predictive astrology compares the the positions of planets in the future to those at the time of birth in order to discover future events or trends. *Synastry* involves comparing the charts of two people to reveal the dynamics of their relationship.

The explanation of astrology favoured by most modern astrologers is that rather than the planets 'causing' things it's more a matter of 'sychronicity'. This is the idea of C G Jung (founder of a major psychotherapeutic school) who believed that what happens in one sphere of existence reflects and is connected to what happens in another - 'As above, so below'.

So far research has largely failed to prove that astrology works, with the exception of the startling results of the Gauqelins, who set out to disprove astrology but through analysis of thousands of charts found a significant link between profession and the position of planets on four major points in the horoscope (see *Written in the Stars* by Michel Gauqelin, Aquarian £6.99).

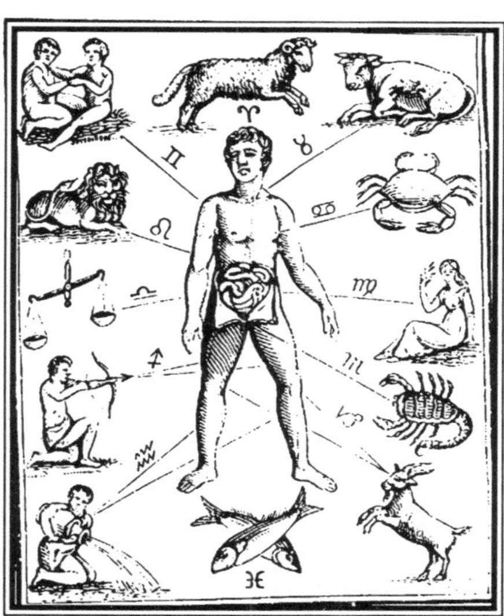

Astrologers have different approaches: some will 'predict the future' but many prefer to use the chart as a tool for character analysis - some in conjunction with counselling.

■ **Astrological Association,** *PO Box 39, North PDO, Nottingham NG5 5PD, (0602 265473).* Professional association publishes bi-mthly journal, lectures, workshops on various aspects of astrology, promotes research. Meetings in London.

■ **Astrological Lodge,** *BM Astrolodge, WC1N 3XX (624 1913).* Classes and lectures (some free), workshops. Publishes Astrology qtly. Meets Mon at *Art Workers' Guild, 6 Queen Sq, WC1.*

■ **Centre for Psychological Astrology,** *PO Box 890, NW3 2JZ (267 5913).* Use Jungian influenced approach to interpretation, founded by Liz Greene whose books are an interesting read even for the non astrological - especially *Relating - an astrological guide to living with others on a small planet* (Aquarian Press £2.99). Seminars Sun.

■ **Company of Astrologers,** *6 Queen Sq, WC1 (837 4410).* Wide range of courses which seek to take in range of approaches from divination, psychotherapy and modern philosophy.

■ **Faculty of Astrological Studies,** *29A Sussex Rd, Hayward's Heath, Sussex RH16 4DZ, (0444 453504).* Reputedly one of the best schools, its diploma (DFAstrolS) is highest qualification available. Seminars in London Sats. Register of consultants available.

■ **Mayo School,** *Alvana Gdns, Tregavethan, Truro, Cornwall TR4 9EN, (0872 560048).* Correspondence course to Certificate and Diploma level (DMS Astrol). List of consultants.

■ **Urania Trust,** *396 Caledonian Rd, N1 (607 4133).* Publishes Astrology Calendar and Directory (free) listing organisations, events, periodicals etc. Sponsors groups and schools to promote education in astrology.

Tarot

No-one knows where Tarot cards came from, Aleister Crowley thought they came from Ancient Egypt, and others have claimed their origins were in the Kabalah, Gnosticism, or the Haiwaian Huna tribe. In the Renaissance they were used as ordinary playing cards of which they are the forebears.

The designs of different packs range from traditional medieval woodcuts (the *Marseilles* version is the most famous) to modern reinterpretations. These modern packs include those of the occultists such as A E Waite (of the Golden Dawn group of magicians), Crowley, or Eliphas Levi, as well as by modern teachers such as Ouspensky and Shree Rajneesh. The Motherpeace Tarot pack uses round cards and reinterprets meanings and positions in an ingeniously non-patriarchal way.

There are 78 cards; the first 22 are known as the Major Arcana and are, according to various commentators, of astrological, numerological and archetypal significance. They can be seen in mythical terms as a journey from innocence through experience to knowledge and wholeness. The Minor Arcana consist of four suites: cups, clubs (or batons), swords and pentacles.

They can be used for meditation, reflection, analysis and fortune telling.

They're sold at Watkins (p160), Mysteries (p155) and Compendium (p153). A classic introduction is A E Waite's *Pictorial Key to the Tarot* (though some interpretations read a bit like something out of Greek tragedy). An in-depth study of the symbolism of the Major Arcana is given in *Jung and Tarot* Sallie Nichols (Weiser), and *The New Feminist Tarot* Jean Freer (Aquarian Press £4.99) gives a creative, contemporary approach.

■ **Faculty of Contemporary Tarot Studies,** *28d Montague St, WC1.* Publish *Arcana* - Tarot, metaphysics, mysticism, magic, astrology sub £3.50 for 4 issues.

Numerology

Each number has a particular quality and indicates the nature of whatever it's attached to: house numbers, dates of events, people. Date of birth or event can be added up. Each letter of the alphabet also has a number value:

1	2	3	4	5	6	7	8	9
A	B	C	D	E	F	G	H	I
J	K	L	M	N	O	P	Q	R
S	T	U	V	W	X	Y	Z	

Allocate each letter of your name together, add together all the numbers, and then add digits of the sum together until reduced to a single digit. Changes to birth name (e.g. nicknames adopted, name changes on marriage etc) indicate changes in character or roles you've adopted, and names can be altered to bring about better 'vibes'. Birth date number is calculated by adding together each digit of birth date. So if you were born on 14th April 1957 your birth number would be calculated by adding 1+4+4 +1+9+5+7 = 31 which gives a birth number of 4. Kabalists use numerology in its more occult significance, and they give letters a different value based on the Hebrew alphabet.

Palmistry

Doctors diagnose certain conditions by observing the state of the nails and hands. Palmistry takes this a lot further and reads lines, shape and proportions of the hands to analyse character and predict destiny. Classic introductions are Cheiro's *The Language of the Hand* (Arrow £2.50) and Beryl Hutchinson's *Your Life in Your Hands.*

Graphology

Handwriting is interpreted to show character, psychological make-up (such as tendencies towards extraversion or introversion), emotional stability, creativity and intellectual capacity. For instance, forward slanting writing shows an outgoing nature, while backwards slanting is shy and introverted. Now almost respectable as some US and European companies use it as part of selection of executives - though there's disagreement about how fair or reliable graphology is. A good introduction is M Gullan-Whur's *What Your Handwriting Reveals* (Aquarian Press).

I Ching

Perhaps the most venerable of all oracles, the 3,000 year old Chinese 'Book of Changes' is based on the philosophy that the basic energy of the cosmos, *Ch'i*, is made up of two opposite elements which constantly change and interact. These elements are *Yin* (receptive, dark, feminine) and *Yang* (active, light, masculine). The 64 *hexagrams* are figures made of six lines: Yin (broken - -) and Yang (unbroken —) which all have different meanings. Each line also has a specific interpretation.

To consult the I Ching usually three coins are thrown, though real afficionados use a more complex system throwing 49 yarrow stalks. Heads has a numerical value of 2, and tails of 3. The total value of a throw gives you either a broken or an unbroken line thus:

6 = - - (moving)
7 = ——
8 = - -
9 = —— (moving)

You throw a total of six times, and at each throw record the line, starting at the bottom to build up a figure of six lines, one on top of the other. This is called a *hexagram*, which you can then look up in the book for its interpretation.

Three heads or three tails makes a 'moving line' which has a special interpretation and changes the hexagram into another.

Steeped in Taoism and Confuscianism, the I Ching can sometimes deliver seemingly cryptic messages. Interpretation relies on receptivity and some objectivity about the situation. Framing the question is important, and it works best with what will happen if I do so and so questions, and not with either/ or questions. It often reveals what you may already subconsciously know.

It was used by C G Jung, who wrote the introduction to the best version, translated by Richard Wilhelm (Arkana £7.99). Some versions have been freely adapted to focus on particular areas, such as *The I Ching on Love* Guy Damian-Knight (Blandford Press), *I Ching on Business and Decision-Making* also by Guy Damian Knight (Century Paperbacks £5.99).

Centres

■ **Merlins 8,** *26 Wardour St, W1 (434 2951).* Tarot, palmistry, astrology, psychometry (divination from an object), graphology, mediums. Bookshop also sells mystical paraphernalia.

■ **Mysteries,** *9 Monmouth St, WC2 (240 3688).* Tarot, palmistry, astrology, graphology, crystal ball readings.

■ **British Astrological and Psychic Society,** *21 Warnham Ct Rd, Carshalton Beeches, Surrey SM5 3LY, (643 2293).* Have register of consultant members, vetted by them. Membership open to public £8, (consultant members £18) includes Mercury newsletter (qtly). Some ad hoc workshops.

▼ PSYCHOTHERAPY ▼ AND GROWTH

There are four main approaches to psychotherapy: psychoanalytic, cognitive, behavioural and humanistic.

The **psychoanalytic** approach developed by Sigmund Freud explains behaviour in terms of the interplay between what is conscious, and what has been repressed into the unconscious mind (especially, according to Freud, sexual and aggressive feelings).

Cognitive psychology argues that we make sense of the world using particular views and assumptions which have been formed by our previous experience. By adopting another point of view, we can change our behaviour.

Behavioural psychotherapy sees people as conditioned by their environment. By being rewarded for behaving in a certain way, and punished for not acting in that way, we can relearn more appropriate ways of acting.

Humanistic psychotherapy, unlike orthodox psychiatry, does not aim to adjust people to society's idea of 'normality'. Instead it seeks to uncover the inner life of the individual, and affirm her unique view and experience of the world. It tends to be less 'illness' based and is more 'growth' oriented.

Bioenergetics

Was developed by Alexander Lowen, a pupil of Wilhelm Reich who believed that we block the flow of life energy through the body by chronically tensing muscles forming a 'character armour' at various stages of childhood development. Physical posture reveal a person's character. Building on Reich's theory, Lowen invented many physical exercises to release this tension and so change the personality. There are stress positions such as the 'grounding position' (legs slightly apart, knees bent and back arched slightly backwards) which are held until muscles begin to vibrate and release energy as well as active cathartic exercises such as hitting cushions with tennis rackets and pounding mattresses.

■ **Open Centre,** *188 Old St, EC1 (549 9583).* Workshops in many different therapies (including encounter, gestalt, various body therapies) as well as bioenergetics.

■ **British Institute for Bioenergetic Analysis,** *22 Fitzjohn's Ave, NW3 (435 1079).*

Biodynamic Psychology

Developed by Gerda Boyesen, also out of Reich's work, uses massage to release chronic muscular and emotional blocks. It emphasises the part played by the intestine in 'digesting' and discharging stress, and a stethoscope is used to listen to the sounds made in this process. Repressed feelings often emerge as physical tension is released.

■ **Gerda Boyesen Centre for Biodynamic Psychology,** *Acacia Hse, Central Avenue, W3 (743 2437).* Fully trained therapists as well as low cost massage from trainees. Short courses in massage and 2-4 year training in massage and psychotherapy.

Co-Counselling

Co-counselling doesn't involve a professionally trained therapist - two people meet together and agree to counsel each other for an equal amount of time each taking turns to be 'client' and 'counsellor'. The client is in charge and determines what she wants to talk about, for how long, and how much she wants the counsellor to intervene. The counsellor's job is to listen to the client, stick with the material she produces and, if requested, reflect back material.

To train you do a basic 40 hour course and then you can join a network of people with whom you can practice.

■ **London Co-Counselling Community,** *17 Lisburne Rd, NW3 (485 0005).*

Encounter

There are different types of encounter group, but all are designed to encourage participants to drop social masks and unnecessary inhibitions so that they can encounter each other in more real ways. Groups members are encouraged not only to express feelings they might normally repress or distort, but to be honest about what they think or feel about other group members.

In 'open encounter' pioneered by Will Schutz, emphasis is placed on physical expression of emotions as well as verbal - for instance if one group member was angry with another and wanted to kick her into action, she might be encouraged to kick a cushion around the room. The Rogerian or basic encounter group aims to create an atmosphere of empathy and honesty, and the leader is not directive.

Groups last from a few hours to several days (called a *marathon* encounter where participants may not get very much sleep).

■ **Open Centre** (see above), Evening on-going groups and weekend 'marathons'.

■ **Spectrum,** *7 Endymion Rd N4 (341 2277).* On-going evening and 'marathon' groups, single sex groups available.

Feminist Therapy

Feminist therapy emerged out of consciousness-raising groups and rape crisis work. Women felt that sexist assumptions were being made by some therapists and they wanted to develop an alternative. Feminist therapists include an awareness of women's conditioning and role in society and often focus on the areas of anger and power, self-care, and sexuality. Feminist therapy also deals with issues which affect women more than men, such as compulsive eating or starving, abortion and fertility, family relationships.

■ **Pellin Feminist Therapy Centre,** *43 Killyon Rd, SW8 (622 0148).* Various weekend workshops and training course in psychotherapy for women.

■ **Women's Therapy Centre,** *6 Manor Gdns, N7 (263 6200).* Wide range of workshops include sexuality, eating problems, racism, assertiveness training. Sliding scale of charges.

Gestalt

Gestalt therapy encourages awareness of body and feelings in the 'here and now', rather than analysing and finding causes in the past. People are seen as fully responsible for their own feelings, ideas and actions. For instance, if you say you are confused the therapist may ask you 'how do you confuse yourself?'.

'Gestalt' means shape or whole in German. In Gestalt therapy the personality is seen as comprising of many different parts, some of which are in conflict or try to dominate each other ('topdog' and 'underdog' parts). All dream elements are thought of as parts of the individual's psyche, and clients may be asked to identify with the elements to find out what the dream means for them. Another characteristic technique is *the empty chair* - for instance, if you had not expressed your feelings to someone close to you, such as your mother, you may be asked to imagine her sitting in an empty chair, and to say the things you wished you had said to her, imagine what she'd say back, and then to continue the dialogue.

■ **Gestalt Centre,** *64 Warwick Rd, St Albans, Herts, (0727 64806).* Runs groups at various locations, including EC1. Concs available. Run long term part-time training.

■ **Gestalt in West London,** *36 Newburgh, W3, (993 0868).* Individuals, groups and couples .

Hypnotherapy

Hypnotherapists guide their clients into a state of deep relaxation where the defences of the conscious mind no longer operate. It is most often used to treat habits, addictions, phobias and anxiety. The therapist may do this by implanting a new, positive suggestion in the client's mind - for instance: 'When you leave here you will want to smoke less', or by uncovering repressed feelings or memories which may be at the root of problems. You can't be made to do anything against your will in hypnosis, or against your code of ethics.

Self hypnosis is also taught by hypnotherapists.

■ **British Hypnotherapy Assn,** *1 Wythburn Pl, W1 (723 4443).* Write stating briefly problem and your age, enclosing £2 for list of practitioners.

■ **UK Training College of Hypnotherapy and Counselling,** *10 Alexander St, W2 (221 1796).*

Neuro-Linguistic Programming (NLP)

Created by studying closely the way outstanding therapists communicated and helped their clients change. NLP therapists and their clients learn a number of techniques. These include *matching* where the therapist watches the eye and head movements, breathing and pupil size of the client to find out whether the client is recalling a memory visually, by hearing or kinesthetically. She can then communicate back using the same sense, and so develop a better rapport. *Anchoring* is creating a good experience or memory as a resource, which can then be connected to an unpleasant memory to lessen its painful associations.

■ **UK Training Centre for NLP,** *11 Buckland Cres, NW3 (483 2384).* Runs proficiency, diploma and advanced courses. 5 day course £395.

Psychoanalytic Psychotherapy & Jungian Analysis

Psychoanalytic psychotherapy holds to the basic theories of Freud in which neurosis is the result of repressed feelings and memories which become 'unconscious'. The relationship which develops between analyst and patient involves 'transference' – feelings and impulses you originally had towards important figures from the past (usually parents) which revive and are redirected towards the analyst who then tries to make you aware of them. In attempting to explore the unconscious, you also encounter 'resistance' - defences (e.g. forgetfulness) which prevent repressed emotions coming into consciousness. Becoming aware of the unconscious and its defences frees the patient from compulsive behaviour and problems.

Jung broke with Freud because he felt the unconscious was not only a 'dustbin' for childhood emotions, but also a source of creativity and growth, and at a deep level reflected the history of the whole of the human race and the cosmic order. He called this the *collective unconscious*. He also invented a system of personality types, part of which is the well known classification of 'extravert' (sociable, outgoing) and introvert' (shy, sensitive, inward-looking), and placed great emphasis on the creative power of dreams.

■ **British Association of Psychotherapists,** *121 Hendon La, N3 (346 1747).* £25 for assessment interview, then £18 per session. Phone them - not a drop in centre.

■ **Tavistock Clinic,** *120 Belsize La, NW3 (435 7111).* NHS referral by GP necessary. Also run family unit, and counselling for young people (up to 27).

■ **Association of Jungian Analysts,** *3-7 Eton Ave, NW3 (794 8711).*

■ **Imprint,** *377 Wimbledon Pk Rd, SW19 (788 1500).* Jungian analysis plus art therapy.

Psychodrama

In Psychodrama group members take turns to work on an issue. The person working on an issue gives a description of the people involved (eg the family), the scene and so on and chooses other group members to act out the parts. The therapist directs the action. Roles may be switched so that you can see the situation from the point of view of the person you're in conflict with (for instance), and get some insight into the situation – the process may also bring strong emotions up. The cast discuss at the end what happened and how they felt playing their roles.

■ **Open Centre,** *(549 9583)* (p 156) runs some w/ end workshops.

■ **Holwell Centre for Psychodrama and Sociodrama,** *East Down, Barnstaple, Devon, (027 182 267).* Workshops in Londo/residentials in Devon.

Psychosynthesis

Psychosynthesis is based on 'transpersonal' psychology, which emphasises the importance of spirituality, the imagination and creativity, as well as resolving conflicts and problems.

The personality is seen as made up of many different parts or roles ('subpersonalities') which need to be harmonised through the 'self', a sense of awareness which is not identified with any one part. Beyond the personality is the higher unconscious (concerned with creativity, joy and vision) and the lower unconscious (concerned with basic drives and memories). Assagioli, who founded Psychosynthesis, also emphasised the importance of the 'will', by which he meant the ability to make conscious choices and take responsibility for one's life. Images and symbols are often used to clarify feelings and situations.

■ **Institute of Psychosynthesis,** *3The Barn, Nan Clark's Lane, NW7, (959 2330).* Counselling service for individual sessions, workshops, training course.

■ **Trust for the Furtherance of Psychosynthesis and Education,** *188-194 Old St, EC1 (608 2231).* Counselling service, workshops, training course.

■ **Moving Line,** *c/o 13 Oldfield Mews, N6* . A group of counsellors covering different areas of London. North: *341 4413;* South East: *656 9209;* East: *790 8146;* South West: *733 7883.* Individual sessions and workshops.

Rebirthing

This is based on the idea that an experience of birth which is painful or traumatic (as most hospital deliveries are) leaves you with emotional scars and sets negative patterns for the rest of life. By reliving your birth these negative attitudes can be changed. You lie in a quiet, comfortable room and do a breathing exercise until memories of birth or experience in the womb come back. The rebirther may give you 'affirmations' afterwards which replace negative beliefs with positive ones, for instance if you believe that life is struggle your affirmation may be 'life is easy and effortless'.

■ **British Rebirth Society,** *18a Great Percy St, WC1 (833 0741).* Will send copy of magazine 'Breathe' which has list of rebirthers.

■ **Holistic Rebirthing Institute,** *23 Albany Terr, Leamington Spa, Warks, (0926 882494).* Training courses in rebirthing.

Transactional Analysis (TA)

Created by Eric Berne, a Canadian psychoanalyst, whose bestseller *Games People Play* describes ways people relate to each other to avoid getting too close. He invented the idea of the *life script* – a life plan which we live out from decisions made in childhood even though we've forgotten about them. He thought we have three ways of functioning which are in constant interaction with each other - the Parent (often based on our actual parents), the Adult who is objective and rational, and the Child who is spontaneous and acts on feelings.

■ **South London Psychotherapy Training Centre,** *106 Heathwood Gdns, SE7 (854 3606).* Also offer training course.

■ **Metanoia,** *13 North Common Rd, W5 (579 2505).* Workshops on a variety of topics - not just TA - as well as a training programme.

■ **Institute of Transactional Analysis,** *BM Box 4104, WC1 (404 5011).* Therapists and counsellors throughout London. Training sessions for teachers.

How to Find a Therapist

As yet there is no official standard of training so anyone can set themselves up - though by 1992 there should be a system of accreditation which will ensure that practising therapists have had a thorough training. Personal recommendation is often best, or you can use or contact one of the groups below.

■ **Association of Humanistic Psychology Practitioners,** *c/o 45 Litchfield Way, NW1.* Write for list of practitioners.

■ **Association for Humanistic Psychology in Britain (AHP(B)),** *c/o Huddlestone Rd, E7.* Lectures, workshops, publishes journal *Self & Society*, runs *Whirl-y-Gig* alternative disco (Sat 8pm, *Notre Dame Hall, 6 Leicester Pl, WC2* £4, £3 concs).

■ **Concessions Register,** *55A Longridge Rd, SW5 9SF (244 7578).* Have list of qualified therapists and alternative medicine practitioners who offer concessions to low/unwaged. Send sae for list.

■ **Help Advisory Service** *(937 7687)* (p71) run free groups for young people.

■ **Minster Centre,** *57 Minster Rd, NW2 (435 9200).* Group and individual sessions, training course includes wide range of approaches.

■ **Open Centre,** *188 Old St, EC1 (549 9583).* Gestalt, psychodrama, encounter, TA, massage, Feldenkrais method, bioenergetics, primal integration, and more. Weekend workshops and ongoing evening groups.

■ **Pathways,** *12 Southcote Rd, N19 (607 7852)* information for the public on therapy, growth and healing. Publicity for therapists. Produce bulletin.

■ **Playspace,** *Short Court Unit, Polytechnic of Central London, 35 Marylebone Rd, W1 (935 3874)* run weekend workshops in psychodrama, gestalt etc.

■ **Spectrum,** *7 Endymion Rd, N4 (341 2277).* Wide range of workshops, including a sexuality programme.

■ **Westminster Pastoral Foundation,** *23 Kensington Sq, W8 (937 6956).* Individual and group sessions. Concs available. Short courses on aspects of counselling and training.

Publications

■ **Human Potential Magazine,** *3 Netherby Rd, SE23 (291 6254).* Qtly. Has some of the most relevant articles in the area of self development and growth, psychotherapy and spirituality. Subjects range from unconditional love, dream interpretation, coping with money, swimming with dolphins, women's and men's issues, relationships to creativity. Includes a comprehensive resource directory plus calendar of events. Subs £5 p.a.

■ *London Guide to Mind, Body and Spirit* (Brainwave £4.95) lists all the centres in London, what they do and gives helpful explanations of different therapies. The best book in the field (we should know, we wrote it!).

■ *Talking to a Stranger - A Consumer's Guide to Psychotherapy* Lindsey Knight (Fontana £2.95) is a good introductory guide to one to one therapy and what to expect.

■ *A Guide to Humanistic Psychology* by John Rowan explains the major humanistic psychologies in Britain (£1.50 + 35p p&p, Association of Humanistic Psychology). *Individual Therapy in Britain* ed. W. Dryden (Harper & Row, 1984, £10.50) and *Innovative Therapy in Britain* eds. Dryden and Rowan (Harper and Row £12.50) are more scholarly work and deals very thoroughly with a number of approaches, including psychoanalytic, cognitive, behavioural as well as humanistic and compares them.

How to Become a Counsellor

There are many trainings in psychotherapy and counselling offered by institutes. Our book *The London Guide to Mind Body and Spirit* £4.95, lists them with details of cost, entry requirements, and length of course.

Therapy Holidays

It may not be your idea of a relaxing time off to spend your holidays baring your soul to others and facing your complexes, but a residential workshop can mean you get much closer to others, build up a sense of community and support, and possibly even enjoy some pleasant countryside as well (but check the schedule to see how much time you get off!).

UK

Residential workshops from a weekend to a week in various approaches.

■ **CAER,** *Rosemerryn, Lamorna, Penzance, Cornwall TR19 6BN, (0736 810 530).*

■ **Grimstone Manor,** *Yelverton, Devon PL20 7QY,* Send 50p in stamps for programme.

■ **Monkton Wyld Court,** *Charmouth, Bridport, Dorset DT6 6DQ, (0297 60342)* sae for programme.

ABROAD

■ **Cortijo Romero,** *72 Meadowsweet Rd, Creekmoor, Poole, Dorset BH17 7XT, (Broadstone 0202 699581).* In the foothills of the Sierra Nevada, Spain.

■ **Skyros Centre,** *1 Fawley Rd, NW6 (431 0867).* On the island of Skyros, Greece. There is also the Atsitsa Centre on the same island which holds body-oriented courses (tai chi, massage, yoga etc).

▼ GENERAL PUBLICATIONS ▼

■ **Human Potential Magazine,** *3 Netherby Rd, SE23 (291 6254).* (See p159). Self-development, psychotherapy, spirituality, plus calendar of events and resource directory listings. Qtly £1.20.

■ **Kindred Spirit,** *(0985 213461).* 'New Age' issues: self development, ecology, holism, spirituality.

■ **Link Up,** *51 Northwick Business Centre, Blockley, Glos GL 56 9RF, (0386 701091).* Ecology, spirituality, self-development. Diary of nationwide events.

■ **New Humanity,** *51a York Mansions, Prince of Wales Dr, SW11.* Political and spiritual 'New Age' issues, 'journal for the creative individual'. Bi-mthly, £1.50.

■ **Resurgence,** Ford House, Hartland, Bideford, Devon, (023 74 293). Covers issues of development, disarmament, appropriate technology, health, education and human scale in all kinds of organisations. Bimthly £1.80.

■ **I-to-I,** *1 Fawley Rd, NW6, (435 1211).* Exciting new mag (out Nov '89) which seeks to combine personal growth with a sensitive political outlook. News, reviews, intelligent but accessible articles, I- catching format (!).

▼ BOOKSHOPS ▼

■ **Compendium,** *(485 8944)* (see p253). Good sections on psychotherapy, spiritual, astrology.

■ **Genesis Books,** *East West Centre, 188 Old St, EC1 (250 1868).* M-F 11.30-7, Sat 11-3. Alternative medicine, New Age, macrobiotics.

■ **H Karnac,** *58 Gloucester Rd, SW7 (584 3303).* M-Sat 9-6. Psychoanalysis and psychotherapy, as well as general books. Also have branch in Finchley Road.

■ **Mysteries,** *(240 3688).*(see p 155). 10-6 M-Sat. Mystical, New Age, divination etc. Second hand, tapes, jewellery and esoteric paraphernalia sold as well.

■ **Mystic Trader,** *60 Chalk Farm Rd, NW1 (284 0141).* Open 11am-6pm, 7 days a week. New Age books and tapes. Room at back where videos are shown.

■ **Quest Bookshop,** *12 Bury Pl, WC1 (405 2309).* Occult, mystical, astrology, religion. Mail order. Wkdays 10-6, Sat 10-4.

■ **Watkins,** *21 Cecil Ct, WC2 (836 2182).* Refurbished and now expanded to include the basement, have a very large range: astrology, mystical, occult, psychology, alternative medicine, tarot, dowsing; s/h section. Mon, Tu, Th, Fri, Sat 10-6, Weds 10.30-6.

■ **Changes Bookshop,** *242 Belsize Rd, NW6 (328 5161).* M-F 10-6, Sat 10-5. Specialises in books on psychotherapy: analytical, body oriented, cognitive, humanistic, self help, transpersonal, spiritual - it's all crammed into this bulging, friendly shop.

▼ FESTIVAL ▼

■ **Festival for Mind-Body-Spirit,** *170 Campden Hill Rd, W8 (938 3788).* Once yearly, 5 day exhibition with stalls promoting various groups and wares, as well as workshops and talks. Started in 1977 and still going strong even if it is the 'New Age' marketplace. Good for buying alternative trinkets, getting your palm read or feet massaged (you'll need it) and bumping into people you know.

▼ STRANGE PHENOMENA ▼

Publications

■ **Brain Mind Bulletin,** *PO Box 42211, 231 S Ave.52, Los Angeles, California 90042, (0101 800 626 4557).* News bulletin covers unusual research - left/right brain function to near death experiences ($45 pa).

■ **Research into Lost Knowledge Organisation, (RILKO),** *8 The Drive, N11 (368 4088).* Sacred geometry, megalithic and Masonic monuments. Lectures; sae for publications list.

■ **No 1 Electronics,** *(328 3861)* (see p66) cheap ionisers, kirlian cameras, organ tuning, time travel machine. Anything electronic to do with healing, or anything electronic that 'will raise people's consciousness'. Sell brain wave machines and IQ increasing machines!

■ **British Society of Dowsers,** *Sycamore Cottage, Hastingleigh, Ashford, Kent TN25 5HW, (0233 75253).* Hold meetings in London. Books by mail order. Send SAE.

■ **Fortean Times,** *96 Mansfield Rd, NW3* covers strange phenomena of all kinds (eg frogs falling out of the sky).

■ **Institute of Pyramidology,** *31 Station Rd, Harpenden, Herts AL5 4XB, (05827 64510).* Founded by Adam Rutherford publishing books which show how the Great pyramid predicted the life of Christ. Religious organisation, (nothing to do with 'pyramid energy') looking forward to the time when 'false religion and erroneous scientific theories will vanish'.

health

At the moment, the state of the nation's health is a live issue on several fronts. Radical changes are planned (as detailed in the Government White Paper on the NHS) to the structure of an already over-worked and underpaid state health service. The changes will, among other things, tie doctors to considerations of how much a treatment costs, rather than how much a patient needs it, as well as severely undermining local hospital provision.

Together with this there is a growing feeling among many people that orthodox medicine, which treats the disease rather than the person with the disease, has its limitations. The last 10 years have seen a tremendous growth in interest in alternative medicine. Perhaps another aspect of this sense that science hasn't got all the answers is a growing awareness of the way in which our environment affects health. We are only just beginning to find out about some of the ways in which pollution causes disease. And of course the greatest threat of all to health is poverty, both in this country and throughout the world. This is health as a world-wide issue, but before becoming overwhelmed by this scale of looking at things, it's important to remember that you can only start from where you are - with your own health. To a large extent, health is a matter of doing the right things, and taking care of oneself; a matter of personal responsibility.

Below we give information on both orthodox medicine as it is in this country (i.e. the National Health Service), and alternative or complementary medicine.

▼ NATIONAL HEALTH SERVICE ▼

Registering with a GP

Every British Citizen has a right to be registered with a General Practitioner. Lists of GPs in your area can be found at local **Family Practitioner Committees** (who administer GP services), **Community Health Councils, Citizens Advice Bureaux** and in clinics and libraries (look in phone book for numbers).

In choosing a GP you are entitled to shop around and to ask for information. GPs are obliged to publicise a certain amount of basic information about their practices but if you need to know more, you can always ask. However, you may find that some practices cover catchment areas and if you are outside these catchments, you are unlikely to be able to join the list.

A GP may also refuse to take a patient and can remove patients from her list. On the other hand, everyone has a right to be placed with a GP. If you have any difficulty in this respect, you should contact the local Family Practitioner Committee who must find a GP who will take you.

If you are only living temporarily in an area, for not more than 3 months, you can be registered with any GP as a 'temporary resident'.

You can change your doctor if you wish and not have to give any reason either to the

New to this country?

For details of health care, see section **People from Abroad (p117)**

GP or the FPC. Under new proposals, patients will be able to change their doctor without having to go through the FPC or have their NHS card signed by their doctors.

GP surgeries are open at varying times. At some surgeries it's necessary to make an appointment in advance (in an emergency the doctor should see you without an appointment), at others you can walk in without an appointment and wait to see a doctor. At any rate, you are entitled to see a doctor when you need to without charge.

Outside surgery hours or if you are too ill to get to the surgery, you can phone the doctor. GPs are obliged to make home visits it they judge that the condition requires it.

Getting Hospital Treatment.

In an emergency, go to your nearest Accident and Emergency Department (in most main hospitals). For non-urgent hospital treatment, you have to be referred through your GP. You can ask to see a particular consultant or go to a particular hospital but there is no absolute right for this request to be met. Once referred to a speciality department, there may be delays due to waiting lists.

Clinics

There are various 'self-referral' and 'walk-in' NHS clinics to be found in most areas. Family Planning Clinics offer advice and provide contraceptive services. For young people wanting family planning advice, there are the **Brook Advisory Centres** (see p72). Most main hospitals will have *Sexually Transmitted Diseases Clinics* which offer tests for Aids, VD etc. (see p83). In most areas there will be *Well Women Clinics* where women can get medical check-ups and cervical smear tests.

Prescriptions and Charges

Basic GP and hospital treatment is free of charge to NHS patients. There are, however, charges for prescriptions except that some groups are exempt from the charges. Men aged 65 or over, women ages 60 or over, children, students in full-time education aged under 19, pregnant women, women who have had a baby in the last 12 months and those receiving income support or family credit, are all entitled to free prescriptions. Others on low income may also be entitled but they have to make a claim; for details see DHSS leaflet AB11 *Help with NHS Costs.*

Those not living in the country who use the NHS may face charges for hospital treatment unless they are covered by reciprocal arrangements between countries as happens within the EEC (see section **People from Abroad** p117).

Dentists and Opticians

Until recently everyone was entitled to a free NHS dental check-up and eye-test but the Government has now introduced charges for these. Other dental treatment is also charged but as with prescriptions, certain groups are exempt (see DHSS leaflet D11 *NHS Dental Treatment - How to get it Free or Get Help with Costs*)

Maternity

Hospitals tend to vary in their approach to birth. Some, for example, will be more open to 'natural birth' than others. It is therefore best to ask about this first and also to state what kind of birth you want in a written 'birth plan'.

If you want a 'home birth', it is necessary

to find a GP and midwife sympathetic to births at home. If your own GP is not willing to do this simply because she is opposed to 'home births' (i.e. not because of any valid medical reason), then try to find a more sympathetic doctor. You can always ask your local Community Health Council or contact the National.Childbirth Trust (see p81 **Maternity** section).

Mental Health

Urgent mental health care is available at hospitals and various clinics/centres. Some areas may have a 'crisis intervention team' which will visit the person's home in an emergency, which can avoid hospitalisation. Some areas also have community mental health centres with 'walk-in' facilities where people can go either for urgent or non-urgent care.

Psychiatric patients can be detained, and in certain circumstances given compulsory treatment, under the Mental Health Act. However there are strict legal conditions surrounding these procedures. For a short summary of the Mental Health Act see Chapter 9 of Which's *A Patients Guide to he NHS*. For more detailed advice concerning individual cases contact **MIND** (The National Association For Mental Health see p213) or your local Community Health Council.

Counselling and Psychotherapy

Counselling and psychotherapy are not widely available in the NHS. However, a growing number of GPs are employing counsellors in their practices. GPs can also refer patients for NHS psychotherapy, but places are limited. There are some community based centres which may offer NHS counselling. (See p156 for details about non-NHS counselling)

Alternative Medicine on the NHS

In the NHS 'alternative treatment' can only be offered by a doctor registered with the General Medical Council. There are a few doctors who practise alternative or complementary therapies such as acupuncture, homoeopathy and hypnotherapy. There are also some hospitals which allow spiritual healers to see patients, if requested.

Medical Records

There is no legal right for patients to gain access to their medical records except where information is stored on computer (under the Data Protection Act). Some hospitals and GPs have a voluntary policy whereby patients are able to see their medical notes.

Complaints

There are various procedures for making complaints. Complaints against a GP should be addressed to the local Family Practitioner Committee. Complaints against hospitals should be sent to the senior person involved (if to do with administration to the hospital administrator, if to do with clinical matters, to the consultant). For assistance and advice about making a complaint contact your local Community Health Council.

■ **Action for Victims of Medical Accidents**, *Bank Chambers, 1 London Rd, SE23 (291 2793)*. Advise people who think they may have had an accident while under under medical care, or who have suffered negligence, on how to seek compensation or appropriate help. Campaign to improve attitudes in the Health Service to victims of medical accidents.

Community Health Councils

Community Health Councils were set up to represent the interests of consumers of the health service. They act on behalf of patients in respect of complaints and they are also called upon to monitor the provision and delivery of services. They have various statutory powers, in particular, the Health Authority must consult them on any major changes such as hospital closures. All CHC meetings are open to the public. Most CHCs will have shop front offices where advice and information can be obtained.

Support Groups / Pressure Groups

In addition to CHCs, there are a whole variety of other pressure groups and support groups campaigning for better health services and providing support for particular care groups. For details see lists that follow or read *Health AHelpline* (Bedford Square Press/ Thames Television) which is an excellent guide to organisations that can help you with your health problems.

For a guide to your rights under the NHS see *Patients Rights*(National Consumer Council), and for a general guide to the NHS read *A Patient's Guide to the NHS* published by *Which?*.

(See also **Advice Centres** p207, **Sex** p71, **Sexually Transmitted Diseases** p83)

■ **Socialist Health Assoc,** *195 Walworth Rd, SE17 (703 6838).*

■ **Tower Hamlets Health Campaign,** *Oxford Ho, Derbyshire St, E2 (729 3686).*

■ **Health Rights,** *344 South Lambeth Rd, SW8 (720 9811).* Independent voluntary group who do research, give advice and information on health care in the NHS. Occasionally take on cases of victims of medical accidents.

■ **National Consumer Council,** *20 Grosvenor Gdns, SW1W 0DH (730 3469).* Publish patients' rights leaflet.

■ **Association of Community Health Councils in England and Wales,** *30 Drayton Pk, N5 1PB (609 8405).* Publish series of booklets including *How to Choose Your Doctor, You and Your Optician etc.*

▼ ALTERNATIVE MEDICINE ▼

There has been a tremendous growth in 'alternative' or 'complementary' medicine in the last few years, and centres offering 'natural therapies' have multiplied. What unites these therapies is that they all attempt to encourage the body's own capacity to heal itself. Most complementary medicines have traditionally treated the whole person - their diet, predominant emotions, life history and environment are all taken into account. Conventional medicine tends to suppress symptoms and, sometimes along with them , much of the body's own power to fight disease. Recently though orthodox medicine has been emphasising the importance of preventing disease rather than treating a fully developed complaint, and studies have been done on temperament and life events as they connect to various diseases.

As yet little alternative medicine is available on the NHS, and with cuts in services it seems that this is less likely happen. However, in a few innovative hospitals and clinics, natural therapies are being introduced to treat drug addiction, cancer and some chronic complaints.

The Therapies

ACUPUNCTURE

Acupuncture is the Chinese healing art, said to date back to the stone age, in which needles are inserted lightly into the skin at particular points in order to affect the organs and energies of the body. There are about 800 points which are linked together in pathways called meridians, down which the life energy, or *ch'i* as it is called, flows to one of the twelve organs. By inserting the needles the acupuncturist stimulates the flow of chi, which is made up of two opposing forces, *yin* (receptive, cold, dark) and *yang* active, warm, light). According to the system, it is the balance of these two forces, and the even flow of energy through the meridians which bring about good health.

Diagnosis is largely carried out by taking the *pulses* at the wrist, which are a more detailed indicator of the condition of the various organs than the single pulse taken in western medicine. Physical characteristics, life history and temperament are also taken into account. Sterilised or disposable needles are inserted lightly into the chosen points, usually in a completely different place from the organ to which they are connected. Sometimes the needles are gently twisted or stimulated, and sometimes moxa (dried mugworth, an aromatic herb) is burnt just over (but not on!) the skin.

The use of acupuncture for analgesia in Chinese hospitals has been widely publicised in films which show patients treated in this way, fully awake and even drinking tea during major surgery. Research has shown that treatment stimulates the production of *endorphins*, hormones manufactured naturally by the brain to relieve pain, and from this evidence some people have put forward the theory that it may work on other conditions by adjusting production of other hormones, though research on the different applications of acupuncture is scant. The World Health Organisation has catalogued 40 disorders which could be helped by this therapy, including asthma, ulcers, colitis, migraine, addiction, period pains and osteoarthritis. A new acupuncture point has been developed in the West to help people give up smoking - a staple is inserted into the ear and twiddled by the patient when she or he feels the urge to smoke. Other recent developments are laser beams instead of needles, and electrical stimulation of points.

■ **British Acupuncture Assoc,** *34 Alderney St, SW1 (834 1012).* Send £1.50 plus postage for handbook giving information about acupuncture and register of qualified practitioners; also runs courses.

■ **Traditional Acupuncture Society,** *11 Grange Pk, Stratford-upon-Avon, Warwicks, (0789 298798).* Send SAE to be put in touch with a local practitioner. Info leaflets.

■ **Chung Sang Acupuncture School,** *15 Porchester Gdns, W2 (727 6778).* Clinic. 3 year part time course for those with 'A' levels in science subjects.

■ **Register of Traditional Chinese Medicine,** *7a Thorndean St, SW18 (883 8431).* Register of practitioners qualified in acupuncture and other branches of Chinese medicine.

■ **College of Traditional Chinese Acupuncture,** *Tower House, Queensway, Leamington Spa, Warks, (0926 422121).* 3-year part-time courses. Phone registrar for details.

■ **International College of Oriental Medicine,** *Green Hedges Hse, Green Hedges Ave, East Grinstead, Surrey, (0342 313106).* 3-year full-time BAc course: costs about £1,950 pa.

■ **Liu Academy of Taoist Therapist,** *13 Gunnersbury Ave, W5 (993 2549).* Runs clinic. Also 3-year part-time courses in traditional Chinese medicine including acupuncture and martial arts.

■ **British College of Acupuncture,** 8 Hunter St, WC1 (833 8164). Register of qualified practitioners. 2-5yr courses for qualified traditional/alternative medical practitioners only.

ALEXANDER TECHNIQUE

This is a way of unlearning habitual misuse of the body by re-educating 'students' in the natural posture and movement which is the foundation of good health. Alexander, who as a young actor formulated the technique to cure his own voice problems. Mis-alignment of the head and body causes stresses, strains and misplacement throughout the whole body. Through awareness, practice and the gentle guidance of the 'teacher' the body, can become freed from constricting habits, and this in turn can affect the mind and emotions.

■ **Society of Teachers of the Alexander Technique,** *10 London House, 266 Fulham Rd, SW10 (351 0828).* Publishes *The Alexander Journal.* Does not put people in touch with practitioners.

■ **Alexander Teaching Associates,** *188 Old St, EC1 (250 3038).* Info on AT. Evening/weekend courses as well as individual lessons (about £15).

ALLERGY THERAPY

While it has been accepted for a long time that some people are allergic to pollen and develop hayfever, allergies to food or substances in the environment have been more controversial, possibly because they are more difficult to trace.

An allergic reaction is caused when the body reacts to a substance which has been eaten, inhaled or touched as if it were harmful, even though the substance is not toxic. Common foods, such as white flour, dairy products and food additives can often be the culprits in food allergies, and symptoms can range from headaches, digestive problems, depression and arthritic pains. The sufferer is often addicted to and craves for the very substance to which she is allergic.

Tracing the allergy can be done in a number of ways. Two methods are to restrict foods to be eaten and reintroduce suspected substances one by one, or the 'scratch test' where the suspected allergen is applied to a scratch on the skin to see if it becomes irritated. Treatment is either to avoid the food, or the 'neutralising dose' where by injecting highly diluted doses of the allergen, the body is trained not to react to it.

■ **Institute of Allergy Therapists,** *Ffynnonwen Natural Therapy Centre, Llangwyryfon, Aberystwyth, Dyfed, (09747 376).* Lists of practitioners, training courses and other information.

APPLIED KINESIOLOGY

This is also sometimes called 'Touch for Health'. According to this system, groups of muscles are thought to be connected to the functions of the various organs of the body. Muscular weakness may show a disturbance in the workings of an organ. This is tested for by applying gentle pressure to extended arms or legs. Bad diet or an allergy may also be the cause of this muscular weakness. Whatever underlying problem is revealed it is treated by strengthening the muscles by working on the reflexes, massaging energy pathways or 'meridians' (see Acupuncture, above), and in some cases by diet.

■ **Association for Systematic Kinesiology,** *39 Browns Rd, Surbiton, Surrey, (399 3215).* Register of practitioners, information, courses for all levels.

■ **British Touch for Health Association,** *78 Castlewood Dr, Eltham, SE9 (856 7717).* Register and information.

AROMATHERAPY

Essential oils extracted from plants are massaged into the skin, inhaled, sprinkled in baths, or, more rarely, ingested. It's most often used with massage as a way of relaxing. The most sensual of the complementary therapies, aromatherapy is becoming very popular - essential oils are now available in high street chemists. The **Body Shop** also stocks them (though these tend to be more diluted and therefore expensive than those from specialist stockists), as do **Baldwin & Co,** *173 Walworth Rd, SE17 (703 5550)* do a good range, and **Neal's Yard Apothecary,** *2 Neal's Yd, (379 7222)* who also have a branch in Chalk Farm Road. Some wholefood shops also stock them.

Courses are run at:

■ **London School of Aromatherapy,** *PO Box 780, NW6 5EQ.* 9 mth part-time course.

■ **Micheline Arcier Aromatherapy,** *7 William St, SW1 (235 3545).* 8 day training. Essential oils sold.

■ **Aromatherapy Associates,** *7 Wardo Ave, SW6 (371 0465).* Five weekends course for those with some massage experience.

BACH FLOWER REMEDIES

These are herbal remedies derived from flowers, which are prescribed to treat the underlying negative emotional states which Dr Edward Bach saw as the cause of disease. These states are: fear, uncertaintyor indecision, lack of interest in the present, despondency and despair, over concern for the welfare of others, loneliness and over-sensitivity. Each of these is sub-divided for prescription of the various flower remedies, so that for instance under the heading of 'over-sensitivity' there are four remedies: *Agrimony* for anxiety and mental torment hidden under a brave face; *Centaury* for weak will and a 'doormat' tendency; *Walnut* for major life changes and *Holly* for jealously and suspicion.

Bach himself discovered the remedies by intuition, and many people use them to treat themselves either by buying a handbook to match their state to a remedies, or by *radiesthesia* - dowsing with a pendulum.

■ **The Dr. E. Bach Centre,** *Mt Vernon, Sotwell, Wallingford, Oxon. OX10 OPZ.* Sells remedies mail-order and books on how to use them.

COLOUR THERAPY

According to the theory of colour therapy, all colours emit vibrational energy which can harmonise with, or disturb, the body's energy. Different colours are introduced into the client's environment, body or awareness to heal the body, and stimulate or calm the mind. This can be done using coloured lights (or liquids that have been bathed in them), foods of particular colours, clothes or decor, or meditation. Studies have shown that blue light lowers blood pressure, while white light puts it up. Colour visualisation is used for pain control, especially for cancer patients.

■ **Living Colour,** *33 Lancaster Grove, NW3 (794 1371).* 'Awareness through colour'. Courses on colour body consciousness, dress; also individual sessions.

■ **Your True Colours,** *12 St Marks Crescent, NW1 (0923 818371 or 937 4426).* Workshops, training course.

FELDENKRAIS METHOD

Like Alexander Technique, the Feldenkrais Method aims to retrain the body through gentle exercises which encourage sensitivity to movement. Moshe Feldenkrais taught Judo for 30 years, and brought together some aspects of the Alexander Technique with Martial Arts body training. The exercises resemble the ways in which babies and young children learn to move. New ways of using the body are explored, and at first, to release the pupil from the pressure of gravity, she is encouraged to do exercises lying on the ground.

In changing negative physical patterns, restrictive mental patterns are believed to change too.

■ **Feldenkrais Method,** *18 Kemplay Rd, NW3 1SY (794 4066).*

■ **Feldenkrais PTP Information Centre,** *188 Old St, EC1 (584 8819).* Individual sessions and training course 4 years (8 weeks full time per year).

■ **British Naturopathic and Osteopathic Assoc,** see **Osteopathy,** 4 yr full-time training course, and register of practitioner.

■ **International Federation of Radionics,** *Memory Seat, Sandy Balls Estate, Godshill, Fordingbridge, Hants, W1 (0425 53677).*

HEALING

Healers use their hands (or their thoughts in the case of 'absent' healing) to direct the force of life energy to cure disease. They may not touch you - some work off the body - but you may feel a sensation of heat or cold under the healer's hands, or pins and needles, or tingling sensations. They may not charge anything, or may ask for a donation. Many spiritualist churches offer this kind of hand healing. Some hospitals are now allowing spiritual healers to treat patients in the wards voluntarily.

■ **Spiritualist Assn of Great Britain,** 33 *Belgrave St, SW1 (235 3351).* No fixed charges - they ask for a donation.

HERBALISM

Using plants to treat illness is probably the oldest and most widespread medical practice. Herbs in the past were not used in isolation to treat specific symptoms, but as part of a process of healing which might also involve investigation of the underlying spiritual causes of the disease, rituals or religious practices. The discovery of particular herbs by intuition or revelation in dreams or altered states of consciousness was sometimes surrounded by folklore.

Now, substances extracted from herbs

have become 'respectable' modern drugs: foxglove becomes digitalis which is used to stimulate the heart; the opium poppy when refined yields morphine; the oestrogen used in the contraceptive pill comes from the yam and so on. However, while modern drugs use one highly concentrated and refined active ingredient of a plant, herbal remedies contain other parts of the plant which, according to herbalists, contain substances needed to balance its effect. Hawthorn, for instance, contains both a substance which decreases the heart rate and one which increases the flow of blood through the heart.

The research which has been done suggests that the healing potential of plants is as yet largely untapped. A few plants have been tested: garlic has been discovered to reduce cholesterol and help prevent infection, liquorice root if taken on an empty stomach is better at healing gastric ulcers than any conventional drug, aloe vera helps wounds heal and reduces inflammation.

While medicines are prescribed in orthodox medicine to suppress the body's own response to disease - the symptoms, herbal remedies are prescribed to support the body's own healing defences, to trigger helpful reactions and add minerals and nutrients that might be lacking. They don't usually have the side effects of modern drugs. However, some of them can be toxic if taken in large quantities, so it's always best to consult a herbalist or herb stockist.

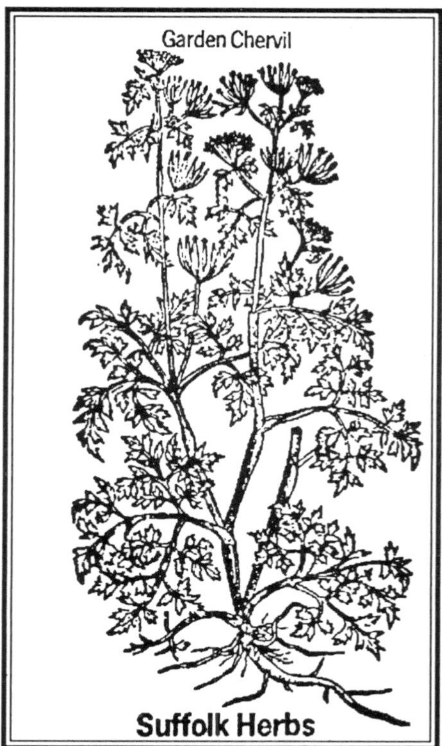

■ **Baldwins,** *173 Walworth Rd, SE17 (703 5550).* Tues-Sat 9-5.30. Established for nearly 150 years, Baldwins stocks a very good range of herbs at reasonable prices. Will give advice too.

■ **Haelen Centre,** *41 The Broadway, Crouch End, N8 (340 4258).* Mon-Fri 9-6.30 Sat 9-6. Wholefood shop which stocks large range of herbs as well as toiletries, alternative medicines, organic wines etc. Will give advice.

■ **Cosmos Herbs,** *124 Chiswick High Rd, W4 (995 7239).* 11-6pm Mon-Sat. Herbs, alternative medicines.

■ **The Herbalists,** *74 Lee High Rd, SE13 (852 9792).* Small local herb shop with good selection of herbs, homoeopathic remedies etc. 9-5.30 Thurs 8.30 till 4.

■ **Culpepers,** *8 The Market, Covent Gdn Piazza, WC2 (379 6698).* Expensive, packaged end of market. Mon-Sat 10-8, Sun 11.30-5.

■ **Herb Society,** *77 Great Peter St, SW1 (222 3634)* can give info on herb shops and suppliers.

■ **Neal's Yard Apothecary,** *2 Neal's Yard, WC2 (379 7222).* Herbs, remedies, essential oils. M-F 10-6, Sun 11-4.

■ **Pierce A. Arnold and Son,** *12 Park Rd, Hackbridge, Surrey, (647 5330).* Wholesale dried herbs only.

■ **Suffolk Herbs,** *Sawyers Farm, Little Cornard, Sudbury, Suffolk, (0787 227247).* Seed suppliers, send sae for catalogue. Open Sat only. Also try *wholefood shops,* many of whom stock a limited range of herbs and alternative medicines.

■ **School of Herbal Medicine,** *148 Forest Rd, Tunbridge Wells, Kent, (0892 30400).* List of practitioners and courses

■ **National Institute of Medical Herbalists,** *41 Hatherley Rd, Winchester, Hants, (228 4417).* Professional body; will send free list of recognised practitioners. Four year training course.

■ **Herb Society,** See above. Information, library and small museum.

HOMOEOPATHY

This is based on the principle of 'like is cured by like'; an illness which produces certain symptoms can be cured by a substance which produces the same symptoms. It was developed over 150 years ago by Dr Samuel Hahnemann when he noticed that quinine, used to treat malaria, causes similar symptoms to the disease itself if taken by a healthy person. Subsequently he went on to carefully test in a series of 'provings' the symptoms produced on himself and volunteers by many other substances, cataloguing them meticulously to match them to diseases. Concerned about the damaging effects that might be produced by some of these substances, he attempted to reduce the dose, and this led to his discovery that the greater the dilution, the stronger its curative effect became. It is this theory of 'potentization' which is controversial, since the remedies are sometimes so diluted that there is not even a molecule of the original substance left. Some homoeopaths believe that its energy is retained, and this is more potent than physical presence.

Homoeopathy is based on the idea that by aggravating the symptoms minutely, the body's own healing mechanism, or 'vital force', is stimulated. Remedies are not prescribed for diseases, but for the whole person - their character, history and environment as well as their symptoms, which means that the same remedy may not be prescribed for two people suffering from the same complaint.

Homoeopathy is available on the NHS, unlike many natural therapies, and there are even homoeopathic dentists and vets. Some members of the royal family use it.

■ **Society of Homoeopaths,** *2 Artizan Rd, Northampton, NN1 4HU (0604 21400).* Keeps a register of professional homoeopaths who conform to the Society's standards of practice. Publishes magazine/newsletter.

■ **College of Homoeopathy,** *26 Clarendon Rise, SE13 (852 0573).* 3-year part-time course; medical qualifications not needed.

■ **British Homoeopathic Assoc,** *27a Devonshire St, W1 (935 2163).* List of medically qualified practitioners and chemists supplying remedies; publishes Homoeopathy magazine.

■ **Faculty of Homoeopathy,** *The Royal London Homoeopathic Hospital, Great Ormond St, WC1N 3HR (837 8833 ex 303 or 234).* Set up by manufacturers of remedies to give advice and info. List of homoeopathic doctors (send sae), also dentists and vets.

■ **Nelsons,** *73 Duke St, W1 (629 3118).* One of the biggest manufacturers; dispensary, bookshop, first aid kit.

■ **Ainsworths,** *38 New Cavendish St, W1 (935 5330).* Set up by staff ex of Nelsons; books and preparations.

■ **Kilburn Chemists,** *216 Belsize Rd, NW6 (328 1030)* and

■ **E. Gould,** *14 Crowndale Rd, NW1 (388 4752)* also stock large range.

IRIDOLOGY

Iridology is a way of diagnosing physical or psychological problems, often before they have become apparent as a disease, by looking at the condition of the iris. The whole body is believed to be reflected in the eye, which is divided into segments corresponding to different organs. The kind of irregularities (unusual colouring or markings, flecking or clouding) in that segment will indicate why that part of the body isn't working properly.

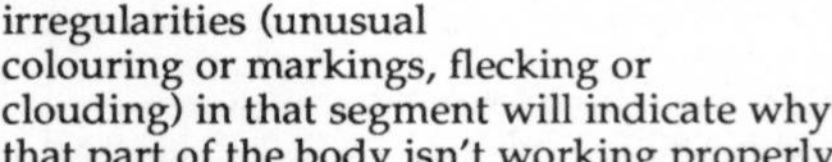

■ **National Council and Register of Iridologists,** *80 Portland Rd, Bournemouth, (0202 529793).* Send SAE for register. Colour therapy

MASSAGE

Massage is something nearly everyone can use, often with little training, as a way of healing, soothing, communicating or getting close.

There are many different types of massage. **Swedish massage** uses a variety of strokes - pummelling, pounding, stroking, rubbing over muscles, joints and nerves.

In **Intuitive massage** the masseuse is guided to areas of tension more by the way the client's body feels, rather than following a course dictated by anatomy.

Shiatsu from Japan is like a form of acupuncture without needles. The acupuncture points are stimulated, soothed or toned with the hands to balance the life energy at points where it may have become blocked, affecting the organs. It's a useful form of self-therapy and some people use it in this way at the dentist's as an alternative form of pain relief. **Acupressure** is the Chinese version of this.

Biodynamic massage was evolved by Gerda Boyesen, who found that when blocked energy in the body is released during massage the intestine makes a spontaneous movement, as if it is 'digesting' and eliminating stress. The therapist uses a stethoscope to listen to the noises inside the abdomen, and interprets these noises to direct the way she massages. Sometimes this technique is used in conjunction with biodynamic psychotherapy, in which case the client is encouraged to talk about or express her feelings.

Reflexology involves massaging the soles and sides of the feet, which are believed to correspond to parts of the body (e.g. part of the big toe corresponds to the pituitary gland, part of the heel to the sexual organs). The reflexologist feels for tiny lumps under the skin, and the presence of these and their location will show which organ is not functioning properly. She then massages these to disperse the lumps, and get that part of the body working properly again.

■ **Churchill Centre,** *22 Montagu St, W1 (402 9475).* Runs a wide range of courses including aromatherapy, reflexology, acupressure, relaxation massage, rolfing. Some free talks, demonstrations. Training for ITEC (recognised qualification in massage) certificate given.

■ **Gerda Boyesen Centre,** *Acacia Hse, Centre Ave, W3 (743 2437).* Biodynamic massage, low cost if given by trainees. Also Swedish massage and ITEC diploma courses.

■ **Liu School of Taoist Therapists,** (see 'Acupuncture') Teach shiatsu.

NATUROPATHY

Naturopathy seeks to help us co-operate with the body's own healing power by removing 'toxins' and bad habits in lifestyle or diet which affect the body adversly. Naturopaths usually treat either with fasting (to clear out the system) followed by establishing healthy diet and giving dietary supplements, or with hydrotherapy (hot/cold baths or showers, increased intake of water). Healthy lifestyle in terms of diet and exercise is seen as most important to maintain health. Osteopathy (see below) is frequently used as well.

■ **British College of Naturopathy and Osteopathy,** *6 Netherhall Gdns, NW3 (435 7830).* Register of practitioners. Training 4 yrs full time mainly for those with science 'A' levels.

■ **Community Health Foundation,** *188 Old St, EC1 (251 4076).* Specialises in oriental therapies/ practices: shiatsu, macrobiotics, nutrition, cookery, yoga and meditation; also western massage and workshops on other aspects of healthy lifestyle. Their large but informal centre houses a macrobiotic restaurant, wholefood shop, bookshop (Genesis) as well as 2 independent groups concerned with growth/therapy. Workshops approx £50 w/end, £4-7 per evening.

■ **Kushi Institute,** which runs intensive courses in macrobiotics, shiatsu, oriental diagnosis and philosophy.

OSTEOPATHY

This uses manipulation of the spine, joints and muscles to restore them to their proper alignment, relieving the patient of pain and disease. The inventor of the technique, Andrew Taylor Still, believed that *lesions* form where the vertebrae have slipped out of position and this blocks the flow of messages from the nerves to the brain and the blood supply, causing disease.

The osteopath will carry out diagnosis by looking at the way you walk, stand and sit and by *palpation* - feeling with the hands for problems areas. Treatment is usually very active and may involve massage or pulling, pushing, articulating or applying pressure to limbs or spine.

It's usually used for bad backs and joint problems, but it can be used to treat a much wider range of disorders.

Cranial osteopathy is based on the idea that the plates of bone in the skull are moving very slightly all the time, and that the circulation of the spinal fluid can be assisted by gentle touch to the head.

Chiropractic is very similar to osteopathy, but X-rays are used for diagnosis more often.

■ **General Council and Register of Osteopaths,** *1-4 Suffolk St, SW1 (839 2060).* Register of practitioners; training school.

■ **British Naturopathic and Osteopathic Assoc,** *Frazer Hse, 6 Netherall Gdns, NW3 (435 8728).* Register of practitioners (send £1.50 and write to secretary).

■ **Ecole Europenee d'Osteopathie,** *104 Tunbridge Rd, Maidstone, Kent, (0622 671558).* 4 yrs full-time course. Entry requirements 2 'A' levels.

■ **Cranial Osteopathy Assoc,** *478 Baker St, Enfield, EN1 3QS (367 5561).* List of qualified practitioners (SAE required).

■ **College of Osteopaths,** *110 Thorkill Rd, Thames Ditton, Surrey, (398 3308).* 6-year 'Open University' style part-time course.

■ **British Chiropractic Assoc,** *Premier Hse, 10 Greycoat Pl, SW1P 1SB (222 8866).* For register of practitioners and info send self-addressed envelope (9" X 6") and cheque or PO for £1 made out to above.

■ **Anglo-European College of Chiropractic,** *13-15 Parkwood Rd, Boscombe, Bournemouth, (0202 431021).* 4-year full-time course for those with science 'A' levels.

■ **McTimoney Chiropractic School,** *PO Box 127, Oxford, (0865 246786).* 3-year part-time (mostly weekends) course in McTimoney Chiropractic. Minimum age 23yrs.

■ **Institute of Pure Chiropractic,** *PO Box 126, Oxford, OX2 8AR, (0865 246687).* Send SAE for list of practitioners.

POLARITY THERAPY

Various techniques are used in polarity therapy to remove blocks to the flow of life energy around the body. The body is seen as having five energy centres which correspond to the elements of earth, water, fire, air and ether (the fifth element in Indian philosophy). The therapist seeks to balance the energies of these points and help the life energy flow

between them, often placing the hands on different parts or massaging in a clockwise or anti-clockwise direction. Stretching postures ('polarity yoga') are also used, as well as fasts and dietary therapy to strengthen the body's own resources by expelling toxins.

■ **Polarity Therapy Association UK,** *33 Dudley Ct, Upper Berkeley St, W1* Register of qualified practitioners.

Natural Health Centres

There are now a large number of natural and alternative medicine centres offering a variety of therapies. These are listed in that invaluable book (though we say so ourselves!) *The London Guide to Mind, Body and Spirit* K Brady and M Considine (Brainwave £4.95), which also lists trainings. Below are some of the larger centres.

■ **South London Natural Health Centre,** *7a Clapham Common Southside, SW4 (720 8817).* Wide range of natural therapies available as well as a floatation tank (an enclosed tank, filled with warm water in which you float to induce relaxation).

■ **Neals Yard Therapy Rooms,** *2 Neals Yd, WC2 (379 7662).* Set in a complex which offers a range of services from the olde worlde to the high-tech including a wholefood shop, bakery, organic greengrocers, herbal shop, cafe and desktop publishing centre. Wide range of therapies available.

■ **City Health Centre,** *36-37 Featherstone St, EC1 (251 4429).* Acupuncture, Alexander technique, counselling, herbalism, homoeopathy, iridology, massage, osteopathy, reflexology etc.

■ **Primrose Healing Centre,** *9 St George's Mews, NW1 (586 0148).* Reflexology, polarity therapy, osteopathy, nutrition, naturopathy, homoeopathy, hypnotherapy, herbalism, colonic irrigation, aromatherapy, acupuncture and Chinese herbalism, shiatsu, holistic massage, psychic consultations, rebirthing, colour healing, reiki, energy balancing.

■ **St James's Centre for Health and Healing,** *197 Piccadilly, W1V 9LF (437 7118/734 4511).*

■ **Bromley Natural Therapies Centre,** *9 Homefield Rd, Bromley, Kent, (464 9939).* Acupuncture, applied Kinesiology, aromatherapy, astrology, biomobility, counselling, herbal medicine, homoeopathy, hypnotherapy, psychotherapy, reflexology, massage, yoga. Also talks, workshops, books.

■ **London Natural Health Clinic,** *Arnica Hse, Campden Hill Rd, W8 (938 3788).* Homoeopathy, osteopathy, naturopathy, reflexology, aromatherapy, hypnotherapy, medical herbalism, massage, Kirlian photographic diagnosis, spiritual healing, acupuncture, allergy diagnosis.

■ **Brackenbury Natural Health Centre,** *30 Brackenbury Rd, W6 (741 9264).* Homoeopathy, acupuncture, herbalism, psychotherapy, Alexander technique, aromatherapy, dietary therapy, hypnotherapy, massage, reflexology, shiatsu.

■ **Bantridge Forest Hill School,** *Highfield, Dane Hill, Haywards Heath, Sussex, (0825 790214).* Correspondence courses in homoeopathy, colour healing, , naturopathy, massage, hypnotherapy etc. Cost about £140.

Resources

■ **Institute for Complementary Medicine,** *21 Portland Pl, W1 (636 9543).* Provides information for the public on complementary medicine, and runs a referral service. Campaigns and researches, publishes *Journal of Alternative and Complementary Medicine,* and yearbook. Gives seminars and talks, runs health assessment clinic.

■ **British Holistic Medical Assn,** *179 Gloucester Pl, NW1 (262 5299).* Mainly for doctors interested in an holistic approach. Self help cassettes, publish newsletter, arrange conferences.

■ **Cancer Help Centre,** *Grove House, Cornwallis Rd, Clifton, Bristol, (0272 743216).* A number of different natural techniques are used in treatment. Also offer seminars for cancer patients and professionals involved in their treatment and care.

■ **Caduceus,** *38 Russell Terrace, Leamington Spa, Warwickshire CV3 1HE (0925) 22388.* Magazine with articles on wide range of issues to do with holistic health, with an emphasis on the spiritual dimension of healing.

martial arts

Martial arts are not only a form of self-defence, but are also steeped in the philosophy, religion and history of the East. Used by monks and nuns both to defend themselves and harmonise the body with the mind, they are often connected with the Zen Buddhist discipline of awareness and *mindfulness*. In Japan they were also practised by the warrior class, the Samurai. Martial arts now can be classified as *hard* or *soft*. *Hard* martial arts develop physical strength, muscle power and use attacking moves. Advanced students may be given weapons training. *Hard* styles include karate, kendo and Chinese temple boxing. *Soft* forms rely on defensive moves to turn the attacker's strength against itself. Tai Chi Chuan and Aikido are *soft* forms. Most martial arts are graded: you take a test to progress to the next *belt* which is differentiated by colour. The highest belt is black, after which gradings are called *dans*. Clubs differ in how much emphasis they place on grading. Many people just practice for fun and don't bother about grading. It's important to go to a club where the teaching is good and the participants are kept in order, otherwise you can get injured - either by doing complicated moves badly or by reckless partners. All reputable clubs are members of the

■ **Martial Arts Commission,** *1st Floor, Broadway Hse, Deptford Broadway, SE8 (691 3433)* who check safety and standards. They will put you in touch with local clubs.

■ **Amateur Martial Arts Assn,** *80 Judd St, WC1 (837 4406)*. Send sae for details of nearest martial arts club.

As well as the following list of clubs, various martial arts are taught at local sports centres. See Time Out's *Guide to Sport, Health and Fitness in London* (£4.95) for a list, or look in the phone book under your local borough.

▼ CHINESE ▼

Kung Fu

Kung Fu (*Kung* means worker or artist, *fu* means man) is the generic term for Chinese martial arts, which are also known as Wu Shu, meaning 'stop fighting' - stressing that they are intended to function as a deterrent to aggression. There are various theories about how they evolved, the most popular of which is that it was introduced into monasteries by Bodhidharma (the legendary figure who brought Zen Buddhism to Japan) in order to toughen up the monks. There are now over 360 styles which are based on the movements of particular animals, or on philosophical ideas. These include:

White Crane The hands are held high above the head in imitation of the bird, or 'peck' at the opponent's vulnerable spots.

Ta Sheng Meng or Monkey style According to the legend this was first used by the monkey bodyguard of a Buddhist monk as he travelled from China to India. Uses rolls, leaps and crouching defensive positions.

Praying Mantis style Characterised by strong grips and clawing movements.

Wing Chung Created by a nun of the same name (it means 'beautiful springtime'), this is the style in which Bruce Lee originally trained, and is typified by efficiency and economy of movement.

■ **British Kung Fu Council,** *c/o Mr Coley, 39 Tower St, Kings Lynn, Norfolk, (0533 761282)*. This governing body will put you in touch with your nearest class.

■ **World Body Mind and Spirit Martial Arts Assn,** *72A Shepherds Bush Rd, W6 (602 8969)*. Teach Wing Chun Kung Fu.

■ **Sifu Kung Fu Club,** *27 Romford Rd, E1 (552 7631)*.

■ **White Crane Fist Kung Fu and Lion Dance Troupe,** *St Stephens Ch, Parkside Rd, Hounslow, Middx, (572 6440).*

Tai Chi

Not so much a martial art, more a system of spiritual development and 'moving meditation', tai chi uses soft, very slow, flowing movements based on those of animals. Its background is the philosophy of Taoism, with its emphasis on not forcing, but 'going with the flow' of universal energy. The student learns to harmonise with the life force within (*Ch'i* energy) through co-operation with gravity and the breath. It's non-competitive and its use as a form of self defence is regarded as a by-product of practice at higher levels - it works on the principle that the soft and yielding overcomes the hard and forceful by turning the aggresor's own strength against itself.

■ **British Tai Chi Assoc,** *7 Upper Wimpole St, W1 (935 8444).*

■ **London School of T'ai Chi Chuan,** *45 Blenheim Rd, W4 (995 4303).*

■ **Liu School,** *13 Gunnersbury Ave, W5 (993 2549).*

■ **International Tai Chi Chuan Assoc,** *The People's Hall, No 8 Oriental Arts Studio, 91/97 Freston Rd , W11 (229 2900).*

■ **Wutan T'ai Chi Ch'uan,** *Jubilee Hall, Tavistock St, WC1 (836 4835).*

▼ JAPANESE ▼

Karate

Meaning 'way of the empty hand', karate was once called 'way of the Chinese hand' until it was renamed because of anti-Chinese feeling in Japan at the turn of the century. It uses the famous chopping movements, kicks, blocks and punches. There are different schools of karate - *Shotokan* is typified by its low, powerful stance, while *Shukokai* uses a higher, speed-motivated stance. The diaphragm is the centre from which karate force comes, and this is helped by powerful yells or 'kiais' uttered for concentration and to distract the opponent.

■ **English Karate Council,** *(250 1584).*

■ **The Fitness Centre,** *10-11 Floral St, WC2 (836 6544).*

■ **London Goju-Ryu Karate Centre,** *188-194 Old St, EC1 (250 1584).*

■ **National College of Karate,** *80 Judd St, WC1 (278 5608).* Ring and go along to see before joining.

■ **School of Japanese Karate,** *Broomfield Sports Hall and Oaktree Gymnasium, 180 Shrewsbury Rd, N11 (368 6249).* Shotokan.

■ **Tora Karate Club,** *Cranford Community School, High St, Cranford, Middlesex, (897 0703).* Mon, Wed, Fri 8-10. Shotokan. £1.50.

Judo

Perhaps somewhat misnamed as 'the way of gentleness' (despite the fact that most of the dangerous moves have been removed) Judo involves trying to get a good grip on your opponent and throw her to the floor. Once there, you keep her there with various locks, or, if you're both on the ground, you try to get on top and apply strangleholds etc. It's highly competitive.

■ **British Judo Assn,** *9 Islington High St, N1 (833 4424).* Holds lists of local clubs.

■ **Britannia Judo Club,** *Britannia Leisure Centre, Hyde Rd, N1 (529 3375).*

■ **Bushido Judo Club,** *Grahame Pk Community Centre, Grahame Pk Estate, Colindale, (959 7034).* M and W 6-8pm.

■ **Croydon Judo Club,** *Tavistock Centre, Tavistock Rd, Croydon, (Mr Rickard 681 6256).*

■ **George Sylvester Judo Club,** *George Sylvester Sport Centre, Wilton Way, E8 (985 2105).*

■ **Southover Judo Club,** *Old Finchleians Memorial Ground, Southover, N12 (444 0156).* M and Th 7pm onwards.

■ **Sparrows Judo Club,** *Sparrows Farm Infant School, Denham Rd, Feltham, Middx, (890 7887).* Tu and Thur 6-7 and 7-8 (children), 8-9 adults. First night free, then 50p.

Aikido

Devised by Morei Uyeshiba who was inspired in post war Japan to teach martial arts in a way which would encourage co-operation, non-violence and the spiritual development of practitioners - 'the way of harmony'. Like tai chi the aim is to turn the opponent's own force against her, using throws and rolls and smooth rolling movements. It's mostly non-competitive, and is particularly popular with women who want to practise a martial art.

■ **London Aikido Club,** *4 Bath St, EC1V 9DX (253 7437).* Full-time professional club, classes day and evening, 7 days a week.

Ju-Jitsu

Uses blows, punches and kicks to the opponent's vulnerable spots for self defence. Can be used to render your opponent unconscious so luckily students also learn various methods of revival. Often taught for self defence.

■ **British Ju Jitsu Assn,** *6 Wash Rd, Hutton, Essex, (0277 224057).* Will put you in touch with nearest club

■ **Medway Ju Jitsu Club,** *Tottenham Sports Centre, 70 Tottenham High Rd, N17 (446 7190).*

Kendo

The art of Japanese swordsmanship, as practised by the Samurai warriors, though now bamboo swords are used and protective clothing worn. Unlike fencing, it's highly formalised, and there are only 8 places where cuts are allowed.Very popular in Japan. Iado is the art of drawing the sword and killing the opponent in one stroke.

Contact **Martial Arts Commission** for details.

Kempo

Mixture of hard and soft styles, derives from Chinese boxing. Rooted in Buddhism, this 'temple boxing' is a registered religion which includes meditation.

■ **British Shorinji Kempo Assn,** *c/o Mr Goodman, 72 Anson Rd, N7 (607 5931).* List of clubs.

Tae Kwon Do

The kick is the most important move in this karate-like Olympic sport, as it is in Tang So Do which is similar.

■ **British Tae Kwon Do Council,** *58 Wiltshire La, Eastcoat, Pinner, Middx HA5 2LU, (429 0878).* Will put you in touch with your local club.

■ **Paragon Centre,** *Pargon School, Searles Rd, SE1 (703 3360).* Tae kwon do and kick boxing.

▼ OTHER ▼

Sul Ki Do

Generic term for Korean martial arts - use kicking and striking techniques.

■ **UK Sul ki do Federation,** *1st Floor, 472 Caledonian Rd, N7 (607 9517).*

Hap Ki Do

This is a korean version of Aikido which concentrates on defence rather than attack.

■ **National Sul Ki Do Academy,** *472 Caledonian Rd, N7 (607 9517).* Hap Ki Do, Sul Ki Do Korean Art of Self Defence. 6pm beginners.

Thai Boxing

■ **British Thai Boxing Council,** *(061 653 3479).* Phone for club in your area.

Tang so do

■ **UK Tang so do Federation,** *44 Holden Way, Upminster, Essex, (04022 25739).* List of clubs.

Wu Shu

■ **Wu Shu Kwan Chinese Boxing Centre,** *1 The Colonnades, Bishops Bridge Rd, W2 (229 6354).* Publish own magazine (£1.20), and put in touch with nearest training centre.

General

■ **Redo,** *c/o 25C Roderick Rd, NW3 (485 0659/737 7571).* Run by founder members of Federation of Women Martial Artists, Kaleghl Quinn method of self preservation is taught, also some Chi-kung, the mother of martial arts. Classes held at various places in London.

■ **Croydon Martial Arts Centre,** *c/o Keith Nicholas, 32 Chaucer Green, Croydon CR0 7BN, (656 2181).* Karate, kick boxing, kendo, judo, self-defence, wu-shu kwan, ju-jitsu, aikido, eiado, Thai boxing. Also aikido and philosophy.

■ **Elite Martial Academy,** *37 Compton St, EC1 (693 9885).*

Bookshops

■ **Atoz Book Centre,** *11 Kenway Road, SW5 (370 0236).*

■ **Paul Crompton,** *102 Felsham Rd, SW15 (780 1063).*

SEXUAL POLITICS: Women, Men, Lesbians & Gays, Transsexuals/Transvestites

women

the network of support, friendship and information provided by women for women has grown over the years into a powerful force for social and political change.

Even though many of the centres have to fight a constant battle for funding they have managed to carry on providing a wide variety of services. The following list will not give you every centre in London but should point you in the right direction for finding out how and where to get what you need.

Services include legal advice, health information, women's history archives, rape crisis counselling, as well as, simply, places to meet and share your experience with other women.

There are many groups now specifically for minorities; black women, lesbians, women with disabilities, Jewish women etc.

There are still many issues which confront women even after the passing of the Equal Pay and Sex Discrimination Acts. Women still earn much less than men and are rarely encouraged to train for higher status jobs unless, of course, there is a shortage of men to do those jobs.

Discrimination is still widespread and a woman's right to choose abortion is constantly under threat. Despite the removal of Cruise missiles the campaign for peace is still very much alive. Also many people are now seeing a connection between the ways in which women have been treated and the destruction of the fragile ecological balance of the planet, and so see the liberation of women as an integral part of the fight for the survival and well-being of the earth.

▼ INFORMATION ▼

Where to go or look for information on women's history, activities, politics, and the current feminist movement:

■ **Feminist Library,** *(930 0715).* Sat-Sun 2-5 Tue 11-8. Includes WRRC (Women's Research and Resources Centre).

■ **Fawcett Library,** *City of London Polytechnic, Calcutta Hse, Old Castle St, E1 7NT (283 1030 x 570).* A lending and reference library with an extensive collection of books for and by women. Subscription £10 yrly , £2 per day (waged) or £5 yrly, £1 per day for students and unwaged. You cannot take books out on a day ticket. Opening times; term time Mon 11-8.30. Wed, Thur, Fri 10-5. closed Tue. Vacation time mon, Wed, Thur, Fri 10-5. Excellent historical resource library covering a broad range of subjects from the early days of women's suffrage to the present day.

■ **Feminist Archive,** *Trinity Rd, St Philips, Bristol BS2 ONW, (0272 350025 (24hrs)).* Wed 2-7.30, Sat 2-5 or by appointment. A library of women's writing, unpublished research and periodicals from all over the world. Including all publications by Virago. Set up to document the development of the movement. Not a lending library. Would welcome additions to their collection. Also houses the Dora Russell collection of memorabilia from her European Peace caravan tour. A sister collection has also been started at Bradford University, contact the library for details.

■ **Women's International Resource Centre,** *173 Archway Rd, N6 (341 4403).* Library (membership £6 (£3) for individuals, £12 for groups), newsletter, also workshops.

▼ PUBLICATIONS ▼

■ **Spare Rib,** *27 Clerkenwell Cl, EC1R OAT (253 9792).* Best known feminist mag. £ .monthly. News, articles, reviews, listings. Good annual diary.

■ **Women for Women,** *3 Kestrel Ave Herne Hill, SE24 OED (737 3250).* Mag of working class women's writing.

■ **Shocking Pink,** *23 Tunstall Rd, SW9 (274 0412),* is an hilarious radical magazine for and by youngish women, produced 'trimenstrually' and covering subjects that are usually ignored in mainstream mags, such as sex, racism, attitudes to women etc. 65p. Subs £2.80 for women, £5.60 for institutions and men.

■ **Women and Computing,** *c/o Microsyster, Wesley Hse, 4 Wild Ct. Kingsway, WC2 5AU (430 0655).* Qtly newsletter (sub £6) for women interested in computers. Also contact address for the **National Women and Computing Network.** (see p 237 **Computers**)

■ **Trouble and Strife,** *Subscriptions c/o Women's Centre 34 Exchange St Norwich NR2 1AX,* Radical feminist mag £6.00 for three issues also available is bookshops. Back issues £1.

▼ RIGHTS ▼

The following organisations will be able to give you information and advice on your rights in all areas of your life; work, home, relationships, education etc. Many of them are also working to improve the rights of women in this country where in spite of legal changes women often have to face discrimination and prejudice .

See also the **Kings Cross Women's Centre, A Woman's Place, Wesley House** and the **London Lesbian and Gay Centre.**

■ **The Rights of Women (ROW),** *52-54 Featherstone St, EC1Y 8RT (251 6575/6/7).* Legal advice line three evenings a week . Bullitin three times a year plus a range of leaflets and publications on aspects of the law concerning women (eg lesbian custody, sexual harassment etc) Always looking for volunteeers in office or on help line . Campaign for the legal profession and leglisaltion to be fairer to women. Can refer women to sympathetic lawyers. They also encourage the setting up of other women's advice centres. *Women's Rights & the EEC - A Guide to women in the UK* from ROW £3.00 Other groups associated with ROW: **The Sexual Violence and the Law Group, The Lesbian Custody Support Group, The Women's Legal Defence Fund and The European Network of Women.**

■ **The Women's Legal Defence Fund,** *Third floor 29 Great James St, WC1 (831 6890).* Info, advice and support specifically to help women fight sex discrimination.

■ **NCCL (below)** publish a range of information and discussion leaflets and books among them: *The Rape Controversy* Melissa Benn, Tess Gill and Anna Coote £1.75 (inc p&p), *Positive Action: Changing the Workplace for Women,* Paddy Stamp & Sadie Robarts £5.35 (inc p&p).

■ **Women's Rights Unit (NCCL),** *21 Tabard St, SE1 4LA (403 3888).* Campaigns for end of sexual harassment and sex discrimination and for maternity rights, equal pay and positive action at work. Newsletter.

■ **EOC Equal Opportunities Commission,** *Overseas House, Quay St, Manchester M3 3HN, (061 833 9244).* Government body set up to ensure effective enforcement of the Sex Discrimination Act and the Equal Pay Act. If you feel you have been unfairly treated at work because of your sex you can contact the EOC who will be able to advise you on how to take your case to a tribunal.

■ **Commission of the European Communities,** *8 Storey's Gate, SW1P 3AT (222 8122).* Has a library (10-1 M-F) and various pamphlets including info on case law resulting from EEC decisions. Can advise on how to campaign to have EEC law recognised here.

■ **Women In Prison,** *25t Horsell Rd, N5 (607 3353609 7463/8167).* Campaigning & lobbying group for the rights of women in prison, also help individual women who have been or are in prison.

■ **Black Female Prisoners' Scheme,** *Black Enterprise Centre, 444 Brixton Rd, SW9 (733 5520).* Aim to help women prisoners (Afro-Caribbean and Asian) back into the community.

■ **Women Against Sexual Harassment,** *242 Pentonville Rd , N1 9UN (833 0222/3883).* Advice sessions Thur eve 6.30-8. Phone for appointment.

▼ CENTRES ▼

These range from umbrella organisations like the Kings Cross Women's Centre which houses a large number of campaigning groups to small women's centres where you can just drop in to meet other women, or take a class in yoga or computing. Services range from provision of creches, libraries, washing machines to counselling and training.
The atmosphere varies from the highly political to groups of chatting mothers and their toddlers. If you can't find what you want don't despair, maybe there are other women out there who feel the same, so how about starting your own group?

■ **Kings Cross Women's Centre,** *71 Tonbridge St, WC1 (837 7509).* T-Th 11-5pm. Multi-racial women's centre. Drop in, resource, advice and survival information for women on a wide range of issues including anti-racism, disability rights, immigration, welfare benefits, housing, prostitution, employment, Restart, divorce, custody, anti-lesbian discrimination, rape and violence. Base for: **Black Women for Wages for Housework Campaign; English Collective of Prostitutes; Wages for Housework Campaign; Legal Action for Women** (see p194 **Law** section); **Peace Collective, WinVisible (Women with Visible and Invisible Disabilities** see p235 **Disabled** section) and **Women against Rape**. The centre is wheelchair accessible but no accessible toilet. Signs in English for the deaf. All materials available on tape on request.

■ **London Women's Centre,** *Wesley Hse, 4 Wild Court, WC2 (831 6946).* Groups based at Wesley Hse:

Akina Mama Wa Afrika *(405 0678)*

Asian Women's Network *post only*

Beach Project *(831 7377)*

Black Women Healers and Mama Sila *(430 1044)*

Camden Black Sisters *(831 7897)*

Clean Break Theatre Company *(405 0765)*

Fleet Street Nursery *(831 9179)*

Kingsway Children's Centre *8(31 7460)*

Lesbian Archives *(405 6475)*

Lespop *(833 4996)*

Microsyster *(430 0655)*

National Abortion Campaign *(405 4801)*

National Childcare Campaign *(405 5617/8)*

Women's Computer Centre *(403 0112)*

Women's Sports Foundation *(831 7863)*

Women's Training Link *(242 6050)*

■ **Deptford and Lewisham Women's Centre,** *74 Deptford High St, SE8 (692 1851).* Mon-Thur 10-4. Drop in info centre, workshops and classes, creche, free pregnancy testing, Lesbian and Black women's groups. Late opening Tues eve, activities include meditation, tarot, video screening and assertion training.

■ **Haringay Women's Centre,** *Tottenham Green Education Centre, Town Hall Approach Rd, N15 (808 1436).* After Sept they hope to be back at *40 Turnpike Lane N8 (881 6090).* Opening hours: Mon, Wed, Thur 10-3, Tue 10-1. Classes; self defence, lesbian and children's groups, Yoga. Library, use of washing machine and dryer, meeting room, creche provided during classes (free).

■ **Hackney Women's Centre,** *20 Dalston Lane, E8 (254 2980).* Help and advice, various classes including craft, massage, assertiveness training, literacy and bi-lingual writing classes. Lesbian and black lesbian groups.

■ **Brent Women's Centre,** *Community Centre 232 High Rd NW10 2NX (459 7660).* W-F 12-6. Drop-in centre, various activities including literacy classes, advice sessions, counselling. Creche. Various evening classes.

■ **Croydon Women's Centre,** *13 Woodside Green South Norwood, SE25 (656 2369).*

■ **Enfield Women's Centre,** *31a Derby Rd Ponders End Enfield Middx EN3 4AJ, (443 1902).*

■ **Hillingdon Women's Centre,** *333 Long Lane Hillingdon Middx, (0895 59578).*

■ **South Camden Women's Centre,** *90 Cromer St, WC1 H8DD (278 0120/837 8774).* Open M-F 10-5 W10-1. Variety of workshops e.g. sign language, herbalism, mask making. Lesbian group Mon7.30 and more. Phone for details.

■ **Southwark Women's Centre,** *2-8 Peckham High St, SE15 (701 2564).*

■ **Sutton Women's Centre,** *3 Palmerston Rd Sutton Surrey, (661 1991).* Various courses, assertion, literacy etc. Open 10-4 M-F.

■ **Waltham Forest Women's Centre,** *109 Hoe St, E17 4SE (520 5318).*

■ **West Hampstead Women's Centre,** *55 Hemstal Rd , NW6 2AD (328 7389).* Advice and info, various workshops, Black and Lesbian groups as well as activities for disabled women (full access).

▼ ETHNIC MINORITIES ▼

Women from ethnic minorities face discrimination, not only on the grounds of their race and ethnicity, but also their sex. As a response, women have established a wide range of self-help groups in order to supplement and often fill the gaps in the provision of services. It is of course impossible to list them all, but here is a sample which should give you an idea of potential resources.

Black Women

■ **Southall Black Sisters,** *52 Norwood Green Southall Middx UB2 4DW, (571 9595).*

■ **Haringay Black Women's Centre,** *Lower Somerset School Lordship Lane , N17 (808 7973).*

■ **Peckham Black Women's Centre,** *69 Bellenden Rd, SE1 5BH (358 1486/7).* Centre for African, Afro-Caribbean and Asian women. Open M-Th. Provide advice and info, free pregnancy testing, qtly newsletter, various courses, library, creche facilities for activities, wheelchair access.

■ **Claudia Jones Organisation,** *103 Stoke Newington Rd, N16 (241 1646).* Afro-Caribbean women's group, advice and info counselling on health issues, hospital visiting, supplementary

school Sats and holidays.

■ **East London Black Women's Organisation,** *ELBWO Centre Clinton Rd Forest Gate , E7 (534 7545).* Courses, Sat school, self-help sessions, advice, info and arts projects.

■ **African Women's Welfare Association,** *c/o Celestial Church of Christ, Stratford Parish Hall Northumbria St, Poplar, E14 (987 0371).* Employment training, info and advice, cultural activities. Open 10-5 M-F by appointment.

■ **Moroccan Women's Project,** *61 Goldbourne Rd, W10 (960 6672).* Info and advice, EFL classes, mother & toddler's group, help with interpreting.

Asian

■ **Asian Women's Forum,** *50 Mayes Rd, N22 (888 2446).* Campaign and discussion group around Asian women's issues. They run a mothers & toddlers club, various classes and have two refuges for battered Asian women.

■ **Asian Women's Action Group,** *18a Edison Rd Crouch End , N8 (341 2351/348 6900).* Resource & drop in centre, advice sessions, counselling, educational and cultural activities as well as self defense classes.

■ **Asian Women's Resource Centre,** *134 Minet Ave , NW10 (961 5701).*

■ **Asian Women's Network,** *London Women's Centre. 4 Wild Court, WC2.* Contact by post only.

■ **ASHA Collective Asian Women's Resource Centre,** *27 Santley St, SW4 (274 8854).* Advice and info. Help for battered women and girls, two refuges. Open 9-5 by appointment.

■ **Bangladesh Women's Association,** *91 Highbury Hill, N5 (359 5836).*

■ **Pakistan Women's Welfare Association,** *226 High St Walthamstow, E17 (520 1603).* Activities for Pakistani women.

Other

■ **London Irish Women's Centre,** *59 Stoke Newington Church St, N16 (249 7318).*

■ **Union of Turkish Women in Britain,** *110 Clarence Rd, E5 (985 4072/986 1358).* Advice and info, counsellors, interpreters, various courses.

▼ WORK ▼

At the centre of the campaign for women's rights is the demand for equality at work, in pay, conditions and opportunities in training and promotion. Whether at home or in the workplace women's contribution to society is often either undervalued or ignored. It is estimated that women do two-thirds of the worlds work in return for only one-tenth of its income and only own 1% of its property. They are not paid for work in the home and are badly paid for traditionally unskilled 'women's work'.

To choose to work outside the home a woman has to overcome many hurdles that few men share, from practical problems such as provision of childcare (see p220 **Kids** section) to dealing with a mostly male environment.

■ **Lambeth Women's Workshop,** *Unit 22, Parkhall Trading Est, Martell , West Norwood, SE21 8EA (670 0339).* Training workshop for women teaching courses in basic carpentry and computing. Priority given to black and working class women and women with kids who otherwise wouldn't be able to train .

■ **Wages for Housework Campaign,** *c/o Kings Cross Women's Centre 71 Tonbridge st, WC1 (837 7509).* Network of black and white women campaigning internationally for wages for housework for all women from all governments - to be paid for by dismantling the military-industrial complex. Circulating international petition *Women Count - Count Women's Work* available in 22 languages and braille. Pressing the government to implement the 1985 UN decision to count all women's waged and unwaged work in the GNP of every country. Have published *All Work and No Pay.* Lists on request.

■ **Black Women for Wages for Housework,** *(As above),* Publications include *Black Women: Bringing It All Back Home, Black women and the Peace Movement, Roots* and*Black Ghetto Ecology.*

■ **Wages Due Lesbians,** *(as above),* Started in 1985 they aim to count lesbian women's work in all situations from housework to fighting violence in all its forms.

■ **Women and Manual Trades,** *52 Featherstone St, EC1 (251 9192).* Qtly newsletter £5 (organisations) £2.50 (tradeswomen). Open 10.30-5.30 (phone first). Run workshops to encourage women to work in this traditionally all-male field. Also lobby training agencies and work with unions.

■ **Women's Motor Mechanics Workshop Ltd.,** *Bay 4R Brixton Estate 1-3 Brixton Rd , SW9 6DE (582*

2574). Free workshops in car mechanics by women for women.

■ **Working Mothers Association,** *(700 5771).* A self-help organisation for working parents and their children.

Books on Women and Work

Available from WEA: *Women At Work,* Chris Aldred (£1.75) - book analysing the problems that women face at work, home and in unions. Pamphlets: *Women and Technology* 95p

The Women's Guide to Starting Your own Business:Where to Begin and How to Make it Work Deborah Fowler (Thorsons £6.99).

▼ PROSTITUTION ▼

■ **English Collective of Prostitutes (ECP),** *c/o Kings Cross Women's Centre, WC1 (837 7509).* A Network of black and white women working in different levels of the sex industry. They campaign for the abolition of all prostitution laws; for human, legal and civil rights for prostitute women and for financial alternatives for women - higher benefits, grants and wages, so that no woman is forced into sex with anyone by poverty. In 1982 they occupied a church in King's Cross to protest police illegality and racism. Publications include *Prostitutes - Our Life, The Hooker and the Beak, Prostitute Women and AIDS* and *Resisting the Virus of Repression.*

▼ HEALTH ▼

Whose body is it? Does it belong to you or the medical profession? Questions many women are coming to grips with in a lot of different ways, as they say NO to authoritarian attitudes within the medical professions. More and more women are turning to alternative medicine in their search for a more human centred approach. For more help with finding a therapist see section on **Self Discovery** (p 156).

Our Bodies Ourselves Angela Phillips and Jill Rakusan (Penguin £8.95) first published in (USA) 1971 and still selling well, regularly updated. Written by feminists for women it is a comprehensive guide to everything you've ever wanted to know about your body - and more. From lifestyles (lesbianism, celibacy, marriage) to health care (pregnancy, periods, menopause).

■ **Women's Therapy Centre,** *6 Manor Gardens, , N7 6LA (263 6200).*

■ **Pellin Feminist Therapy Centre,** *43 Killyon Rd, SW8 2XS (622 0148),* for workshops, training courses, individual and group therapy.

■ **Women's Reproductive Rights Information Centre,** *52-54 Featherstone St, EC1Y 8RT (251 6332/ 6580).* For info on all women's health issues from pregnancy to menopause, genital warts to artificial insemination. Also sell pamphlets and books and have a quarterly newsletter. Library and phone line open 11-5pm Mon, Wed, Thur & Fri. Wheelchair access. Send sae for publications list which include *Women's Health Teaching Pack* (£5.00). *The Menopause - A Guide for Women of All Ages* (£2.50).

■ **Women's Health Information Centre,** *52-54 Featherstione St, EC1Y 8RT (251 6580).* Library, factsheets and newsletter and info on all aspects of women's health-support groups.

■ **National Abortion Campaign,** *Wesley Hse 4 Wilde Court, WC2 5AU (405 4801).* Produces mag, info/education pamphlets and videos.

■ **Abortion Law Reform Ass/A Women's Right to Choose Campaign,** *88a Islington High St , N1 8EG (359 5200).*

■ **Women's Dept,** *London Borough of Hammersmith & Fulham Town Hall King St, W6 9JU (748 3020).* Do a free leaflet on *Women And Aids.*

■ **Women's Alcohol Centre,** *254 St Paul's Rd, N1 2LJ (226 4581).* Info, counselling and support including some residential facilities.

■ **Breast Care and Mastectomy Association,** *26a Harrison St Kings Cross, WC1H 8JG (837 0908).* Support and counselling for women with breast cancer. They aim to get women 'back to normal' as soon as possible after treatment. Open 9-5 Mon-Fri phone first for appointment. *The Cancer Journals* Audre Lorde Sheba £2.95 - personal experience of mastectomy.

■ **Sisters Against Disablement,** *241 Albion Rd , N16 (241 2263).* Campaign for the rights of women with disabilities.

■ **WinVisible (Women with Visible and Invisible Disabilities),** *King's Cross Women's Centre (see p235,* Campaigning for economic independence, mobility, access and housing, abortion/the right to have children, and against welfare cuts, racism,

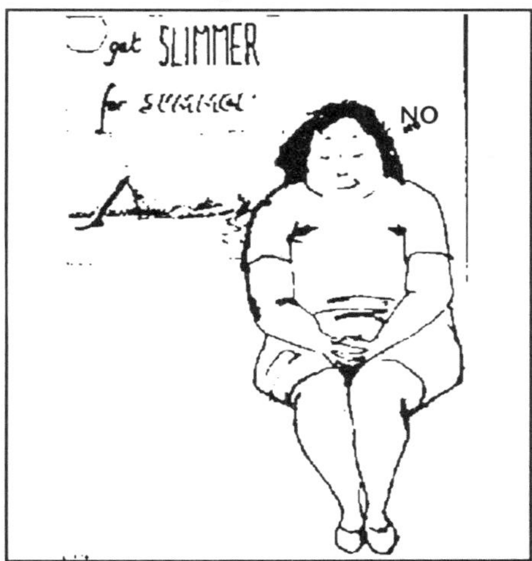

(Leeds Postcards)

rape and military-industrial pollution. Publications include *True Confessions of a Raspberry/Message to Bhopal* by Claire Glasmen and WinVisible. List on request. *Able Lives: Women's Experience of Paralysis* Edited by Jenny Morris (Women's Press £5.95) - contributions from women with spinal cord injuries describing their experiences.

■ **Overeaters Anonymous,** *c/o Manor Gdns Centre 609 Manor Gdns , N7 (868 4109).* Regular meetings. Phone for details.

■ **Fat Women's Group,** *c/o Wesley Hse 4 Wild Court Kingsway, WC2B 5AU (831 6946).* Support group challenging negative stereotypes and prejudice against fat women. *Women's Secret Disorders* Mira Dana & Marilyn Lawrence(Grafton Books £3.50/ '89) on Bulimia Nervosa, how to give it up and guide to setting up and running a self-help group. *Fed Up and Hungry* Marilyn Lawrence(Ed) (Women's Press 1987). Essays on eating problems.

■ **Positively Women,** *333 Grays Inn Rd, WC1X 8PX (837 9705).* Fortnightly Support group for women who have Aids/ARC/HIV, also info and advice service and counselling.

■ **Women's Natural Health Centre,** *1 Hillside Hghgate Rd, N5 1QT (482 3293).* Homoeopathy, massage, osteopathy, acupuncture, reflexology for women on a low income. Phone for appointment Mon-Fri 9-1.

■ **The Rainbow Net,** *151 Rye La, SE15 (639 5945).* Counselling and growth centre for women: individual counselling (hypnotherapy, client-centred or transpersonal), workshops, yoga, support groups.

■ **Moving Line Counselling Service** (See p158). A group of women counsello

See for **Sex** section (p71) for sex therapy and contraception.

▼ HELP ▼

CENTRES

■ **London Rape Crisis Centre,** *PO BOX 69, WC1X 9NJ (837 1600 (24 hours) 278 3956 (Office hours)).* Free confidential service for any woman or girl who has been raped or sexually assaulted. They can provide support, info on prevention of pregnancy after rape, abortion and VD. They'll go with you to the police, court, doctors or clinics. They can inform you about police procedures and how to apply for compensation.

■ **Women Against Rape,** *c/o Kings Cross Women's Centre 71 Tonbridge St, WC1 (837 7509).* Campaigns against rape in all its forms, can provide help with court cases, compensation and info.

A good book on the subject is*Surviving Sexual Violence* Liz Kelly (Polity Press £8.95).

Rape

WHAT TO DO IF YOU ARE SEXUALLY ASSAULTED OR RAPED.

If you decide to report to the police-

- Report to the police as soon as possible - delay may go against your case.
- If at all possible tell someone what has happened as soon as you can - a witness to your distress and early complaint will help.
- Do not wash, tidy yourself or change clothing because you may destroy valuable evidence.
- Do not take any drugs or alcohol.
- Call a friend or call the Rape Crisis Centre (see number below) so that someone can give you support during police and medical procedures.
- Take a change of warm clothing with you - the police may keep some of your original clothing for tests and evidence.
- Making notes about the rape may help you when you give your statement, but don't worry if you can't do this. Important things to remember are the sequence of events, details, and what was said. Thre is no reason why you should talk to any police officer except the one in charge of your case.

Medical examination, internal and external.

- You can ask for your own GP or a woman doctor, if you prefer. The sole purpose of this examination is to collect medical evidence of rape or sexual assault.
- You may be asked to look at mug shots, accompany the police to the scene of the crime, or identify your assailant/s.
- You can ask for your name not to be read out in court.
- If you feel you are not being treated well, ask to see the officer in charge of the station.
- Whether or not you report to the police- talk to someone about what has happened - you need a friend at this time.
- See a doctor to check for: VD, Aids pregnancy and possible injury.

Reproduced with the permission of the Rape Crisis Centre, London.

Women's Refuge

■ **National Women's Aid Federation (Battered Women's Refuges),** *52-54 Featherstone st , EC1 (251 6537 National Helpline 0272 428368).* Referral and advice agency with 200 affiliated refuges. You can also contact your local refuge through the Samaritans, Citizens Advice Bureau, Advice centres or the police.

■ **ASHA,** *27 Santley St, SW4 7QF (274 8854), (see p 178* Asian women's groups.

▼ GETTING HOME SAFELY ▼

Women's Safe Transport (WST) schemes are popping up all over London (funding permitting) They've been created in response to the increasing harassment and violence towards women in the capital. Most of them are operated by women for women. If there isn't one for your area contact your local authority and they'll be able to let you know if there is one. There are also commercially run taxi services for women. If you want to set up a taxi scheme for women contact

■ **London Community Transport Association (LCTA),** *c/o Finsbury Business Centre, 40 Bowling Green Lane, EC1(278 0333/837 0081)* do an excellent (free) booklet on how to set up a safe transport scheme for women.

Taxis for Women by Women:

■ **Stockwell Women's Lift Service,** *46 Kepler Rd, SW4 (274 4641).* West Lambeth area. Sat 9.30pm-1.30am. M-F 7-11pm F daytime 9-5 Sat 9pm-1am Car and 11 seater minibus. No fixed fee, donation according to what you can afford.

■ **Safe Women's Transport Service,** *Palingswick Hse 241 King St, W6 (748 6036).* Run by Hammersmith & Fulham Council for women and girl. Available Wed/Thur 6.30-12pm. 50p anywhere in the Borough. Women drivers.

■ **Ladycabs Mini-Cab Service,** *150 Green Lanes, N16 (254 3501/254 3314).* Women-only drivers (mainly for women and children but will take men passangers as well) operates up to 12.30 wkdays, 1 am Fri, 2 am Sat. £2 for first 2 miles 70p thereafter.

■ **Ladybirds,** *Ladybirds Hse 458 Ewell Rd Surbiton Surrey KT16 7EL, (390 3518).* 24hr service, women drivers available on request. Opening times to book Thur/Fri/Sat all night, Mon/Tue/Wed until 7pm. 24hr ansaphone available for night service. 75p a mile

■ **Gainsborough Ladies Car Service,** *173 South Ealing Rd , W5 (568 3333/560 2377).* Women drivers 24hrs on request. 80p a mile.

■ **Ladycare Cabs,** *Walthamstow, (521 2012).* Women drivers. £1.60 1st two miles then 75p a mile.

▼ MATERNITY ▼

Since April 87 maternity benefits have only been available to a minority of women. Women's right to maternity leave and employment rights after maternity have been reduced. See p### for info on maternity rights, pregnancy, birth, breastfeeding and post-natal depression. See p 220; **Kids** for daycare etc.

■ **Maternity Alliance,** *15 Britannia St , WC1X 9JP (837 1265),* for info on campaigns for maternity rights. See **Sex** section (p71). Books available from NCCL (see p215) on maternity rights; *Maternity Rights at Work* (£1.75 incl p&p) and *Maternity Rights Handbook* £5.35 incl p&p).

See also *The Politics of Breastfeeding,* Gabrielle Palmer (Pandora Press £6.95) which puts breastfeeding into its political, environmental and historical context (did you know that for every 3 million bottle fed babies 70,000 tonnes of metal are used up in discarded milk tins?). *Multi-Racial Initiatives on Maternity Care* Asma Ahmed & Maggie Pearson (£3) - directory of 34 projects for black & ethnic minority women wanting to improve maternity care. *Maternity Rights Handbook* (Penguin £4.95)

▼ EDUCATION AND MEDIA ▼

In these days of 'equality' there is still a large difference between the education of girls and boys.

While you may see girls wielding a saw in woodwork lessons and boys battling with bobbins and thimbles in needlework classes, when it comes to employment training the difference is more obvious. For example in 1987 82% of young women on YTS schemes were doing clerical, catering or selling work compared with 18% of young men, and 50% of young men on the scheme were involved in manufacturing compared with only 8% of young women.

■ **Women's Education Group (WEDG),** *Women's Resource Centre ILEA Drama and Tape Centre, Princeton St, WC1R 4BH (242 6807).* Run support groups, courses, give advice and info to women in order to encourage and support anti-sexist and anti-racist initiatives. Open M-F 11-6.

■ **Workers' Educational Association,** *9 Upper Berkeley St, W1H 8BY (402 5608/9).* Publish *Women's Studies Newsletter* (£5 yr for two issues) a forum for exchanging ideas and experiences of putting on courses for and about women. Also available from

I TOLD NIGEL THAT I NEEDED HIS INTEREST AND SUPPORT - AND AS USUAL HE DIDN'T UNDERSTAND WHAT I MEANT

WEA: *Women At Work*, Chris Aldred £1.75 - analysing the problems that women face at work, home and in unions. Pamphlet: *Women and Technology* 95p

■ **National Union of Students Women's Campaign**, *461 Holloway Rd, N7 6LJ (272 8900).* Provides info, advice and support. Researches and campaigns on issues of women's liberation within the student movement such as sexual harassment in colleges, creche provision, child sexual abuse etc.

■ **Gender and Mathematics Assn (GAMMA)**, *c/o Dept of Mathematical Sciences, Goldsmiths College Lewisham Way, SE14 6NW (692 7171 ex 2179).* National network concerned with gender bias in mathematics. Membership £5 (£2concs).

■ **Women's Media Resources Project**, *The Rio Cinema ,107 Kingsland Rd, E8 (254 6536).* Women only sound studio, film/video shows and discussion.

■ **Women Artists Slide Library**, *Fulham Palace, Bishops Ave, SW6 6EA (731 7618)*, reference library of women artists work, old and new, from all over the world. It has over 20,000 slides. Open Tue-Fri 10-5.

■ **Women in Music**, *Battersea Arts Centre Old Town Hall , Lavender Hill, SW11 5TF (978 4823).* Raising profile of women in music by lobbying, running workshops, networking etc. Membership between £2-£10.

■ **Women in Publishing**, *12 Dyott St, WC1* see **Printing and Publishing section** (p262).

■ **Clio Co-op**, *91c Mildmay Rd, N1 4PU (249 2551)*, women's oral history group documenting older women's lives. Can provide speakers and run courses.

■ **Ova Music Studio**, *Highgate Newtown Community Centre 25 Bertram St, N19 5DQ (281 2528).* Women only recording studio and music resource centre. Also voice, rhythm and percussion workshops.

■ **Drill Hall Arts Centre**, *16 Chenies St, WC1E 7ET (631 1253).* Women only bar (Mon eves) and workshops. Creche. Theatre. Vegetarian cafe downstairs.

■ **Aphra Workshop**, *99 Leighton Rd Kentish Town, NW5 2RB (485 2105)*, offer workshops for women on script writing, concentrating mainly on writing for television.

■ **Cinema of Women**, *31 Clerkenwell Close, EC1R OAT (251 4978).*

■ **Cinistra Pictures**, *The Co-op Centre,11 Mowll St, SW9 6GB (793 0157).* Training in all aspects of video production. Reductions for unwaged. Phone for details.

■ **Circles Women's Film & Video Distribution Ltd**, *113 Roman Rd, E2 OHU (981 6828).* Distributes films and videos by women. They have over 230 titles in stock including rare archive material of early films by women, as well as contemporary material from all over the world. Catalogue (£3.50 for individuals £6 for groups). Previews Weds, book in advance. Educational packs available. Regular screening and discussions. Publications.

▼ POLITICS ▼

■ **300 Group**, *9 Poland St, W1 (734 3457).* Support group for women who want to stand in elections, both local and national, regardless of party. There are only 41 women MPs out of 650. They want 325.

■ **Feminist Review**, *c/o Rachel Maund, Routledge Promotion Department, 11 New Fetter La, EC4.* Socialist, feminist journal published three times a year (£15). Interesting back issues (£6.95 each) including *The Past Before Us: 20 Years of Feminism. & Family Secrets: Child Sexual Abuse Today.*

▼ PEACE AND ENVIRONMENT ▼

■ **The Women's Environmental Network**, *287 City Rd, EC1V 1LA (490 2511).* See **Green Environment** (p275).

■ **Women's International League for Peace and Freedom**, *29 Great James St, WC1N 3ES (242 1521).* The oldest women's peace organisation, born 1915 in response to WW1, and a belief that women's vote was important to stop the killing. National and international pressure group. Sub £8 pa, concs.

■ **Maypole Fund**, *Box 25, 136 Kingsland High St Hackney, E8 2SN.* Small scale funding for women's activities. Especially those projects concerned with disarmament and action against the arms trade; anti-militarism and action against male violence; nuclear and environmental issues; promoting women's economic and political autonomy around

the world and international links between women for these purposes.

▼ BOOKSHOPS ▼

■ **Sisterwrite,** *190 Upper St, N1 (226 9782).* Mon-Sat 10-6, Thur 10-7. Also pamphlets, postcards, records, cassettes, crafts, women only noticeboard, info. Monthly booklist (mail order) £1.75 for six months (UK) £2.25 Europe, £2.50 elsewhere.

■ **Silver Moon Women's Bookshop,** *68 Charing Cross Rd, WC2 (836 7906).*

■ **Feminist Audio Books,** *52-54 Featherstone St, EC1Y 8RT (251 2908/0713).* Can provide feminist and women oriented books on tape for women who are blind or partially sighted. Welcome volunteers to read books onto tape.

▼ PUBLISHERS ▼

These publish books for, by and about women and women's experience. They cover a range of subjects including history, art, politics, physical and mental health, poetry and literature. Unsolicited manuscripts are not usually read, so it's best to send them a synopsis of the work and ask if they'd be willing to read it. If you want to get your work published see **Printing and Publishing** section (p255) . Most of them also do mail order and publications lists send sae for details.

■ **Virago Press Ltd,** *Centro House 20-23 Mandela St Camden Town, NW1 0HQ (383 5150/sales 379 6637).* Founded in '73 is now famous for discovering and publishing long forgotten women authors. Appeals to a wide audience also recently brought out books for girls and young women called *Virago Upstarts.*

■ **The Women's Press,** *34 Great Sutton St, EC1 (251 3007 Book club 253 0009).* Interesting and varied titles. Also fund a book-club giving 25-50% discount on their own and other's titles. £15 life sub, or £7.50 pa (£10 and £5 for students, claimants and pensioners); minimum purchase 4 books a year.

■ **Pandora Press,** *15-17 Broadwick St , W1V 1FP (439 3126).* A feminist press which publishes a range of fiction and non-fiction by women.

■ **Onlywoman Press,** *38 Mount Pleasant, WC1X OAP (837 0596).* Lesbian, radical, feminist publishers.

■ **Sheba Feminist Publishers,** *10a Bradbury St, N16 8JN (254 1590).* Feminist co-op publishing anti-sexist, anti-racist children's books, They give priority to work by black women, working class women and lesbians. Desperately need donations (or loans).

■ **Zed Press,** *57 Caledonian Rd , N1 9BU (837 4014).* Publish books on third world issues including politics, history, culture, women's studies, environmental issues. 50 titles a year.

▼ MISCELLANEOUS ▼

■ **Compulsive Eaters Group,** *c/o K, Noble, 86 Holmleigh Rd, N16 (800 9099).* Connected with Spare Tyre theatre group and based on *Fat is a Feminist Issue* S Orbach (Arrow Books £2.25p). Details of shows and workshops on eating problems.

■ **Advertising Standards Authority,** *Brook House Torrington Pl, WC1 (580 5555).* For complaints about press, posters, direct mail, cinema and video (not TV or radio). Always write to the manufacturer as well.

■ **Everywoman,** *34A Islington Green, N1 8DU (359 5496).* Feminist current affairs mag, co-operatively run. Also do a directory of women's Co-ops and are pioneering new ways of organising co-ops. Managed to survive legal battle with the Mirror group after daring to criticise Marje Proops.

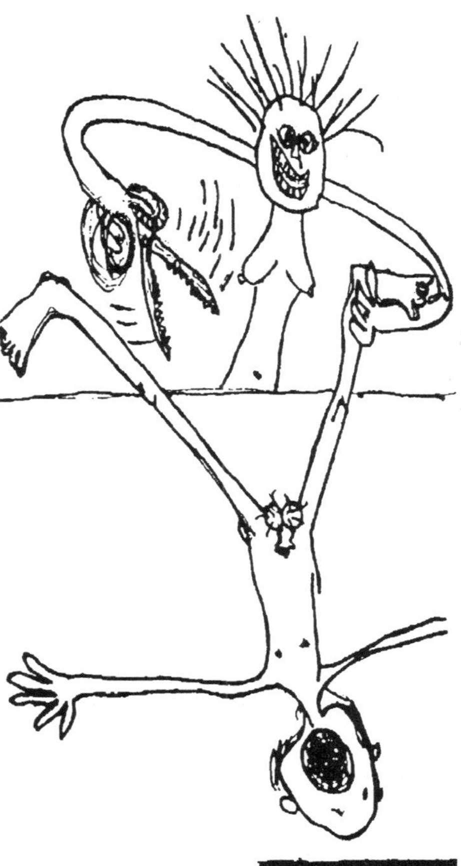

men

It's hard to say whether there is such a thing as the men's movement. Unlike organisations for women which are tied together with a common bond of freedom from oppression and a struggle for liberation, men's organisations have no such political unity. Organisations for men that deal with the emotional issues of divorce, becoming a widower, lone fathers, relationship difficulties, fatherhood, retirement and sexual identity are growing (see under 'Groups'). However, organisations that lobby and campaign, and deal with men's rights in these areas are few.

▼ PUBLICATIONS ▼

■ **Achilles Heel,** *79 Pembroke Rd, E17 (607 0365).* (£1.50). Irregular. An anti-sexist pro-feminist collective, concerned with men's sex role stereotyping and issues of masculinity and being a man. Welcome material for their mag.

▼ READING ▼

For Men Against Sexism, ed. John Snodgrass, Times Change Press. Covers anti sexist practice, male sexuality, male supremacy, men's liberation, gay, working class and third world men. *Fathers A Psychological Perspective,* Ed. Nigel Beail/J McGuire (Junction Books), covers pregnancy, childbirth, father child relationship, fathers in society. *Men in Love* by Nancy Friday (Belacourt Press 1980) is a book about male sexual fantasies. *Male Initiation: The Grief of its Absence* by Robert Bly (1989) addresses the issue of how young males are not initiated into adult manhood in our society, and it's subsequent effects.

▼ DIVORCE AND CHILDREN ▼

■ **Both Parents Forever,** *39 Cloonmore Av, Orpington, Kent BR6 9LE, (0689 54343).* Give and advice and info to the divorced/divorcing on what their rights are in relation to their children. Info pack £5 incl p&p gives info on legislation, rights, joint custody, access and their children's education. Most of their clients are men.

▼ FATHERHOOD ▼

■ **Families Need Fathers,** *BM Families, London WC1N 3XX, (886 0970)* is a national society primarily concerned with the problems of maintaining a child's relationship with both its parents during and following separation and divorce. Believe joint custody should be the norm after separation. Subs £10 pa inc journal *Access*. Publish some helpful booklets *Divorce and Your Child, Custody and Access Guidelines, Schools and the Non-Custodial Parent*. Group counselling sessions. Members/non members drop in at Conway Hall, Red Lion Square, WC1, 7.30-9.30pm on the first and third Fri evening of every month.

Lone Fathers

Lone fathers make up 10% of one parent families.

■ **Gingerbread,** *(240 0953).* (See p213) are good at giving advice to lone fathers and can put you in touch with a local support group.

■ **National Council for One-Parent Families,** *(267 1361).* (See p213).

▼ GROUPS ▼

The following is a list of men working specifically with men. Most produce literature which they will be happy to send.

■ **Dave Findlay,** *(639 9372).* Trained in Psychosynthesis, runs a programme of 6 workshops through the year entitled 'Brothers: Embodying the Masculine' and including 'The Wild Man', 'Fathers and Sons,', and 'The Men's Lodge'.

■ **Nick Gregor, Spectrum,** *(340 0426).* Works individually and runs mixed groups for adult children of alcoholic parents. Would be open to starting a men only group. Also focuses on male sexual abuse and incest.

■ **The Men's Centre,** *(267 8713).* Aims to stop domestic violence. Will help men to take responsibility for their violence and to find ways other than physical and emotional abuse of their partners to cope with conflicts or problems in the relationship. Once a week group for the six months. £ Neg, concs.

■ **Malcom Sterne, Monkton Wilde Court,** *Charmouth Bridport Dorset, (0297 60342).* Runs men's groups in Dorset and occasionally in London at St James's Church, Piccadilly

■ **Piers Partridge,** *(241 0018).* Works to help men become more aware of their needs and to be able to articulate them more clearly. Uses existential approach, Transactional Analysis and bodywork.

■ **Gerry Popplestone and David Simpson,** *(739 0754 and 692 5097).* Run groups and day workshops for men on men's issues including *Owning up* assertiveness training for men.

■ **Re-Evaluation Counselling,** *(291 4108 (Gale Burns)).* Hold men's events and include men's issues in their workshops. Also regular support groups around London.

■ **Spectrum,** *7 Endymion Rd , N4 1EE (341 2277/ 340 0426).* Offer a broad range of group and individual work for men & women, including focus on sexuality, child abuse and incest. Rex Bradley and Terry Cooper are directors. Rex Bradley works with men on raising their awareness and self-esteem. Terry Cooper, founder of Spectrum, pioneered men's sexuality and consciousness-raising groups in this country. Runs on-going group 'Men for Men'.

■ **John Witt, Spectrum,** *(340 0426).* Existential therapist, runs therapy groups for men focusing on 'how we present ourselves as men', self image and sexuality and learning to give and take constructive feedback.

■ **Paul Wolf-Light,** *(388 0947).*

Other

■ **London Bisexual Group,** *Box BM/ BI, London WC1N 3XX.* Regular Friday meetings 8pm at *London Friend, 86 Caledonian Rd, N1.* For men and women (mostly men) who are not sure where they stand in relationship to straight and gay stereotypes.

lesbians and gays

One person in ten is said to be lesbian or gay and very few of them would fit the stereotypical role that the media has set out for them. Often it's hard enough for lesbians and gays to be recognised by each other let alone by 'outsiders'. In spite of the visible and invisible prejudice that abounds in this country men and women in London have come together to form one of Europe's most flourishing gay communities outside of Berlin or Amsterdam.

▼ INFORMATION AND HELP ▼

■ **Lesbian and Gay Switchboard,** *BM Box 1514, WC1N 3XX (837 7324)* for info on the lesbian and gay scene: where to go to meet people, get advice, find a lesbian carpenter etc. The only drawback is that it's often engaged! Unless you're in a hurry write with an sae. They also do a good flatshare service. It's also the contact address for the **Gay Bereavement Support Group.**

■ **Gay Bereavement Project,** *c/o Unitarian Room Hoop Lane, NW11 8BS (837 7324 24 hrs).* N. London group offering support to gays whose partners have died. They can usually find clergy in sympathy with gay relationships to conduct the funeral service. Also Bereavement groups for Lesbians run at **Rainbow Net** Peckham see **Women's** section p178.

■ **GLLAD (Gay and Lesbian Legal Advice),** *(T-F 7-10 p.m. 253 2043).*

■ **Albany Trust,** *24 Chester Sq, SW1W 9HS (730 5871).* Provide a personal counselling service for people with all types of sexual identity & relationship problems (not just Lesbian or Gay) and educational programmes.

■ **London Friend,** *86 Caledonian Rd, N1 (837 3337* (Women's Line, T & Th, 7.30-10, 837 2782)). Offers counselling to men and women by phone or on a one-to-one basis with counsellors who are trained to help you cope with any problem - from thinking you may be lesbian or gay to a relationship break-up. Provide a range of groups to help people come together. A good way to meet people if you're not fond of 'the scene'.

■ **The Jewish Lesbian and Gay Helpline,** *BM Jewish Helpline, WC1 3XX* ((Mon & Thur 7-10) 706 3123). For information on Jewish Lesbian and Gay events and for support and counselling.

■ **Terrence Higgins Trust,** *BM AIDS , WC1N 3XX (242 1010).* Aids helpline 3-10 pm, 7 days. See **Sex** section p###.

■ **London Lighthouse,** *111-117 Lancaster Rd, W11 1QT (792 1200).* Counselling and support for men and women with HIV, Aids or ARC. Courses, workshops, drop in centre as well as residential facilities. Cafe open Mon-Fri.

■ **Black HIV/AIDS Network (BHAN),** *BM MCC, WC1 3XX (848 8700 ext 216 (Hong Tan)).* Aims to provide support and care for black people affected by HIV/Aids, also education and training.

■ **Gay London Policing Group (GALOP),** *38 Mount Pleasant, WC1X OAP (278 6215).* Counselling, support and advice for lesbians and gays in trouble with the police. Mon-Fri 10-6

■ **Lesbian & Gay Employment Rights (LAGER),** *Rm 203 Southbank Hse, Black Prince Rd, SE1 7SJ (587 1643 (Lesbians 587 1636)).* Advice and support particularly in cases of unfair dismissal whether on the grounds of sexual orientation or being HIV positive.

■ **Piccadilly Advice Centre,** *100 Shaftsbury Ave, W1 (434 3773)* for single homeless people in the West End.

■ **Housing Advice Switchboard,** *7a/b Fortess Yard, Fortess rd , NW1 (482 3837).* 24 hours. General housing advice during the day. Emergency service from 6pm if you're stuck for somewhere to stay the night. For people without children, or single, both have a very helpful attitude to lesbians and gays.(see **Somewhere to Live** p2) Also do books and pamphlets on housing.

■ **Stonewall Housing Association,** *(885 2305 and 263 3238).* Hostel accommodation for young lesbians and gays.

■ **Lesbian and Gay Alcohol Problem Service,** *34 Electric Lane, SW9 8JT (737 3570).* One to one counselling (free) phone for

appointment. Tue eve for les & gays only.

■ **PACE (Project for Advice, Counselling and Education),** *(251 2689).* Offers free counselling and art therapy for individuals, couples and groups. Training in Aids and HIV issues, counselling skills and heterosexism awareness. Services provided by lesbians and gay men.

There are local authority Lesbian and Gay Units which can often help with matters of housing, harassment or problems at work. They are keen to offer support to lesbians and gays from ethnic minorities.

■ **Camden L.G.U.,** *(405 2675).*

■ **Ealing L.G.U.,** *(579 2424 Ext 55028).*

■ **Haringay L.G.U.,** *(801 8981).*

■ **Southwark L.G.U.,** *(703 0911 Ext 2166/7).*

▼ CAMPAIGNS ▼

In 1988 many lesbians and gays were angry and in action against Section 28 of the local Government Bill (which prohibits local government or anyone funded by them from 'promoting homosexuality')

We marched, wrote to M.P's and organised ourselves. But the anger has subsided and once again the numbers of women and men involved in helping to build the lesbian and gay community have dwindled. Giving time, money or effort will not only help others but you will indirectly help yourself and you will most likely make friends too. Whatever you have to offer - a friendly manner, cheque book or practical skills - some group out there needs you. Local social groups depend on their members enthusiasm. There are still some areas of London without a support group so you could help to set one up.

■ **Organisation for Lesbian and Gay Action (OLGA),** *Room 3, Panther Hse, 38 Mount Pleasant, WC1X OAP (833 3860).* Founded in 1987 to campaign for Lesbian and Gay rights, particularly against Clause 28, violence towards Lesbians and Gays and discrimination against Lesbian mothers. One of the results of the introduction of Clause 28 is the strengthening of ties between Lesbians and Gays in Europe as a whole. OLGA is now part of *Pink Angle a European Activists Network* who organised a successful European tour against the Clause and who are planning a European Lesbian And Gay festival for 1992. Details from OLGA.

■ **CHE (Campaign for Homosexual Equality),** *CHE 38 Mount Pleasant, WC1X OAP (833 3912).* A campaign group for anyone Gay or Straight who believes in equality for all, regardless of sexual orientation. Membership £5 (£2).

■ **The Stonewall Group,** *5 Rector St, N1.* Formed in 1989 to influence and promote legislation towards equality for lesbians and gays.

■ **Act Up (Aids Coalition to Unleash Power),** *LLGC (See p#188,* meets every Tues 7.45. Organises direct action against companies and institutions which discriminate against people with Aids or HIV.

■ **The Gay and Lesbian Humanist Association,** *34 Spring Lane, Kenilworth CV8 2HB, (0926 58450).* National organisation promoting a rational humanist attitude to sexuality and lesbian and gay right as human rights. Open meetings every 2nd Fri of the month at *Conway Hall Red, Lion Sq WC1.*

▼ PARENTS OF LESBIANS ▼ OR GAYS

For many parents it may be the first time they've ever had to think about their attitude to homosexuality when their daughter or son 'comes out' as lesbian or gay. Both parents and their offspring need support at this time. There are two organisations set up to help: **Parents Enquiry,** *c/o Rose Robertson, 16 Hamlet Rd, SE16 2HZ (698 1815)* who offer counselling for parents of young lesbians and gays and **Parents & Friends of Lesbians & Gays,** *Eve Semple-Arnett, 98 Spruce Court, Hazelway, Chingford, E4 8RW (523 2910)* 24hr Helpline. Aims to keep families together and encourage acceptance of the children and generally working to change negative

attitudes towards Lesbians and Gays. Booklet *Parents Guide To Homosexuality* (suggested donation £1.50 + p&p) from **Parents Friend,** *c/o CVS 1st floor, 19-25 Sunbridge Rd, Bradford , BD1 2AY (0532 674627)*

▼ YOUTH GROUPS ▼

(See also **Kids** section p220)

No, you are not alone, although it may feel like it sometimes. There are now a number of groups specifically for young lesbians and gays where you can go to meet each other and not feel like a fish out of water.

■ **Lesbian and Gay Youth Movement (LGYM),** *BM/GYM, WC1N 3XX (317 9690).* Contacts, info and advice for those under 26 *Lesbian and Gay Youth Magazine.*

■ **Lewisham Gay Young People's Group,** *(697 7435).* Contact Dennis or Geraldine. For 16-21s, mixed. Mon 7-10.

■ **South London Lesbian & Gay Young Peoples Group,** *17 Brownhill Rd Catford, SE6 (461 4112).* Mon 7-10 for 16-21 yr olds.

■ **Westminster L & G Youth Group,** *St Martins in the Field, 12 Adalaide St, WC2 (930 1037).* 16 up to 25. Contact Marcia or Rob between 5-10 Fri's. Meets Fri 7.30-10.

■ **N London Line,** *Old School Building, Highbury Station Rd, N1 (359 2884).* L & G Youth Project Camden/Islington Mon 6-8.30. Also Counselling & support groups throughout the week.

■ **Portobello Project,** *(221 4413)* see p 230 Kids Section but also do writing workshops every Thu 7-10 for Lesbian and Gay 16-25 yr olds.

■ **Lesbian and Gay Teenage Group,** *7 Manor Gdns, N7 (272 5741).* Wed 7-10, Sun 3-7.

■ **Young London Group,** *Kings Cross Neighbourhood Centre, Argyle St, WC1 (254 5791).* Mon 7.30-10.

■ **NUS Lesbian & Gay Section,** *461 Holloway Rd, N7 6LJ (272 8900).* Can put students on to their nearest soc.

▼ SOCIAL ▼

■ **LLGC (London Lesbian and Gay Centre),** *67-69 Cowcross St, EC1M 6BP (608 1471).* Bar & restaurant open: Tue 5.30-11pm, Wed & Thur 12-11pm, Fri & Sat 12-12, Sun 12-10.30. Members free, non-members 30p/15p. As well as the bar there are lots of different things going on, discos, tea dances, theatre, counselling, community groups and more. Phone for details. Also houses *The Hall-Carpenter Archives*, a collection of history and current news.

■ **Oval House,** *Kennington Oval, SE11 (735 2786).* Diverse mixed gay events, workshops, theatre groups etc. Phone for details.

■ **Black Lesbian and Gay Centre Project,** *BM 4390, WC1N 3XX (885 3543).* Library, drop in centre, magazine *Blackout*. Membership £2.50 (£1.50).

■ **SHAKTI South Asian Lesbian and Gay Network,** *BM Box 4390, WC1N 3XX Men phone 837 2782 (daytime ask for Atul) 993 9001(eves/wkends, ask for Shiva). Women Phone 885 3543 (Office hours ask for Savi) or 802 8981 (Office hours ask for Gilli).* For South Asian lesbians, gays and bisexuals, regular meetings every 2nd and 4th Sun of the month at **London Friend.** Newsletter.

■ **Jewish Lesbian and Gay Group,** *BM JGLG, WC1N 3XX (706 3123 (helpline Th 7-10pm)).* Weekly religious/social events for Jewish lesbians and gay men.

For pubs, clubs and other meeting places see listings in *City Limits*, *Time Out* or some of the papers listed under Publications. A couple of the most well established commercial places are:

■ **First Out,** *52 St Giles High St, WC2 (240 8042)* is a very pleasant cafe just behind Centre Point, an ideal place to sit alone to eat or read or to visit with a friend. Vegetarian.

■ **The Fallen Angel,** *65 Graham St, N1 (253 3996).* Bar/cafe near Regents canal. Vegetarian. One night a week women only. Entertainment.

▼ MISCELLANEOUS ▼

■ **Lesbian & Gay Christian Movement,** *BM 6914, WC1N 3XX (283 5165).* Counselling and befriending for lesbian and gays of all ages. Send sae for details.

■ **Metropolitan Community Church,** *The Institute Room, 4th Floor, Bloomsbury Baptist Church, Shaftesbury Ave, WC2 (Hong Tan 485 6756, Gill Storey 670 2619).* Sun 7.30. Christian Church that welcomes Lesbians and Gays. Have women ministers.

■ **Lesbian and Gay Immigration Group, LGIG** *BM WELCOME, WC1 3XX (388 0241).* Advice and referral service for lesbians and gays with immigration problems. Campaigning to have lesbian and gay relationships recognised within the Immigration Laws, to abolish abusive immigration practices and to ensure that lesbians and gays can be granted refugee status on the grounds of their sexual orientation.

■ **At Ease,** *c/o St John's Church, Waterloo Rd, SE1 (928 2003 (M 4.30-6.30)).* Help for those in the armed forces.

■ **Gay Business Association,** *BCM GBA London, WC1N 3XX (622 2130).* Publishes a directory of Lesbian and gay businesses.

■ **Gay Authors Workshop,** *Kathryn Byrd, BM Box 5700, WC1N 3XX* was formed in 1978 to encourage lesbian and gay creative writers. Monthly meetings, friendly and informal, w-chair accessible. Qtly newsletter, print and tape. Subs £4/£2 unwaged. SAE.

■ **Gay Vegetarians & Vegans**, *GV, c/o Gemma, BM Box 5700, WC1N 3XX.* Friendly informal groups of women and men, all ages. Regular meetings. SAE.

■ **Quest**, *(792 0234)*. For homosexual Catholics (or Catholic homosexuals) (mostly men). Meetings, newsletter. Fri/ Sat/Sun 7-10pm.

▼ BOOKS AND PUBLICATIONS ▼

■ **Gay's the Word**, *66 Marchmont St, WC1N 1AB (278 7654)*. Mon-Sat 11-7 and Sun 2-6pm. Bookshop for gay, lesbian and feminist literature. Extensive second hand section, good detective section as well as imported American books that you can't get any where else. Is also a contact address for: The Black Gay Group, British Airways Lesbian group, and Capital Gay on tape. Is also the venue for a Lesbian discussion group every Wed 8.00, friendly meeting place for those new to scene.

■ **Gay Men's Press Publishers Ltd**, *PO Box 247, N17 9QR (365 1545)*. Largest gay book publishers. 10 years old. Mail order book service 'Male Image'. Write for free catalogue.

■ **Capital Gay**, *38 Mount Pleasant, WC1 (278 3764)*. Weekly (Thur) newspaper published by gay men. News, views, ads and gossip mostly for Gay men. Well established and has had particularly good coverage of HIV/Aids issues as well as keeping diligently up to date with the pub and club scene.

■ **Square Peg**, *BM Square Peg , WC1N 3XX* Glossy arts and culture mag for Lesbians and gays.

■ **Gay Times**, *283 Camden High St , NW1 7BX (482 2576)*. Glossy, monthly mag incorporating Gay News, mainly for men.

"Darling! How many times have I got to tell you? With lamé you can wear the pearls, with *leather* you wear the *chains!*"

■ **The Pink Paper**, *42 Colebrooke Row, N1 8AF (226 8905)*. 'Britains only national newspaper for Lesbians and Gay men'. Offers news, listings, humour, ads and info, weekly. Distributed free to most Lesbian and Gay venues. Subs 35p a copy. Is also available on tape, free, to the visually handicapped (contact 935 8433 after 5pm)

Compendium *234 Camden High St, NW1* do a good selection of books for and on lesbians and gays. As do **Housemans**, *5 Caledonian Rd, N1*.

▼ GAY MEN ▼

Friendship & Relationships

Gay men's London can seem very unfriendly. Yet everyone is looking for friends (and maybe 'more' as they say in the small ads). British reserve, plus the superficiality of much of the *scene* can smother opportunities for gays to get to know one another. Many men are afraid to be open about their sexual orientation for fear of prejudice and so find it hard to meet other gays. There are alternatives.

■ **Chinwag Gayline**, *(0898 200 888)* and **Grapevine**, *(0898 444 800)* give you a chance to talk, one to one, to a stranger, but remember these chats are charged at 25p a minute off peak (38p peak), so they can be costly.

Small personal ads in *Capital Gay, Pink Paper* and *Loot* (60p at newsagents, Mon & Thur) are free except for the box number charges and give you a chance to specify who you want to meet. The man you meet will probably not be precisely what he claimed - but could well turn out to be better! Remember that answering an ad means divulging your address and phone number.

Some gay venues are friendlier than most. **London Friend** (see p186) has various get togethers for gay men in it's coffee bar. Usually there's a discussion, speaker or video too and volunteers will welcome you and help you mix.

■ **Royal Vauxhall Tavern**, *372 Kennington Lane , SE11 (582 0833)*.

■ **The William IV**, *75 Hampstead High St, NW3 (435 5747)* a long established gay pub with garden.

■ **The Phoenix**, *37 Cavendish Sq , W1*. Downstairs Fri, Sat and Sun from 10pm.

■ **The Copa**, *180 Earls Court Rd, SW5 (373 3407)*. Open every night except Sun.

New to the Scene

For men new to being gay there are **London Friend's** *Turning Points* (Weds) *New Beginnings* at the **LLGC** and the befriending group which goes to pubs and discos on Fridays and can be contacted through the lesbian and gay switchboard (see p186).

The telephone equivalent of a contact ad is available on various lines which are advertised in the gay press. Hearing a voice can be both a plus and a minus. If you do decide to call to record your own ad, write down your lines and practice first - that way you'll give a better impression.

Sport and Recreation

There are sure to be gay men working out at any sports centre in London. The fun is also to work out who is gay- or if gays are the majority- who isn't. Many London boroughs have Leisurecard schemes which give residents discounts in local centres.

Weight training and body building attract many gays but require dedication. Swimming may do you as much good, without taking your life over. The men's bathing pond at Parliament Hill, Hampstead Heath (Bus C2 from Oxford Circus or Camden Town) attracts swimmers, gay or not, all the year round. Be careful - it's deep. On a sunny day the grass bank behind the pool will be full of gays, many of whom cannot swim.

The Dolphin Swimming Club (see Gay Times for current details) meets weekly in central London. The **London Central YMCA**, *Great Russell St, WC1 (Tottenham Court Rd tube station)* has one of Londons best pools. Membership required. There are exclusively gay gyms, usually with weights and sauna but no pool. Check the ads in *Capital Gay* or ring the switchboard for details.

For soccer fans **The Gay Football Supporters Network**, *10 Uist Cres Stepps Glasgow G33 6AF*, is based in Scotland but has plenty of members in London who socialise and attend matches together.

Services

Amongst the best known and the longest-established holiday firms are **Man Around**, *(376 5361)* and **Uranian Travel**, *(332 1022)*

For sports clothing, leather, cards and books try **Zipper**, *283 Camden High St*, or **Studio 40**, *40 Berwick St, W1*

▼ LESBIANS ▼

There have been some big changes for lesbians during the past year - financial cutbacks in welfare benefits and services as well as new government legislation. Section 28 of the local Government Act describes lesbian mothers and their families as 'pretended', trying to make them even more invisible while encouraging discrimination and attacks against lesbians.

While resources for lesbians in London remain limited, there has been an increase in services by and for lesbian women: massage, self-defence, advice and counselling, phone lines, alternative health and discos. A few lesbian campaigning groups have been going a long time, others sprang up in response to Section 28. You can find groups for lesbians from varying backgrounds, including Black lesbians, young lesbians to lesbian women with disabilities and lesbian mothers.

Advice & Info

■ **Wages Due Lesbians,** *c/o King's Cross Women's Centre. Mail: PO Box 287, NW6 5QU (837 7509).*

■ **Lesbian Line,** *LLL BCM Box 1514, WC1N 3XX (251 6911).* M-F 2-10, T,W, Th 7-10. Advice and info (not counselling but can refer you). Run by a voluntary collective of feminists. Friendly voices down the line for info on events, groups, rights or just for a chat. Organise regular socials where you can meet other women.

■ **Southwark Lesbian Line,** *(703 3849).* Tue 2-4 Thu 7.30-10 for advice or a chat.

■ **Lesbian Employment Rights,** *Rm 203 Southbank House Black Prince Rd, SE1 7SJ (587 1636).* Part of LAGER (see p186) providing practical support and advice for lesbians on anything to do with employment. If you want to put in a claim for unfair dismissal you need to do it within three months of leaving the job.

■ **Lesbian Archive & Information Centre,** *LAIC, BCM 7005, WC1N 3XX (405 6475).* Open Mon, Thu & every 2nd Sat. Phone for details.

■ **Women's Tapeover***c/o 66 Oakfield Rd, N4* Monthly taped mag of articles from lesbian and feminist press.

■ **Lambeth Womens Helpline,** *(274 1213 (Weds 6.60-9.30, Suns 3-6)).* Support and info for women.

Centres

Many of the centres listed in the women's section also cater for lesbian women, there are more centres listed under lesbians and gays.

■ **Camden Lesbian Centre and Black Lesbian Group,** *54-56 Phoenix Rd, NW1 (383 5405).* Drop in, workshops, library and creche facilities, group for mature lesbians (40+).

■ **London Irish Lesbian Group,** *c/o LIWC, 59 Stoke Newington Church St, N16 (249 7318).*

■ **Chinese Lesbian Group,** *PO Box 47, Sisterwrite, 190 Upper St, N1.*

Social

Where can you go to meet other lesbians, relax and feel free to be yourself? Apart from **Friend** and the **LLGC** (see p188) other places to meet other lesbians are changing all the time. For an update see listings in *City Limits* or *Time Out*. Some of the longer lasting ones are:

■ **Drill Hall,** *(631 1253).* See p 182

■ **Older Lesbian Network,** *BM 5700, WC1N 3XX.* Meets every 3rd Sat of the month 12-5.30pm.

■ **Reeves Hotel,** *48 Shepherd's Bush Green, W12 (740 1158).* Private hotel for women. Bar, sauna, restaurant. Mixed crowd not just lesbians.

■ **Women's Theatre Cafe,** *Lauderdale Hse Waterlow Park Highgate Hill, N6 (348 8716).* Women only, licensed. 7-10pm 2nd Fri of the month. Admission £1.50-£3.

■ **The Fallen Angel,** *65 Graham St, N1.* Tues night is lesbian night.

■ **Medea's Last Stand,** *Royal Oak 95 Tooley St , SE1.* Thursdays 9.30- 2am £3 (£2).

■ **Gemma,** *c/o BM 5700, WC1N 3XX.* National friendship/ information group of lesbians with or without disabilities. All ages. Network of pen-, tape- and phone friends. Qtly newsletter (print and tape). Monthly socials in Camden, good access. Enquiries -SAE/tape/braille.

Young Lesbians

■ **Notting Hill Young Lesbian Group,** *(Thurs 7.30-10pm 229 3266).*

■ **South West London Young Lesbian Group,** *(274 7215).* Phone Tricia or Eddy Tue 6.30-8 or Thur 4-6. Meets Mon 7.30-10pm.

■ **Camden Young Lesbian Group,** *c/o Kentish Town Project, 4 Caversham Rd, NW5 (267 1298).* Wed 6.30-10pm.

■ **Shelburne Young Lesbian Group,** *6th Form Centre, Chillingworth Rd, N7 (607 7527).* Tue 6.30. Also *Blackchat* group for young black lesbians.

■ **Young Black Lesbian Club,** *(387 7450).* Camden Tue 6-9.

■ **Kentish Town Young Lesbian Group,** *(267 0688).* Thurs.

■ **Open Door,** *Women's Resource Centre, 308 Brownhill Rd, Catford, SE6 (698 9453).* Group for young Lesbians Wed 7-9. Black women only 1st Wed of each month. Also run Open Line advice line for young lesbians on Wed 7-11pm.

Reading

Lesbian Mothers on Trial report from ROW £2.00. *Lesbian Mothers Legal Handbook* (Womens Press £3.95). *Lesbian Passion* Joanne Loulan.

Sisterwrite and Silver Moon women's bookshops (see **Women's** section p183) has a good selection of books for and by lesbians.

transsexuals/ transvestites

While it is easy these days for women to dress as men if they want to it's not the same for men who want to dress as women. There are few places where they can go and feel safe to express themselves in the way they want. While 'cross dressing' remains socially unacceptable more people take the drastic step to becoming a transsexual (known as gender re-assignment) than would do if society were more tolerant. The following societies offer services for transvestites and transsexuals of whom the majority are men. They offer support, advice and friendship. Reported cases of male transvestism in this country are 1 in 1000 and for transsexuals (male to female) the figure is 1 in 30,000.

▼ CONTACTS ▼

■ **Beaumont Society,** *BM 3084, WC1N 3XX* A self-help group established in 1965 which is at pains to point out that they are heterosexual men, most of whom are married with children. Over 4000 members nationwide. Provides fortnightly mag, social events, library and a confidential contact system for sponsored members. Membership is open to heterosexual transvestite men, transsexuals can join but may be referred on.

■ **Beaumont Trust,** *BM CHARITY, WC1N 3XX (730 7453).* Works in conjunction with the Beaumont Society to provide counselling and an educational service. Helpline Tue (Transvestites) & Th (Transsexuals) 7-11pm.

■ **Women of the Beaumont Society (WOBS),** *BM Wobs, WC1N 3XX (0606 871984 London Helpline 0293 545656).* Helping wives and girlfriends of transvestites to come to terms with, and understand, what their partners are doing. Telephone counselling service Mon evenings 5-11.

■ Leaflets and book to inform and help wives and partners of TVs/TSs by Yvonne Sinclair (£5) available from **TV/TS Support Group,** *2 French Pl, off Bateman's Row, E1 6JB (729 1466)* Helpline M-F 10.30-4, Sat, Sun 8-10pm. Regular social evenings.

■ **Gender Dysphoria Trust,** *BM Box 7624 , WC1N 3XX* for those men and women who want 'surgical and hormonal sex re-assignment'.

■ **Self-Help Association for Transsexuals (SHAFT),** *106 Barton ave Keyham Plymouth Devon PL2 1NZ* , Counselling, support and friendship for transsexuals or those who are thinking of 'gender re-assignment'.

HELP: Law, Prisons, Advice Centres

the law

Ignorance of the law can be a great disadvantage, and is not a defence to criminal charges. A general awareness of the law and an understanding of how it works is very useful and may save time and trouble. Common legal problems include family law and domestic violence, landlord and tenant, and unfair dismissal. But this chapter deals mainly with criminal legal problems. The last section deals with some common domestic legal problems, and suggests some strategies that may be helpful when problems arise.

▼ POLICE AND ▼ CRIMINAL LAW

Police and the Public

Police in Britain have always enjoyed extensive powers. They have a great deal of discretion when dealing with members of the public. How people are treated by the police tends to depend on whether police sympathise with them or respect them. In general, young, poor, black people are treated worse than people from the white middle class, and find it more difficult to exercise their rights. But increasingly, police are in conflict with new groups - journalists, professional staff, middle class activists, for example. When dealing with the police, it's important to have your wits about you. Insisting on theoretical rights can be difficult without support, information, and some insight into how the police are likely to react.

INITIAL CONTACT

When dealing with the police while driving, or on the street, the best strategy is to be polite as far as possible, but keep conversation to a bare minimum. Aggression towards the police is unhelpful, and likely to lead to trouble. Different circumstances will require a different response. If you're hoping to persuade an officer not to prosecute over a broken car light, it's best to be charming. It may get you out of trouble. If, however, the police look as though they have decided to take action anyway, and want to ask difficult questions, silence may be the best strategy. Try not to appear nervous, don't volunteer information, and avoid making matters complicated.

Try to look and behave like a reasonable person, and make sure the police understand that you're able to take an intelligent interest in what's going on.

RIGHTS

Many people think they have *rights* that they can insist on. It's an unpleasant surprise to find that there are few enforceable rights in the U.K. Illegally obtained evidence can be produced at court. Judges and magistrates generally ignore irregularities in police behaviour, and exclude very little improperly obtained evidence. If police are behaving improperly, it's unlikely that you'll be able to do anything effective about it on the streets or while in custody. It's best to argue later in court with the help of a lawyer.

KEY LEGISLATION

In the early 1980s the government felt that the police needed extensive new powers to improve public co-operation. There had been concern about maltreatment of people detained in police stations, and juries were often failing to believe police evidence. There was concern that the police had too much influence over the prosecution in the criminal courts. In 1984, the *Police and Criminal Evidence Act* (PACE) was passed by Parliament, introducing comprehensive reforms, and increasing police powers. The Act sets out police powers to stop, search and arrest, conditions of detention in police stations, and codes of practice governing treatment of prisoners. It's a most important piece of legislation dealing with police powers to stop, search, arrest and detain ordinary citizens and affects almost every aspect of detention procedure. The police now have to keep detailed records about people detained. Custody officers have been introduced to deal with detainees. Continued detention must be reviewed periodically. There is a strict limit to the maximum period of detention before charge.

ON THE STREET - STOP AND SEARCH

Police can stop and question people whenever they wish. Although they are supposed to rely on public co-operation, it may be very difficult for individuals on the street to avoid initial police questioning without looking very suspicious.

Police are supposed to ask questions in order to decide whether or not grounds exist for a search. A satisfactory explanation for *suspicious* behaviour should, according to police codes of practice, make a search unnecessary. In practice, the police stop and search at will, and justify their action later.

Police can stop to search for firearms and ammunition, poaching equipment, or stolen goods. They can also search under powers designed to protect certain kinds of wildlife and for prohibited articles such as weapons, and tools adapted as offensive weapons and for housebreaking, for example. Police can search for alcohol at sporting events such as football matches, and, of course, for illegal drugs.

Police often try to get consent for searches describing a search as *just routine*. In fact, *routine* searches are illegal unless they are done with consent. Searches without consent can only be done on *reasonable suspicion*.

Grounds for *reasonable suspicion* may be based on furtive or other unusual behaviour, time or place of activity, and tip offs, among other things. Belonging to a particular ethnic group, unusual dress, and police knowledge of previous convictions do not count as reasonable grounds.

Before searching someone against their will, police must:

• identify themselves
• explain grounds for suspicion
• explain exactly what they are looking for
• inform the person searched that a copy of the record of the search will be available if requested within a year.

A public search should only be a superficial inspection of outer clothing. A more detailed search should be done by a police officer of the same sex. Searches for drugs may involve a detailed search at a police station. Special legal provision for drugs searches allow the police to take suspects to a police station without a formal arrest.

STRATEGY ON BEING STOPPED ON THE STREET

• ask the police officer for identification
• try to avoid being searched by being polite if you are asked to consent to a search, politely refuse. Say that you will co-operate, but will not give your consent
• if you asked to go to the police station to be searched, politely make it clear that you are not going of your own free will
• keep conversation short
• ask for the reason for the search, and for a record

SEARCHES OF VEHICLES

Vehicles can be stopped under Road Traffic legislation, and under PACE, on the basis of similar *reasonable* suspicion. Police often claim to be making routine checks of vehicles, but these are not recognised as adequate grounds for a check in law. Police can stop and search cars near the scene of a particular crime, or having regard to *patterns of crime* in a particular area. Drivers and cyclists must give their names to the police, although passengers are entitled to remain silent.

SEARCH OF PREMISES

Police can search at any time with consent. But without consent, police can only enter and search if they want to:

• execute a warrant (an authority from court)
• arrest someone for a serious offence or an offence that is visibly taking place, or are in hot pursuit
• prevent a breach of the peace (could be violence threatened from a house)
• protect life and limb

• to recapture someone at large (for example an escaped prisoner)
Or if the premises are in the immediate vicinity of a *serious arrestable offence* (such as rape, robbery, supply of drugs, serious wounding).

A search warrant is a form signed and dated by a magistrate (or judge), specifying the premises to be searched, what police are looking for, and the grounds for the warrant. They are valid for up to a month, and should be returned to the court when they have been used, or have expired unused. It's worth checking the warrant to make sure that all the details are correct.

It's difficult to know what to do if the police knock at the door. They can just burst in if they feel that delay in entering will lead to disposal of evidence (drugs, for example). Evidence acquired during an unlawful search will be admissible in court. In practice, police often claim that they had consent before searching. Inviting police into premises may imply consent to unforeseen actions. An invitation onto premises to discuss, say the loss of a bicycle, could become a search for drugs if police become suspicious.

If you believe that the police have no legal power of entry, in theory you can use physical force to prevent them entering, or throw them out. But this could be risky, and charges of assault, obstruction, or worse could result.

Once police are inside, they should not damage property or cause unnecessary disturbance. They can remove numerous items - not only stolen property and illegal drugs, but anything believed to be evidence of an offence, or that may have been obtained through criminal activity. Quantities of cash, jewellery and other goods are frequently removed by police, even when there is strong evidence that they were acquired legally. Documents like bank books and address books are often taken, causing great inconvenience. Police should provide receipts for property seized. They often retain property while investigations are made, and sometimes until court proceedings are concluded.

When police search premises, they often search individuals, even visitors on premises. Usually they have the legal power to do so. They often ask questions which may amount to an interrogation (see section on questioning p197).

Special rules apply to searches of journalists working with confidential material, and people with confidential personal counselling and welfare responsibilities. Under PACE, some categories of confidential material are not available to the police.

However, people taking work home with them may find that files that would have been legally protected at work are unprotected at home.

STRATEGY ON POLICE ENTERING PREMISES

• if police approach without a search warrant, keep them talking at the door, and open the door on the chain
• check the warrant, if there is one
• make it clear that you do not consent to a search
• be aware of what's happening and make notes of things taken away
• avoid answering questions. Conversations may be recorded by the police.

Arrest and Detention

Many people held at police stations are not under arrest at all. They are said to be *helping police with their enquiries*. If they want to leave, however, they find themselves under arrest. Arrest means being under forcible detention. Under PACE, the most important rules governing detention apply only if the person is under arrest. Generally speaking, it is an advantage to have been arrested. Strict time limits to detention apply, and you can sue if you have been wrongly arrested.

Police arrest people in order to hold them while they investigate offences and gain evidence with which they can prosecute. The length of time people can be held depends on the kind of offence police suspect they have committed. Under PACE, offences are divided in to:
• *arrestable offence* e.g. shoplifting, possession of drugs, possession of offensive weapons.
• *serious arrestable offence* e.g. supply of drugs, robbery, large scale theft, murder.

Traffic and other trivial offences seldom result in prolonged detention. But offences where people are likely to be detained and questioned are usually governed by PACE.

RULES ON DETENTION

A custody officer is responsible for the welfare of prisoners, and is responsible for filling in forms which act as a check on procedure. The officer is independent of the investigation. Anyone booked into a police station should make sure that the arrival time is logged correctly. Don't sign for property that doesn't belong to you. If you suffer from a medical problem that needs attention, tell the custody officer immediately. If you're not sure whether or not you're under arrest, check with the custody officer.

If you can't leave the station on request, you should insist that you are arrested and booked in by the custody officer.

ARRESTABLE OFFENCES

People suspected of an arrestable offence are entitled to:

• have a friend or relative informed of arrest
• consult a *Duty Solicitor* or other solicitor for advice
• consult police codes of practice

Many people detained sign a form saying that they do not want to see a solicitor. This is usually a mistake. But police can't always find enough duty solicitors to see everyone in custody, and this can lead to delays. Solicitors are often reluctant to deal with trivial offences.

After 24 hours, people suspected of minor offences must either be charged, or released.

SERIOUS ARRESTABLE OFFENCES

People suspected of serious arrestable offences may be:

• held up to 36 hours without having anyone informed
• held up to 36 hours without access to legal advice (on authority of the superintendent).

After 36 hours, access to a solicitor is guaranteed. Continued detention can be authorised by a magistrate in a series of stages up to a maximum of 96 hours.

After 96 hours (4 days) suspects must either be charged or released. (Different rules apply under the Prevention of Terrorism Act, under which people can be held for up to 7 days).

HELPING SOMEONE UNDER ARREST

If a relative or friend has been arrested, you can help by getting a solicitor involved immediately. **Release** (see p103) can put you in touch with solicitors. You will not be asked to pay for the solicitor's fees. Most help is covered under legal aid. You will need to know the name of the person arrested before you can get much legal help. Don't be tempted to go down to the police station. You won't be able to give much help, and are unlikely to get access. After someone has been charged, it is possible to send cigarettes, food, and clothing into the police station. Before charge it's usually very difficult.

Parents of young people under 17 should be careful if they attend the police station. The police are usually anxious to have them present, as they can then record interviews. The right to silence is important, and young people should understand that they too have this right. It's best to go to the police station with a solicitor. Otherwise, you may be brought into witness an interview when the young person could have had the benefit of legal help.

QUESTIONING

At present, you have the right to remain silent. The right to silence in court is to be abolished. But the best strategy to adopt while in police custody is always likely to be silence. If you are innocent, say so, and if there is a simple explanation that is likely to satisfy the police, obviously, give it. Remember that it's easier to say nothing from the start rather than stop answering questions when they get difficult. And be careful about what you say: things that seem harmless and innocent can be twisted in court.

Many people are convicted of offences through signing statements of guilt, without a solicitor present. Often no other evidence is needed. What you say during questioning will be of critical importance during your trial, even though you may not have been formally cautioned.

The police are trained in interrogation. They are aware that people in custody are disorientated, and will play on this. Most people are prepared to do almost anything to get out of the police station - even to sign false statements admitting guilt. They bitterly regret what they have said later, in court. The best approach to questioning in custody is to insist that a solicitor is called. If police persist in questioning, it's best to say something like 'I'd like to help, but I won't say anything until I have seen a solicitor'. Although silence will probably lead to longer detention and perhaps some harassment, remember that there are strict time limits on detention, and eventually the police will have to release you or charge you.

Young people under 17 should not be questioned without an appropriate adult being present (a parent, solicitor or social worker). Interviews taken without an appropriate adult present are *never* admissible in court.

GETTING A LAWYER IN CUSTODY

If you are allowed access to a solicitor, you can call in your own, you can phone **Release** for advice and a solicitor, or you may want to rely on the Duty Solicitor. Duty Solicitors are independent of the police, although police are sometimes accused of referring serious cases to solicitors who don't cause trouble. Most criminal solicitors are members of the Duty Solicitor scheme, but this is no guarantee of competence. Some solicitors are more effective than others. Insist that you're advised fully on your rights, don't be afraid to ask questions, and ask to talk in private. The solicitor won't be able to speak on your behalf during the interview, but will make notes.

Legal Aid is available to cover solicitors attending police stations and advising before court appearances. Lawyers can arrange sureties, negotiate bail with the police and the courts, and contact relatives and friends on your behalf.

STATEMENTS

Damaging signed statements are difficult to explain away in court. It's hard to establish that statements were only signed because of pressure. People often regret making statements when they are read in court. They also reveal lines of defence to the police, who prepare the prosecution case accordingly.

A written statement denying allegations, or saying 'I have said nothing about this charge' may impress a jury and cast suspicion on police evidence of verbal admissions of guilt. If there is important defence information - an alibi or independent witness - it may be to your advantage to make a statement establishing that you have informed the police. But if you have any doubt at all don't make a statement until you have had access to independent legal advice.

Police offer a great deal of harmful legal advice to people in custody. Don't listen to it.

DEALS WITH THE POLICE

Don't make deals with the police except through a solicitor. Make sure that you *know* that the deal is to your advantage. Police often offer deals about reduced charges if you make a statement, particularly when a group of friends have been arrested together. Often they don't have enough evidence to lay any charges at all, and are hoping that you will convict yourself.

FINGERPRINTS, PHOTOGRAPHS, BODY SAMPLES AND INTIMATE SEARCHES

Police are entitled to take fingerprints, by force if necessary, if a superintendent has reasonable grounds for thinking that fingerprints would prove or disprove involvement in a criminal offence. Fingerprints can also be taken if a suspect is charged or convicted of an offence.

Photographs can't be taken without consent unless needed to record the circumstances of the arrest, or if a suspect has been charged or convicted of a criminal offence. Force should not be used.

Samples of saliva and urine need not be taken by consent, but other intimate body samples - blood, semen, tissue and swabs from body orifices should only be taken with consent, and by a doctor, with written authorisation from a police superintendent.

Non-intimate samples such as fingernail scrapings, hair and footprints can be taken with written consent, or without consent when a superintendent has reasonable grounds to suspect involvement in a serious arrestable offence.

Intimate searches of body orifices can be authorised by a police superintendent who suspects that a Class A drug (e.g. heroin, cocaine) has been concealed, or some other object that could cause injury. The search must be conducted by a doctor or nurse in a hospital or clinic. Police superintendents can authorise a police officer to conduct an intimate search at a police station if they suspect a weapon is concealed in a body orifice, and it is impracticable to have the search carried out by medical staff.

Charge and Police Bail

Eventually, after 24 hours or 96 hours, the police must either charge or release suspects. A charge is usually read out with a formal caution. After the charge, you will be asked how you respond. You don't have to say anything, but your answer will be recorded - you may want to record any difficulties that have occurred during detention. Police can either arrange for you to appear in court at the next hearing, or release you on police bail.

Police can also release you on bail while their enquiries continue. Sometimes, they set conditions, such as a surety guaranteeing appearance in court (and facing a financial penalty for non-appearance). If you have no permanent address, you may need to stay at a fixed address with relatives or friends.

Police can refuse bail or object to bail in court on the following grounds if they believe that you will:

- abscond because the charge is serious or you have no fixed address
- commit another offence
- interfere with witnesses

If the police refuse bail, you can apply at court to magistrates. If they refuse, you can apply to a judge in chambers if you are prepared to pay for private representation.

A Duty Solicitor should be available to make an initial bail application, but if you find yourself alone in court, stress the following points:

- you have a good record or haven't absconded before
- you can live at a fixed address
- you have a job which you may lose if held
- you have family responsibilities
- you intend to plead not guilty
- you have *sureties*

Sureties must be over 18, prove that they have the sum required by the police or court, and preferably, are without previous convictions. They can sign up at any police station, but it is less complicated if they attend court.

Defence Lawyers and Legal Advice

Solicitors can advise on how to plead (people often think they are guilty when they are not). They can present cases at magistrates court, and gather evidence on behalf of the defence. This may be important even in guilty pleas, when there are extenuating circumstances for the court to consider.

Anything told to a solicitor is supposed to be confidential. Solicitors work to certain professional rules. They cannot represent a client who admits guilt privately but wishes to plead not guilty in court.

If you need urgent criminal advice, you can contact **Release** *(306 8654 24hrs)*. They can also help with defence solicitors.

PLEADING IN COURT

Magistrates courts are very busy, and cases are often heard very fast. On your first appearance, if you fail to make contact with a duty solicitor, you will want to play for time to get representation and advice. You will be asked how you plead. Always plead 'Not Guilty' at first - you can change your mind later without facing a penalty. Ask for the case to be put off so that you can get legal advice. The case will always be adjourned to another day unless you plead guilty.

Cases can be heard either at Magistrates Court or Crown Court. Serious offences have to be heard at Crown Court, but some types of cases, theft, possession of drugs, can be heard in either court. Some minor offences can only be heard in Magistrates Court. Magistrates can refer cases to Crown Court for sentence. The maximum sentences that magistrates can normally impose are 6 months imprisonment and £2,000 fine.

Magistrates Courts are very busy, and cases are heard either by three lay magistrates, or one professional magistrate. Magistrates Courts often deal with cases quickly, and often accept police evidence without question. There are strict limits to their power to sentence.

Crown Court cases are heard by judges, and in 'Not Guilty' cases, juries. There is a higher acquittal rate than in Magistrates Court. Judges can impose greater penalties.

It is possible to appeal against conviction and sentence by magistrates. The Crown Court hears the case, and has the direction to impose as well as reduce sentence.

Don't agree to have a case heard at magistrates court unless you have had advice. Never plead guilty because the police tell you that you will get a better result. They are often wrong, and certainly aren't defence experts!

If Legal Aid is refused, you may end up representing yourself. Write down the important points you want to make. A friend can sit by you in court to advise, make notes, and give moral support. Apply to the magistrates quoting the 'Court of Appeal ruling in McKenzie v McKenzie'. Attend court a few times to familiarise yourself with procedure and cross examination.

LEGAL AID

The Duty Solicitor scheme operates in most courts, providing emergency representation for people without a lawyer. They are often very busy and unable to represent all the people up in court. If you do have to appear in court without a solicitor, ask immediately to see the Duty Solicitor so that they know that you need help.

Preliminary advice is available from solicitors under the *Green Form* scheme if you have a low income. You may want a solicitor to fill in a full Legal Aid application form, to advise on litigation, or to recover some property from the police. The Green Form scheme does not cover representation in court.

For help in court, you need to apply for full Legal Aid, which is a government scheme run through the courts. Help is discretionary, and often refused if the court thinks a case is trivial. The scheme is means tested, and often you are asked to make a contribution. Legal Aid is often turned down for cases in magistrates courts, but rarely at Crown Court. Getting Legal Aid does not restrict your choice of solicitor, but it can be difficult to change solicitors if you are dissatisfied. Don't sign Legal Aid forms with the Duty Solicitor unless you are sure that you want to be represented throughout the case by that firm.

To apply for Legal Aid you have to fill in several forms which are available from the local magistrates court. One is a 'statement of means' (how much money you have) and one is the application form, where you have to specify the reasons for applying. Try to get advice from a solicitor on filling the form in. Legal Aid is granted if there is a risk of prison (i.e. the case is serious, or you have previous convictions). It should be granted if there will be difficulty in understanding proceedings, if you will have to trace witnesses, or if there is a complex legal argument. Bear this in mind when filling in the form. Previous convictions, language difficulties, or a 'Not Guilty' plea to a serious case should be mentioned when filling in the form. Send the forms back to the court, and you'll be notified by post of the result. Allow some days for the application to be processed. Green form advice is available but the means test takes account only of income. Full Legal Aid takes account of expenditure as well as income - mortgage and HP payments, and more people are eligible.

If legal aid is refused, a solicitor may be willing to argue that it should have been granted to the magistrates, but you can argue yourself if necessary.

Changing solicitors can be complicated. You will have to give reasons in writing. Get advice from **Release**, a local Law Centre or Citizens Advice Bureau.

Complaints against the police

If you want to make a complaint against the police, you will face a number of difficulties. Police officers from the same force investigate most of the complaints themselves, and people who have complained often describe a feeling of bias against the public. The police Complaints Authority oversees the complaints process, which can range from rudeness through to allegations of serious criminal misconduct. The proportion of complaints upheld is very low. Only 14% of recorded complaints result in disciplinary procedure, and 2% in criminal charges.

If you are facing criminal court proceedings, or want to sue, don't even write to the police outlining your complaint without consulting a solicitor first. You may end up disclosing information that is important to your case in court.

Solicitors can help with complaints against the police. For people on low incomes, legal aid may cover expenses under the Green form scheme. If there are grounds for believing that the police have broken the law (e.g. through assault, false imprisonment, trespass, wrongful damage to goods or malicious prosecution) seek legal advice. It is usually better to sue through the civil courts than to rely on the complaints procedure. Of course, there's nothing to stop you from suing and complaining, but get advice first. Legal Aid may be available.

▼ OTHER AREAS OF LAW ▼

It's possible to get involved in a variety of legal disputes while trying to lead a quiet life. Common problems include divorce and family law, employment problems, housing law, and debt. It's impossible to deal with all these areas in this chapter, but some common problems are outlined here.

Divorce and domestic violence

There's only one ground for divorce - irretrievable breakdown of marriage. This is considered to have happened if

- both consent and have lived apart for 2 years
- you've been deserted for 2 years
- Your spouse's behaviour is so unreasonable

that you cannot be expected to live with it (could include adultery)

• You've been separated for 5 years

No matter what the circumstances, you can only get divorced after a minimum period of 1 year.

Undefended divorce is simple where there is an agreement about property and there are no children to consider. Everything can be done by post. If you are on a low income you could get advice under the Green Form scheme. All you have to do is to get forms from the registry, together with your marriage certificate and a small fee. The court will check that the forms ('petition') are correctly filled in and will send them on to your partner who will be asked whether they want to defend the divorce. If there are no problems, the court will examine the petition and grant a *decree nisi*. The process takes about 8 weeks if the matter is straightforward. After a further 6 weeks, you can apply for the decree to be made *absolute*.

The court has to satisfy itself that appropriate arrangements have been made for the children, and may want to discuss matters with them if they are over 9 years old.

If both parties agree on the divorce, the best way to show irretrievable breakdown is on the basis of living apart for 2 years. To show adultery or unreasonable behaviour will involve making accusations and providing proof. This can be time consuming and expensive. Take legal advice if the divorce is likely to be defended, or if you can't agree on the arrangements for children.

Matrimonial property

Problems often arise in agreeing maintenance payments. Both wife and husband can apply. Owner occupiers may find that they need to work out arrangements about housing. The courts take account of the living standards of the couple before they separated, and try to allocate resources to minimise hardship. In practise, this is very difficult. If children are involved their needs will be considered, particularly with regard to housing.

If the property is in one partner's name, the other partner will probably still have rights relating to it. If one partner moves out of the matrimonial home, it's sensible to register a 'Right of Occupation' to the District Land Registry.

Magistrates and County Courts deal with maintenance payments and financial provision. Get advice on where to have your case heard. They can order regular maintenance payments (where money is lodged with the courts), and lump sum payments.

It's important to work out your likely entitlements with help from a lawyer. Amicable divorces can run into trouble over finances. Having taken advice, you may want to negotiate your own settlement. Where one partner is legally aided, there can be difficulties when lump sum payments are made. When lump sum payments are awarded over a certain sum, legal aid costs can be deducted from the award. This often comes as an unpleasant surprise, and is a no-win situation, particularly when the money was earmarked for purchase of a house.

When working out financial arrangements, try to be realistic, and avoid prolonged and expensive battles where lawyers' fees eventually eat into relatively small amounts of capital.

Domestic violence

If you have been assaulted by your partner, go to the doctor to record the assault. It will be helpful in court. If you have been verbally abused, you should go to your doctor for the same reason.

You can telephone the police and ask them to come round. An assault at home is a criminal offence. Police are starting to respond more actively to assaults on women. If they refuse to come round, telephone **Women's Refuge**(see p180) and ask them to call the police.

You can take out an injunction at the County Court. If you are married, you can apply to the Magistrates Court for a similar order, but County Court injunctions are more flexible. A violent partner can be ordered out of the home, usually for a few months to adjust housing arrangements. Terms of injunctions may include that:

• the person should not assault or interfere with you or your children

• the person should leave home by a certain

date
• the person must keep a certain distance from home
• that you should be let back into the home.

It is possible to get injunctions with a power of arrest, useful if the harassment continues. Without power of arrest, police can only request that a person obeys an injunction.

Civil Actions

A civil action is where one individual sues another, and must show their case to be 'more probably true than false'. This is a lower standard of proof than in the criminal courts. If you lose a civil case, you may be liable to pay damages and legal costs. Civil law covers a huge variety of different areas. Ordinary people usually take action over accidents, debts, landlord and tenant disputes, contracts and divorce. Most actions are heard in the County Court.

SMALL CLAIMS

If you sue for less than £500, the legal costs won't be awarded even if you win, so it is best to handle small claims for things like faulty goods, unreturned deposits, yourself.

Decide whether or not it's worth suing - it's rarely worth it just to be proved right. Try to come to an agreement before you start legal action, by writing to the person or company concerned a number of times over a few weeks. Keep all copies of the correspondence. Then write to them giving them a deadline of 7 days after which you will issue proceedings if they don't give satisfaction. If you don't hear from them start your action.

Write out a full statement detailing circumstances, your loss, expenses etc. and collect all letters and receipts concerning the matter. Take two copies of your statement to the County Court nearest to the person or company that you are suing, and ask for the Clerk's Office. The clerk will go through your claim, and advise you on the kind of summons you need, who to serve it on, and will help you fill in a request form. When you get a summons issued, you have to pay a fee on a sliding scale - approximately 10% of your claim. Many people pay up when a summons is issued.

If your claim is not settled, then it's likely that a registrar will suggest that you go to arbitration (an informal hearing) to settle the claim. If both parties agree, claims larger than £500 can also go to arbitration. Arbitration is held in private, and both parties can argue their case in front of a arbitrator (usually the registrar) who decides the outcome.

LARGER CLAIMS

Contested claims for larger amounts are heard in the County Court. You can conduct the case yourself, and judges who hear cases often allow a lot of leeway and give advice to people representing themselves. Both sides present their arguments and call witnesses, if there are any, who can be cross examined. Witnesses have to attend court - their statements can't be taken into account without mutual agreement.

If you win, you can recover damages (loss and expenses, but not punishment for the loser), and you may win an injunction telling the loser to stop doing something (or to do something) connected with the case.

COSTS

If you win, you'll usually recover some of your costs. People on legal aid can get a large proportion of their legal costs covered. But be careful, if the courts think that you have acted unreasonably, costs can be used as a hidden weapon. Take advice from the Clerk of the Court or a solicitor before you start an action. If you have represented yourself, you may be entitled to claim a sum up to two thirds of the cost of solicitors fees. (See *Small Claims in the County Court*, HMSO 1984).

No matter what your means, solicitors can give a 1/2 hour fixed fee interview for £5 under Legal Aid.

▼ CONTACTS ▼

■ **Release,** *169 Commercial St , EC1 (603 8654 377 5905, 24 hr emergency service).* Office 10-6 Mon-Fri. Release is an independent national agency concerned with the welfare of people using drugs, including people with legal problems over their drug use. They offer a confidential national advice, information, referral and counselling service to drug users, dealing with illegal and prescribed drug use, drugs and the law, and general criminal legal problems. Will refer people onto specialist groups/agencies if necessary.

■ **Police Complaints Department**, *New Scotland Yard, SW1 (230 1212).*

■ **The Divorce Counselling and Advisory Service** *38 Ebury St, SW1 (730 2422).* Initial interview £20 for one partner, £35 a couple. People on Income Support , or are unemployed or eligible for legal aid are seen free. Can refer you to a suitable solicitor, but not over the phone. Not marriage guidance. Advise on custody of children, access, maintenance etc.

■ **Legal Action Group,** *242 Pentonville Rd, N1 (833 2931)* seek to improve legal services for the community. Publish *Legal Action Bulletin,* Monthly, £3.20.

prisons

this section is mainly to help first time offenders or people who have never been in custody before, as anyone who has been in the bin will already know the ropes.

▼ NEW ARRIVALS ▼

Prison is a punitive measure taken by society against an individual for breaking the law - so expect your stay to be geared towards this. There are very few rehabilitation or educational opportunities for short/medium-stay prisoners (except by other prisoners). Things are a little different for long-stay prisoners (10 yrs +).

The Cells

Probably your very first encounter with prison and confinement will either be in police cells or magistrates court cells. In both cases, facilities are inadequate. In police cells the lights are kept on 24hrs a day, there are no exercise facilities (for your exercise you will be walked handcuffed around the police car park) and you will share a cell which was originally designed for one person. The magistrates' cells are generally underground with only a bench in the cell. You might think you're going nuts. Fear not - things can only get better.

If you get remanded at Magistrates' Court you are sent to a holding prison for the duration of your remand (7-28 days), until committal proceeding for Crown Court can be completed. Usually, this is a wing of a prison called a magistrates' remand wing, but with the present situation in the prison service you might well find yourself in a police cell for the duration of your remand. A real piss off.

As a remand prisoner you are allowed one visit a day. You can wear your own clothes and get clothes, books, tobacco and food from your visitor/s. Visiting time varies in length from 15-30 minutes depending on which prison you're in. In police stations it can be even longer (a small recompense).

Prisoners Number

If you're sent to a magistrates' remand wing, you immediately come under the jurisdiction of the prison authorities. This means that you will be processed and allocated a number. Yes the dreaded number! This is your very own number for your entire stay in prison whether it be two weeks or fifty years.

This number is also the number that must accompany virtually every aspect of prison life: letters, getting a bar of soap, a new razor and shaving equipment, visits, newspapers, books, etc, etc, the list is almost endless! To do almost anything you have to make an *application*. You generally hand it in first thing in the morning to your landing officer or senior officer. Depending on what the application is, it will be processed within 1-5 days - you hope!

As you probably gather by now this makes doing even the most menial thing time consuming and gives you writer's cramp. But once again each prison will have a slightly different system, but they do the same job - just.

Keeping Quiet

When you arrive in prison do not to talk to anyone except your brief (barrister or solicitor) about your case, as 'grassing' or 'going Queen's Evidence' is not unheard of, though generally speaking very rare! (Life expectancy for squealers can be very short). Squealers tend to go Section 43 (segregation) and are much hated by the rest of the prison community.

At any rate be careful who you talk to about your case (this includes prisoners and prison officers). Certain crimes (child molesting for instance) are a real 'no-no' and you could be making a lot of trouble for yourself.

Prison Life

After (if you get committed to crown) committal, if you have not received bail you will go on to a remand wing at a prison until your case comes up. This tends to be between 2-3 months, but can be longer in serious cases.

Things tend to be a lot better in long-stay remand

wings. Because you have a routine you can get to know people over the period of a few weeks or months and so have a social life, or what goes for one in prison. Again all the same rules apply i.e. applications for everything. You can cell up with a friend if things can be arranged between you and the landing officers. This certainly helps break the monotony of 23 hours banged up in your cell.

You have a right to see your brief as many times as necessary and the duration of these visits are not timed.

The main social event of the day is the exercise period which tends to be an hour or so long, and you can talk to your mates if you have any, or play cards, or whatever takes your fancy. If the weather is bad though, you may not get the exercise period, and in winter it can get cold because once you're out on exercise you have to stay out till the end of the period.

Some prisons have gymnasiums where you can play basketball or do physical exercise. This is usually for an hour a week though in some prisons it may be more.

Your cell is likely to be fairly small, 10-12 ft long x 6-8 ft wide, with a ceiling that may be as low as 8ft. These cells in Victorian prisons were designed for single occupancy. However, nowadays they generally hold two people, and increasingly, three people. There are no sanitation arrangements as such and all washing, shaving, pissing, shitting are done in the cell in the utensils provided. You piss in the bucket and then during 'slopping out' time you pour the contents of the bucket down a big sink with a large hole in it. If you can get a warden to open the cell up for you, you can shit in a toilet (miracles!). But after 8 pm at night this is impossible so most guys do it on a piece of paper and chuck it out of the cell window (it's called a shit parcel).

The furnishings of a cell generally consist of two beds, two tables, two chairs, two cabinets and other bits and pieces picked up from friends and other cells.

Visitors will be searched at some prisons, not others. *You* will be searched before and after the visit. No letters can be given to visitors during a visit.

When you arrive you are issued with a blanket, two sheets, one plastic knife, one plastic fork, one plastic jug, one plastic washing bowl, one plastic bucket for slopping out (with lid!). These are your very own eating, drinking, washing utensils and as such should be looked after, as replacements tend to be hard to come by.

The regime of all establishments is routine and a prisons routine is time-based. A typical day is as follows:

7.45 am wake up
8.00-8.15 slop-out and applications
8.30 breakfast
9.00 slop-out
10.00-11.00 exercise
12.00 visits
1.00-1.15 pm dinner
2.00-3.30 slop-out
8.00 pm bang up

Slop-out periods generally last 10-15 minutes four times a day. Once a week there is *evening association* when prisoners can watch TV (generally a video), or play snooker or some such games. Showers tend to be once a week either allocated by rota to individual landing or integrated into association time.

Clothes

It gets cold in winter even though there is a primitive form of central heating in all prisons, so clothing is important. If you're wearing prison issue clothes they are changed once a week along with bedding during either showers or a special laundry call out. The exchange of garments and bedding is on a one-for-one basis. With a little judicious haggling and borrowing off friends you can end up with two complete sets of clothing or bedding, but beware if you're caught on a 'spin' (cell search). Your extra garments can be confiscated from you, and you can get withdrawal of privileges though this is generally speaking rare. Usually you just get bollocked and asked where you got them from.

Food

Along with clothing, food the other staple is pretty basic. It is very bland and generally speaking badly cooked though there is usually enough of it. Certain things such as sugar and butter are rationed: sugar to two teaspoonfuls a day and butter to a small pat with each meal.

Tea is served with all meals but is really bad (usually it tastes as if it has been made with old potato peelings and such leftovers).

Last thing at night (7pm) there is a tea round where you may have either a cup of tea or hot water so you can brew up yourself, but again if you're on the tail end of the tea round it tends to be lukewarm or gone.

Vegetarian food is generally better than the normal diet (Wandsworth prison is the exception), so when you first arrive in prison and are asked if you are vegetarian, say 'Yes'. If you have any other special dietary needs you should inform the prison authorities as soon as you arrive (it's harder to change your diet later). Those with medical reasons for special diets might be asked to supply information or certificates from their G.P. or some authorised body before their diet is sanctioned. The prison authorities tend to be amenable to special diets on religious grounds (they have to be so by law), especially if you're obviously a member of religious or ethnic minority (e.g. a Moslem, Jew, Sikh).

Medical

At reception you should make all medical problems known to the doctor who will interview you. If your complaint is serious the doctor will ask for medical records of your illness from hospital or your G.P. (this may take some time if you allow the prison authorities to work at their own pace, so shout and persist).

Prison medical facilities are fairly basic. You can see a doctor every morning by application, but the remedies are usually of the aspirin and band-aid type. The doctors themselves are able to diagnose you through brick walls so don't expect a consultation such as you have with your G.P!

Getting in to see a specialist is difficult but persist and after 6-12 weeks you may get a chance to see one in a prison hospital. You may have to visit another prison which has a suitable facility which means that if you do have a serious medical condition you should start the ball rolling as soon as you enter prison, so beware!

Gays

Gay prisoners and people with AIDS will probably be on *Section 43* which means segregation. If you are gay *do not* ask to be put with the regular prisoners. Don't be surprised to find an intense dislike of gays in prison and anyone who is found to be gay, or engaging in those activities, can expect savage and severe treatment, not to mention frequent beatings and brutality from the inmates!

Work

When all inmates arrive in prison they are interviewed by an Assistant Governor who asks whether they wish to work or not. You should answer 'Yes', otherwise you lose your canteen allowance which is £1.40-£1.60 a week. With this money you can buy the basics of life once a week at the prison 'canteen' (shop).

For most inmates this is the only source of income for things like tea, tobacco, sugar, dried milk, shampoo, soap, etc. The prices charged in the 'canteen' are the same as on the outside so £1.60 does not go a long way, but it's better than nothing.

Most inmates stay 'unemployed' during their stay in nick but some get asked to, or apply for jobs themselves. The jobs available are as cleaners, laundry staff, kitchen workers, gardeners etc, but the good jobs tend to go to inmates on long term sentences. This state of affairs is only applicable to remand prisoners. If you are convicted and sent down you could be sent to a prison where work is compulsory and you may end up sewing mailbags for eight hours a day, but that is *very* unlikely. Even though all prisoners have to work by law there are just not the facilities to achieve this and a lot of convicts remain locked up for their entire sentence.

However, if you do work you get an increase in your wages of between £2.50-£5 per week and you get out of your cell for a few hours a day.

Money can also be handed to remand prisoners by their friends on visits or by post. If you are receiving it by post make sure it's recorded delivery as things tend to get lost (transistor radios rarely get through).

All mail is censored, both coming in and going out of prison, so be careful about what you say (it could affect your trial), though having a few lewd thoughts of, and about your loved one, ain't going to go amiss with the censor.

There are many things that have not been gone into in detail and some not discussed at all, but the use of common sense and judgment will smooth your stay in prison. It's no joy ride but it can be tolerable if you make an effort.

▼ LONDON'S PRISONS ▼

There are four main men's prisons and one women's prison (Holloway) in London.

■ **Brixton Prison,** *Jebb Av, SW2 (674 9811).* Rough and a generally unpleasant prison. The guards are unhelpful. Visiting facilities are appalling. It's the main allocation prison, when convicted you are likely to be held here for 2-3 weeks before being sent to a prison elsewhere in the country.

■ **Wormwood Scrubs,** *Du Cane Rd, W12 (743 0311).* A rigourous regime. Only basic facilities for inmates. Mixture of long term convicted, short term convicted and magistrates remand. Visitors searched going in and out.

■ **Pentonville,** *Caledonian Rd, N7 (609 1121).* Relaxed regime. Very good visiting facilities. Mixture of long term remand and short to medium term convicted. Probably the best of the four men's prisons.

■ **Wandsworth Prison,** *Heathfield Rd, SW18 (874 7292).* Only for convicted criminals with sentences two years or longer and convictions of a serious nature. Very tough regime for inmates and bad facilities.

■ **Holloway Prison,** *Parkhurst Rd, N7 (607 6747).* Is the only remand prison for women in the London area, and holds long term prisoners too. Mother and baby unit. Visiting quite good, but waiting can be long.

▼ CONTACTS ▼

■ **Prisoners' Wives Services,** *51 Borough High St, SE1 (403 4091).* Info and advice to prisoners' wives throughout the country, as well as support, practical help, home visiting and self help groups to women in, or returning to London.

■ **The New Bridge,** *1 Thorpe Clse, Ladbroke Grove , W10 (969 9133).* Voluntary befriending scheme offering prison visits and help on getting work when released. Employment (London only) and advisory service: at the above office and at *135 Stockwell Rd, SW9. (733 7853).*

■ **Apex Trust,** *1-4 Brixton Hill Pl, SW2 (671 7633).* Job placement service for ex-prisoners or offenders who have special difficulties in finding employment - lifers, sex offenders, those who've offended against their employer or who've been forced to change the type of work they can do because of the nature of their offence - e.g. disqualified HGV drivers.

■ **Prisoners' Wives and Families Society,** *254 Caledonian Rd, N1 (278 3981).* Advice and info for prisoners' families, dependents and friends. Drop in, phone or write. Small hostel in London.

■ **NACRO (National Assoc for the Care and Resettlement of Offenders),** *169 Clapham Rd, SW9 (582 6500).* Promotes the care and resettlement of offenders in the community, and community involvement in the prevention of crime. It runs housing, employment, youth training, education and advice projects for ex-offenders as well as providing research, information and training services for people concerned with offenders and the criminal justice system. Wide range of publications. Ask for the information dept.

■ **Prisoners Abroad,** *82 Rosebery Av, EC1 (833 3467).* Provides advice, information and welfare services to prisoners (normally UK residents) who are in prisons abroad; send reading and educational material to them. If you're travelling abroad they can provide details of prisoners wanting visits. Also provide info and advice to friends and relatives of prisoners abroad. Provide help with resettlement for returning ex-prisoners.

■ **Howard League for Penal Reform,** *322 Kennington Park Rd, SE11 (735 3317).* Independent lobbying group. Campaign and research for better conditions and alternatives to prison. Concerned with a broad range of criminal justice issues. Publish *Howard Journal of Criminal Justice* which provides in-depth analysis of current issues, and *Criminal Justice* which is a membership magazine with short articles and letters. Memb £17pa includes both publications.

■ **Prisoners Advice and Information Network (PAIN),** *BM PAIN, London , WC1N 3XX (542 3744).* Answers enquiries. Info regarding all aspects of prisoners' treatment. Maintains an info and advice network for the following organisations: **Black Female Prisoners Scheme, Women in Prison, PROP (Protection of the Rights of Prisoners)** and **RAP (Radical Alternatives to Prison).**

■ **Prison Reform Trust,** *59 Caledonian Rd, N1 (278 9815)* is a charity which is mostly a campaigning organisation, but can provide non legal advice to prisoners and their families. Provide a free information pack to prisoners and their families (£2.95 to organisations) which includes a book *Visiting Prisons* listing all the prisons in England and Wales, with info on visiting times, transport, creche facilities, disabled access etc. Leaflets on visits, letters, welfare, remand, release, parole etc. Free publications list and manifesto.

■ **Women in Prison,** *25 Horsell Rd, N5 (609 7463).* Voluntary organisation that specialises in working with women in custody. Child care, fostering, homelessness, DSS, employment. Help prisoners, ex-prisoners and their families. Also a campaigning organisation.

■ **Women's Prisoners Resource Centre,** *Room 1, 1 Thorpe Close, Ladbroke Grove, W10 (968 3121).* An advice and information service for women in prison and help when they are released to London. Advice on housing, education, employment, training, legal rights, benefits etc. Will refer if they can't help.

▼ BOOKSHOPS ▼

■ **News from Nowhere,** *112 Bold St, Liverpool 1, (051 708 7270).* Radical Bookshop which specialise in law, prisons and crime. Will advise you on relevant books over the phone. Mail order.

advice centres

hopefully you will not need this section.However, if the landladywon't do the repairs, or if you're being discriminated against at work because of your sex or race, or if the DSS (otherwise known as the Department of Stealth and Social Obscurity) are obstructive then you may find the help you need listed here. The centres we've included will provide free confidential help or they will refer you to someone who will give you the advice you need. There are three types of centres - ***Law Centres, Legal Advice Centres and General Advice Centres.*** *Legal advice centres are staffed by volunteer lawyers and have limited opening hours. They usually give advice free of charge, but only to a limited extent.*

Law centres (marked LC) employ full-time staff, including lawyers. They may take your case up from beginning to end, including representation at court or at a tribunal. The service is usually free unless they explain otherwise. Law centres usually require that you should live (sometimes work) in the area where the centre is located and not be able to afford the solicitors' fees. They will only take on work in which they specialise, mostly housing, juvenile crime and care, employment, immigration and nationality, sex discrimination and welfare rights. Some centres work with groups and do very little casework.

General advice centres vary greatly. Some are set up by local authorities others are independent (and have grown out of the needs of the community where they play a strong role). **The Federation of Independent Advice Centres (FIAC),** *13 Stockwell Rd, SW9 (274 1878) publish a directory of independent advice centres (£8.95). The directory is indexed by area, advice offered, representation services, languages, translators, advice user, and wheelchair access.*

▼ LEGAL ADVICE CENTRES - LAW CENTRES ▼ GENERAL ADVICE CENTRES

The centres below are listed by area. The exception is the first category 'All London' where advice is given to all Londoners, not just those who live in the area of the office (unless otherwise stated).

All London

■ **Citizens Advice Bureau** (CABx). They have offices in most areas (see phone book). Are often busy and you usually have to queue if no appointment. For legal matters they can offer preliminary advice and refer you, though there are a number of volunteer solicitors attached to a few of them. The staff are trained volunteers and are generally very helpful.

■ **Citizen's Rights Office,** *4th Floor, 1-5 Bath St, EC1 (253 6569).* Only deal with enquiries from advice workers and organisations. So don't ring if you are an individual and want information on your own case as they are very busy. Advice on welfare benefits, welfare rights, income support, NI, disability. M-Th 2-4.

■ **Samaritans,** *46 Marshall St, W1 (439 2224)* is the main centre and there are 13 other London branches (see phone book), all 24-hour. Ring the above number or any of the branches, is does not matter where you live in London. Will encourage you to talk about any problem and provide emotional support. It's free and confidential. If you want to talk face to face they will see you. Can refer you to a counsellor if you wish. The admin offices are at *17 Uxbridge Rd, Slough, SL1 1SN (0753 32713).*

■ **Legal Advice Bureau,** *104 Roman Rd, E2 (980 4205).* Mon-Thur 10-12.00, 2-4.30; Wed also 5.30-8. Legal advice and representation, advice on welfare rights, etc. Max. discretionary charge of £5 to people outside the Green Form scheme.

■ **National Council for Civil Liberties (NCCL),** *21 Tabard St, SE1 (403 3888).* Independent voluntary organisation. Advise on abuse of police powers,

invasion of privacy, human rights and all types of discrimination.

■ **Release,** *(603 8654, (24 hr emergency) 377 5905).* (see p103)

■ **Central London Community Law Centre (LC),** *(437 5854).* Employment, housing - for tenants only, immigration. For those who live or work in Covent Garden, Soho, West End. Telephone advice for London enquiries. Cantonese, Bengali (Sylheti).

■ **Clerkenwell Citizens Advice Bureau,** *EC1 (253 2155).* M, Tu, Th, F 10.30-1. Free legal advice Tu 6.30-7.30.

■ **Fitzrovia Neighbourhood Association,** *39 Tottenham St, W1 (580 4576).* General advice. Mon 3-6.30, Tu and Th 10-1.30, Fri 10-5. Legal advice W 6-7. Also works with local groups on planning and housing issues. Mostly local people but will advise others. Bengali.

■ **Inquire Neighbourhood Centre,** *NW1 (388 0094).*

■ **Legal Action for Women (LAW),** *King's Cross Women's Centre, 71 Tonbridge St, WC1 (837 7509).* M-Th 11-5. Legal advice service for all women. Italian, Spanish, French, some Indian languages and Turkish on request. Phone first for appointment. See **Women** section (p177).

■ **Mary Ward Legal Centre,** *42 Queen Sq, WC1 (Legal 831 7009, Financial 831 7079).* Appt only. M-F 9.30-5.30. Evening Appts available. Recently burnt out, so won't be at the above address till perhaps April 1990. Temporary premises in the WC1 area in the meantime. Financial help: debt, tax, bankruptcy, pension. Legal help: matrimonial, personal injury, employment, housing, consumer. Do not cover probate and conveyancing.

East

■ **The Aid Centre,** *807 High Rd, Leyton, E10 (558 0033/6).* Advice, help and representation for people living or working in Waltham Forest. Debt, welfare, housing and employment, and can advise battered women. M-F 10-5 closed W, Sat 9-1. Interpreter can be arranged.

■ **Hackney Citizens People's Advice Centre,** *Centerprise, 136-138Kingsland High St , E8 (254 9632/254 8941).* Tu 10.30-12.30. Th 6.30-7.30, Legal advice for those who live or work in Hackney. Housing, welfare benefits, representation to social security tribunals. Interpreter by app.

■ **Hackney Law Centre (LC),** *(985 8364).* Give free legal advice over the phone, M, W, F 10-1.

■ **Hackney Council for Racial Equality,** *1 Crossway, Stoke Newington, N16 (241 0097).* M-F 9.30-5.30. Matrimonial, housing, crime, employment, and personal injury.

■ **Information Advice,** *Wally Foster Centre, Homerton Rd, E9 (985 3804).* M-F 9-5. Advice bureau.

■ **Newham Rights Centre (LC),** *285 Romford Rd, Forest Gate, E7 (555 3331).* Without appt: M, Tu, W and F 10-12.30, 2-5. Tu 6.30-7.30. Limited to those who live or work in Newham. Do not advise on divorce, conveyancing, car and traffic problems, business and commercial, or consumer. Urdu, Punjabi, Hindi and Bengali.

■ **Tower Hamlets Law Centre (LC),** *(791 0741).*

■ **Waltham Forest Community Relations Council,** *25 Church Hill, E17 (521 8851/2/3).* M-F 9.30-5.15, Thur also 6-8. Appt preferred. Advice on anything.

North

■ **Carila,** *29 Islington Park Rd, N1 (359 2270).* Welfare group for people from Latin America. Will give advice on housing, immigration, welfare etc. Interpreting service for visits to DHSS, law courts etc. Free of charge . Phone for appointment. M, Tu, W, Th, F 10-4. Mail order books.

■ **Family Centre,** *50 Rectory Rd, N16 (249 8334).* M-F 9.30-5.30. Advice, mainly on welfare rights, and referral to other groups. Also has meeting rooms for community groups. Legal advisory service 9-8.30. Urdu, Hindi, Bengali. Health classes for women.

■ **Hoxton Centre,** *Hoxton Hall, 130 Hoxton St, N1 (739 5431).* Wed 7pm.

■ **Islington People's Rights,** *2 St Paul's Rd, N1 (359 7627).* M Tu Th 10.30-12.30 and 2-4.30. Tu 6.30-8.30. Welfare benefits, debts, council evictions. Bengali.

■ **North Islington Law Centre (LC),** *(607 2461).*

■ **South Islington Law Centre (LC),** *131/132 Upper St, N1 (354 0133).* M, Tu, W and F 9.30-5.30 (outside these times by appt). Mainly housing, employment, immigration. Gujrati, Hindi, Punjabi, Urdu, Farsi and Bengali.

■ **Stoke Newington Advice Group Service,** *Manor Rd United Reform Church, 102 Manor Rd, N16 (802 7949 (during sessions)).* M & W 7-8.

■ **Tottenham Advice Bureau,** *290 High Rd, N15 (808 6555).* General advice service with limited representation at

tribunals. Gujrati. Limited to those who live or work in Haringey.

■ **Tottenham Law Centre (LC),** *15 West Green Rd, N15 (802 0911 (24 hr emergency outside office hrs)).* M 12-6, F 10-1, Th 10-1, Wed 4-7, or by appt. Will advise people in Tottenham on almost anything, but specialise in housing, juveniles, employment, welfare and immigration. Gujrati, Hindi, Bengali and Ibo by appt.

North-West

■ **Brent Community Law Centre (LC),** *190 High Rd, Willesden, NW10 (451 1122).* By appointment only. Residents or workers in Brent. Most languages.

■ **Brent Young Peoples Law Centre (LC),** *272 High Rd, Willesden, NW10 (451 2428).* M-F 9.30-5.30. Prefer appt. For under 21s in Brent. Gujerati, French, Urdu, Punjabi.

■ **Brent Community Centre,** *190 High Rd, NW10 (451 1122).* App only. Any subject. French.

■ **Camden Community Law Centre (LC),** *2 Prince of Wales Rd, NW5 (485 6672* (not Thur morn)). Mon, Wed 10-5, Fri 10-4. For those who live or work north of Euston Rd and east of Finchley Rd. Housing, employment, race and immigration, family, mental health, education and general advice. Bengali, Punjabi and Hindi (appointment advisable).

■ **Camden Town Neighbourhood Centre,** *12 Greenland Rd, NW1 (267 5279).* M 1-4, Tu 10-1, W 11-2, Fri 10-1. Mainly welfare rights, housing and fuel debt. Community worker helps set up tenants' associations and community groups. Provide meeting room.

■ **Community House Information Centre,** *Derry Hse, Penfold, NW8 (402 6750).* Tu-F 10-4, legal advice W 6-9 by appt. Serves N. Marylebone but will refer or help if you're desperate. Youth worker. Advise mainly young Asian people. Bengali, Chinese, Morrocan.

■ **Harlesden Advice Centre,** *25 High St, NW10 (965 2590/7305).* M, W 10.30am - 12.30 pm, Tu, Th 2-4. For those who live and work in Brent. Housing, immigration, fuel debts, nationality, welfare rights and employment. Gujerati.

■ **West Hampstead Community Centre,** *62 Mill Lane, NW6 (794 9034).* M-Th 11-6, F 11-4. General advice - good on the elderly and children (under 5s as well). Welfare rights, crisis, counselling. Community cafe. Social events including festival. Hire out rooms to community groups. For W Hampstead residents, but others welcome.

■ **West Hampstead Community Law Centre (LC),** *59 Kingsgate Rd, NW6 (328 4501/ 4523 (not Wed morn)).* M, Tu, Th, 11-2 F 11-1.30, W, 2-5. W and Th 6-8 for housing and immigration respectively. For those who live or work in the area. Gujarati, Kutchi, Hindi, Punjabi, Urdu.

South-East

■ **Advice Centre in The Blue,** *190 Southwark Pk Rd, SE16 (231 2471).* W, Th, F 11-12.M, W, F 1-3.

■ **Afro-Asian Advisory Service,** *Cambridge House, 137 Camberwell Rd, SE5 (701 0141).* Open M-F 9-12.30 by appt only. Give advice and info over the phone M-F 9.30-5.30. Immigration and nationality only but will refer. Interpreters can be provided.

■ **Albany Rights and Information Centre,** *Douglas Way, SE8 (692 0231).* M 10-12.30, W 10-1, Th 10-12.30 (women only), F 10-12.30. Will give advice over the phone M-F 9.30-5.30. Income Support, employment/industrial tribunals.

■ **Bellenden Neighbourhood Advice Centre,** *Copleston Rd Centre, Copleston Rd, SE15 (639 8447).* M, W 6.30-8.30 and Sat 11-1. Drop in. Advice on most areas. Cantonese, Vietnamise, Iranian.

■ **Blackfriars Advice Centre,** *Blackfriars Settlement, 44 Nelson Sq, SE1 (928 9521).* Appts only 10-12. Tu 5.30-7.30 and F 10-12 drop in. Also do campaign work (including fuel issues and the poor service given by local DHSS offices).

■ **Brixton Advice Centre,** *167 Railton Rd, SE24 (733 4674).* M, Tu and Th. 6.30-7.30 for legal advice to Londoners. M, Tu and Thur 2-4 (local people only). Tribunal representation, employment, social security.

■ **Cambridge House Legal Centre (LC),** *137 Camberwell Rd, SE5 (703 3051).* M, Tu, W, F 10.30-12.30, 2.15-4.30; Tu, Th 7-8.30. By appt only. Independent law centre covering most legal matters except conveyancing and adult criminal matters. They represent some cases, otherwise refer to outside lawyers. Green Form scheme for low income.

■ **Greenwich Community Law Centre (LC),** *187 Trafalgar Rd, Greenwich, SE10 (853 2550).* Tu-F 10-1, M 2-4.

■ **Romany Neighbourhood Council,** *97 Clive Rd, SE21 (761 2222).* M-F 10-1. F 7-8. Ward councillors (can deal with legal matters). General advice.

■ **North Lambeth Law Centre (LC),** *381 Kennington Lane, SE11 (582 4425/4373).* By appt. Limited to those who live or work in N Lambeth from Thames to the Oval. Advice limited to tenants, employees, claimants; housing, immigration, nationality, employment and welfare rights. Creole and Yoruba.

■ **North Lewisham Law Centre (LC),** *28 Deptford High St, SE8 (692 5355).* Tue 3-7, W 10-12 women's only advice, F and Sat 10-12, or by appt. Serves Deptford but has good booklets of wider interest including two guides to employment rights (free). They also take students on placement. Punjabi and French.

■ **Plumstead Community Law Centre (LC),** *105 Plumstead High St, SE18 (855 9817 Mon-Fri 10-*

1.30). M and W 6.30-8pm, F 10-12 noon. General advice to Greenwich workers or residents but casework limited to housing, employment, welfare, race and immigration for SE2 and SE18 residents. Variety of Asian languages by appt. Wheelchair accessible.

■ **Southwark Law Project (LC)**, *29-35 Lordship Lane, SE22 (299 1024)*. Tu 4.30-6.30, F 10.30-12.30 (by appt for further visits). For residents of SE22 and borders of SE24/SE15. Also run an advice session at **Beormund Community Centre**, *177 Abbey St SE1* (Mon 2-4), for residents of SE16 and part of SE1. Also a session at **CAB**, *97 Peckham High St, SE15* (Wed 2-4 for those in SE15/5). French.

■ **New Cross Legal Advice Centre**, *170 New Cross Rd, SE14 (732 9716)*. Th 6.30pm-8pm (get there before 7). Will try to arrange interpreter.

■ **Walworth Project Advice Centre**, *186a Crampton St, SE17 (701 1038)*. M 9.30-12.30, Tu 6-8 (fortnightly), Th 9.30-12.30 . Can arrange representation at tribunals. Housing and welfare rights and general advice.

■ **Waterloo Legal Advice Service**, *Waterloo Action Centre, 14 Baylis Rd, SE1 (261 1404)*. Th 6.30-8.30pm. Limited primarily to those who live or work in the area. Advice on employment, compensation and housing.

South-West

■ **Battersea Neighbourhood Aid Centre**, *22 Battersea Park Rd, SW11 (720 9409)*. M and W 10.30-12.30, Th 2-4, Tu by appt. Legal advice sessions Th 7-8, by appt. Representation at social security appeal tribunals, CICB hearings, rent officer assessments, and occasionally industrial tribunals. Participate in a duty representation scheme for Income Support appeals at Battersea tribunals. Legal advice session deals with tenancy problems, insurance/ compensation claims, personal injury claims. Wandsworth residents or those who work there. Interpreter if necessary.

■ **Brixton Neighbourhood Community Association**, *71 Atlantic Rd, SW9 (274 0011)*. M 6-7 and Sat 11-1 by appt. Tribunal representation, employment.

■ **Centre 70 Community Association**, *138 Christchurch Rd, SW2 (674 6671)*. Mon, Tu, Th 10-12. Mon 7-8.30 legal sessions and Th 7-8 at at 22 Norwood High St, SE27. Advice on benefits, housing, employment, consumer; representation at tribunals.

■ **Clapham Community Project**, *St Anne's Hall, Venn St, SW4 (720 8731)*. Mon, Wed 1-4 drop in. Legal advice Tu 7-8 drop in.

■ **Earls Court Advice Centre**, *282 Earls Court Rd, SW15 (373 7837)*. M-F 10-1 and 2-4 by appt. only. Can drop in (emergency) at the same times, but you may have to wait. Tribunal representation. Family, social security, nationality and immigration, education, housing, nationality, employment, personal debt counselling. Interpreter in Arabic can be provided (ring first).

■ **Friendship House**, *200 Wandsworth Rd, SW8 (622 4897)*. Tu 7.30-9.

■ **Fulham Legal Advice Centre**, *510 Fulham Rd, SW6 (731 2401)*. M, Tu and Th 6.30pm-8pm. Limited to those who live and work in the area. No appt necessary. Personal callers only.

■ **Brixton Law Centre (LC)**, *506 Brixton Rd, SW9 (733 4245)*. M, Tu, F 10.30am-12pm Wed 6-8. For housing, employment and immigration. Give initial advice on most matters. A lot on kids rights and crime, also complaints about the police. For those who live and work in Brixton. French.

■ **Nucleus**, *298 Old Brompton Rd, SW5 (373 4005)*.

■ **Roehampton and Putney Community Law Centre (LC)**, *162 - 164 Upper Richmond Rd, SW15 (789 8232)*. M-F 10-6, by appt only. Immigration housing employment, welfare rights.

■ **Stockwell and Clapham Law Centre (LC)**, *337 Wandsworth Rd, SW8 (720 6231 (24hr emergency outside office hrs))*. W 6pm-7.30pm, Tu 4.30-6, education advice. Low pay clinic Tu 6.30pm-7.30pm. Low pay, employment, social security, public sector housing, nationality, immigration, racial and sex discrimination. Limited to those who live or work in SW4-8, some of SW2.

■ **Battersea and Wandsworth Law Centre (LC)**, *Top Floor, 248 Lavender Hill, SW11 (228 9462/ 228 2566)*. M-F 10-6 appt only. Evening advice sessions held at different locations in the borough. Housing, immigration, welfare rights, employment. Farsi spoken.

West

■ **Ealing Law Centre (LC)**, *Steyne Hall, Rectory Rd, W3 (993 7801)*. M-F 10-6 app only, immigration law, landlord and tenant rights and employment law only. Wed 3-7.30 drop in for general advice.

■ **Hammersmith and Fulham Law Centre (LC)**, *106-108 King St, W6 (741 4021/741 8288)*. W 10.30-1: women's advice session (by appt). Tu 5.30-7.30: immigration and nationality (drop in). Homelessness, possession, illegal eviction in private sector, race and sex discrimination, equal pay,

mental health, health and safety, care and juvenile crime. Hammersmith and Fulham residents/ workers only. French and Italian by appt, other interpreters by arrangement. Phone for advice M, W and Th 10-1 or M, Tu, Th and Fri 2-5.

■ **North Kensington Law Centre (LC)**, *74 Golborne Rd, W10 (969 7473)*. M, Tu, F 10-6. Wed 1-6. Th 10-1. Housing, juvenile crime, employment, immigration. Spanish, Moroccan.

■ **Paddington Advice and Law Centre (LC),** *439 Harrow Rd, W10 (960 3155).* Drop in sessions: Mon 11-1 for housing, Tu 7-8 on anything, Th 11-1 employment and immigration. Urdu.

■ **Shepherds Bush Advice Centre,** *338 Uxbridge Rd, W12 (743 6953).* M Th F 9.30-12, Tu 2-4, M and W 6-8. Evenings by appt for workers only. Welfare rights, housing, consumer, employment, representation at DHSS tribunals. No foreign languages. Hammersmith and Fulham residents and workers.

■ **Croydon Community Relations Council,** *70 Park Lane, Croydon, (686 8014).* Legal advice W 6.30-8. Can refer you to a solicitor. Free and confidential.

■ **Hillingdon Legal Resource Centre (LC),** *12 Harold Ave, Hayes, Middx, (561 9400).* M - F 10-5, F 6-8 by appt. Limited to those who live or work in Hillingdon. Free. Employment, housing, welfare rights, race and immigration, juvenile crime. Punjabi.

■ **Northolt Village Community Legal Aid Service,** *(845 0643).*

■ **Phipps Bridge Advice Centre,** *South Mitcham Community Centre, Cobham Ct, Haslemere Ave, Mitcham, (648 3740).* Legal advice Tu 10-12, Th 2-4. Drop in. Wed 9.30-12 for mums and children to discuss family life.

■ **Southall Rights & Legal Advice Centre,** *54 High St, Southall, (571 4920).* M-F 10-6 by appt. Drop in M W Th 6-8. Fri 6-8 (immigration): fortnightly Tu women's session: Sat 11-2 Tribunal representation. Urdu, Punjabi, Gujerati and Hindi.

▼ YOUTH ▼ ADVISORY SERVICES

The following centres specialise in young people's problems. Some make a charge but most are free. Some want you to make an appointment first, others let you drop in. This section has been divided into two - advice and counselling which deals mostly with emotional/ relationship issues and advice on homelessness.

Advice and Counselling

■ **Acorn Youth Information Centre,** *55 High St, Acton, W3 (992 8182).* Age 12-25. Drop-in centre. Counselling. Unemployment, DSS, social activities.

■ **Apex Trust Wandsworth,** *168-170 Battersea Park Rd, SW11 (627 3726/3882).* M-F 9.30-5.30. Computing, office skills, photography and a 'job club' helps unemployed find work.

■ **Basement Youth Project,** *227 Earls Ct Rd, SW5 (373 2335).* Drop-in. M-F 10-2, Tu 1-4, W 2-5, Th 1-4 (women only). SS, education, gays, employment etc.

■ **Brent Consultation Centre,** *Johnston House, 51 Winchester Ave, NW6 (328 0918).* Drop in M 7.15-9.30, Tue 4.30-7, Th 12-2.30; or phone 9.30-5.30. For 15-23 yr olds; long-term counselling.

■ **Capital Radio Helpline,** *PO Box 194, Euston Rd, NW1 (388 7575).* M-F 9.30-5.30 & W till 9. Offers advice and assistance to its listeners on any subject.

■ **Central Wandsworth Youth Advisory Service,** *97 East Hill, SW18 (870 5818/6574).* Age 15-23. Advice, information and counselling. Free pregnancy testing.

■ **Chelsea Pastoral Foundation,** *155a King's Rd, SW3 (351 0839).* Age 17-24. Counselling centre only. App necessary.

■ **Community House Information Centre,** *Derry Hse, Penfold, NW8 (402 6750).* Tue-F 10-12, legal advice W 6-9 by appt. Serves local community but will refer or help if you're desperate. Youth worker. Welfare rights, housing, immigration. Bengali, Chinese, Morrocan.

■ **Harambee II Project,** *106 Downham Road, N1 (249 4741).* (see p230). Has grown from a youth club to an organisation which provides short life housing, temporary hostels for the homeless, counselling, workshops in building, tailoring, computer skills and silk screen printing. Phone for details. M-F (not Sat & Sun) 10-7.30. Also an advice centre during office hours.

■ **Help Starts Here,** *168 Battersea Park Rd, SW11 (720 0753).* For under 21s in Wandsworth.

■ **Just Ask,** *YMCA, 112 Gt Russell St, WC1 (636 4308/637 1333 x 4241).* M-F 2-8 drop in or make an appt. Help with emotional problems, referrals for legal/ accommodation/drug/ contraception problems and enquiries. 24-hr answerphone.

■ **Kaleidoscope,** *40 Cromwell Rd, Kingston-upon-Thmes, (549 2681).* All night club Fri from 10pm - 6am Sat with medical clinic (also on Wed from 7pm). Hostel for 16-22 yr olds. (18 residents). 24 hour staff cover. Coffee-bar Tu-F 12-4 . Also run art workshops, education unit and training bakery.

■ **Kings Corner Project,** *92 Central St, EC1 (253 6776).* Age 16-25. M-Th 10-10, F 10-6 appt. Counselling. Male and female counsellors. Computer training. Basketball and badminton. Housing advice. Women's independent cinema showing films by or about women (can bring male guests), fantasy role playing group.

■ **London Youth Advisory Centre,** *26 Prince of Wales Rd, NW5 (267 4792).* M W Th 9.30-8, Tu and F 9.30-5; appt preferred. Drop in Th 2-5. For 12-25s. Counselling, psychotherapy and family planning.

■ **New Grapevine,** *416 St John St, EC1 (278 9157. Helpline : 278 9147).* For those aged 25 or under. Weds 2.30-6.30 drop in or helpline. Office hours Mon-Thurs 10.30-5. Phone first if possible. Long term counselling also available, and counselling on sexual problems.

■ **Newham Young People's Counselling Service,** *252 Katherine Rd, E7 (552 5171).* Age 14-25. Therapeutic counselling centre. 14-16 yr olds must have parental consent. Handle problems such as child abuse, anxiety about leaving home, fears of madness and anxieties about drugs. Confidential service. Can refer.

■ **Off Centre,** *25 Hackney Grove, E8 (985 8566 or 986 4016/7).* M-F 10-6 or phone for appt. Advice, help and counselling. Also run specific programmes for kids leaving care and in counselling. You can just drop in for tea and are made to feel comfortable. Age 13-25.

■ **Off the Record,** *5 Woodhouse Rd, N12 (445 0888).* Phone for appt (day or evening). M-F 10-4.30. Set up for teenagers though most clients are 16-25.

■ **Open Door,** *12 Middle Lane, Crouch End, N8 (348 5947).* Drop in for general enquiries or phone for appt.

■ **Portobello Project,** *49/51 Porchester Rd, W2 (221 4413).* Exists to make information easily available to any person under 25. Provide benefits info and help in looking for work. Give info on housing, grants, setting yourself up in business. Will help with training and college courses.You can write your CV up on a computer with laser print out for high quality. Short workshops 6-8 weeks (one evening a week) in word processing, personal finance, journalistic/creative writing, interviewing techniques, music recording techniques, voluntary work. Write their own booklets about what they consider to be missing in the market, such as on finding casual work, Afro-Caribbean groups in West London and *How to Be Your Own Boss, All You Ever Wanted to Know About Accommodation in London But Were Afraid to Ask,Bed and Breakfast Directory, Being Lesbian or Gay in London.* Languages spoken Greek, Spanish and French. Noticeboards with ads for education, employment training and counselling. Drop in. Informal basement atmosphere with easy armchairs. Can talk about absolutely anything, including personal problems. They helped in writing parts for this book.

■ **Soho Project,** *12 Adelaide St, WC2 (930 3453 (Soho Project),* 930 3440 (London Connection)). For young homeless. Call in M, Tu, Th F between 11.30-1 and W 10-12 or phone 10-6 M-F except W afternoon. Downstairs the **London Connection** run a cafe which opens early morning and will welcome you. Cheap food and drink and you can sit and talk. **London Connection** also run various youth activities M-F 8-4, M 6-9 women only, Tu W Th 6-9. Lesbian and Gay F 7.30-9-30.

■ **Teenage Information Network (TIN),** *102 Harper Rd, SE1 (403 2444).* Phone Mon, Wed, Thu 12-6, Tu 10-6, Fri 10-2; drop-in times M 4-7, Tu 1-4, Th 3-6, F 10-1. For people who have a connection with Southwark aged 13-25. Advice and contacts for personal/sexual problems, laws, work, education, training, housing, rights etc. Will refer if they can't help.

■ **Unity Care,** *112 Palace Garden Terrace, W8 (221 1316).* M-F 10am-12.30pm. No age limit. Independently funded. Offer free social work and counselling. Home visits. Mostly young adults, who, for one reason or another are under stress. You can refer yourself.

■ **Upstairs Project,** *182 Hammersmith Rd, W6 7DJ (741 3335).* Age up to 25. Counselling on any problems, phone for appointment. Groups for women and young black people.

■ **Walk-In,** *42 Turnpike Lane , N8 (888 3138/3198).* Drop-in centre open M-Tu 2-5, Fri 12-4. Funding uncertain at time of going to press.

■ **Westminster Youth Advisory Service,** *(969 3825).*

■ **Young People's Counselling Service,** *Tavistock Centre, 120 Belsize Lane, NW3 (435 7111 x 251/326).* By appt only. Self referral. Up to 4 free sessions for 16-30 yr olds with emotional problems.

■ **Youth Aid - The Hearsay Centre,** *17 Brownhill Rd, SE6 (697 2152).* Drop in Mon 10.30-1, Tue and Th 10.30-1.30 and Th 4-7. Advice, info and groups. Phone for details.

Homelessness

■ **Alone In London Service,** *(278 4224).* Open M, Tu, Th, Fri 9-4, Wed 9-12.30. Advice on accommodation over the phone for homeless young people.

■ **Centrepoint,** *65a Shaftsbury Ave, W1 (434 2861).* Males 16-19, females 16-21. Dormatory accomodation avaialble on a daily basis, free. Must be at the gate at 8pm.

■ **Melting Pot,** *361 Clapham Rd, SW9 (274 9566. Hostel 733 7694).* Give support and advice on housing in the area and run a hostel for young black people.

■ **New Horizon Youth Centre,** 1 *Macklin St, WC2 (242 0010/242 2238/405 1126).* In Central London for 16-21 yr olds who are unemployed and are either

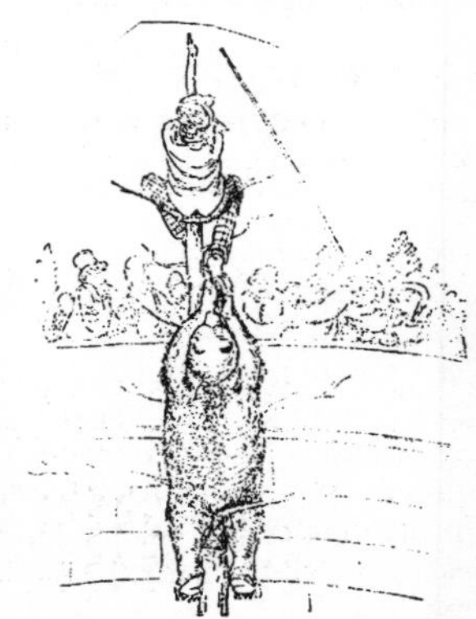

homeless or living in b & b accommodation or hostels. Open M-F 8-5 (not Thur morns). Info and advice on welfare rights and housing. A range of activities including discussion groups, video-making and photography.

■ **Piccadilly Advice Centre,** *100 Shaftsbury Av, W1 (437 1579).* Gives advice to young homeless people on any problem they might have - health, rights, employment.Drop in centre open M-Th 10-9, Fri-Sun 1-9, (closed between 1-2 and 6-7pm).

■ **Soho Project,** *12 Adelaide St, WC2 (930 3453 (Soho Project),* 930 3440 (London Connection)). (see p212).

■ **Message Home,** *(799 7662).* Open 24 hrs. For those who have left home and want to let relatives or friends know they're OK. This is a confidential service.

▼ MENTAL HEALTH▼

■ **Arbours Association,** *55 Dartmouth Pk Rd, NW5 (340 8125)* run a crisis centre.

■ **Mind,** *22 Harley St, W1 (637 0741)* campaigns for the rights of the mentally ill or handicapped and their families. Advice and info 2-4 daily. Will give list of local centres around London. Publications include *Open Mind* (70p mthly).

■ **Tavistock Clinic,** *120 Belsize Lane, NW3 (435 7111)* is an NHS out-patient clinic devoted to psycho-analytic therapy where you can refer yourself to the Young Peoples Counselling Service or to the Child and Family Dept, otherwise you have to be referred by a doctor.

■ **Depressives Associated,** *PO Box 5, Castle Town, Portland, Dorset. DT5 1BQ,* For £5.00/yr you can get information, list of contacts, qtly newsletter *(A Single Step)* and advice on setting up a local group. If there's no local group they can, at least, put you in touch with a penfriend. Send sae (9x6) for info.

■ **Philadelphia Assn,** *14 Peto Pl, NW1 (486 9012).* Run community households where those suffering from mental illness can live.

▼ PARENTS ▼

■ **Parents Anonymous,** *6 Manor Gdns, N7 (263 8918 - 24 hours)* for someone to talk things over with if you're under a lot of strain and think you're going to take it out on your kids. Will only contact the social services at your request. You can also write to them at the above address.

■ **National Council for One Parent Families,** *225 Kentish Town Rd, NW5 (267 1361).* Comprehensive adivice on SS, tax, maintenance, law, housing transfers and mortgages, pregnancy and daycare. Telephone advice M, Tu, Th, F 10-2 and 2-4, or write. Free booklist incl. own publications. Qrtly newsletter *One Parent Times* (50p per copy or free to members). Membership £14 pa (sub) or send £7. If a one parent family or if you are an individual it's £22 (members) a year for everything they publish. Range of advice leaflets for single parents. Reading list. Statistics and reports. Library.

■ **Gingerbread,** *35 Wellington St, WC2 (240 0953)* is a self-help organisation of and for single parents with kids of all ages. Phone to find out your local group. Advice on welfare rights, housing, etc. They provide holidays which focus on activities for parents and kids. Memb £4 pa. Sae for booklist.

▼MISCELLANEOUS▼

■ **Gamblers Anonymous,** *17/23 Blantyre St, SW10 (352 3060).* 'A unique spiritual movement' that produces pamphlets about the nature of compulsive gambling and their recovery programme.

■ **At Ease,** *(928 2003 on Mon 4.30-6.30)* is a counselling service for conscientious objectors (see p188 **Lesbian and Gay** section).

■ **Motor Insurers Bureau,** *New Garden Hs, 78 Hatton Gdn, EC1 (242 0033).* If you are the victim of a hit and run driver or the victim of a driver who is uninsured you can get personal injury compensation so long as the accident is reported within three years. You can also claim for damage to any of your property if caused by an uninsured driver (though not by a hit and run driver). The case will be investigated by insurers and compensation is worked out on the same basis the courts use. The scheme is funded by the motor insurance market.

■ **British Dyslexia Assoc,** *98 London Rd, Reading, Berkshire RG1 5AU., (0734 668271).* Advice and support. London group is at *Flat 2, 20 Wellesley Rd, Chiswick, W4, (747 4648).*

■ **Terrence Higgins Trust,** *BM AIDS, London, WC1N 3XX (831 0330 office; 242 1010 helpline; 405 2381 legal line).* Provides practical support, help, advice and counselling for anyone with, or concerned about Aids or HTLV III infection. Run counselling helpline from 3-10pm daily as well as individual and group counselling for those worried about Aids, those diagnosed as HIV positive, those with Aids and those who care about them. Legal line for legal advice on Aids and HIV issues; welfare rights advice, support and services for those with Aids; drugs and health education; runs an interfaith group to bring together people of different faiths over the issue of Aids. Excellent leaflets.

ORGANISING: Agitation, Kids, Ethnic Minorities, Disabilities

agitation

▼ CIVIL LIBERTIES ▼

■ **National Council for Civil Liberties, (NCCL),** *21 Tabard St, SE1 4LA (403 3888).* Pressure group established in 1934 to fight the use of 'agent provocateurs' during a hunger march in '32. Now aims to combat: racial harassment, abuse of police poweras well as discriminatory immigration laws, and campaign for rights in the areas of mental health, gay/ women's rights, etc. Seeks law reform through a Parliamentary Civil Liberties Group. Will take up an individual case if it's likely to have repercussions on rights generally. M'Ship £12 pa (£6 concs); affiliation on request. Publish many books inc. *Decade of Decline: Civil Liberties in the Thatcher Years*: £3.95 (inc p&p), also a series of pamphlets: Civil Liberty Briefings including such titles as *The Civil Liberties of the Zircon Affair* (95p) and *The Privacy Implications of the Poll Tax* (60p). Also have a Women's Rights Unit. (See p 176)

▼ OVERSEAS ▼ SUPPORT/CAMPAIGN GROUPS

General Groups

■ **Amnesty International (British Section)** , *99-119 Rosebury Ave, EC1R 4RE (278 6000).* Campaigns on behalf of all those who are *prisoners of conscience* - people detained anywhere in the world for their beliefs, colour, sex, ethnic origin, language or religion who haven't used or advocated violence. It also campaigns for an end to the death penalty and torture. It monitors the state of human rights throughout the world, and publicises abuses. Publish *Amnesty International Newsletter* mthly £5pa.

■ **Baby Milk Action Coalition,** *6 Regent Terrace, Cambridge, CB2*

1AA, (0223 464420). International network organising boycott of Nestles and others (Boots, Cow & Gate, Milupa and Wyeth) who continue to promote powdered baby milk in developing countries. Also promotes awareness among professionals on the effects of bottle feeding and of the World Health Organisations Code.

■ **British Refugee Council,** *Bondway Hse, 3-9 Bondway, SW8 1SJ (582 6922).* Aims to support refugees from other countries arriving and living in Britain.

■ **Partizans,** *218 Liverpool Rd, N1 (609 1852).* Stands for People against RTZ (a multinational corporation) and its subsidiaries.

■ **The Onaway Trust,** *275 Main St, Shadwell, Leeds LS17 8LH , (L (0532) 659611).* Formed to help native peoples (particularly Native American) restore and preserve their cultural and

spiritual heritage and to prevent their absorption into mainstream western life. They fund self-help projects and produce a magazine *The Onaway Mag* (£5.50 sub) (well worth reading) with articles on American Indian, aboriginal and other endangered minorities.

■ **Survival International,** *310 Edgware Rd, W2 1DY (723 5535).* Founded in 1969 to help Brazilian Indians. Helps aboriginal peoples all over the world protect their rights, and promotes international recognition of their needs. Now campaigning mainly for land rights but also act as an intermediary for groups seeking funding; carry out some fieldwork among threatened groups. Publish the lucid *Survival International Review* (newsletter).

■ **International Coalition for Development Action,** *(ICDA), c/o WDM, 4th Floor, Bedford Chambers, Covent Gdn, WC2E 8HA (836 3672).* Membership organisaton. Campaigning for improvements in UK & EEC policy towards poorest groups in third world countries. Headquarters in Brussels. Their *ICDA News* has info on the conflicts between rich and poor countries.

■ **Minority Rights Group,** *29 Craven St, WC2 (930 6659).* Investigates plight of persecuted cultural, ethnic and religious miniorites. Publishes wide ranging reports of its findings (£1.80 each). Promotes human rights education, especially for young people. Have speakers at the UN each year. Postcards and posters (e.g. of Pastor Niemoeller's poem p216).

■ **Returned Volunteer Action,** *1 Amwell St, EC1 (278 0804).* Helps overseas volunteers and development workers returning to this country to reorientate and use what they've learned abroad.

■ **World Development Movement**, *Bedford Chambers, Covent Gdn, WC2E 8HA (836 3672)*. Is a network of local action groups campaigning for political changes in Britain's policies towards the Third World. Among their successful campaigns: '86; change of British restrictions to Bangladesh textiles creating more jobs particularly for women; '87; doubling of government's contribution to UNICEF. Membership £9 (£4). Newspaper *Spur*.

Latin America

■ **Chile Solidarity Campaign,** *129 Seven Sisters Rd, N7 7QG (272 4298)*. Despite the 'no' vote in the plebicite of Oct '88 the regime of Pinochet remains fundamentally unchanged. The CSC provides a focus for campaigns for democracy and against violations of Human Rights. Organises boycotts (i.e. of Chilean fruit and wine), demos and help for refugees and political prisoners. Also campaigns against the British Government's resumption of arms sales to Pinochet (under Thatcher). Publishes *Chile Fights* (qrtly) M/ship £8.00 (£3.00).

■ **El Salvador Solidarity Campaign (ELSSOC),** *20/21 Compton Terrace, N1 2UN (704 9849)*. According to the Human Rights Commission 37,000 civilians were murdered by the El Salvador regime between 1979 and 1983. The Campaign works to raise public awareness about the regime and runs aid projects and is working to change the attitude of UK and US governments towards El Salvador.

■ **Latin American Bureau,** *1Amwell St, EC1 R1UL (278 2829)*. Research and publications on development issues and human rights in Latin Amarica. Can advise and arrange contacts for groups and individuals working in LA or over here.

■ **Latin American Newsletters,** *61 Old St, EC1B 9HX (251 0012)*. Reports on the political and economic climate of Latin America - aimed at people in business.

■ **Nicaragua Solidarity Campaign,** *23 Bevenden St , N1 6BH (253 2464)*. Support group for the revolutionary Government (Sandinistas) which ousted the right wing dictator Somoza in'79. Includes **Environmental Network for Nicaragua.** Publishes *Nicaragua Today* (Qtly) M/ship £10 (£4).

Middle East

■ **Committe against Repression and for Democratic Rights in Iraq, (CARDRI),** *PO Box 210, N16 5PL*. Fight for democracy and an end to torture and murder in Iraq, and for autonomy in Iraqi Kurdistan. Publish bulletin *Iraq Solidarity Voice*.

■ **Palestine Liberation Organisation,** *4 Clareville Gro , SW7 (370 3244)*. HQ of government in exile. Acts as a diplomatic service.

Africa

■ **Africa Centre,** *38 King St, Covent Gdn, WC2E 8JT (836 1973)*. Independent cultural, educational and social centre for Africans and people interested in Africa.

■ **Anti-Apartheid Movement,** *13 Mandela St, NW1 ODW (387 7966)*. Launched 30 yrs ago, campaigns against segregation on grounds of race in South Africa. Wants comprehensive sanctions against SA: campaigns to get people to stop buying their goods, going on holiday there, and banking with banks with major financial involvement in SA. Successses include the arms embargo, and sporting boycott - continue to oppose sporting tours of SA. Campaign for release of political prisoners e.g. Nelson Mandela, and those on death row. Publish *Anti Aparthied News* 10 times pa (30p) which aims to break news boycott of events in South Africa. Membership (30,000 nationally) costs £10 p.a.

■ **Committee on South African War Resisters,** *(COSAWR-UK),*

'First they came for the Jews
and I did not speak out -
because I was not a Jew.

Then they came for the communists
and I did not speak out -
because I was not a communist.

Then they came for the trade unionists
and I did not speak out -
because I was not a trade unionist.

Then they came for me -
and there was no one left to speak out for me.'

Pastor Niemoeller (Victim of the Nazis)

BM Box 2190, WC1N 3XX (287 3786). Formed in '79 by South African exiles who have refused to serve in the army. Campaigns against apartheid and militarism, helps war resisters who come to this country. Advocates the total isolation of the apartheid regime.

■ **African National Congress,** *(ANC), PO Box 38, 28 Penton St, N1 (837 2012)*. Oldest of SA's liberation movements, aims to get total isolation of SA.

■ **Namibia Support Committee,** *PO Box 16, NW5 2LW (267 1942)*. Provides support for *SWAPO (South West Africa People's Organisation)*, which is the main movement fighting for Namibian independence from SA. Publishes *Action on Namibia* (qtly) and *International News Briefing* on Namibia (£10 yrly sub for the two).

■ **Britain-Tanzania Society,** *6d East Heath Rd, NW3 1BN*.Non-political Society promoting understanding between the two countries by organising cultural activities and managing a programme of aid to small rural projects. Can provide info, contacts and literature.

Asia

■ **Society for Anglo-Chinese Understanding,** *152 Camden High St, NW1 ONE (485 8241)*. Seeks to promote understanding between Britain and China.

USSR and Eastern Europe

■ **Albanian Society,** *26 Cambridge Rd, Ilford, Essex IG3 8LU*. Non-party organisation which provides information about Albania and fosters friendship between British and Albanian people. Lectures, concerts, films and publishes *Albanian Life* 3 times a year.

■ **Committee for the Defence of Ukrainian Political Prisoners in the USSR,** *49 Linden Gardens, W2 (229 8392)*. Publishes *Ukrainian Review*.

Europe

■ **Common Market Monitoring Assoc,** *14 Carroun Rd, SW8 (582 3996)*. Campagins to replace EEC with wider international trade links, including the Third World.

▼ UK & EIRE ▼ CAMPAIGN GROUPS

Ireland

■ **The Connolly Association,** *c/o Four Provinces Bkshop 244/246 Greys Inn Rd , WC1X 8JR (833 3022)*. Based at Irish bookshop. Members are mosty Irish people working in the Labour movement for a United Ireland. They follow the theory of James Connolly (founder of the Irish Citizens Army and leader of the Easter Uprising). Publish *Irish Democrat*.

■ **Troops Out Movement,** *PO Box 353, NW5 4NH (609 1743)*. Started in 1974. Sees the British military presence as the cause of the 'troubles' in Ireland. Over 100 publications. Mthly paper *Troops Out*. Subs £8pa, £4 unwaged.

Separatist Movements

■ **The Fourth World,** *24 Abercorn Pl, NW8 (286 4366)*. Founded by the same person who started *Resurgence* (see p 160) supporting groups working for independence at all levels - from local to national. Committed to decentralist ideas and locally based political strategies. Publish *The Fourth World Review* (which now includes *Green Options*), surprisingly unpurturbed by criticism of its lack of feminist perspective.

■ **Cornish Nationalist Party,** *61 Church Way, Falmouth, Kernow*, Publish *An Baner Kernewek (The Cornish Banner)* qtly. Memb £3 pa.

■ **Plaid Cymru,** *134 Gipsy Rd, Welling, Kent, DA16 1JG*, Welsh Nationalist Party, London branch. Campaigns for an independent Wales in Europe. Also involved in such things as the peace tax campaign, CND and human and ethnic rights. Meets once a month.

Gypsies

■ **Romany Guild,** *50-56 The Farm Temple Mill Ln, E15 (555 7214)*. Run by gypsies dealing with all aspects of welfare and trying to get proper provision of sites.

▼ PACIFISM AND ▼ ANTI-MILITARISM

■ **War Resisters International,** *55 Dawes St, SE17 (703 7189)*. Campaigns for disarmament and against conscription and provides support for conscientious objectors. London office can put enquirers in touch with overseas peace movements. Bimnthly newsletter *Broken Rifle* (£6 uk pa), women's newsletter (every 6 mths.)

■ **Peace Pledge Union,** *6 Endsleigh St, WC1H ODX (387 5501)*. Section of **WRI (War Resisters International)** Seeks and practises 'nonviolent approaches to the very real problems facing all of us who want a world without war'. Current work includes: the

development - of Peace education, publication of material for Peace campaigning, the promotion of co-operative games, support for conscientious objectors, as well as campaigning against nuclear power and the arms trade. Material available for exhibitions, will provide speakers and visit schools. Introduced the controversial White poppy for Rememberance Day. Mag *The Pacifist*. M/ship £5-£25 sliding scale. Publications, posters, badges and postcards.

■ **Campaign Against the Arms Trade,** *(CAAT) 11 Goodwin St, N4 38Q (281 0297)*. Coalition of groups and individuals committed to ending the international arms trade and advocating the conversion of military industry to socially-useful production. Provides speakers, slide shows etc. Meetings all over the country. Excellent publications list; free newsletter.

■ **National Peace Council,** *29 Gt James St, WC1N 3ES (242 3228)*. Peace information service and umbrella organisation which links 170 affiliated groups. Promotes co-operation between them. Monthly mailing list and topical bulletin. Individual m'ship £16-20 pa (£10-15 concs).

■ **United Nations Association,** *3 Whitehall Ct, SW1A 2EL (930 2931/2)*. (Not to be confused with the UNO) Supplies speakers, fact sheets and disarmament info. Publications include *Peaceworking* (£1.50 + p&p) - a handbook for branches, with a detailed list of info sources, groups. Also posters, badges etc. List on request.

■ **Peace Tax Campaign,** *1a Hollybush Pl, E2 9QX (739 5088)*. 'Defence' expenditure per taxpayer per week in '88 was £14.52. The projected military budget for '89 is over £19 thousand million. The Peace Tax Campaign works for a change in the law so that those opposed to paying for war preparations can choose to have part of their taxes allocated to a Peace fund. Bi-monthly newsletter, advice leaflets for lobbying and war tax resisters. Suggested membership rate £1 per £1,000 annual income.

■ **Fellowship Party,** *Woolacombe Hse, 141 Woolacombe Rd, SE38 qp (856 6249)*. Works to elect MPs pledged to non-violence, social justice and total disarmament. Put up candidates for parliamentary and council elections. Publishes *Day by Day* (38p plus p&p /UK sub £30 pa). M'ship £10pa. (50% reduction for unwaged, students, pensioners)

■ **Quaker Peace Service,** *Friends Hse 173-177 Euston Rd, NW1 2BJ (387 3601)*. Produces books and pamphlets.

■ **Peace News,** *8 Elm Ave, Nottingham NG3 4GF, (0602 503587)*. 50p Fortnightly. (Sub 6 months £7 (£5) 5 trial issues £2) Well-established voice covering campaigns of all those working for peace. International and local news and info. Also feminism, civil liberties, nukes, good events diary.

▼ NUCLEAR ▼ DISARMAMENT

Groups

■ **Campaign for Nuclear Disarmament,** *22-24 Underwood St, N1 7JG (250 4010)*. Britain's largest Peace organisation advocating unilateral nuclear disarmament as a first step to 'general and complete disarmament' - and world peace. It's activities have grown massively in recent years, along with membership (currently 85,000 paid up; 250,000 affiliated; 1300 local groups). There's a growing network of regional groups and specialist sections, among them Labour CND, Christian CND, Ecology CND, Youth CND, Teachers for Peace, and The Medical Campaign Against Nuclear Weapons. The national office has a bookshop and provides general info, campaign materials, speakers and advice on setting up local groups. Publish many books, leaflets and factsheets (sae for list). M'ship £9; students, unwaged, pensioners £3; under-21s £2; Mag *Sanity*. £9.50 (£7) extra.

■ **Bertrand Russell Peace Foundation,** *Bertrand Russell Hse, Gamble St, Nottingham NG7 4ET, ((0602) 784 504)*. Campaigning for human rights and social justice and peace. In particular they promote research into nuclear disarmament. Publish *END Papers* 3 times a year (£12 sub) and various pamphlets and books .

■ **World Disarmament Campaign,** *45-47 Blythe St, E2 6LX (729 2523).* In Sept '88 the 159 countries that make up the UN voted overwhelmingly for disarmament measures, notable exceptions were, USA and Britain. The WDC works to see that nations carry out the disarmament resolutions made by the UN. Mainly local group activity; HQ provides bulletin *World Disarm* (40p) badges, leaflets etc.

Reading

Prospectus for a Habitable Planet ed. by E.P.Thompson & Dan Smith Penguin £3.95. *Defended to Death* Ed. by Gwyn Prins Pelican £3.50

Research and Info Groups

■ **Stockholm International Peace Research Institute (SIPRI),** *Pipers vag 28, S-171 73 Solna, Stockholm, Sweden.,* Independent research centre monitoring the world weapon situation. Publishes various brochures as well as the comprehensive *SIPRI Yearbook. World Armaments and Disarmament* available from Oxford University Press.

▼ ANIMAL ▼ LIBERATION

Groups

■ **Animal Aid,** *7 Castle St, Tonbridge, Kent TN9 1BH, (0732 364546).* Campaigning for total abolition of animal exploitation . Formed in 1980, now 12,000 strong; m'ship £5, £3 unwaged, includes *Outrage* (bimthly).

■ **BUAV (British Union for the Abolition of Vivisection),** *16A Crane Grove, N7 8LB (700 4888).* M'ship £8 (£5), including mag *Liberator.*

■ **Hunt Saboteurs Assoc,** *PO Box 87, Exeter, EX4 3TX, ((0392) 430521).* Use non-violent, direct action to sabotage all forms of bloodsports - usually hunts. Several London groups. Membership £5 pa waged, £3 concs. Publish *Howl* qtly, £30p.

■ **League Against Cruel Sports,** *83 -87 Union St, SE1 1SG (407 0979).* Campaigns for wildlife protection and the abolition of hunting and coursing. Buys land for sanctuaries which hunts can't enter. Will give advice on how to sue hunts for damage to property or pets. M'ship £5, includes *Wildlife Guardian* (qrtly).

From *Freedom* (see Freedom Bookshop below)

Books

Animal Liberation Peter Singer presents the moral case against animal experimentation. (£6.95)

Cured to Death Arabella Melville & Colin Johnson (New English Library).

▼ POLITICAL▼ BOOKSHOPS

■ **Freedom Press,** *Angel Alley, 84b Whitechapel High St, E1 (247 9249).* M-F 10-6, Sat 10-4pm. Bookshop specialising in anarchist publications. Also publish a range of anarchist books, and newspaper *Freedom,* as well as the newer journal *Raven* qtly. Noticeboard for events and groups.

■ **121 Bookshop and Collective,** *121 Railton Rd, SE24 (274 6655).* M-F 1-5. Squatted the above address on Brixton's 'front line' (as it came to be known in the days of the riots) in 1981. Help local publishing groups in the area. Distribution point for anarchist mag *Black Flag,* which is in its fifteenth year of life and *Crowbar* the anarchist squatters magazine. Cafe on the premises.

■ **Bookmarks,** *265 Seven Sisters Rd, N4 (802 6145).* 10-6 M-S, Weds 10-7. Bookshop of **Socialist Workers** party, but stock is not restricted to their publications and covers a wide range including politics, academic books in social sciences and related areas, economics, social work, psychology, women's studies, Trades Union studies and fiction. Posters, postcards, T-shirts. Magazines and newspapers Mail order, and TU book service, catalogues available. Quarterly bookclub offers books at reduced prices. Noticeboard.

■ **Central Books,** *37 Gray's Inn Rd, WC1 (242 6166).* 10-6 M-F, 10-5 Sat. Politics, feminism, international, ecology, cultural politics, fiction. Secondhand books. Posters, T shirts, postcards, badges. Noticeboard. Bookshop of the **Communist Party of Great Britain.**

■ **CND Bookshop,** *22-24 Underwood St, N1 (250 4010).* 10-4 Tu-Thur. Peace studies, nuclear disarmament, postcards, posters, T-shirts etc. Bookshop of the **Campaign for Nuclear Disarmament.**

■ **Collets International Bookshop,** *129 -131 Charing Cross Rd, WC2 (734 0782).* M-F 10-6.30, Sat 10-6. Social science books, politics, feminism, politics, philosophy, travel guide books, fiction. Also Russian and Slavonic dept - books in Russian and English published in Soviet Union and books published in UK about Soviet Union. Language teaching aids for Russian and Eastern European languages (and others), news-papers, travel guides, records. T shirts, postcards, posters, badges. Opening Oct '89, after having been firebombed earlier in the year.

kids

there is plenty in this book that will concern those under 18 but this section is specifically for you (and for the parents of very young children). It tells you about your rights, the law, education, youth projects, activities in London and lots more.

▼ DAYCARE FOR UNDER 5S ▼

Full time

Finding somewhere for your child to go, if you need or want to work, can be a job in itself. There are not nearly enough places to fill the demand. Britain lags behind other countries when it comes to childcare provision; in fact it has the lowest level of publicly funded childcare in Europe e.g. 44% of under 3s get day-care compared to 2% in this country.

NURSERY PROVISION

There are three types of nurseries; council, voluntary and private. They can all provide complete daytime care including play and learning activities, outings and meals. They all have to adhere to Social Service standards. There are also childminders who will look after children in their own homes.

Work Arrangements

Other alternatives are to get together with other parents in the same situation and share time and resources. Job-sharing is another possibility, as more and more employers are open to this idea. *New Ways to Work* (see p 40 **Jobs** section) keeps a register of people who are looking for others to job share with. You could also share your home with other parents and share the child- care. There are also quite a few jobs that can be done at home. Some employers might be happy for you to take young kids with you to work. More employers are beginning to set up workplace creches to encourage women back to work now there is a shortage of school leavers to fill up jobs. There is a campaign to have housework and child-rearing recognised as a valuable job worthy of payment See **Wages for House work** p178.

Setting up a Voluntary Nursery

If you want to set up your own voluntary nursery in your area you can get help (for setting up but not the running costs) in the form of an I.P.C. grant from your local council. To find out about local facilities ask your *health visitor*, **Citizens' Advice Bureau, Social Services, Area Health Authority** or look in your local library.

■ **The National Childcare Campaign**, *Wesley Hse, 4 Wild Court, Kingsway , WC2B 5AU (405 5617/8)* is working for under fives childcare provision.

You can find a list of Under 5s associations and parents groups in your area at your local library

A variety of play and daycare schemes are run by **The Save the Children Fund**, *Goldhawk Hse, 49 Goldhawk Rd, W12 8QP (743 3311)* and **Dr Barnardo's**, *Tanners Lane, Barkingside, Essex, (551 0011).*

Council Nurseries
These are cheap (free to those on benefits), but there are very few places. They take children up to 5. To get your child in you need to show you're either a single working parent or that both parents have to work.

Private Nurseries
These are either businesses or charities. Fees and age range vary and there is often a waiting list. Usually open from 8am -6pm. Prices range from £20-50 for 5 days (though sometimes much higher).

Nursery Education
Many under 's can go into the reception classes of schools. Known as 'rising 5s' if they are coming up to the age of 5 in the term they are admitted. But this is not the best alternative for very young children as staffing levels are often much lower than in nurseries.

■ **The National Campaign for Nursery Education,** *33 High St, SW1 (828 2844)* is campaigning for better nursery provision and can advise on setting up a local campaign.

■ **The Montessori Society,** *26 Lyndhurst Gdns, NW3 5NW (435 7874)* run nursery schools based on the teaching methods of Maria Montessori (born 1870). Fundamental to her approach was a great respect for the child as an independent individual; aims are to develop learning skills rather than to teach knowledge for its own sake. The schools provide an environment which encourage the childrens' interest in tasks which have been carefully selected for their stage of development. Materials used have been specially designed to enable the child to correct her own mistakes. The kids are helped to see themselves as part of a group: 'The Liberty of the child should have as its limit the collective interest'. There are several schools in London though you may have to book a year in advance.

WORKPLACE CRECHES
Some companies and colleges provide free or cheap creches for their employees' children. If there are a lot of you with children why not ask your employer to set one up.

■ **Workplace Nurseries Ltd,** *Room 205, Southbank Hse, Black Prince Rd, SE1 7SJ (582 7199/587 1456)* will be able to help with all aspects of setting up a workplace nursery, whether you are an employer or employee. They also do research into the educational and welfare needs of the children.

■ **The Kingsway Children's Centre,** *70 Great Queen St, WC2 (831 7460)* is a workplace creche which you can visit to see how it's done.

■ **Workplace Nurseries Campaign** *77 Holloway Rd, N7 (700 0281),* will be able to help you with practical advice. Your trade union should be able to give you advice and information about childcare while you work.

If you're a student you can contact the **National Association of Teachers in Further & Higher Education,** *27 Britannia St , WC1 (837 3636)* for a free leaflet; *Nurseries and Playgroups, Plan for Action.* The NUS should also be able to give advice. (see p129).

CHILDMINDERS
These have to be registered and approved of by the council. Lists can be obtained from your local Social Services dept. It's not a good idea to use an unregistered child-minder unless you're sure they're trustworthy.

■ **The National Childminding Association,** *8 Masons Hill, Bromley, Kent BR2 9EY, (01 464 6164).* Can provide info packs on finding a childminder and on setting up childminding schemes, also run training programmes.

HOME HELPS
If you can afford it you can hire a home help or a nanny. Getting one through an agency will make it more expensive but you could reduce the expense by getting together with other parents and sharing the cost.

BABYSITTING
Again this is expensive (£2-£4 an hour see *Yellow Pages*) but there are endless possibilities of time or skill sharing with friends or neighbours to get round the problem. Your local university or college might be a good source of cheap babysitters. You could advertise but ask for references and meet them first.

■ **Babysitters Unlimited,** *271-273 Kings St, Hammersmith, W6 (741 5566).* £30 Annual mem, or £5 each booking. Charges; £3.50 hour (day) Eves Sun-Thur £2.50, Fri-Sat £2.90.

■ **Universal Aunts,** *250 Kings Rd, SW3 (351 5767).* Can deal with any crisis and provide babysitters to meet children from trains etc or take them out for the day. From £3.50 an hour.

Part-time Care

Many women's centres provide creches (see p176 **Women's** section). Most boroughs now have mobile creches, usually a converted bus with workers, toys and other equipment, they often provide a multi-cultural, anti-sexist approach. Book well in advance.

Playgroups

Sessions are usually from 9.30-12.30 you can stay and help out or leave your child there. There is a small charge (about 50p) for each session.

■ **The Pre-School Playgroups Association (PPA),** *61-63 Kings Cross Rd, WC1X 9LL (833 0991)* can give you info on groups in your area. They also give advice and have local support groups. They can arrange training and do a useful leaflet *Starting a Playgroup* (50p inc p&p) and other publications.

One O'Clock Clubs

Free, run by the council, open between 1 and 4.30 on weekdays mostly term time only. You stay to help or just chat with other parents.

Parents and Toddlers Clubs

As much a meeting place for parents as a place for the kids (0-3 yrs old only) to play. Parents must stay with the kids.

Special Needs

HOME VISITING

Home visitors offer support to parents of under 5s with special needs who would otherwise feel isolated. They come to listen, talk and bring toys and equipment to your home. Contact Social Services or your local Under 5s group. There are also home visiting schemes for children with special needs run by the **National Portage Association,** *(0962 60148)*. Can bring educational toys to the home to encourage the child's intellectual development.

Most boroughs also run *Respite Care* schemes where volunteer families can regularly have handicapped children to stay in their homes for short periods to enable their parents to have a break. Ask the Social Services.

Check the attitude of the group that you choose, some parents and carers have had to complain or even set up their own groups to ensure an environment free of racism and sexism for their children. *Boys and Girls Come Out To Play* (£2.50 from **Play Board NI,** *136 University Street Belfast BT7 1HH*) is an illustrated booklet exploring such issues as how to create a play environment that does not reinforce stereotypes.

Play

There are usually local play associations which can offer support and advice - you can find out about them from your local library.

■ **The National Playing Fields Association (NPFA),** *25 Ovington Sq, SW3 1LQ (584 6445)*. Gives advice and technical information on anything to do with playgrounds, training equipment and resources. They will also advise on the safe construction of equipment for adventure playgrounds. Sometimes give small grants to self-help groups

■ **The National Children's Bureau,** *8 Wakley St, EC1 V7QE (278 9441)*. They deal mainly with professionals (social workers etc) but can refer you to other organisations.

■ **Play Matters/The National Toy Libraries Association,** *68 Churchway, NW1 1LT (387 9592)*. Can tell you how to set up a toy library.

■ **Dalston Children's Centre,** *76 Shacklewell Lane Dalston, E8 (254 9661)*. Alternative childcare for under fives and after school. Also collect kids from school.

■ **Islington Play & Recreation Training Unit,** *345 Holloway Rd, N7 (607 7331)*. Resource and training centre with a wide range of facilities, from crafts and building tools to video, for registered recreation groups in the borough (non-ILEA).

■ **The Children's Scrap Project,** *137 Homerton High St, Hackney, E9 (985 6290)*. See **Green Environment** p727.

■ **The Handicapped Adventure Playground Association,** *c/o Fulham Palace, Bishop's Ave, SW6 6EA (736 4443)*. Gives advice and info on how to set up an adventure playground for handicapped children.

■ **The National Playbus Association(NPA)/ Mobile Projects Association,** *Unit G, Arno's Castle Estate, Junction Rd, Brislington, Bristol BS4 5AJ , (0272 775375)*. Help with consultancy, design, general info and grantsfor those who want to convert a double-decker bus for use as a mobile community space.

■ **Woodcraft Folk,** *13 Ritherdon Rd, SW17 (767 2457)*. The 'alternative' scouts and guides - they aim to foster co-operation, equality of races and sexes, care for the environment and peaceful resolution of conflict. Everyone takes part in the decision-making. Activities for 6-16 year olds include games, drama, dancing, crafts, hiking. As seen on CND demos.

Out of School Schemes

LATCHKEY SCHEMES

These are schemes where school age children are looked after before (8am) and/or after school (till 6pm. They are for kids whose parents are working. There is usually a long waiting list and a small charge. Some of the centres also operate during the school holidays.

AFTER SCHOOL CARE

Much the same as the latchkey schemes but only providing care at the end of the school day (up to 6pm).

HOLIDAY PLAY SCHEMES

Lots of fun for kids during school holidays with inflatables, face painting, theatre and outings organised by local council with experienced playleaders.

■ **BASSAC (British Assoc of Settlements & Social Action Centres),** *13 Stockwell Rd, SW9 9AU (733 7428).* A network of independent local centres providing things such as playgroups and advice centres. Can give help and advice on setting up your own local projects also provide factsheets and booklist. Qtly newsletter *Social Action.* Also provide a training programme for workers and volunteers in local centres.

■ **National Out of School Alliance,** *Oxford House Derbyshire St, E2 6HG (739 4787).* Gives advice, training and info to groups and individuals about the needs of school age children and their parents. Publishes a directory of out of school schemes in London, (£2), and a Mag *School's Out.* Membership costs range from £5 for individuals up to £40 for commercial organisations..

■ **Mencap London Division,** *115 Golden Lane, EC1Y OTJ (250 4105).* Run Gateway Clubs for mentally handicapped children.

■ **PHAB (Physically Handicapped and Able-Bodied),** *Tavistock House North (2nd Floor) Tavistock Sq, WC1H 9HX (388 1963).* Run groups for the physically handicapped.

▼ EDUCATION ▼

By law parents are obliged to see that their children are educated. In theory they have a choice about how this is done though in practice many parents find that they have little choice and the children even less. The choice is between state schools, direct grant schools (which are actually state aided private schools), independent schools and 'otherwise' (as defined by the 1944 Education Act).

Small ('Free') Schools

There are a few schools around the country, which used to be known as *Free schools.* They are usually run jointly by the children, teachers (known as workers) and parents, there are no head teachers. Lessons are not compulsory but the children are strongly encouraged to take part. There are not many in London as they are easier and cheaper to run in smaller communities, but there is a growing movement in quite a few areas to start such ventures up again. The most notable in London were **The Kirkdale School** which has now folded and the **White Lion Free School** which is still struggling for survival. They offer many advantages, such as direct parent involvement, small intimate classes and an absence of the anonymity that often exists in larger schools.

■ **The White Lion Free School,** *York Way Premises, Delhi St, N1 (833 2780)* has 36 pupils (all local), aged 3-16. No compulsory learning. School is run by the kids, 'workers' (not called teachers) and parents. They have weekly meetings. No head teacher.

SETTING UP AN INDEPENDENT (OR SMALL) SCHOOL.

Defined by the 1944 Education Act (Section 114) as any institution which provides full-time education for more than 5 pupils of compulsory school age, other than one maintained by a *Local Education Authority* or a non-

maintained special school. It must be registered with the *Dept of Education and Science* as soon as it opens.

There are minimum standards that you'll have to meet in order to be approved by the DES.

Premises.
These need to be broadly comparable to those in maintained schools. The inspectors use *The Education (School Premises) Regulations 1981* (£2.90) from the DES (ask for SI 1981/909). Make sure that fire safety standards are adhered to.

Curriculum
The White Paper *Better Schools* 1985 (£6.40) (DES Cmnd 9469) sets out the general requirements fro teaching standards. The new national curriculum will not be mandatory for independent school but they will be asked to 'take account of its principles'. What this will mean exactly is still unclear. A circular advising independent school of their position regarding the national curriculum has yet to appear.

Staff
Teachers in independent school do not have to be formally qualified but at least some of them will be expected to have appropriate qualifications or experience. They must not have a criminal background and not be on the teachers blacklist *List 99*.

If the DES don't give their approval you have the right of appeal to an *Independent Schools Tribunal*.

Other Rules.
You must keep an attendance register for morning and afternoon and tell the authorities of truancy. By law children must attend at least 200 days a year (or 400 sessions morning and afternoon). If you provide meals you must also comply with public health standards.

If you're interested in helping to set one up, the following people are the ones to contact:

■ **Poppy Green**, *15 Bellvue Clifton Bristol BS8 1DB, (0272 735091)*. Networking for holistic education movement. Is compiling *New Education Directory*.

■ **Human Scale Education Movement**, *Quincecote, Cheristow, Hartland, Devon EX39 6DA*. Founded in 1987. Emphasise the need for quality of relationship between teacher and pupil and the need to foster, among other things, sensitivity, creativity and a sense of responsibility. They have three main areas of work: schemes that allow large schools to restructure on human scale, small schools which are non-fee paying and have a high adult/child ratio and 'Flexi-schooling' which encourages schools to combine school with home-based or community based education. Membership £12 (£8 & £4). London contacts North: Muriel Hall, *50 Bendysh Rd, Bushey, Herts WD2 2HY*. South: Ruth Goffe, *11 Veronica Rd, SW17 8QL*.

■ **Dept of Education and Science**, *Mowden Hall,*

my mother says I have to go to school to learn how to deal with the world

I wish there was somewhere I could go where I could learn how to deal with school

Staindrop Rd, Darlington, Co Durham DL3 9BG, (0325 460155). Ask the independent schools team for info pack on setting up an independent school.

Home Teaching

One way round the system if you don't want to set up a school of your own, is to educate your kid/s at home.

By law if you have fewer than 5 pupils or only provide part time education it's known as 'education otherwise' and it will come under the jurisdiction of the Local Education Authority who, basically, will want to be satisfied that parents (or guardians) are 'conforming with their duty to ensure sufficient and suitable education for their children.'

You will need to inform your LEA. They will send round an inspector who will want to see that the curriculum is satisfactory. She will check that the child is learning basic skills, a broad range of subjects, is getting enough exercise and has the chance to mix with other kids.

Some LEAs will insist that the child is taught by a DES recognised teacher. If they are not happy with what you are doing they can order you to send her to a school. If you have any problems the **Children's Legal Centre,** (see p228) will be able to help you. For help, advice and support contact **Education Otherwise,** *25 Common Lane, Hemingford Abbots, Cambridgeshire PE18 9AN, (0480 63130)* which is a support and advice service for people educating their children out of school. Of their 500 members, 120 are practising education out of school, mostly working from home using local community resources. They publish a booklet *School is Not Compulsory* (£3.00) which sets out the legal aspects and other costs for people harassed by the authorities.

■ **The World-Wide Education Service,** *Strode Hse, 44-50 Osnaburgh St, NW1 3NN (387 9228).* Set up to help families abroad but also help those educating their child at home in this country. Supply teaching packs for all ages including nursery level. Rather expensive (from £580 a year)

■ **Growing without Schooling,** *2269 Massachusetts Avenue Cambridge MA 02140 USA, (617-864-3100).* An American mag for people interested in education out of schools. Much of the info isn't relevant here but there are lots of ideas and learning resources as well as a directory, booklets and correspondence. Sub $20 pa.

■ **Association of British Correspondence Colleges,** *6 Francis Grove, SW19.* Have a list of correspondence courses (from accountancy to yachting) available from accredited member colleges. Their leaflet lists subjects, colleges and exams.

Rudolph Steiner Schools.

The first Steiner School was the Waldorf free school in Stuttgart. Based on the ideas of Rudolf Steiner (philosopher and scientist see p151)There are now more than 20 in this country. They are concerned with seeing and fostering the spiritual qualities in children and developing what they see as the three basic faculties; thinking, feeling and willing.

In kindergarten (4-6) they encourage children to develop their will through imitation rather than telling the child what to do. In lower school (6-14) feelings and imagination are emphasised. At this stage the children are guided mostly by the same teacher throughout the eight years. In the upper school (14-18) The emphasis shifts to encouraging rational thinking and a clear critical faculty. Here specialist teachers are brought in. Each school is autonomous, there is no hierarchy, no heads, decisions are made collectively by the teachers. Subjects taught include the standard curriculum as well as crafts and eurythmy a form of movement set to speech and music). The schools are private but try to help those on low income as much as possible by providing bursaries and a sliding scale. If you can't afford it but really want your child to go maybe there are some other skills you can exchange? All children are interviewed before being accepted. Classes are co-educational and unstreamed. The teachers are committed to providing an education that helps the growth of tolerance and awareness of others and emphasise the connection between the different subjects that they study.

■ **The Steiner Schools Fellowship,** *Kidbrooke Park, Forest Row, Sussex RH18 5JB, (0342 82 2115).* Phone or write for any info on Steiner schools.

The Steiner Fellowship can also give info on how to train to be a teacher in Steiner schools. They look for maturity and life experience rather than formal qualifications. Their training is not recognised by the education authorities in Britain. There is no fixed pay in Steiner Schools, pay varies and is often according to need. Posts are not advertised; you need to contact the individual schools. There is a two year part time course in Rudolf Steiner House London - for details contact The London Waldorf Teacher Training Seminar at the address above.

For other information on Steiner activities contact **Rudolph Steiner House,** *35 Park Rd , NW1 6XT (01 723 4400).*

STEINER SCHOOLS IN LONDON

Kindergartens

■ **Mulberry Bush Kindergarten,** *c/o 19 Jeffreys Place, NW1 9PP (485 9859).* 3-6 yr olds. £4 for one session 9.30-12.30 (fees negotiable).

■ **Primrose Nursery,** *Glenills Rd, NW3 4AP (794 5865).* Phone for details.

New schools

At the moment they are only taking kids from nursery age up to 12 but will expand as their pupils get older.

■ **The North London Rudolph Steiner School,** *P.O.Box 280, N8 7HT (348 5050).*

■ **Waldorf School of South-West London,** *12 Balham Park Rd, SW12 8DR (675 4443).*

Reading

Steiner:The Way of the Child A.C. Harwood £4.50. *Education of the Child* Steiner £2.70. *Rudolf Steiner Education-The Waldorf Schools* L. Francis Edmunds tells you all about it. £4.50; available from the Steiner Fellowship, or from **Rudolf Steiner Bookshop,** *35 Park Rd , NW1 6XT.*

State Schools

THE 'IFS' AND 'BUTS' OF EDUCATION

The new national curriculum lays down country-wide standards for subjects taught and the means of assessing them. With its gradual introduction (to be completed in 1991) there is a general air of unsettledness in the educational world as it is still unclear what the changes will mean.

London faces even greater uncertainty with the abolition of the ILEA (Inner London Education Authority). By April 1990 each local education authority (LEA) will be responsible for organising its own educational facilities. They will eventually set up their own LMS (Local Management of Schools) systems which will devolve more and more responsibility to the schools themselves.

It will probably be years before the full effect of these changes will be seen. While it is hoped that the changes will allow greater administrative efficiency and improve educational facilities it is also feared that the poorer boroughs will be the losers from an unequal distribution of wealth across London.

■ **The London Residual Body (LRB),** *(633 5000)* will be the transition vehicle in the transfer of powers from the ILEA to the local authorities.

CHOOSING A SCHOOL

In theory you have a right to choose the school that you or your child goes to. In practice it will depend on the *catchment* area that you're in. In other words you'll be restricted to a choice from schools that are within a certain distance from your home. There are some exceptions to this for special cases, for example if you are a Catholic or you want your child to attend a single sex school and there is no appropriate school in your area. When making your choice it's important to find out as much as you can about the school. Shop around, visit them, take a list of questions about such things as discipline, streaming, sex equality, racial mix and teaching methods.

If you're choosing a primary school finding out which secondary school the children move on to may be an important consideration.

Involve you child in the decision, she'll be more likely to be happy about attending a school if she has a choice about which one she goes to. If your choice is refused you can appeal.

You can get advice from:

■ **ILEA Information Service,** *(633 1066).*

■ **Advisory Centre for Education** *(ACE), 18 Victoria Park Sq, E2 (980 4596).* They inform and guide parents and children on their rights to do with state education. Publications.

■ **Afro-Caribbean Education Resource Centre (ACER),** *Wyvil School Wyvil Rd, SW8 2TJ (627 2662).* Set up in 1978 to design learning materials for use in schools which recognise racial and cultural differences. Has a reference library, runs an annual young Black writers competition, runs courses and can give advice and info. Publications from ACER:

Black Voices Anthology (£7.70 incl p&p) writing by young Black people on unemployment, education etc. *Roots in Britain Booklet* (70p incl p&p), outline of contributions made by Black and Asian people to Britain through the ages.

■ **Gabbitas-Thring Educational Trust,** *6 Sackville St, W1 (734 0161 (advisory service 439 2071/1771)).* Will give info on independent schools in London.

■ **The Independent Schools Info Service,** *56 Buckingham Gate, SW1E 6AH (630 8793).*

READING

Parents Guide to Secondary Schools in London's Commuter Land John Howson ('86 Macmillan £6.95).

PTAS

Most schools now have a PTA (Parent Teacher Association) where you can meet other parents and get involved in the running of the school. You can get advice on starting one from the **National Confederation of Parent-Teacher Associations**, *2 Ebbsfleet Ind Est, Stonebridge Rd, Gravesend, Kent, DA11 9DZ, (Gravesend(0474) 560618).*

TRUANCY

These days schools are so big that you might not be missed for a while if you're not there. While they may be a lot more human and even fun than they used to be, they can still be scary places. If you don't go (and, by law, you should) the school will eventually have to inform the LEA (Local Education Authority) who will send round a *Truancy Officer* to find out why you haven't been attending. If you still don't go they have the power to prosecute your parents or even start proceedings to have you taken into care.

If you find you really can't stand school and you can't talk to your parents about it, don't give up. Try and talk to a sympathetic teacher about your difficulties, you might find that they can do something to help with you hadn't thought of. If you get together with other kids, you may find that they feel the same way you do and together you could get some changes made. If you can't, at least you can support each other. Remember in a school of anything up to 2,000 pupils *you are not alone!*

There are some projects set up for kids who have had difficulty in 'normal' schools though there are very few places.

■ **The Basement Project Intermediate Education Centre,** *St Georges Town Hall, Cable St, E1 (790 4020)* is an alternative education project which has all kinds of activities, including horse riding, video and photography, as well as teaching basic skills.

■ **School House Alternative Education Project,** *10 St Johns Vale , SE8 4EW (691 7102).*

GIFTED CHILDREN

■ **The National Association for Gifted Children (NAGC),** *1 South Audley St, W1Y 5DQ (499 1188).* Advice on how to tell if your child is gifted (it's not that easy, the signs can often be misleading). Trying to raise public awareness of the difficulties faced by gifted children. Also run support groups for parents and teachers and provide activities through their *Explorers Clubs* (46 all over the country) as well as running some inner city projects for disadvantaged gifted children.
The Social, Educational and Emotional Needs of Gifted Children Patricia Mason & Juliet Essen (NAGC £5.00).

BOOKS

The Playbook for Kids about Sex Joanie Blank & Marcia Quackenbush (Sheba £2.00) for 8-11 yr olds.

Girls are Powerful Susan Hemmings (Ed) (Sheba). Extracts from *Spare Rib* and *Shocking Pink* by young women.

Black Girls in Britain Audrey Osler due out in Autumn '89 Asian and Afro-Caribbean girls from Birmingham interviewed, telling a story of what it's like to be young, black and British.

Watch Out World Dynamic Careers for Young women. Alice Henry & Ruth Wallsgrove. More than just a career book it also gives advice on what it's like to work in non-traditional jobs as well as how to cope with unemployment and looking for work.

Relationships, Guy Dauncey. Simple exercises to help adolescents to learn more about themselves and how to improve their relationships. A sensitive book. For both kids and parents. Also teachers' pack with 10 or more copies. £3.95 from **Hobsons Pubs** *PLC Bateman St Cambridge* .

■ **Virago (Women** Section p183) do a range of books for kids called Virago Upstarts and have recently published a new series of books for girls and young women.

■ **Campaign to Impede Sex Stereotyping in the Young, (CISSY),** *177 Gleneldon Rd, SW16* produce two lists of non-sexist kids books; Non-sexist picture books 75p. *Seven plus Stories* £1.25 (both inc p&p) The campaign is now folding but still functions as a contact address for the few publications they have left.

■ **Letterbox Library,** *8 Bradbury St , N16 8BR (254 1640).* A women's co-op providing non-sexist, multi-cultural, children's books.

■ **Children's Bookshop,** *29 Fortis Green Rd, N10 (444 5500).* Books for kids from 0-teens. Mail order as well.

■ **Bookspread,** *58 Tooting Bec Rd, SW17 8BE (767 6377/4551).* Books for up to 18,

▼ KIDS' RIGHTS ▼

Contacts

■ **Message Home,** *(799 7662).* If you've run away and want to get a message home without anyone knowing where you are you can phone this

In the eyes of the courts not knowing the law is no excuse for having broken it.
At 10 • You can be arrested for breaking the law.
At 14 • You can be held responsible for breaking the law and if you're a boy, you can be sent to a detention centre.
• Girls and boys can be sent to remand centres to wait for their trial.
• You can own an air rifle and go to a pub (but not drink alcohol).
• You have to pay full fare on public transport.
At 15 • Girls and boys can be sent to a youth custody centre.
• Boys can be sent to prison to await trial.
• You can leave school on an approved leaving date.
• You can work part-time.
At 16 • You can: get a full time job (but not work nights), join a union, claim benefits choose your own religion or doctor, drink beer, wine or cider with a meal in a pub or restaurant, buy cigarettes or tobacco, drive a moped, tractor or invalid car.
• You can leave home, get married or get a passport with your parents permission.
• Girls can consent to sexual intercourse with men.
• Boys can join the armed forces with their parents' permission.
At 17 • You can: drive a car or motorbike, apply for a pilot's licence, be a street trader (except on Sundays), buy a firearm (with a licence) and be sent to prison.
• Girls can join the armed forces with their parents' permission.
At 18 • You can: leave home, get married, give blood, change your name, vote, buy property, get a mortgage, drink in a pub, sit on a jury, apply for a passport, buy goods on H.P. (Hire Purchase), sue and be sued and be tattooed (but don't try and join the army if you're a girl with tattoos, they won't have you).
At 21 • You can: adopt a child, stand for elections, apply for an HGV (Heavy Goods Vehicle) licence, hold a licence to sell alcohol and be sentenced to life imprisonment for certain crimes.
• Men can legally have sex with with other men in private.

number and leave a message on their answerphone and they'll make sure it's passed on.

■ **Childline,** *Addle Hill Entrance, Faraday Building, Queen Victoria St, EC4V 4BU (0800 1111).* National 24 hour helpline for kids you can phone them with any problem. They have a team of experienced counsellors and volunteers who can provide support and advice and can refer you to other helping agencies if that's what you need. The phone call won't cost anything.

■ **The Children's Legal Centre,** *20 Compton Terrace, N1 2UN (359 6251/2).* Advice service 2-5pm weekdays. Advice by phone and post also monthly bulletin (sub £25.00) about children and young peoples rights in all areas of law and policy. Useful publications include *Social Security for Young People*(1.20) and *Legal Aid and Getting Help*(£1.50)

■ **Justice for Children,** *2 Garden Court, Temple, EC4 (353 1633).* Can refer you to useful organisations.

Care

If you persistently skive off school, get into trouble with the police, are thought to be in 'moral danger' (e.g. involved in sex, drugs, homosexuality) or if the authorities think your parents aren't looking after you properly then you could be taken into care.

Alternatively, if it's not so serious, you could be made a ward of court. This means that you stay at home but the courts have the right to make the important decisions in your life, for example about medical treatment, or which parent you stay with if they are separated.

■ **Family Rights Group,** *6-9 Manor Gardens Holloway Rd, N7 6LA (272 7308 (Mon, Wed, Fri, 9.30-12.30) for advice), or phone 263 4016/9724 for general enquiries, Mon-Fri 9.30-5.30 (not Tue morn).* Give advice and practical help for families with children in care or on child protection registers. Can refer you to a solicitor. Have advice worker to help with problems of access to children in care. Publications incl *101 Questions and Answers, A Guide for those with Kids inCare* 75p . *A Guide to Care and Related Proceedings* Mary Ryan £3.00.

■ **Voice of the Child in Care,** *Interchange 15 Wilkin St , NW5 3NG (267 9421).*

Adoption

If you're adopted, when you're 18 you can get a copy of your birth certificate (which will have the names of your natural parents on it) and if you want you can also ask the court which made the adoption order to let you see the records about your adoption. If you were adopted before 12th November 1975 you will have to have counselling from a social worker before you can get the information. If you were adopted after that date it's up to you to decide if you want the counselling. Either way it's a good idea as they'll be able to help you if you choose to try and trace your natural parents.

To get an application form for access to your birth records write to **The General Register Officer (CA Section),** *Titchfield, Fareham, Hants PO 15 5RU.*

Sex

See **Sex** section p71.

GIRLS

You can consent to sex with a man at 16. If you're under 16, in some circumstances you could be taken into care or made a 'ward of court'. You can be charged with indecent assault if you're over 16 and the boy you sleep with is under 16.

Under 16 you are entitled to contraceptives on prescription without your parents consent, but some doctors are not happy with this so check with the doctor that the consultation will be confidential or go to a clinic.

LESBIANS

See **Lesbian and Gay** section p186.

Sex between girls over 16 is legal (unless you're in the armed forces). If one of you is over 21 and the other under 16 the older one could be charged with indecent assault.

(Leeds Postcards)

BOYS

It is illegal for any male over 14 to have sex with a girl under 16, even if she agrees. Boys under 14 could be charged with indecent assault. Any male over 14 who has sexual intercourse with a woman without her consent has committed rape. This is true even within marriage. This is a very serious offence for which the maximum penalty is life imprisonment.

GAYS

See **Lesbian and Gay** section p186.

Any sex between men under 21 is illegal. Over 21 both men must consent and they must be alone, in private.

▼ ACTIVITIES FOR KIDS ▼

City Limits and *Time Out* have a good Kids section.

■ **London Tourist Board,** *(730 3488).* M-F9-6 Sat 9-5 info on events.

■ **Westminster Play Assoc,** *147 Church St , W2 1NA (258 3817).* Run playgrounds for 5-12 yr olds and publish *Capital Radio London for Kids* £1.50 from bookshops.

■ **Central Bureau for Educational Visits and Exchanges,** *(486 5101).* Puts UK schools in touch with partners abroad. A penfriend service for individuals in the 10-18 age group offered (write to *Central Bureau, 16 Malone Rd, Belfast BT9 5BN*). Publish a termly newsletter for schools (free with SAE).

▼ THEATRE ▼ AND ARTS

See also **Arts and Media** section p107

■ **Battersea Arts Centre,** *Old Town Hall Lavender Hill , SW11 5TF (223 2223).* The Clapperboard Club shows kids' films on Sat afternoon. M/ship £3 or £5 for families, tickets £1.50 (adults), £1 for under 18s also kids classes on Sat - drama, dance and photography. Youth Theatre for 15-21yr olds Tue eves 7.30. They produce 3 plays a year.

■ **Islington Arts Factory,** *2 Parkhurst Rd, N7 (607 0561).* Classes in ballet, dance theatre, visual arts etc. £7.50 a term for under 12s, 12s-18s £12 a term.

■ **Lauderdale House,** *Waterlow Park, Highgate Hill, N6 5HG (348 8716).* Sat am shows for under-10s, from 11.30 for up to an hour £1.50 (80p unwaged).

■ **The ICA,** *The Mall, SW1 (930 0493).* Kids' club with films and events every weekend.

■ **Little Angel Marionette Theatre,** *14 Dagmar Passage, Cross St, Islington, N1 (226 1787).* Weekend puppet shows 11am; adults £3.00 kids £2.00. 3pm: adults £3.50, kids £2.50. Morning shows for 3-6 yr olds, afternoons for over 6s.

■ **Young Film-makers' and Actors' Club,** *167 Clarence Gate Gdns, NW1 (262 6803).* For 12-21yr-olds. Members share equipment and learn from each other - some are hobbyists, others are looking for a career. Membership £10. You don't need to own equipment to join.

■ **National Youth Theatre,** *443-445 Holloway Rd, N7 6LW (281 3863).*

■ **Royal Court Young People's Theatre,** *309 Portobello Rd, W10 9PD (960 4641).* Runs workshops

to encourage young writers and performers. Mems £10 (£6 for unwaged or students), includes all workshops and cheap entrance to plays at the Royal Court (£1).

■ **Oval House,** *54 Kennington Oval, SE11 (735 2786).* Workshops for over-15s including modern dance, acrobatics, theatre and cinema. Membership £4 pa (for 15-18 yr olds). They also put on experimental theatre and there's a cafe open during performances where a lot of young people go.

■ **Greenwich Young People's Theatre,** *Burrage Rd, SE18 (854 1316).* Workshops in music, drama and dance for 7-25s

■ **Nomad Puppets,** *Nomad Studio, 37 Upper Tooting Rd, SW17 (767 4005)* put on shows on Sun 11.30 & 2.30. Also do private parties by arrangement (all bookings by phone please).

■ **Unicorn Theatre,** *6 Gt Newport St, WC2 (836 3334).* Plays for children and the young at heart.

▼ YOUTH PROJECTS ▼

Community Centres often have facilities and projects for kids. See your local library or CABx for lists of local clubs. ILEA information (p226) can tell you about other projects. The following is a list of non-commercial groups that have various activities for teenagers.

■ **Harambee II Project,** *106 Downham Road, N1 5BE (249 4741)* has grown from a youth club to an organisation which provides short life housing, temporary hostels for the homeless, counselling, workshops in building, tailoring, computer skills and silk screen printing. Phone for details. M-F (not Sat & Sun) 10-7.30. Also an advice centre during office hours.

■ **Portobello Project,** *49-51 Porchester Rd, W2 (221 4413).* Advice and info on anything from Income Support to finding a place to live. They also have a mobile info service that goes around North Kensington. They have regularly updated housing and job lists. Open 10-6 M-F (T 10-4). Also run cartoon workshops and classes in computing accounts and book-keeping. Info booklets free from them include *The Complete Saturday Job Book, All You Want to Know About Accommodation* and *Be Your Own Boss.* For people 25 and under. They wrote the **Jobs** section of this book.

■ **Inter-Action,** *HMS President ,Victoria Emb, nr Blackfriars Bridge, EC4 OHJ (583 2652).* Provides training and resources for voluntary groups. In the past they have helped to set up projects such as children's theatre, city farms, mobile play facilities and are now pioneering a computer network for youth clubs and schools. Publish handbooks on youth and community projects and creative play techniques as well as computer and media training. They also sets up projects such as 'Work to Play' a self help environmental improvements scheme for school playgrounds. *New Game Songs Activities and Projects* focuses on co-operation and sharing while encouraging self-esteem and *Healthy Learning Songs* R.L.Dogg (Ed) are both available from Inter-Action, £4.25 each.

■ **Youthaid Research/Pressure Grp,** *9 Poland St, W1 (439 8523).* Help and advice.

■ **Camden Girls' Centre Project,** *4 Caversham Rd, NW5 2DU (267 2898).* Mon-Fri 10-5.30. Leisure activities like games and workshops; resource centre and library. Anti racist/sexist approach. Building not suitable for the disabled.

■ **Shelburne Young Women's Centre,** *6th Form Centre, Chillingworth Rd, N7 (607 7527).* Wide range of activities for girls and young women including groups for the disabled, young mums, lesbians and lots more.

For where to go to get help on variety of problems see **Advice Centres** p211.

Help for young children and their parents:

■ **Earls Court Child Guidance Unit,** *25 Stratford Rd, W8 6RA (937 4561).* Under 16 usually with parents.

■ **The Notre Dame Child Guidance Clinic,** *63 Lancaster Rd , W1 (221 4656).* Centre for psychotherapy.

ethnic minorities

London has the greatest concentration of Britain's ethnic minorities. Before its abolition, the GLC estimated that in 1986 1 in 7 of all Londoners were of Asian or Afro-Caribbean descent. Many of these people have been here some time and have made a significant contribution to the economic, social and cultural life of the city.

Literally hundreds of voluntary, community-based groups have been established and it is beyond the scope of this book to attempt to list and do justice to them all. An invaluable guide has been produced by

■ **London Voluntary Services Council,** *68 Charlton St, NW1 (388 0241).* Most of London's Local Authorities now have Ethnic Minorities Units/Race Relations Units from which information on local resources can be obtained. *Bridges* (£5 inc postage from them) is a comprehensive directory which lists over 800 community groups in London. Recommended.

Listed below are some useful organisations which can be starting points to steer you in the right direction.

▼ HARASSMENT ▼ DISCRIMINATION

The Race Relations Act 1976 makes it unlawful to discriminate on grounds of Race. Despite such legislation, racism and racial discrimination is rife.

■ **Commission for Racial Equality,** *Elliot Hse, 10-12 Allington St, SW1 (828 7022).* Government funded body which helps people fight discrimination, will give legal advice and representation in courts if appropriate. Works closely with the network of local voluntary Community Relations Councils - they have a list of them nationwide. Monitors and campaigns against discrimination, gives some grants for self-help groups. Community Relations Councils give legal and immigration advice, promote equal opportunities and campaign for changes in policy and practice at a local level.

■ **Greater London Action for Race Equality,** *Room 312, Southbank Ho, Black Prince Rd, SE1 (587 0740).* Co-ordinating body for London Community Relations Councils. Also runs research projects

■ **Runnymede Trust,** *11 Princelet St, E1 (375 1496).* Anti-racist publication. Library (open to the public, ring first) of publications, press cuttings.

■ **Institute of Race Relations,** 2-6 Leeke St, WC1 (837 0041). Reference library and info on 3rd world struggles and anti-racism in Britain - it's origins and patterns. Publishes *Race and Class* (qtly), books, and a variety of political and analytical pamphlets. Films available.

■ **All London Teachers Against Racism and Fascism,** *(ALTARF), Panther Hse, Rm 216, 38 Mount Pleasant, WC1X OAP (278 7856).* Supports community action against racist attacks, deportations and police harassment. Develops strategies to challange racism in the classroom and the racism of institutions. Supports national and international campaigns to combat racism and publishes anti-racist resources for schools. Membership £5 students £1.

■ **Community and Race Relations Unit,** *Inter church Hse 35-41 Lower Marsh, SE17 (620 4444).* Christian oranisation set up to inform Churches and Christians about different aspects of racial oppression (inc. police harassment and the threat of Fascism). Grants are available from their project fund to support the racially oppressed and their organisations. Literature available on request.

▼ RACIST ATTACKS ▼

■ **CAPA (East London) Limited,** *Oxford Ho, Derbyshire St, E2 (729 2652).* 24-hour emergency service for victims of racial harrasment and attack and domestic violence. Can put you in touch with solicitors, and liaise with police. Open 9-6. Emergency line after 6pm staffed with volunteers (they are looking for more volunteers).

■ **Greenwich Action Committee Against Racial Attacks,** *78 Sandy Hill Rd, SE18 (855 4343).* Monitor racial attacks and attitudes of the police in Greenwich and help victims. **Newham Monitoring Cttee** *(555 8151)* performs a similar function in Newham.

▼ IMMIGRATION AND ▼ NATIONALITY

For details of the law and advice centres see **People From Abroad** section (p119).

▼ THE RIGHT TO BE ▼ UNDERSTOOD

The majority of statutory and voluntary organisations have very little information translated into languages other than English. Fewer still have interpreters available. Consequently, many people whose first language is not English face additional difficulties when approaching organisations for assistnace.

Some London boroughs have their own translation/interpreting services (e.g. Camden).

■ **Greater London Translation Unit,** *5 Westminster Bridge Rd, SE1 (928 9889).*

▼ HEALTH ▼

People from ethnic minorities can suffer discrimination in their treatment by the NHS. For instance many more black people get diagnosed as 'schizophrenic', often because workers in the psychiatric services don't take into account different cultural standards. Less emphasis is given to research into diseases such as Sickle Cell Anaemia, which particularly affects black people.

■ **Black and Ethnic Minority Development Team,** *MIND South East, 24-32 Stephenson Way, NW1 (387 9070).* Have produced comprehensive directory of black and ethnic minority community mental health services in London.

■ **Afro-Caribbean Mental Health Assn,** *35-37 Electric Ave, SW9 (737 3603/6333).* Phone for appointment 9.30-5.30. Mental healh centre offering counselling, housing advice, legal advice and befriending. For Lambeth, Lewisham and Southwark redsidents. Referrals by self, or statutory/voluntary bodies.

■ **Nafsiat Inter-Cultural Therapy Centre,** *278 Seven Sisters Rd, N4 (263 6394).* Psychotherapy and counselling service.

■ **Sickle Cell Society,** *Green Lodge, Barretts Green Rd, NW10 (961 7795/961 8346).* Advice and counselling service. Information on local NHS Sickle Cell Centres. Can offer financial help to those with Sickle Cell disease.

■ **London Black Women Health Action Project,** *Bethnal Green Hosp, Cambridge Heath Rd, E2 (980 3503).* Promoting Black women's health generally but their special area of concern is genital mutilation (female 'circumcision').

■ **Latin American Health Group,** *Mawbey Brough Health Centre, 39 Wilcox Cl, SW8 (627 4444).*

■ **Medical Foundation for Care of Victims of Torture,** *National Temperance Hosp, 110 Hampstead Rd, NW1 (388 8204).* Medical care for those who have suffered torture and their families.

▼ CULTURAL ▼

■ **Africa Centre,** *38 King St, WC2 (836 1973).* Regular music events, meetings, restaurant, bookshop and crafts shop.

■ **Arts Media Group,** *90 De Beauvoir Rd, N1 (254 6256/249 0994).* Campaigns on behalf of black and minority arts community.

■ **Bahia Radar Projects,** *39 Foxley Rd , SW9 (582 0981).* Classes, workshops concerned with Carnival.

■ **Black Cultural Centre,** *St Pauls Ct, Gliddon Rd, W14 (741 1119).* Social events and cultural activities for young people.

■ **Black Dance Forum,** *24 Cranbourn St, WC2* promotes development of minority dance groups.

■ **Black Music Assn UK ,** *146 Manor Pk Rd, NW10 (961 4857).* Consultations, advice and education for Black musicians

■ **Black Peoples Entertainment,** *Flat 9, 216 Finchley Rd, NW3 (328 5362).* Arrange leisure and entertainment for black community.

■ **Black Theatre Co-op,** *8 Bradbury St, N16 (249 9150).* National touring company which seeks to bring plays to public that reflect various aspects of black life.

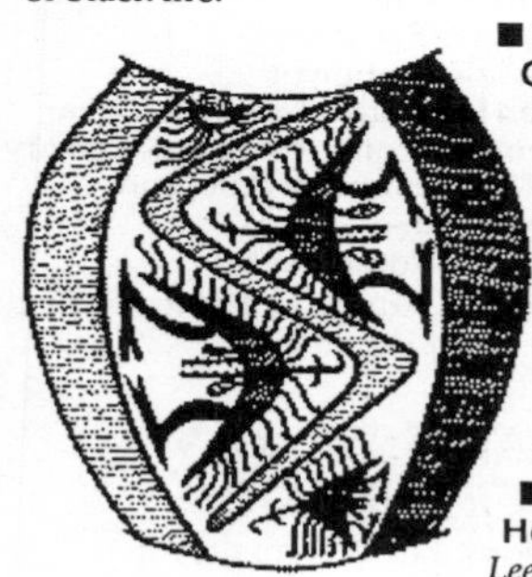

■ **Caribbean Cultural International,** *Karnak Hse, 300 Westbourne Park Rd, W11 (221 6490).* Promotes Caribbean and African cultural activity. Karnak House dancers and singers.

■ **Caribbean Heritage Group,** *Lee Community Education Centre, 1 Aislibie Rd, SE12 (852 4700).* Exploring language, history and culture.

■ **Commonwealth Centre,** *Kensington High St, W8 (603 4535).* Cultural centre with particular interest in Black Commonwealth communities. Cinema, theatres, bookshop and restaurant.

■ **Festival of Chinese Arts,** *PO Box 892, NW1.* Has register of Chinese artists and performers.

■ **Foundation for African Arts,** *Old George Orwell Bldg, Holland Wk, N19 (263 8141).* Promotes African arts, info for schools and colleges.

■ **Foundation for African Arts,** *Archway Annexe, 16 Highgate hill, N19 (263 8141).* Bring groups from Africa to do concerts here, and organise workshops in African music, drumming, dance, ceramics and sculpture for groups - can tailor to your requirements. Shop selling crafts.

■ **Indian Arts Council in UK,** *70 Marchmont St, WC1 (837 1431).* Art gallery holding exhibitions of asian artists' work and literary society.

■ **East African Assn,** *120 Squires La, N3 (349 1412).* Promotes Kenyan, Tanzanian and Ugandan culture meetings every 6 weeks.

■ **East London African Arts,** *c/o T.H.A.P. Bookshop Whitechapel Rd, E2 (247 0216).* Classes in African dance, music and drama for children and unemployed people.

■ **Latin American Community Project,** *14 Brixton Rd, SW9 6BU (582 5590).* Give general advice and interpreting service to Latin American/Spanish speaking people.

■ **Minority Arts Advisory Service,** *25-31 Tavistock Pl, WC1 (254 7295).* Give advice and information on all aspects of finance, training, venues, contacts, arts policies to artists and performers. Also consultancy for organisations, and development of minority arts in general. Runs training courses in arts management, publicity, arts law, accounting, committee skills, and some technical courses.

■ **Tara Arts Group,** *356 Garratt La, SW18 (871 1458/9).* As well as being an national touring company, they have a centre which hosts Asian arts events and a community group for those who want to learn acting skills (see p110 **Arts and Media** section).

■ **Ujamaa Centre,** *14 Brixton Rd, SW9 (820 1855).* M-S 10-6.30. Co-op selling crafts from 3rd world countries, and books. Noticeboard.

■ **Yaa Asantewa Workshops,** *1 Chippenham Mews, Marylands Rd, W9 (286 1656).* Projects include black writing, dance, drama, music.

■ **Zuriya Theatre Co,** *38 Brixton Rd, SW9 (582 9479).* Performances and workshops in African dance, drama, music, story-telling.

▼ GROUPS ▼

Again, only a small sample appears below, as an indication of what is available - consult *Bridges* above for a comprehensive (although still by no means exhaustive) list.

■ **Afro Carribean Project,** *422 Seven Sisters Rd, N4 (809 3071).*

■ **Afro-Asian Advisory Service,** *Cambridge Hse, 137 Camberwell Rd, SE5 (701 0141).* Appointment only 9.30-12.30. Immigration and nationality advice only.

■ **Afro-Caribbean Organisation,** *335 Grays Inn Rd, WC1X (837 0396).* Self-help drop-in centre staffed by workers who can give advice on immigration, housing, education and legal matters. (M-F 10-5). Run by volunteers in the evenings. Classes in word processing (Amstrad).

■ **African Peoples Movement South East,** *226 Camberwell Rd, SE5 (701 7121).* M-F 9-5, legal, housing and benefits advice. Drop in.

■ **Asian Forum,** *63 Montepelier Rd, SE15 (639 5168).* Acts as a federation of Asian organisations. May be able to provide information on local projects.

■ **Chile Democratico,** *95 Old St, EC1 (253 8404).* National organisation of Chilian exiles. Counselling and welfare advice, projects.

■ **Chinese Community Centre,** *2nd Floor, 44 Gerrard St, W1 (439 3822).*

■ **Chinese Information and Advice Centre,** *152 Shaftesbury Ave, WC2 (836 8291).* Advice and legal help on welfare benefits, housing, racial harassment, matrimonial issues etc. M-F 10-6. Tues by appointment only.

■ **Carila,** *(358 2270)* see p208, advice for Latin American people.

■ **East European Advice Centre POSK,** *238 King St, W6 (748 3085).* Welfare, legal and general advice, and help on translation. M-F 10-4 drop in, or make an appointment if you want a more private interview.

■ **Eritrean Community in the UK,** *244 Upper St, N1 (704 9272).*

■ **Ghana Welfare Assn,** *541 High St, E11 (558 9311).* Advice on immigration, education, centre for Ghanaian culture, legal issues. Also information for general public on Ghana. Legal advice Tues - Th 4-9.

■ **Indian Workers Assn,** *12a The Green, Southall, Middx, (574 7283).* Advice and casework sessions - legal, immigration, housing, welfare etc. Also run some community projects.

■ **Iranian Community Centre,** *465a Green Lanes, N4 (341 5005).* Advice on welfare, women, housing, education, employment, rights, immigration, refugees. Representation at tribunals, courts etc. Help people arriving at the port of entry into Britain.

■ **Jewish Welfare Board,** *221 Golders Green Rd, NW11 (458 3282).* This and the **Jewish Blind Society** will be called **Jewish Care** as from 1989. For local services ring Edgware Jewish Family Services: *(951 0166),* North East: *(809 2889),* Ilford Redbridge Jewish Family Service: *(554 8299).* South London ring Golders Green branch.

■ **Kurdish Cultural Centre,** *14 Stannary St, SE11 (735 0918).* M-F 10-6. Appointment preferred. Assist Kurdish refugee people, focus on issues such as housing, social security, education, detention centres. Also cultural activities, including open courses on the Kurdish Language, for beginners and mother tongue speakers.

■ **London Irish Centre,** *50/52 Camden Sq, NW1 9XB (485 0051).* A social/cultural club. Also provides help and advice especially to newly arrived Irish in London. Irish language classes. Two hostels.

■ **Moroccan Workers Assn,** *c/o Dame Colet Ho, Ben Johnson Rd, E1 (790 9077).*

■ **North London Bangladesh Welfare Assn,** *251 Pentonville Rd, N1 (278 0877).* Open M-F 10-5.

■ **Pakistan Welfare Assn,** *18 Trinity Rd, SW17 (767 6474).*

■ **Philippine Resource Centre,** *1 Grangeway, NW6 (624 0270).*

■ **Portuguese Community Centre,** *Thorpe Cl, W10 (969 3890).* Advice session Thurs. Also translation and interpreting service. Teach English as a second language one evening a week. Also open in the evening as a community centre.

■ **Rastafarian Advisory Service,** *17a Netherwood Rd, W14 (602 3767).* General advice service as well as business advice.

■ **Somali London Community & Cultural Assn,** *12 Wickford St, E2 (791 3045).* Advice on employment, housing, immigration etc. Translation for those with language difficulties. Also run educational project - teach english as a second langauge, employment training. Appointments preferred.

■ **Theatro Technis: Cypriot Advisory Service,** *26 Crowndale Rd, NW1 (388 7971).* M-F 10-5 except Thur 10-1. Appointments only. Mainly for elderly people and those who don't speak English - advice on welfare benefits, medical, housing, interpreters, holiday trips, legal problems.

■ **Turkish Community Centre,** *92 Stoke Newington Rd, N16 (249 6980).* Interpreting service.

■ **Ugandan Assylum Seekers Assn,** *200 The Grove, E13 (519 0893).* Appointments only (Tues, Wed, Thurs). Help for refugees, and on immigration, political assylum, welfare benefits, marriage problems, housing, education. Training. Sell cultural goods, and centre for Ugandan music.

■ **West African Welfare Assn,** *98 Craven Pk, NW10 (586 1080/453 0299).*

▼ PUBLICATIONS ▼

■ *Front Line, Karnak Hse, 300 Westbourne Pk Rd, W11 (221 6490).* Publish books of essays on Caribbean and African culture/affairs.

■ *Race Today, 165 Railton Rd, SE24 OLU (737 2268).* Independent paper with articles on the Asian and West Indian community here and abroad. 'The voice of the black community in the UK'. Mthly.

▼ BOOKSHOPS ▼

■ **Africa Book Centre,** *38 King St, WC1 (240 6649).* M-F 11-5.30m, Sat 11-5. Books about Africa covering: women, children and education, history, politics, economics, sociology, art, music, fiction, criticism, cookery, health. Magazines, records, cassettes, t -shirts, badges and more!

■ **East Asia Books,** *101-103 Camden High St, NW1 (388 5783).* Chinese medicine, art, philosophy, culture, acupuncture and alternative medicine.

■ **Grassroots Storefront,** *61 Golborne Rd, W10 (969 0687).* M-Sat 10-6.30. Black literature, Third world, left, feminist. Mail order, catalogue in production. Noticeboard. Crafts - African carvings and batiks.

■ **Green Ink,** *8 Archway Mall, Junction Rd, N19 (263 4748).* M-Sat 10-6 (is behind Archway Tube). A wide selection of books by Irish authors and about Ireland. Also stock magazines and periodicals, videos, tapes, badges, tapes, cards and crafts. Writers group meets every 2 weeks on Thurs. Noticeboard.

■ **Hellenic Books,** *122 Charing Cross Rd, WC2 (836 7071).* M-F 9-6.30, Sat 9-6. History, culture, politics, religion, travel and cookery of ancient and modern Greece, books in Greek and postcards.

■ **Headstart Books & Crafts,** *25 West Green Rd, N15 (802 2838).* M-F 9.30-6.30, Tu 9.30-9.30, Sat 9.30-7. Black interest material from Africa, Caribbean, North and South America, Europe and the World. Also sell cards, magazines, newspapers, posters, dress and dress material, African musical instruments, woodcarvings, crafts, jewellery and cosmetics. Supply libraries, schools, nurseries. Bookclub.

■ **New Beacon,** *76 Stroud Green Rd, N4 (272 4889).* Tu-Sat 10.30-6. African, Afro-American, Caribbean, Black British and European writers, multi-ethnic children's books. Free list, mail order. Community/cultural noticeboard.

■ **Orbis Bookshop,** *66 Kenway Rd, SW5 (370 2210). M-F 9.30-5.30,* Sat 9.30-4.30. Books on Eastern Europe, as well as books in Czech, Urkranian, Polish and Russian.

■ **Walter Rodney Bookshop,** *5A Chignall Pl, W13 (579 4920).* 10.30-5.30. African, Carribean, Latin American, Asian and general titles. Mail order. Organise book exhibitions in schools, advise teachers on books/reading lists for classes.

disabled

Disabled people face all the difficulties common to the rest of us - problems with housing, employment, getting around, and on top of this they have their disability to contend with.

There are many organisations that deal with the disabled, but like society, they often deal with the disability rather than the person. Whilst well meaning in providing special treatment for tdisabled paople such as special employment centres and segregated housing, this treatment can often increase the sense of isolation of disabled people.

To combat this isolation and stigma of being disabled (often associated by many with mental disability) pressure groups and social groups have formed. These groups are often run by the disabled themselves.

▼ SELF-HELP GROUPS ▼

■ **Gemma,** *BM 5700, WC1N 3XX* *(see p 191).* Support group for disabled lesbians.

■ See also **Winvisible** (Women with Visible and Invisible Disabilities) p 179 **Women's** section.

■ **Spinal Injuries Assoc,** *Newpoint Hs, 76 St. Jame's La, N10 (444 2121).* Run by paraplegics and tetraplegics for other spinal cord injured people and their families. They give information and have holiday facilities, including two converted narrow boats and caravans. Publications include *So You're Paralysed* (A consumers guide to spinal cord injury) (£4.50 inc p&p). M'ship (£8) includes info-packed qtly newsletter. Services include a care attendant agency, confidential welfare service and comprehensive information service.

■ **Assoc of Disabled Professionals,** *The Stables, 73 Pound Rd, Banstead, Surrey SM7 2HU, (0737 352366).* Aims to improve education, training and employment opportunities at professional level (most other programmes focus on semi-skilled and clerical work). Register of professional advisers. M'ship (£6, students £2) includes qtly bulletin and irregular newsletter.

■ **Outsiders Club,** *Box 4ZB, W1A 4ZB (499 0900).* To help physically and socially handicapped people form good personal relationships.

▼ SERVICES ▼

■ **Grants** Details of trusts giving grants for people in need are given in *The Guide to Grants to Individuals in Need* (Directory of Social Change), and *The Charities Digest* (Family Welfare Association) – both should be available at local libraries.

■ **Feminist Audio Books,** *52-54 Featherstone St, EC1 8RT (251 2908/ 0713).* See Women's section p. 183

■ **Motability,** *2nd floor, Gate Hs, West Gate, Harlow, Essex EM20 1HR, (0279 635666).* Sell or lease cars to those receiving Mobility Allowance to enable them to get the best deal for their money. Many manufacturers offer discounts to people getting a Mobility Allowance. Ask your dealer.

■ **Holiday Care Service,** *2 Old Bank Chambers, Station Rd, Horley, Surrey, (0293 775137)* info and advice on holidays for people with special needs - elderly, disabled, one parent families or people with difficult circumstances. Have details of accommodation, transport, guides, sources of financial help. Try to provide a volunteer to help on the holiday (free). Write stating details and needs. Sae.

■ **RADAR,** *25 Mortimer St, W1 (637 5400).* Publishes *Holidays in the British Isles* (1989) a *Guide for Disabled People* annually (£4.50 inc p&p), and *Holidays and Travel Abroad 1989 Guide for Disabled People* (£3 inc p&p) and various access guides.

■ **RNIB (Royal National Institute for the Blind),** *224 Gt Portland St, W1 (388 1266).* You can send tapes or braille free to blind people and groups anywhere in the country and at a reduced rate to the rest of the world.

▼ORGANISATIONS▼

■ **Network for the Handicapped,** *16 Princeton Street, WC1 (831 8031/7740).* Advice and info for disabled people and their families.

■ **The Greater London Ass for Disabled People (GLAD),** *336 Brixton Rd, SW9 (274 0107).*

■ **Handicapped Helpline,** *81 High St South, E6 4EJ (472 6652).* Telephone advice for people with disabilities and their carers.

■ **Disabled Living Foundation,** *380-384 Harrow Rd, W9 (289 6111).* Masses of info and a permanent exhibition of equipment and aids for disabled people (please phone for appointment, don't just turn up). Also info on work, education, accommodation and leisure facilities. Free publications list.

■ **Disabled Advice Service,** *305 Garrett Ln, SW18 (870 7437).* M-F 11-1, 2-4. Info and referralsfor welfare benefits, equipment etc.

COMMUNICATION: Computers, Phone, Networks, Finding Info, Printing/Publishing

computers

the purpose of this chapter is to tell you some basics about computers, to give an idea about the computer and **peripherals** *which are currently available and finally to help you decide what you need and how to buy it.*

Personal computers have come a long way in the last eight to ten years. The price has stayed about the same (decreased if you take inflation into account) but the power you get for your money has increased massively. One rider to this statement is that the machines at the leading edge of technology are always dearer for the first year or so after introduction. Once the development costs have been recouped the manufacturer only has to cover the cost of manufacture and the price drops (by then there will be a new leading edge of technology machine). When personal computers first came out, it was such a challenge to do anything useful on them that only hobbyists and technofreaks really bothered but today nearly anyone can learn to use a microcomputer profitably.

One of the biggest problems associated with buying a computer to suit your needs is getting past the bullshit and jargon. Probably the worst offenders are sales people. At the low end (e.g. Dixons) it is likely to be a spotty eighteen year old eager to impress you with her vast knowledge of acronyms before she sells you a video games machine with a rubbery keyboard which she will insist is *the* ideal word processor. On the other hand, the rep selling serious business machines to serious business people will be very good at *selling*, having spent most of her life selling office furniture or photocopiers before starting work for the computer company; after two weeks of in-house training she is released onto an unsuspecting world. She will be much more plausible than the spotty person (she will probably be older and wearing a nice suit for starters) but she is just as likely to sell you a lemon.

One way around this problem is to define why you want a computer and exactly what you want it to do (another solution is to be very rich and buy top of the range everything).

To get anywhere in the computer jungle you need to understand at least a smattering of the jargon, there is no way out of it. At the end of this section, there is a glossary covering most of the important terms; all the terms covered in the glossary are in **bold type** in the main text. Read it from beginning to end, or look up terms as you come across them. Read some of the specialist magazines (see *magazines*). Pretty soon it will start to make sense.

▼ REASONS FOR WANTING A COMPUTER ▼

There are a number of reasons for wanting a computer.

i) The executive toy.

Playing with a nice computer can be fun, and if it does some word processing and accounting as well, so much the better. I have to admit that, apart from the executive bit, this is my reason for having a computer. Now, of course, I could not live without one.

ii) The video games freak.

If you are one of those people who spends pounds on video arcade games, then the best thing for you would be to buy a computer designed primarily for games. The quality is on a par with arcade games and there is more variety.

iii) The programmer.

For most people this is a subset of (i). In a few months, you can learn to programme in your spare time and have fun writing little programmes to bounce balls round the screen, sort the titles of your record collection into alphabetical order and accomplish other such useful tasks. The days when you could buy a computer, learn programming and write a best selling programme in six months are long gone (if they ever existed). Today's programmes are, for the most part, written by teams of professional programmers and take many years to write.

iv) The 'serious user'.

This is a horrible term much loved by copywriters which I am using for anyone who has any of the following needs: to write anything from form letters to a best selling novel; to manage household accounts or to do cost projections for a medium sized company; to keep track of information such as a recipe file or an address list, or a need for drawing, graphic design, layout (pamphlets to national newspapers have been laid out using personal computers) or statistical analysis.

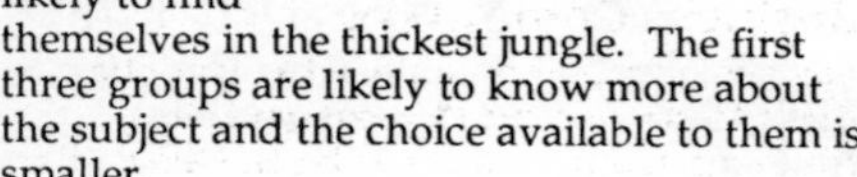

Most of this chapter is aimed at the needs of the latter group because they are likely to find themselves in the thickest jungle. The first three groups are likely to know more about the subject and the choice available to them is smaller.

▼ WHAT IS A COMPUTER? ▼

A computer has the following components. Its brain is the **microprocessor** which does all the calculations and stores the results of those calculations in the **memory (RAM)**. This is a temporary (dynamic) **memory** and it only lasts until you turn the computer off. The computer also has a permanent **memory** which can be a **hard disc**, a **floppy disc** or a cassette tape. The computer also needs to communicate with you in the outside world. It sends information to you via the **monitor** (screen) and printer and you return information to the computer using the keyboard.

So at the minimum, a computer system consists of a **microprocessor** with some dynamic **memory**, a permanent **memory**, a keyboard, a **monitor** and a printer.

Microcomputers can be be broadly divided into three generations; 8, 16, and 32 **bit microprocessors**. Each generation is approximately 4 -10 fold more powerful than the previous one. The 8-**bit** machines are those of the late seventies and the early eighties and they consist of machines like the Acorn BBC (featured on TV and found in many schools and colleges), the Sinclair Spectrum and the original IBM PC; there are very few new 8 **bit** machines sold today. Sixteen **bit** machines date from the mid eighties and typical sixteen **bit** machines are the Atari ST, the Apple Macintosh Plus and SE, and the IBM AT and its **clones**. These machines are still sold and probably represent the bulk of the machines in use today. They are powerful enough for most applications and this is the area where the best bargains are to be found as companies switch to the newer 32 **bit** machines. Thirty-two **bit** machines started to arrive in the last 2 years or so, examples are the IBM 80386 and PS/2 ranges and the Apple Macintosh II family; the Acorn Archimedes, while not having a true 32 **bit** processor, is of comparable power. These machines are very powerful and the distinction between the more advanced of these machines and a mini computer (that would have its own room and acolytes to run it) is starting to blur. The 16 **bit** machines are useful if you want to run a medium size company or a large database, or simply would like to have the biggest toy on the block (like me). They tend to be expensive, although the expense can be alleviated to some extent (see Computers on the Cheap below).

▼ WHICH COMPUTER ? ▼

In general, microcomputers can be broadly split into two groups, business computers and home computers. Home computers normally support colour, have excellent graphics and sound and are capable of using a domestic television set as a **monitor** and, in the older models, a cassette player is used instead of a **disc** drive for storage. Business computers often have poor or nonexistent sound and poor graphics, but this is compensated for by their expandability, robust construction and the sort of high quality keyboard and **monitor** which are needed for a machine in constant use.

The prices quoted below are for the basic machine and exclude VAT; beware that some programmes, particularly non-games programmes, will require the purchase of a **monitor** which is of higher resolution than a television screen, additional **memory**, **floppy** or **hard disc** drives; the cost of these additions can soon double the cost of the computer system. The prices quoted are the prices at which the machines are selling in June 1989 and are generally lower than the recommended retail price; and the prices will almost certainly have changed (downwards in some cases) by the time this book is published.

Home computers

This is a relatively brief section because most people who want to buy a home computer will already know the market reasonably well. This section will also be incomplete as there are just too many machines in this category to mention them all.

The *Acorn BBC* is an obsolete 8 **bit** machine. However, it was an excellent machine for its time and there is a reasonable number of games and educational software for it. If you just want learn about computers and try some programming, this is an excellent place to start. Second-hand models in reasonable condition can be picked up for under £100.

The *Atari ST* is a sixteen **bit** machine with excellent colour and graphics. It includes a **floppy disc** drive as standard and it has a 'graphical interface'. This means that directories and subdirectories are represented by pictures of folders, documents by pictures of typewritten pages and they are manipulated by moving a pointer around on the screen with a mouse. Despite what some of its advocates might claim, it is primarily a machine for games. It has probably the widest choice of games available for any machine and they are of excellent quality. There is also 'serious' software available for it, some is excellent and low priced. However, if your main use for it is business, then I recommend that you spend a little more and buy a business machine; by the time you have purchased the second **floppy** or **hard disc** and **monitor** necessary to use your Atari, there is not much saved. Also, the Atari keyboard is poor quality and the casing has a cheap feel to it. The beefed up (and more expensive) versions have better keyboards and casings. At the time of writing (August 1989) the basic (single **floppy** drive, no **hard disc** or **monitor**) Atari ST FM system can be had for as little as £260+VAT new, or less second-hand.

The *Comodore Amiga* is another 16 bit machine. It has superlative sound and graphics, it even has a special chip (a 'blitter') which can handle the sideways movement of animated figures. It is a very well made and powerful machine. Again, the main market is for 'entertainment' software, the software quality is high but there is less choice than for the Atari ST and there is dearth of serious software. The basic machine can be bought for about £320.

The *Acorn Archimedes* is a very powerful machine indeed, when it was released in 1988 it was the most powerful microcomputer available. It uses a different type of **microprocessor** than the other computers discussed, but the chip is equivalent in power to a fast 32 **bit microprocessor**. This is the machine for the enthusiast or hobbyist. Because it is manufactured and sold predominantly in Britain, there is not the quantity nor quality of software available on the other machines, and the unfortunate consequence is that most of this power stays locked up due to the lack of good software. If you want to write your own programmes, and you need this sort of power, this could be the machine for you. The machine comes in two versions. The cheaper, less expandable A3000 version is poor value with a recommended retail price of £649 (too new at the time of writing to have a 'true' price but probably £Z350-400). The full blown machine can be had for £750 without a **monitor**. Only buy an Archimedes if you know that you want one (in which case you don't need to read this section).

Business Computers

Business computers come in two varieties: *Apple Macintosh* and *IBM* **compatible**. Although my preference is for the Mac, I'll try not to let that influence my discussion too much. In theory (and to some extent it is true in practice) all Macs can run the same Mac software and all IBMs can run all IBM software. This is one of the biggest advantages of business machines. With only two major players, the software houses can dedicate a lot of effort to writing the perfect program secure in the knowledge of a large number of potential customers. Because the software houses are competing amongst themselves for your custom, the products are very good. If there are only one or two word processors for a computer (e.g. the Archimedes) then you can be sure that neither will have all the features you want. Anyway back to the Mac and the IBM, the philosophy of these two machines is very different, both in design and marketing. The Macintosh has a graphical interface and very strict interface guidelines for programmers. **Files** and programmes are represented by little pictures (called icons) which can be manipulated with a pointer on the screen controlled by a mouse.

Directories are represented by a picture of a folder and **files** are deleted by 'dragging' them into waste-basket icon. Commands are accessed from menus at the top of the screen and the strict guidelines ensure that, wherever possible, the same command (e.g. save or print) is in the same place for all programs. A further consequence of these guidelines is that information can very easily be 'copied' and 'pasted' between different programmes (e.g. a drawing to a word processing or database file). The whole operating system is an analogy to an office and desk top. This operating system has evolved over the past 8 years and is consequently very smooth, sophisticated, intuitive and easy to use. The graphical nature of the Mac means that all machines have a potentially vast range of styles and sizes of typefaces available. The upshot of this is that the Mac is relatively simple to use and is especially recommended for computer phobes; the standardisation of the software layout means that once you have mastered one Mac programme, you've mastered 80% of all other Mac programmes. The Mac is also the king of Desk Top Publishing (**DTP**). The Daily News paper (now defunct) was laid out using a Mac **DTP** system and this book was completely typeset using a Macintosh. As always there is a price to be paid for this ease of use, that price is monetary. A Mac is at least double the price of a comparably powered IBM **clone**. Similarly, the software is more expensive. This is mainly due to Apple's policy of not allowing Mac **clones** and operating a policy of selling only through authorised dealers. There are ways to alleviate the cost (see *Computers on the Cheap*).

The IBM is more like everyone's traditional idea of a microcomputer. In order to make it do things, one has to use non-intuitive commands typed in exact order to manipulate **files**. Programmes too are often not intuitive with obscure keystrokes required to use the software. There have been some attempts to implement a graphical interface on the IBM microcomputers but because different programs have different ways of implementing it, many of the advantages of the Mac are lost. The upshot of this is that it takes a lot longer to learn to use an IBM and the various programmes that run on it. Once this learning is over the IBM machines can do all that a Mac can and sometimes more. The only exception to this is perhaps in the area of **DTP** where the Mac is far ahead. The real advantage of IBM machines is their price and the price of their software. Unlike Apple, IBM have a policy of encouraging other manufacturers to make **clones** which are completely **compatible** with the IBM product. This element of competition leads to much cheaper prices than for the comparable Macintosh.

Once you've decided between IBM or Macintosh, how do you decide which one?

The choice of Macintosh is easier to make because there are less of them. There are two 16 **bit** machines: the Mac Plus and the SE 20. The former comes with 1 mega**byte** of **RAM** (expandable to 4), an integral **monitor** and one **floppy disk** drive; it is not at present possible to upgrade it to a more sophisticated machine. In order to use it to any effect either a second **floppy** drive or preferably a **hard** drive is essential. The cost of all this (if you pay full price) is about £2000. For £300-£400 pounds more you can have the SE 2/20. This comes with 2Mb of **RAM**, a 20Mb **hard disc** and (by the time you read this) a **floppy** drive capable of reading and writing to IBM 3.5 inch **disk**c. It is also capable of being upgraded (for a price) and having a Fax card installed (see **Scanners and Faxcards**) and large screens, etc. added. Prices for both the Mac Plus and SE 20 are likely to fall in the near future.

The next group of Macs are the 32 **bit** machines. The first of these is the Mac II; this is a large and expensive machine and, due to a policy decision by Apple, is more or less obsolete only 2 years after being launched. The price for a new Mac II with a black and white **monitor** is about £5000 pounds. This machine should be avoided new at all costs whatever the salesperson tells you. However, it is a buyers' market and you could find some excellent second-hand bargains (I would not pay more than £2000). The other 32 **bit** Macs are the SE 30, the Mac IIcx and the Mac IIx range (others may have been released by the time you read this). The SE 30 is a very powerful machine in the same cute and compact box as the Mac Plus and SE 20. In common with them it has a 9 inch integral black and white **monitor** and it is luggable. It comes with either 2 or 4 Mb of **RAM** and a 40 Mb **hard disc**. It can also have colour screens and other **peripherals** added. The list price is £3,500-£4000. The Mac IIcx is a modular computer with a separate screen, the choice of size and colour is yours. Its innards are essentially the same as the SE 30 although it also has industry standard 'NuBus' slots which allow the addition of third party cards. Cost is about £700-£800 more than the comparable SE 30. The Mac IIx is the company flagship, it is a large modular machine externally like the Mac II. Internally it is identical to the IIcx except that it has extra NuBus slots. Expect to pay up to £8000 for this one.

If the high prices listed here compared to the IBM **compatibles** have scared you away, see **Computers on the Cheap** (below), because the dearer the machine, the greater the potential for discounts.

With IBM **compatible** machines it is not possible to list every thing on the market. The choices run into hundreds if not thousands. It is very much a case of mix and match; what processor, **maths coprocessor, clock speed, graphics card, monitor, disc** drive and **hard disc** do you want in your machine? The first rule is, unless you are large company afraid to buy anything without a major brand name, do not buy IBM; they can cost over double the price of an equivalent **clone**.

The choice of **microprocessor** is essentially: the 8 **bit** (Intel 8086 or equivalent), the 16 **bit** (Intel 80286), or the 32 **bit** (Intel 80386). The 8 **bit** machines are equivalent to the original IBM PC and XT. These can be got very cheaply second-hand (£150-400); or a similar price for a new Amstrad, about which I'll say more later. The 8 **bit** machine is a good entry point and ideal if your needs do not run to much more than a bit of word processing. The 16 **bit** machines are equivalent to the IBM AT and this is the type of machine I would recommend you to go for. They are fast enough for most applications and some real bargains can be had. The 32 **bit** machines are ideal for the real 'Power Users'. They are good in **networks** and for fast, colour, graphics applications. Most 32 **bit** machines use AT (16 **bit**) architecture but there also exists a high priced MCA architecture (IBMs PS/2 machines) for use with the 32 **bit microprocessor** and the OS/2 operating system; this is widely tipped to flop by industry pundits. Be aware of its existence but I do not recommend that you buy it.

The next thing to consider is the display system which consists of a graphics card inside your machine and a **monitor** screen outside it. This decides what you see, at what resolution you see it, and in how many colours. The choices boil down to MDA, CGA, Hercules EGA and VGA. MDA and Hercules are monochrome only. MDA displays text only and is obsolete, Hercules displays text and graphics and is the card of choice with a mono system. For colour, the choice is CGA, EGA and VGA; all display text and graphics. CGA has the lowest resolution and is painful to look at for any length of time. For not much more, you can have EGA, this is a good choice if you are watching your budget. Finally, VGA is becoming the *de facto* standard and is recommended if you can afford it, it will give really stunning colour graphics with the appropriate **monitor**. The final choice depends on how much you can afford and the intended use for your computer; if you are primarily doing word processing, then a mono display with a Hercules card is probably the most cost effective choice. Remember that most printers will only output in black and white. The **monitor** will depend to a large extent on the graphics card and it is often sold with the computer. If you are not buying a complete package your best bet is to look at the choices available at a dealers' and see which one looks best to you.

For storage, you would ideally have two **floppy disc** drives and a **hard** drive. The IBM standard is for 5.25 inch drives which can have a variety of capacities, viz single density (360kb), and high density (1.2 Mb). Drives of higher capacity can usually read **discs** formatted at a lower capacity but not vice versa. The IBM also supports 3.5 inch drives which are becoming more popular and also come in a range of storage capacities. **Hard discs** come in anything from 10-300 Mb and a variety of access speeds (the time it takes to get the data from the **hard disc** into the computer). Again, it is a case of buying the best you can afford. The ideal system might have one 3.5 inch and one 5.25 inch drive (both at the highest 1.4 Mb capacity) and a 40 Mb **hard disc** (300Mb for a massive data base). The minimum which I would aim for is a single 5.25 inch double density drive and a 20Mb **hard disc**. The increase in performance to be gained from a **hard disc** is well worth the relatively small additional cost.

Clock speed is just like the speed of car, double the **clock speed**, (approximately) and double the speed at which the computer runs. I do not think that this is something to worry too much about unless you are going to run number crunching programmes like big spread sheets. In most cases you will be working at a much slower rate than the computer.

Maths coprocessors are chips dedicated to doing arithmetic, they have to be matched to the **microprocessor** and can massively speed up processor intensive calculations. Typically cost between £100 and £300. The same comments apply here as for **clock speed**.

Let's take a number of different systems and look at typical prices (note typical not lowest). An 80286 machine with a mono

monitor and Hercules graphics card running at 12 MHz with a double density drive (3.5 or 5.25 inch) and a 30MB **hard disc** would now sell at £870, the same system with EGA card and colour **monitor**, £1000, and with VGA card and **monitor**, £1200 and an 80386 machine, additional **RAM**, VGA graphics card and **monitor**, running at 20MHz, with a high density drive (3.5 or 5.25 inch) and a fast 40MB **hard disc**, (OS/2 MCA **compatible** in addition), for £2700. All these will be cheaper second-hand. The price you pay is dependent on whether the manufacturer is a big well known company like Olivetti and Epson, or a small company buying parts in from the far east and assembling them in the UK. Things to look out for are the quality of the keyboard and casing. If they've skimped on five quid's worth of plastic who knows what has been skimped on inside. The feel of the keyboard is also very important for anyone who types at speed.

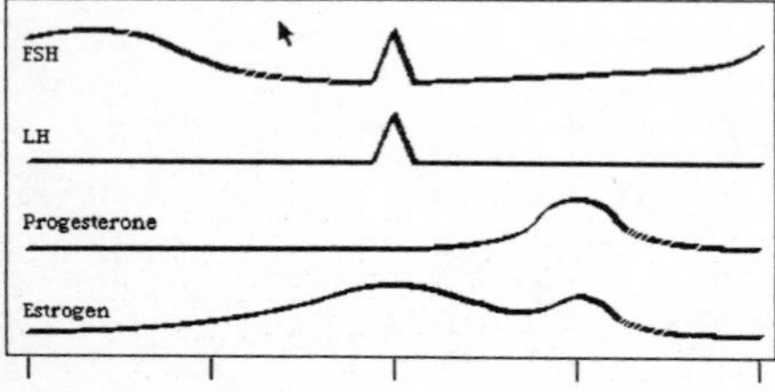

A menstrual cycle worked out on the computer whilst playing chess on the same computer (below)

This brings me on to *Amstrad* who have made their name by supplying at low cost. Here you have advantages of a large company product combined with low cost. The caveats are poor quality keyboards and **monitors**, but this is not such a problem with the newer Amstrads. Note that the PCW series are not IBM **compatible** and use 70's technology; they are very cheap (£315 to £439) and are great if all you need is a simple word processor, but if you want anything more, forget it. There is the PC 1512 range which have only 512k of **memory** rather than the more usual 640K. These are **compatible** with the 8 **bit** (8088 chip) (IBM XT) and, for a model with a single sided drive and mono **monitor**, the cost is £375. For slightly more money there is the 1640 range which have 640K of **memory**. There is also a range of Amstrad machines with the 16 **bit** (80286) chip and 32 **bit** (80386) chip. Prices for the 286 machine without **hard disc** start at £550, the 386 machines are less of a bargain, starting at £2400. As with all machines, try before you buy.

Hand held, Portable and Laptop Computers

The *Psion Organiser* is a good example of the hand held computers. They are about the same size as a FiloFax and serve much the same purpose: diary, financial planner, address book, etc. The basic machine costs £80 but cards can be purchased to add extra utilities such as financial functions or a dictionary. The cards cost between £12 and £50 each. In my opinion, you would be better off with a filofax and a French-English dictionary. By the time you've dug it out of the bag and worked out how to use it, you've forgotten what you wanted it for; they look stupid too. There are other hand held computers as well but Psion is the leader. One advantage is that you can (in theory) transfer data to a larger computer.

Portables and laptops can be divided into two groups. The first is the battery-operated, light-weight, fully-functional IBM **clone**; it is the size of a small briefcase and is comprised of an integral **hard disc**, a **floppy disc** drive, and full-size, fold-out, liquid-crystal screen. In general, portables and laptops tend to be more expensive than the full sized equivalent. Between these and the Psion, lie products like the *Cambridge Z88*. This is an A4-sized, less than 2lb computer with a 3 or 4 line screen on the same plane as the full size keyboard. It has a built in diary, alarm, calculator, word processor and spreadsheet. All are reasonably basic, but for about £200 you get a nicely laid out computer which is easy to use and data can be simply transferred to a full size computer. If you need a portable computer but cannot afford a laptop this is recommended option (though it helps to have access to a full-sized machine because the small screen of the Z88 renders some tasks tiresome).

▼ PRINTERS ▼

Once you have decided on a microcomputer, the next task is to chose a printer. This decision will be based on a combination of budget and intended use. If you want to produce booklets, newsletters or publicity material then, obviously, you will need a better quality printer than if you are primarily using it to print out invoices and keep track of the accounts.

The resolution of a printer is defined in terms of dots per inch (**dpi**); 70 **dpi** is about the minimum for computer printout and 300 **dpi** is near typeset quality. The principal options are as follows: a dot matrix (9 to 24 pin) printer, a daisywheel printer, an inkjet printer or a laser printer.

The cheapest is a 9 pin dot matrix printer; these are priced from £100 pounds. The dot matrix print head contains an array of 9 pins which, like a typewriter, make their impact on the paper through a ribbon; the characters or graphics are made up of a pattern of small dots. This leads to the slightly jagged quality of text printed by these printers, so called 'near letter quality' (NLQ). The resolution of this type of printer is typically of the order of 70 dots per inch (**dpi**). These printers are also slow and noisy.

Dot matrix printers with 24 pins print at 180-300 **dpi**; they have a much higher resolution than the 9 pin printers and they are faster. Prices for the 24 pin printers start at around £300 but most of the printers are in the £700-800 range.

A possible budget solution for high quality print is the daisy wheel printer. The daisy-wheel is analogous to the golf ball on an electric typewriter and the print quality is correspondingly good. The major drawback of this type of printer, other than its noise and slowness, is that, because one is limited to the characters on the daisy-wheel, the printer cannot handle any graphics. The cost of a new daisy-wheel printer starts at around £400, but second-hand printers are plentiful and considerably cheaper.

The lower cost alternative to a laser printer is an ink jet printer. The ink jet printer works by squirting a stream of ink onto the page. They are relatively fast, quiet and produce output of 200 - 300 **dpi**. Its main drawbacks are the high cost of ink cartridges (about 4p/page) and the water soluble ink which smudges easily unless a spray fixative is applied. The printers cost £250 to £600.

Laser printers are at the top of the line with output at 300 **dpi** and a speed of 6 to 12 pages per minute. The same technology used for photocopiers is employed for laser printers and the running costs are comparable (2-3p/page). They have their own **microprocessor** and **memory** and the more sophisticated laser printers use a page description language called **Postscript** which allows very complex, high quality typesetting and is **compatible** with typesetting machines. Prices start at about £800 for a not-very-robust machine, while most cost over £1,200 and £20,000 will buy a colour **Postscript** laser printer.

On a Macintosh the choice of printer is, for the most part, limited to Apple's own machines. However, printer drivers for other printers do exist, don't be put off by bullshit from the dealer. Look at advertisements in the specialist magazines.

▼ SOFTWARE ▼

The utility of the computer lies in the software (as opposed to the hardware which is the machine itself). Software is also referred to as the programmes or the applications. A very important part of deciding what computer to buy must lie in what software is available for it. If you have only a single or limited use for a computer, this should be your major deciding factor. Go to a dealer's and see the software in action. Talk to other people who have used the programmes and read the software reviews (see magazines).

Word processors are programmes which allow you to type documents. The text appears on the screen and is saved on **disc**. You can change portions of text, move them round, print out multiple copies with slight variations and do 'mail merge' (where 500 people will get the same letter but addressed to them personally). The more sophisticated packages will allow multiple columns, mixed text and graphics, '**w**hat **y**ou **s**ee (on screen) **i**s **w**hat **y**ou **g**et (on the printer)' (wysiwyg), a built in thesaurus and a spelling checker, find and replace utilities, contents and index generator and more. Word processors cost anywhere between £30 and £300

Page layout programmes are used to typeset text, graphics and photographs for output on a laserprinter or typesetting machine. You get fine control over all aspects of the page layout. These programmes tend to be expensive if they are any good. Expect to pay over £200 for anything worth having, even though there are products available for as little as £20.

Graphics programmes This covers a multitude of sins, from drawing programmes which will let you make a plan of your house to full fledged **CAD/CAM** which will let you produce complete blueprints for an international airport. Prices vary accordingly, from £30 to £3000. Whereas drawing programmes are object based (manipulation of lines, squares, circles, etc), painting programmes are pixel based; the manipulation is at the level of the smallest dot on screen or printer. Output from this sort of package is usually more 'organic' looking, more like a painting than a technical drawing. Prices are in the range of £20 to £300, £100 is about average. There are also specialist programmes for graph drawing, printed circuit board design, yacht sail design and who-knows-what-else.

Database programmes allow large quantities of information to be accessed easily. For example, if you had the details of 20 thousand employees and their favourite recipes, you could retrieve the names of people working for you who earn over £20,000 pa and whose favourite food is beans on toast. Database costs vary with capabilities: £50-£600 and £100 worth should serve most purposes.

Spread sheets are like dynamic graph paper. With a properly set-up spreadsheet any sort of financial accounting can be done neatly and accurately with a huge saving in time. Spread sheets are also ideal for statistical and data analyses. They cost about £50-£300, with the most useful being at the higher end of this range.

Programming Languages are how you write your own software which you or other people can use. It is easy to write small programmes but anything remotely commercial will almost certainly take a lot of experience and development time. There is a plethora of languages, but the most common microcomputer languages are BASIC, PASCAL and C. These either come free with the machine (usually BASIC) or can be bought. BASIC is a good place to start, but if you have to buy a language I would suggest PASCAL because it is a more powerful language although is not much more difficult to learn than BASIC. Languages cost in the range of £30-£100, though obscure languages can be more.

Emulators are deserving of at least an honourable mention in this section. Emulators are software packages which allow one brand of computer to behave like another: to make an Archimedes or an Atari behave like a Mac. The problem with much of this software is that the emulation is never perfect and the **floppy** drives may not be **compatible** so you have to connect the machine you are emulating to the machine doing the emulating in order to transfer the programme. Some emulators are not worth the bother. Try before you buy.

There are plenty of other types of software packages from text recognition to astrology and pools predictors, but most of the commonest types are described above. In all cases before buying, try to find someone who uses the package, or at least read the reviews in the computing press (see magazines).

At this point, I would like to give a mention to Shareware, Freeware and Public Domain (PD) software. This, in contrast to commercial software, is freely distributed on bulletin boards and user groups or sold by the **disc** full for a nominal sum by specialist companies. This is usually (but not always) software that is not written to as high a standard as commercial software. PD and Freeware are, as the names suggest, free; PD is in the public domain and you can do with it whatever you want, including changing the code; although Freeware is free, the copyright still resides with the author and there are are limitations on what you can do with it. Shareware is software sold on an honesty system. You are encouraged to try it and if you continue to use it you are expected to send some money to the author.

▼ COMPUTERS ON THE CHEAP ▼

There are a number of ways to decrease the cost of your computing. One place to look for low priced hardware is in the back of computer magazines (see the *Magazine* section below). The prices will be up to 50% less than the recommended retail price (RRP) and it is often possible to reduce the cost even further by ringing round and playing one dealer off against another. (Ring Shop A and say "B offered me £X for this product, what can you do?", then ring Shop B back or Shop C and say "A will sell it for £X. . .").

Educational discount is also an excellent way of getting inexpensive computers. If you are in an educational institution (even evening classes will do), or have a friend who is, you are in business. Some companies require an official order from the institute, or one on the institutetion's headed notepaper, while others (e.g. Apple) only require you to fill in one of their forms and get it signed by a professor or head of department (people who attend the University of Life have been known to try using their flat mate). The savings can be substantial. Here are a couple of Apple examples. Mac Plus RRP £1250, educational price £850; Mac SE 30 4/40, RRP about £4300, educational price £2500. The second-hand prices for Macs are higher than the educational prices. Normally educational prices can only be obtained from authorised dealers. An alternative way to purchase from the big name brands like IBM and Apple is to buy from 'grey importers'. These grey import companies buy from the United States where prices are lower and resell in the UK for less than UK authorised dealers. If you use these companies the warranty and after sales service may be reduced (but the money you save will probably offset this).

If you really know what you are doing then it is possible save a lot of money by building your own IBM **compatible** from the various component boards; many of the smaller **clone** makers are doing just this themselves. One way to start **clone** building is by reading the article "Build your own PC" in issue 17 (July 1989) of *Computer Shopper*.

If you know what you are looking for and its second-hand price you should be able to find some real bargains at computer auctions. Auctions are advertised in the *Micro Computer Mart* magazine and catalogues can normally be obtained for a SAE. Be warned that not all that is sold at an auction is as described in the catalogue (I recently bought a so-called **modem** that turned out to be a printer sharing device) so examine carefully anything you are planning to purchase. Because there are a lot of idiots about who will bid more than the item is worth, it is really important to decide beforehand how much you should to spend. Auctioneers often sell stuff independently of their auctions. The prices tend to be trade wholesale and are often very good value. If you are not sure what you are doing, this is probably a better bet than bidding at an auction.

Another source of inexpensive, new and second-hand, computer equipment is

■ **Morgan Computers**, *64-72 New Oxford Street, London WC1, (01-255-2115)* (at their other shop they sell cameras). Examples: new, discontinued dot matrix printers, RRP £460, for £75, new Postscript laser printers, RRP £4000, selling for £2000. Be aware that not everything that Morgan sells is a bargain; learn the retail prices before making a purchase.

Second-hand bargains can also be found in the classified advertisements in various magazines.

For some reason software is invariably dearer in the UK than in the USA. One way around this is to buy directly from the USA. Look in the magazine advertisements for mail order companies. You can purchase by phone if you are willing to quote your credit card number and packages are delivered by Federal Express (3 days) or Airmail (10-18 days). The advantage of airmail is that, in addition to being cheaper, there is chance that you won't get billed for the 7% duty and the VAT; if Federal Express deliver you will be sure to pay these. Price differentials between the UK and USA can be horrendous, the worse I have seen is a five-fold difference between the US mail order price and the UK price. More typical is a $=£ equivalence between US and UK prices.

▼ COMPUTER MAINTENANCE ▼

Computer maintenance is expensive, but if your computer breaks down, what can you do? For better or worse, here are a couple of companies:

■ **Da Vinci Computers**, *Unit 3, Graham Park Way NW9 5QY(200-8787.* charge £50/hour for rapid on site repair.

■ **Bell & Watson**, *Technology House, Unit 4, Sheraton Business centre, Wadsworth Close, Perivale Middlesex, UB6 7JB (997-6068).* Offer maintenance contracts Eg £275/year for IBM and printer. Promise to get you up and running in 24hrs and this fee includes the cost of all parts and labour.

▼ COMPUTER SECURITY ▼ VIRUSES AND BACKING UP

Many types of systems for keeping data private and secure involve passwords but perhaps the best way to keep sensitive material secure is simply by saving it on a

floppy disc and locking it in a safe place.

Of more concern to most people will be secure backing up of data and programmes. Both **hard** and **floppy discs** are fallible and, if the data on them is lost, you may lose hours, days or years of work. Never use the original programme **disc**, keep it in safe place; always work from a copy of the programme (the exception to this rule is copy protected software). Make copies of anything important on at least two **discs** and keep them in separate places (the editors of this book keep their back-up **discs** in a safe deposit box). There are programmes which will copy the contents of a **hard disc** onto a series of **floppy discs** so that they can be restored to a reformatted **hard disc** if necessary. Hard **disc** back-up should be a weekly exercise, thus no more than a week's work could be lost. A more expensive solution to backing up is a 'tape streamer'. Anything written to the **hard disc** is automatically copied to the tape, the oldest material is written over, in this way, there is always an up to date copy of the **hard disc** available on tape. These systems start at about £200.

There are companies which specialise in recovering data from damaged **discs**. You pay on the basis of the results and they are expensive.

Viruses and **Trojan Horses** are something to worry about if your computer is promiscuous (most are). Written by malicious people, these nasty programmes copy themselves onto your **disc** and cause varying degrees of damage, ranging from a happy Christmas message on Christmas day to wiping your **hard disc** while showing you some animated naked women. There are programmes available which protect you from **viruses** and check **discs** for their presence. It is always worth checking any new software or **disc** you are given for the presence of **viruses**.

▼ RENTAL▼

Computer renting is a better deal for companies who can write the whole cost off against tax, than for individuals. However, if you need a scanner or laser printer for that important project, rental may be a more cost effective solution than a bureau which charges by the page.

■ **CCA MicroRentals**, *Unit 7&8, Imperial Studios, Imperial Rd. SW6 2AG; phone (731-4310.)* Will rent or lease an IBM or Mac. Prices depend on rental period. MacII £500 per month.

■ **MicroRent**, *Unit 1, St.Marks Studios, Chillingworth Rd, N7 8QJ; (700-4848).* This is an excellent company who will rent you a **memory** upgrade for your Macintosh or rent you a complete **networked** system. If you are an existing customer they will often let take equipment or software out for a day or two on evaluation. IBM PS2/30 £39/day or £79/week.

▼ NETWORKS ▼

Networks are the connection of several microcomputers in order that a person working on one machine can access **files** and software held on another. In some cases one machine serves as a 'file server' and is dedicated to distributing **files** between the other machines. Networking is worthy of an article on its own and there is not space to go into it here. If you need to set up a **network** , it is a case of reading reviews and talking to different dealers. For a large system (bigger than 4 machines say), it might be worth hiring a **network** consultant.

▼ COMMUNICATION ▼ BULLETIN BOARDS AND MODEMS

If you want your computer to talk to the outside world, you will need a **modem** (short for modulator/demodulator) and a phone line (the cost is about 50p/hour for off-peak local calls). A **modem** is a device that sits between your computer and a phone socket. With the appropriate software, which is usually in the public domain or comes free with the **modem**, the **modem** allows you to communicate with other remote computers, to access remote databases such as Prestel and Telecom Gold, to play multi-user games (an expensive pastime) and connect to computer bulletin boards (**BBS**s). **BBS**s are computers set up to receive and store messages. After you have connected to a **BBS** you will see a welcome screen and a list of 'rooms', the areas containing discussions on different topics. You can read the messages which previous callers have left and then you can leave your own contributions for subsequent callers to read and reply to. Discussions take place on a very wide variety of subjects from computer hardware and programming to lonely hearts and philosophy; the choice of topics depends on the sysop (system operator who runs the **BBS**) and the interests of the callers. **BBS**s also give you access to a wealth of computer expertise; if you have a computer problem, leave a message describing it and there is a good chance that someone who knows the solution will read and reply to your message. Another aspect of bulletin boards is 'downloading' or transferring programs and other **files** from the **BBS** to your own computer. Many of the programmes will be Shareware and some will be written by the **BBS** callers themselves. Be especially wary of **virus**es though, don't download a **virus** with your new programme). **BBS**s can be divided into three broad categories: non-commercial, semi-commercial and commercial. The non-commercial **BBS** is likely to be set up by an enthusiast in his bedroom just for the fun of it. This variety of **BBS** often have special interest 'echoes' which range from cooking to astronomy to women's issues (plus the usual computer stuff). These echoes go round the world, normally to the USA, but often to the rest of Europe and Australia as well, according to the diligence/wealth of the sysop running the **BBS**. The semi-commercial category will either exist primarily as a vehicle for selling or will only allow limited access to non-subscribers (e.g. free access to the mail and discussion areas but no downloading privileges). The commercial **BBS**s such as CIX and Telecom Gold are often held on mainframe computers and let you access huge amounts of information. With Telecom Gold you can send private electronic mail to other subscribers, find the cheapest airline tickets, order train tickets and flowers by InterFlora, and many other useful services. There is normally a monthly subscription charge (£5 for Telecom Gold) and an additional charge for every minute that you are connected.

The **modem** is needed to connect your computer to the phone line and a number of types of **modem** are available. The speed of the **modem** determines the rate at which you can transmit and receive information. The standard speeds (in baud or **bits**/second) are V21 (300 baud), V23 (1200 baud in/ 75 baud out), V22 (1200 baud), V22bis (2400 baud) and higher. At present most systems support V21, V23 (UK only), V22 and V22bis. Higher speed **modem**s are not so widely supported because of their greater cost (£600-£1500). Another consideration in choosing a **modem** is Hayes compatibility. Hayes is a manufacturer of (expensive) **modem**s and their **modem** control language has become a standard. Only the very cheapest **modems**, manual **modems**, do not have any degree of Hayes compatibility. A Hayes **compatible modem** supporting V21 and V22 is a good beginner's **modem**, and they are priced from about £100. Because these cheaper **modems** are often imported, they do not usually support the UK, V23 standard; this is not really a problem as most services which support V23 also support V22. A **modem** that also supports V22bis will cost from £200. **Modems** are connected to the telephone system and therefore are legally required to be British Telecom approved. The prices quoted above (V22 and V22bis) are for non-BT approved **modems**; BT approved **modem**s cost considerably more. When buying a **modem** from the USA, be certain that it supports the CCIT standard. Most **modem**s support both the UK CCIT and the US Bell standard; however, some of the cheapest Hayes **compatible modem**s from the USA ($60!) only support the Bell standard.

Telephone numbers

- **Telecom Gold and Prestel** *(voice): 0800-200700(both), (822-1122(Prestel)), (406-6777(TG).)*

On line numbers

- **Body Matters** (medical **BBS**)*: (603-7581)*
- **CIX** (expensive computer freak and financial service, asks for your credit card number the first time you log on)*:(399-5252.)*
- **Co-Op Board** (Co-operatives **BBS**): *(316-6488)*
- **Crystal Tower** (good general **BBS**): *(886-2813)*
- **Kybernesis** (Church and Charity **BBS**): *(673-7294)*
- **MacTel Metro** (Macintosh **BBS**): *(543-8017)*
- **Organic Garden** (Gardening **BBS**): *(464-3305)*
- **Pink Triangle** (Gay and Lesbian **BBS**): *(963-0496)*
- **Star Base One** (Astronomy **BBS**): *(738-7225)*

See Listing at the back of *Personal Computer World* for more numbers.

▼ SCANNERS AND FAX CARDS ▼

Fax cards are related to **modem**s. They allow you to turn your computer into a budget Fax machine. Some will only let you send Faxes, others let you both send and receive and more sophisticated models will also function as a Hayes **compatible modem**. Costs for Fax cards are between £200 and £350.

Fax cards will only send material that you have typed or drawn on the computer, unless you have a scanner. A scanner is a device to digitise documents and transfer them into the computer where they can be manipulated or sent as a Fax. The most basic scanners are hand-held and only read in black and white. The major limitations with this scanner are the steady hand needed to scan and the problem that images over 4 inches wide cannot be entered in a single scan. However, scanners are more than toys, a good portion of the art work in this book was scanned using a hand-held scanner. Prices are between £150 and £300. Flat bed scanners can cope with A4 size images; like a photocopier, the document is placed on top of the scanning device. The cost of a basic black and white flat bed scanner starts at about £600 and scanners capable of many grey scales and/or colour can cost up to £3000 or £4000.

▼ MAGAZINES ▼

There are a number of microcomputer magazines that are worth reading, either for learning current prices or to familiarise yourself with the technology and jargon. There are also specialist magazines for individual machines.

For prices and some reviews the monthlies, *What Micro* and *Computer Shopper* are good. More in the mold of *Exchange and Mart* and a little down market, is the fortnightly, *Micro Computer Mart*.

For general reading and reviews, there is nothing to touch *Personal Computer World*. This magazine also includes a monthly *Focus* supplement which deals in depth with a particular topic and gives a detailed product list. Another excellent general magazine is *Byte* from the US.

Most magazines are produced for users of specific brands of computers such as Atari, Amstrad, Macs, Acorn etc. They are useful to look at if you are thinking of buying a particular computer, or if you have bought the computer and want to know more about getting the most from it.

Specifically for Macintosh fans, there is *MacUser* and a number of free subscription magazines. None of them are very good and your money would be better spent on the US magazine *MacWorld*. Both *MacWorld* and *Byte* are available from **Harrods** and the larger branches of **W.H.Smiths**.

▼ USER GROUPS ▼

There are a number of user groups dedicated to individual machines or interests. These are invaluable if you wish to get the most out of your machine, particularly if you are an isolated computer user. They are normally non-profit organisations run by enthusiasts and you will probably get much more help from them than from your dealer. There is not enough space here to list all of them but there is an extensive list at the back of the *Personal Computer World* magazine.

▼ SPECIAL NEEDS ▼ EDUCATIONAL, ELDERLY & DISABLED COMPUTER USERS

There are a number of computer aids to help the mentally and physically handicapped. Examples are touch boards, educational software and large displays for partially sighted people. More information can be obtained from charities and support groups. Also contact Jeff Hughes at the **Special Needs User group**, *39 Eccleston Gardens, St Helens, WA10 3BJ; phone 0744-24608*.

Educational users can contact Charles Shannon, **TECUG**, *35 Wellington St., Gravesend, Kent, DA12 1JG; phone 0474-567931*.

Older people who have not previously come into contact with computers will probably benefit from using a computer with a graphical interface such as a Macintosh, Atari or Amiga. For more information contact Mark ramsden, Computer Manager, **Age Concern England**, *60 Pitcairn Road, Mitcham, Surrey, CR4 3LL; (640-5431)*.

▼ THE JARGON ▼

In order to defend yourself from the bullshit artists, you have to know the jargon. So here are some of the common buzz words.

BBS are computers set up to receive and store messages. After you have connected to a **BBS** you will see a welcome screen and a list of 'rooms', the areas containing discussions on different topics. You can read the messages which previous callers have left and then you can leave your own contributions for subsequent callers to read and reply to. Discussions take place on a very wide variety of subjects from computer hardware and programming to lonely hearts and philosophy; the choice of topics depends on the sysop (see **Communications** Section p246).

Bit See **memory**.

Byte See **memory**

CAD/CAM Term applied to computer aided design, usually of sophisticated nature.

CPU This stands for central processor unit, the brain of a computer. The more sophisticated the **CPU** is, the more it can do and the faster it can do it. There are two main players in the game. Motorola have a series of CPUs 68000, 68020, 68030. These are found at the heart of Atari and Apple Macintosh computers. Intel (and Intel copiers) make the CPU series found in IBM PCs and **clones**; these are the 8088, V20, V40, 8086, V30, 80186, 80286 and 80386.

Clock speed This is measured in MHz (megaHertz) or millions of cycles per second and it is simply the speed at which the computer runs. If two machines have the same CPU, one running at 24 MHz should perform an operation twice as fast as one running at 12 MHz. This is only a rule of thumb because other factors such as **disc drive speed** also affect the speed.

Clone A **clone** is the term applied to a computer made by one manufacturer which is a copy of another manufacturer's machine; they are often cheaper and/or faster than the original. The word **clone** is most often applied to copies of IBM PCs.

Compatible Another word for **clone**. An IBM **compatible** is an IBM **clone**.

Disc See hard and floppy discs.

dpi A measure of screen or printer resolution, dots per inch.

DTP Desk top publishing, producing publication quality material using a computer and peripherals. A system that really lives up to the name will cost between £5000-£10,000.

Hard and floppy discs Both **hard** and **floppy discs** are magnetic **discs** which spin rapidly to allow fast transfer of information between the computer and the **disc**. **floppy discs** are about ten times slower than **hard discs**; typically they hold 0.4-1.5 Mb. They are cheap (50p-£2.50 depending on format) and, by virtue of being removable from the 'drive' mechanism that reads them, they are portable. Hard **discs** are fast and have a much higher storage capacity, typically 10-300 Mb. They are not normally portable and they are relatively expensive (£150-£2000, depending on capacity, and on which computer they are designed for). On the other hand, you normally only need one **hard disc** per computer. There are storage devices called Bernoulli boxes which combine the portability of floppies with the capacity of **hard discs**, but they are expensive and not as fast as **hard discs**.

Maths Coprocessor are chips dedicated to doing arithmetic, they have to be matched to the **microprocessor** and can massively speed up processor intensive calculations.

Memory is where a computer stores the results of its calculations. Computer **memory** is usually measured in **bits** or **bytes**, there are 8 bits to one **byte** (one **byte** will often store one typewritten character or one pixel on the screen) and is normally quoted in multiples of (approximately) a thousand, (kilo**bytes**) kb, a million, (mega**byte**) Mb, or more rarely, a thousand million, (giga**byte**) Gb. There are three types of **memory** associated with all computers, **RAM**, **ROM** and storage.

Microprocessor is the part of a computer which does all of the calculations, the brain of the computer.

Modem is a device that sits between your computer and a phone socket. With the appropriate software a **modem** allows you to communicate with other remote computers.

Monitor The screen that is used with a computer; it is usually of higher resolution than a television set. Also called video display unit (VDU).

Network See *Networks*.

Peripheral Any device that connects to the computer, e.g. scanners, printers, **monitors** etc.

Postscript A page description language licenced by Adobe inc. which is used in high resolution printers and typesetters to give very high resolution printed output independent (to some degree) of the computer software outputting the information.

RAM stands for random access **memory** and is like words written on a blackboard. They can be rewritten and erased over and over again. This is the **memory** that the computer uses to store the results of its calculations, its instructions and what to print on the screen. As a general rule the more **RAM** that you have in your computer the more it can do (there are exceptions, sometimes the computer does not realise that there is extra **RAM** available). The more colours you have on your screen the more **memory** you need. If you have a black and white **monitor**, the computer only has to store '0 or 1' for each pixel. If you have 256 colours available the computer has to store 0 or 1 or 2 . . . 256. **RAM** is erased when you turn your computer off.

ROM stands for 'read only **memory**'. It is like the printed word; it cannot be erased and **ROM** is put into the computer by the manufacturer so that the machine knows what to do when you first turn it on and can do the necessary 'internal housekeeping'.

Scanner A device for digitising two dimensional images so that they may be put into a computer for manipulation.

Storage Although there are other more arcane media, the term storage is most often applied to **floppy discs** and **hard discs**. This is where the computer stores the results of its calculations (it 'writes to' and 'reads from' its storage medium). **Discs** work in the same way as audio tape and, in the early days, ordinary cassette tape was often used as computer storage. Data stored on **disc** does not disappear when the power is turned off and stays until you 'write over it' or wave a dirty great electro-magnet (like a ringing phone) over it. Unlike audio tape, where an extraneous crackle in the middle of a song is a minor irritation, the data on a **disc** can easily be corrupted and rendered unreadable by an extraneous crackle. This means that you should always back-up (make duplicates of) any important work or programs.

Trojan Horse See virus.

Virus A small programme which is designed to copy and attach itself to other programmes in order to cause varying of damage. A **Trojan Horse** is a similar programme to a virus. It looks as if it does one thing but when it is run it does something completely different, usually to destroy or severely damage the system.

phone

*f**rom the 6th May 1990* 01 *for London will disappear. Either* 071 *)or (*081*) will replace* 01. 071 *will be the new prefix for all exchanges in the inner zone, an area of roughly four miles radius from Charing Cross, extended in the east to include the Docklands. All exchanges in the outer zone will be prefixed by* 081. *You will have to use the prefix when dialling out if the zone you are dialling from is different from the zone of the number you are dialling e.g. if you wish to dial an* 071 *number and your prefix is* 081 *then you must use the prefix* 081 *before you dial the seven figure London number. For a period after the change, recorded announcements will inform callers who have neglected to dial the prefix. British Telecom (BT) have already issued a leaflet showing the new prefix for each exchange. For further information call (0800 800873).*

▼ INSTALLATION ▼

The time it takes to have a new line installed varies from exchange to exchange. Businesses have priority over residential subscribers, and in some areas a new business line can be installed in as little as 7 days. It is also possible to wait nine months for a residential line.

BT has exclusive rights to supply the master box when a new residential line is installed. New residential subscribers, particularly tenants, will in all probability have to pay a deposit, returnable after one year provided that bills have been paid. A new residential line costs £105 + VAT to install and £13.95 + VAT per quarter rental. You do not have to rent your phone from BT. The quarterly rental for the phone itself is £3 + VAT, so buying one pays for itself in a few years. However if the phone handset breaks down, if it's not rented from BT, they won't fix it. The cheapest place we've found to buy a telephone handset (and answering machine) is:

■ **Age Electronics,** *Galaxy Audio Visual, 230 Tottenham Court Rd, W1 (631 0036).*

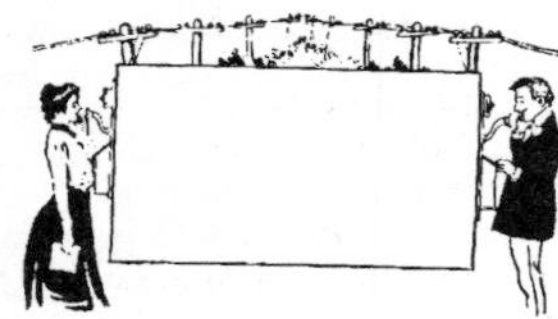

Charges

If your phone has been out of order, then remember to claim credit on the rental charge for that period. You should ask the operator at the time it occurs for credit on mis-connections.

When an existing subscriber moves house, transfer of the old number costs £21 + VAT.

Business subscribers pay more than domestic subscribers: installation of line costs £115 + VAT and £22.55 + VAT per quarter rental. If your business moves it costs £100 + VAT for a new number. But business subscribers have an alternative to BT which is Mercury.

Mercury

Mercury offer residential, business, telex, fax and paging services like BT, only 15% to 20% cheaper. For £8 a year, residential subscribers can join Mercury. With a phone supplied by, or compatible, with Mercury (i.e. one equipped with a special button), domestic phone users can plug into Mercury via a *pin* number in the telephone's memory, and make trunk and international calls cheaper than BT calls. However, Mercury cannot be used by residential subscribers for local calls. Mercury's bills are itemised. For more information contact

■ **Mercury Communications Ltd,** *90 Long Acre, WC2 (528 2000).*

▼ OBSCENE ▼
PHONE CALLS

These can be extremely distressing and there are about 8 million a year in Britain. To minimise the risk, women are advised not to give their forenames in the phone book or other publicly available directories. Unless it is absolutely essential, don't be gender specific if placing an advert. Better still use a box number which most newspapers and magazines offer to advertisers even though it costs more than quoting a phone number. Avoid saying the number to incoming callers. Do not answer a caller who asks 'what number is this?'. Instead ask which number the person dialled, then say whether she is right or wrong. Never give your address unless you are sure of the caller's identity. If an obscene caller does ring, hang up without saying anything or communicating any emotion (e.g. indrawn breath) which might play along with his fantasy. Some obscene callers begin with an apparently innocent conversation, such as pretending to be market researchers. Again hang up *gently* as soon as the obscenity starts.

If troubled by a persistent pervert, an answering machine with a speaker helps. Set the machine to come on after several rings, so that you know there is an incoming call. The obscene caller is unlikely to leave a message. If it's a friend and she starts to leave a message you will be able to hear her through the speaker. Pick up the receiver and talk to her, the machine should cut off automatically. Alternatively, BT will intercept calls you ask them, but only on phones on digital exchanges. This service is free if the obscene caller is persistent. BT's definition of persistent is once a day over three or four days, or once or twice a week over a few weeks. The police say they treat reports of obscene calls 'seriously' and can ask BT to trace calls where the system is digital. The last resort for women harassed by a persistent caller is to pay BT to change their number. It will be at least ten years before equipment used in the USA to show the number from which an incoming call originate will be available in the UK. Two other useful tactics are:

• Keep a whistle by the phone and give a good blast down the line.

• Pretend the line is very bad and you can't hear what he is saying, 'You've got a twelve inch *what*?'. This tactic empowers you, by giving you more control over the situation.

▼ FREEPHONE ▼

Calls to numbers listed as freephone or beginning with 0800 are free. 0800 numbers can be dialled direct: for Freephone numbers call the operator on 100 and ask for the freephone number.

▼ COMPLAINTS ▼

Two independent organisations deal with complaints.

■ **The Office of Telecommunications,** *Atlantic Hse, Holborn Viaduct, EC1 (353 4020).*

■ **Telephone Users Association,** *48 Percy Rd, N12 (445 0996)* (write rather than phone).

▼ CORDLESS PHONES ▼

These cost between £80 and £140 but can be operated legally only within 200 metres of their base. They may be taken into the garden or even to the corner shop, but not in the car or to the office if these are likely to be more than 200m away. Cordless phones are both receivers and transmitters and are consequently the easiest system to intercept.

▼ CELLULAR PHONES ▼

Racal Vodephone and Cellnet, which is part of BT, operate the cellular networks,which are not compatible. The phones cost anything between £300 and £2000 and will work all over the country, topography permitting. Calls cost 46p minute to dial out and to dial into a cellular phone costs 33p minute.

▼ GADGETS ▼

Almost all the incredible array of gadgets currently available are BT approved. Among the most useful are:

• **Call logging equipment** which prints out all numbers called, duration and cost of each call. (It does not solve disputes over bills in shared houses as effectively as pay phones though, but it is less expensive than pay phones and if you can come to amicable agreements are therefore cheaper).

• **Connecting kits and socket doublers,** costing around £10.50, allow old style answering machines to be fitted to new style sockets. This is cheaper than asking BT to refit the machine (call out charge around £15) and much cheaper than buying new one.

• **Headsets** - so hands can be kept free and callers can be heard in noisy environments.

There are many adaptions for callers with special needs, though some seem pricey for those on disability pensions. A nodule on the figure 5 in the middle of the pad on push button phones helps blind people to dial out. For the partially sighted there are extra large pads and 10 number memory in the phone.

• **For the hard-of-hearing,** phones are fitted with a flashing light instead of a bell, or the bell can be amplified. For people who cannot speak loudly enough to be heard on the phone the *Claudius Converse* has coded messages including requests for assistance programmed into the machine, and the messages can be adapted, at a price, for each user.

• **Carephones** are for frail, usually elderly people living alone. There is a device you can wear round your neck with a button on it and a special button on the phone itself. When either is pressed, three selected people are phoned automatically and given the message that assistance is needed. Details of these and other equipment are available from

■ **Alternative Telephones,** *Shop 1, The Shopping Centre, Shepherds Bush, W12 (740 7733).*

International Directories

■ **Westminster Central Reference Library,** *35 St. Martins St, WC2 (798 2034)* has international directories for most big cities throughout the world; they'll give you numbers over the phone.

networks

everyone has met someone who met someone who met someone - and that chain of contacts potentially reaches everyone else on the planet. Networking is the use of formal informal links to exchange information, which may be the sort regarded as subversive or cranky by official organisations and withheld by the mainstream media.
See also Computers p###.

▼ WHAT ARE ▼ NETWORKS

Networks can be so loose as to be invisible, or formal. The formal ones, such as those listed below, exist to bring together people who have interests or experience in common, locally, nationally and globally. At their most mundane, networks resemble clubs, and may offer little more than a monthly meeting with a guest speaker. They also parallel the 'old boy network' by providing opportunities to work for or with other members. Goods and services obtained through networks are as variable in quality as those obtained any other way. At their best, networks combat isolation, promote co-operation and shared action.

▼ HOW THEY ▼ WORK

Networks generally charge an annual subscription to cover the costs of circulating information and, in some cases, an administrator's time. Ideally, they are non-hierarchical and flexible, though inevitably the most active members exert the strongest influence. Contacts are established and maintained through newsletters, directories of members, conferences, workshops etc. Additional charges are usually made for events.

▼ STARTING A ▼ NETWORK

• Check it does not already exist

• Be clear what it is about and who it is for, but

• Be prepared to start small and grow organically - if it expands beyond your initial vision, the way the network operates may need to change.

• set a subscription rate that covers administration time as well as direct costs, and have the subs paid by standing order

• set up a bank account and keep full financial records as members need to know what happened to their money

• connect as much as possible with other networks

■ **GreenNet,** *26 Underwood St, N1 (490 1510)* is a 'global computer network for environment, peace and human rights'. For people with a personal computer and a modem, its services include electronic mailing, computer conferences and databases. £30 deposit, monthly minimum charge of £5 and connect time at 9p per minute. M'ship over 3000). Open to groups and individuals.

■ **Business Network,** *18 Well Walk, NW3* founded in 1982, 'aims to develop a more holistic approach to business practice and informs and encourages those seeking to humanise and to green their business lives'.

■ **Findhorn Foundation,** (see p###).

■ **One Earth Network of Resource People,** comprises over 170 people in 34 countries who have been part of the Findhorn Community and provide information about the Foundation and 'new consciousness' activities. London resource people include *David Platts, 25 Chomeley Lodge, N6* and *Andrew Ferguson, The Breakthrough Centre, 7 Poplar Mews, Uxbridge Rd, W12.*

■ **Women's Environmental Network,** *287 City Rd, EC1* is 'a non-profit organisation, educating, informing and empowering women who care about the environment.' Men are welcome to join, but the organisation is staffed by women and examines issues of environment, health, ecology and aid from a woman's perspective.

■ **Sophia Network,** *2 Gondar Mansions, Mill Lane, NW6* 'brings together women who are interested in symbol myth and archetype, who draw from it in their creative work, or who want to explore what lies behind the power of the mythic.'

■ **Scientific Medical Network,** *The Old School House, Hamnett, Northleach, Glos GL54 3NN, (0451 60869).* Doctors, scientists, philosophers and others interested in 'Acknowledging the relevance of intuitive and spiritual scientists, insights...' thinking beyond orthodox materialism'. Run the annual *May Lectures* on parapsychology. Issues around health , mysticism and forces for change. Newsletter. M'ship by invitation. Also address for **IANDS (UK) The international Association for Near-Death studies.**

finding information

Its possible to find information on just about anything if you persist. Not only are there regular public libraries and specialist libraries there are also commercial organisations willing to supply information free and over the phone. If you can't find the information from organisations listed elsewhere in this book then you may find it through one of the organisations listed here.

▼ BOOKSHOPS ▼

There are hundreds of bookshops in London - general, secondhand and those who specialise in subjects from Eastern Europe to detective fiction. Many of the large general bookshops are chain stores and have a number of branches within London (generally in the town centre): the bright and snappy **Books etc**, the well-stocked **Waterstones**, the populist **Claude Gill**, and the upper-crust **Hatchards**. It's difficult to miss these if you are in town. However, below we list some of the independent, smaller bookshops which offer specialist sections in radical or unusual subjects.

For specialist bookshops see also relevant section: **Green Environment** (p280); **Ethnic Minorities** (p234); **Lesbian & Gay** (p186); **Kids** (p227); **Martial Arts** (p173); **Agitation** (p219); **Self Discovery** (p155).

General

■ **Compendium,** *234 Camden High St, NW1 (485 8944/267 1525).* 10-6 M-S, Sun 12-6. Mail order. Large selection of books on a large range of subjects: philosophy, politics, ecology,

modern music, media, women's studies, poetry, psychology, astrology, occult, and they stock 'small press' titles. The staff here are surely among the friendliest and most helpful of the large London bookshops. Noticeboard.

■ **Bush Books and Records,** *113 Shepherds Bush Centre, W12* (749 7652). Mon -Fri 10-6, Sat 10-5.30. General books in wide area. Classical records, mostly CD's.

■ **Collets International,** *129 Charing Cross Rd, WC2 (734 0782).* 10-6.30. Large range: feminism, left politics, international sections. Branch in Gt Russell St.

■ **Crouch End Books,** *60 Crouch End Hill, N8 (348 8966).* 9-6. Large s/h section. General, fiction, feminist, politics, gay sections.

■ **Fagins,** *76 Upper St, N1 (359 4699).* M-Sat 10-10. Good general range.

■ **Kilburn Bookshop,** *8 Kilburn Bridge, Kilburn High Rd, NW6 (328 7071).* 9.30-5.30. Children's multicultural books, feminist, black studies, Irish, gay. Noticeboard for community concerns.

■ **Red and Green Books,** *144 Churchfield Rd, W3 (992 6029).* M-Sat 10-6 closed 2.30-3.30. Politics, ecology, peace, socialism, women's issues, fiction, lesbian and gay fiction, children's multi-cultural books, bargain books. OU set books. T-shirts, cards. Noticeboard.

■ **Village Books,** *17 Shrubbery Rd, SW16 (677 2667).* M-Sat 10.30-7 except Weds when closed. Strong on fiction, women. S/h books. Noticeboard.

Community

■ **The Bookplace,** *13 Peckham High St, SE15 (701 1757).* 10-6, shut Th. Black literature, kids, welfare rights, women, local books . Kids booklist free with sae. Small s/h section.

■ **Centerprise,** *136-138 Kingsland Rd, E8 (254 9632).* Tu-Sat 10.30-5.30. Women's fiction/ non fiction, sociology, politics, black fiction/non fiction, specialises in children books, especially multicultural, and local books published by their own project. Will do bookstalls. Coffee bar, advice centre and meeting rooms on premises.

■ **East End Bookshop,** *178 Whitechapel Rd, E1 (247 0216).* T-F 9.30-5.30, Sat 9.30-5. Only general bookshop in Tower Hamlets which specialises in books about the area by local people, as well women's, ethnic minority sections. S/h section, prints and cards.

Miscellaneous

■ **Oxfam Bookshop,** *91 Marylebone High St, W1 (486 4111).* Second-hand books and Oxfam publications.

■ **Sun Power,** *198 Blackstock Rd, N4 (704 0247).* 10-6. Women, health, ecology, anarchy. Also stock non-exploitative crafts, wholefood. Worker's co-op. Noticeboard.

Arts

■ **Arts Bibliographic,** *37 Gt Russell St, WC1 (636 5320).* M-F10-6. 20th century visual arts. Mail order, cat £7.50 for 6 issues for new customers.

■ **Battersea Arts Centre,** *Old Town Hall, Lavender Hill, SW11*

(223 6557). Tu, W 10-8, Th, Fri, Sat 10-8, Sun 12-6. General, fiction, women, travel, art, health, 'upmarket paperbacks'. Noticeboard.

■ **ICA**, *Nash Hse, The Mall, SW1Y 5AH (930 3647)*. T-Sun 12-9pm. Good selection of magazines, some imports.

Second hand/ Antiquarian/ Specialist

Many of these are clustered in Charing Cross Road, and around the British Museum. For second hand, you will be extremely lucky to get any bargains here, but try also:

■ **Skoob**, *15 Sicilian Ave, Southampton Row, WC1 (404 3063)* which sells a lot of heavyweight books (it's near London University),

■ **Books of Charing Cross Rd**, *56 Charing Cross Rd, WC2 (836 3697)*. 10.30-7.30 7 days a week. Large and seemingly chaotic secondhand bookshop, with bargain basement.

■ **Primrose Hill Books**, *134 Regent's Pk Rd, NW1 (586 2022)*. M-F 10-6.30, Sat 10-6, Sun 11.30-6.30. Secondhand, but also carries some new stock.

■ **Response Community Bookshop**, *300 Old Brompton Rd, SW5 (244 8787)*. M-Sat 10-6.30. Secondhand and a few new art books.

■ **Walden Books**, *38 Harmood St, NW1 (267 8146)*. Th-Sun 10.30-6. Large stock of secondhand.

The Bookshops of London Diana Stephenson (Lascelles £3.95) is a good guide, arranged by postcode, to the same, even though quite a few shops have come and gone since its last update in 1985.

If you are looking for a particular book,

■ **Whitaker's**, *(836 8911)*. Can answer up to three queries by phone, and give you the publisher, price and where to get hold of a book. Publish *Books in Print*. Otherwise, you can look it up on microfiche at a reference library.

▼ LIBRARIES ▼

Public libraries are free. To join you must live, work or study in the borough and you will have to show identity (which must include your address). Often an envelope with postmark with your name and address will suffice. Public libraries are listed in the Yellow Pages, but not all libraries are included. It's best to look under borough headings in the phone book. You can use your ticket at *any* public library.

Non fiction books are shelved in subject order, then by author. Fiction is shelved by author.

If you can't find the book you want at that library then you can use their inter-library loan scheme (25p).

College and university libraries are good for reference. You can usually walk straight in even if you are not a student, though you may have to brazen it out if questioned.

The *Directory of London Public Libraries* should be available at your local reference library, and lists all the libraries in London. For the whole of Britain see *Libraries in the UK and Republic of Ireland* (produced by the Library Association, this also lists academic libraries. For more specialist information, government departments often have libraries which are listed in *The Guide to Government Department and Other Libraries*, as do firms (including law firms). These are listed in *ALSIB Directory of Information Sources in the UK* - which has a subject index in back. Entrance to all of these will usually be a matter of convincing them that you have a legitimate reason for wanting to use it.

■ **The Library Association**, *7 Ridgemount St, WC1 (636 7543)* publishes list of public and academic libraries.

■ **British Library,** *Gt Russell St, WC1 (636 1544)* they keep a copy of all publications in the UK. It's hard to become a member/ get a readers ticket. The more obscure your research, the more likely you are to get a ticket.

■ **London Library**, *14 St James Sq, SW1 (930 7705)*. Private collection, covering the humanities, 1 million titles, some out of print books. Membership £75 pa.

Specialist Libraries

■ **London Sound and Video Archive,** *London History Workshop, 42 Queen Sq, WC1 (831 8871)* 2,000 hours of audio tape and 500 videotapes, plus related transcripts, letters, and over 5,000 photographs covering aspects of everyday life on the history of London. Runs workshops, exhibitions, produces resource packs. Open M-F 10-4, ring for appointment.

■ **National Sound Archive,** *29 Exhibition Rd, SW7 (589 6603).* Has around 750,000 discs. Useful for film-makers, broadcasting agencies, the recording industry - and it's open to the public. Have recordings dating back to the 1890's, including the voices of Florence Nightingale, Gladstone, Tennyson and Browning. Recordings of poetry, all kinds of music, theatre, parliamentary sessions, language and dialogue collection and industrial sounds. Open by appointment.

■ **British Newspaper Library,** *Colindale Ave, NW9 (636 1544).* International newspapers and magazines, the earliest of which dates back to 1645. You need to be over 21 to join and to produce identification.

■ **Central Music Library,** *160 Buckingham Palace Rd, SW1 (798 2192).* M-F 9.30-7, Sat 9.30-5. Books, orchestral sets, sheet music, periodicals.

■ **City Business Library,** *106 Fenchurch St, EC3 (638 8215).* Reference only. UK and overseas trade directories, business newspapers, periodicals, company information, market research, info on company law etc.

■ **Mark Longman Library,** *7 Ridgemount St, WC1 (636 7543).* Specialises in books about books. Useful to publishers and booksellers.

■ **Marx Memorial Library,** *37a Clerkenwell Grn, EC1 (253 1485).* M and Fri 2-6, Tu, W, Th 2-9, Sat 11-1. (Visiting non-members call 2-6). Membership £5 + £1 joining fee, £1 OAPs. History of socialism and communism internationally: Marx, Engles, Lenin, Labour movement. Specialist collections: International Brigades Spanish Civil War Archives, John Williamson American Labour Movement Collection, JD Bernal Peace Library, Klugman Collection of Chartist and early radical material. Regularly hold education classes.

■ **St Bride Printing Library,** *St Bride Inst, Bride Ln, EC4 (353 4660).* Public reference library - typography, graphic design, illustration etc.

■ **University College Library,** *Little Magazines Collection, Gower St, WC1 (387 7050).* Collection of current little magazines, underground and alternative press material and small press publishing, mainly from the UK, US, Commonwealth and other countries. By arrangement only. M-F 10-5.

■ **UN Information Centre/ Library,** *20 Buckingham Gate, SW1 (630 1981).* M,W,Th 10-1; 2-5. Holds all UN reports.

▼ BOOK FINDING ▼

■ **The Book Information Service,** *Book Hse, 45 East Hill, SW18 (874 8526).* Will try to give answers to any queries about books - e.g. whether out of print. Write in if your question is simple in which case the service is free (send SAE). If complicated then £10 + VAT. Will take phone queries if quick and simple. Very helpful. One enquiry only per call/letter.

■ **Twiggers,** *Book Finding Service, 108 Reedley Rd, Stoke Bishop, Bristol BS9 1BE, (0272 682155).* Will try to find any book out of print. They advertise the book you are looking for in trade journals and second hand bookshops throughout the world. They do an 'ordinary' search; you pay if they find the book. They also do a more thorough 'extended' search which costs £1.50 extra per title.

■ **Bibliagora,** *PO Box 77, Feltham, TW14 8JF, (898 1234).* Out of print book tracing service £7 per title, and they will look indefinitely till they find the book.

▼MISCELLANEOUS▼

■ **The Daily Telegraph Information Service,** *(538 5000)* they will give you information on almost anything, but it costs. Phone the number (you pay in advance or by credit card). Min £3 for five minutes research, £15 + VAT for 30 minutes.

■ **Public Records Office,** *Ruskin Ave, Kew, Surrey, (876 3444).* Holds all government records, which become available to the public after 30 years. Bring proof of identity to join. Law Courts records are held at Chancery Lane branch.

■ **Companies Registration Office,** *55 City Rd, EC1 (253 9393).* Annual accounts of all limited companies have to be deposited here. You can see them for £2.50 per company.

■ **Business Info Service,** *25 Southampton Buildings, WC2 (323 7979).* M-F 10-7. For business users who need to know market figures and information on companies and products. They operate a quick (5 minute) enquiry service on *323 7454.*

■ **House of Commons Information,** *(219 4272)* gives info on House of Commons - proceedings, history etc.

■ **Labour Research Dept,** *78 Blackfriars Rd, (928 3649).* Primarily for trade unions, but individuals can become affiliated for £41.50. Information on companies, health and safety, privatisation, employment law, pay etc. Publications.

■ **Stone,** *45 Westwood Hill, SE26 (767 1715).* Information on alternative festivals - phone between 6pm and midnight or send sae for list.

printing/publishing

▼ GETTING INTO PRINT ▼

There are many different ways of preparing and getting material printed. Which way you choose depends very much on a number of factors: how large the job is (i.e. whether it's a leaflet or a book) and how many you want printed, how much skill you have or can muster, how much money you want to spend and what quality of design or printing you want.

There are four main ways of getting into print:

Duplicating: This is a cheap way of producing leaflets without graphics, but it's poor quality. You type text onto a stencil sheet and then this forms a kind of plate which is then put into the duplicator which you can easily learn to operate yourself.

Photocopying: This is another cheap method for leaflets etc. which is suitable if you've got graphics, but is still relatively poor quality. It's not economical for colour work, as copies made by special colour copiers are expensive.

Screen Process: This is used for printing on fabrics (e.g. T shirts), or posters. It's best for short runs (when you don't want to print many posters/things), when you need large areas of colour, and haven't got much text. The equipment is cheap, but it's fairly time-consuming to do yourself.

Litho Printing: This involves heavy printing equipment so can only be done by a printer. It's good for long runs, for colour and gives good quality - for books, magazines, pamphlets etc. but is the most expensive method.

The Process

First you edit your *copy* (your text or manuscript) so that you don't need to make any more changes. Then you or someone else needs to design it — to decide what it should look like on the final, printed page. Then you need to convert your copy to the right size and layout, either by getting it typeset or using one of the help-yourself methods suggested below. If you are using traditional typesetting you will then need to get it *pasted up* - stuck down on a layout grid (a sheet of paper with guidelines for the printer, to show what size you want the page to be) with any graphics or pictures you want to use. If you are using a desk top publishing system you will typeset your text straight onto a page the right size, and you will need to do very little, if any, paste-up.

If you are using litho printing, the printer will then take the page(s), and, by a photographic process, make a 'plate' from each page. (A plate is a sheet of metal, paper or sometimes plastic on which all the areas which should be printed black are etched away. This lets the superfluous ink through onto the paper.)

For books, magazines or pamphlets, after printing the pages have to be 'bound' — stuck, sewn or stapled together in the right order.

The golden rule for all of these processes is shop around - prices can vary enormously. Some firms will only do one part of the process, and some will do everything from design to printing. Design and printing co-ops, who tend to be more helpful to the novice than some commercial firms can be, are listed at the end of this section.

DESIGN

Get what you want to say (the text or *copy*) ready and edited so that it's perfect — don't try to change it unless it's essential after this stage as this can prove very expensive. Now you will need to think about design. You can do two things, either:

Get a Designer - If you want a very stylish production and have some money to spend you may want to look for a designer. You can either use a freelance designer, go to a design

studio (which can be expensive) or to a printing co-op (listed below) where they can take care of the whole job. If you go to a designer, she will discuss how you want it to look, and can organise the typesetting, and even the printing if you want.
Or you can:
Design it Yourself - If you haven't got much money you may want to do the design. To get some ideas, look at similar publications/ leaflets/brochures, find one you like and copy their style. Keep it fairly simple, and be clear about what you want to stand out - don't use too much bold or large type.
Books and Pamphlet: The spine is important, it should have title, author and name of press on it reading top to bottom, in clear print. Put blurb on the back as well as the ISBN number and bar code if you have one (see below), and price.

Typestyles

This book is typeset in a typeface called Palatino
and the headings are in Stone Sans bold
This is a typeface called Times
And this is another common typeface called Helvetica
If you want something fancy, this is Zapf Chancery

Typefaces also come in
Roman
Italic and
Bold
and different 'point' sizes
This book is in 8 and 7 point (or thereabouts)
Most books and magazines are in 8, 9 or 10 point.
This is 11 point

This text is ragged right which means that the right hand margin is uneven and the left hand margin is straight, like the text in this book.

This text is ragged left which means that the left hand margin is ragged, and the right hand margin is straight.

This text is justified which means that the text is straight on both sides, and the words are hyphenated or broken up when they don't fit on the line.

This text is centred which means that the text is ragged on both sides. This is often used for large headings, posters etc.

TYPESETTING

This is the process of putting your words into the right typeface (style of lettering) and making them the right size and looking as they will on the printed page. There are various ways of doing this.

To save money you can hand write, using a black pen, felt-tip or ballpoint, though this isn't very readable. Another cheap way is to use a typewriter - use one with a newish carbon ribbon if possible as this gives the cleanest type. Cloth ribbons aren't so good, and dot matrix printers reproduce very badly, though if you have to use one quality can be improved by photocopying the printout. You can do the headings in letraset. This is sheets of letters in different sizes and styles which you can buy in art or graphics shops. These are put onto the page like transfers. However, this can be fiddly and time consuming if you have a lot of headings.

For the best quality print, though most expensive, you have either to go to a typesetter who will set your copy using a photographic process onto 'bromides'. A cheaper alternative is to use a desk top publishing system (see below).

First you will need to pick a 'typeface' (the style of lettering you want). You can look through a letraset catalogue for ideas or the typesetter should have a catalogue of faces they offer. Remember some typefaces take up little space, and some take up more. The typesetters will show you about sizes and faces and should be able to tell you approximately how much space it will take up. If you are pasting up yourself, and you find your text is too big or long after typesetting, you can reduce it on a good photocopier. The other main consideration is whether you want your text straight on the left and right hand margins ('justified'), straight on the left but ragged on the right ('ragged right'). 'Centred' text is ragged on both sides and in the centre of the column (see box).

Typesetting comes from the typesetters in long sheets (*bromides* or *galleys*). Proof reading is done from these and you need to use standard marks to indicate corrections. Helpful typesetters may supply you with a sheet which shows these, otherwise *Hart's Rules for Compositors* (OUP) has them. Typesetters will do corrections without these marks, but a correction that looks obvious to you may be ambiguous to someone else. Typesetters correct their mistakes free, but if you start making big changes it could become expensive.

PASTE-UP/ARTWORK

When you get the final corrected bromides back you will need to cut them up and stick them down onto a layout sheet, usually bigger than a page or a double page spread. You can buy these ready made at some places (see **Redesign** below). If you are making your own, use a light blue pencil to rule any guidelines you make (to show page size and to help you stick things down straight) as these don't show up when the artwork is photographed to make the printing plates. Small layout boards with parallel motion bars can be bought for about £25 at graphics shops, and these help you get things straight. The best glue is Cow Gum (vegetarians take heart - not so named because it's made out of ground up cows but after its inventor, Mr Cow) - it enables you to slide the artwork about to get it into the right position. Aerosol glues can be bad for your lungs and the ozone layer. Clean the artwork up with lighter fuel, which removes excess cow gum, or peel it off using a ball of dried-up cow gum.

Photos and Illustrations: If these are not the right size you'll need to get it reduced or enlarged. If you are using a printer, she can do this or go to a high street print shop that does *PMTs*. For a cheaper reduction (black and white only), use a photocopier which has a reducing facility - this can give a fairly respectable reproduction. If you are using a litho printer, photos and illustrations with 'halftones' (shades of grey) need to be 'screened' (broken up into tiny dots) using a process camera. The printer can do this. Indicate clearly where you want the photo and what size you want it. A simple way of finding out how high a picture will be when it has been reduced to your column width is shown below.

How to find out how high a picture will be when it's reduced to fit the width of your columns.

- Draw a diagonal line from one corner of your picture to the other on tracing paper **(1)**
- From the foot of the diagonal line, mark off the width you want the picture to fit. **(2)**
- The vertical line **(3)** shows how high your picture will be when reduced.

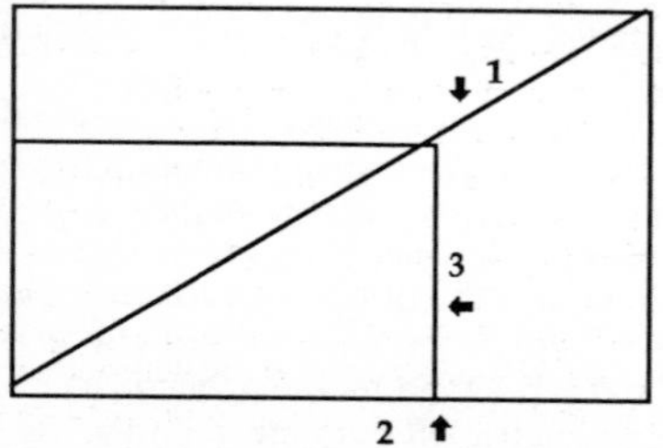

Invaluable tip: there are some books of out of copyright pictures you can use free - as seen in this very book. Available from

■ **Dover Books,** *18 Earlham St, WC2 (836 2111).* Publishes books of old etchings, woodcuts and prints, (Victorian, medieval, and present day) which can be used very effectively - they allow you to use up to 10 from any one book without permission. Museums and picture libraries charge for reproduction of images. Photo libraries are quite expensive. If you know an amateur photographer you could use her, but remember that photos can sometimes reproduce badly in print, especially if they are very grey, or slightly out of focus and they don't photocopy *at all* well.

DESK TOP PUBLISHING

One way of bypassing the paste-up stage is to use a desk top publishing (DTP) system. This also has the advantage that you can see what you're doing and how it looks before it gets typeset. People who have few design skills can produce much more sophisticated designs than they would be able to using the traditional methods. This book was produced in this way using a DTP system.

The main DTP systems are for use on either Apple Macintosh or IBM computers (see also **Computers** section p237). You can buy a computer and a desk top publishing programme but it will cost a few thousand pounds, though there's a substantial discount on Apple and IBM computers for students, teachers, lecturers and educational establishments, and Apple also offer discounts for registered charities, journalists and publishers (you have to be a member of the NUJ or have had something published in something people pay for) - apply to them for details of eligibility. Another way of getting your hands on one is to go to one of the community resources centres or desk top publishing bureaux that allow you to use their machines. You will probably be charged by the hour. You'll need to know something about how to use them first though. **Neal's Yard DTP Studio** (below) runs training courses and has published a booklet on DTP called *Publish!* Nicholas Saunders (50p). This booklet will also tell you how to translate disks from other computer systems onto Apple Macintosh, which is what most DTP bureaux use.

Photos and illustrations can be *scanned* (copied in digitised form onto disc) so that you can enlarge them and shrink them on screen, and do text *wrap arounds* (where the text fits itself round the outline of the picture - see this page where the text follows the outline of the picture of the computer). Scanning costs extra and photos don't come out as well as those screened by the printer the traditional way - they look 'dotty' like a video picture because there are fewer dots per inch. However you can play about with the photo to get special effects (stretching, high contrast etc).

Once you have done the design, you have a choice about how to produce your text.
Laser Printout: This is a cheap alternative to bromides. Prints out at 300-600 dots per inch compared with 1200-2400 dots per inch on standard typesetting. This means that the letters are slightly fuzzier round the edges, but if you need better quality you could do the laser printout twice the size and photocopy reduce it to the size you want it. This only works if your finished product is going to be less than A4 size, because laser printout only goes up to A4 size. Laser printout costs from 40p per page (300 dots per inch) to £1 or over (600 dots per inch).
Linotron: This produces best quality printout on photographic paper ('bromides') but is expensive (approx £5 a page).

Bureaus are

■ **Neal's Yard DTP Studio**, 2 *Neal's Yard, WC2 (379 5113).* It costs £5 an hour to use one of their Apple Macintosh computers (£20 if you need full assistance/tuition). Laser printouts are 50p + VAT each. Also scan graphics and translate discs - IBM to Apple and vice versa. No linotronic output.

■ **Copyart**, *41 Culross Bldgs, Battle Bridge Rd, NW1 (833 4417).* Apple Mac Computer with laser printer (30p per sheet) plus charge per hour (£6, £4 concs). Other facilities available - see below.

■ **The Printing Centre**, *30 Store St, WC1 (636 8723).* Two Apple Macs, £4.50 per hour. Printouts 35p + VAT per sheet.

■ **Union Place**, *122 Vassall Rd, SW9 (735 6123).* Apple Macs - sliding scale for community groups/ commercial concerns.

■ **Data Layout**, 36 Cornwall Rd, SE1 (401 2299). Not a do-it-yourself place - for linotronic output (bromides) if you must have it (£5 per page plus VAT).

WHICH PRINTER?

If you just want some stationery or a leaflet printed, and you want under 1,000, you may be as well going to a high street 'instant' print shop where they print short runs fast and cheaply with a process using plastic or paper plates which don't last long so can't be used for reprinting. The numbers are in the yellow pages under printing, or try:

■ **The Printing Centre**, *(636 8723).* (See above). 1000 A4 leaflets printed both sides on white paper cost £29 + £2 for coloured paper. Also cheap do-it-yourself photocopying (A4 3p per sheet).

■ **Instant Print**, *12 Heddon St, W1 (734 6205).* 1000 A4 leaflets printed both sides cost £29.

For book publishing try

■ **Anthony Rowe**, *Bumber's Farm, Bristol Rd, Chippenham, Wilts SN14 6QA, (0249 659706).* Specialise in very short runs.

■ **A Wheaton**, *Hennock Rd, Marsh Barton, Exeter EX2 8RP, (0392 74121).* Specialise in book printing: cheap, friendly and will give you help and advice because they print a lot of books for small or do-it-yourself publishers. We used them for this book.

You might also consider photocopying - cheap rates are offered at community print shops and some do it yourself places.

If you want a bigger job done (more pages, or poster size, or a lot of leaflets) you should get some quotes from litho printers.

For more than 1000, especially if you may want a reprint, or if you have a larger job - a magazine, booklet or book, as always it pays to shop around - ask for a 'quote' on price telling them number of pages, quality of paper, colours, number of photos, etc. London printers are on the whole very expensive, so try outside London - printers can arrange delivery though this may cost extra. For bigger jobs *Exchange & Mart* lists cheap printers, or you can look at papers and mags similar to yours to see who prints them. Printers also vary in terms of quality - get samples of work to check this out.

Don't use a printer who seems unwilling to give clear advice about what they can do cheapest, and how they want artwork presented. Always check the price after the printer has seen your artwork. Check that there will be no hidden extras. Get your quote from the printer in writing.

If you are doing a book or magazine you need to decide how many pages. Printers print in multiples of 2, 4, 8 or 16 on a single sheet then fold them down. If you have colour on the cover and/or different paper this will probably be printed separately. If you want best value for money, make sure you have the number of pages that fits their system.

Finishing/Binding: Newspaper pages don't need fixing together but just have to be collated (put in order). Magazines and booklets can be stapled or stitched, large magazines and books can be perfect bound (glued). Your printer will organise this.

▼ PUBLISHING ▼

ISBN/ISSN

ISBN and ISSN are free reference numbers which make it easier to trace the publication. To get an ISBN (books) number write to the **Standard Book Numbering Agency**, *12 Dyott St, WC1* - apply six months in advance of publication. An ISBN number means you get listed in Whitaker's *Books in Print* (see below). For an ISSN Number (magazines) to **UK National Serials Data Centre**, *The British Library, 2 Sheraton St, W1* sending description, photocopy of contents page or similar for their records. If you change the title in any way you may need a new number.

Getting a Book Publisher

If you decide not to do it yourself you will need a publisher who will take your manuscript and produce and distribute your book. You will get 7-12% of the cover price (royalties). However, 95% of unsolicited manuscripts are turned down. Choose publishers you know print your kind of book. Send a synopsis of the book, rather than the whole manuscript, in a letter asking whether the publisher would be prepared to read the manuscript. You can try getting an agent, who will market your work for you if she thinks it's sellable, and take a cut if it's accepted. Publishers and agents are listed in *The Writers' & Artists' Yearbook* (A C Black)

Vanity Publishers: Beware publishers who ask you to pay for publishing your work. This kind of publisher rarely provides any services worth the money they charge. If you want to publish, have some cash and can't find a publisher, it's better to do it yourself. For some specialist books, the publisher may ask you to pay a *proportion* of the costs, in which case both you and the publisher will be responsible for selling the book.

Pricing

Make sure you've priced your magazine or book right. Consider the price of similar items, how much it cost you to put together, how many you think you'll sell, bookshops cut (25-40%) plus distributor's cut if you're using one - (15-35%).

Distributors

Having a distributor means that you don't have to go round the shops yourself. But they take a large cut, and may not be that bothered about pushing your book or magazine as one among many.

You will need to sign a distribution contract which will detail who has what distribution rights: you could try to keep distribution within London, for instance, and mail order rights (though most small distributors will want all or nothing). Be clear about who pays for promotion, and what form this will take.

■ **Airlift Book Co,** *26 Eden Gr, N7 (607 5792).* Small press distribution.

■ **Turnaround,** *27 Horsell Rd, N5 (609 7836).* Small press distribution, specialise in social and political issue books.

■ **Counter Productions,** *PO Box 556, SE5 (274 9009).* Distributor of small press and imported books - mostly unusual stuff.

■ **Feminist Book Fortnight,** *c/o 7 Loddon Hse, Church St, NW8 (402 8159).* Takes place annually in May.

■ **A Distribution,** *84b Whitechapel High St, E1 (558 7782).* Publishers' co-op rather than a service. It's a non-wages, non-profit collective which promotes anarchist and liberation books, pamphlets and periodicals. Co-publish New Anarchist Review.

■ **Aphoria Press and Counter Distribution,** *PO Box 556, London, SE5* 0RL Counter Distribution are very efficient distributors of books about experimental culture, obscure literature and bizarre political tracts.

■ **Independent Press Distribution,** *12 Stevenage Rd, SW6 (736 5059).* represents small presses, mainly poetry and prose. Mail order to individuals and shops.

■ **Ultra Violet Enterprises,** *25 Horsell Rd, N5* Consultations to individuals and groups on getting material pulished: how to find a printer or publisher, publicity etc. Specialises in non-fiction (no poetry). Write for details.

Distributing It Yourself

This means going round to bookshops/ newsagents to sell. Magazines are usually taken *sale or return,* books may be bought or sale or return. Items taken on sale or return are returned to you if they aren't sold - you only get the money for what has been sold. You will also need to check when you think they will have sold out to see if they need any more. You can refuse to take back copies that are very shop soiled. With magazines, don't be niggardly about how many you give the shop - they look and sell better if there are a pile of them.

You will need to set up a good system to record orders/returns from bookshops, and to invoice them. You can post orders if you haven't got transport or the orders are small - use air-filled envelopes, particularly for books. The post office will collect large consignments for £2.70.

For a list of bookshops, *The Bookshops of London* Diana Stephenson (Lascelles) is a bit out of date but does London, or you could try asking a friendly distributor for their list.

Target any specialist bookshops likely to sell your book/magazine. Exhibitions and bookfairs are another outlet.

To sell to libraries you have to apply to the headquarters library in each borough. Find these in the *Directory of London Public Libraries* which should be available - in your local library! For the whole of Britain see *Libraries in the UK and Republic of Ireland* (produced by the **Library Association**) You can also get people to sell your book freelance, at markets, in the street, among friends, at conferences etc.

Promotion

You don't necessarily have to fork out a lot of money on expensive advertising. Swap ads with other publications for mail order sales. When your book or magazine is published, make sure you send a review copy to relevant magazines and newspapers, and to local radio - ring up first to get the name of the book reviewer otherwise the review copy may go astray. Send a press release – your own review of the book - magazines etc are more likely to review it if they can use ready-made copy. Make this as interesting as possible.

Mail Order

You don't have to give a cut to a third party on mail order, but you do have to advertise. Subscriptions are most important for magazines - much easier and more profitable than time-consuming sale or return.

■ **Small Press Group,** *SPG, BM Bozo, London,*

WC1N 3XX Aims to promote small presses, to get wider distribution of their work, and exchange information. Represents members at bookfairs. Is aiming to set up Small Press Centre. Publish *Small Press Yearbook* (£5.99 + 70p p&p) full of all manner of weird and wonderful publishers and their books, from the anarchic to the avant garde, and *Small Press Monthly*, free to members. M'ship £12 pa.

■ **Women In Publishing,** *12 Dyott St, WC1* Speakers and discussions, training courses to develop personal and professional skills. Meetings second Weds of month at the **Publishers Assn,** *19 Bedford Sq, WC1* at 6.30. Mthly newsletter *Wiplash*.

Copyright

To establish your copyright print © with the year and your name or press name after it. Legally you are supposed to send a copy of your publication to the **Copyright Receipt Office,** *2 Sheraton St, WC1* within one month of publication, though they are years behind with their cataloguing. If it hasn't been published yet, and you are looking for a publisher, you can send a copy of your publication or work to yourself. Leave it sealed in the envelope - the post office date stamp will show when you completed it so that in case of dispute about authorship you can prove you wrote it first.

Using copyright material: You are allowed to quote up to 400 words without the author's or publisher's permission. However, you should indicate where the quote came from. If you want to quote more, many people will let you use their material for nothing or next to nothing, but check with them.

For non copyright graphics see **Graphics** in the **Printing** section above.

■ **Publishers Assn,** *19 Bedford Sq, WC1 (580 6321)* can be persuaded to give advice for publishers.

■ **Patent Office,** *Copyright Enquiries, Room 1504, State Ho, 66-71 High Holborn, WC1 (829 6145).* will answer queries about copyright.

Books about Books

■ **International Directory of Little Magazines & Small Presses,** *Dustbooks, Len Fulton, Publisher, PO Box 100, Paradise, CA 95969,* Dubbed 'The Bible of the Business' by Wall St Journal, covers US. $22.95 + postage.

▼ CENSORSHIP ▼

Censorship is not only a matter of laws which restrict the kind of material which can be published. It begins with who owns and controls the media and what they want us to know or not to know - of the 11 national daily newspapers for instance, 7 are owned by 4 companies; of the 9 national Sunday papers, 4 are owned by 2 companies (figures from the Labour Party discussion paper, *Freeing the Press*). Almost all of these are politically pro-Conservative. The press also operates a system of voluntary self-censorship on defence and intelligence information, called the D-Notice system.

Television is to be censored by Lord Rees-Mogg who

will decide what we can see on the screen - though a number of programmes have been withdrawn by the TV companies themselves because of their political content or because they might be 'shocking'.

Then there are laws which restrict what you can publish. The Obscene Publications Act makes it illegal to publish material which is thought likely to 'deprave and corrupt' - though definition of these words is a matter of subjective interpretation, so whether you get convicted or not can be a matter of luck. (It's also illegal to bring 'obscene' material into the country even for your own consumption, and to send it through the post or ask for it to be sent through the post). There are also some Common laws (laws which aren't written down but are based on previous cases and judgements) which have been invoked to prosecute people. The Law of Blasphemous Libel was used against *Gay News* in 1978 when they published a poem describing a homosexual Roman soldier's response to the dying Christ - proving at least that art can still be radical. Recently a sculptor, Richard Gibson and and the owner of the gallery in which his *Fetus Earrings* were shown were found guilty of 'Conspiracy to outrage public decency' and fined.

What we are allowed to know about the workings of government is similarly restricted. The Official Secrets Acts (1911) makes it illegal for any pubic official or civil servant to give any information to the public about government activity unless authorised. The Police and Criminal Evidence Act (1984) makes it possible for the police to get a court order to force journalists, photographers and newspapers to hand over unpublished confidential material - their photos have been then used to convict demonstrators. Clause 28 of the Local Authorities Bill (1988) makes it illegal for local authorities to 'promote' homosexuality, or for teachers to 'promote... the acceptability of homosexuality as a pretended family relationship'.

There are also restrictions imposed by the law on our public behaviour which may have little to do with others' safety. The Public Order Act (1986) restricts or censors demonstrations and how people act in the street - police can move marches or impose conditions on them (e.g. move them to a quieter part of town where few people will see them). It also makes it an offence to use words or behaviour which are threatening, abusive, insulting or disorderly, and likely to harass, alarm or distress another - even if no-one *is* actually distressed (this includes shouting four letter words in the direction of Number 10 Downing Street).

Though not an aspect of censorship by the state, the Libel laws, which are meant to work in a way that is protective of the public, can also operate in an unfair way. Record-breaking awards against the press recently could have the effect of restricting or breaking smaller newspapers and magazines, while tabloids owned by large companies can continue to publish scandalous stories because they can afford to pay if a libel judgement goes against them.

For an wide ranging-study of censorship in Britain in all its aspects, see *Index on Censorship* September 1988, Vol 17 No 8 which is available from

■ **Index on Censorship**, *39c Highbury Pl, N5 (359 0161)*. Keeps tabs on censorship throughout the world, and publishes articles by silenced writers whatever their politics. Issue on the worstening situation in Britain is worth reading (Sept '88, vol 17 no 8). 10 issues pa, £1.65 ea.

■ **National Campaign for the Reform of the Obscene Publications Acts (NCROPA)**, *15 Sloane Ct West, Chelsea, SW3 4TD (730 9537)*. Campaigns for the freedom to read, view and listen without censorship.

■ **Campaign Against Pornography and Censorship**, *PO Box 844, SE5 (801 4204)*. Campaign for the repeal of the Obscenity Laws, and the formation of new sex discrimination legislation to regulate how women can be portrayed sexually.

Miscellaneous

■ **London College of Printing**, *Elephant and Castle, SE1 (735 8484)*. Run wide range of courses in design, layout, printing, DTP, computer graphics etc.

■ **Colebrook, Evans & McKenzie**, *5 Quality Ct, WC2 (242 1362)*. Hold auctions of printing machinery all over the country. Ring for catalogue.

■ **Danes**, *1 Sugar Hse Ln, E15 (534 2213)*. Sell a wide range of silk screen inks.

Silk Screen Printers

■ **Debruis**, 8 Blenheim Rd, Raynes Pk, SW20 (542 4106). Silk Screen, fabric printing, T shirts etc. Print on vinyls and plastics.

Badge Makers

■ **Better Badges**, *97 Caledonian Rd, N1 (837 0509)*. 500 minimum. Fast turnaround.

■ **Fly Press**, *52 Acre Ln, SW2 (274 5181)*. Badges and litho printing. Min order 500 badges.

■ **Pawson Promotions**, *PO Box 664, London E5 0JW*. 25mm badges, 100 for £12, 500 for £45. Will make up badges from your art work (write for layout sheets) or can produce artwork for you. Also catalogue of badge designs. Write for details.

■ **Universal Button Co**, *1 Birbeck St, E2 (739 8309)*. Minimum order 500. Sizes from 19mm-3in. Also sell badge making equipment.

Litho Printers

Most of the printers listed below will also do design and typesetting if you need it.

■ **Blackrose**, *30 Clerkenwell Cl, EC1 (251 3043)*. Up to A2, also design. Co-op.

■ **Calverts Press**, *31-39 Redchurch St, E2 (739 1474)*. Up to A2 offset litho, in house typesetting and design. DTP, and WP conversion. Full colour printing. Most competitive on short run full colour and long run single and multicolour. Co-op.

■ **Inkwell**, *713 Seven Sisters Rd, N15 (802 9884)*. Offset litho up to A1, colour work, darkroom, photocopying (1/10p, 10/83p). Badges and promotional items.

■ **Lithosphere Printing Co-op**, *203 Pentonville Rd, N1 (833 2526)*. Design, typesetting, printing up to A2. Co-op.

■ **Oval Printshop**, *54 Kennington Oval, SE11 (582 4750)*. Phone for details.

■ **Redesign**, *9/11 London Ln, E8 (533 2631)*. Design service and advice to clients doing their own stuff, fully equipped darkroom. Print up to A2. PMTs, platemaking and finishing equipment. Photocopy up to B4. Do standard A4 & A5 grid sheets.

■ **Shac-Shac**, *25 All Saints Rd, W11 (229 2844).* Reasonable rates. Up to A3. Photographic work.

■ **Spiderweb Offset**, *14/20 Sussex Way, N7 (281 3033).* Will give advice on launching your publication. Design, typesetting, printing up to up to A5, distribution. Co-op.

■ **Trojan Printing** , *25 Downham Rd, N1 (249 5771).* Litho printers, DTP. Can convert WP disks. Co-op.

Community Print Resources

■ **Camden Arts Centre**, *Arkwright Rd, NW3 (431 1292).* Etching, silk screen printing classes (£45 for Camden residents, £65 non residents).

■ **Copyart**, *41 Culross Bldgs, Battle Bridge Rd, NW1 2TH (833 4417).* Photocopying, dot screening for photographs, DTP (see DTP section above). Also light table, layout space, typewriter (use of facilities charge 50p hour concs, £1 waged).

■ **Greenwich/Bexley Resource Centre**, *8 Vincent Rd, SE18 (854 9092).* Provide media resources for community groups in Greenwich mainly, but also for those from all over London. Artwork facilities, duplicating , photocopying, litho, DTP. Will teach people how to do it themselves. Also do some commercial work for small businesses. Affiliation fee: £5 for local groups, £8 for London-wide organisations, £10 small businesses. Also have video camera and tape slide projector for loan.

■ **Horizon**, *Shop 8 Taplow, Aylesbury Estate, SE17 (708 1280).* Silkscreening, A3 Litho printing, darkroom, process camera, layout area. Also have a number of projects: a 16 track recording studio and rehearsal room; photography project with darkroom facilities; drama project, theatre seating 100; radio project where people make their own radio programmes; and a publishing project for local people to get their work into print. Run short courses, and also open days. For Southwark residents.

■ **InterChange**, *15 Wilkin St, NW5 (267 9421).* High speed photocopier, electronic stencil cutters, duplicators, silkscreen, metal sign-making, badge-making. Monthly training courses for community groups. Arts and theatre centre, cafe.

■ **Island Arts Centre**, *Tiller Rd, E14 (987 7925).* For use by people living in Tower Hamlets and Isle of Dogs. Courses in screenprinting.

■ **Lenthall Rd Workshop**, *81 Lenthall Rd, E8 (254 3082 or 241 6584).* Screen printing and darkroom. You pay a sessional charge and for materials - concessions available.

■ **Moonshine Community Arts Workshop**, *Victor Rd, NW10 (960 0055).* 16-track recording studio, fully equipped, video workshop with editing facilities, printshop providing training and printing.

■ **Paddington Printshop**, *Basement 1 Elgin Ave, W9 (286 1123).* Give advice and information to voluntary organisations in graphic design and printing. Develop training courses in graphic design for community groups. Set up and run projects which aim to use printmaking in new and innovative ways. Co-publish artists prints with artists, market and sell them. Undertake projects to develop access to printing facilities for the disabled.

■ **Print Place**, *351 Southwark Pk Rd, SE16 (237 3881).* Drawing board, process camera, darkroom. A3 offset. Facilities for use by community groups in Southwark area only. Take on trainees and volunteers.

■ **Response**, *300 Old Brompton Rd, SW5 (370 4606).* Printshop for Earl's Court residents, community photocopier and computer workshop. Also runs one of the few remaining community newspapers.

■ **Tottenham Community Project**, *628 High Rd, N17 (808 4754).* Litho printing, desktop publishing, community languages. Duplicating, photocopying. Community groups only.

■ **Union Place Community Resource Centre**, *122 Vassall Rd, SW9 (735 6123).* Offset litho, A4 and A3. Silkscreen posters to A1. DTP, and can convert WP discs. DTP on Apple Macintosh (£5 per hour plus charge on sliding scale for laser). Layout and design, photocopying, duplicating. Open for use by individuals, community groups and businesses, but charges differ.

■ **Selby Site**, *Selby Rd, N17 (801 2589).* DTP and printing facilities. New and large project which houses many community groups and has meeting rooms available for local groups. Also space for rehearsal, training, arts.

Typesetters

Note that with all typesetting, there's a different rate for *straight text* (straightforward text with perhapss a few headings), and *display* work (e.g. tables, posters, anything with a lot of changes of typeface and size). Straight text is usually charged by the 1000 words, sometimes by the 1000 *ems*, which are more or less equivalent to characters.

■ **Bread'n Roses Typesetting and Design**, *Tenants Corner, 46a Oval Mansions, Vauxhall St, SE11 (582 7286).* Photosetting, IBM composers, disc conversion, also machines for use by community groups. £12 per 1000 words for IBM. £16-20 per 1000 for photosetting. Co-op.

■ **Leveller Graphics**, *52 Acre La, SW2 (274 2288).* Design, typesetting (£18.50 per 100 words), word processing, disc conversion (IBM or compatible), and work with Fly Press (listed under printers) for printing.

■ **Lasso**, *18 Sussex Way, N7 (272 9141).* Design, typesetting, artwork. £18 per 100 words for text, £30 hour display work. Women's co-op.

■ **Windhorse Photosetters**, *119 Roman Rd, E2 (981 1407).* Design and paste up, PMTs, photosetting, upwards of 118 typefaces, £17 per 1000 for straight text and £28 per hour for more complicated setting plus small galley charge. £20 min charge for typesetting. Women's co-op.

ENVIRONMENT: Community, Green Environment, Alternative Technology

community

Community action is one way of bringing about the changes you would like to see in your local area. Rather than hoping for the bureaucrats to come and make changes, committed groups of ordinary people have come together to challenge the social and environmental deprivation in their neighbourhoods

There are examples in London of a whole range of practical developments which provide creative responses to such problems as poor quality, high cost housing, high unemployment and inadequate social and recreational facilities. Community initiatives have shown that anonymous dwelling areas can be transformed into living neighbourhoods. Some projects fail due to inertia and conflicts of interest or become bogged down in bureaucracy and inadequate financial resources. There are, however, outstanding successes like the Coin St. development scheme on the south Bank where community groups fought a 15 year campaign to have their community plan implemented on a 13 acre derelict site. When the scheme is finished it will provide low cost housing for 1,300 people and a major light industrial development employing 1,200. There will be a new car park and riverside walk, cafes, shops and other social and leisure facilities.

There are many other examples of smaller scale projects ranging from community gardens, adventure playgrounds, workshops and social centres.

In the many and varied forms which community action takes there is the potential for people to establish their rights to be consulted, to determine how they want their environments to be, and to tap unused skills and resources to achieve what they want.

▼ COMMUNITY ACTION ▼

The following organisations are the representative bodies for the numerous voluntary and community organisations who provide services in the community.

■ **London Voluntary Services Council,** *68 Chalton St, NW1 (388 0241).* Co-ordinate the voluntary sector in London. Publications about management, law etc. Train those involved in the voluntary sector in a range of skills, eg computing, management, media skills, assertiveness.

■ **National Federation of Community Organisations,** *8/9 Upper St, Islington, N1 (226 0189).* Represent the interests of neighbourhood groups and community associations and encourages further development. Publishes *Community* magazine Qtly (£2.50 pa).

■ **National Council for Voluntary Organisations,** *(NCVO), 26 Bedford Sq, WC1 (636 4066).* The National representative body for voluntary organisations. Provides advice and info, has a large library and publishes books and pamphlets.

■ **BASSAC (British Association for Settlements and Social Action Centres),** *13 Stockwell Rd, SW9 (733 7428).* There are thirty cantres in London offering a wide range of projects and activities which serve the needs of their areas - pensioners clubs, women's activities, creches, arts and crafts and leisure facilities. Contact above address for a list of centres.

Starting a Project

Before taking action spend some time getting clear about your ideas. This will make it easier to express them to others. Tell your friends about it and put up some notices to get people interested, advertise in the local library, community centre or local paper. Arrange a meeting to discuss your ideas and establish whether there is local support. Encourage people to bring some food and leave time for socialising afterwards. See if it's possible to get somebody else to arrange the next meeting. Your local community centre may be willing to provide some facilities for you.

Some useful publications and sources of info for start up:

• *At Work In The Community* - a resource pack to stimulate discussion on identifying and meeting local needs with suggested activities. (£3 from NFCO).

• *Community Start Up* - a common sense guide to starting a community group and keeping it going. (£4.95 NFCO).

• *Education for Neighbourhood Change* (Resource Packs). Survival skills for community Action Groups - how to sort out problems and possibilities and decide on priorities for taking action. Publications list available from

■ **Adult Education Research Centre,** *Block B, Cherry Tree Buildings, Nottingham University, Nottingham NG7 2RD.*

Nutshell Training Pack offers ideas and skills to

groups and individuals for community activities, based on the experiences of people who have developed successful projects. Available from

■ **Nutshell (Neighbourhood Use of Time & Space for Homes, Environment, Livelihood & Leisure),** *318 Summer Lane, Newtown, Birmingham, B19 3RL, (021 359 3562).*

■ **Neighbourhood Initiatives Foundation,** *Chapel Hse, 7 Gravel Leasowe, Lightmoor, Telford, Shropshire, TF4 3QL, (0952 590902).* Supports initiatives for neighbourhood renewal by putting groups in touch with each other. Provides resources for Start-up, advice on funding and dealing with bureaucracy.

■ **Community Projects Foundation,** *60 Highbury Gr, N5 (226 5375).* Provides resources, info, training and advice to community projects.

Community Transport

■ **London Community Transport Association,** *40 Bowling Green Lane, EC1 (278 0333).* Association of groups providing transport facilities for the community - advice, info and training. See **Getting Around** p138.

Funding

For Credit Unions see **Co-op** section p270.
The main sources of money for community projects are grants from government agencies, charitable trusts and the business sector.

Funding from government is increasingly difficult to obtain because social schemes are given low priority. It often has strings attached and can be subject to long delays.

Charitable trusts give away around £300 million a year to various projects. You will need to do some research to find the trusts whose requirements your project is most likely to meet.

There is an increase in the amount of money available to community projects from business and industry. Particularly where the donor stands to gain good P.R. from its investment. About £100 million a year is donated by companies with further £50 million in social sponsorship schemes. Most of this money goes into sport and the arts but there is untapped potential there for community action projects.

Further info and funding is available from the organisations listed previously.

The following guides may be available in your local library:

• *A Guide To The Major Trusts* published by the **Directory of Social Change** (£12.50) - lists the policies of over 400 grant making trusts, tells you how much money they have to spend and what projects they have supported in the past.

• *A Guide To Company Giving* -D.O.S.S. (above) (£12.50) - the major companies and their policies for funding.

• *London Grants Guide* is the best source of information for all types of funding, covering government trusts and companies with background articles on their respective approaches. It also lists the agencies which provide support and assistance in making applications. Published by **DoSC** (below). (£9.95).

DoSC also provides information and training for the voluntary organisations on fund raising, financial management and communications. They publish a series of useful leaflets at 50p each plus 50p per order, these include *Setting up, Planning a Capital Project, Drawing Up a Budget, Fundraising Sources, Developing A Fundraising Strategy, Writing An Application* and *Raising Money Locally.* Apply to:

■ **Directory of Social Change (DoSC),** *Radius Works, Back Lane, , NW3 (435 8171)*

■ **Voluntary Service Unit,** *Home Office, 50 Queen Anne's Gt, SW1 (273 3000).* gives advice on grants from central government. Will fund projects covered by more than one department, made by national organisations (and exceptionally for innovatory or nationally important projects).

■ **Community Accountancy Project,** *485 Kingsland Rd, E8 (249 7109).* Gives advice to community groups on accounts

Making use of Empty Buildings and Space

(See also **Green Environment** p272).

Tapping unused resources in your community can include bringing derelict land into use for housing, gardens, playspace, green areas and creating jobs .

Derelict buildings can be done up to provide space for social and recreational activities.

At Camley Street close to Kings Cross there's now a pond with coots and ducks. Wildflowers bloom where a coalyard used to be. In Vauxhall a community garden has transformed a derelict site at Harleyford Road. In Camden Town residents have created seedbed workshops, a community hall, creche and small garden on one site. These and many more projects enhance the quality of life in the city. They are made possible by collaboration between groups of residents and the many support organisations which exist to expand skills and know how in the community.

For information on how to raise awareness in your neighbourhood, celebrate green spaces and create new areas contact:

■ **Think Green,** *Premier Hse, 43/8 New St, Birmingham, B2 4LJ, (643 8899).* A national organisation which campaigns for environmental improvements. They've produced a DIY guide for interested groups on *Community Landscape* (£2.50 + £1 p&p) and *Green Celebrations* a guide for practical action (£4.99 + £1 p&p).

Community Architecture

If you know of empty buildings or derelict sites in your neighbourhood and can form a group of residents with ideas for how they could be used for community projects, you will find that there is expert help available. You'll need expertise in acquiring the site, developing your plans and finding funds. *Technical Aid Centres* have developed in the past two decades to provide such expertise. They are independent organisations funded by government grants, providing architectural and landscaping services. They will explain the design and construction process so that you can make your own decisions. The first step is to approach them for a feasibility study to see if your plan could work out in practice. Their initial services are usually free to groups.

If you have difficulty in acquiring funds for the feasibility study there is a *Community Projects Fund* which provides 50% of the cost up to £1,000 inc VAT. Make sure you apply for funding before you start the study.

A full list of Technical Aid Centres in London is available from: **ACTAC Royal Institution,** *Colquitt St, Liverpool, LI 4DE, (051 708 7607).*

For information on Self-Build Housing: **Walter Segal Self-Build Trust,** *PO Box 542, SE1 1TX (357 7674).*

■ **RIBA Community Architecture Resource Centre,** *66 Portland Place, W1 (580 5533).*

■ **Community Action,** *PO Box 665, SW1X 8DZ (251 3008).* An independent magazine produced by and for tenants' and action groups and community campaigns.

■ **Education for Neighbourhood Change,** *Adult Education Research Centre, Block B, Nottingham University, NG7 2RD, (0602 484848 x3699 (mornings only)).* provide a number of 'packs' and 'fact banks' for use by self-help community info and action groups. They cover neighbourhood, planning, work and energy. Want to encourage community-based decision-making. Sae for list.

■ **Support,** *Unit 3, Cottons Studios, 7-13 Cottons Gdns, E2 (739 7969).* Established co-op with a lot of experience of catering to needs of Community Projects/ Tenant's groups, and of liaising with the different committees involved in this kind of work.

Planning for People

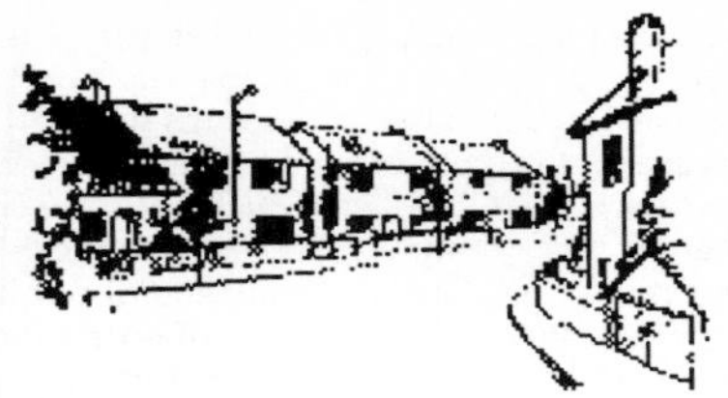

Planning legislation has tended to favour commercial interests in London to the detriment of local people. Many derelict sites, which could be used for much needed facilities, are developed in a way which helps to destroy community life rather than adding to it. Community associations, particularly in Central London, have been campaigning for 20 years to preserve their neighbourhoods for people. Their efforts are beginning to bear fruit. In the process they have developed a lot of skills and experience, making it possible for them to come up with their own plans and an alternative vision for the future of community life in London.

■ **TCPA,** *17 Carlton Hse Terr, SW1 (930 8903).* Pressure group which gives general advice on planning problems. Membership £24 pa includes journal, *Community Network*. Bookshop.

■ **Campaign For Homes in Central London,** *5 Dryden St, WC2 (240 2430).*

■ **Planning Aid for London,** *100 Minories, EC3 (702 0051).* Free and independent advice to individuals and groups who can't afford consultancy, from those finding it hard to get planning permission, to groups campaigning against major developments. Can arrange home visits if necessary.

▼ CO-OPS ▼

The co-operative movement was born out of an essential human survival skill - that of coming together with others to pool skills and resources, share responsibility and achieve a common aim. It started during the 'Industrial Revolution' in the 19th century when it offered an alternative to the exploitation of workers by the owners of the factory or business they worked in. There has been a revival in recent times spurred on by the renewed desire for personal freedom, community with others and the need to bring value and meaning to life and work.

Co-operatives can have differing aims but share, at least in theory, the following basic principles:

Membership is open to all who can use the co-ops services and are willing to share the responsibility. There is no artificial restriction or discrimination.

Democracy Members enjoy equal voting rights.

Share Capital Interest, if paid, is strictly limited.
Profit Any trading surplus belongs to the members and is distributed in a fair and agreed way.
Education Co-ops should provide for the education of members and the general public in the principles and techniques of economic and democratic co-operation.
Inter-Co-op Co-operation All co-ops should actively co-operate with each other at the local, national and international levels.

These principles can operate in practically all aspects of life - work, housing, consuming and finance.

Types of Co-ops

Workers' co-ops People who come together to create employment by sharing skills, resources and management on an equal basis. (See **Jobs** Section p36).
Housing co-ops Where tenants or homebuyers group together to buy or rent and manage good quality housing at low cost. (See **Somewhere to Live** p2).
Marketing Co-ops Producers of goods join together to sell their products.
Consumers Co-ops consumers share and run a service which enables them to pool their buying power to buy reasonably priced food or goods.
A Credit Union a co-operative of savers and buyers where members can have the use of finance at reasonable interest rates. Credit unions are multiplying fast in local communities, workplaces or as a means to finance neighbourhood projects.
Neighbourhood Co-ops A co-op run by employees allowing non-emloyee members from the neighbourhood to participate. The aim is to make use of local skills in getting community based businesses going.
Community Co-op a set up whose members come from business and the local community with aims that meet business and social needs.

Joining a Co-op

The success of a co-operative enterprise depends on good working relationships between members who share a common aim and can agree on the means of implementing it. For this reason Co-ops usually set a probationary period for potential members of between 1-6 months.
You can find out about vacancies through the *London Co-op News* a bi-monthly publication from **London ICOM** or by contacting your local **CDA (Co-operative Development Agency** see below).

Starting A Co-op

Legally you will need seven people to register a workers co-op. However if you can gather together two or more people who have an idea in common, complimentary skills and abilities and a commitment to co-operative principles you will find that the agencies listed below will provide the necessary information and resources to develop your idea further. CDAs are usually controlled by their local workers' co-ops. They provide:
• basic business training and start up advice
• advice on drawing up a business plan
• advice on obtaining funds
• access to a range of specialist consultants who can help you with business problems
• contacts with other co-ops who can share their experience and skills with you

Before you go ahead do as much research as possible, from the publications below and with other established co-ops, particularly with regard to the decision making process and management structures you intend to adopt. Conflicts within co-ops can arise when the way in which power is shared and decisions are taken is not sufficiently well worked out.

USEFUL PUBLICATIONS

• The best introduction to setting up a *Co-op is the Workers' Co-operative Handbook* Peter Cockerton and Anna Whyatt (ICOM Co-publications 1986 £4.25).
• *Everywoman Directory of Women's Co-ops* (ICOM Co-production with Everywoman) (75p inc p&p).
•*Co-operative Learning Packs* developed by the Open University Co-operative Research Unit : *Introducing Co-ops* (£3.50), *Launching a Co-op* (£7.50), *Improving Co-op Performance* (£7.50), all from:
■ **Turnaround,** *27 Horsell Rd, , N5 (609 7836).*
• *Casting Off - A Guide To Setting Up a Co-operative Business* Malcolm Corbett and Anna Lamacraft. This guide was produced to accompany the Thames TV series of the same name. Available free from
■ **Members Relations Dept,** *CRS South Eastern Ltd, 78-102 The Broadway, Stratford, E15 (534 4201).*
Directory of Co-ops in the UK available from
■ **The Co-operative Research Systems Group,** *Open University, Waltham Hall, Milton Keynes, Bucks, MK7 6AA.,* This is the most up to date listing for co-ops but it costs £25. Many of the organisations mentioned in this section will have a copy and may let you use it for reference.

CONTACTS

■ **ICOM (The Industrial Common Ownership**

Movement), *7-8 The Corn Exchange, Leeds LS1 7BP, (0532 461737)* is the national federation for workers co-operatives. Most Co-ops use model rules drawn up by ICOM. There is a legal registration service for co-ops which takes approx. 3 months and costs in the region of £275-£325 plus VAT. Provide support and info together with some useful publications.

■ **ICOM (London),** *8 Bradbury St, N16 (249 2837)* provides info packs for prospective co-ops in London. Gives advice on registration although the paperwork is sent to national ICOM. Publishes *London Co-op News* a quarterly mag. Organises a open meetings (qtly) for people interested in the co-operative movement in London.

■ **Co-operative Development Agency,** *Broadmead Hse, 21 Panton St, SW1 (839 2988).*

■ **Kingston & Richmond CDA,** *58b London Rd, Kingston, Surrey, KT2 6QA.*

■ **Latin American CDP,** *The Co-op Centre, Mowll St, SW9 (582 4482).*

■ **Lambeth CDA,** *The Co-op Centre, Mowll St, , SW9 (582 0003).*

■ **Croydon CDA,** *46 High St, Croydon, Surrey, CRO 1YB, (686 1966).*

■ **Hackney Co-op Developments,** *16 Dalston Ln, E8 (254 4829).*

■ **Hammersmith CEDA,** *Palingswick Hse, 241 King St, W6 (741 2304).*

■ **Newham CDA,** *375 High St, Stratford, E15 (519 2377).*

■ **SSBA,** *170 Brick Lane, Tower Hamlets, E1 (247 1892).*

■ **Tower Hamlets CDA,** *84 Whitehorse Rd, E1 (791 0450).*

■ **Islington CDA,** *177 Upper St , N1 (226 2783).*

■ **Ealing CDA,** *Charles Hse, Bridge Rd, Southall Middx, UB2 4BD, (574 4724).*

■ **GERU,** *311 Plumstead High St, Greenwich, SE18 (310 6695).*

■ **Southwark CDA,** *135 Rye Lane, SE15 (639 0134).*

■ **National Federation of Housing Co-operatives,** *88 Old St, EC1 (608 2494).*

CREDIT UNIONS

■ **Association of British Credit Unions Ltd,** *48 Maddox St, W1 (408 1699).*

■ **Community Economy Ltd,** *Essex Hse, 375 High St, Stratford, E15 (519 6447)* an independent non-profit making company set up to research the potential for community based economic development. Among other activities it provides for training and guidance in the setting up of community based credit unions.

▼ COMMUNAL LIVING ▼

Communal Living is by no means an easy option. Those who choose this way of life need to devote a lot of time, energy and willingness to overcome the emotional and practical obstacles which inevitably arise. Nonetheless it remains an attractive option to people who want to try to develop a sense of belonging, companionship and a supportive atmosphere with a number of others, and there are also the obvious practical advantages of sharing resources.

There are known to be at least 100 communes in Britain today differing greatly from each other according to their size and location. Set-ups vary from single households in towns and cities to rural land based arrangements with large sprawling mansions, to village sized communities. For further details contact the

■ **Communes Network,** *c/o Lifespan Community, Townhead, Dunford Bridge, Sheffield S30 6TG,* an informal network of communal groups in Britain. They produce a newsletter and info about communities worldwide.

There are as many different models of communal living as there are communes. Each group tends to evolve its own unique way of working, depending on it's size, location and philosophy.

The following gives some indication of how aspects of life are shared.

Decision making: group decision making is an important feature of communal living. The 'consensus' (everyone has to agree) method is usually favoured because it takes everybody's opinion into account and the final decision is the best possible solution acceptable to all. However it is time consuming and subject to abuse unless everyone is very much committed to "the good of the whole". It is not suitable for quick, day to day decisions nor for those which require a lot of technical know-how.

Income Pooling
Communes usually have a system for distributing or re-distributing income among members. Some pool all

income to cover expenses and re-distribute pocket money to individuals. Others survive without any need to pool income. In groups where people have different jobs outside, income is often equalised by a percentage contribution. Other communes which provide separate living facilities operate a 'rent difference' where individuals or families pay according to such things as income or size of accommodation.

Work Some communities set up co-operative businesses together as a means of generating income. Others make a living from the land and share all but the most highly skilled tasks. Within the household there is usually a rota system in operation.

Childcare Most income sharing communities have some form of structured childcare facilities where children are looked after by the whole group.

Publications

• *Diggers and Dreamers* - an invaluable source of information on all aspects of communal living. With advice on getting started and a directory listing 50 communities in Britain. (Published by the **Communes Network** at £4.95).

• *Building Communities the Co-operative Way* J Birchall (Routledge Kegan & Paul 1988).

Communities in London:

Some of these communities welcome visitors and are open to new members, but contact them first to arrange a visit.

■ **Double Helix,** *44 Josephine Ave, SW2*. Members have private accommodation and shared communal space in four large houses. Socialist/ Feminist ideology.

■ **Mornington Grove,** *13-14 Mornington Grove, Bow, E3*. A group of 16 people sharing two large houses and a garden. Vegetarian household with people with various ideologies.

■ **Root Groups,** *USPG Partnership Hse, 157 Waterloo Rd, SE1*. Christian communities who experiment with lay ministry and work alongside local churches in the inner city or outer estates. Groups are financially self-supporting and encourage a simple lifestyle.

■ **Some Friends,** *128 Bethnal Green Rd, E8*. An international community with 17 members of Quaker and other complimentary persuasions.

▼ VOLUNTEERING ▼

Volunteering can be a rewarding experience - you can increase your skills and know how, get to know people in your neighbourhood and contribute your efforts to worthwhile projects.

It is important, however, to be clear about your motives and expectations. Make sure the organisation you choose to work for meets your requirements. Before contacting an agency, spend some time thinking about what you have to offer. How much time can you give? How often? What skills and experience do you have to offer? What do you need to know about them?

For info on what's available in your area you can contact the following:

■ **Local Volunteer Bureaux** act as a volunteers 'job-shop', matching people to voluntary groups' needs. Look in the phone book or *Yellow Pages* under *Volunteers* or *Voluntary*.

■ **Councils for Voluntary Services** will know about most of the voluntary organisations in your area.

■ **BASSAC** (See **Community Action** p266) to see if there are volunteering opportunities in your local social action centre.

■ **London Voluntary Services Council** (See Community Action p###) provides advice and publishes *Voluntary Action Across London* a directory of community and voluntary agencies operating in the city. Try your local library for a copy, you may find there is a reference file there for local voluntary projects.

■ **The Volunteer Centre UK,** *29 Lower Kings Rd, Birkhamstead, Hertfordshire, HP4 2AB,* provides an info sheet on volunteering opportunities throughout the UK.

RESIDENTIAL WORK

■ **Community Service Volunteers,** *237 Pentonville Rd, N1 (278 6601)*. Placements are full time, away from home - opportunities in London and outside. You get board, lodging and £18 pw and placements are 4-12 months. They accept everyone. Work is with people in need: handicapped, young, elderly etc. Contact Louise Baxter.

■ **National Youth Bureau,** *17 Albion St, Leicester, (0533 471200)*. Youth and community resource centre which provides info and youth volunteering opportunities nationwide.

■ **British Trust for Conservation Volunteers,** *36 St Mary's St, Wallingford, Oxfordshire, OX 10 OEU, (0491 39766)*. The trust operates holiday work camps throughout Britain as well as weekend environmental conservation work in the Greater London area. Volunteers pay a membership fee and a donation towards the running costs of the camp (this varies according to the facilities offered). In return accommodation, food and catering equipment are provided.

■ **The Central Bureau for Educational Visits and Exchanges,** *Seymour Mews Hse, Seymour Mews, W1H 9PE (486 5101)*. Publish *Working Holidays 1989* (£7.70 incl p&p) which lists thousands of short term (2 wks to 1 year) paid and voluntary jobs in Britain and overseas. Also publish *Home from Home* (£3.95 incl p&p) which is an international guide to home stays and exchange visits with detailed info on organisations which arrange the swap.

green environment

If you're someone who believes officialdom is finally admitting to the depth of the global crisis you could be right - but are they doing anything about it?

Now we are beginning to become aware of the toll humankind is taking on the planet and finding ourselves on the edge of a precipice. We all know it's going to need active will power, individual and organisational responsibility to stop and reverse the damage done.

It is very encouraging to report on and list the extent of the work being done by Londoners, by groups and individuals dedicated to working to publicise, prevent and solve some of the huge environmental problems we face.

There has been encouraging progress in this area and what is equally apparent is that people are finding more and mpre imaginative ways to express the value of protecting our blue planet.

▼ LONDON HABITATS AND ▼ CITY WILDLIFE

When green spaces and habitats are lost to developers, wildlife suffers and people suffer as well by losing contact with open green spaces.

There is an estimated 30 sq. miles of wasteland in inner London which could support birds, insects (such as butterflies and bees - London honey wins national prizes), many kinds of wild flowers, trees and small mammals, all of which are declining in the wild.

There are organisations which help volunteers turn areas into nature reserves, ecological parks and community gardens. Some councils offer start-up grants to help people reclaim waste land and some property developers have been persuaded to lend a site until they decide what to do with it, and this can sometimes be a long time.

The London Wildlife Trust is the city's leading urban wildlife organisation and manages over 45 sites across London and liaises with the 32 London Boroughs. One of the biggest and richest sites is **Camley Street Natural Park,** *12 Camley st, NW1 ONX (833 2311).* This has a meadow, wildlife garden, pond, bird hide, bog and tree planting area.

Currently Camley St is under threat from a proposed new development by British Rail under the existing Kings Cross Station. It appears there are alternatives to this site and there is a 'Save Camley Street Campaign.'

Another interesting site is ***Ainslie Wood,*** a four acre mixed oak woodland at Chingford Mount in Waltham Forest borough. It is quite ancient in origin having been continuously wooded since 1600 and has many interesting old plants and a variety of woodland birds. Enter via *Woodside Gardens E4.*

For more details of special ecological parks contact the **London Wildlife Trust,** *80 York Way, N1 (278 6612/3)* which campaign and manage various sites for wildlife conservation in the city. They publish a newsletter *Wild London* (qtly) Membership £11 (£6 conc).

Action

There are plenty of sites which could be claimed for local people which would maintain and build the delicate ecological infrastructure in London as well as providing education and recreational sanctuaries.

Certainly before-and-after pictures of these natural sites are impressive and show what develops in a very few years. Dragonflies and nesting water birds and kestrals appear even in central London natural sites.

Gardens

These have great potential as wildlife habitats and they amount to a vast area of land. Help turn the city into a nature reserve, scatter wild flower seeds, plant native trees, leave old wood to rot as a home for fungi and forget about regular grass cutting (a spring and autumn cutting is enough). Avoid pesticides and herbicides which destroy the self-regulating balance that develops.

■ **Nature Conservancy Council (NCC),** *Northminster Hse, Northminster Rd, Peterborough PE1 1UA, ((0733) 40345)* for posters, publications and teaching packs.

▼ ORGANIC GROWING ▼

Every year more gardens and farms go organic and as the demand for organic produce increases in the city it will help the countryside environment and also increase supply. Organic wholesalers at New Covent Garden early morning fruit and veg market are increasing and large supermarkets are beginning to stock organic produce , as do health food stores.

Although obviously every organic garden helps, growing your own food in London has its problems. For a start it is very time consuming and there is the pollution from lead in the air and soil. Experts give a lot of contradictory advice. Small quantities of lead don't do much harm but children are particularly vulnerable.

There are some guidelines to follow: Don't grow anything within 25 yards of a busy road (most London roads are busy!). If possible, concentrate on fruiting veg like peas, beans, tomatoes, courgettes and cucumbers. Grow root veg only if you are in the outer suburbs.

Leafy veg are not such a good idea, even bought leafy veg should be washed thoroughly and the outer leaves removed. Scrub roots and don't reuse the water for soups. Cloches and greenhouses reduce contamination.

Use your food waste in the garden as compost. It improves the soil and helps moisture retention.

A compost tumbler which is claimed to make compost in 21 days and is made from recycled plastic barrels is available price £39.95 incl. delivery from **Blackwall Products Ltd.,** *Unit 4, Riverside Industrial Estate, 150 Riverway, SE10 OBH.* Information on composting and composters can be obtained from **The Soil Association,** *86-88 Colston St Bristol BS1 5BB, (0272 290661).*

Indoor Gardening

You don't need to have a garden to grow food. Window boxes indoors or out can be planted with fast growing salad crops. Sunny windows are good for pots of tomatoes or peppers. Herbs, radishes, spring onions and lettuce will grow well under artificial light. You will need to keep the plants free from draughts and use humidifiers if you're lucky enough to have central heating. Help pollination by using a fine mist spray or do it manually. Mushrooms need no light - they grow all year round in an attic, or cupboard, kept at 50-60 C. Most seed shops sell cheap kits with instructions. Sprouting beans are very easy and a good cheap protein source.

Hydroponics

This is growing food, in or out of doors, using nutrient solutions instead of soil. You can get fantastic yields from very little space using either organic or chemical means. Best introduction (and the funniest) is *Hydro-Story: The complete Manual of Hydroponic Gardening at Home* C Sherman (Nolo Press). You can get ready mixed nutrient solution from **Phostrogen Limited,** *Corwen, Clwyd, LL21 OEE.*

Allotments

If you don't have a garden contact your local council or **FOE (Friends of the Earth** p275) for the nearest allotment. They're cheap but there's usually a long waiting list.

■ **Henry Doubleday Research Assn (Sales),** *National Centre for Organic Gardening, Ryton-on-Dunsmore, Coventry CV8 3LG, ((0203) 303517)* researches and encourages organic gardeners. Members get free gardening advice, magazine, use of reference library as well as access to vegetable varieties outlawed under recent EEC regulations. Sae for organic gardening catalogue: seeds, fertilisers, organic pest and disease control devices and applications, gardening supplies and books. Also organic wines.

▼ CITY FARMS ▼

City Farms have been expanding and growing in London since the 70s. They are projects which involve local people in farming in the city, often on derelict land. They are charities planned and managed by local people and operate throughout the year.

Children get a lot from city farms and they are not the only ones! They are educational, recreational and to a certain extent commercial businesses.

They have a variety of different functions which vary from farm to farm e.g. producing small crops, herbs, wild flowers, hay, crafts, rearing animals, composting and hydroponics. As well as providing training they are often very therapeutic places for young people and adults who find urban life hard.

City Farms now have a sister project setting up 'country farms' within 50 miles of the city to link the city and country and generate jobs and training opportunities.

There are 14 farms in London and 6 community gardens. For a full list ring the **National Federation of City Farms,** *The Old Vicarage, 66 Fraser St, Windmill Hill, Bristol BS3 4LY, (0272-660663)* who hold meetings and conferences also training courses in animal husbandry, animal welfare and homoeopathy for livestock.

The farms are often open 7 days a week for visitors and groups. It is best to book if you are bringing a small group so you can be shown around and have pony rides etc.

Vauxhall City Farm is very well established and is just getting new buildings, and is famous for her exceptionally huge and gentle sow'Muriel'.

Hackney City Farm has unique fundraising Pig-Racing. The manager moved the feeding trough further away each morning and now the pigs enjoy a gallop (?) down the length of the farmyard. Pig-Racing takes place quite often on a Sunday afternoon.

Put 20p on 'Streaky Lightning'.

The following farms are open to visitors. They all cater for school groups. Some of them can offer teaching in animal care, crafts and other skills such as building and carpentry. Run as working farms, many of them also offer farm produce for sale. Phone for details.

■ **Surrey Docks Farm,** *Rotherhithe St, SE16 (231 1010).* Closed Mon. Open 10.00-5pm.

■ **Mudchute Community Farm,** *Pier St, Millwall, E14 (515 5901).* Open 7.30-5.30.

■ **Stepping Stones Farm,** *Stepney Way, Ben Jonson Rd, E1 3DG (790 8204).* Closed Mon. Open 9.30-1.00 and 2.00-6.00.

■ **Kentish Town City Farm,** *1 Cressfield Cl, NW5 (485 4585).* 9.30-6.00.

■ **Spitalfields Farm Assn Ltd,** *Weaver St, E1 (247 8762).* 9.00-6.00.

■ **Freightliners,** *Paradise Pk, Sherinham Rd, N7 (609 0467).* 11.00-1.00 and 2.00-5.00. Closed Mon.

■ **Hackney City Farm,** *1a Goldsmiths Row, E2 (729 6381).* 10.00-4.30. Closed Mon.

■ **Vauxhall City Farm,** *24 St Oswald's Pl, SE11 (582 4204).* 10.30-5.00. Closed Mon & Fri.

■ **Peoples Farm,** *Shacklewell Lane, E8 (806 5743).* 9.30-5.00.

■ **Thameside Park Assn,** *40 Thames Rd, Barking, Essex, (594 8449).* 8.30-5.00.

■ **Corams Fields,** *93 Guilford St, WC1 (837 6138).* 8.00- 8.00 every day of the year except Xmas and Boxing day.

■ **Elm Farm,** *Gladstone Terrace, Lockington Rd, Battersea, SW8 (627 1130).* 8.30-5.00. Closed Mon & Fri.

■ **Dean City Farm,** *1 Batsworth Rd, Mitcham, Surrey, (648 1461).* 8.00-6.00.

■ **Walworth City Farm,** *230 Amelia St, SE17 (582 2652).* The newest of London City farms. 8.30 - 4.00.

■ **Wellgate Community Farm,** *Collier Row Rd, Romford, Essex, (599 0415).* 9.00-4.00. (9.00-12.00 Wk/ends)

■ **Spelthorne Farm Project for the Handicapped,** *6 Burrows Hill Clse, Heathrow, Houndslow, Middlesex, (0753 680330).* Access by the farm's minibus from Heathrow.

▼ ENVIRONMENTAL GROUPS ▼

London has many groups which spearhead different environmental concerns and each has its own approach and style.
Some organisations are multi-issue pressure groups (like **Friends of the Earth which** runs at least 10 different campaigns), some are single issue pressure groups with local or national interest (e.g. the **Countryside Commission** and **World Wildlife Fund**) and some are just one specific issue like the **Woodland Trust** and the **Noise Abatement Society.** All these groups are non-party political and their function is to influence politicians and voters of all persuasions.

Below are a few of the contact points. If you need more specialist information there is a comprehensive directory called *The Directory for the Environment*, Michael Barker (ed) (Routledge and Kegan Paul 1986).

■ **Friends of the Earth Ltd,** *26-28 Underwood St, N17JQ (490 1555)* now has over 100,000 supporters in the UK and is international with groups in 35 different countries co-ordinated through FOE International. It has an excellent track record of campaigning and battles won. The work is more on land based campaigns e.g. ozone layer, rain forests, acid rain and energy. The well-organised local group network co-ordinates actions such as the successful boycott of ozone damaging aerosols forcing the phasing out of CFCs as propellants.

In London FOE have a *Cities for People* lobby, campaigning for the rights of cyclists, pedestrians, users of public transport and protecting green spaces in the city and reducing pollution.

They have a large range of publications, posters, badges,T-shirts, exhibitions and slide sets for loan and a good bookshop. They do a neat little publication called the *A-Z of Local Pollution* with a London directory for Environmental Health departments etc. This will be an invaluable aid in your battle against dog fouling in your local park, or any of those other small things you can do to improve the environment.

■ **Greenpeace,** *30-31 Islington Gn, N1 8XE (351 5100).* This is one of the largest organisations and has at the time of writing 218,000 UK supporters, a number which is growing by some 2,000 new supporters every week. It specialises in sea campaigns which were spearheaded by the famous voyages of the *Rainbow Warrior* in protest against nuclear testing and whaling. It is powerful because it is international - it has established a base in Antarctica to claim the continent as a World Park. There are various UK and local activities which range from the scaling of Big Ben with a huge banner TIME TO STOP TESTING to scientific research on water pollution in British rivers.

■ **The ARK Trust,** *500 Harrow Rd, W9 3QA (968 6780).* New non-political organisation offering practical solutions to environmental problems. Advocates individual responsibility towards the environment such as using lead free petrol, recycling, eating less meat and buying organically grown products. Membership £10 (£5).

■ **The Women's Environmental Network,** *287 City Rd, EC1V 1LA (490 2511).* Founded in 1988 to campaign on and highlight environmental issues that specifically affect women and to mobilise the power women have as consumers to affect change. Membership £10 (£7).

■ **Living Earth Foundation,** *10 Upper Grosvensor St, W1 (499 0856).* Promotes the sustainable use of the Earth's resources in business and educational fields.

■ **Ecological Studies Institute (ESI),** *50 Chandos Place, WC2N 4HG (836 0341/8570).* Looks at the impact of environmental issues on electoral politics and checks up on the environmental record of Britain's major companies.

■ **National Association for Environmental Education,** *West Midlands College of Higher Education, Gorway, Walsall WS1 3BD, (0922 31200).* For lecturers, teachers and others concerned with education and the environment. Runs conferences and has a wide range of practical publications including its journal *Environmental Education;* a series of guides to courses in Environmental Studies; school study aids; and occasional papers. Sae for list.

■ **Earth Resources Research,** *(ERR), 258 Pentonville Rd , N1 9JY (278 3833).* Independent organisation carrying out research into environmental concerns (e.g. recycling, transport planning and various aspects of nuclear power) and publishing its results in book or pamphlet form.

■ **Council for the Protection of Rural England (CPRE),** *4 Hobart Place, SW1W OHY (235 9481).* One of the country's leading conservation groups

which has helped to create National Parks, Green Belts and campaigned on energy and transport issues.

■ **Town and Country Planning Association, (TCPA),** *17 Carlton House Terr, SW1Y 5AS (930 8903/4/5).* TCPA campaigns for a standardised planning framework for the regions and for measures to tackle inner city decay and the growing North/South divide. Originally part of the 'garden city' movement which set up towns like Welwyn Garden City. Runs conferences, training and projects such as the Lightmoor new community, a self-managed community financed by a 'community mortgage'. Publish planning aid manuals for community groups and monthly magazine, *Town and Country Planning* as well as *Community Network* and *Planning Bulletin.* Wide range of titles sold at bookshop - send sae for catalogue.

■ **The Environment Council,** *80 York Way, N1 9AG (278 4736).* National coalition of non-government organisations meeting to discuss environmental issues and to coordinate the use of scarce resources. Publishes *Habitat* (£10.00/yr). Recently implemented the Business and Environment Programme which aims to educate companies about the commercial benefits of taking care of the environment.

■ **Countryside Commission,** *John Dower Hse, Crescent Pl, Cheltenham, Glos GL50 3RA, (0242 521381).* Publish a free directory of training opportunities in countryside conservation and recreation *The Countryside Education and Training Directory.* Are proposing a path along the Thames from its source to the Thames barrier.

■ **British Waterways Board,** *Melbury Hse, Melbury Terr, NW1*. Responsible for canals and rivers. Info on navigation, walks and history.

▼ GREEN POLITICS ▼

The inspiration for green politics springs from a different source from traditional politics: it is not so much concerned with having control over 'things' but more with fostering a relationship of mutual respect between people, and their environment.

Voting Green no longer has that wasted vote stigma and more and more people are acknowledging that environmental concerns should now come first on the political agenda.

In Europe, the Green Party has had a small but significant voice for some time and the percentage growth in votes at each election is greater than any other party. We are just beginning to see this emerging in Britain as people question our economic system. Even the *Daily Telegraph* reviewed the Green Party Election Manifesto in 1987 as 'an election manifesto of disarming frankness'.

However, without proportional representation it is an uphill battle to get green candidates elected. An important role for the Greens at present is to stand outside the system and to deliberately and systematically challenge the major parties.

It is true to say that even at this time green politics and increasing environmental awareness has had a profound effect on all political parties. The danger is of being duped into thinking that if a party produces a document on an issue they have the will and understanding to do something.

So far most efforts on any environmental issues from the main parties either fall short of acknowledging the full seriousness of the situation or underestimate the enormous difficulties ahead with unrealistic optimism.

Green politics requires a fundamental shift of thinking. Rather than an unquestioning acceptance of unlimited economic growth and competition what is called for is a view of economics based on careful use of resources and co-operation.

■ **Green Party,** *10 Station Parade, Balham High Rd, SW12 9AZ (673 0045)*. Formerly the Ecology Party, with close links with the Green Parties in the rest of Europe.

■ **Green Alliance,** *60 Chandos Place, WC2N 4HG (836 0341)*. An alliance of people from different political backgrounds, but who share a concern for the environment.

■ **Green Democrats,** *Cranmore, 3 Chessington Road, Ewell, Surrey, KT17 1TS , (394 0644)*. For members of the Social and Liberal Democratic Party.

■ **Liberal Ecology Group,** *77 Dresden Road, N19 3BG.*

■ **SDP Greens,** *69 Cambridge Rd, Oakington, Cambridge, CB4 5BG.*

■ **SERA, (Socialist Environment and Resources Association),** *26 Underwood St, N1 7JQ (490 0240)*. Founded in '73, is a valuable link between reds and greens. Calling for decentralisation, they advocate changes in the management of the environment and encourage awareness of environmental issues by policy and decision makers. Current campaigns include action against the destruction of rain forests, and the London Environmental Charter. *New Ground* mag (£1).

Reading

BOOKS

Jonathon Porritt's *Seeing Green* (Blackwell 1984) is still by far the best introductory book on Green Politics in Britain. It is clear, honest, witty, fearless and is particularly good at exploring the perspective on economics and industrialisation.

Sara Parkin *Green Parties - An International Guide* (Heretic books1989) examines established Green parties in the 15 West European countries giving addresses, publications and other references.

MAGAZINES.

■ **The Ecologist**, *Worthyvale Manor, Camelford, Cornwall.*

■ **Green Line,** *34 Cowley Road, Oxford OX4 1HZ.*

■ **New Internationalist,** *42 Hythe Bridge Street, Oxford OX1 1EP.*

■ **Resurgence,** *Ford House, Hartland, Bideford, Devon.*

■ **i to i** *1 Fawley Rd NW6 435 3350.*

▼ CONSERVATION ▼

Land is our most basic asset and because it is a limited resource it has always been the subject of struggle between those who have conflicting ideas about how to use it.

A strong voice is needed to counter those who speak loudly for financial concerns; 80% of the land surface in Britain is countryside but rural affairs are controlled by a tiny group of people who own the land and make the laws. The land in Britain is owned by a very small proportion of the population (9% own 84% of the land). So nature conservation groups are a very important way in which people can get their voices heard.

Some of the issues conservation groups are dealing with in Britain:

• Hedgerow loss has accelerated to 4,000 miles a year in the 80s.

• Ordinary citizens can be treated as trespassers on more than 1.2 million of the 1.5 million acres of the so called 'common land' in England and Wales.

• The Ramblers Association state that around 66% of public footpaths across England are ploughed up.

Organisations

The groups listed cover rural concerns and some urban issues such as wasteland reclamation, planning and architecture.

■ **British Trust for Conservation Volunteers (BTCV),** *36 St. Mary's St, Wallingford, Oxon OX10 OEU, (0491 39766).* Organise conservation volunteers (fancy a working holiday?), publications include handbooks on *Drystone Walling* and *Footpaths*. Membership £10 (£5.50 students and unwaged).

■ **Civic Trust,** *17 Carlton Hse Terr, SW1 (930 0914).* Semi-official body concerned with planning and architectural ('heritage') aspects of the environment. Will help form local amenity societies and 'co-operative street improvement schemes'. Publishes *Heritage Outlook* £7.50 per yr (bi-monthly) Produces the excellent *Environmental Directory* (3.50+50p) which lists all public and private groups concerned with the environment.

■ **National Trust,** *36 Queen Anne's Gate, SW1H 9AS (222 9251).*

■ **Royal Society for the Protection of Birds,** *The Lodge, Sandy, Beds, SG19 2DL, (0767 80551).* The largest conservation society .

■ **Ramblers Association,** *1/5 Wandsworth Rd, SW8 (582 6878).* Campaign for the protection of footpaths and wildlife. Oversee network of 300 local groups which organise walks. Membership £9.75 or £12.20 for two members at the same address. Bi-mnthly mag, handbook with bed and breakfast addresses and info, map library.

Trees

■ **Tree Council,** *35 Belgrave Sq, SW1 (235 8854).*

■ **Woodland Trust,** *Autumn Park, Dysart Road, Grantham, Lincolnshire NG31 6LL,* National charity concerned with conservation of native woodland and broadleaved trees.

■ **Men of the Trees,** *Sandy Lane, Crawley Down, Crawley, Sussex RH10 4HS, (0342 712536).* International society dedicated to the planting of trees. Membership, presumably open to women too, (£10).

▼ POLLUTION ▼

Polluters, whether individuals or businesses, do so because they gain financially or personally at the expense of others. They will continue to do so until they are forced to stop.

Most of the environmental groups campaign against various types of pollution. Overall it is more effective if groups diversify and each focus on a single issue. Don't feel powerless because there is so much to do. Just put your back into one small area you feel strongly about and contribute a little of your life for the benefit of everyone!

Certainly the British Government is exceptionally blind when it comes to pollution, they pay lip service to the idea that whoever causes pollution should pay for the damage they cause but enforcement of the law is very weak. Many businesses will try to get away with waste dumping wherever possible. British pollution affects Europe and it has taken great pressure from Germany (where 52% of the trees are dead or dying) and Sweden (where a quarter of the lakes are suffering from acidification which has killed most aquatic wildlife) to get the government to start pollution control in the power stations, which emit the pollution responsible. Even then the gesture they made was surely a token when in 1986 they announced that 12 (out of 41) power stations were going to fit scrubbers in the smoke stacks, reducing sulphur emissions by 30% by the year 2000! The annual UK investment in cleaning up power stations is a thirtieth of that made by West Germany.

What Can You Do?

In addition to spearheading environmental lobbying there is a lot you can do as an individual.

• Try to use biodegradable chemicals wherever possible. Such cleaners (e.g. Ecover) are now sold in large supermarkets. Get your store to stock them.

• If you have a car, check if it will run on unleaded petrol and get it fitted with a catalytic converter, which reduces the emission of harmful substances. Use the car as little as possible and encourage your friends to do the same.

- Avoid using *any* spray cans that are not 'ozone friendly'.
- Work towards making your home and workplace energy efficient. There is a host of things you can do from effective insulation which will cut down on your heating bills, to not leaving taps running or lights on unnecessarily. Challenge the management about improvements in your working environment.
- Don't buy products which are wastefully packaged (e.g. many fast foods).
- Recycle whatever is possible and see what can be done at your workplace. Badger your local council to improve facilities for collection.
- Buy organically grown food. Increased demand will improve supply and prices.
- Make your voice heard - challenge those who litter and pollute.

Organisations

■ **Campaign Against Lead in Petrol,** *171 Barnett Wood Lane Ashtead Surrey KT21 2LP, (0372 275977).* In spite of the recent introduction of lead free petrol at our stations Britain still lags behind other European countries when it comes to the use of lead free petrol. The percentage of vehicles using unleaded petrol in Britain is 22% compared to Germany's 60%, Holland's 50%.

■ **Royal Commission on Environmental Pollution,** *Church Hse, Gt Smith St, SW1 (276 2080).* Advises the government and carries out independent studies.

■ **Noise Abatement Society,** *PO Box 8, Bromley, Kent, (460 3145).* Campaigns to reduce noise pollution - from lawnmowers to juggernauts. Free booklet on how to complain about noise.

■ **Greenpeace,** (see p###).

▼ WASTE AND RECYCLING ▼

Did you know:

- Greater London produces over 13.5 *million* tonnes of rubbish a year - *enough to fill up the Huses of Parliament every three days!*
- We each produce a tonne (2240lbs) of rubbish every year.
- British people pay £720 million annually through rates and taxes to get rid of all that rubbish.
- There's £750 million's-worth of re-useable refuse thrown away each year on the enormous British waste heap.

Recycling can save money, create jobs, preserve the countryside and conserve the valuable resources of our world - so go out and start rummaging around in your dustbin.

This section is to give some idea of our wastage and what can be done by you in London.

If it is well organised recycling can be very profitable, either for the council or small firms. Ring your local council to find out where the collection points are. If they provide a limited service it's because of poor organisation which should be complained about.

Richmond-upon-Thames borough sets a good example with a scheme where the money they obtain from recycling pays the salary for a full-time recycling officer and also provides a good fund for local charities. There is no reason why other boroughs shouldn't follow suit.

Packaging

Around 70% of domestic waste is packaging materials and manufacturers are using it as a means of making their product more attractive. A revolution in what we eat has already occurred. Consumer pressure has led to additive free foods being freely available. This is starting to happen on tin cans. If consumers start refusing environmentally irresponsible packaging the manufacturers, designers and retailers will have to respond.

Bottles

Have you ever counted how many glass containers you empty each week? Probably at least 7. That's your share of the six billion glass containers used each year.

Bottle banks are familiar to most people. They were first introduced by the **GMF (Glass Manufacturers Federation)** after **Friends of the Earth** campaigned against the decline of non-returnable bottles.

Sadly large supermarket chains have little interest in the returnable bottle but many are sympathetic to bottle banks which can be found increasingly in supermarket car parks.

Make sure you save your bottles at home and at work and perhaps share taking them to the bottle banks with others for whom transport is more difficult.

Lack of transport is obviously limiting for some people. In some parts of the country (e.g. Scotland) councils do different collections on different days for glass, paper etc. It would seem if they can do it in Scotland we should be able to develop similar schemes in London.

Paper

Every person in Britain uses up about 2 trees' worth of paper products each year. In 1985 Britain used a forest the equivalent size of Wales. Recycling can make a major contribution to the conservation of resources.

There is an energy saving of up to 50% in the production of paper from waste rather than virgin pulp. 29% of paper and board is recycled in the UK.

WASTE PAPER OR RECYCLE IT?

The piles of papers we produce daily are one of the most obvious displays of absurd and needless waste. It is not difficult to keep paper separate and recycle it with ease. The difficulty is that the value of waste paper fluctuates greatly and varies according to grade, making it very difficult for groups to run a viable collection scheme.

A stable market for waste paper and board is, therefore, necessary if recycling paper is going to be worthwhile. The paper industry could provide this market by guaranteeing a minimum price for waste paper.

An alternative way of developing the market for waste paper is to expand the demand for recycled paper products.

The quality of recycled paper is improving all the time and the greater the demand, the better it will get. See if you can use more recycled products and start discussing photocopying and toilet paper at work. Most people know it makes sense!

OUTLETS

■ **Books for a Change,** *52 Charing Cross Road, WC2 (836 2315).*

■ **Ecology Centre,** 42 Shelton Street, Covent Garden, WC2 (379 4324).

■ **Oxfam,** *7 Astoria Parade, Streatham High Road, SW16 (769 0515).*

■ **TREES Recycled Products,** *c/o D Kemball-Cook, 9 Horsford Road, SW2 5BW (737 6015).*

MAIL ORDER

■ **The Conservation Foundation,** *Lowther Lodge, Kensington Gore, SW7 2AR (823 8844).*

■ **Forest Saver,** *228 London Road, Reading. Berks RG6 1AH , (0734 668611).*

■ **Standard Continuous,** *Forms House 473 Stratford Road, Shirley, Solihull, West Midlands E90 45AD , (021-733 3131).*

■ **Traidcraft,** *Kingsway, Gateshead, Tyne on Wear NE11 ONE , (091-491 0591).*

WHOLESALE

■ **City Paper Supplies Ltd,** *1 Vandy Street, EC2 (377 5112). (Paper not envelopes).*

■ **Impact Business Forms,** *128 Regent Road, Leicester LE1 7PF , (0533 541597).* (Computer listing paper).

■ **Paperback Ltd,** *Bow Triangle Business Centre, Unit 2 Eleanor Street, E3 4NP (980 2233).*

Cans

The scrap metal industry is well established but very little domestic waste is recovered. Every household throws away about 95 kilos of food and beverage cans each year. Britain's waste cans placed end to end would reach the moon. We only recycle a measly 1%.

Two schemes exist for recycling cans:

■ **Save-a-Can,** *Elm House 19 Elmshott Lane Cippenham Slough Berks SL1 5QS, (06286 66658).* Operated by the **Can Makers Association.** Skips are placed in car parks or near supermarkets. They collect all types of cans and make a donation from the profits to local charities.

■ **Ali-can Scheme Aluminium Can Recycling Association,** *PO Box 57 Newport, Gwent., (0633-892722).*

Scrap dealers may pay £15 - £20 per cwt for crushed, bagged aluminium cans.

Aluminium ring pulls and foil: Ring pulls are always made of pure aluminium. They are clean and easy to store and lots of charities now collect them to raise funds. Aluminium foil from kitchen foil, milk bottle tops, yoghurt tops, frozen food, take-away containers must be washed and flattened before sending to charities like **Guide Dogs for the Blind**.

Coins and Stamps

Foreign Coins are worth money! All those old francs and rupees left in the bottom of drawers provide a very useful fund raiser for charities. Stamps are also welcomed.

The following charities are among those who take coins and stamps:-

■ **Arthritis Care,** *6 Grosvenor Crescent , SW1X 7ER (235 0902).*

■ **Chest Heart and Stroke Association,** *Tavistock*

House North, Tavistock Square, WC1H 9JE (387 3012).

■ **Green Party,** *10 Station Parade, Balham High Road, SW12 9AZ (235 0433).*

■ **Leukemia Research Fund,** *43 Great Ormond St, WC1 (405 0101).* Coins only.

■ **Projects for the Blind - Wandsworth,** *Yukon Road SW12, (675 3900).* Stamps only.

■ **Save the Children Fund,** *Mary Datchelor House, 17 Grove Lane, SE5 5JS (703 5400).*

Craft Materials

The **Children's Scrap Project** is a non-profit making voluntary organisation which collects safe, clean, industrial waste from local factories and offices for redistribution to children's and community groups for use in their art, craft and play activities.

■ **Childrens Scrap Project,** *137 Homerton High Street, Hackney, E9 (985 6290).*

■ **South London Children's Scrap Scheme,** *The Spike Complex, off Consort Road, SE15 (698 9280).*

Furniture/White Elephant Goods

The amount of old furniture which ends up on skips, dumped on the road or taken to the council tip is incredible. Most of it is probably worth a little to the second-hand shop, try the *Yellow Pages* or advertise in the local paper or shop window. You can advertise for free in *Loot* (60p in Newsagents Mon and Thu).

Oil

Oil can be recycled easily. Pouring used motor oil down the drain or dumping it is illegal. Garages usually collect waste oil or the Council site will have a collection point.

Local oil reclaimation companies are:

■ **Sharpes,** *Arlington Road, Twickenham TW1 2BB , (892 0502).* (Charge £10 for under 100 gallons if collection required).

■ **A1 Waste Oil Recovery,** *Darenth Industrial Park, Erith, Kent, (0322-347402).*

Plastics

The durability of most plastics makes them a waste disposal problem. They don't degrade and expanded plastic containers for fast food are made with CFC gases which contribute to the destruction of the ozone layer. Nearly 3/4 of the plastic going into our dustbins is packaging and the use of plastics is still increasing.

At present there are no large scale schemes to collect post-consumer waste plastic. One of the main problems is that there are many different types of plastic which cannot be mixed.

Vast amounts of plastics are being dumped in the rapidly decreasing landfill sites. They are a legacy that will remain with us for hundreds of years.

The only real answer is to use *biodegradable* plastics. While research in this area is still in the early stages, look out for products using biodegradable plastic.

Try to use glass containers, or re-use plastic ones. Plastic bags can be re-used or take them to shops. The Body Shop use refillable plastic bottles.

Start by looking in your rubbish and work from there. If you want more comprehensive information get *The Recyclers Guide to Greater London.* Kim Castle (£4.50 1986) from the **London Energy and Employment Network (LEEN),** *99 Midland Road, NW1 2A1 (387 4393).* **Friends of the Earth** produce a comprehensive information package *Recycling - The Way Forward.*

▼ SPECIALIST BOOKSHOPS ▼

Listed below are a few of the best known alternative bookshops which should be able to help you.

■ **Housmans Bookshop,** *5 Caledonian Rd, N1 9PX (837 4473).* Just around the corner from Kings Cross tube station, it has the most comprehensive range of books on peace and related issues.

■ **C.N.D. Bookshop,** *22-24 Underwood St, N1 7JG (250 4010).* Comprehensive range of books and publications.

■ **Books For A Change,** *52 Charing Cross Rd, WC2H OBB (836 2315).* Jointly organised by CND, FOE, The United Nations Association and War On Want; a good range of books for quite a small shop plus recycled commercial stationary. Has a comprehensive catalogue available (send sae).

■ **Compendium,** *234 Camden High St, NW1 8QS (485 8944).* See Bookshops p###. Well worth a special effort to visit, in many people's opinion, Britain's best alternative bookshop. It produces catalogues and will do mail order. Open Sun.

■ **Sunpower,** *198 Blackstock Rd, Finsbury Park , N4 2JW (704 0247).* More than just a bookshop, Sunpower also sells wholefoods and crafts, has a community noticeboard, a 'campaign box' and space for leaflets - it's a real Alladins cave.

■ **Centreprise,** *136-138 Kingsland High St, E8 2NS (254 9632).* See **Bookshops** p###. As well as a good bookshop they run a coffee bar and take-away.

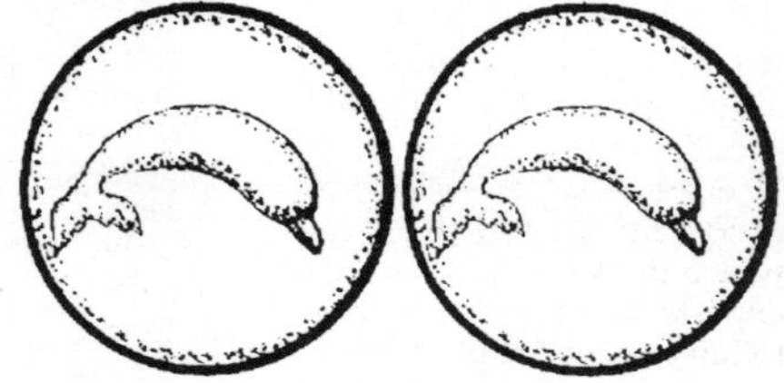

alternative technology

alternative, or appropriate, technology for a long time derided by 'the Establishment' is now assuming a higher profile. No longer just a means of helping third world countries to manufacture bricks without the use of huge industrial complexes, alternative technology is now being seen as as a vital weapon in the battle against ecological devastation. It is now being recognised that if 'under-developed' countries continue to follow the Western road to industrialisation then there will be no possible way we can reverse the destruction caused by pollution and continued use of limited resources. However it is no good pointing the finger at less 'developed' countries when we continue to see our own wealth as dependant on the use of non-renewable, highly toxic fuels and energy inefficient industrial complexes.

Alternative technology is not only environmentally friendly it also aims to be 'user friendly'. It is a way of producing and using energy which does not rely on experts, and which allows us to have some measure of control. One of the major obstacles to the use of renewable energy is the problem of how to make money out of it. If we can recycle our waste to produce heating, or generate our own electricity from wind or solar power who's going to rake in the profit? It is not surprising that the development of AT has been the province of small, fringe organisations. There has been little encouragement on the part of the government to research and develop AT; in 1988 Britain spent over £300 million on nuclear energy and only £14 million on researching new sources of power.

▼ORGANISATIONS▼

■ **NATTA (Network for Alternative Technology Assessment),** *c/o Energy & Environment Research Unit, Faculty of Technology, Open University, Milton Keynes, Bucks, MK7 6AA, ((0908) 653197).* Independent national coalition of people concerned with AT development. Holds national conferences, can supply speakers and slides, reports on projects, discussion papers, technical advice and careers advisory service. Local London group. Bi-mthly newsletter. Membership £10 (£8 concs).

■ **Centre for Alternative Technology (CAT)** *Machnynlleth, Powys , Wales, (0654 2400).* Started in 1974, now one of the largest and best known centres attracting thousands of visitors each month. Variety of weekend residential courses in AT where you can learn such things as solar panel construction and self build energy housing. Displays of AT for the public with working examples of renewable power - solar, wind, water, biomass and also conservation techniques. Lots on organic gardening and self-sufficiency. Bookshop carries a 1000 titles - send 70p in stamps for catalogue. If you're in the area, don't miss it.

■ **Energy and Environment Research Unit,** *Open University,*

Walton Hall, Milton Keynes, MK7 6AA, (0908 274066). Publish research on renewable sources of energy and its use, assessing its environmental impact (wind generators may not produce radiation or use up finite supplies of fuel but is the prospect of acres and acres of huge, state-of-the-art windmills across the Yorkshire moors the answer?).

■ **Commonwork**, *Bore Place, Chiddingstone, Edenbridge, Kent TN8 7AR, (0732 463255).* Experimental community/demo centre for organic farming and AT which encourages the 'creative development of natural resources'.

■ **SCRAM**, *11 Forth St, Edinburgh EH1 3LE, (031 557 4283)* is an anti-nuclear Scottish organisation which publishes *SCRAM: The Safe Energy Journal*. It covers nuclear issues and also gives coverage to electricity privatisation, the greenhouse effect and alternative technology.

■ **Neighbourhood Energy Action**, *2/4 Bigg Market, Newcastle NE1 1UW, (091 261 5677).* Promotes self-help energy projects. Publications on request.Workshops for low-income groups. Aims to develop a national network of locally based projects to insulate the homes of people on low incomes. If all the homes and buildings in Britain were effectively insulated we could reduce our consumption of energy by as much as two thirds.

■ **British Wind Energy Association**, *c/o Royal Aeronautical Association 4 Hamilton Place, W1V OBQ (499 3515).* Membership is mainly for professionals involved in the field of wind energy, but they also have associate and student membership. Newsletter *Windirections*.

■ **Northumbrian Energy Workshop**, *Wind Energy Works, Acomb, Hexham, Northumberland NE46 4SA, (0434 606737).* Co-operative research/consultancy/design company who make, supply and install renewable energy systems. Invented the 'Windlogger' for automatic long-term surveys of the wind resources in a given spot. Newsletter.

■ **The Energy Technology Support Unit**, *AER, Harwell Laboratory, Didcot, Oxon OX11 ORA, (0235 834621 ext 3518).* Publishes a guide to all official projects in renewable energy sources.

■ **Parliamentary Alternative Energy Group**, *c/o Tony Speller, MP, Hse of Commons, SW1 (219 5489).* All party discussion and lobbying group.

■ **Intermediate Technology Development Group**, *103 Southampton Row, WC1 (436 9761 Head office 0788 60631).* Founded by E.F. Schumacher, author of *Small is Beautiful*, this is a 'charity that helps the rural poor of the Thrid World to acquire the tools and techniques they need to work themselves out of poverty'. Runs own projects and consultancy to organisations. Publish *Small World*. Large bookshop. Young people's wing is **Youth Technology Action Group (Youthtag)**, *Myson Ho, Railway Terr, Rugby CV21 3BR*, publish magazine, run fund-raising events.

■ **Green Deserts**, *Rougham, Bury St Edmunds, Suffolk, (0359 70265).* One third of the Earth's usable land is at risk of turning into desert. The work of Green Deserts is to share their knowledge and practical skills in an effort to revitalise the arid land. Projects include: networking with local communities, planting trees and research. Membership £10 (incl info pack and newsletter). Info pack on its own £1.50.

■ **CSV (Community Service Volunteers)**, *237 Pentonville Rd, N1 9NJ (278 6601).* Do info pack for teaching AT.

▼ BOOKSHOPS ▼

■ See **Centre for Alternative Technology** p281.

■ **Intermediate Technology Bookshop**, *103 Southampton Row, WC1 (436 9761).* Specialises in areas of energy, transport and materials. Booklist.

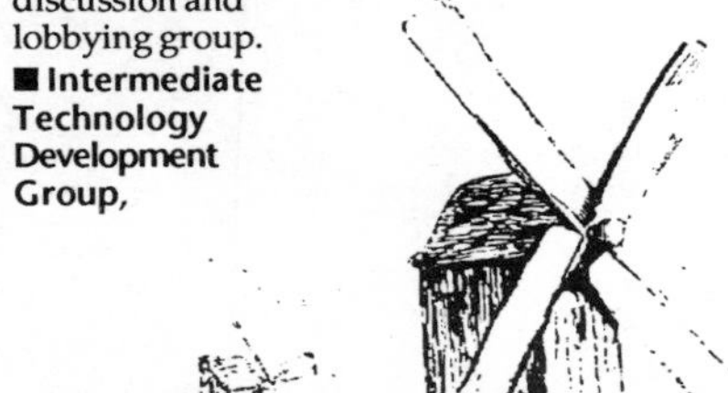

index

About this Book
How this book managed to get finished I do not know. I am writing this on the morning of the day the book is due to go to the printers, whilst feverishly pasting up the last remnants of the art work. One of the two hard discs, which holds the main files, has just packed up so I am writing this final page on the other computer.
Kate and I had previously written a book *The London Guide to Mind Body and Spirit*. We had learnt how to write and how to publish, and we thought we could manage a bigger challenge but...
The office is always a mess. Paper, coffee cups, pens and bits of paper litter the desks and carpet. Whenever we tidied up, the next day it looked just the same. The phones never cease to ring adding to the general chaos in which we work.
We live in a housing co-operative house and the licence expires this year so we're forced into getting this book finished before we are thrown out and must find somewhere else. The roof leaks and when we have a downpour the buckets and saucepans collect the rainwater. There are pigeons in the loft which is just above the office and sometimes their chorus is so loud we cannot hear our phone conversations. I have to climb into the loft and shoo them away through the holes in the roof.
We do not belong to any organisation, nor do we tow any political party line. We met as friends and our intention was to write a book that would empower the individual. We've indicated wherever possible how you can do it yourself, from plumbing to making a claim in a small claims court. We've also refrained from taking advertising which would have compromised our freedom to edit.
We initially obtained the names of organisations listed in this book from a variety of sources; directories, friends, other organisations, magazines and books. We either sent letters to them or phoned them. We then pooled our own and friends' knowledge on these organisations and contacted anyone who could enlighten us about them. The database started to mushroom out of all proportion. We were trying to write at the same time as calls were pouring into our hectic office. If we were not sure of anything we would use our informal network of friends and acquaintances to provide us with the information. As the book developed the number of friends and acquaintances who began to contribute grew. For more specialist and technical help we contacted organisations in those fields and asked them to contribute. Only when a number of contributions started to come in did the book start to take shape and gave us hope that we might get it finished.
Although one of our hard discs has just keeled over and died I must say that this book would have been impossible without the computer system, and a plug here must be given to Hypercard, an amazing programme which comes free with Apple Macintosh computers. It is a programme which allows mixing of database, text and graphics and it was the backbone for our work.
Many thanks here to all those who contributed to this book, whether you gave us help over the phone, sent in information, provided us with financial assistance or wrote for us.

Mike Considine
London

Dodges and Tips
If you have any dodges or tips you would like to get into print in the next edition of this book send them to us at Alternative Press, BCM Raft, London WC1N 3XX. If we use them we will reward you with a small amount of money or something more exotic perhaps.

Further Copies of this Book
If you want further copies of this book send £4.95 + £1 p&p (£2 p&p overseas) to Alternative Press, BCM Raft, London WC1 3XX.